FX Options and Smile Risk

Antonio Castagna

WILEY
A John Wiley and Sons, Ltd., Publication

Registered office
John Wiley & Sons Ltd, The Atrium, Southern Gate, Chichester, West Sussex, PO19 8SQ, United Kingdom

For details of our global editorial offices, for customer services and for information about how to apply for permission to reuse the copyright material in this book please see our website at www.wiley.com.

Library of Congress Cataloging-in-Publication Data

Castagna, Antonio.
FX options and smile risk / Antonio Castagna.
p. cm.
ISBN 978-0-470-75419-1
1. Foreign exchange options. 2. Risk management. I. Title.
HG3853.C37 2009
332.4′5–dc22
2009036554

A catalogue record for this book is available from the British Library.

ISBN 978-0-470-75419-1 (H/B)

Typeset in 10/12pt Times by Aptara Inc., New Delhi, India
Printed in Great Britain by CPI Antony Rowe, Chippenham, Wiltshire

Fato sive Caso dicatum

For other titles in the Wiley Finance Series
please see www.wiley.com/finance

Contents

Preface **ix**

Notation and Acronyms **xiii**

1 The FX Market **1**
1.1 FX rates and spot contracts 1
1.2 Outright and FX swap contracts 4
1.3 FX option contracts 10
1.3.1 Exercise 11
1.3.2 Expiry date and settlement date 11
1.3.3 Premium 13
1.3.4 Market standard practices for quoting options 14
1.4 Main traded FX option structures 16

2 Pricing Models for FX Options **21**
2.1 Principles of option pricing theory 21
2.1.1 The Black–Scholes economy 21
2.1.2 Stochastic volatility economy 26
2.1.3 Change of numeraire 27
2.2 The black–scholes model 29
2.2.1 The forward price to use in the formula 30
2.2.2 BS greeks 31
2.2.3 Retrieving implied volatility and strike 35
2.2.4 Some relationships of the BS formula 38
2.3 The Heston Model 41
2.3.1 Time-dependent parameters in the Heston model 42
2.4 The SABR model 44
2.5 The mixture approach 45
2.5.1 The LMLV model 45
2.5.2 The LMUV model 48

2.5.3 Features of the LMLV and LMUV models and a comparison between them 50
2.5.4 Extension of the LMUV model 51
2.6 Some considerations about the choice of model 53

3 Dynamic Hedging and Volatility Trading 57
3.1 Preliminary considerations 57
3.2 A general framework 59
3.3 Hedging with a constant implied volatility 61
3.4 Hedging with an updating implied volatility 63
3.4.1 A market model for the implied volatility 66
3.5 Hedging Vega 68
3.6 Hedging Delta, Vega, Vanna and Volga 70
3.6.1 Vanna–Volga hedging with one implied volatility 71
3.6.2 Vanna–Volga hedging with different implied volatilities 71
3.7 The volatility smile and its phenomenology 75
3.8 Local exposures to the volatility smile 79
3.8.1 Retrieving the strikes of the main structures 79
3.8.2 ATM straddle exposures 81
3.8.3 Risk reversal exposures 81
3.8.4 Vega-weighted butterfly exposures 83
3.9 Scenario hedging and its relationship with Vanna–Volga hedging 84
3.9.1 Scenario hedging with constant Delta options 86

4 The Volatility Surface 91
4.1 General definitions 91
4.1.1 Arbitrage opportunities under the three different rules 92
4.2 Criteria for an efficient and convenient representation of the volatility surface 94
4.3 Commonly adopted approaches to building a volatility surface 96
4.4 Smile interpolation among strikes: the Vanna–Volga approach 97
4.4.1 The Vanna–Volga approach: general setting 97
4.4.2 Computing the Vanna–Volga weights and option prices 99
4.4.3 Limit and no-arbitrage conditions 102
4.4.4 Approximating implied volatilities 102
4.5 Some features of the Vanna–Volga approach 104
4.5.1 Hedging error for longer expiries 105
4.5.2 The implied risk-neutral density and smile asymptotics 106
4.5.3 Two consistency results 108
4.6 An alternative characterization of the Vanna–Volga approach 110
4.7 Smile interpolation among expiries: implied volatility term structure 112
4.8 Admissible volatility surfaces 115
4.9 Taking into account the market butterfly 116
4.10 Building the volatility matrix in practice 120

5 Plain Vanilla Options **131**
5.1 Pricing of plain vanilla options 131
5.1.1 Delayed settlement date 131
5.1.2 Cash settlement 133
5.2 Market-making tools 134
5.2.1 Inferring the implied volatility for a given strike 134
5.2.2 Inferring the implied volatility for a given Delta 135
5.2.3 Quoting the Vega-weighted butterfly and the risk reversal 136
5.3 Bid/ask spreads for plain vanilla options 139
5.4 Cutoff times and spreads 141
5.5 Digital options 142
5.5.1 Digital options pricing: the static replica approach 143
5.5.2 Digital options pricing in specific model settings 148
5.5.3 Delayed cash settlement date 150
5.5.4 Bid/ask spreads 150
5.5.5 Quotation conventions 152
5.6 American plain vanilla options 152
5.6.1 Valuation of American plain vanilla options in a BS setting 152
5.6.2 Pricing of American plain vanilla options with the volatility smile 153

6 Barrier Options **155**
6.1 A taxonomy of barrier options 155
6.2 Some relationships of barrier option prices 156
6.3 Pricing for barrier options in a BS economy 157
6.3.1 The diffusion equation under single absorbing boundaries 158
6.3.2 Dealing with a constant barrier 159
6.4 Pricing formulae for barrier options 160
6.5 One-touch (rebate) and no-touch options 162
6.6 Double-barrier options 164
6.6.1 Two absorbing states 164
6.6.2 Pricing formula for double-barrier options 165
6.7 Double-no-touch and double-touch options 167
6.8 Probability of hitting a barrier 167
6.9 Greek calculation 168
6.10 Pricing barrier options in other model settings 169
6.11 Pricing barriers with non-standard delivery 170
6.11.1 Delayed settlement date 170
6.11.2 Cash settlement 170
6.12 Market approach to pricing barrier options 171
6.12.1 Inclusion of the smile: the Vanna–Volga approach for barrier options 171
6.12.2 The Vanna–Volga approach for barrier options: variations on the theme 177
6.12.3 Slippage at the barrier level 181
6.12.4 Delta-hedging near the barrier level 183
6.12.5 Implicit one-touch and gearing 184
6.12.6 Vega-hedge rebalancing 186

6.13 Bid/ask spreads 188
6.14 Monitoring frequency 191

7 Other Exotic Options 195
7.1 Introduction 195
7.2 At-expiry barrier options 195
7.3 Window barrier options 197
7.4 First–then and knock-in–knock-out barrier options 199
7.5 Auto-quanto options 202
7.6 Forward start options 204
7.6.1 Including the volatility smile in the pricing 207
7.6.2 Forward implied volatility smiles 210
7.6.3 Forward start barrier and bet options 210
7.6.4 Dealing with notional amounts expressed in numeraire currency 211
7.7 Variance swaps 212
7.8 Compound, Asian and lookback options 215

8 Risk Management Tools and Analysis 217
8.1 Introduction 217
8.2 Implementation of the LMUV model 217
8.2.1 The forward volatility surfaces 221
8.2.2 Calculating the sensitivity to the movements of the volatility surface 223
8.3 Risk monitoring tools 227
8.3.1 FX spot rate-related Greeks 227
8.3.2 Cash-settled options 229
8.3.3 Volatility-related Greeks and sensitivities 229
8.3.4 Barrier implicit one-touch, bets and digitals 231
8.3.5 Interest rate-related Greeks 234
8.4 Risk analysis of plain vanilla options 236
8.4.1 ATM straddle 236
8.4.2 Risk reversal 239
8.4.3 Vega-weighted butterfly 241
8.5 Risk analysis of digital options 244
8.6 Risk analysis of exotic options 249
8.6.1 Barrier options 249
8.6.2 Double barrier options 258
8.6.3 Bet options 262

9 Correlation and FX Options 269
9.1 Preliminary considerations 269
9.2 Correlation in the BS setting 269
9.3 Contracts depending on several FX spot rates 275
9.4 Dealing with correlation and volatility smile 278
9.4.1 Vanna–Volga extension 278
9.5 Linking volatility smiles 283

References 287

Index 291

Preface

When I first proposed writing a book on FX options, I could not help thinking that the final result would produce in the reader that disappointing, yet typically human, feeling caused by the recognition of what the Qoelet expresses in such a condensed way: "Quod factum est, ipsum est, quod faciendum est: nihil sub sole novum", which in slightly more modern words, and in accordance with the situation, means "Many books on options have been written in the past and this one is just telling the same old stories everybody knows". This fear was also sharpened by the fact that some very good books have already been written on the subject, so that just trying to be at the same level would be a titanic task. In this respect, I would like to mention here the excellent book by Uwe Wystup [63], which covers many areas, from pricing to regulation issues.

My scepticism about the likely outcome of my efforts was then partially reduced when, by chance, I read an aphorism of that solitary Colombian thinker (still inexplicably not too much known), Nicolas Davila, in his *Escolios a un texto implicito*, which stated: "Nobody thinks seriously until he cares about being original". I started to become aware that actually I did not have to search for new areas to analyse, and that I did not necessarily have to be original about the choice of subjects: "simply", I had to explore them deeply. Two questions naturally arose in my mind: Do I have the knowledge and expertise to undertake such a thorough inquiry? Besides, and probably more importantly, even if we assume that knowledge and expretise just for the sake of argument, why should I do it?

As far as the first question is concerned, I could not conceitedly say that my expertise derived from theoretical studies or technical skills, or from the fact that I was a smart trader capable of understanding the markets on any occasion, simply because none of that was true. Yet, in the year 2000, when I was working as a market maker on the interest derivatives (caps, floors and swaptions) market in Banca IMI, Milan, I was asked by the two heads of the dealing room to start a desk, market making in FX options. I had no experience in such a market, and nobody who could teach me about how it worked, or had ever worked, in the bank. So I began setting up pricing systems and risk management tools by relying only on my intuition and reasoning. Then, I started to make prices and manage the book, and so started to learn. I learnt in the only way living beings learn on earth, that is: by suffering. In the market-making context suffering means basically two things: losing money in its phenomenal aspect (which mainly concerns the financial institution) and feeling depressed in its psychological aspect (which mainly concerns the trader). Ultimately, I can say I achieved my expertise on FX options by suffering, so that I have no fear in claiming that my knowledge and understanding of FX options is not purely academic or theoretical, in which case I should admit my manifest inferiority to many people. Alternatively said, my knowledge is entirely due to the principle that the eighteenth-century philosopher Vico stated in his *Principi di Scienza Nuova*, according to which one really and fully knows something only if he has made it.

As far as the second question is concerned, it is relevant that in the year 2006 I stopped being in charge of the FX options desk in Banca IMI. I can safely say that (to use the scholastic philosopher's categories) if I was, in a more or less unconscious way, the efficient cause of the FX options desk, I was also, again in a more or less unconscious way, the final cause of it (at least in the way I liked it to operate). After two years I had stopped the market-making activity in FX options, but I did not want to forget and lose for ever all that I had assimilated during those six years. Writing a book is likely the best way to firmly fix all the concepts and the know-how that I absorbed from my experience.

As should be clear from all that has been said above, this book is written from a market-maker perspective and is focused mainly on problems related to pricing and risk management. I prefer to start with a list of what this book is not meant to be: it is not a mathematical finance textbook, although some basic options pricing theory will be presented and in general much mathematical formalism will be used; it is not aimed at showing all the possible structures that can be traded in the FX market, especially with a bank's customers (corporates, speculators, investors, etc.). Hence, I do not deal with aspects referring to the sell side. As a consequence of the previous point, I will not analyse all the possible existing kinds of contracts. Namely, I will not deal with Asian options, basket options and correlation contracts (range mountain options, for example). These options are typically used to build structured products for investors and they are very common in the equity options market. When currencies are considered as an asset class, then the same kind of options can have them as an underlying. Anyway, many books have been written on how to price such contracts, and how to manage their risk and, although they have their main reference to equities, their result can easily be extended to the FX market. In a few words, this book is not a collection of pricing formulae. Besides, I will not enter into details of the interest rates market and I will not examine how to build a discount factor curve by bootstrap procedures: I assume that we are already provided with discount factors for any maturity, even if I am aware that I am neglecting a very momentous subject, at least at the time of writing.

This book is aimed at examining all the relevant issues a market maker has to cope with, both in terms of pricing different kinds of contracts and managing their related risks. Many details, often overlooked in most textbooks or articles, will be examined explicitly. Actually, they represent the link between the theory and practice, and they have a dramatic impact on the profitability of an FX options desk. I will also provide many examples: since in most cases one must resort to numerical procedures, they will be described step-by-step and then worked out in practice.

After this preliminary warning, an overview of the outline of the book is in order. I will start, in the first chapter, with the basic definitions of the FX market: the definition of pairs and the description of the main contracts are presented. I will also illustrate the main conventions operating amongst professional market makers. The second chapter is devoted to a quick review of the main concepts of the option pricing theory and their application within a Black–Scholes (BS hereon) economy, and then a stochastic volatility environment. I introduce some models that could be implemented to price and manage FX options, although in subsequent chapters I will use only one of them as an example of the alternatives to the BS setting.

Managing the volatility risk is the main task of the options trader, so the entire third chapter is devoted to the effects of volatility on the profits and losses arising from the hedging activity. It is in this regard that the volatility smile is first introduced and examined. The fourth chapter extends the analysis to the building of a consistent volatility smile from a few options' market prices. Here I take the chance to remember that much of the work related to these topics has been conducted together with Fabio Mercurio, an exceptional colleague from the quantitative department in Banca IMI, and a good friend of mine too: it was a great intellectual pleasure to work with him and I thank him for sharing with me his experience and skills.

The fifth chapter dwells on the pricing of plain vanilla options and digital options, with much attention paid to some details and market conventions whose impact on the pricing is significant. In the sixth chapter barrier options are examined; they probably form the vast majority of the exotic options dealing in the FX market, so that they deserve an in-depth analysis and many tools and methods devised by practitioners will be described. By the same token, in the seventh chapter the other less common exotic options are examined.

The eighth chapter illustrates the tools for monitoring the main risks of an FX options book; besides, it shows and comments at some length on the behaviour, in terms of volatility risks, of the plain vanilla hedging instruments and of the main exotic options. The ninth and final chapter offers a quick analysis of the links among three currencies, and sketches an extension of the methods examined in the previous chapters to the contracts depending on many pairs.

One noteworthy feature of most of the methods and approaches described is that they hinge mainly on the BS model, which is still the main working tool in the market, although its flaws have been identified and discussed abundantly during the last 30 years. The reason for the striking inconsistency between the ascertained deficiencies of the BS model, and its widespread use in the FX market, is not due to the fact that market makers are stupidly stubborn (or, at least, they are not completely stupidly stubborn): on the contrary, they are aware of the risks that the model is not able to consider and include them in the pricing by resorting to sophisticated, yet definitely empirical (mis-)uses of the model, sometimes designed in a very clever way, even if from a theoretical perspective the adopted solutions may make academicians turn their noses up. I would like to define this as a "Dionysian" approach to the problems related to FX options: the complexity and even the inconsistency of the real world is accepted and faced with all the means we have at our disposal, although a reasonable rigour is needed in the choice of them. In contrast, I would see an "Apollonian" approach as aimed at the perfection of the formal theory, at the elegance of the derivation of the results and the beauty of the internal consistency of the models: the fascination for all of these is manifestly congenital to human nature (at least the most noble part of it) but, alas, they are not enough to account for all the noxious details of the real world. As usually happens, a combination of the two approaches, an "Apollonian" vision of a "Dionysian" experience, as someone wrote somewhere, is likely to produce the best results. I believe this is what actually occurs in the FX options market (and in other markets too, to be honest). On the other hand, if they say that options trading is an art, then FX options trading is the *Oedipus Rex*, or the Sistine Chapel if you prefer visual works.

I do not mean to start from the origin of the universe to thank all the people and events that made possible the writing of this book, but I cannot help mentioning my parents, who wanted me to study at LUISS University in Rome; there I took a degree in Financial Markets' Economics, under the supervision of Professor Emilio Barone, with a thesis on the pricing of American options. Professor Barone, whose bright mind I admire, was the first to encourage my studies in finance and I was honoured to write with him two articles. I would like to thank all the people who worked with me on the FX options desk in Banca IMI, even if for a short time: Roberto Binello, Marek Fogiel, Giuseppe Levato, Michele Lanza (who succeeded me as the head of the desk and who contributed greatly to its development), Andrej Mariani, Cristina Castagner and Alessandro Gavazzeni. I would also like to mention my colleagues and friends from the interest rate options desk: Luca Dominici, Stefano De Nuccio, Pierluigi D'Orazio and Davide Moresco. In the same bank I had the lucky chance to work in a stimulating environment with an exceptional quantitative department: besides the already mentioned Fabio Mercurio, I had interesting discussions with Francesco Rapisarda, Andrea Bugin, Damiano Brigo, Giulio Sartorelli and Lorenzo Bisesti. I have to acknowledge also the illuminating talks that I had with my colleagues and friends Cristiano Cosso, Francesco Fede, Raffaele Giura and Sergio Grasso.

Paola Mosconi deserves special thanks for proofreading the manuscript and for suggesting many improvements. The suggestions of anonymous reviewers are greatly acknowledged as well.

Although not directly related to the ideas and concepts discussed in this book, still all my friends in Milan (many of whom I have known since I was at the university) had a more or less hidden role: I would like to thank them for all their support and affection.

Finally, I must thank the last two top managers I had as my bosses in Banca IMI: Andrea Crovetto and Gianluca Cugno, whose decisions, unconsciously and unwittingly according to the utmost perfect heterogenesis of ends, ultimately allowed me to write this book.

Notation and Acronyms

- S_t : spot price of the exchange rate at time t
- $F(t, T)$: forward price of the exchange rate at time t for a contract expiring at time T
- $r^d(t)$,r_t^d : domestic spot rate at time t. It may be continuous, simple or annual compounded according to the context
- $r^f(t)$,r_t^f : foreign spot rate at time t. It may be continuous, simple or annual compounded according to the context
- $P^d(t, T) = E^Q[e^{-\int_t^T r^d(s)ds}]$: domestic zero-coupon bond price expiring at time T prevailing at time t
- $P^f(t, T) = E^Q[e^{-\int_t^T r^f(s)ds}]$: foreign zero-coupon bond price expiring at time T prevailing at time t
- $D^d(t) = D_t^d = e^{\int_0^t r^d(s)ds}$: domestic deposit (bank account) accruing interest at the domestic rate r^d with initial value in domestic currency units $D^d(0) = 1$
- $D^f(t) = D_t^f = e^{\int_0^t r^f(s)ds}$: foreign deposit (bank account) accruing interest at the foreign rate r^f with initial value in foreign currency units $D^f(0) = 1$
- H_t : barrier level at time t
- τ : time between t and T expressed as a year fraction, i.e. $\tau = \frac{T-t}{365}$
- $T_1, T_2, ..., T_i - 1, T_i$: set of maturities
- ς_t : instantaneous volatility of exchange rate spot process at time t
- $\sigma(K, T), \sigma(K)$: implied volatility to plug into the Bl formula for an option struck at K and expiring in T
- Q : risk-neutral measure
- Q^T : forward risk-adjusted measure (the domestic zero-coupon $P(t, T)$ is the numeraire)
- $E[x]$: expected value of x under the physical measure
- $E^Q[x]$: expected value of x under the risk-neutral measure
- $E^T[x]$: expected value of x under the forward risk-adjusted measure
- $\mathcal{N}(\mu, \sigma)$: normal distribution with mean μ and variance σ
- $\Phi(x)$: cumulative distribution function of a standard Gaussian distribution calculated in x
- W_t, Z_t : Brownian motions under the real-world measure
- W_t^Q, Z_t^Q : Brownian motions under the risk-neutral measure
- $\mathcal{O}(\cdot)$: price of a European contingent claim, such as a plain vanilla European option
- $\text{Bl}(S_t, t, T, K, P^d(t, T), P^f(t, T), \sigma, \omega)$: price of a plain vanilla European option at time t and expiring at time T, struck at K and evaluated according to the BS model with a forward price of the exchange rate $F(t; T)$, an implied volatility equal to σ and with the price of the

domestic zero-coupon bond equal to $P^d(t, T)$. If the option is a call then $\omega = 1$, if it is a put then $\omega = -1$

- **C**$(\cdot)$: price of a plain vanilla European call option. The function's arguments vary according to the context
- **P**$(\cdot)$: price of a plain vanilla European put. The function's arguments vary according to the context
- p : an option's premium
- $\mathcal{E}(\cdot)$: price of a generic exotic option
- $\mathcal{B}(\cdot)$: price of a generic European barrier option, such as an up&out call option
- $\mathcal{D}\mathcal{B}(\cdot)$: price of a generic European double-barrier option
- **KOC** : price of a knock-out call option
- **KOP** : price of a knock-out put option
- **KIC** : price of a knock-in call option
- **KIP** : price of a knock-in put option
- **UOC** : price of an up&out call option
- **DOC** : price of a down&out call option
- **UIC** : price of an up&in call option
- **DIC** : price of a down&in call option
- **UOP** : price of an up&out put option
- **DOP** : price of a down&out put option
- **UIP** : price of an up&in put option
- **DIP** : price of a down&in put option
- **OTH** : price of a one-touch option whose nominal amount is paid at the hit of the barrier level
- **OTE** : price of a one-touch option whose nominal amount is paid at the expiry of the contract
- **NT** : price of a no-touch option
- **DKOC** : price of a double-knock-out call option
- **DKOP** : price of a double-knock-out put option
- **DKIC** : price of a double-knock-in call option
- **DKIP** : price of a double-knock-in put option
- **DNT** : price of a double-no-touch option
- **DTE** : price of a double-touch option, paid at expiry
- **Fw**(t, T) : value of a forward contract (outright) at time t, expiring at time T
- **Fsw**(t, T) : value of an FX swap contract at time t, expiring at time T
- **STDL** : ATM straddle, i.e. a trading strategy (structure) involving the buying of a call and of a put struck at the same ATM level
- **RR** : risk reversal, i.e. a trading strategy (structure) involving the buying of a call against the selling of a put
- **VWB** : Vega-weighted butterfly, i.e. a trading strategy (structure) involving the buying of a strangle against the selling of an ATM straddle in such an amount as to make the total (BS model) Vega position nil
- **stdl** : ATM straddle price, in terms of BS implied volatility
- **RR** : risk reversal, i.e. a trading strategy (structure) involving the buying of a call against the selling of a put
- **rr** : risk reversal price, in terms of BS implied volatility

- **VWB** : Vega-weighted butterfly, i.e. a trading strategy (structure) involving the buying of a strangle against the selling of an ATM straddle in such an amount as to make the total (BS model) Vega position nil
- **vwb** : Vega-weighted butterfly price, in terms BS of implied volatility
- ATM : at-the-money level of the strike price of an option
- OTM : out-of-the-money level of the strike price of an option
- ITM : in-the-money level of the strike price of an option
- SDE : stochastic differential equation
- PDE : partial differential equation
- BS : Black–Scholes
- SV : stochastic volatility
- UV : uncertain volatility
- MIX : lognormal mixture

1
The FX Market

The foreign exchange (FX) market is an OTC market where each participant trades directly with the others; there is no exchange, though we can identify some major geographic trading centres: London (the primary centre, where the primary banks' market makers are located; its importance has increased in the last few years), New York, Tokyo, Singapore and Sydney. This means that trading activity is carried out 24 hours a day, though in practice during London working hours the market has the most liquidity. Needless to say, the FX market experiences fierce competition amongst participants.

Most trades are currently carried out via interbank platforms (EBS is the most important). Anyway, the major market makers offer Internet platforms to their clients for quick trades and for leaving orders. The Reuters Dealing, which was the main platform in the past, has lately lost much of its pre-eminence. Basically, it is a chat system connecting the participants, capable of recognizing the deal implicit in typical conversations between two professional operators, and transforming it into an automatic confirmation for the transaction. Nowadays, the Reuters Dealing is used mainly by option traders.

1.1 FX RATES AND SPOT CONTRACTS

Definition 1.1.1. ***FX rate****. An exchange (FX) rate is the price of one currency in terms of another currency; the two currencies make a* ***pair****. The* ***pair*** *is denoted by a label, made up of two tags of three characters each: each currency is identified by its tag. The first tag in the exchange rate is the base* ***currency****, the second is the* ***numeraire currency****. So the FX is the price of the base currency in terms of the numeraire currency.*

The numeraire currency can be considered as domestic: actually, in what follows we will refer to it as domestic. The base currency can be regarded as an asset whose trading generates profits and/or losses in terms of the domestic currency. In what follows the base currency will also be referred to as the foreign currency. We would like to stress that these denominations are not related to the perspective of the trader, who can actually be located anywhere and for whom the foreign currency may turn out to be indeed the domestic currency, from a "civil" point of view.

Example 1.1.1. *The euro/US dollar FX rate is identified by the label EURUSD and it denotes how many US dollars are worth 1 euro. The domestic (numeraire) currency is the US dollar and the foreign (base) currency is the euro.*

For each currency specific market conventions apply, and two of them are also important for the FX market: the *settlement date* and the *day count*. The settlement date (or delivery date) is the number of business days needed to actually transfer funds (if any are due) amongst interbank market participants after the closing of a deal; for most currencies it is two business days, but there are exceptions. In the market lore it is commonly referred to as "T + *number of days*", where "T" stands for the time (day) when the deal is closed. The *day count* is the

Table 1.1 *Settlement date* and *day count* conventions for some major currencies

Tag	Currency	Settlement (T +)	Day count
AUD	Australian dollar	2	act/360
CAD	Canadian dollar	2	act/360
CHF	Swiss franc	2	act/360
CZK	Czech koruna	2	act/360
DKK	Danish krone	2	act/360
EUR	Euro	2	act/360
GBP	UK pound	0	act/365
HKD	Hong Kong dollar	2	act/365
JPY	Japanese yen	2	act/360
NOK	Norwegian kroner	2	act/360
NZD	New Zealand dollar	2	act/360
PLN	Polish zloty	2	act/360
SEK	Swedish krona	2	act/360
USD	US dollar	2	act/360
ZAR	South African rand	2	act/365

time factor used to calculate accrued interest between two dates in the money market of the relevant currency; it usually applies for simple compounding. A list of some currencies and their related settlement date and day count conventions is given in Table 1.1.

The settlement date and the day count for each currency are useful to price forward (outright) and FX swap contracts. There is a settlement date specific for the spot contract though, and it is the number of days, after the trade date, when the two amounts denominated in the currencies involved are exchanged between the counterparties. The rules to determine the settlement date for a spot contract are a little more complex, since they need the intersection of three calendars: we list them below when we define the spot contract.

The FX rates are expressed as five-digit numbers, with no regard for the number of decimals; the fifth digit is named *pip*: 100 pips make a *figure*. As an example, the major FX rates for spot contracts (we will define *spot* below) as of 29 October 2007 are shown in Figure 1.1. Regular trades are for fixed amounts of the base currency. For example, if a trader asks for a spot price via the Reuters Dealing in the EURUSD, and they write

"I Buy (or Sell) 2 mios EURUSD at 1.3597"

this means that the trader buys (or sells) 2 million euros against 2 719 400 US dollars (1.3597 × 2 mios). Clearly, should one need exactly 1 million US dollars, it has to be specified as follows:

"I Buy 1 mio USD against EUR at 1.3597"

This means that the trader buys 1 million US dollars against 735 456 euros (1/1.3597 × 1 million). The two contracts closed in the examples are *spot* and the employed FX rate is also said to be *spot*. We define the spot contract as follows:

Definition 1.1.2. ***Spot.*** *Two counterparties entering into a spot contract agree to exchange the base currency amounts against an amount of the numeraire currency equal to the spot FX rate. The settlement date is usually two business days after the transaction date (but it depends on the currency).*

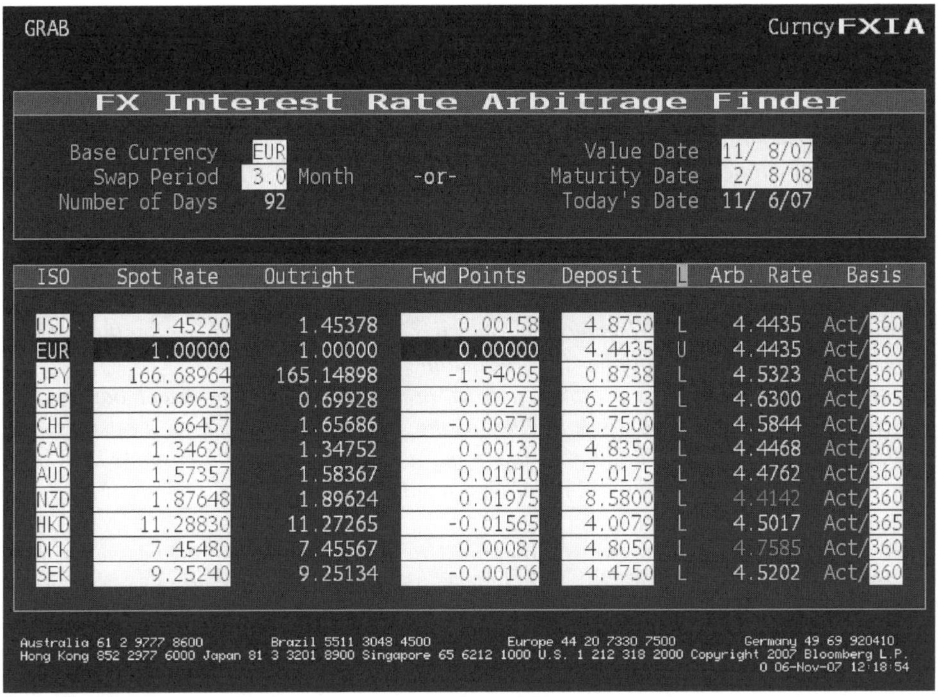
GRAB Curncy FXIA

FX Interest Rate Arbitrage Finder

Base Currency EUR
Swap Period 3.0 Month -or-
Number of Days 92
Value Date 11/ 8/07
Maturity Date 2/ 8/08
Today's Date 11/ 6/07

ISO	Spot Rate	Outright	Fwd Points	Deposit	L	Arb. Rate	Basis
USD	1.45220	1.45378	0.00158	4.8750	L	4.4435	Act/360
EUR	1.00000	1.00000	0.00000	4.4435	U	4.4435	Act/360
JPY	166.68964	165.14898	-1.54065	0.8738	L	4.5323	Act/360
GBP	0.69653	0.69928	0.00275	6.2813	L	4.6300	Act/365
CHF	1.66457	1.65686	-0.00771	2.7500	L	4.5844	Act/360
CAD	1.34620	1.34752	0.00132	4.8350	L	4.4468	Act/360
AUD	1.57357	1.58367	0.01010	7.0175	L	4.4762	Act/360
NZD	1.87648	1.89624	0.01975	8.5800	L	4.4142	Act/360
HKD	11.28830	11.27265	-0.01565	4.0079	L	4.5017	Act/365
DKK	7.45480	7.45567	0.00087	4.8050	L	4.7585	Act/360
SEK	9.25240	9.25134	-0.00106	4.4750	L	4.5202	Act/360

Australia 61 2 9777 8600 Brazil 5511 3048 4500 Europe 44 20 7330 7500 Germany 49 69 920410
Hong Kong 852 2977 6000 Japan 81 3 3201 8900 Singapore 65 6212 1000 U.S. 1 212 318 2000 Copyright 2007 Bloomberg L.P.
0 06-Nov-07 12:18:54

Source: Bloomberg.

Figure 1.1 FX rates as of 29 October 2007 (Reproduced with permission)

As mentioned above, the settlement date for a spot contract is set according to specific rules involving three calendars (collapsing to two if the US dollar is one of the currencies of the traded pair). Here they are:

1. As a general rule, the settlement date for a spot contract is two business days after the trade date ($T + 2$), if this date is a business day for each of the two currencies of the pair. If this is not the case, the date is shifted forward until the condition is matched. An exception to this rule is the USDCAD (i.e., the US dollar/Canadian dollar pair), for which the settlement date is one business day after the trade date.
2. The settlement date set as in (1) must also be a business day in the USA, otherwise the date is shifted one day forward and the condition that the new date is a business day for each currency has to be checked again.
3. When the date after the trade date is a holiday in the USA (except for weekends), but not in other countries, then this date is counted as a business day to determine the settlement date. In this case it happens that for two days spot contracts will be settled on the same date, and in the market lore we say that the "settlement date is repeated".

We provide an example to clarify how to actually apply these rules.

Example 1.1.2. *Assume we are on Tuesday* 20 *November* 2007*; from market calendars it can be seen that Thursday* 22 *November is a holiday in the USA and Friday* 23 *November is a holiday in Japan. Consider three currencies: the US dollar, the euro and the yen. We consider the following possible trades with the corresponding settlement dates:*

- *On* 20 *November we close a spot contract in EURUSD. The settlement date will be* 23 *November: two business days would imply* 22 *November, but this is a holiday in the USA, so the settlement date is shifted forward one day, a "good" business day for both currencies.*
- *On* 21 *November we close a spot contract in EURUSD. The settlement date will be* 23 *November (repeated): the holiday in the USA is one day after the trade and is not a weekend, so it is taken as a business day.*
- *On* 20 *November we close a spot contract in USDJPY. The settlement date will be* 26 *November:* 22 *November is a holiday in the USA, so the settlement date is shifted forward one day, but* 23 *November is a holiday in Japan, so the settlement date is shifted forward to the first available business day, which is Monday* 26 *November, after the weekend. The same calculation also applies if we traded in EURJPY.*
- *On* 21 *November we close a spot contract in USDJPY. The settlement date will be* 26 *November:* 22 *November is a holiday in the USA but it is taken as a business day; anyway,* 23 *November is a holiday in Japan but it is not counted as a business day, so the settlement date is shifted forward to the first available business day, which is Monday* 26 *November, after the weekend.*
- *On* 22 *November we close a spot contract in EURUSD; it is a US holiday but we can trade in other countries. The settlement date will be* 26 *November:* 23 *November is a "good" business day for both currencies, then there is the weekend, and Monday* 26 *November is the second business day.*
- *On* 22 *November we close a spot contract in EURJPY. The settlement date will be* 27 *November:* 23 *November is a good business day for the euro, but not for the yen, so we skip after the weekend, and Tuesday* 27 *November is the second business day, "good" for both currencies and the US dollar as well.*

The rules for the calculation of the settlement date are probably the only real market-related technical issue a trader has to know, then they are ready to take part in the fastest game in town.

1.2 OUTRIGHT AND FX SWAP CONTRACTS

Outright (or forward) contracts are a simple extension of a spot contract, as is manifest from the following definition:

Definition 1.2.1. ***Outright****. Two counterparties entering into an outright (or forward) contract agree to exchange, at a given expiry (settlement) date, the base currency amounts against an amount of the numeraire currency equal to the (forward) exchange rate.*

It is quite easy to see that the outright contract differs from a spot contract only for the settlement date, which is shifted forward in time up to the expiry date in the future. That, however, also implies an FX rate, which the transaction is executed at, different from the spot rate and the problem of its calculation arises. Actually, the calculation of the forward FX price can easily be tackled by means of the following arbitrage strategy:

Strategy 1.2.1. *Assume that we have an XXXYYY pair and that the spot FX rate is S_t at time t, whereas $F(t, T)$ is the forward FX rate for the expiry at time T. At time t, we operate the following:*

- *Borrow one unit of foreign currency XXX.*

- *Change one unit of XXX (foreign) against YYY and receive S_t YYY (domestic) units.*
- *Invest S_t YYY in a domestic deposit.*
- *Close an outright contract to change the terminal amount back into XXX, so that we receive $S_t \frac{1}{P^d(t,T)} \frac{1}{F(t,T)}$ XXX.*
- *Pay back the loan of one YYY plus interest.*

To avoid arbitrage, the final amount $S_t \frac{1}{P^d(t,T)} \frac{1}{F(t,T)}$ XXX must be equal to the value of the loan of 1 XXX at time T, which can be calculated by adding interest to the notional amount.

This strategy can be translated into formal terms as:

$$S_t \frac{1}{P^d(t,T)} \frac{1}{F(t,T)} = 1 \frac{1}{P^f(t,T)}$$

which means that we invest the S_t YYY units in a deposit traded in the domestic money market, yielding at the end $S_t \frac{1}{P^d(t,T)}$ ($P^d(t,T)$ is the price of the domestic pure zero-coupon bond), and change then back to XXX currency at the $F(t,T)$ forward rate. This has to be equal to 1 XXX units plus the interest prevailing in the foreign money market ($P^f(t,T)$ is the price of the foreign pure zero-coupon bond). Hence:

$$F(t,T) = S_t \frac{P^f(t,T)}{P^d(t,T)} \tag{1.1}$$

In Chapter 2 we will see an alternative, and more thorough, derivation for the fair price of a forward contract. The FX rate in equation (1.1) is that which makes the value of the outright contract nil at inception, as it has to be since no cash flow from either party is due when the deal is closed.

A strategy can also be operated by borrowing money in the domestic currency, investing it in a foreign deposit and converting it back into domestic currency units by an outright contract. It is easy to see that we come up with the same value of the fair forward price as in equation (1.1), which prevents any arbitrage opportunity.

The careful reader has surely noticed that in Strategy 1.2.1 the prices of pure discount bonds have been used to calculate the present and future value of a given currency amount. Actually, the market practice is to use money market conventions to price the deposits and hence to determine the forward FX rates. The use of pure discount bonds (also known as discount factors) is perfectly consistent with the market methodology as long as they are derived by a *bootstrap* procedure from the available market prices of the deposits.

Remark 1.2.1. *Strategy 1.2.1 is model-independent and operating it carries the forward price $F(t,T)$ at a level consistent with the other market variables (*i.e.*, the FX spot rate and the domestic and foreign interest rates), so any arbitrage opportunity is cleared out. It should be stressed that two main assumptions underpin the strategy: (i) counterparties are not subject to default risk, and (ii) there is no limit to borrowing in the money markets.*

Assume that the first assumption does not hold. When we invest the amount denominated in YYY in a deposit yielding domestic interest, we are no longer sure of receiving the amount $S_t \frac{1}{P^d(t,T)}$ at time T to convert back into XXX units since the counterparty, to whom we lent money, may go bankrupt. We could expect to recover a fraction of the notional amount of the deposit, but the strategy is no longer effective anyway. In this case we may have a forward price

F(t, T) trading in the market which is different from that determined univocally by Strategy 1.2.1, and we cannot operate the latter to exploit an arbitrage opportunity, since we would bear a risk of default that is not considered at all.

Assume now that the second assumption does not hold. We could observe a forward price in the market higher than that determined by Strategy 1.2.1, but we are not able to exploit the arbitrage opportunity just because there is a limited amount of lending in the market, so we cannot borrow the amount of one unit of XXX currency to start the strategy.

In reality, both situations can be experienced in the market and actually the risk of default can also strongly affect the amount of money that market operators are willing to lend amongst themselves. Starting from July 2007, a financial environment with a perceived high default risk related to financial institutions and a severe shrinking of the available liquidity has been very common, so that arbitrage opportunities can no longer be fully cleared out by operating the replication Strategy 1.2.1.

In the market, outright contracts are quoted in forward points:

$$\mathbf{Fpts}(t, T) = F(t, T) - S_t$$

Forward points are positive or negative, depending on the interest rate differentials, and they are also a function of the level of the spot rate. They are (algebraically) added to the spot rate when an outright is traded, so as to get the fair forward FX rate. In Figure 1.2, forward points

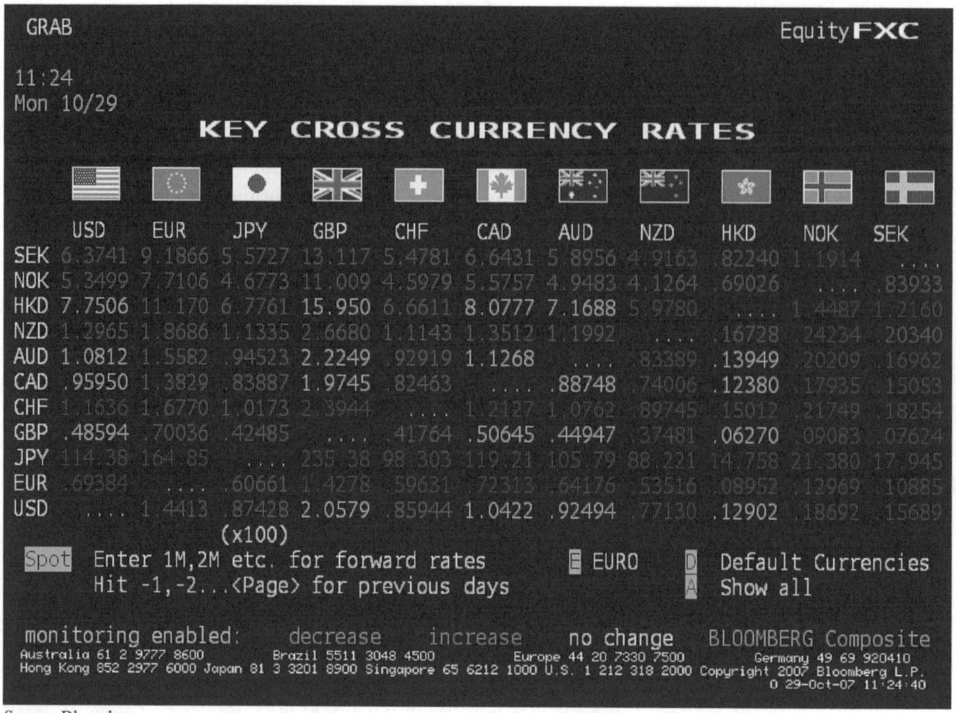
GRAB EquityFXC

11:24
Mon 10/29

KEY CROSS CURRENCY RATES

	USD	EUR	JPY	GBP	CHF	CAD	AUD	NZD	HKD	NOK	SEK
SEK	6.3741	9.1866	5.5727	13.117	5.4781	6.6431	5.8956	4.9163	.82240	1.1914	....
NOK	5.3499	7.7106	4.6773	11.009	4.5979	5.5757	4.9483	4.1264	.69026	....	.83933
HKD	7.7506	11.170	6.7761	15.950	6.6611	8.0777	7.1688	5.9780	....	1.4487	1.2160
NZD	1.2965	1.8686	1.1335	2.6680	1.1143	1.3512	1.1992	....	.16728	.24234	.20340
AUD	1.0812	1.5582	.94523	2.2249	.92919	1.1268	....	.83389	.13949	.20209	.16962
CAD	.95950	1.3829	.83887	1.9745	.82463	....	.88748	.74006	.12380	.17935	.15053
CHF	1.1636	1.6770	1.0173	2.3944	....	1.2127	1.0762	.89745	.15012	.21749	.18254
GBP	.48594	.70036	.42485	....	.41764	.50645	.44947	.37481	.06270	.09083	.07624
JPY	114.38	164.85	....	235.38	98.303	119.21	105.79	88.221	14.758	21.380	17.945
EUR	.69384	....	.60661	1.4278	.59631	.72313	.64176	.53516	.08952	.12969	.10885
USD	....	1.4413	.87428	2.0579	.85944	1.0422	.92494	.77130	.12902	.18692	.15689

(x100)

Spot Enter 1M,2M etc. for forward rates E EURO D Default Currencies
Hit -1,-2...<Page> for previous days A Show all

monitoring enabled: decrease increase no change BLOOMBERG Composite
Australia 61 2 9777 8600 Brazil 5511 3048 4500 Europe 44 20 7330 7500 Germany 49 69 920410
Hong Kong 852 2977 6000 Japan 81 3 3201 8900 Singapore 65 6212 1000 U.S. 1 212 318 2000 Copyright 2007 Bloomberg L.P.
0 29-Oct-07 11:24:40

Source: Bloomberg.

Figure 1.2 Forward points at 6 November 2007 (Reproduced with permission)

at 6 November 2007 for a three-month delivery are shown – they are the same points used in FX swap contracts, which will be defined below. The base currency is the euro and forward points are referred to each (numeraire) currency listed against the euro: in the column "Arb. rate" the forward implied no-arbitrage rate for the euro is provided and it is derived from the formula to calculate the forward FX rate so as to match the market level of the latter.

For the sake of clarity and to show how forward FX rates are actually calculated, we provide the following example:

Example 1.2.1. *Assume we have the market data as in Figure* 1.2. *We want to check how the forward points for the EURUSD are calculated. We use formula* (1.1) *to calculate the forward FX rate, but we apply the money market conventions for capitalization and for discounting (i.e., simple compounding):*

$$F(0, 3M) = 1.4522 \frac{\left(1 + 4.875\% \frac{92}{360}\right)}{\left(1 + 4.4435\% \frac{92}{360}\right)} = 1.45378$$

where $3M$ *stands for "three-month expiry". Hence, the FX swap points are calculated straightforwardly as:*

$$\mathbf{Fpts}(0, 3M) = F(0, 3M) - S_0 = 1.45378 - 1.4522 = 0.00158$$

so that both the forward FX rate and forward points are verified by what is shown in the figure.

The FX swap is a very popular contract involving a spot and an outright contract:

Definition 1.2.2. ***FX swap.*** *Two counterparties entering into an FX swap contract agree to close a spot deal for a given amount of the base currency, and at the same time they agree to reverse the trade by an outright (forward) with the same base currency amount at a given expiry.*

From the definition of an FX swap, the valuation is straightforward: it is the sum of a spot contract and the value of a forward contract. So, we just need the spot rate and the forward points, which are denominated (FX) swap points when referred to such a contract. A typical request by a trader on the Reuters Dealing (which is still one of the main platforms where FX swap contracts can be traded) might be:

"I buy and sell back 1 mio EUR against USD in 3 months"

This means that the trader enters into a spot contract buying 1 million euros against US dollars, and then sells them back at the expiry of the FX swap in three months' time. We use market data provided in the Bloomberg screen shown in Figure 1.2 to see, in practice, how the FX swap contract implied by the request above is quoted and traded. Besides, in the example the difference between a *par* (alternatively an *even*) FX swap and a *non-par* (alternatively an *uneven* or *split* or *change*) FX swap is stressed.

Example 1.2.2. *We use the same market data as in Example* 1.2.1 *and in Figure* 1.2. *The current value of a* 3M *FX swap "buy and sell back 1 mio EUR against USD" has to be split* *into its domestic (US dollar in our case) and foreign (euro) components:*

$$\mathbf{Fsw}^d(0, 3M) = -S_0 + \frac{1}{(1 + r^d \tau)} F(0, 3M)$$

$$= -1.4522 + 1.45378 \frac{1}{\left(1 + 4.875\% \dfrac{92}{360}\right)} = -0.0163 \text{ USD}$$

$$\mathbf{Fsw}^f(0, 3M) = 1 - \frac{1}{(1 + r^f \tau)}$$

$$= 1 - \frac{1}{\left(1 + 4.4435\% \dfrac{92}{360}\right)} = 0.0112 \text{ EUR}$$

In the two formulae above we just calculated the present value for all the cash flows provided by the FX swap contract, separately for each of the two currencies involved. An outflow of S_0 US dollars against 1 euro at inception and an inflow of $F(0, 3M)$ on the delivery date against 1 euro again. The two final values are expressed for each leg of the corresponding currency. This is a par FX swap contract, since the notional amount (1 million euros) exchanged at inception via the spot transaction, and the final amount exchanged back at expiry, via the outright transaction, are the same. It is manifest that a par FX swap engenders a position different from 0 in both currencies. Professional market participants prefer to have nil currency exposure (we will see why later), so they prefer to trade non-par FX swaps. In this trade the amount of the base currency exchanged at the forward expiry is modified so as to generate a zero currency exposure. It is easy to see that the amount to be exchanged (so as to have a par FX swap) has to be compounded at the numeraire (foreign) currency interest rate. Hence, if we set the amount of euros to be exchanged on the delivery date equal to $(1 + 4.4435\% \frac{92}{360}) = 1.0114$ instead of 1, we get:

$$\mathbf{Fsw}^d(0, 3M) = -S_0 + \frac{(1 + r^f \tau)}{(1 + r^d \tau)} F(0, 3M)$$

$$= -1.4522 + 1.45378 \frac{\left(1 + 4.4435\% \dfrac{92}{360}\right)}{\left(1 + 4.875\% \dfrac{92}{360}\right)} = 0 \text{ USD}$$

$$\mathbf{Fsw}^f(0, 3M) = 1 - \frac{(1 + r^f \tau)}{(1 + r^f \tau)}$$

$$= 1 - 1 = 0 \text{ EUR}$$

which clearly shows no residual exposure to the FX risk.

The quoted price of an FX swap contract will be simply the forward points. They are related to the FX spot level, to be specified when closing the contract. When uneven FX swaps are traded, the domestic interest rate has to be agreed upon as well.

After this short analysis, we are able to sum up the specific features of outright and FX swap contracts:

1. An outright contract is exposed to an FX rate risk for the full nominal amount. It also has exposure to interest rates, although this is very small compared to the FX risk.

2. In an FX swap contract the FX rate risk of the spot transaction is almost entirely offset by the outright transaction. In the case of non-par contracts, the FX risk is completely offset, and only a residual exposure to the interest rate risk is left.
3. For the reasons above, outright contracts are mainly traded by speculators and hedgers in the FX market.
4. The FX swap is rather a treasury product, traded in the interbank market to move funds from one currency to another, without any FX risk (for par contracts), and to hedge or get exposure to the interest rate risks in two different currencies. Nonetheless, it is used by options traders to hedge exposure to the domestic and foreign interest rates.

Remark 1.2.2. *If we assume that we are working in a world where the occurrence of default of a counterparty is removed, then by standard arbitrage arguments we must impose that the forward points of an outright contract are exactly the same as the swap points of an FX swap contract. Things change if we introduce the chance that market operators can go bankrupt, so that the mechanics of the two contracts imply great differences in their pricing.*

We have seen before that the arbitrage argument of the replica Strategy 1.2.1 can no longer be applied when default is taken into account, so that the actual traded forward price can differ substantially from the theoretical arbitrage price, since a trader can suffer a big loss if the counterparty from whom they bought the deposit defaults. Now, we would like to examine whether removing the no-default assumption impacts in the same way both the outright and the FX swap contract.

To this end, consider the case when the FX swap points for a given expiry imply a tradable forward price $F'(t, T)$ greater than the theoretical price $F(t, T)$ obtained by formula (1.1). *To exploit the possible arbitrage, we could borrow one million units of foreign currency, say the euro, and close an FX swap contract "sell and buy back 1 mio EUR, uneven amount", similar to that in Example 1.2.2, but with a reverse sign. Basically, we are operating Strategy 1.2.1 with an FX swap, instead of an outright contract. Assume also that, after the deal is struck, our counterparty in the FX swap deal might be subject to default, in which case they will not perform their contractual obligations, so we will not receive back the one million euros times $(1 + r^f \tau)$, against $F'(t, T)$ million US dollars times $(1 + r^f \tau)$ paid by us. In such an event, we will not have the amount of money we need to pay back our loan in euros, whose value at the end of the contract is equal to $(1 + r^f \tau)$ million euros. Nevertheless, we still have the initial exchanged amount in USD, equal to S_t (the FX spot rate at inception of the contract), and we could use this to pay back our debt. In this case, assuming we have kept the amount in cash, we can convert it back into euros at the terminal FX spot rate S_T, which might be lower or higher than S_t, so that we can end up with a final amount of euros greater or smaller than one million (the euro amount will be S_t/S_T). The terminal economic result could be a profit or a loss, depending on the level of the FX spot rate S_T and on how much we have to pay for the interest on the loan in euros. Nonetheless, we may reasonably expect not to lose as much as one million euros, and the total loss (or even profit) is a function of the volatility of the exchange rate and the time to maturity of the contract.*

Assume now that we operated Strategy 1.2.1 with an outright contract. We borrow one million euros, convert it into dollars at S_t, buy a deposit in dollars, and convert the terminal amount by selling an outright at the rate $F'(t, T)$. If our counterparty defaults, they will not pay back the amount of money we lent to them (supposing there is no fraction of the notional amount recovered) and we will end up with no money to sell via the outright, so as to convert it into euros and pay back our loan. In this case we are fully exposed to the original amount *of one million euros and we will suffer a loss for sure equal to this amount, plus the interest on the loan.*

From the two cases we have described, we can see that the FX swap can be considered as a collateralized loan. The example shows a situation just as if we lent an amount denominated in euros, collateralized by an amount denominated in dollars. Clearly, the collateral is not risk-free, since its value in euros is dependent on the level of the exchange rate, but it is a guarantee that will grant a presumably high recovery rate of the amount lent on the occurrence of default of the counterparty, and we could possibly end up with a profit. In the other case we examined, that is the outright contract, we see that we have no collateral at all as a guarantee against the default of the counterparty, so we are fully exposed to the risk of losing the amount of dollars we lent to them. This loss can be mitigated if we assume that we can recover a fraction of the notional amount we lent, but the recovery will very likely be much smaller than the fraction of notional we can recover via the collateral.

There are two conclusions we can draw:

1. *The forward rate $F(t, T)$ determined as in equation* (1.1) *does not identify the unique arbitrage-free price of an outright contract, if we include the chance of default of the counterparty.*
2. *The forward price implied by an FX swap contract can be different from that of an outright contract when default of the counterparty is considered, because Strategy 1.2.1 operated with an FX swap is less risky than the same strategy operated with an outright contract.*

1.3 FX OPTION CONTRACTS

FX options are no different from the usual options written on any other asset, apart from some slight distinctions in the jargon. The definition of a *plain vanilla European* option contract is the following:

Definition 1.3.1. ***European plain vanilla FX option contract.*** *Assume we have the pair XXXYYY. Two counterparties entering into a plain vanilla FX option contract agree on the following, according to the type of option traded:*

- *Type* ***XXX call YYY put****: the buyer has the right to enter at expiry into a spot contract to buy (sell) the notional amount of the XXX (YYY) currency, at the strike FX rate level K.*
- *Type* ***XXX put YYY call****: the buyer has the right to enter at expiry into a spot contract to sell (buy) the notional amount of the XXX (YYY) currency, at the strike FX rate level K.*

The spot contract at expiry is settled on the settlement date determined according to the rules for spot transactions. The notional amount N in the XXX base currency is exchanged against $N \times K$ units of the numeraire currency. The buyer pays a premium at inception of the contract for their right.

The following chapters are devoted to the fair calculation of the premium of an option, the analysis of the risk exposures engendered by trading it, and the possible approaches to hedging these exposures. Clearly, this will be done not only for plain vanilla options, but also for other kinds of options, usually denoted as *exotics*. A very rough taxonomy for FX options is presented in Table 1.2; this should be considered just as a guide to how the analysis will be organized in what follows. Besides, it is worth noticing that the difference between

Table 1.2 Taxonomy of FX options

Group	Name	Exercise	Monitoring
Plain vanilla	Call/put	E/A	E
First-generation exotic	Digital	E	E
First-generation exotic	Knock-in/out barriers	E/A	E/C/D
First-generation exotic	Double-knock in/out barriers	E/A	E/C/D
First-generation exotic	One-touch/no-touch/ double-no-touch/double-touch	A	C/D
First-generation exotic	Asian	E/A	D
First-generation exotic	Basket	E/A	D
Second-generation exotic	Window knock-in/out barriers	E/A	E/C/D
Second-generation exotic	First-in-then-out barriers	E/A	E/C/D
Second-generation exotic	Forward start plain/barriers	E/A	E/C/D
Second-generation exotic	External barriers	E/A	E/C/D
Second-generation exotic	Quanto plain/barriers	E/A	E/C/D

Exercise: European (E), American (A). Monitoring: at expiry (E), continuous (C), discrete (D).

first-generation and second-generation exotics is due to the time sequence of their appearance in the market rather than any reference to their complexity.

It is worth describing in more detail the option contract and the market conventions and practices relating to it.

1.3.1 Exercise

The exercise normally has to be announced by the option's buyer at 10:00 AM New York time; options are denominated *NY Cut* in this case, and they are the standard options traded in the interbank market. The counterparties may also agree on a different time; such as 3:00 PM Tokyo time; in this case we have the *Tokyo Cut*. The exercise is considered automatic for a given percentage of in-the-moneyness of the options at expiry (e.g., 1.5%), according to the ISDA master agreement signed between two professional counterparties before starting any trading activity between them. In other cases the exercise has to be announced explicitly, although it is market fairness to consider exercised (or abandoned) options manifestly in-the-money (or out-of-the money), even without any call from the option's buyer.

1.3.2 Expiry date and settlement date

The expiry date for an option can be any date when at least one marketplace is open, then the settlement date is set according to the settlement rules used for spot contacts. Some market technicalities concern the determination of the expiry and settlement (delivery) dates for what we call *canonic* or *standard* dates. In more detail, in the interbank market daily quotes are easily available for standard expiries expressed in terms of time units from the trade date, i.e., overnight, weeks, months and years.

Day periods. Overnight is the simplest case to analyse, since it indicates an expiry for the next available business day, so:

1. In normal conditions it is the day after the trade date or after three days in case the trade date is a Friday (due to the weekend).

2. The expiry is shifted forward if the day after the trade date is not a business day all around the world (e.g., 25 December). On the contrary if at least one marketplace is open, then the expiry date is a good one.
3. Once the expiry date is determined, the settlement date is calculated with the rules applied for the spot contract.

If the standard expiry is in terms of number of days (e.g., three days), the same procedure as for overnight applies, with expiry date initially and tentatively set as the number of days specified after the trade date.

Week periods. This case is not very different from the day period one:

1. The expiry is set on the same week day (e.g., Tuesday) as the trade date, for the given number of weeks ahead in the future (e.g., 2 for two weeks).
2. At least one marketplace must be open, otherwise the expiry is shifted forward by one day and the open market condition checked again.
3. Once the expiry is determined, the usual rules for the spot contract settlement date apply.

Month and year periods. In these cases a slightly different rule applies, since the spot settlement date corresponding to the trade date is the driver. More specifically:

1. One moves ahead in the future by the given number of periods (e.g., 6 for six months), then the same day of the month as the spot settlement date (corresponding to the trade date, in the current month) is taken as the settlement date of the option (e.g., again for six-month expiry, if the trade date is the 13th of the current month and the 15th is the settlement date for a corresponding spot contract, then the 15th day of the sixth month in the future will be the option settlement date). If the settlement date of the future month is not a valid date for the pair involved, then the date is shifted forward until a good date is achieved.
2. If the settlement determined in (1) happens to fall in the month after the one corresponding to the number of periods considered (e.g., the six-month expiry yields a settlement actually falling in the seventh month ahead), then the *end-of-month* rule applies. From the first settlement date (identified from the spot settlement of the trade date), the date is shifted backward until a valid (for the contract's pair) settlement date is reached.
3. The expiry can now be calculated by applying backward from the settlement date the rules for a spot contract.
4. The year period is treated with same rules simply by considering the fact that one year equals 12 months.

We provide an example to clarify the rules listed above.

Example 1.3.1. *Assume we trade an option EUR call USD put with expiry in one month. We consider the following cases:*

- *The trade date is* 19 *October 2007. From the market calendars the spot settlement date for such a trade date can be calculated and set on* 23 *October so that the settlement of the option has to be set on* 23 *November (i.e., the same day one month ahead). This date can be a settlement date for the EURUSD pair and the corresponding expiry date is* 21 *November, since the 22nd is a holiday in the USA but is counted as a business day according to the spot date rules. Actually, we know from Example 1.1.2 that the spot trades dealt on* 20 *November also imply a settlement date on the 22nd. When the expiry date is calculated working backward from the settlement, the first possible trade date encountered is taken (i.e., the 21st in this case).*

- *The trade date is 19 October 2007. From the market calendars the spot settlement date for such a trade date is 24 October, thus the option's settlement date is 24 November, which is a Saturday, so it is shifted forward to the first available business day for both currencies: Monday 26 November. Working backward to calculate the expiry date, we would take 22 November but this is a US holiday, so we move one more day backward and set the expiry on the 21st, which agrees with spot settlement rules.*

After analysing the rules for standard expiries, for the sake of completeness we just remark that if a specific date is agreed upon for the expiry (e.g., 7 January 2008), then the standard spot settlement rules apply to calculate the option's settlement date (9 January, if the contract's pair is EURUSD).

1.3.3 Premium

The option's premium is paid on the spot settlement date corresponding to the trade date. It can be paid in one of either currencies of the underlying pair and it can be expressed in four different ways, which we list below:

1. *Numeraire currency units* (p_{numccy}). This is the standard way in which, for some pairs, premiums are expressed for plain vanilla options in the interbank market after the closing of the deal. It is worth noticing also that this is the natural premium one calculates by a pricing formula. The actual premium to pay is calculated by multiplying the currency units times the notional amount (in base currency units): $N \times p_{numccy}$.
2. *Numeraire currency percentage* ($p_{numeccy\%}$). This is the standard way in which premiums are expressed and quoted for exotic (one-touch, double-no-touch, etc.) options in the interbank market, when the payout is a numeraire currency amount. It can be calculated by dividing the premium in numeraire currency units by the strike: $p_{numccy\%} = \frac{p_{numccy}}{K} \times 100$. The actual premium to pay is equal to the notional amount in numeraire currency units ($N \times K$) times the numeraire currency percentage premium: $N_{numccy} \times \frac{p_{numccy\%}}{100}$.
3. *Base currency units* ($p_{baseccy}$). This way of quoting may be useful when the numeraire currency amount is fixed for all the options entering into a given strategy (e.g., in an EUR call USD put spread). It can be calculated by dividing the premium in numeraire currency units by the spot FX rate and then by the strike: $p_{baseccy} = \frac{p_{numccy}}{S_t K}$. The actual premium to pay is equal to the notional amount, expressed in numeraire currency (that is: $N \times K$), times the base currency units premium: $N_{numccy} \times p_{baseccy}$.
4. *Base currency percentage* ($p_{baseccy\%}$). This is the standard way in which premiums are expressed and quoted for exotic (barrier) options, and for some pairs also for plain vanilla options, in the interbank market. It can be calculated by dividing the premium in numeraire currency units by the spot FX rate: $p_{baseccy\%} = \frac{p_{numccy}}{S_t} \times 100$. The actual premium to pay is equal to the notional amount times the base currency percentage premium: $N \times \frac{p_{baseccy\%}}{100}$.

In Table 1.3 we report some market conventions for option premiums; usually, the numeraire currency premium is multiplied by a factor such that it is expressed in terms of pips (see above for the definition of the latter), or as a percentage of either notional rounded to the nearest quarter of 0.01%. We will see later that the way markets quote premiums has an impact on the building of the volatility matrix, so that it is not just a curiosity one may lightly neglect.

Table 1.3 Market conventions for option premiums for some pairs

Pair	p_{numccy}	$p_{baseccy}\%$
EURUSD	USD pips	
EURCAD	CAD pips	
EURCHF		EUR %
EURGBP	GBP pips	
EURJPY		EUR %
EURZAR		EUR %
GBPCHF		GBP %
GBPJPY		GBP %
GBPUSD	USD pips	
USDCAD		USD %
USDCHF		USD %
USDJPY		USD %
USDZAR		USD %

Example 1.3.2. *Assume we want to buy* 2 000 000 *EUR call USD put struck at* 1.3500, *with a reference EURUSD spot rate equal to* 1.2800. *The notional amount in USD is* $2\,000\,000 \times 1.3500 = 2\,700\,000$. *The premium can be quoted in one of the four ways we have examined and we have that:*

1. *If the premium is in numeraire currency units and it is* $p_{USD} = 0.0075$ *US dollars per one EUR unit of option, we will pay* $2\,000\,000 \times 0.0075 = 15\,000$ *USD.*
2. *If the quotation is expressed as a numeraire currency percentage, the premium is* $p_{USD\%} = \frac{0.0075}{1.3500} \times 100 = 0.5550\%$ *(rounded to the nearest quarter of* 0.01%*) for one USD unit of option dollar, and we pay* $0.5550 \times \frac{2\,700\,000}{100} = 14\,985$ *USD (the small difference of* 15 000 *is due to rounding conventions).*
3. *If the quotation is in base currency units, the premium is* $p_{EUR} = \frac{0.75}{1.2800 \times 1.3500} = 0.00435$ *EUR per one USD unit of option dollar, and we pay* $0.55 \times \frac{2\,700\,000}{100} = 11\,750$ *EUR.*
4. *Finally, if the premium is expressed as a base currency percentage, it is* $p_{EUR\%} = \frac{0.0075}{1.2800} \times 100 = 0.5875\%$ *of the EUR notional (rounded to the nearest quarter of* 0.01%*) and we pay* $0.5875 \frac{2\,000\,000}{100} = 11\,750$ *EUR.*

1.3.4 Market standard practices for quoting options

FX options can be dealt for any expiry and also for any level of strike price. Amongst professionals, options are quoted according to standards: some of them are actually rather clever, and make FX options one of the most efficient OTC derivatives markets.

Let us start with plain vanilla options. Firstly, options are usually quoted for standard dates, although it is possible to ask a market maker for an expiry occurring on any possible date. Secondly, quotations are not in terms of (any of the four above) premiums but in terms of implied volatilities, that is to say, in terms of the volatility parameter to plug into the BS model (given the values of all the other parameters and the level of the FX spot rate, retrievable from the market). Once the deal is closed, the counterparties may agree to actually express the premium in any of the four ways listed above, although the standard way is in numeraire currency pips (p_{numccy}). Thirdly, strike prices are quoted in terms of the Delta[1] of the option: this means that before closing the deal, the strike level is not determined yet in absolute terms. Once the deal is closed, given the level of the FX spot rate and the implied volatility agreed upon (the interest rate levels will be taken from the money market), the strike will be set at a level yielding the BS Delta the two counterparties were dealing. This way of quoting is smart: it allows us not to worry about small movements of the underlying market during the bargaining process, because the absolute strike level will be defined only after the agreement on the price (in terms of implied volatility), so that the trader is sure to trade an option with given features in terms of exposures both to the underlying pair and to the implied volatility.[2]

If not otherwise specified when asking for a quote, the option is considered to be traded Delta-hedged ("with Delta exchange"), i.e., a spot trade offsetting the BS Delta exposure is closed along the option's transaction. Usually, for strikes very far OTM with a very tiny premium (p_{numccy}) and a negligible Delta exposure, options are quoted at an absolute level of premium and with no Delta hedge ("without Delta exchange").

For popular exotic options[3] some other conventions are in force for ordinary market activity. For barrier options, contrary to plain vanilla options, when a trader asks for a price, strikes and barrier levels are asked for in absolute terms, by specifying the reference spot FX rate, and also an ATM implied volatility level. The quote will be assumed to be valid for those levels, and it will be provided in terms of the premium as a percentage of the base currency notional. Also, for barrier options it is assumed that the deal includes a Delta-hedge transaction and in most cases a Vega-hedge[4] transaction (by dealing a spot contract and an ATM straddle[5] to offset the related exposures). The amounts dealt in those transactions are calculated according to the BS model, using as inputs the reference FX spot and implied volatility levels.

Other very common exotics are the bet options,[6] i.e., one-touch, no-touch, double-no-touch, double-touch, digitals. They are quoted as a percentage of the notional amount (which is the payout of the bet, usually in base currency), given reference levels of the FX spot and implied volatility. After the agreement on the price, the deal will include the Delta-hedge and Vega-hedge transactions (to be defined according to the BS model).

In the following example we provide some customary conversations between professional traders. We just mean to clarify the conventions we have described above, and are aware that we are anticipating many of the issues that will be investigated in detail in the following chapters. So, the reader should not be worried if they feel somewhat lost.

Example 1.3.3. *On the Reuters Dealing, which we have already mentioned to be the main trading platform for FX, options are traded via conversations like those below:*

- *Plain vanilla*
  > Please, 3M EUR call USD put 25D, in 30.
  > 7.5 7.7
  > 7.7 pls, spot ref 1.4575.

[1] The Delta of an option will be defined in Chapter 2, where the BS model is presented.

[2] This statement will become clearer with the analysis in Chapter 3.

[3] The definition for each of the options we mention below will be given in the chapters devoted to their analysis.

[4] Vega will be defined in Chapter 2.

[5] This structure is described later on in this chapter.

[6] More details about the definition of bet options can be found in Chapter 6.

The first trader asks for a price for EUR call USD put expiring in three months with a strike level not yet defined in absolute terms, but referred to in terms of 25% *Delta EUR call, with a notional amount of* 30 *million euros. The second trader quotes a bid/ask in terms of BS implied volatility and the first trader is buying the options paying* 7.7% *and providing also the FX spot level (set reasonably near to the market level), which will be used to calculate the strike level corresponding to the* 25% *EUR call, the premium (in USD pips) and will also be the level of the Delta-hedge transaction. In fact, since there was no mention of it in the request for the quote, it is assumed to be included in the deal.*

- *Barrier option*

  > Please, 6m EUR put USD call 1.4500 RKO 1.3800, spot ref 1.4576, in 50 with VH.
  > 0.20 0.25
  > 0.25 pls.

  The first trader asks for a quote in an RKO barrier EUR put USD call expiring in six months. The strike (1.4500) *and the barrier* (1.3800) *are specified right from the start of the request. The notional amount is* 50 *million euros and the asked quote is for a trade including the Vega hedge ("with VH"), besides the Delta hedge. The second trader's quote is in absolute premiums, in terms of a percentage of the notional amount, so that when the first trade accepts to buy by applying the offer, they will pay* 0.25% *of* 50 *million euros.*

- *Double-no-touch*

  > Please, 1Y EURUSD DNT 1.3500 1.4500, in 1 mio EUR with VH.
  > 20 25
  > 20 pls.

  The first trader asks for a quote in a double-no-touch expiring in 1Y on the EURUSD pair, with lower range level at 1.3500 *and upper range level at* 1.4500*. The payout is in* 1 *million euros and the trade will include the Vega hedge. The second trader's quote is in absolute premium, expressed as a percentage of the payout, so that the first trader will cash in* 200 000 *euros since they are selling the options by applying the bid (20%).*

1.4 MAIN TRADED FX OPTION STRUCTURES

Although the FX option market is very liquid for options with any kind of strike level and expiry, nonetheless it is possible to identify some structures that are very popular amongst professional market participants. We will understand why later on, when we examine how to manage the volatility risk of an options portfolio, and we will also study the features and behaviour of their risk exposure.

The first structure is the ATM *straddle* (**STDL** hereafter): that is, the sum of a (base currency) call and a (base currency) put struck at the at-the-money level. The quotes for this structure on standard expiries are the most liquid ones.

One has to pay some attention when defining the exact strike the market is referring to in trading ATM options, since several definitions exist. The first kind of ATM is the *at-the-money spot*: in this case, the strike of the option is set equal to the FX spot rate; the expiry is immaterial in determining the strike. The second kind is the ATM *forward*: the strike is set equal to the forward price of the underlying pair for the same expiry of the option; in this case, we have different ATM strikes for each maturity (recall formula (1.1)). The third kind is the 0 *Delta* **STDL**: the strike is chosen so that, given the expiry, a put and a call have the same Delta but with different signs. This implies that no Delta hedge is needed when trading the straddle. We will see later how to retrieve this strike. The ATM implied volatility quoted in the FX option market is the one referring to a 0 Delta **STDL** strike, and hence it is the implied volatility to plug into the BS formula when trading an ATM **STDL**.

The amount of an ATM **STDL** is traded as the sum of the (base currency) amounts of two component options.

Example 1.4.1. *Suppose we want to buy an ATM* **STDL**. *On the Reuters Dealing we can ask a broker or a market maker for this structure, and can experience a conversation like the following:*

> *Please, 1M EURUSD ATM straddle in 50.*
> *8.10 8.30*
> *8.30 pls, spot ref 1.4575.*

The first trader asks for an ATM **STDL** *in* 50 *million EUR, meaning that if the deal is struck they will trade in a straddle made up of* 25 *million EUR put and* 25 *million EUR call. The words "ATM straddle" are actually redundant, since "1M in* 50*" will unequivocally indicate an ATM* **STDL**. *The second trader makes a quote and the first trader applies the offer at* 8.30%, *thus buying the structure, suggesting also the reference level for the FX spot rate at* 1.4575, *upon which the ATM strike will be set and the premium is calculated by using the dealt implied volatility* (8.30%). *Clearly, by definition, no Delta hedge will be exchanged since the* **STDL** *will engender no exposure to the FX rate.*

Besides the ATM **STDL**, there are at least two other structures frequently traded: they are the 25% *Delta risk reversal* (**RR** hereafter) and the 25% *Delta Vega-weighted butterfly* (**VWB** hereafter).[7]

The **RR** is a structure set up when one buys a (base currency) call and sells a (base currency) put both featured with a symmetric Delta (long **RR**), or the reverse (short **RR**). Delta can be chosen equal to any level, but the 25% is the most liquid one so that the call and the put entering into the **RR** will have a strike level yielding a 25% Delta, without considering its sign (actually, for puts it will be negative). The **RR** is quoted as the difference between the two implied volatilities to plug into the BS formula in order to price two legs of the structure, and we indicate this price in volatility as **rr**. A positive number means that the call is favoured and that its implied volatility is higher than the implied volatility of the put; a negative number implies the opposite. For example, if the three-month 25% Delta **rr** for the EURUSD pair is −0.5%, then the implied volatility of the EUR call is 0.5% lower than the EUR put (both struck at a level yielding 25% Delta, without considering the sign). At time t, we can write the price (in implied volatility terms) of a 25% Delta **RR** with maturity in T as:

$$\mathbf{rr}(t, T; 25) = \sigma_{25C}(t, T) - \sigma_{25P}(t, T) \tag{1.2}$$

where $\sigma(t, T)$ is the implied volatility at t for an option expiring in T and struck at the level indicated in the subscript.

The amount of an **RR** is typically denominated in terms of base currency units, and it is referred to the amount of base currency call that will be traded against the equal amount of base currency put.

[7] It is worth noticing here that in market lore traders refer to options struck at a level implying a 25% Delta, without considering the sign, indistinctly as a 25 or 0.25 or finally 25% Delta call or put.

Example 1.4.2. *We present a market conversation to deal a* 25 *Delta* **RR***:*

> *Please, usdjpy 6M 25D RR in 100.*
> *1.70 1.80 P*
> *1.70 pls, spot ref 108.35.*
> *OK, vols 11.85 10.15*

The first trader asks for a 25 *Delta risk reversal in USDJPY, in an amount of* 100 *million US dollars. If the deal is closed, it will be traded in* 100 *million USD call JPY put against* 100 *million USD put JPY call. The second trader makes a quote and the deal is struck because the first trader hits the bid at* 1.70%. *The* **rr** *is favouring the USD put, as indicated by the "P" after the quotes. This is usually disregarded amongst professionals when there is no possibility of misunderstanding (as in this case, where the* **rr** *is far from* 0 *and the market makers are supposed to know what type of options are favoured). The suggestion of the reference for the USDJPY spot rate at* 108.35, *if accepted, will allow us to determine the strikes corresponding to the* 25 *Delta USD call and USD put, by also using the two volatilities. These are determined starting from the ATM level dealing in the market when the* **RR** *is closed, and then adding half the dealt price of the* **RR** (0.85% *in the example) for the USD put since it is favoured, and subtracting half the price for the USD call. Should the USD call be favoured instead of the put, then the addition would be for the call (and the subtraction for the put, clearly). In fact, the second trader suggests* 11.85% *implied volatility for the USD put and* 10.15% *for the USD call and from this, we can infer that the ATM volatility is dealing in the market at a mid price of* 11.00%.

The **VWB** is the other notable structure: it is built up by selling an ATM **STDL** and buying a symmetric Delta strangle, if one wishes to be long the **VWB**. On the contrary, by buying the straddle and selling the strangle, one is short the **VWB**. The strangle is just the sum of a (base currency) call and put both struck at a level yielding the specified level of Delta (without any consideration of its sign). The 25% Delta is the most traded **VWB**.

Since the structure, as already mentioned, has to be Vega-weighted and since the Vega of the straddle is greater than the Vega of the strangle, the quantity of the former has to be smaller than the quantity of the latter. Indicating as **vwb** the butterfly's price in volatility terms, at time t we can write the price of a 25% Delta **VWB** expiring in T as:

$$\mathbf{vwb}(t, T; 25) = 0.5(\sigma_{25C}(t, T) + \sigma_{25P}(t, T)) - \sigma_{ATM}(t, T) \tag{1.3}$$

This is how quotations for **VWB** appear in the interbank market.

The amount of the **VWB** is, as usual, expressed in terms of base currency units and referred to the amount of the ATM **STDL** (with the same convention as above) that is traded against the Vega-weighted amount of the strangle (whose total is evenly split between the 25 Delta call and the 25 Delta put).

Example 1.4.3. *Hereafter a conversation is shown between two traders to deal a* 25 *Delta* **VWB***:*

> *Pls, EURJPY 1Y 25D fly in 250.*
> *0.275 0.375*
> *0.375 pls, spot ref 158.25.*
> *OK, vol for atm 10.90.*

The first line is the request for a quote for a EURJPY 25 Delta **VWB** *("fly" is the shorthand used for it in conversations) in an amount of 250 million EUR for the ATM* **STDL**. *The quote is in the second line and it is the amount that has to be added to the ATM volatility to get the implied volatility for the 25D EUR call and EUR put. The first trader buys the* **VWB** *by applying the offer at 0.375% and suggesting the reference for the FX spot rate EURJPY. So they will buy the strangle and sell the straddle. The second trader indicates the implied volatility they will use to calculate the premium for the ATM* **STDL** *and the 25 Delta strangle (with an implied volatility set equal to* $10.90\% + 0.375\% = 11.275\%$*). The strikes will be determined by means of the FX spot rate used as reference and the implied volatilities above. The amount on the strangle will be calculated so that the total Vega of the structure is nil. Assume that 1.5 times the ATM* **STDL** *amount is needed for the strangle, hence the first trader buys* $375/2 = 187.5$ *million EUR per leg on the 25 Delta strangle and sells* $250/2 = 125$ *million EUR per leg in the ATM* **STDL**.

We will later examine in more detail the **RR** and **VWB**: they deserve special attention since they allow us, together with the ATM **STDL**, to take exposures to the shape of the volatility matrix.

2
Pricing Models for FX Options

2.1 PRINCIPLES OF OPTION PRICING THEORY

We will shortly review the theory of option pricing with a strict reference to the FX world. First, we introduce a (slightly extended) BS economy, then we relax one of the basic assumptions: we will allow the volatility of the FX rate process to be stochastic. These principles will pave the way to the analysis of some well-known models employed in practice to price FX options.

2.1.1 The Black–Scholes economy

We work in continuous time and assume that W_t is a standard Brownian motion, and a martingale with respect to a filtered probability space $(\Omega, \mathcal{F}, F, P)$ for the time set $[0, \infty)$. We assume also that the filtration F satisfies the usual conditions,[1] and that we have a perfect frictionless market, with one domestic and foreign interest rate (at which interest accrues continuously). In the economy, one risky asset is traded: an FX pair whose price process is the following stochastic differential equation (SDE):

$$dS_t = \mu_t S_t dt + \varsigma_t S_t dW_t \tag{2.1}$$

where μ_t and ς_t are time-dependent parameters. A second traded asset is a riskless (domestic) deposit,[2] whose price changes according to the following differential equation:

$$dD_t^d = r_t^d D_t^d dt \tag{2.2}$$

An FX pair can be considered as an asset yielding a continuous cash flow equal to the foreign interest rate. In fact, when a trader buys one unit of a given pair, they sell S_t quantity of domestic currency: this quantity can be invested in a money market deposit and earn accrued interest at the rate r_t^f.

We have described a BS economy, since it is basically the same economy assumed by Black and Scholes [9] (apart from time-dependent parameters).

The two assets can be employed in a trading strategy, and we are interested in designing a strategy with the following specific feature:

Definition 2.1.1. ***Self-financing strategy.*** *Assume that we establish a trading strategy by holding, at time 0, the quantity α_0 of the risky asset (i.e., the FX pair) and the quantity β_0 of the deposit. A trading strategy is defined as self-financing if:*

$$\alpha_t S_t + \beta_t D_t^d = \alpha_0 S_0 + \beta_0 D_0^d + \int_0^t \alpha_\tau dS_\tau + \int_0^t \beta_\tau r_\tau^d D_\tau^d d\tau + \int_0^t r_\tau^f S_\tau d\tau \tag{2.3}$$

[1] The approach we describe in this section is based on the works by Harrison and Pliska [34, 35], and we refer to them also for a more formal treatment of the foundations.

[2] Hence we are assuming that the interest rate is a deterministic (possibly time-dependent) variable.

Equation (2.3) simply states that the total value of the portfolio at time t (left-hand side) equals the sum of (i) the initial value, (ii) all the losses/gains generated by the trading between time 0 and t and (iii) the interest earned on the foreign currency[3] (right-hand side). No additional cash flow is injected besides the initial one needed to start up the strategy.

We define a new process $\widetilde{S}_t = S_t e^{\int r_t^f dt}$ and, applying Itô's lemma, we obtain

$$d\widetilde{S}_t = \widetilde{\mu}_t \widetilde{S}_t dt + \varsigma_t \widetilde{S}_t dW_t \tag{2.4}$$

where $\widetilde{\mu} = \mu + r_t^f$. The self-financing trading strategy can thus be written:

$$\alpha_t e^{-\int_0^t r_\tau^f d\tau} \widetilde{S}_t + \beta_t D_t^d = \alpha_0 \widetilde{S}_0 + \beta_0 D_0^d + \int_0^t \alpha_\tau e^{-\int_0^\tau r_s^f ds} d\widetilde{S}_\tau + \int_0^t \beta_\tau r_\tau^d D_\tau^d d\tau \tag{2.5}$$

Suppose we have a claim whose value at time T is V_T. If we are able to start up a self-financing strategy whose terminal value is $\alpha_T S_T + \beta_T D_T^d = V_T$, then the claim is defined as *redundant* and its value at time 0 must be set to equal the value of the portfolio which must be paid to enter into the strategy. In fact, by a no-arbitrage argument, it is easy to ascertain that a sure profit can be made at time 0 by selling the higher between the claim and the portfolio, and then continuing the self-financing strategy until time T. The terminal value of the portfolio equals that of the claim, so that the liabilities match the assets. We apply this idea to the pricing of a European option $\mathcal{O}$ expiring at time T.[4] We aim to define a self-financing trading strategy (α, β) such that:

$$\begin{aligned}\mathcal{O}(S_T, T) &= \alpha_T e^{-\int_0^T r_\tau^f d\tau} \widetilde{S}_T + \beta_T D_T^d \\ &= \alpha_0 \widetilde{S}_0 + \beta_0 D_0^d + \int_0^T \alpha_\tau e^{-\int_0^\tau r_s^f ds} d\widetilde{S}_\tau + \int_0^T \beta_\tau r_\tau^d D_\tau^d d\tau \end{aligned}\tag{2.6}$$

As above, equation (2.6) simply states that the terminal value of the option equals the terminal value of the portfolio, including the two assets of the strategy carried out. The latter, in turn, is the sum of the initial value of the portfolio and the trading proceeds. By direct application of Itô's lemma, we have:

$$\mathcal{O}(S_T, T) = \mathcal{O}(S_0, 0) + \int_0^T \mathcal{L}^{\mu,\varsigma}\mathcal{O}(S_\tau, \tau) d\tau + \int_0^T \frac{\partial \mathcal{O}(S_\tau, \tau)}{\partial S_\tau} \varsigma_\tau S_\tau dW_\tau \tag{2.7}$$

where $\mathcal{L}^{\mu,\varsigma}\mathcal{O}(S_\tau, \tau)$ is defined as:

$$\mathcal{L}^{\mu,\varsigma}\mathcal{O}(S_t, t) = \frac{\partial \mathcal{O}(S_t, t)}{\partial S_t}\mu_t S_t + \frac{1}{2}\frac{\partial^2 \mathcal{O}(S_t, t)}{\partial S_t^2}\varsigma_\tau^2 S_t^2 + \frac{\partial \mathcal{O}(S_t, t)}{\partial t} \tag{2.8}$$

Substitution of equation (2.7) into equation (2.6) yields

$$\begin{aligned}&\int_0^T [\mathcal{L}^{\mu,\varsigma}\mathcal{O}(S_\tau, \tau) - \alpha_\tau \widetilde{\mu}_\tau e^{-\int_0^\tau r_s^f ds} \widetilde{S}_\tau - \beta_\tau r_\tau^d D_\tau^d] d\tau + \\ &\int_0^T \left[\frac{\partial \mathcal{O}(S_\tau, \tau)}{\partial S_\tau} \varsigma_\tau S_\tau - \alpha_\tau \varsigma_\tau e^{-\int_0^\tau r_s^f ds} \widetilde{S}_\tau\right] dW_\tau = 0\end{aligned}\tag{2.9}$$

[3] For the sake of clarity we note that, at any time t, one unit of foreign currency equals S_t units of domestic currency, so that in equation (2.3) interest is instantaneously converted into the domestic currency.

[4] We are assuming $\mathcal{O}(S, t)$ is a function sufficiently differentiable for the application of Itô's lemma.

To solve equation (2.9) it suffices to set both integrands equal to zero, by taking α and β as (recalling also the definition of $\widetilde{S}$):[5]

$$\alpha_t = \frac{\partial \mathcal{O}(S_t, t)}{\partial S_t} \tag{2.10}$$

$$\beta_t = \frac{\mathcal{L}^{\mu,\varsigma}\mathcal{O}(S_t, t) - \dfrac{\partial \mathcal{O}(S_t, t)}{\partial S_t}\widetilde{\mu}_t S_t}{r_t^d D_t^d} \tag{2.11}$$

Since at any time t we must have that $\mathcal{O}(S_t, t) = \alpha_t e^{-\int_0^t r_\tau^f d\tau}\widetilde{S}_t + \beta_t D_t^d = \alpha_t S_t + \beta_t D_t^d$, we have that

$$\mathcal{O}(S_t, t) = \frac{\partial \mathcal{O}(S_t, t)}{\partial S_t} S_t + \frac{\mathcal{L}^{\mu,\varsigma}\mathcal{O}(S_t, t) - \frac{\partial \mathcal{O}(S_t, t)}{\partial S_t}\widetilde{\mu}_t S_t}{r_t^d}$$

which, after rearranging, finally yields

$$\frac{\partial \mathcal{O}(S_t, t)}{\partial S_t}(r_t^d - r_t^f)S_t + \frac{1}{2}\frac{\partial^2 \mathcal{O}(S_t, t)}{\partial S_t^2}\varsigma_t^2 S_t^2 + \frac{\partial \mathcal{O}(S_t, t)}{\partial t} - r_t^d \mathcal{O}(S_t, t) = 0 \tag{2.12}$$

Equation (2.12) is the PDE whose solution is the price of the European option, provided suitable terminal and boundary conditions are met. Actually, the self-financing strategy argument can be used for any contingent claim whose terminal value can be set equal to the terminal value of the portfolio of the two basic assets (i.e., for any *attainable claim*). Each claim is the solution to equation (2.12) with specific terminal and boundary conditions determined by the payoff (possibly not only at expiry, but also occurring during the life of the claim).

The solution to equation (2.12) can also be expressed in terms of an expectation. In fact, by means of the Feynman–Kac formula, we have

$$\mathcal{O}(S_t, t) = E^Q\left[e^{-\int_t^T r_s^d ds}\mathcal{O}(S_T, T)\right] \tag{2.13}$$

where S_t is the solution to the SDE (2.1) with $\mu_t = r_t^d - r_t^f$. The drift is the continuously compounded domestic interest rate, net of the continuous flow equal to the foreign interest rate, and it is named *risk-neutral*. Actually, one can calculate the value of a contingent claim (and hence also of a European option) simply by calculating the present expected value (by discounting at the domestic interest rate) of the terminal payoff, which is a function of S. The process commanding the dynamics for S, however, is not the original one but the risk-neutral one. The superscript Q in equation (2.13) means that the expectation has shifted from a real-world measure of probability to a risk-neutral one. This is a valuable result, since one does not have to worry about the actual drift of the underlying asset and can safely determine it with quantities much more easily retrievable from market data, such as interest rates.

We will now try to examine in more depth the link between the self-financing trading strategy and the risk-neutral expected value of the terminal value of the contingent claim. We start by defining the discounted FX rate process $\widetilde{S}^* = \widetilde{S}/D^d$, whose dynamics by Itô's

[5] It is easy to check that the strategy is actually self-financing (see, for example, Bergman [6]), although the property is also manifest by the choice of α and β.

lemma is

$$d\widetilde{S}_t^* = (\widetilde{\mu}_t - r_t^d)\widetilde{S}_t^* dt + \varsigma_t \widetilde{S}_t^* dW_t$$

If we are able to find a probability measure such that the process in equation (2.1) is a martingale, then we will get the following result:

Proposition 2.1.1. *A probability measure Q on $(\Omega, \mathcal{F})$, equivalent to the real-world measure P, is a martingale measure if $\widetilde{S}^*$ is a martingale. Besides, under the equivalent martingale measure the discounted process of the self-financing strategy is a martingale. The trading strategy in this case is called admissible.*

Proof: Let $V_t = \alpha_t S_t + \beta_t D_t^d$, the value at time t of the strategy involving a position in α_t spot contracts and an amount of β_t domestic deposit. Let $V_t^* = V_t / D_t^d$. By Itô's lemma:

$$\begin{aligned} dV_t^* &= d(V_t(D_t^d)^{-1}) = V_t d(D_t^d)^{-1} + (D_t^d)^{-1} dV_t \\ &= (\alpha_t \widetilde{S}_t + \beta_t D_t^d)(dD_t^d)^{-1} + (D_t^d)^{-1}(\alpha_t d\widetilde{S}_t + \beta_t dD_t^d) \\ &= \alpha_t((D_t^d)^{-1} d\widetilde{S}_t + \widetilde{S}_t (D_t^d)^{-1}) = \alpha_t d\widetilde{S}_t^* \end{aligned}$$

Hence

$$V_t^* = V_0^* + \int_0^t \alpha_s d\widetilde{S}_s^*$$

which is a martingale from the local martingale property of Itô's integral. □

If a claim can be replicated via an admissible strategy, then there exists one arbitrage-free price:

Proposition 2.1.2. *Let $\mathcal{O}_T$ be the value of a European contingent claim that can be replicated via an admissible strategy. Its price at time $0 < t < T$, $\mathcal{O}_t$, is given by the risk-neutral expectation of the terminal value:*

$$\mathcal{O}_t = D_t^d E^Q[(D_T^d)^{-1} \mathcal{O}_T | \mathcal{F}_t] \tag{2.14}$$

Proof: Assume V_t is an admissible trading strategy. Then, by definition:

$$(D_t^d)^{-1}\mathcal{O}_t = V_t^* = E^Q[V_T^* | \mathcal{F}_t] = E^Q[(D_T^d)^{-1}\mathcal{O}_T | \mathcal{F}_t]$$

The second equality is derived from Proposition 2.1.1, whereas the others are simply based on the definition of no-arbitrage price. □

From the definition of D_t, it is straightforward to see that equation (2.14) is the same as the Feynman–Kac formula (2.13), thus establishing a link between the two approaches. Now we are left with only one problem: how to calculate an equivalent martingale measure for the FX rate. We can resort to standard results of stochastic calculus, which yield the following:

Proposition 2.1.3. *Given the BS economy setting, a unique martingale measure for the discounted FX rate exists and is given by the Radon–Nikodym derivative:*

$$\frac{dQ}{dP} = \exp\left(\int_t^T \frac{r_s^d - \widetilde{\mu}_s}{\varsigma_s} dW_s - \int_t^T \frac{1}{2} \frac{(r_s^d - \widetilde{\mu}_s)^2}{\varsigma_s^2} ds \right)$$

Under the probability measure Q, the discounted FX rate process is

$$d\widetilde{S}_t^* = \varsigma_t \widetilde{S}_t^* dW_t^Q \tag{2.15}$$

where $W_t^Q = W_t - \int_0^t [(r_s^d - \widetilde{\mu}_s)/\varsigma_s]ds$ *is a standard Brownian motion in* (Ω, F, Q). *Recalling the definition of* $\widetilde{S}$, *by applying Itô's lemma, we can write the risk-neutral evolution of the FX rate process as*

$$dS_t = (r_t^d - r_t^f)S_t dt + \varsigma_t S_t dW_t^Q \tag{2.16}$$

whose solution is

$$S_t = S_0 e^{\int_0^t (r_s^d - r_s^f - \frac{1}{2}\varsigma_s)ds + \int_0^t \varsigma_s dW_s^Q} \tag{2.17}$$

Proof: The proposition is a direct consequence of Girsanov's theorem. □

To recapitulate the results above: there is a connection between the existence of a self-financing trading strategy, replicating the final value of the contingent claim, and the existence of an equivalent martingale measure. They both guarantee that an arbitrage-free price of the contingent claim is unequivocally determined. That can be calculated as the current value of the related replica strategy, or alternatively as the expected value of the discounted final payoff of the claim, under the risk-neutral probability measure.

Example 2.1.1. ***Forward FX price.*** *A forward contract (outright) has been defined in Chapter 1, and the fair forward FX rate has been derived with standard no-arbitrage arguments. We now aim to obtain the forward price using the tools we have presented above, since a forward contract is a contingent claim* ($\mathcal{O} = F$).

Let $\mathbf{Fw}(t, T)$ *be the value of a forward contract at time* t, *expiring at* T. *From the definition of the contract, we have*

$$\mathbf{Fw}(T, T) = S_T - F(t, T) \tag{2.18}$$

where $F(t, T)$ *is the forward FX price set at inception of the contract. A self-financing strategy can be established as explained above, and its current value can be determined by solving the PDE* (2.12) *with the terminal condition expressed in equation* (2.18). *As an alternative, we may calculate the risk-neutral expected discounted payoff* (2.18). *We know from the Feynman–Kac formula* (2.13) *that this is the same as finding the solution of the PDE* (2.12):

$$\begin{aligned}\mathbf{Fw}(t, T) &= D_t^d E^Q[(D_T^d)^{-1}(\widetilde{S}_T - F(t, T))|\mathcal{F}_t] \\ &= D_t^d E^Q[\widetilde{S}_T|\mathcal{F}_t] - D_t^d E^Q[(D_T^d)^{-1} F(t, T)|\mathcal{F}_t] \\ &= S_t P^f(t, T) - P^d(t, T)F(t, T)\end{aligned}$$

The last equality follows from the martingale property of S^* *and from the definition of the discounted price. Moreover, from the definition of a pure discount bond it follows that* $D_t^d / D_T^d = P^d(t, T)$, *considering also that we are working in a deterministic interest rate environment. Finally, we have used* $P^f(t, T) = e^{-\int_t^T r_s^f ds}$.

The fair forward price at time t *is the value which makes nil the value of the contract (since no cash flow is due at inception by either counterparty):*

$$F(t, T) = S_t \frac{P^f(t, T)}{P^d(t, T)}$$

which clearly agrees with the price we derived in Chapter 1.

2.1.2 Stochastic volatility economy

The main flaw of a BS economy concerns the assumption of a deterministic (though possibly time-dependent) instantaneous volatility ς_t. We will relax this assumption by assuming the following dynamics for the FX rate process:

$$dS_t = \mu_t S_t dt + \varsigma_t S_t dW_t$$

where

$$d\varsigma_t = \phi(\varsigma_t, t)dt + \nu(\varsigma_t, t)dZ_t \tag{2.19}$$

The Brownian motions W_t and Z_t are defined in a probability space $(\Omega, \mathcal{F}, F, P)$ and have cross-variations $d\langle W, Z\rangle_t = \rho_t dt$ for some $\rho_t \in [-1, 1]$.

Suppose we want to price, at time t, a contingent claim expiring at T. We try to start a self-financing strategy with terminal value equal to the payoff of the claim, $\mathcal{O}(S_T, \varsigma_T, T)$, as in equation (2.6). We use once more the process $\widetilde{S}_t$ and, by application of Itô's lemma, we have

$$\begin{aligned}\mathcal{O}(S_T, \varsigma_T, T) &= \mathcal{O}(S_0, \varsigma_0, 0) + \int_0^T \mathcal{L}^{\mu,\rho,\phi,\nu}\mathcal{O}(S_\tau, \varsigma_\tau, \tau)d\tau \\ &\quad + \int_0^T \frac{\partial \mathcal{O}(S_\tau, \varsigma_\tau, \tau)}{\partial S_\tau}\varsigma_\tau S_\tau dW_\tau + \int_0^T \frac{\partial \mathcal{O}(S_\tau, \varsigma_\tau, \tau)}{\partial \varsigma_\tau}\nu_\tau dZ_\tau\end{aligned} \tag{2.20}$$

where $\mathcal{L}^{\mu,\rho,\phi,\nu}\mathcal{O}(S_\tau, \varsigma_\tau, \tau)$ is defined as

$$\begin{aligned}\mathcal{L}^{\mu,\rho,\phi,\nu}\mathcal{O}(S_t, \varsigma_t, t) &= \frac{\partial \mathcal{O}(S_t, \varsigma_t, t)}{\partial S_t}\mu_t S_t + \frac{1}{2}\frac{\partial^2 \mathcal{O}(S_t, \varsigma_t, t)}{\partial S_t^2}\varsigma_t^2 S_t^2 \\ &\quad + \frac{\partial \mathcal{O}(S_t, \varsigma_t, t)}{\partial \varsigma_t}\phi(\varsigma_t, t) + \frac{1}{2}\frac{\partial^2 \mathcal{O}(S_t, \varsigma_t, t)}{\partial \varsigma_t^2}\nu(\varsigma_t, t)^2 \\ &\quad + \frac{\partial^2 \mathcal{O}(S_t, \varsigma_t, t)}{\partial S_t \partial \varsigma_t}\rho\varsigma_t S_t \nu(\varsigma_t, t) + \frac{\partial \mathcal{O}(S_t, \varsigma, t)}{\partial t}\end{aligned}$$

Substitution of equation (2.20) into equation (2.6) yields

$$\begin{aligned}&\int_0^T [\mathcal{L}^{\mu,\rho,\phi,\nu}\mathcal{O}(S_\tau, \varsigma_\tau, \tau) - \alpha_\tau \widetilde{\mu}_\tau e^{-\int_0^\tau r_s^f ds}\widetilde{S}_\tau - \beta_\tau r_\tau^d D_\tau^d]d\tau \\ &+ \int_0^T \left[\frac{\partial \mathcal{O}(S_\tau, \varsigma_\tau, \tau)}{\partial S_t}\varsigma_\tau S_\tau - \alpha_\tau \varsigma_\tau e^{-\int_0^\tau r_s^f ds}\widetilde{S}_\tau\right]dW_\tau \\ &+ \int_0^T \left[\frac{\partial \mathcal{O}(S_\tau, \varsigma_\tau, \tau)}{\partial \varsigma_t}\nu(S_\tau, \tau)_\tau\right]dZ_\tau = 0\end{aligned} \tag{2.21}$$

It is clear that it is not possible to choose α and β such that equation (2.21) can be solved. The replication argument via the self-financing strategy cannot be applied, and the market is defined as *incomplete* in this case. Moreover, as a consequence of the market incompleteness, there is no unique equivalent martingale measure under which an arbitrage-free price can be calculated. One possible approach to make up for this situation is to assume that an equivalent probability measure Q exists, under which the discounted price $\widetilde{S}_t^* = \widetilde{S}_t / D_t^d$ is a martingale for some time T. Thus, by an application of Girsanov's theorem, we have

$$dS_t = (r_t^d - r_t^f)S_t dt + \varsigma_t S_t dW_t^Q$$

where

$$d\varsigma_t = \widetilde{\phi}(\varsigma_t, t)dt + \nu(\varsigma_t, t)dZ_t^Q$$

with

$$\widetilde{\phi}(\varsigma_t, t) = \phi(\varsigma_t, t) - \lambda(\varsigma_t, t)\nu(\varsigma_t, t)$$

The additional term $\lambda(\varsigma_t, t)\nu(\varsigma_t, t)$, though a direct aftermath of the application of Girsanov's theorem, can be chosen in different ways. In practice, it will be specified in such a way that it allows for a convenient treatment of the model one wishes to design. It represents the *volatility risk premium*. As a result of the assumptions above, we have

Proposition 2.1.4. *Given a stochastic volatility economy setting, the martingale measure for the discounted FX rate is given by the Radon–Nikodym derivative:*

$$\frac{dQ}{dP} = \mathcal{Y}^T \mathcal{U}^T \tag{2.22}$$

$$\mathcal{Y}^T = \exp\left(\int_t^T \frac{r_s^d - \widetilde{\mu}_s}{\varsigma_s} dW_s - \int_t^T \frac{1}{2}\frac{(r_s^d - \widetilde{\mu}_s)^2}{\varsigma_s^2} ds\right) \tag{2.23}$$

$$\mathcal{U}^T = \exp\left(\int_t^T \lambda(\varsigma_s, s)dW_s - \int_t^T \frac{1}{2}\lambda(\varsigma_s, s)ds\right) \tag{2.24}$$

Under the probability measure Q the discounted FX rate process, whose solution is

$$\widetilde{S}_t^* = \widetilde{S}_0^* \exp\left(\int_t^T \varsigma_s dW_s^Q - \frac{1}{2}\int_t^T \varsigma_s^2 ds\right) \tag{2.25}$$

is a martingale.

We can derive the PDE whose solution, provided suitable terminal and boundary conditions are met, is the price of the contingent claim in a stochastic volatility world. In fact, we can still use the Feynman–Kac formula (2.13) for the new risk-neutral process and then infer the PDE, which is

$$\mathcal{L}^{(r_t^d - r_t^f),\rho,\widetilde{\phi},\nu}\mathcal{O}(S_\tau, \varsigma_\tau, \tau) - r_t^d \mathcal{O}(S_\tau, \varsigma_\tau, \tau) = 0 \tag{2.26}$$

2.1.3 Change of numeraire

The main point of the theory examined above is to find an equivalent probability measure under which the discounted price of the FX rate (net of the foreign accrued interest) is a martingale. We have implicitly assumed changing the numeraire of the original price and expressing it with respect to another one that, in the specific case, is the domestic deposit. This approach can be extended (and actually, has been, see Geman *et al.* [31] and Jamshidian [40]) to include any kind of numeraire, so as to make as convenient as possible the pricing of contingent claims according to their distinctive features. The theory of change of numeraire is particularly useful in the interest rate derivatives' evaluation, but it turns out that we will occasionally resort to it, so it is worth reviewing briefly here. We present the main concepts and results, whereas for a more thorough treatment we refer, for example, to Brigo and Mercurio [14].

As mentioned above, a numeraire can be any traded (non-dividend-paying) asset, and it can be used to normalize the prices of all other assets and contingent claims. The main result, due to Geman *et al.* [31], is that any self-financing strategy remains self-financing under any possible numeraire. In fact, if V_t is the value of a self-financing strategy:

$$dV_t = \alpha_t S_t + \beta_t D_t^d$$

implies

$$d\frac{V_t}{Z_t} = \alpha_t \frac{S_t}{Z_t} + \beta_t \frac{D_t^d}{Z_t}$$

so that any attainable claim can be replicated under any numeraire. We then have the following fundamental result:

Proposition 2.1.5. *If there is a numeraire Q and a related probability measure P^Q (equivalent to the real-world measure P) under which any asset's price S is a martingale:*

$$\frac{S_t}{Q_t} = E^Q\left[\frac{S_T}{Q_T}|\mathcal{F}_t\right]$$

then there exists a numeraire asset U and a related probability measure P^U (equivalent to the real one P), such that any attainable claim, whose price is $\mathcal{O}$, normalized by U, is a martingale under P^U:

$$\frac{\mathcal{O}_t}{U_t} = E^U\left[\frac{\mathcal{O}_T}{U_T}|\mathcal{F}_t\right]$$

The Radon–Nikodym derivative defining the new probability measure P^U is

$$\frac{dP^U}{dP^Q} = \frac{U_T Q_0}{U_0 Q_T}$$

The proof of the proposition is in Geman *et al.* [31]. As an immediate consequence, a useful formula can be derived, which allows us to compute in a very simple way the drift of any asset shifting from a numeraire Q to another numeraire U:

Proposition 2.1.6. *Assume we have two asset prices Q and U, evolving under the probability measure P^U according to the SDEs*

$$dQ_t = \mu_t^Q(Q_t)dt + \varsigma_t^Q C dW_t^U$$
$$dU_t = \mu_t^U(U_t)dt + \varsigma_t^U C dW_t^U$$

where ς_t^Q and ς_t^U are $1 \times n$ vectors, W_t^U is a standard Brownian motion, and $CC' = \rho$. The drift of a claim X is $\mu^Q(X)$ under the probability measure Q. Moving from the probability measure P^Q to the probability measure P^U implies a new drift equal to

$$\mu_t^U(X_t) = \mu_t^Q(X_t) - \varsigma_t^X \rho \left(\frac{\varsigma_t^Q}{Q_t} - \frac{\varsigma_t^U}{U_t}\right) \tag{2.27}$$

This formula was derived in Brigo and Mercurio [14], and we refer to them for the complete proof. We would like only to stress that it is a simple and powerful tool that can be employed when it is more convenient to change the numeraire to allow for a less painful achievement of a pricing formula.

2.2 THE BLACK–SCHOLES MODEL

In Section 2.1 we examined how to evaluate a contingent claim in a BS economy, so here we can provide the pricing formula for FX plain vanilla options derived within that environment. The formula was derived for the first time by Black and Scholes [9], although it was generalized by Merton [51] and this generalization is used to evaluate FX options (actually, just for historical precision's sake, the application of the BS framework to the FX markets was studied by Garman and Kohlhagen [30]).

Assume that at time t we want to price a European FX option expiring at time T, the spot FX rate being S_t. By formula (2.14), evaluating the (risk-neutral) present value of the terminal payoff (i.e., $\max[S_T - K, 0]$ for a call and $\max[K - S_T, 0]$ for a put), we have

$$\begin{aligned} \mathcal{O}(S_t, t) &= \mathrm{Bl}(S_t, t, T, K, P^d(t,T), P^f(t,T), \sigma, \omega) \\ &= P^d(t,T)\,[\omega F(t,T)\Phi(\omega d_1) - \omega K\,\Phi(\omega d_2)] \end{aligned} \tag{2.28}$$

where

$$d_1 = \frac{\ln \frac{F(t,T)}{K} + \frac{\sigma^2}{2}(T-t)}{\sigma\sqrt{T-t}}$$

$$d_2 = d_1 - \sigma\sqrt{T-t}$$

and $\Phi(x)$ is the normal cumulative distribution function calculated in x.[6] We are still working in a deterministic interest rate setting, so that $D^n_t / D^n_T = P^n(t,T)$, for $n \in \{d, f\}$. Formula (2.28) can be used to price call options by setting the parameter $\omega = 1$; if one needs to price a put, then $\omega = -1$. The FX spot rate enters into the formula via the FX forward price (outright):

$$F(t,T) = S_t \frac{P^f(t,T)}{P^d(t,T)}$$

where the price of the zero-coupon bond maturing at the option's expiry can be retrieved and calculated from the money market rates. The parameter σ is the implied volatility, and is equal to

$$\sigma = \sqrt{\frac{\int_t^T \varsigma_s^2 ds}{T-t}}$$

It is important because it is a tool to express the market prices of the options, since the BS formula is monotone in σ. In the following chapters much analysis will be devoted to the implied volatility and the implications of market practices related to it. In what follows, to lighten the notation, we will omit the arguments of the Bl function where this can be done with no loss of precision.

Although the BS model suffers many flaws, it is still often used, at least for quoting purposes. In the FX options market, option prices are quoted in terms of implied volatilities. The Delta hedge to be exchanged between counterparties is calculated according to the BS formula, and this is true also for the Vega hedge for exotic options. In many cases, the model is also employed to run the trading books. Thus, we also provide below the derivatives and sensitivities of the BS formula to the relevant variables and parameters (also known as the "Greeks''), since they are commonly used in market activity.

---

[6] The evaluation of $\Phi(x)$ can be performed by means of numerical integration or analytical approximations; see, for example, Abramowitz and Stegun [1].

2.2.1 The forward price to use in the formula

We have seen in Chapter 1, Remark 1.2.2, that when the default risk is taken into account, the forward prices implied by the FX swap prices can be (significantly) different from those implied by the outright contracts and set as in formula (1.1). In this formula we use the zero-coupon prices derived from the deposit interest rates (e.g., Euribor for the EUR, or Libor for the USD), but we should be aware that these rates are referring to a contract by which one party lends an amount of money for a given period to another party, and is fully exposed for the entire amount to the risk of default of the latter. We saw that an FX swap contract can actually be considered as a collateralized loan, by either party, so we can expect that interest rates to set the forward price will be different from those to set the forward price of an outright contract. This reflects the specific (lower) risk borne for default in an FX swap contract.

In the pricing formula (2.28) we have to use the forward price implied by the FX swap contract, since we can use them for hedging purposes (and actually we should use them, since they are less risky than an outright contract). Although it is beyond the scope of this book, we sketch here a method to include the default risk in the analysis and determine the "pure'' interest rates and then those related to the FX swap contracts, and which of them we have to input in formula (2.28). We start by assuming the following:

- All market operators (i.e., counterparties) have the same probability of default in a given period of time, starting from t and ending at T.
- The loss $L_{\{.\}}$ borne on the notional amount of the contract is the same for each counterparty, so the recovery rate is $R_{\{.\}} = 1 - L_{\{.\}}$ and depends on the currency the notional is denominated in (the subscripts will then be d or f, depending on whether the loss (or recovery) refers to the domestic or the foreign amount).

These assumptions are quite reasonable if we consider financial institutions participating in the interbank market as counterparties. We denote by $Q(t, T) = E[\mathbf{1}_{\tau_t > T} | \mathcal{F}_t]$ the survival probability of the generic counterparty at time t up to time T (τ_t is the default time, which could be time-dependent). The probability of default is simply $1 - Q(t, T)$.

We want to determine the fair forward price of an FX swap starting at t and expiring at T. We just choose to evaluate the present value of the contract in domestic currency units, and sum all the cash flows of the "buy and sell back 1 unit of foreign currency" contract. In calculating the present value of the cash flows, we consider also the default risk related to the counterparty:

$$\mathbf{Fsw}^f(t, T) = +1 - P^f_{rf}(t, T)[1\ Q(t, T) + R_f(1 - Q(t, T))] \tag{2.29}$$

Equation (2.29) is the sum of one unit of foreign currency today, plus the expected value at time T of one unit of foreign currency discounted at the risk-free rate (whence the subscript rf for the zero-coupon price). The expected value at T is in square brackets and is equal to one, weighted by the survival probability, plus the recovery received if the counterparty goes bankrupt, weighted by the default probability. The domestic currency leg's present value is similarly derived:

$$\mathbf{Fsw}^d(t, T) = -S_t + F(t, T)P^d_{rf}(t, T)[1\ Q(t, T) + R_d(1 - Q(t, T))] \tag{2.30}$$

The net present value in domestic currency units at time t is

$$\begin{aligned}\mathbf{Fsw}(t,T) = S_t\big(1 - P^f_{rf}(t,T)[1\,Q(t,T) + R_d(1-Q(t,T))]\big) \\ -S_t + F(t,T)P^d_{rf}(t,T)[1\,Q(t,T) + R_f(1-Q(t,T))]\end{aligned} \tag{2.31}$$

By setting equation (2.31) equal to zero, we have that the forward price of an FX swap contract is

$$F(t,T) = S_t \frac{P^f_{rf}(t,T)[1\,Q(t,T) + R_d(1-Q(t,T))]}{P^d_{rf}(t,T)[1\,Q(t,T) + R_f(1-Q(t,T))} \tag{2.32}$$

We can draw some conclusions from equation (2.32):

1. If the recovery rates are equal for the two counterparties involved, then the forward price has the same value as that determined by just using risk-free zero-coupon bonds. In other words, the default risks of the two counterparties are symmetrical and perfectly counterbalance each other, so that the net result is the same as in an economy with no default risk.
2. The risk-free zero-coupon bonds can be computed by means of the OIS swap rates. The rate underlying these contracts is the overnight interbank rate, which embeds the risk of default for just one day, so that it can safely be neglected and the rate considered risk-free.
3. It is possible to retrieve from market prices the (FX swap) forward prices $F(t,T)$ for different expiries and the risk-free zero-coupon bonds, so that calibrating to all the available prices (under the given assumptions), in theory one could derive the market-implied default probabilities, recovery rates and zero-coupon prices.

In conclusion, we just apply the following rules to identify the inputs of formula (2.28).

- The forward price is that calculated (in theory) as in formula (2.32) and implied from FX swap prices.
- The discounting (by means of the domestic zero-coupon price outside the square brackets in formula (2.28)) is performed with the zero-coupon prices $P^d(t,T)$ based on the Euribor rates. In this case we are assuming that the default risk borne by the buyer of the option is the same as that for the buyer of a deposit in the interbank market.
- If we think that the default risk is not the same as that of a deposit, then we should use a different interest rate. For example, amongst professional operators (mainly financial institutions), daily or weekly margining agreements, for OTC contracts, are usually active so that the counterparty risk is dramatically, or even totally, removed. So, for options traded in the interbank market, it could be more appropriate to substitute $P^d(t,T)$ with $P^d_{rf}(t,T)$ (where $P^d_{rf}(t,T)$ is extracted from the OIS swap prices) outside the square brackets in formula (2.32).

2.2.2 BS Greeks

We start with Delta, or the first derivative of the option price with respect to the underlying FX spot rate:

$$\Delta(S_t, t, T, K, P^d(t,T), P^f(t,T), \sigma, \omega) = \Delta_t = \frac{\partial \text{Bl}}{\partial S_t} = \omega P^f(t,T)\Phi(\omega d_1) \tag{2.33}$$

Mathematically speaking, Delta is the ratio of the variation of the price of the option to an infinitesimal variation of the FX spot rate. Financially speaking, Delta is the amount of base currency units, expressed as a percentage of the (base currency) notional, equivalent to the position in the option. If a trader wants to be hedged against the movements of the underlying FX rate, they have to trade on the market a spot contract with equal amount and opposite sign to Delta.

It is probably worth making some more remarks on the relationships between the base and numeraire currency amounts. Firstly, suppose we are dealing in the XXXYYY pair. It is clear that Δ_t XXX units (i.e., Delta in equation (2.33)) are worth $-\Delta_t S_t$ YYY. If a trader wishes to express this as a percentage of the numeraire currency amount, it suffices to divide it by the strike price, i.e., $-\Delta_t S_t/K$.

Secondly, in Chapter 1 we listed the different ways to express the premium of an FX option. Market conventions are to have premiums as p_{numccy} for some pairs and $p_{baseccy\%}$ for others. Delta in equation (2.33) is referred to as the p_{numccy} case, and determines the amount of the base currency in the hedge FX spot transaction. If premiums are traded as $p_{baseccy\%}$ things change slightly, since now the premium (i.e., the option's value) to be hedged is in base currency (XXX) units, so that the hedging instrument should no longer be the XXXYYY pair (whose trading generates profits and losses in YYY units) but the reverse YYYXXX pair (whose trading generates profits in XXX units) as we need to cover variations in XXX units. Let $S' = 1/S$ and assume the premium is $p_{baseccy\%}$. Delta with respect to S' is then (recalling also the definition of $p_{baseccy\%}$):

$$\frac{\partial(0.01p_{baseccy\%})}{\partial S'_t} = \frac{\partial[\text{Bl}(1/S'_t)S'_t]}{\partial S'_t} = -\Delta_t \frac{1}{S'^2_t} S'_t + \text{Bl}(1/S'_t) = -\frac{\Delta_t}{S'_t} + \text{Bl}(1/S'_t)$$

This quantity indicates how much a trader has to hold in YYY units to hedge the option's value, $0.01p_{baseccy\%}$. When trading the option, it is a market convention to still express the spot hedge transaction as a percentage of the base (according to the standard quotation of the pair) currency notional, so that we convert the amount above into XXX (clearly reversing the sign also) and finally yield

$$\Delta_t^{pi} = -\frac{1}{S_t}\left[-\frac{\Delta_t}{S'_t} + \text{Bl}(1/S'_t)\right] = \Delta_t - \frac{\text{Bl}(1/S'_t)}{S_t} = \Delta_t - 0.01p_{baseccy\%} \tag{2.34}$$

Hence, if the premium is quoted in $p_{baseccy\%}$, this amount (divided by 100) is deducted from the standard Delta. This is usually called the *premium-included Delta* (whence the superscript pi). Equation (2.35) can be written explicitly as

$$\Delta_t^{pi} = \omega\frac{K}{S_t}P^d(t,T)\Phi(\omega d_2) \tag{2.35}$$

Remark 2.2.1. *The premium-adjusted Delta is used amongst professionals when the premium is expressed as $p_{baseccy\%}$ to determine the amount of the hedge spot transaction (and the absolute levels of the strike corresponding to Delta, in this case). One may wonder which Delta should be used when rebalancing the hedging after the initial trade. In this case, market conventions can be disregarded and the trader has to consider what they are really trying to hedge. We will make this point clear with the following example.*

Suppose we are trading a EURUSD option. We know that the market standard for plain vanilla options is to express the premium as p_{numccy} so that the exchanged Delta amount will be with no premium adjustment. We also know that all the variations in the option's value and the terminal payoff (i.e., all the profits and losses) are in the numeraire (domestic) *currency – US dollars. If a trader's book is revalued in US dollars and its profits and losses are computed in US dollars (as is the case if they are located in the USA), then they can keep on hedging their book according to the standard Delta hedge in equation* (2.33)*, since in this case this is exactly the amount of euros to trade (with opposite sign) to match the changes in option values in US dollars.*

If the trader is located in Europe, then their book's profits and losses are very likely computed in euros, so what they really aim at is hedging the option values converted into euros. Hence, if $\mathbf{bv}$ *is the book value in US dollars and S is the EURUSD FX spot rate,* $\mathbf{bv}/S$ *is the book value converted into euros and the Europe-based trader wishes to hedge the changes in the latter amount:* $\partial(\mathbf{bv}/S)/\partial S$*. But this is just what the premium-adjusted Delta in equation* (2.35) *measures, and this amount should be used when rebalancing the hedge amount in euros.*

In summary, apart from the market standards that will command the initial FX spot amount to trade for hedging, in the running of the book the two different kinds of Delta can be used according to the actual hedging targets of the traders. In the example above, the US-based trader will hedge by the standard Delta's indications, whereas the Europe-based trader will hedge the premium-adjusted Delta's suggestions.

Delta is a good approximation for the change of the value only for small movements of the FX spot rate. Gamma (i.e., the second derivative of the option's price with respect to the underlying price) is used to gauge how much Delta would change according to the FX rate:

$$\Gamma(S_t, t, T, K, P^d(t,T), P^f(t,T), \sigma, \omega) = \Gamma_t = \frac{\partial^2 \mathrm{Bl}}{\partial S_t^2} = \frac{\omega P^f(t,T)\varphi(d_1)}{S_t \sigma \sqrt{T-t}} \tag{2.36}$$

with

$$\varphi(x) = \Phi'(x) = \frac{1}{\sqrt{2\pi}} e^{-\frac{x^2}{2}}$$

If the premium is included in Delta, then Gamma is

$$\Gamma^{pi}(S_t, t, T, K, P^d(t,T), P^f(t,T), \sigma, \omega) = \Gamma(S_t, t, T, K, P^d(t,T), P^f(t,T), \sigma, \omega)$$
$$-\frac{\Delta(S_t, t, T, K, P^d(t,T), P^f(t,T), \sigma, \omega)}{S_t} + 2\frac{0.01 p_{baseccy\%}}{S_t} \tag{2.37}$$

Usually, Gamma is expressed so as to indicate how much Delta changes given a variation of the FX spot rate. Typically, this will be taken equal to 1%, so we have

$$\Gamma_t^{tr} = \Gamma_t \frac{S_t}{100} \tag{2.38}$$

which is sometimes referred to as the *trader's Gamma*.

Delta and Gamma are tools to hedge exposure to the FX rate changes. In the BS model that should be enough to perfectly match all the sources of risk. In reality, market operators use the BS formula in more elaborate, and somehow inconsistent, ways due to their scepticism about the ability of the model to fully and exhaustively depict the complexity of the true world. That is why traders resort to derivatives with respect to the parameters of formula (2.28) (besides the variable S_t), so as to cover the exposure to them although, according to the starting assumptions of the model, they are not variables and should not be hedged at all.

The main source of risk is originated by the volatility. In the BS model it is simply considered a deterministic function of time, but actually implied volatilities change in a manner not consistent with this hypothesis (without considering at the moment the smile effect that we will introduce later on in the analysis). As such, traders wish to calculate the exposure to the implied volatility by Vega:

$$\mathcal{V}(S_t, t, T, K, P^d(t,T), P^f(t,T), \sigma, \omega) = \mathcal{V}_t = \frac{\partial \mathrm{Bl}}{\partial \sigma} = P^f(t,T)S_t\sqrt{T-t}\varphi(d_1) \tag{2.39}$$

The hedging can be carried out via other instruments whose value depends on the implied volatility as well, mainly other options. Nonetheless, since an option's Vega changes when the implied volatility varies, traders want to estimate the stability of their hedge and they employ Volga, i.e., the derivative of Vega with respect to the implied volatility:

$$\begin{aligned}\mathcal{W}(S_t, t, T, K, P^d(t,T), P^f(t,T), \sigma, \omega) = \mathcal{W}_t &= \frac{\partial^2 \mathrm{Bl}}{\partial \sigma^2}\\ &= \frac{P^f(t,T)S_t\varphi(d_1)d_1d_2\sqrt{T-t}}{\sigma}\end{aligned} \tag{2.40}$$

Volga is analogous to Gamma for the volatility (in fact, the name stands for "volatility Gamma"). But there is still another dependence of Vega on market variables; that is, it changes along with the FX spot rate movements. This relationship is measured via Vanna:

$$\begin{aligned}\mathcal{X}(S_t, t, T, K, P^d(t,T), P^f(t,T), \sigma, \omega) = \mathcal{X}_t &= \frac{\partial^2 \mathrm{Bl}}{\partial \sigma \partial S_t}\\ &= -\frac{P^f(t,T)\varphi(d_1)d_2}{\sigma}\end{aligned} \tag{2.41}$$

When the premium is included in Delta, Vanna is modified as follows:

$$\begin{aligned}\mathcal{X}^{pi}(S_t, t, T, K, P^d(t,T), P^f(t,T), \sigma, \omega) &= \mathcal{X}(S_t, t, T, K, P^d(t,T), P^f(t,T), \sigma, \omega)\\ &\quad -\frac{\mathcal{V}(S_t, t, T, K, P^d(t,T), P^f(t,T), \sigma, \omega)}{S_t}\end{aligned} \tag{2.42}$$

These three volatility-related derivatives are fundamental tools; their relation to the volatility smile, their use in the volatility plays and their application in the global hedging of an option's book will be examined in depth in the next chapters.

Another two sensitivities are momentous for risk management: the domestic and foreign Rhos. These are derivatives of the option price with respect to, respectively, the domestic and foreign interest rates:

$$\begin{aligned}\mathrm{Rho}^d(S_t, t, T, K, P^d(t,T), P^f(t,T), \sigma, \omega) = \mathrm{Rho}_t^d &= \frac{\partial \mathrm{Bl}_t}{\partial \overline{r}^d}\\ &= \omega K(T-t)P^d(t,T)\Phi(\omega d_2)\end{aligned} \tag{2.43}$$

$$\begin{aligned}\mathrm{Rho}^f(S_t, t, T, K, P^d(t,T), P^f(t,T), \sigma, \omega) = \mathrm{Rho}_t^f &= \frac{\partial \mathrm{Bl}}{\partial \overline{r}^f}\\ &= -\omega(T-t)P^f(t,T)S_t\Phi(\omega d_1)\end{aligned} \tag{2.44}$$

It is worth noticing that we have calculated the derivatives with respect to an average rate $\overline{r}^c = (\int_t^T r_s^c ds)/(T-t)$, with $c \in \{d, f\}$. This is possible since, in the BS model, the interest rates are deterministic functions of time. The approach is exactly the same as in the implied volatility case, which can be considered as an average instantaneous volatility.

2.2.3 Retrieving implied volatility and strike

As already mentioned, the BS formula is used as a benchmark in the market to calculate the price of plain vanilla options and to some extent also in trading barrier options. Premiums of European options are generally quoted in terms of implied volatility σ to plug into formula (2.28), but it may happen that we receive a quote in terms of premiums, so one wants to know which is the corresponding implied volatility, all other variables and parameters being fixed at given levels.

Unfortunately, formula (2.28) cannot be inverted to calculate σ analytically, and a numerical procedure must be employed to back it out. A Newton–Raphson or secant method can be implemented, and the result within a given degree of accuracy can be achieved in a few steps. The starting point may be set as follows:[7]

$$\sigma = \sqrt{\frac{2}{\tau}\frac{F(t,T)}{K}}$$

where $\tau = T - t$. Alternatively, one may choose the following:[8]

$$\sigma\sqrt{\tau} = \frac{\sqrt{2\pi}}{S_t P^f(t,T) - KP^d(t,T)}\Bigg(\mathcal{O}_t - \frac{1}{2}(S_t P^f(t,T) - KP^d(t,T)) + \sqrt{\left(\mathcal{O}_t + \frac{1}{2}(S_t P^f(t,T) - KP^d(t,T))\right)^2 - \frac{1}{\pi}(S_t P^f(t,T) - KP^d(t,T))}\Bigg)$$

In Chapter 1 we mentioned that FX options are usually quoted with reference to a strike level expressed in terms of Delta. Once the option is traded and the FX spot reference rate and the implied volatility are fixed, then the absolute level of the strike can be retrieved by setting

$$\omega P^f(t,T)\Phi(\omega d_1) = \overline{\Delta} \tag{2.45}$$

which immediately leads to

$$K = F(t,T)\exp\left[-\omega\sigma\sqrt{\tau}\Phi^{-1}\left(\left|\overline{\Delta}\right|/P^f(t,T)\right) + 0.5\sigma^2\tau\right] \tag{2.46}$$

where, as usual, $\omega = 1$ (respectively, $\omega = -1$) if a call (put) option is involved, Φ^{-1} is the inverse of the normal distribution function, and the values σ and $\overline{\Delta}$ are the required inputs. It is worth noticing that Delta enters into the formula as its absolute value.

Formula (2.46) yields the correct result when Delta is the standard one in equation (2.33). If the market quoting conventions imply a premium-included Delta, then one must resort to a numerical, though fast, procedure (based on the Newton–Raphson scheme), since the option

[7] This starting point was proposed by Manaster and Koehler [47].

[8] This approximation was proposed by Corrado and Miller [23].

premium entering into Delta is a function of the strike itself. We outline the procedure as follows:

Procedure 2.2.1. *To retrieve the strike corresponding to a given level of premium-included Delta* $\Delta_t^{pi} = \overline{\Delta}$ *and a given level of volatility* $\overline{\sigma}$*:*

1. *Set the initial strike at a given level* $K^i = \overline{K}$ *for* $i = 0$*. This is the value calculated by equation* (2.46).
2. *Calculate the option's value*

$$\mathcal{O}^i = Bl(S_t, t, T, K^i, P^d(t,T), P^f(t,T), \overline{\sigma}, \omega)$$

   and the corresponding Δ^i *(this is the usual Delta and not the premium-included one).*

3. *Calculate the option's premium-adjusted Delta derivatives with respect to the strike. We do this numerically by evaluating the option at a slightly different strike (say* $1.01K^i$*):*

$$\widetilde{\mathcal{O}}^i = Bl(S_t, t, T, 1.01K^i, P^d(t,T), P^f(t,T), \overline{\sigma}, \omega)$$

   and the corresponding $\widetilde{\Delta}^i$*, so that:*[9]

$$Delta = \frac{\partial \Delta^{pi}}{\partial K} = \frac{\widetilde{\Delta}^i - \widetilde{\mathcal{O}}_t^i / S_t - (\Delta^i - \mathcal{O}_t^i / S_t)}{0.01K^i}$$

4. *Calculate the strike* K^{i+1} *as*

$$K^{i+1} = K^i - \frac{\Delta^i - \mathcal{O}^i / S_t - \overline{\Delta}}{Delta}$$

5. *Iterate until* $|K^{i+1} - K^i| < \epsilon$*, where* ϵ *is a tolerance error parameter. Usually, three iterations are enough to achieve a satisfactory degree of accuracy for practical purposes.*

Example 2.2.1. *Assume we want to calculate the strike corresponding to the 25D USD put JPY call for six-month expiry* ($\tau = \frac{182}{365}$)*. The spot rate is* 103.00 *and the implied volatility used is* 10.25%*. We also set the domestic and foreign discount factors (zero-coupon bonds) equal, respectively, to* $P^d(0, 6M) = 0.99482$ *and* $P^f(0, 6M) = 0.98508$*. The strike is equal to* 97.47 *if the premium is in JPY units, and* 97.22 *if it is in USD %, as it actually is according to market conventions.*

Remark 2.2.2. *The inclusion of the premium into Delta has some consequences that are worth considering. In Figure 2.1 we plot the standard BS Delta and the premium-included Delta for a base currency call, with the following data:* $S_t = 1.5000$, $\tau = T - t = 0.5$, $P^d(t,T) = 0.97531$, $P^f(t,T) = 0.98265$ *and* $\sigma = 10\%$*. The figure shows that the premium-included Delta can never be higher than a standard Delta, and some levels are produced by two strikes, since the function is not monotonic. This could engender a problem when running Procedure 2.2.1, since for some premium-included Delta values it may converge to one of the two possible solutions. Although in mathematical terms this is true, in practice the procedure converges to the one strike that is also accepted in the market as referred to the given level of Delta. In fact, either (i) we search for a level never achieved by the premium-included Delta function (for example,* 95% *in the figure), so that no strike exists yielding such a value; or*

[9] One can actually calculate the derivative of Delta analytically with respect to the strike, although there is no real improvement in the efficiency of the procedure since all the inputs we need at step i have already been computed at step $i - 1$.

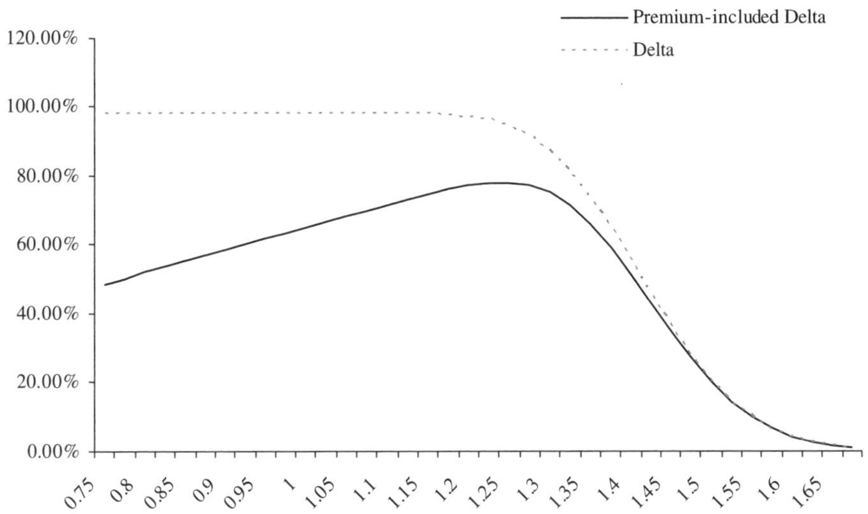

Figure 2.1 Standard BS Delta and premium-included Delta for a base currency call option

(ii) we search for a value that is in the range of the premium-included Delta function (for example, 75% in the figure). In this case the first guess (the strike corresponding to a standard Delta) is always higher than the solution(s) we are looking for, and the procedure will always stop at the nearest lower level of strike yielding the desired premium-included Delta value. This is the strike accepted in the market and the second (mathematically valid) solution is discarded (actually it is never reached by the procedure, setting the starting value of the strike as prescribed).

When a base currency put option is considered, we have no such problem. Figure 2.2 shows the standard BS Delta and the premium-included Delta for this kind of option, using the same data as above for the base currency call. It is manifest that the monotonic behaviour of both functions poses no ambiguity in the convergence of Procedure 2.2.1.

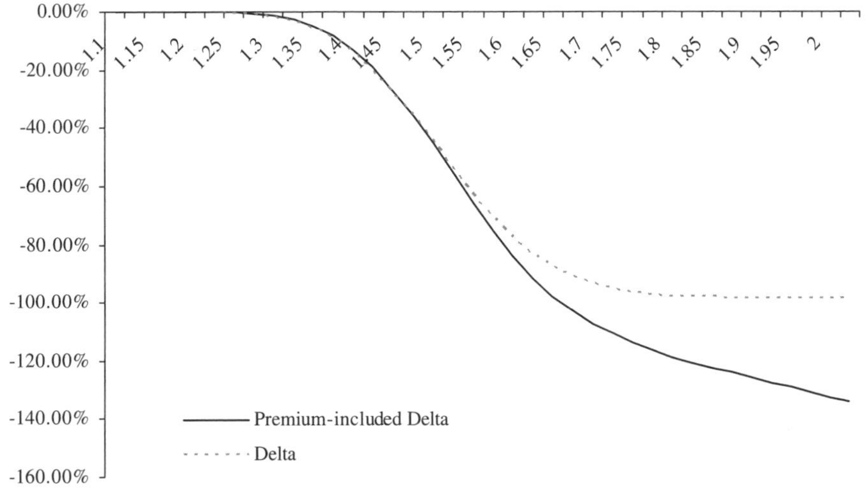

Figure 2.2 Standard BS Delta and premium-included Delta for a base currency put option

2.2.4 Some relationships of the BS formula

There is a simple relationship linking the call and put option, also known as *put–call parity*:

$$\mathbf{C}(K, T) = \mathbf{P}(K, T) + S_t P^f(t, T) - P^d(t, T)K \tag{2.47}$$

This can be proved directly by the pricing formula for call and put (2.28), or by a no-arbitrage argument: the put–call parity is model-independent. A similar relationship is the *put–call symmetry*:[10]

$$\begin{aligned}\mathrm{Bl}(S_t, t, T, K, P^d(t, T), P^f(t, T), \sigma, 1) = \\ \mathrm{Bl}(K, t, T, S_t, P^f(t, T), P^d(t, T), \sigma, -1)\end{aligned} \tag{2.48}$$

This relationship may seem a rather idle mathematical trick, but it can actually be useful in some situations to derive the pricing formula of particular kinds of options and to hedge knock-in options (although under a number of restrictive assumptions), as we will show later on. In fact, in practical applications, it is more effective to employ the following version of the put–call symmetry:

$$\begin{aligned}\mathrm{Bl}(S_t, t, T, K, P^d(t, T), P^f(t, T), \sigma, 1) = \\ \frac{K}{S_t}\mathrm{Bl}(S_t, t, T, S_t^2/K, P^f(t, T), P^d(t, T), \sigma, -1)\end{aligned} \tag{2.49}$$

which is a direct consequence of equation (2.48) and of the straightforward manipulation: $\max[S_t - K, 0] = K/S_t \max[S_t^2/K - S_t, 0]$. The reason why equation (2.49) is much more useful to practitioners is clear: it is possible (although sometimes not easy) to trade an option struck at S_t^2/K in an amount (K/S_t) with an FX spot rate equal to S_t, whereas it would be impossible to trade it with the FX spot set equal to K (unless $K = S_t$).

A relationship specific to the FX options market is the *foreign–domestic symmetry*, which is an application of the put–call symmetry:

$$\begin{aligned}\frac{1}{S_t}\mathrm{Bl}(S_t, t, T, K, P^d(t, T), P^f(t, T), \sigma, 1) = \\ K\mathrm{Bl}(1/S_t, t, T, 1/K, P^f(t, T), P^d(t, T), \sigma, -1)\end{aligned} \tag{2.50}$$

Financially speaking, two traders trading the same option must agree on the value, even if each one considers the FX rate from their own perspective. For the sake of clarity, consider an FX spot rate S_t for the pair XXXYYY and an XXX Call YYY Put option struck at K, whose price is $p_{numccy} = \mathrm{Bl}(S_t, t, T, K, P^d(t, T), P^f(t, T), \sigma, 1)$ in YYY units, which can be converted into base currency units, yielding $\frac{1}{S_t}\mathrm{Bl}(S_t, t, T, K, P^d(t, T), P^f(t, T), \sigma, 1)$ XXX. Assume now that a trader is based in the country where the base currency is in use (the foreign country) and that they want to express the FX rate as if the original base currency were the numeraire one. Then they have the FX rate YYYXXX $= 1/S_t$, with the domestic bond now being P^f and the foreign bond being P^d. The option above can now be considered a YYY put XXX call struck at $1/K$ and in an amount equal to K YYY (=1 XXX). The option can be priced by the same σ parameter since the processes of S_t and $1/S_t$ both have the same volatility, thus justifying equation (2.50), because the two prices of the option must be equal under economic and mathematical points of view.

The BS enjoys some other properties that can sometimes be useful. We just focus on a couple of them, which we will make use of in the subsequent analysis. Firstly we notice that

[10] The put–call symmetry was derived for the first time by Bjerksund and Stensland [8].

the formula is time-homogeneous, since it depends on time t only via the time to maturity $\tau = T - t$. Then we have

$$\frac{\partial \mathrm{Bl}}{\partial t} = -\frac{\partial \mathrm{Bl}}{\partial \tau} \tag{2.51}$$

Secondly, replacing $\overline{r}^d$, $\overline{r}^f$, σ and τ with

$$\overline{r}^d \rightarrow \overline{r}^d \varphi \tag{2.52}$$
$$\overline{r}^f \rightarrow \overline{r}^f \varphi \tag{2.53}$$
$$\sigma \rightarrow \sigma \sqrt{\varphi} \tag{2.54}$$
$$\tau \rightarrow \frac{\tau}{\varphi} \tag{2.55}$$

where φ is a strictly positive real number, the option's price does not change:

$$\begin{aligned}\mathrm{Bl}(S_t, t, T, K, P^d(t, T)\ \ , P^f(t, T), \sigma, \omega) = \\ \mathrm{Bl}(S_t, t/\varphi, T/\varphi, K, P^d(t, T; \phi), P^f(t, T; \phi), \sigma\sqrt{\varphi}, \omega)\end{aligned} \tag{2.56}$$

where $P^c(t, T; \varphi) = e^{-\overline{r}^c(T-t)/\phi}$, for $c \in \{d, f\}$, is calculated with the rescaled parameters. Differentiating both sides with respect to φ and setting $\varphi = 1$ yields

$$\frac{1}{2}\sigma\frac{\partial \mathrm{Bl}}{\partial \sigma} + \overline{r}^d \frac{\partial \mathrm{Bl}}{\partial \overline{r}^d} + \overline{r}^f \frac{\partial \mathrm{Bl}}{\partial \overline{r}^f} - \tau \frac{\partial \mathrm{Bl}}{\partial \tau} = 0$$

or equivalently by equation (2.51):

$$\frac{1}{2}\sigma\frac{\partial \mathrm{Bl}}{\partial \sigma} + \overline{r}^d \frac{\partial \mathrm{Bl}}{\partial \overline{r}^d} + \overline{r}^f \frac{\partial \mathrm{Bl}}{\partial \overline{r}^f} + \tau \frac{\partial \mathrm{Bl}}{\partial t} = 0 \tag{2.57}$$

This relationship was derived by Reiss and Wystup [56]. It is quite easy to verify, by direct calculation, that the following *interest rate symmetry* also holds:

$$\frac{\partial \mathrm{Bl}}{\partial \overline{r}^d} + \frac{\partial \mathrm{Bl}}{\partial \overline{r}^f} + \tau \mathrm{Bl} = 0 \tag{2.58}$$

Finally, we derive the *Vega–Gamma relationship*. From equation (2.12), and substituting the time-dependent interest rates with the average constant ones and the time-dependent instantaneous volatility with the implied volatility (i.e., an average constant parameter also in this case), we have

$$\frac{\partial \mathrm{Bl}}{\partial t} = \overline{r}^d \mathrm{Bl}(S_t, t) - \frac{\partial \mathrm{Bl}}{\partial S_t}(\overline{r}^d - \overline{r}^f)S_t - \frac{1}{2}\frac{\partial^2 \mathrm{Bl}(S_t, t)}{\partial S_t^2}\sigma S_t^2$$

which can be plugged into equation (2.57) to yield

$$\begin{aligned}&\frac{1}{2}\sigma\frac{\partial \mathrm{Bl}}{\partial \sigma} + \overline{r}^d \frac{\partial \mathrm{Bl}}{\partial \overline{r}^d} + \overline{r}^f \frac{\partial \mathrm{Bl}}{\partial \overline{r}^f} \\ &+\tau\left[\overline{r}^d \mathrm{Bl}(S_t, t) - \frac{\partial \mathrm{Bl}}{\partial S_t}(\overline{r}^d - \overline{r}^f)S_t - \frac{1}{2}\frac{\partial^2 \mathrm{Bl}(S_t, t)}{\partial S_t^2}\sigma^2 S_t^2\right] = 0\end{aligned}$$

Rearranging:

$$\frac{1}{2}\sigma\frac{\partial \mathrm{Bl}}{\partial\sigma} = \frac{\tau}{2}\frac{\partial^2 \mathrm{Bl}(S_t,t)}{\partial S_t^2}\sigma^2 S_t^2 + \frac{\partial \mathrm{Bl}}{\partial S_t}(\bar{r}^d - \bar{r}^f)\tau S_t - \bar{r}^f\frac{\partial \mathrm{Bl}}{\partial \bar{r}^f} - \bar{r}^d\left[\frac{\partial \mathrm{Bl}}{\partial \bar{r}^d} + \tau \mathrm{Bl}(S_t,t)\right]$$

and hence, by interest rate symmetry (2.58), we get the Vega–Gamma relationship

$$\frac{1}{2}\sigma\frac{\partial \mathrm{Bl}}{\partial\sigma} = \frac{\tau}{2}\frac{\partial^2 \mathrm{Bl}(S_t,t)}{\partial S_t^2}\sigma^2 S_t^2 + (\bar{r}^d - \bar{r}^f)\left[\tau S_t\frac{\partial \mathrm{Bl}}{\partial S_t} + \frac{\partial \mathrm{Bl}}{\partial \bar{r}^f}\right] \tag{2.59}$$

Equation (2.59) also holds for any claim with a path-dependent payoff (e.g., barrier options) as long as the interest rates and the volatility are constant.[11] For claims with a European payoff the trick of averaging the parameters does not impact on the pricing, so that a time dependency can be allowed. Actually, a further simplification is possible for European claims; in fact it can be checked that

$$\frac{\partial \mathrm{Bl}}{\partial \bar{r}^f} = -\tau S_t\frac{\partial \mathrm{Bl}}{\partial S_t}$$

so that equation (2.59) simplifies to

$$\frac{1}{2}\sigma\frac{\partial \mathrm{Bl}}{\partial\sigma} = \frac{\tau}{2}\frac{\partial^2 \mathrm{Bl}(S_t,t)}{\partial S_t^2}\sigma^2 S_t^2 \tag{2.60}$$

Many other relations for the BS formula can be found. Amongst them we deem rather useful to future analysis what we name the *Delta–Vega relationship*. In more detail, it can be stated that a call and a put option expiring at the same time T and struck such that the absolute value of Delta is the same for each, also have the same Vega:

$$\begin{aligned}&\left|\Delta(S_t,t,T,K_C,P^d(t,T),P^f(t,T),\sigma_C,1)\right| = \left|\Delta(S_t,t,T,K_P,P^d(t,T),P^f(t,T),\sigma_P,-1)\right|\\ &\longleftrightarrow\\ &\mathcal{V}(S_t,t,T,K_C,P^d(t,T),P^f(t,T),\sigma_C,1) = \mathcal{V}(S_t,t,T,K_P,P^d(t,T),P^f(t,T),\sigma_P,-1)\end{aligned} \tag{2.61}$$

Proof: From equation (2.45) we have, for a put option with a given Delta $\overline{\Delta}$, that

$$\omega d_1^P = \Phi^{-1}\left(\frac{\Delta}{P^f(t,T)\omega}\right) = \Phi^{-1}(\alpha) \tag{2.62}$$

or

$$d_1^P = -\Phi^{-1}(\alpha) \tag{2.63}$$

since $\omega = -1$ for put options. On the other hand, for a call option

$$d_1^C = \Phi^{-1}\left(\frac{\Delta}{P^f(t,T)}\right) = \Phi^{-1}(\alpha) \tag{2.64}$$

[11] In Chapter 6 we will show how to include time-dependent parameters in the BS setting, so that equation (2.59) still holds. We just hint here at the fact that the resulting formulae are only an approximation of the true price.

α is the same value in both cases, since $\omega = -1$ for put options and this always makes positive the ratio in the argument of the inverse normal distribution function, a put's Delta being negative. On the other hand, $\omega = 1$ for call options and it enters into the ratio with Delta always being a positive number. Therefore, d_1^c and d_1^p are equal in absolute value and have opposite sign. When plugged into formula (2.39) to calculate Vega, it is straightforward to check that the Delta–Vega relationship holds. □

Remark 2.2.3. *The Delta–Vega relationship holds only for strike levels entailing equal absolute pure Delta values. This means that when we consider a parity whose conventions provide for a premium-included Delta, equation* (2.61) *does not hold any more. This also has a practical impact on hedging policies, as we will see later on.*

2.3 THE HESTON MODEL

In Section 2.1 we examined how to extend the BS economy so as to allow for a stochastic instantaneous volatility. This feature will make the model more suitable to fitting market prices that, contrary to the BS assumption, do not exhibit a constant flat implied volatility with respect to strikes for a given expiry, thus implying a (possibly) stochastic instantaneous volatility. The specification of the process (2.19) may be manifold, and we focus on a few options amongst those commonly accepted by practitioners.

Heston [37] suggested a specification of the process (2.19) as follows:

$$d\varsigma_t^2 = \kappa[\theta - \varsigma_t^2]dt + \nu\varsigma_t dZ_t \tag{2.65}$$

This is a mean-reverting process for the instantaneous variance (ς^2) of Cox, Ingersoll and Ross [24]. It prevents negative values and this is a critical feature, since variance cannot be negative by its definition. The instantaneous correlation between the Brownian motion dZ_t and that entering into the FX spot process dW_t is ρ. If the volatility risk-premium is assumed to be equal to $\lambda\varsigma_t/\nu$, then the risk-adjusted process for the variance is

$$d\varsigma_t^2 = \{\kappa[\theta - \varsigma_t^2] - \lambda\varsigma_t^2\}dt + \nu\varsigma_t dZ_t^Q$$

We have to impose the constraint $2\kappa\theta > \nu^2$ so that the variance process never reaches zero and is always positive. We can apply formula (2.14) and yield the formula to value a call option. Actually, it is not easy to calculate the expected value of the terminal payoff, since the marginal (and also the transition) distribution of the FX spot rate is unknown in the Heston model. Anyway, the characteristic function can be derived and hence – by means of a numerical integration – the probabilities can also be calculated:[12]

$$\mathcal{O}(S_t, t, T, K, P^d(t,T), P^f(t,T), 1) = S_t\Pi_1 - K\frac{P^d(t,T)}{P^f(t,T)}\Pi_2 \tag{2.66}$$

where

$$\Pi_j = \frac{1}{2} + \frac{1}{\pi}\int_0^\infty Re\left[\frac{e^{-i\phi\ln[K]}f_j(x, \varsigma_t^2, \tau; \phi)}{i\phi}\right]d\phi$$

[12] For the complete derivation we refer to the article by Heston [37]. We use a simplified version of the FX call option shown there, in that the prices of the domestic and foreign bonds are not stochastic.

$$f_j = e^{L(\tau;\phi)+M(\tau;\phi)\varsigma_t^2+i\phi x}$$

$$L(\tau;\phi) = (r_t^d - r_t^f)\phi i\tau + \frac{a}{\nu^2}\left\{(b_j - \rho\nu\phi i + d)\tau - 2\ln\left[\frac{1-ge^{d\tau}}{1-g}\right]\right\}$$

$$M(\tau;\phi) = \frac{b_j - \rho\nu\phi i + d}{\nu^2}\left[\frac{1-e^{d\tau}}{1-ge^{d\tau}}\right]$$

$$g = \frac{b_j - \rho\nu\phi i + d}{b_j - \rho\nu\phi i - d}$$

$$d = \sqrt{(\rho\nu\phi i - b_j)^2 - \nu^2(2u_j\phi i - \phi^2)}$$

$$u_1 = 1/2; \quad u_2 = -1/2; \quad a = \kappa\theta; \quad b_1 = \kappa + \lambda - \rho\nu; \quad b_2 = \kappa + \lambda$$

for $j = \{1, 2\}$ and $x = \ln S_0$. The integral to evaluate the probability must be computed numerically. Some attention should be paid to avoiding instabilities: Albrecher *et al.* [2] show that if d is replaced by $d^* = -d$,[13] numerical problems are almost entirely solved and the integration procedure is robust. The put options can be priced from equation (2.66) by means of put–call parity (2.47).

The quickest and easiest way to compute sensitivities to the model's variables is by numerical differentiation. Delta and Gamma are directly comparable to those of the BS model. This is true for the domestic and foreign Rhos as well. Vega, Vanna and Volga have no direct relationships to the Heston model's sensitivities, although it is possible to find some equivalences. In fact, the Heston model's parameters depend on the shape of the volatility smile and a link between the latter and the Vega-related Greeks of the BS model can be established. We postpone a more thorough discussion of these issues to Chapters 3 and 4, where the concepts are analysed in more detail. The Heston model is rich enough to capture real-world smiles for one expiry, but it will not in general be able to satisfactorily fit an entire volatility surface with a shape commonly observable in the market. Just to provide some intuition behind the model's parameters, the term structure of the ATM volatilities is affected by the starting value of the instantaneous variance ς_t^2, by the mean reversion speed κ and the long-term variance θ. The volatility of the variance ν commands the curvature of the surface, whereas the correlation between the FX spot rate and the instantaneous variance ρ affects its slope: a positive (negative) value yields positively (negatively) sloping surfaces.

2.3.1 Time-dependent parameters in the Heston model

As mentioned above, unfortunately the shapes of the volatility surface produced by a constant-parameter Heston model are too regular compared with the real market ones. A possible solution is to enrich the model by allowing for time-dependent parameters.[14] Some of the (already poor, actually) analytical tractability gets lost in this case, but the fitting power is greatly strengthened. We will show how to extend the Heston model so as to allow for time-dependent parameters, namely, for piecewise-constant parameters.

[13] We refer to the article by Albrecher *et al.* [2] for a more thorough discussion about the origin and the reasons for this choice.

[14] See also Mikhailov and Noegel [52] for more details.

We start from the characteristic functions f_j embedded in equation (2.66) (the notation is the same as above, and we set $t = 0$). They too are a solution of equation (2.26); if we assume there are functions of the kind

$$f_j(S_0, \varsigma_0^2, \tau; f) = e^{L_j(\tau;f)+M_j(\tau;f)\varsigma_0^2+if\ln(S_0)}$$

by direct substitution into equation (2.66) we have

$$\frac{dL_j(\tau;\phi)}{d\tau} - \kappa_t\theta_t M_j(\tau;\phi) - (r_t^d - r_t^f)\phi i = 0$$
$$\frac{dD_j(\tau;\phi)}{d\tau} - \frac{\nu_t^2 M_j(\tau;\phi)}{2} + (b_j - \rho_t\nu_t\phi i)M_j(\tau;\phi) - u_j\phi i + \frac{\phi^2}{2} = 0$$

with initial conditions

$$L(0;\phi) = L_j^0, \quad M(0;\phi) = M_j^0 \tag{2.67}$$

The solutions are very similar to those shown above for the constant-parameter case. More specifically:

$$L(\tau;\phi) = (r_t^d - r_t^f)\phi\tau + \frac{a}{\nu^2}\left\{(b_j - \rho\nu\phi i + d)\tau - 2\ln\left[\frac{1-ge^{d\tau}}{1-g}\right]\right\} + L_j^0 \tag{2.68}$$

$$M(\tau;\phi) = \frac{b_j - \rho\nu\phi i + d - (b_j - \rho\nu\phi i - d)ge^{\tau d}}{\nu^2(1-ge^{d\tau})} \tag{2.69}$$

with

$$g = \frac{b_j - \rho\nu\phi i + d - \nu^2 D_j^0}{b_j - \rho\nu\phi i - d - \nu^2 D_j^0} \tag{2.70}$$

and the rest of the notation is as above. We are now able to calculate M_j and L_j for each interval of time in which the parameters are constant. They will jump to different values in the next interval of time. First, we start by dividing the entire interval $\tau = T - t$ into n sub-intervals $[t_0 = t, t_1]$, ..., $[t_{n-1}, t_n = T]$. In each of these the parameters of the Heston model are constant, but they are different in different sub-intervals. We decide to start from the end of the total interval τ, and we define the first sub-period as $[0, \tau_1]$, where $\tau_k = T - t_{n-k}$, for $k = 1, ..., n-1$. For this sub-interval the initial conditions in equation (2.67) are zero, so that the solutions for (2.68) and (2.69) are the same as in the time-constant Heston model provided in equation (2.66). Moving to the next sub-period $[\tau_1, \tau_2]$, we use the general solutions in (2.68) and (2.69), by imposing the initial conditions (2.67) to be equal to

$$L_j^0 = L^H(\tau_1, \phi), \quad M_0^j = M^H(\tau_1;\phi)$$

where we indicate by $L^H(\tau_1, \phi)$ and $M^H(\tau_1, \phi)$ the solutions used in equation (2.66). The same procedure can be applied for each sub-period τ_k, and we derive the entire set of piecewise-constant parameters. The solution will not be too different from the constant-parameter version of the model, but we are able to significantly enhance its fitting ability.

2.4 THE SABR MODEL

We assumed in the BS economy above, and then in the extended stochastic volatility economy, a particular kind of evolution for the FX spot rate: the geometric Brownian motion in (2.1). Actually, a more general evolution can be adopted, such as

$$dS_t = \mu_t S_t dt + \varsigma_t S_t^\beta dW_t \tag{2.71}$$

This is a *constant elasticity of variance* (CEV) process. For different values of the parameter $\beta \in [0, 1]$, it encompasses the geometric Brownian motion ($\beta = 1$) and a normal model *à la* Bachelier ($\beta = 0$) as special cases. If we further postulate that the instantaneous volatility process in equation (2.19) is specified by setting $\phi(\varsigma, t) = 0$ and $\nu(\varsigma, t) = \nu\varsigma$, and that the correlation between dW_t and dZ_t is equal to ρ, then we have the so-called SABR model, introduced by Hagan *et al.* [33].

This model has several interesting features, and it has been used mainly in the interest rate derivatives market (to model swaptions', caps' and floors' smiles), although it can easily be extended to the FX market. Its most interesting property is that, by means of the β parameter, it preserves a basic downward-sloping shape of the volatility smile (as typically observable in the interest rate markets) subsequent to a movement in the underlying asset price, although this is not necessarily a desirable feature in the FX market.

The other parameters, like in the Heston model, affect the curvature of the smile (ν) and the slope of the smile (ρ). It is clear that two parameters (ρ and β) in the SABR model play a similar role, nevertheless, it is possible to disentangle their effects. The β actually affects the smile via the distribution of the asset price it implies: since $\beta \in [0, 1]$, it produces a distribution ranging from the normal one (generating the maximum negative slope for the volatility smile) to the lognormal one (generating a flat smile). The ρ parameter affects the smile via the correlation between the underlying asset and the instantaneous volatility: it can be negative (engendering a negative-sloping smile, adding its effects to those of β) or positive (engendering a positive effect on the slope of the smile, thus mitigating β's effects and offsetting them).

Amongst the other nice properties of the SABR model, which will be studied to some extent later on, we reckon the availability of a closed-form formula approximation for plain vanilla options. In fact, if we want to price at t an option with expiry at T and struck at K, we can simply use the standard BS model formula (2.28), by plugging in the implied volatility parameter $\sigma = \sigma(K, T)$ set as follows:

$$\sigma(K, T) \simeq \Xi(K)\frac{z}{x(z)}\Psi(K) \tag{2.72}$$

where

$$\Xi(K) = \frac{\alpha}{(F(t,T)K)^{\frac{1-\beta}{2}}\left[1 + \frac{(1-\beta)^2}{24}\ln^2\left(\frac{F(t,T)}{K}\right) + \frac{(1-\beta)^4}{1920}\ln^4\left(\frac{F(t,T)}{K}\right)\right]}$$

$$\Psi(K) = 1 + \left[\frac{(1-\beta)^2\alpha^2}{24(F(t,T)K)^{1-\beta}} + \frac{\rho\beta\nu\alpha}{4(F(t,T)K)^{\frac{1-\beta}{2}}} + \nu^2\frac{2-3\rho^2}{24}\right]\tau$$

$$z = \frac{\nu}{\alpha}(F(t,T)K)^{\frac{1-\beta}{2}}\ln\left(\frac{F(t,T)}{K}\right)$$

$$x(z) = \ln\left[\frac{\sqrt{1-2\rho z + z^2} + z - \rho}{1-\rho}\right]$$

When the option is ATM forward (i.e., struck at the forward price level), equation (2.72) collapses to the particular case

$$\sigma(F(t,T),T) \simeq \frac{\alpha}{F(t,T)^{1-\beta}} \Psi(F(t,T)) \tag{2.73}$$

Also the SABR model, in its constant-parameter version shown above, is in general not rich enough to adequately capture real-world volatility surfaces. Once again, the solution would be to extend the model by introducing time-dependent parameters,[15] but we will not present this here, since the SABR model will be used in the following chapters only in a limited way.

2.5 THE MIXTURE APPROACH

The need for a model capable of capturing the market volatility smile and allowing for analytical tractability has in recent years led to what we name here the mixture approach. It was presented by Brigo and Mercurio [12] and extended by Mercurio [48] and Brigo *et al.* [45]. We start by designing the *lognormal mixture local volatility* (LMLV) model and then present a *lognormal mixture uncertain volatility* (LMUV) model. We stress the relationships and the differences between them.

2.5.1 The LMLV model

Assume[16] the risk-neutral evolution for the FX rate is that given in equation (2.16), and consider N diffusion processes of the kind

$$dS_t^i = (r_t^d - r_t^f)S_t^i dt + \varsigma_i(S_t^i, t)dW_t^Q \tag{2.74}$$

for $i = 1, \ldots, N$. The marginal density of the FX spot rate, under the risk-neutral distribution, is determined by the weighted average of the marginal densities associated with the N processes above, with W being a standard Brownian motion under the risk-neutral measure Q. We denote by $\wp_t^i(x)$ the density function of the process S_i^t at time t: $\wp_t^i(x) = d(Q\{S_t^i < x\})/dx$. We would like to find a *local volatility*[17] function $\varsigma(S_t, t)$ associated with the FX spot rate process in equation (2.16), such that the risk-neutral density function Q is

$$\wp_t(x) = \frac{dQ\{S_t < x\}}{dx} = \sum_{i=1}^{N} \lambda_i \frac{dQ\{S_t^i < x\}}{dx} = \sum_{i=1}^{N} \lambda_i \wp_t^i(x) \tag{2.75}$$

where we set $S_0^i = S_0$ for each i and λ_i is a positive constant with $\sum_{i=1}^{N} \lambda_i = 1$. By applying the Fokker–Planck equation (satisfied by any density function) to equation (2.75), we get

$$\frac{\partial \wp_t(x)}{\partial t} = -\frac{\partial \wp_t(x)}{\partial x}(r_t^d - r_t^f)x + \frac{1}{2}\frac{\partial^2 \wp_t(x)}{\partial x^2}\varsigma(x,t)^2 x^2$$

---

[15] Hagan *et al.* [33] examine such an extension.

[16] Our derivation of the model strictly follows Brigo and Mercurio [13], which we also refer to for the more technical details we omit here.

[17] We define as local volatility the instantaneous volatility when it is a deterministic function of the FX spot rate and of time. This definition is standard in financial theory.

which must also be satisfied by each $\wp_t^i$:

$$\frac{\partial \wp_t^i(x)}{\partial t} = -\frac{\partial \wp_t^i(x)}{\partial x}(r_t^d - r_t^f)x + \frac{1}{2}\frac{\partial^2 \wp_t^i(x)}{\partial x^2}\varsigma_i(x,t)^2$$

From the linearity of the derivative operator, this yields

$$\sum_{i=1}^{N}\lambda_i\left[\frac{\partial^2 \wp_t^i(x)}{\partial x^2}\varsigma_i(x,t)^2\right] = \sum_{i=1}^{N}\lambda_i\left[\frac{\partial^2 \wp_t^i(x)}{\partial x^2}\varsigma(x,t)^2 x^2\right]$$

or equivalently:

$$\left[\frac{\partial^2 \sum_{i=1}^{N}\lambda_i \wp_t^i(x)}{\partial x^2}\varsigma_i(x,t)^2\right] = \left[\frac{\partial^2 \sum_{i=1}^{N}\lambda_i \wp_t^i(x)}{\partial x^2}\varsigma(x,t)^2 x^2\right]$$

The general solution to the last equation is of the kind

$$\frac{\partial^2 \sum_{i=1}^{N}\lambda_i \wp_t^i(x)}{\partial x^2}\varsigma_i(x,t)^2 + A_t x + B_t = \frac{\partial^2 \sum_{i=1}^{N}\lambda_i \wp_t^i(x)}{\partial x^2}\varsigma(x,t)^2 x^2$$

The RHS of the equation above tends to zero for $x \to \infty$, so that the LHS must have zero limit as well: this is true only if $A_t = B_t = 0$ for any t. Hence, it is straightforward to imply the $\varsigma(S_t, t)$:

$$\varsigma(x,t) = \sqrt{\frac{\sum_{i=1}^{N}\lambda_i \varsigma_i(x,t)^2 \wp_t^i(x)}{\sum_{i=1}^{N}\lambda_i x_i^2 \wp_t^i(x)}x} \tag{2.76}$$

Equation (2.76) defines a class of local volatility functions which are consistent with the assumption that the marginal density Q satisfies equation (2.75), that is to say, it is the mixture of N densities each weighted by λ_i. If we further specify the diffusion for each S^i as

$$\varsigma_i(S_t^i, t) = \varsigma_i(t)S_t^i$$

then the marginal density for each S^i, conditional on $S_0^i = S_0$, is

$$\wp_t^i(x) = \frac{1}{x\sigma_i(t)\sqrt{2\pi}}\exp\left\{-\frac{1}{2\sigma_i^2(t)}\left[\ln\frac{x}{S_0} - \int_0^t (r_s^d - r_s^f)ds + \frac{1}{2}\sigma_i^2(t)\right]^2\right\} \tag{2.77}$$

where

$$\sigma_i(t) = \sqrt{\int_0^t \varsigma_i^2(s)ds}$$

and we have the LMLV model. Applying equation (2.77) to (2.76), we can state the following:

Proposition 2.5.1. *(Brigo and Mercurio* [13]*) Let us assume that each ς_i is continuous and that there exists an $\varepsilon > 0$ such that $\varsigma_i(t) = \varsigma_0 > 0$, for each t in $[0, \varepsilon]$ and $i = 1, \ldots, N$.*

Then, if we set

$$\varsigma(x,t)=\sqrt{\frac{\sum_{i=1}^{N}\lambda_i\varsigma_i^2(t)\frac{1}{\sigma_i(t)}\exp\left\{-\frac{1}{2\sigma_i^2(t)}\left[\ln\frac{x}{S_0}-\int_0^t(r_s^d-r_s^f)ds+\frac{1}{2}\sigma_i^2(t)\right]^2\right\}}{\sum_{i=1}^{N}\lambda_i\frac{1}{\sigma_i(t)}\exp\left\{-\frac{1}{2\sigma_i^2(t)}\left[\ln\frac{x}{S_0}-\int_0^t(r_s^d-r_s^f)ds+\frac{1}{2}\sigma_i^2(t)\right]^2\right\}}} \tag{2.78}$$

for $(x,t)>(0,0)$ *and* $\varsigma(x,t)=\varsigma_0$ *for* $(x,t)=(S_0,0)$*, the SDE* (2.74) *has a unique strong solution whose marginal density is given by the mixture of lognormals*

$$\wp_t(x)=\sum_{i=1}^{N}\lambda_i\frac{1}{x\sigma_i(t)\sqrt{2\pi}}\exp\left\{-\frac{1}{2\sigma_i^2(t)}\left[\ln\frac{x}{S_0}-\int_0^t(r_s^d-r_s^f)ds+\frac{1}{2}\sigma_i^2(t)\right]^2\right\} \tag{2.79}$$

Moreover, for $(x,t)>(0,0)$ *we have*

$$\varsigma^2(x,t)=\sum_{i=1}^{N}\Lambda_i(x,t)\varsigma_i^2(t) \tag{2.80}$$

where

$$\Lambda_i(x,t)=\frac{\lambda_i\wp_t^i(x)}{\sum_{i=1}^{N}\lambda_i\wp_t^i(x)}$$

and for each (x,t) *and* i, $\lambda_i\geq 0$ *and* $\sum_{i=1}^{N}\lambda_i=1$*. As a direct consequence:*

$$0<\underline{\varsigma}\leq\varsigma(x,t)\leq\overline{\varsigma} \tag{2.81}$$

$$\underline{\varsigma}=\inf_{t\geq 0}\min_{i=1,\dots,N}\varsigma_i(t)$$
$$\overline{\varsigma}=\sup_{t\geq 0}\max_{i=1,\dots,N}\varsigma_i(t)$$

The LMLV model is interesting because it allows us to define a local volatility function in principle capable of fitting market prices of options with a virtually infinite number of parameters (in fact, we have not specified the number N of probabilities contributing to the FX marginal distribution function). Besides, the dynamics of the FX spot rate is fully explicit, so that it is possible to resort to Monte Carlo methods to price contingent claims. Finally, the model allows for a simple pricing formula for European-type payoffs, such as European plain vanilla options. To see this, we apply formula (2.14) and get

$$\begin{aligned}\mathcal{O}(S_t,t)&=D_t^dE^Q\left[(D_T^d)^{-1}\mathcal{O}(S_T,T)\right]\\&=P^d(t,T)\int_0^\infty\mathcal{O}(x,T)\sum_{i=1}^{N}\lambda_i\wp_T^i(x)dx\\&=\sum_{i=1}^{N}\lambda_iP^d(t,T)\int_0^\infty\mathcal{O}(x,T)\wp_T^i(x)dx\\&=\sum_{i=1}^{N}\lambda_i\mathcal{O}^i(S_t,t)\end{aligned} \tag{2.82}$$

where $\mathcal{O}^i$ denotes the price of the contingent claim associated with the process S^i for $i = 1, \ldots, N$. In the lognormal case above, plain vanilla options can be valued by the BS formula, so that the final price will be a weighted (by λ_i) average of BS premiums:

$$\mathcal{O}(S_t, t) = \sum_{i=1}^{N} \lambda_i \mathrm{Bl}(S_t, t, T, K, P^d(t, T), P^f(t, T), \sigma_i, \omega)$$

$$\sigma_i = \sqrt{\frac{\int_t^T \varsigma_i^2(s) ds}{T - t}}$$

2.5.2 The LMUV model

Assume[18] the FX spot rate evolves, in the risk-neutral world, according to the following dynamics:

$$dS_t = \begin{cases} S_t[(r^d(t) - r^f(t)]\, dt + \varsigma_0\, dW_t^{Q^W}] & t \in [0, \varepsilon] \\ S_t[(r^d(t) - r^f(t)]\, dt + \varsigma(t)\, dW_t^{Q^W}] & t > \varepsilon \end{cases} \tag{2.83}$$

with $S(0) = S_t > 0$, and where $\varsigma(t)$ is a random variable that is independent of W (the usual standard Brownian motion on $(\Omega, \mathcal{F}_T, Q^W)$), ς_0 and ε are positive constants, and the risk-neutral drift rate is a deterministic function of time. The random variable ς takes values in a set of N (given) deterministic functions $\varsigma_i(t)$ with real-world probability $\widehat{\lambda}_i$, and $\varsigma(t)$ denotes its generic value We thus have:

$$t \mapsto \varsigma(t) = \begin{cases} t \mapsto \varsigma_1(t) & \text{with probability } \widehat{\lambda}_1 \\ t \mapsto \varsigma_2(t) & \text{with probability } \widehat{\lambda}_2 \\ \vdots & \vdots \\ t \mapsto \varsigma_N(t) & \text{with probability } \widehat{\lambda}_N \end{cases}$$

where the $\widehat{\lambda}_i$ are strictly positive and add up to one. If $\mathcal{F}_t^W$ is the σ-field generated by W up to time t and $\mathcal{F}^\varsigma$ the σ-field associated with $\varsigma(t)$ then, since W and ς are independent, the underlying filtration $\mathcal{F}_t = \mathcal{F}_t^W \otimes \mathcal{F}^\varsigma : t \geq 0$. Define P^ς as the probability function for the discrete random variable ς, so that $P^\varsigma(\varsigma_i) = \widehat{\lambda}_i$; we set $\Omega = \Omega^W \otimes \Omega^\varsigma$ and $P = Q^W \otimes P^\varsigma$. The probability space for the FX is $(\Omega, \mathcal{F}_T, P)$.

The idea underpinning the assumptions above is the following: the FX spot rate process evolves, during an infinitesimal interval of time, according to a geometric Brownian motion as in equation (2.1), with a constant instantaneous volatility ς_0. After this period, at time $t = \varepsilon$, the instantaneous volatility can take the value $\varsigma_i(t)$ drawn from a given number N of possible outcomes. From this time on, the FX rate evolves according to a geometric Brownian motion with a deterministic time-dependent instantaneous volatility. Hence the volatility is stochastic, although in the simplest possible way. No specific dynamics is designed for it, but its future values are extracted from a set of N scenarios and afterwards any source of uncertainty related to the volatility is fully removed. Moreover, this removal occurs in an infinitesimal interval after the initial time, so that stochasticity affects the volatility only for a very short period. This idea leads to some nice results, as will soon be evident.

The existence of a risk-neutral probability Q is proved by the following proposition:

[18] Our presentation of the LMUV model follows Brigo *et al.* [15] and Mercurio [50].

Proposition 2.5.2. *(Mercurio* [48]*) Define a new probability measure on* $(\Omega^\varsigma, \mathcal{F}^\varsigma)$ *such that*

$$\frac{dQ^\varsigma}{dP^\varsigma} = \frac{\lambda_i}{\widehat{\lambda}_i} \quad i = 1, ..., N$$

where the new probabilities λ_i *are strictly positive and sum to* 1. *There exists a risk-neutral probability measure* Q *on* $(\Omega, \mathcal{F}_T)$*, associated with the numeraire* D_t^d*,*

$$\frac{dQ}{dP} = \frac{dQ^\varsigma}{dP^\varsigma} \exp\left\{ -\frac{1}{2}\int_0^T \left(\frac{\mu(t) - r^d(t) + r^f(t)}{\varsigma_i(t)}\right)^2 dt - \int_0^T \left(\frac{\mu(t) - r^d(t) + r^f(t)}{\varsigma_i(t)}\right) dW_t^{Q^W} \right\} \tag{2.84}$$

such that the drift of the process in equation (2.83) *is* $\mu(t) = r^d(t) - r^f(t)$.

Proof: Under each scenario ς_i, S evolves as a geometric Brownian motion with volatility $\varsigma_i(t)$. Applying both Girsanov's theorem and a change of measure for discrete random variables yields that the process $Se^{\int_0^t (r^f(s) - r^d(s))ds}$ is an $(\mathcal{F}_T, Q)$-martingale; in fact, for each $0 \leq t < T$

$$\frac{E\left[S_T e^{\int_0^T (r^f(s)-r^d(s))ds} \frac{dQ}{dP} | \mathcal{F}_t\right]}{E[\frac{dQ}{dP}|\mathcal{F}_t]}$$

$$= \frac{\frac{dQ^\varsigma}{dP^\varsigma} E\left[S_T e^{\int_0^T (r^f(s)-r^d(s))ds - \frac{1}{2}\int_t^T \left(\frac{\mu(t)-r^d(t)+r^f(t)}{\overline{\varsigma}}\right)^2 ds - \int_t^T \left(\frac{\mu(t)-r^d(t)+r^f(t)}{\overline{\varsigma}}\right) dW_s^{Q^W}} |\mathcal{F}_t\right]}{\frac{dQ^\varsigma}{dP^\varsigma}}$$

$$= S_t e^{\int_t^T (r^f(s)-r^d(s))ds}$$

where $\overline{\varsigma}$ is a volatility function extracted from the possible outcomes. Besides:

$$E\left[S_T e^{\int_0^T (r^f(s)-r^d(s))ds} \frac{dQ}{dP} |\mathcal{F}_t\right] = E^{P^\varsigma}\left\{\frac{dQ^\varsigma}{dP^\varsigma} X\right\} = \sum_{i=1}^N \widehat{\lambda}_i \frac{\lambda_i}{\widehat{\lambda}_i} S_0 = S_0 < +\infty$$

where

$$X = E^{Q^W}\left[S_T e^{\int_0^T (r^f(s)-r^d(s))ds - \frac{1}{2}\int_t^T \left(\frac{\mu(t)-r^d(t)+r^f(t)}{\varsigma_i(t)}\right)^2 ds - \int_t^T \left(\frac{\mu(t)-r^d(t)+r^f(t)}{\varsigma_i(t)}\right) dW_s^{Q^W}} |\varsigma_i(t)\right]$$

□

Finally, by setting $\varsigma_i(t) = \varsigma_0$ for each $t \in [0, \varepsilon]$ and each i, and once more

$$\sigma_i(t) = \sqrt{\int_0^t \varsigma_i^2(s)ds}$$

we have that the density function for S at time $t > \varepsilon$ is

$$\wp_t(x) = \sum_{i=1}^N \lambda_i \frac{1}{x\sigma_i(t)\sqrt{2\pi}} \exp\left\{ -\frac{1}{2\sigma_i^2(t)}\left[\ln\frac{x}{S_t} - \int_0^t (r_s^d - r_s^f)ds + \frac{1}{2}\sigma_i^2(t)\right]^2\right\} \tag{2.85}$$

This is a direct consequence of the fact that

$$P^Q\{S_t \le x\} = \sum_{i=1}^{N} P^Q\{\{S_t \le x\} \cap \{\varsigma(t) = \varsigma_i\}\} = \sum_{i=1}^{N} P^Q\{S_t \le x | \varsigma(t) = \varsigma_i\}$$

It is worth noticing that the marginal probability function of the FX spot rate in the LMUV model is the same as that of the LMLV model, although the starting assumptions of the two models are quite different. This will lead to remarkable differences in the pricing of exotic options, but for plain vanilla options the valuation formulae are exactly the same. In fact, in the LMUV model we also have

$$\begin{aligned} \mathcal{O}(S_t, t) &= D_t^d E^Q\big[(D_T^d)^- 1\mathcal{O}(S_T, T)\big] \\ &= P^d(t, T) \sum_{i=1}^{N} \lambda_i E^Q\big[\mathcal{O}(S_T, T) | \varsigma = \varsigma_i\big] \\ &= \sum_{i=1}^{N} \lambda_i \mathrm{Bl}(S_t, t, T, K, P^d(t, T), P^f(t, T), \sigma_i, \omega) \\ \sigma_i &= \sqrt{\frac{\int_t^T \varsigma_i^2(s) ds}{T - t}} \end{aligned} \tag{2.86}$$

which is equal to equation (2.82).

2.5.3 Features of the LMLV and LMUV models and a comparison between them

The two models we have described above share many nice features that make them suitable for their employment, in a convenient way, in pricing FX options (also of the exotic kind) in a market environment with the presence of a smile for plain vanilla options prices. In fact, these features are:

1. Explicit dynamics of the FX spot rate.
2. Explicit marginal densities – they actually turn out to be the same in both models, *at the initial time* (this point must be stressed).
3. Explicit formulae for European-style payoffs *at the initial time* – they are also the same, as a direct consequence of the point above.

These features enable an easy calibration to market data, and hence the pricing of more complex derivatives' payoffs once the model's parameters are implied. There are two more desirable properties of the LMUV model, which are not shared by the LMLV model but which are very useful in the actual and effective use of the model:

1. Analytical tractability is extended *at the initial time* also to all other kinds of payoffs that have explicit pricing formulae in the BS model.
2. Analytical tractability is preserved *after the initial time*, since future prices can also be obtained explicitly where that is similarly possible in the BS model.

The last two properties make the LMUV model much more appealing from a practical point of view, since they make possible the use of all the analytical tools developed in the BS environment, simply by applying the usual conditioning on the possible states of the discrete random variable $\varsigma(t)$ and then averaging over them. In this way we can use the explicit formulae for exotic options available in the BS world. To better understand the importance of this point, one should just consider that in the LMLV model all the analytical tractability gets lost as the FX initial spot rate S_0 changes. This means that explicit formulae are no longer available, even for plain vanilla options, and so for the basic Greeks such as Delta and Gamma. On the contrary, in the LMUV model, all analytical tractability is retained for different levels of the FX spot rate and the averaging of the correspondent BS values, under each volatility scenario, can always be performed consistently.

The analogies between the two models, which originate in the common properties observable at the initial time, follow from the fact that the LMLV model is a projection of the LMUV model onto the class of local volatility models.[19] Basically, this implies the equivalence of the marginal densities and hence of the pricing formulae for European-style payoffs. Moreover, in both models the FX spot rate is perfectly decorrelated from the (squared) instantaneous volatility.[20] This property impacts significantly on the smile's shape, which can possibly be engendered. In fact, perfect decorrelation between the spot rate and the (squared) volatility only allows for the production of symmetric (in the logarithm of the strike) smile shapes, so that some extensions are needed to accommodate real market conditions where the presence of a skew (asymmetric smile) is usually detectable.

The differences arise from the starting assumptions of the two models. In the LMLV model, the marginal density of the FX spot rate is supposed to be a mixture of basic marginal densities, then a local volatility function of the spot process, consistent with that, is derived. The local volatility function links (in a deterministic fashion) the level of the instantaneous volatility with the level of the FX spot rate and with time. Hence, the instantaneous volatility is stochastic in that the underlying FX spot rate is so, but it has no stochastic process of its own and the only source of randomness, in the model, is given by the spot rate. As a consequence, the model is still *complete*, in the sense that a self-financing strategy (involving trading the FX spot rate and the bank deposit) can be carried out to perfectly replicate the terminal payoff of the contingent claim.

In contrast, the LMUV model is a true stochastic volatility model, although of the most simple kind. This means that the market is not complete and that a self-financing strategy (involving only the underlying FX rate and a bank deposit) cannot be designed so as to perfectly replicate the contingent claim. Actually, the market can be completed (as in any other stochastic volatility model) via the introduction of another asset (for instance, an option). In fact, this is usually what happens in real market activity, so market incompleteness is not an important issue. All in all, we prefer to use the LMUV model in practice, although it lacks market completeness, for its more extended analytical tractability. We will discuss the choice of model further in Section 2.6. For the moment we just extend the LMUV model so as to make it more suitable and effective to cope with real market conditions.

2.5.4 Extension of the LMUV model

As mentioned above, the need to extend the LMUV model arises from its inability to generate asymmetric volatility smiles. One possible solution is to shift the Brownian motion dynamics under each volatility scenario. This yields closed-form pricing formulae for plain vanilla options as a displaced BS model, and some exotic options can also be priced explicitly.

[19] Brigo *et al.* [15] formally prove this point.

[20] This point is also formally proved by Brigo *et al.* [15].

Unfortunately, to keep the model analytically tractable, the displacement cannot be chosen arbitrarily, so the fit to market prices is not always satisfactory.

A second approach is to consider a stochastic foreign interest rate.[21] This will grant some freedom in the fitting to asymmetric volatility smiles, since the requirement that the expected FX spot rate be equal to the current forward price applies only in the corresponding forward measure, and the constraint is somewhat relaxed. Besides, this extension allows for a different shift associated with different options' expiries, which should also cater for a better fit.

The simplest way to introduce stochastic interest rates is to assume that the instantaneous domestic and foreign rates r^d and r^f are known at time 0: $r^d(0) = r_0^d$, $r^f(0) = r_0^f$ and at time $t = \varepsilon$ they are drawn from a discrete number, similar to the instantaneous volatility, so as to produce N scenarios. Thus, the risk-neutral dynamics of the FX spot rate is

$$dS_t = \begin{cases} S_t[(r_0^d - r_0^f)\,dt + \varsigma_0\,dW_t^Q] & t \in [0, \varepsilon] \\ S_t[(r^d(t) - r^f(t))\,dt + \varsigma(t)\,dW_t^Q] & t > \varepsilon \end{cases} \tag{2.87}$$

where the notation is the same as that used above and (r^d, r^f, ς) is a random triplet that is independent of W and is drawn from the set of N (given) triplets of deterministic functions:

$$t \mapsto (r^d(t), r^f(t), \varsigma(t)) = \begin{cases} t \mapsto (r_1^d(t), r_1^f(t), \varsigma_1(t)) & \text{with probability } \lambda_1 \\ t \mapsto (r_2^d(t), r_2^f(t), \varsigma_2(t)) & \text{with probability } \lambda_2 \\ \vdots & \vdots \\ t \mapsto (r_N^d(t), r_N^f(t), \varsigma_N(t)) & \text{with probability } \lambda_N \end{cases}$$

where the λ_i are strictly positive and add up to one. The random value of the triplet is drawn at time $t = \varepsilon$. The interpretation of the model is similar to the basic LMUV model: at time 0 the domestic and foreign interest rates and the instantaneous volatility start from a known value, but in the next infinitesimal instant $t \in [0, \varepsilon]$ they can take the values extracted from one of the N possible triplets. After the triplet manifests, the uncertainty of the model is completely removed, since the dynamics of the FX spot rate is the usual Brownian motion with time-dependent (but not stochastic) parameters.

The extended LMUV model enjoys all the features we have listed above for the basic version, and explicit valuation formulae are still retained everywhere they are available in the corresponding BS model. In fact, for plain vanilla options we have

$$\begin{aligned} \mathcal{O}(S_t, t) &= \sum_{i=1}^{N} \lambda_i E\left\{\mathcal{O}(S_T, T) \middle| (r^d(t) = r_i^d, r^f(t) = r_i^f, \varsigma(t) = \varsigma_i)\right\} \\ &= \sum_{i=1}^{N} \lambda_i \mathrm{Bl}(S_t, t, T, K, P_i^d(t, T), P_i^f(t, T), \sigma_i, \omega) \end{aligned} \tag{2.88}$$

where

$$\sigma_i = \sqrt{\frac{\int_t^T \varsigma_i^2(s)ds}{T - t}}, \quad P_i^d = e^{-\int_t^T r_i^d(s)ds}, \quad P_i^f = e^{-\int_t^T r_i^f(s)ds}$$

Formula (2.88) applies analogously wherever BS explicit formulae are available.

---

[21] Both the displacement of the FX spot rate process and the stochastic foreign interest rate extensions are proposed by Brigo *et al.* [15].

The extension is rich enough to capture a wide range of volatility smile shapes that may be found in the market. Actually, for our purposes, we will see that a restricted version of the extension described above can be employed with good results, namely, we allow only the foreign interest rate to be stochastic, whereas the domestic interest rate will be a deterministic function of time as in the BS model. So, at time $t = \varepsilon$, a couplet instead of a triplet will be extracted from the N possible scenarios.

2.6 SOME CONSIDERATIONS ABOUT THE CHOICE OF MODEL

We have presented above some models to cope with a market environment more complex than that supposed in the BS model, particularly with reference to the presence of a volatility smile. These models can be more or less elegant from a mathematical point of view, they can be more or less realistic about their assumptions regarding the dynamics for the FX spot rate and the instantaneous volatility, and they can be more or less effective in capturing options' prices trading in the market. Nevertheless, in our opinion (and based also on our experience), we think that any model must satisfy a number of requirements to be really useful in quoting and managing the risk of a portfolio of options. In more depth, a model should:

1. Be able to perfectly capture at least the basic market quoted options (the most liquid and actively traded options are usually used for risk management purposes and play an important role also in the pricing of exotic payoffs).[22]
2. Be rich enough to be able to also fit small perturbations of the volatility smile for a given expiry, so as to identify a clear hedging policy for the subsequent variations in the portfolio's value.
3. Have closed-form formulae for at least plain vanilla options, so as to guarantee a fast calibration procedure.
4. Ideally, have closed-form formulae for a wide class of exotic options, more specifically for barrier options. They are likely to make up 90% of the exotic options in the book of a typical market maker and, given the characteristics of the FX market, have to be re-evaluated and their sensitivities computed in the shortest possible time.
5. Allow for the design of efficient numerical procedures to be employed when closed-form formulae are not available.
6. Imply a behaviour of the volatility smile (and, more generally, surface) consistent with what is actually observed in reality.

To our knowledge, the only model fulfilling all the requirements above is the (extended) LMUV, and for this reason we will spend much time in what follows on examining in more detail this model and its implications and presenting some solutions for the implementation of a risk management tool hinging on it.

In the last few years the model has engendered some debate about the reasonability of its starting assumptions and its possible drawbacks. Probably the most heavy criticism of the model was put forward by Piterbarg [53]. He argues that the LMLV is the only consistent model amongst those proposed in a mixture approach, whereas any other model leads to

[22] We have already seen in Chapter 1 the three basic instruments (ATM straddle, risk reversal and butterfly) for each expiry. Their price implies the price also for the three basic options used to build them. More will be said about this is the following chapters.

incorrect pricing of contingent claims except for plain vanilla options.[23] We would like to stress here that the LMUV model is not at all perfect, and its basic assumptions are probably the farthest from reality, but we think that more emphasis should be put on the effectiveness of its use in practice instead of pointing out the flaws in the starting assumptions or even its poor mathematical formalism (although it is quite understandable that a financial quant cannot find any great gratification in the design of such a model).

To be clearer, no model is blindly accepted by any market maker to hedge their book. The model is always regarded suspiciously as far as its ability to predict future evolution of market prices, so that in practice not only the sensitivities of the options to the explicit sources of risk (for instance, in the Heston model, the FX spot rate and the instantaneous volatility) will be hedged, but also all the implicit risks (as far as possible) that can be collectively referred to as *model risks*.

As an example, if a market maker adopts the Heston model, as a first step they will Delta hedge their book; then they should use an instrument to hedge the exposure of their book to the instantaneous volatility. Actually, if all the parameters of the model (however estimated) are correct and constant, this policy is sufficient to correctly hedge all the exposures. The correctness of the model implies that it produces a given volatility surface now (that should agree as far as possible with market prices, and we assume here it is perfectly fit to them), and correctly predicts its future evolution also in the next instant of time.

In reality, nobody believes that the model is able to correctly predict the evolution of the volatility surface; that is the same as saying that nobody trusts the stability of the parameters over time. Periodically (for example, daily or even more often), parameters have to be re-estimated so as to match market prices again. Should a market maker hedge only along the prescription of the model, they would have unexpected profits or losses arising from the new values of the parameters, which in turn imply values of the plain vanilla options (i.e., of the volatility surface) and of the exotic options different from the ones predicted by the model before the recalibration (we will study these sources of profit and loss in more depth in the next chapter). So, market makers will also hedge against all the variations of the model parameters; that is to say: they hedge against the model risk. Clearly, should this hedge require additional costs to bear, they will be transferred in the pricing of contingent claims.

The considerations above mean that a model is never chosen just because it is believed to correctly predict the future. It is readily admitted that no model can describe the complexity of the real world exhaustively. It will therefore be chosen also on the basis of other criteria, such as those we have listed above, amongst which there will surely be the reasonable (yet not perfectly predicted) implicated evolution of options' market prices (i.e., of future volatility surfaces). The LMUV can certainly be criticized for many reasons, but the expected future volatility surface is no less reasonable than that implied by a more sophisticated stochastic volatility model such as Heston's. Although the model assumes that after an infinitesimal time the uncertainty about the instantaneous volatility will be resolved and hence a flat (time-dependent) volatility surface will manifest, nevertheless, at the initial time the *expected* volatility surface is not at all flat. The Delta hedging suggested by the model is affected by the *expected* shape of the surface, not by the fact that it is assumed that in fact it will be flat once one of the possible scenarios is determined.

[23] A part of the debate between the author of this book and M. Gatarek on the one side and V.V. Piterbarg on the opposite side is still publicly available, at the time of writing, at Wilmott's website (www.wilmott.com), Forum section, in the "A Simple Model" thread.

The only difference between a true stochastic volatility model and an LMUV is that in the latter case the hedger is almost completely sure they will have to recalibrate the model after the infinitesimal time elapses (unless one of the flat smile scenarios actually occurs), whereas in the former case one has more chance that the starting configuration of parameters produces a future volatility surface perfectly fitted to the future market surface. But in both cases the profits and losses due to model risk derive from the differences between the *expected* future option's prices and the *actual* market ones (or, alternatively, between the future model's and market's volatility surfaces).

We hope we have provided a sound grounding to the adoption of an LMUV model, although it may appear at first sight to be a naive model from a mathematical perspective and completely unreasonable for the starting assumptions. We will see later on that it can be very useful in practice, and its performance in both pricing and hedging FX options is comparable to a true stochastic volatility model such as the Heston model.

3 Dynamic Hedging and Volatility Trading

3.1 PRELIMINARY CONSIDERATIONS

We have shown in Chapter 2 how to build a portfolio replicating the terminal payoff of a contingent claim via a dynamic trading strategy, with the additional requirement for it to be self-financing. The effectiveness of the strategy hinges on the starting assumptions regarding the dynamics of the FX spot rate. If the assumptions are met in the real world, in the sense that they correctly describe the basic features and behaviour of the market, then it can be argued that the theoretical results hold and the profits and losses originated by the strategy exactly match those arising from a position in the contingent claim. If the assumptions do not hold (or only hold partially), then residual profits and losses result from the strategy so that the contingent claim's replication will be inaccurate.

In this chapter we present a general framework[1] to examine the possible sources of profits and losses when a dynamic trading strategy is implemented and the starting assumptions do not (fully) hold. We will extend the range of possible financial instruments entering into the trading strategy, by including not only the FX spot rate and the domestic deposit but other (actively) traded contingent claims (i.e., in practice, other plain vanilla options). The reason why we are interested in analysing such strategies is that market makers hedge their books not by adhering strictly to how, in theory, the replication strategy should be implemented, but by trying to hedge all the risks they deem relevant, even if they are not taken into account explicitly by the adopted model. That is to say market makers, basically, try to hedge the model risk by means of some rule.

We would like to stress the difference between the *hedging rule* and the *revaluation rule*.

Definition 3.1.1. ***Hedging rule.*** *By a hedging rule is meant the set of: (i) all the trading actions indicated by a given model to hedge against the risk factors it takes into account ("financial risk hedging") and (ii) all the trading strategies implemented to hedge the factors that are not considered risky in the model, but may actually be so ("model risk hedging").*

It is evident from this definition that the hedging rule is identified only after the choice of a model.

Definition 3.1.2. ***Revaluation rule.*** *The criteria embraced to revalue the (possibly derivatives) securities in a trading book are encompassed in the revaluation rule. They can be based on the market prices or, alternatively, on a model that is (more or less) exactly fitted to a given set of market data such as indices (for example, interest rates), variables (for example, implied volatility) and their interpolation.*

Remark 3.1.1. *A financial institution has to establish some rules regarding the revaluation of the derivatives books. One rule can be to perfectly mark-to-market the prices when the derivative securities are actively traded and prices can be easily recovered from the market,*

[1] The framework and many of the results presented here are based on a private communication from Giulio Sartorelli of Banca IMI [57].

as is the case, for instance, for FX plain vanilla options. For these options, in fact, volatility surfaces can be built with a reasonable degree of accuracy, even starting from a few prices for each expiry. For less actively traded derivatives (for instance, barrier options), the revaluation rule can be to price them by means of a model, possibly calibrated to more liquid derivatives (i.e., plain vanilla options). In this case the guiding principle is to deduce the value of the less liquid security consistently with the more liquid ones, and use the latter as hedging tools (so-called market-to-model).

It should be stressed, anyway, that even if prices are easily found in the market, this does not mean that the "mark-to-market" principle is necessarily adopted, since this can be considered less important than the efficient hedging that can be performed by means of a model that is fully consistent but unable to fit market prices exactly. For example, a book of FX plain vanilla options can be revalued by the BS model and a volatility surface provided giving the implied volatility to plug into the formula according to the strike and the expiry of a given contract. Nevertheless, this approach is theoretically inconsistent and will suggest misleading hedging policies,[2] although it allows for a rather perfect mark-to-market of the book. A consistent choice would be to use a BS model with a flat volatility smile and, since the revaluation rule is often set equal to the hedging rule for many practical reasons, the choice could be to keep the theoretical consistency of the BS model by adopting a flat smile revaluation rule alongside a similar hedging rule.

Whereas the model's choice is a prerequisite for the hedging rule, it is not so when the revaluation rule is considered. Actually, at least in principle, no model at all could be adopted if market prices were easily retrievable and/or interpolation of missing prices could be computed satisfactorily. As a consequence, by generalizing the previous statement, the model used for hedging purposes does not have to be the same as the model used for revaluation purposes. Clearly, the two models must agree on the terminal value of the claims priced in each specific framework, but until maturity a divergence between the two values may be experienced, even if it cancels out at expiry.

In theory, only the hedging model should matter since in the end the effectiveness of the hedging rule stems from its aptitude at identifying financial risks and clearly showing model risks. This is true, though, only if the book has an end together with the expiry of the longest contract, and all the assets employed for hedging purposes have the same longest expiry as well. In this case the hedging and revaluation models agree on the pricing of the book at its end. The above-mentioned possible divergences may affect the profits and losses of a given period (for example, a quarter), but the total cumulative economic result is the same in both cases at expiry.

In practice, trading books have no specified end of activities, so the reasoning above no longer applies. The divergence between the revaluation and the hedging model has a deep impact on the yearly performance, on the definition of the balance sheet's items and (last but not least) on the traders' bonuses, obviously. Thus, in general, the revaluation model is chosen to be the same as the hedging model. And even if this is not the case, there is a (human, we dare say) market makers' bias to look carefully at the revaluation model, which might be poorly significant in the long run as far as hedging effectiveness is concerned, but may turn out to be momentous as far as periodic performance is concerned.

[2] Later on we will examine in more depth why the BS model is not consistent with the presence of a smiled volatility surface.

In fact, it should be noted that the revaluation rule determines the unrealized profits and losses. Trading activity generates realized profits and losses, which are given by (loosely speaking) the difference between the initial (selling/purchasing) price and the final price of the considered security. Besides, trading activity generates unrealized profits/losses given by the revaluation rule that assigns a value to a portfolio which is only supposedly what the financial institution will earn should all the positions be dismantled.

All these preliminary considerations seem likely to take us far from the main object of the analysis, but in our opinion they offer a picture of how the real (imperfect) world works. And they should be kept in mind also in the subsequent inquiry.

3.2 A GENERAL FRAMEWORK

Consider the following set-up: we assume we are in a perfect market with no transaction costs and no constraints to trading. We build a portfolio Z_t containing β_t units of a domestic deposit with market value D_t (its dynamics is the same as in equation (2.2), α_t^i quantity of the security C_t^i, for $i = 1, ..., n-1$ and finally a short position $\alpha_t^n = -1$ in the nth (derivative) security C_t^n expiring in T (or, alternatively, a European contingent claim). If a security C_t^i is an option, it is supposed to be a European one with expiry at T. We assume that the market value of the nth security is not known, since it is not actively traded so must be hedged via a replication strategy including the other available (liquid) assets. Clearly, although a price is not retrievable from the market, the security is nonetheless booked at a price $C_t^n = V_t$ calculated by some model and hedged accordingly. This means that the revaluation rule clashes with the hedging rule.

It is worth stressing that, relative to the nth security, no realized profit or loss occurs during the life of the portfolio, since it is involved in no trading activity and the quantity is kept fixed ($\alpha_n = -1$). Thus, at expiry T the total profits/losses associated with it are simply the difference between the selling price and the terminal payoff, which is the same in any model. All the differences between the model price and the "true" price potentially arising during the life of the contingent claim are immaterial in determining the total profits/losses. In order to lighten the notation and allow for the compact Einstein summation convention,[3] we drop the time subscript for the portfolio's weights and the securities' prices. So, we have that the value of the portfolio is

$$Z_t = \beta_t D_t^d + \alpha_i C^i$$

We assume that the portfolio is built at time 0, when the derivative security C^n is sold, and at expiry T of the latter it is wound up. At inception, we employ the revenues originated by selling the nth security in setting up the portfolio, so that $Z_0 = 0$. By imposing the self-financing condition:[4]

$$dZ_t = \beta_t dD_t^d dt + \alpha_i dC^i$$

[3] Remember that the Einstein summation convention implies that when, in some expression, an index appears twice in a single term (as a subscript and as a superscript), then one must sum over all its possible values. For example, $z = a_i x^i$, in the Einstein convention, is equivalent to the classical notation $\sum_{i=0}^{n} a_i x_i$. The index runs from 0 to n by convention.

[4] See Chapter 2 for a discussion of self-financing strategies.

and by recalling that $dD_t^d = r_t^d D_t^d dt$ and that, from the definition of Z_T, $\beta_t D_t^d = Z_t - \alpha_i C^i$, we get

$$dZ_t = (Z_t - \alpha_i C^i) r_t^d dt + \alpha_i dC^i$$

or

$$dZ_t = r_t^d Z_t dt + (\alpha_i dC^i - \alpha_i C^i r_t^d dt)$$

This ODE can be solved by standard techniques,[5] and the solution is ($Z_0 = 0$):

$$Z_T = \int_0^T e^{r_t^d(T-t)}(\alpha_i dC^i - \alpha_i C^i r_t^d dt) \tag{3.1}$$

Equation (3.1) can be interpreted as follows: the portfolio terminal value Z_T is equal to the discounted sum[6] of all the differences, in each instant t, between the *actual* variation of the portfolio's value ($\alpha_i dC^i$) and the *risk-neutral* variation of the portfolio's value ($\alpha_i C^i r_t^d dt$). If the trading strategy replicates the contingent claim C^n perfectly, then we know from Chapter 2 that we can pretend we are in a risk-neutral world (i.e., an equivalent martingale measure exists). This means that the two variations in the portfolio's value are the same: $\alpha_i dC^i = \alpha_i C^i r_t^d dt$. Hence, the total portfolio's value (and profit/loss) at expiry T, is nil. If the hedging strategy is not perfectly replicating, we can no longer pretend we are in a risk-neutral world, and actually the two variations in the portfolio's value are different: $\alpha_i dC^i \neq \alpha_i C^i r_t^d dt$. The terminal portfolio's value is $Z_T \neq 0$. We will investigate further under which conditions we can expect a profit or a loss at expiry arising from a not perfectly replicating strategy. Alternatively, we will examine the extent and sign of the hedging error considering some hedging trading strategies.[7]

It is worth noticing also that the prices, and their variations, in equation (3.1) are certainly those calculated according to the hedging (and revaluation) model for the nth contingent claim. For the other $n-1$ securities, they are actual prices and variations, but we will be more precise about this in each of the cases we examine. We further assume that the prices of the $n-1$ hedging instruments can be expressed by means of a BS pricing formula, with the implied volatility retrieved from the market for a corresponding strike, and that they are call options: $C^i = \text{Bl}(S_t, t, T, K, P^d(t,T), P^f(t,T), \sigma_K, 1)$. The revaluation rule for the nth security is to use the BS model with the implied volatility set in a way depending on the hedging rule implemented.

Assume we have a set of m risk factors including the FX spot rate and all the possible implied volatilities: $\mathcal{S} = (s^0, \ldots, s^m)$, such that $s^0 = S_t$ and the other $m-1$ risk factors s^j are implied volatility processes. In this setting, each hedging instrument can be considered as a function of time and risk factors, $C^i = C^i(t, \mathcal{S})$, and applying Itô's lemma[8] we have:

$$dC^i = \partial_t C^i dt + \partial_j C^i ds^j + \frac{1}{2}\partial_{jk} C^i d\langle s^j, s^k\rangle \tag{3.2}$$

[5] Lagrange indeterminate coefficients, for precision's sake.

[6] The discounted integral, actually, since we are in a continuous time setting.

[7] It is quite obvious that the terminal value of the portfolio Z is the total hedging error, or the total profit/loss, engendered by the replicating strategy adopted.

[8] Recall that $s^0 = S_t$.

where ∂_t denotes the partial derivative with respect to time, ∂_j the partial derivative with respect to risk factor s^j (for $j = 0, ..., m$), and ∂_{jk} the second partial derivative with respect to the risk factors s^j and s^k (for $j, k = 0, ..., m$). The brackets $\langle s^j, s^k \rangle$ denote the covariation of s^j with s^k. It is worth stressing that ds^j and $\langle s^j, s^k \rangle$ are the variations/covariations of the risk factors actually occurring in the market.

Since we assumed also that all the prices can be expressed in terms of the BS pricing function, they solve the basic PDE for the BS model, so that for any C^i:

$$r_t^d C^i = \partial_t C^i + \partial_0 C^i r_t^d s^0 + \frac{1}{2}\partial_{00} C^i (\sigma^i s^0)^2 \tag{3.3}$$

where σ^i is the implied volatility[9] dealing in the market for a plain vanilla option with the same strike as C^i.

Tying up all the results above finally yields

$$\begin{aligned} \alpha_i dC^i - \alpha_i C^i r_t^d dt = {} & \alpha_i(\partial_t C^i dt + \partial_j C^i ds^j + \frac{1}{2}\partial_{jk} C^i d\langle s^j, s^k \rangle) \\ & - \alpha_i(\partial_t C^i + \partial_0 C^i r_t^d s^0 + \frac{1}{2}\partial_{00} C^i (\sigma^i s^0)^2)dt \end{aligned}$$

which, simplifying further the time derivatives, becomes

$$\begin{aligned} \alpha_i dC^i - \alpha_i C^i r_t^d dt = {} & \alpha_i(\partial_j C^i ds^j + \frac{1}{2}\partial_{jk} C^i d\langle s^j, s^k \rangle) \\ & - \alpha_i(\partial_0 C^i r_t^d s^0 + \frac{1}{2}\partial_{00} C^i (\sigma^i s^0)^2)dt \end{aligned} \tag{3.4}$$

We will choose the quantity α_i so as to make equation (3.4) equal to zero. We can anticipate that this will not be entirely possible.

3.3 HEDGING WITH A CONSTANT IMPLIED VOLATILITY

We start by analysing the performance of a very simple hedging rule, strictly sticking to the BS model. The nth contingent claim is continuously Delta hedged according to the BS formula calculated with a constant implied volatility $\sigma^1 = \overline{\sigma}$. Hence, $n = 1, C^0 = S_t = s^0$ and $C^1 = C^1(t, S_t, \overline{\sigma}) = V_t$; under this hedging rule, the only risk factor considered is the FX spot rate, which is also the hedging instrument. More formally:

$$\begin{aligned} \alpha_i \partial_i C^j ds^j &= \sum_j (\alpha_0 \partial_j S_t ds^j - \partial_j V_t ds^j) \\ &= \alpha_0 \partial_0 S_t ds^0 - \partial_0 V_t ds^0 \\ &= \left(\alpha_0 - \frac{\partial V_t}{\partial S_t}\right) dS_t \end{aligned}$$

$$\alpha_i \frac{1}{2}\partial_{jk} C^i d\langle s^j, s^k \rangle = \frac{1}{2}\sum_{jk} (\alpha_0 \partial_{jk} S_t d\langle s^j, s^k \rangle - \partial_{jk} V_t d\langle s^j, s^k \rangle)$$

[9] Although in what follows the implied volatility should be considered a stochastic process, to lighten the notation we will suppress the dependence on time.

$$= -\frac{1}{2}\partial_{00} V_t d\langle s^0\rangle$$
$$= -\frac{1}{2}\frac{\partial^2 V_t}{\partial S_t^2} d\langle S_t\rangle$$

where, as usual, $\langle\cdot\rangle$ are the quadratic variation brackets and $\langle S_t, S_t\rangle = \langle S_t\rangle$. Besides:

$$\alpha_i \partial_0 C^i r_t^d s^0 = \alpha_0 \partial_0 S_t r_t^d - \partial_0 V_t r_t^d$$
$$= \left(\alpha_0 - \frac{\partial V_t}{\partial S_t}\right) r_t^d S_t$$

$$\alpha_i \frac{1}{2}\partial_{00} C^i (\sigma^i s^0)^2 dt = \frac{1}{2}(\alpha_0 \partial_{00} S_t (\sigma_0 s^0)^2 - \partial_{00} V_t (\sigma_1 s^0)^2 dt)$$
$$= -\frac{1}{2}\partial_{00} V_t (\sigma^1 s^0)^2 dt$$
$$= -\frac{1}{2}\frac{\partial^2 V_t}{\partial S_t^2}(\overline{\sigma} S_t)^2 dt$$

Summing up all the terms and using equation (3.4) yields

$$\alpha_i dC^i - \alpha_i C^i r_t^d dt = \left(\alpha_0 - \frac{\partial V_t}{\partial S_t}\right)(dS_t - r_t^d S_t dt) - \frac{1}{2}\frac{\partial^2 V_t}{\partial S_t^2}(d\langle S_t\rangle - (\overline{\sigma} S_t)^2 dt)$$

If we set $\alpha_0 = \partial V_t / \partial S_t$, which is exactly what is prescribed by the Delta-hedging rule chosen above, the first term disappears. Then we plug the remaining term into equation (3.1) and, considering that $d\langle S_t\rangle = \varsigma_t^2 S_t^2 dt$ (ς_t^2 being the realized instantaneous variance), we finally come up with the total profits/losses generated by the hedging strategy:[10]

$$Z_T = -\int_0^T e^{r_t^d (T-t)} \frac{1}{2}\frac{\partial^2 V_t}{\partial S_t^2} S_t^2 (\varsigma_t^2 - \overline{\sigma}^2) dt \tag{3.5}$$

Equation (3.5) manifestly shows that the total profits/losses (or, equivalently, the total hedging error) generated by the constant volatility hedging rule is not nil. Actually, it is a random process depending on two factors:

- The difference between the instantaneous variance actually realized (ς_t^2) and the chosen fixed implied volatility ($\overline{\sigma}^2$).
- The Gamma of the options. This depends, in turn, on the FX spot rate level and the time to expiry of the options in the portfolio.

The following considerations can be made:

- Continuous Delta-hedging of a single option revalued at a constant volatility generates a profit/loss directly proportional to the Gamma of the option.
- In general, the profit/loss of a short position in a European option, continuously rehedged, is positive if the realized volatility is, on average during the option's life, lower than the constant implied volatility; it is negative in the opposite case.
- The previous statement is not always true, since the total hedging error is dependent on the path followed by the underlying. If periods of low realized volatility are experienced when

[10] The result is in accordance with that of Carr and Madan [20].

Gamma is high, whereas periods of high realized volatility are experienced when Gamma is negligible, then the total profit/loss is positive, though the realized volatility can be higher than the implied volatility for periods longer than those when it is lower.

To clarify the last point, assume we have sold an OTM option at a price calculated with the implied volatility $\overline{\sigma}^2$. If this is lower than the realized volatility for most of the time to maturity but suddenly the latter drops as the FX spot rate approaches the strike and the expiry is in a short period, then in this case the total hedging error can turn out to be positive for the seller of the option although one may intuitively think at first glance that it would yield a loss.

In conclusion, we can affirm that, given the fixed implied volatility, the constant volatility hedging rule produces a hedging error whose sign and size are extremely dependent on the path followed by the FX spot rate up to the maturity of the option and on the realized volatility of the path itself.

3.4 HEDGING WITH AN UPDATING IMPLIED VOLATILITY

We extend the previous case slightly: the hedging rule is to Delta hedge the nth contingent claim according to the BS formula calculated with an updating implied volatility σ. In other words, σ is (continuously) marked to market, which implies that the nth security is actually quoted in the market, so that the perfect (and trivial) hedge would be to take exactly the opposite position by trading it in the marketplace. Nevertheless, since we are interested in examining the source of profits and losses produced in implementing replicating trading strategies, we disregard the straightforward hedge and focus instead on the hedging rule depicted above. The risk factors in this case are the FX spot rate and the implied volatility. We assume that the contingent claim is a function of both these and time too, $C^1(t, s^0, s^1) = V_t$. As a hedge instrument we still have the FX spot rate only, $C^0 = S_t$. Hence:

$$\begin{aligned}\alpha_i dC^i - \alpha_i C^i r_t^d dt &= \alpha_i(\partial_t C^i + \partial_j C^i ds^j + \tfrac{1}{2}\partial_{jk} C^i d\langle s^j, s^k\rangle) \\ &\quad - \alpha_i(\partial_t C^i dt + \partial_0 C^i r_t^d s^0 + \tfrac{1}{2}\partial_{00} C^i (\sigma^i s^0)^2)dt\end{aligned}$$

where

$$\begin{aligned}\alpha_i \partial_j C^i ds^j &= \sum_j (\alpha_0 \partial_j S_t ds^j - \partial_j V_t ds^j) \\ &= \alpha_0 \partial_0 S_t ds^0 - \partial_0 V_t ds^0 + \alpha_0 \partial_1 S_t ds^1 - \partial_1 V_t ds^1 \\ &= \left(\alpha_0 - \frac{\partial V_t}{\partial S_t}\right) dS_t - \frac{\partial V_t}{\partial \sigma} d\sigma\end{aligned}$$

and

$$\alpha_i \partial_0 C^i r_t^d s^0 = \left(\alpha_0 - \tfrac{\partial V_t}{\partial S_t}\right) r_t^d S_t$$

$$\begin{aligned}\alpha_i \tfrac{1}{2}\partial_{jk} C^i d\langle s^j, s^k\rangle &= -\tfrac{1}{2}\partial_{jk} C^1 d\langle s^j, s^k\rangle \\ &= -\tfrac{1}{2}\left[\partial_{00} C^1 d\langle s^0\rangle + 2\partial_{01} C^1 d\langle s^0, s^1\rangle + \partial_{11} C^1 d\langle s^1\rangle\right]\end{aligned}$$

$$= -\frac{1}{2}\left[\frac{\partial^2 V_t}{\partial S_t^2} d\langle S_t\rangle + 2\frac{\partial^2 V_t}{\partial S_t \partial\sigma} d\langle S_t, \sigma\rangle + \frac{\partial^2 V_t}{\partial\sigma^2} d\langle\sigma\rangle\right]$$

$$\alpha_i \frac{1}{2}\partial_{00} C^i (\sigma^i s^0)^2 dt = -\frac{1}{2}\partial_{00} V_t (\sigma^1 s^0)^2 dt = -\frac{1}{2}\frac{\partial^2 V_t}{\partial S_t^2} d(\sigma S_t)^2 dt$$

Cropping all the equations above, we have

$$\alpha_i dC^i - \alpha_i C^i r_t^d dt = \left(\alpha_0 - \frac{\partial V_t}{\partial S_t}\right)(dS_t - r_t^d S_t dt) - \frac{\partial V_t}{\partial\sigma} d\sigma$$
$$-\frac{1}{2}\left[\frac{\partial^2 V_t}{\partial S_t^2}(d\langle S_t\rangle - (\sigma S_t)^2 dt) + 2\frac{\partial^2 V_t}{\partial S_t \partial\sigma} d\langle S_t, \sigma\rangle + \frac{\partial^2 V_t}{\partial\sigma^2} d\langle\sigma\rangle\right]$$

We set $\alpha_0 = \partial V_t / \partial S_t$, in accordance with our Delta-hedging rule (Delta is computed at each time t with the proper implied volatility σ), and finally:

$$\alpha_i dC^i - \alpha_i C^i r_t^d dt = -\frac{\partial V_t}{\partial\sigma} d\sigma$$
$$-\frac{1}{2}\left[\frac{\partial^2 V_t}{\partial S_t^2}(d\langle S_t\rangle - (\sigma S_t)^2 dt) + 2\frac{\partial^2 V_t}{\partial S_t \partial\sigma} d\langle S_t, \sigma\rangle + \frac{\partial^2 V_t}{\partial\sigma^2} d\langle\sigma\rangle\right] \quad (3.6)$$

Adopting the notation for the Greeks of the BS model introduced in Chapter 2, we can rewrite equation (3.6) as follows:

$$\alpha_i dC^i - \alpha_i C^i r_t^d dt = -\frac{1}{2}\Gamma_t (d\langle S_t\rangle - (\sigma S_t)^2 dt)$$
$$-\frac{1}{2}\left[2\mathcal{V}_t d\sigma + 2\mathcal{X}_t d\langle S_t, \sigma\rangle + \mathcal{W}_t d\langle\sigma\rangle\right] \quad (3.7)$$

We can inspect equation (3.7) to understand how the instantaneous hedging error is generated. We identify the following factors:

- The difference between the instantaneous quadratic variation of the FX spot rate actually realized ($d\langle S_t\rangle$) and the same implied by the changing implied volatility ($(\sigma S_t)^2$).
- The variation of the implied volatility ($d\sigma$), the covariation between the FX spot rate and the implied volatility ($d\langle S_t, \sigma\rangle$), and the quadratic variation of the implied volatility ($d\langle\sigma\rangle$).
- The Gamma, Vega, Vanna and Volga of the options. They depend on the FX spot rate level, the implied volatility level and the time to expiry of the options in the portfolio.

It can be seen that the first part of equation (3.7) is exactly the same hedging error produced by a constant volatility rule, and it is proportional to Gamma and the difference between the realized and implied volatility. There is a difference in this case, though: the implied volatility is not kept constant.

The second part of equation (3.7) in square brackets relates the hedging error to the volatility-related Greeks. It depends on the variation of the implied volatility times the level of Vega, on the covariation between the FX spot rate and the implied volatility times the level of Vanna, and finally the quadratic variation of the implied volatility times half the level of Volga. It is hard to identify general rules, as the total hedging error is the result of the combined effect of all these factors, whose sign and entity are not determined unambiguously. In fact, Vanna and Volga change sign as the FX spot rate moves.

Although equation (3.7) offers an effective picture of how all the factors contribute to the generation of the hedging error, nonetheless it is worth exploring some alternative way to express it so as to have a deeper and more unequivocal insight. To this end, consider the following: the differential of the discounted value of the contingent claim V_t is

$$dV_t - r_t^d V_t dt = \frac{\partial V_t}{\partial t}dt + \frac{\partial V_t}{\partial S_t}dS_t + \frac{\partial V_t}{\partial \sigma}d\sigma + \frac{1}{2}\left[\frac{\partial^2 V_t}{\partial S_t^2}d\langle S_t\rangle + 2\frac{\partial^2 V_t}{\partial S_t \partial \sigma}d\langle S_t, \sigma\rangle + \frac{\partial^2 V_t}{\partial \sigma^2}d\langle \sigma\rangle\right] - r_t^d V_t dt$$

Under the equivalent martingale (risk-neutral) measure[11] we know also that the drift of the process followed by the process of the discounted value V_t must be zero, so that by Itô's lemma:

$$\frac{\partial V_t}{\partial t}dt + \frac{\partial V_t}{\partial S_t}r_t^d S_t dt + \frac{\partial V_t}{\partial \sigma}\widetilde{\phi}dt + \frac{1}{2}\left[\frac{\partial^2 V_t}{\partial S_t^2}d\langle S_t\rangle + 2\frac{\partial^2 V_t}{\partial S_t \partial \sigma}d\langle S_t, \sigma\rangle + \frac{\partial^2 V_t}{\partial \sigma^2}d\langle \sigma\rangle\right] - r_t^d V_t dt = 0 \quad (3.8)$$

where $\widetilde{\phi}$ is the drift of the process for the implied volatility σ under the risk-neutral measure. Substituting the equation above in equation (3.6) immediately yields

$$\begin{aligned} &\alpha_i dC^i - \alpha_i C^i r_t^d dt \\ &= -\frac{\partial V_t}{\partial \sigma}d\sigma + \frac{1}{2}\frac{\partial^2 V_t}{\partial S_t^2}(\sigma S_t)^2 dt + \frac{\partial V_t}{\partial t}dt + \frac{\partial V_t}{\partial S_t}r_t^d S_t dt + \frac{\partial V_t}{\partial \sigma}\widetilde{\phi}dt - r_t^d V_t dt \\ &= -\frac{\partial V_t}{\partial \sigma}d\sigma + \frac{\partial V_t}{\partial \sigma}\widetilde{\phi}dt \end{aligned} \quad (3.9)$$

where we used the fact that V_t is a BS price and thus satisfies the PDE related to the BS model (see equation (3.3)).

We can now plug equation (3.9) into equation (3.1) and finally obtain the total profits/losses generated by the hedging rule:[12]

$$Z_T = -\int_0^T e^{r_t^d(T-t)}\mathcal{V}_t(d\sigma - \widetilde{\phi}dt) \quad (3.10)$$

Equation (3.10) is, rather surprisingly, extremely simple and similar to the constant volatility hedging total profits/losses equation (3.5). Besides, it gives the opportunity to easily understand where the total hedging errors spring from, by identifying the following factors:

- The actual variation of the implied volatility $d\sigma$ and the risk-neutral expected variation $\widetilde{\phi}dt$ (or, the drift of the risk-neutral process of the implied volatility).
- The level of Vega of the option.

[11] We recall that $C^n = V_t$ is a market price by assumption.

[12] This result is the same as in Forde [29].

In general terms we can state:

- Continuous Delta-hedging of a single option revalued at an updating implied volatility generates a profit/loss proportional to the Vega of the option.
- The profit/loss of a short position in the option, continuously re-hedged, is negative if the realized variation of the implied volatility is, on average during the option's life, lower than its expected risk-neutral variation; it is positive in the opposite case.
- The previous statement is not always true, since the total profit/loss is dependent on the path followed by the underlying. If periods of large realized variations of implied volatility are experienced when Vega is high, whereas periods of small realized volatility are experienced when Vega is negligible, then the total profit/loss could be negative, although the implied volatility may move less than expected, for periods longer than those when it moves more than expected.

3.4.1 A market model for the implied volatility

A byproduct of the above result is that we can derive, in a fairly straightforward way, the dynamics for the implied volatility for a given fixed expiry T and a strike K. To lighten the notation, we drop these dependencies in what follows.[13]

In equation (3.8) the drift of the process for the discounted price of the contingent claim, which we here assume to be a European plain vanilla option, is set equal to zero, by definition of the equivalent martingale measure. We can derive the drift of the implied volatility process under an equivalent martingale measure starting from here. In fact:

$$\begin{aligned}\frac{\partial V_t}{\partial \sigma}\widetilde{\phi} dt &= -\frac{\partial V_t}{\partial t}dt - \frac{\partial V_t}{\partial S_t} r_t^d S_t dt \\ &\quad -\frac{1}{2}\left[\frac{\partial^2 V_t}{\partial S_t^2} d\langle S_t\rangle + 2\frac{\partial^2 V_t}{\partial S_t \partial \sigma} d\langle S_t, \sigma\rangle + \frac{\partial^2 V_t}{\partial \sigma^2} d\langle \sigma\rangle\right] dt + r_t^d V_t dt\end{aligned}$$

From the BS PDE (3.3), we have

$$\begin{aligned}\frac{\partial V_t}{\partial \sigma}\widetilde{\phi} dt &= -r_t^d V_t dt + \tfrac{1}{2}\frac{\partial^2 V_t}{\partial S_t^2}\sigma^2 S_t^2 dt \\ &\quad -\frac{1}{2}\left[\frac{\partial^2 V_t}{\partial S_t^2} d\langle S_t\rangle + 2\frac{\partial^2 V_t}{\partial S_t \partial \sigma} d\langle S_t, \sigma\rangle + \frac{\partial^2 V_t}{\partial \sigma^2} d\langle \sigma\rangle\right] + r_t^d V_t dt\end{aligned}$$

and hence

$$\widetilde{\phi} dt = -\frac{1}{2\frac{\partial V_t}{\partial \sigma}}\left[\frac{\partial^2 V_t}{\partial S_t^2} S_t^2(\varsigma_t^2 - \sigma^2)dt + 2\frac{\partial^2 V_t}{\partial S_t \partial \sigma} d\langle S_t, \sigma\rangle + \frac{\partial^2 V_t}{\partial \sigma^2} d\langle \sigma\rangle\right] \quad (3.11)$$

where, as before, ς_t is the instantaneous realized variance. We assume that the implied volatility is a process of the kind[14]

$$d\sigma = \widetilde{\phi}(S_t, \sigma, \varsigma_t, t)dt + \sigma \sum_{i=1}^{n} \nu_i dZ_i^Q \quad (3.12)$$

[13] Market models for implied volatilities have been studied, amongst others, by Brace *et al.* [10], Ledoit and Santa-Clara [44], Schonbucher [58].

[14] The dynamics for the implied volatility as in equation (3.12) has been proposed by Daglish *et al.* [25].

where Z^i are n Brownian motions, each correlated with the Brownian motion of the FX spot rate dW_t^Q with correlation ρ_i. Then the correlation between two Brownian motions Z^i and Z^j is $\rho_i \rho_j$. Thus, we have that the drift of the implied volatility is

$$\widetilde{\phi}(S_t, \sigma, \varsigma_t, t) = -\frac{1}{2\mathcal{V}_t}\left[\Gamma_t S_t^2(\varsigma_t^2 - \sigma^2) + 2\mathcal{X}_t S_t \varsigma_t \sigma \sum_{i=1}^{n} \nu_i \rho_i \right.$$
$$\left. + \mathcal{W}\sigma^2\left(\sum_{i=1}^{n} \nu_i^2 + \sum_{j \neq i} \nu_i \nu_j \rho_i \rho_j\right)\right] \tag{3.13}$$

It is possible to simplify equation (3.13) massively, by recalling the definition of the Greeks appearing therein. First define

$$\varrho = \sum_{i=1}^{n} \nu_i \rho_i$$
$$\upsilon = \sum_{i=1}^{n} \nu_i^2 + \sum_{j \neq i} \nu_i \nu_j \rho_i \rho_j$$

and $\tau = (T - t)$. We then have

$$\widetilde{\phi}(S_t, \sigma, \varsigma_t, t) = \frac{1}{2\sigma\tau}\left[(\sigma^2 - \varsigma_t^2) - \left(\frac{1}{2}\sigma\tau + \frac{\ln\frac{K}{F_t}}{\sigma}\right)\varsigma_t\sigma\varrho + \left(\frac{1}{4}\sigma^2\tau^2 - \frac{\ln^2\frac{K}{F_t}}{\sigma^2}\right)\upsilon\right]$$

where F_t is the forward price at time t and maturity T. Hence

$$\widetilde{\phi}\,(S_t, \sigma, \varsigma_t, t) = \frac{1}{2\sigma\tau}\left[\sigma^2 - \varsigma_t^2 + \frac{1}{4}\sigma^4\tau^2\upsilon - \sigma^2\tau\varsigma_t\varrho - \ln\frac{K}{F_t}\varsigma_t\sigma\varrho - \ln^2\frac{K}{F_t}\upsilon\right] \tag{3.14}$$

which is quite easy to read. When the time t approaches the expiry T, the drift in equation (3.14) must remain finite and this is possible if

$$\sigma^2 = \varsigma_t^2 + \ln\frac{K}{F_t}\varsigma_t\sigma\varrho + \ln^2\frac{K}{F_t}\upsilon$$

By the above condition it is possible to immediately infer the instantaneous volatility from the option prices (assuming also very short times-to-maturity are available). In fact, for the ATM forward ($F_t = K$), the condition becomes

$$\sigma^2 = \varsigma_t^2 \tag{3.15}$$

which shows that the instantaneous volatility of the FX spot rate process is the implied volatility quoted in the market for an option struck ATM forward and with an expiry in the next instant of time.

Equation (3.12), with $\widetilde{\phi}$ defined as in equation (3.14), could in theory be used to create a market model for the evolution of the entire volatility surface.[15] In practice, there are so many constraints that must be imposed to prevent arbitrage that it turns out to be extremely toilsome, if not impossible, to implement such a model. Nonetheless, it can still be used in the subsequent examination to gain better understanding of some hedging strategies or the congruity of some market practices.

[15] The definition of a volatility surface will be introduced in the next chapter.

3.5 HEDGING VEGA

We go further and add another instrument into our hedging toolkit: an actively quoted option whose implied volatility σ is supposed to be stochastic over time. This volatility is used to calculate the Greeks of the nth security, so that the variations we are going to hedge are not true market ones, although at the expiry of the contingent claim both the market and revaluation prices must converge to the specific payoff. We would like to detect the source of possible profits and losses for such a hedging rule, which we name *Vega hedging*. To fix things, we have three securities ($n = 2$): $\mathcal{C}^0 = S_t$, $\mathcal{C}^1 = \mathcal{O}(t, S_t, \sigma)$, $\mathcal{C}^2 = \mathcal{C}^2(t, S_t, \sigma) = V_t$ and two risk factors ($m = 1$): $s_0 = S_t$ and $s_1 = \sigma$. Performing the required calculations, we get

$$
\begin{aligned}
\alpha_i \partial_j \mathcal{C}^i ds^j &= \sum_j (\alpha_0 \partial_j S_t ds^j + \alpha_1 \partial_j \mathcal{O} ds^j - \partial_j V_t ds^j) \\
&= (\alpha_0 \partial_0 S_t ds^0 + \alpha_1 \partial_0 \mathcal{O} ds^0 - \partial_0 V_t ds^0) \\
&\quad + (\alpha_0 \partial_1 S_t ds^1 + \alpha_1 \partial_1 \mathcal{O} ds^1 - \partial_1 V_t ds^1) \\
&= \left(\alpha_0 + \alpha_1 \frac{\partial \mathcal{O}}{\partial S_t} - \frac{\partial V_t}{\partial S_t}\right) dS_t \\
&\quad + \left(\alpha_1 \frac{\partial \mathcal{O}}{\partial \sigma} - \frac{\partial V_t}{\partial \sigma}\right) d\sigma
\end{aligned}
$$

$$
\begin{aligned}
\alpha_i \partial_0 \mathcal{C}^i r_t^d s^0 &= (\alpha_0 \partial_0 S_t r_t^d s^0 + \alpha_1 \partial_0 \mathcal{O} r_t^d s^0 - \partial_0 V_t r_t^d s^0) \\
&= \left(\alpha_0 + \alpha_1 \frac{\partial \mathcal{O}}{\partial S_t} - \frac{\partial V_t}{\partial S_t}\right) r_t^d S_t
\end{aligned}
$$

According to the hedging rule, we choose α_0 and α_1 so as to make the total portfolio Delta and Vega-hedged. We then solve the following system:

$$
\begin{aligned}
\alpha_0 + \alpha_1 \frac{\partial \mathcal{O}}{\partial S_t} &= \frac{\partial V_t}{\partial S_t} \\
\alpha_1 \frac{\partial \mathcal{O}}{\partial \sigma} &= \frac{\partial V_t}{\partial \sigma}
\end{aligned}
$$

so that we have

$$
\begin{aligned}
\alpha_i d\mathcal{C}^i - \alpha_i \mathcal{C}^i r_t^d dt &= \frac{1}{2} \alpha_i (\partial_{jk} \mathcal{C}^i d \langle s^j, s^k \rangle - \partial_{00} \mathcal{C}^i (\sigma S_t)^2 dt) \\
&= \frac{1}{2} \sum_{i=1}^{2} \alpha_i \left(\sum_{j,k=0}^{1} \partial_{jk} \mathcal{C}^i d \langle s^j, s^k \rangle - \partial_{00} \mathcal{C}^i (\sigma^i s^0)^2 dt \right) \\
&= \frac{1}{2} \left(\sum_{i=1}^{2} \alpha_i \sum_{j,k=0}^{1} \partial_{jk} \mathcal{C}^i d \langle s^j, s^k \rangle - \sum_{i=1}^{2} \alpha_i \partial_{00} \mathcal{C}^i (\sigma^i s^0)^2 dt \right)
\end{aligned}
$$

We expand the summations:

$$\alpha_i dC^i - \alpha_i C^i r_t^d dt = \frac{1}{2}\left[\sum_{j,k=0}^{1}(\alpha_1 \partial_{jk}\mathcal{O} - \partial_{jk}V_t)d\langle s^j, s^k\rangle - \left(\alpha_1\frac{\partial^2\mathcal{O}}{\partial S_t^2} - \frac{\partial^2 V_t}{\partial S_t^2}\right)(\sigma S_t)^2 dt\right]$$
$$= \frac{1}{2}\left[\left(\alpha_1\frac{\partial^2\mathcal{O}}{\partial S_t^2} - \frac{\partial^2 V_t}{\partial S_t^2}\right)d\langle S_t\rangle + \left(\alpha_1\frac{\partial^2\mathcal{O}}{\partial\sigma^2} - \frac{\partial^2 V_t}{\partial\sigma^2}\right)d\langle\sigma\rangle\right.$$
$$\left. + 2\left(\alpha_1\frac{\partial^2\mathcal{O}}{\partial S_t\partial\sigma} - \frac{\partial^2 V_t}{\partial S_t\partial\sigma}\right)d\langle S_t, \sigma\rangle - \left(\alpha_1\frac{\partial^2\mathcal{O}}{\partial S_t^2} - \frac{\partial^2 V_t}{\partial S_t^2}\right)(\sigma S_t)^2 dt\right]$$

Rearranging terms:

$$\alpha_i dC^i - \alpha_i C^i r_t^d dt =$$
$$= \frac{1}{2}\left[\left(\alpha_1\frac{\partial^2\mathcal{O}}{\partial S_t^2} - \frac{\partial^2 V_t}{\partial S_t^2}\right)(d\langle S_t\rangle - (\sigma S_t)^2 dt) + \left(\alpha_1\frac{\partial^2\mathcal{O}}{\partial\sigma^2} - \frac{\partial^2 V_t}{\partial\sigma^2}\right)d\langle\sigma\rangle\right.$$
$$\left. + 2\left(\alpha_1\frac{\partial^2\mathcal{O}}{\partial S_t\partial\sigma} - \frac{\partial^2 V_t}{\partial S_t\partial\sigma}\right)d\langle S_t, \sigma\rangle\right] \tag{3.16}$$

In Chapter 2 we showed the Vega–Gamma relationship (see equation (2.60)). We can use this to simplify the equation above. In fact, since we set α_1 so as to zero the Vega exposure, as a direct consequence the Gamma terms (second derivatives of the securities' prices with respect to the FX spot rate), in brackets, also sum to zero:

$$\alpha_i dC^i - \alpha_i C^i r_t^d dt =$$
$$= \frac{1}{2}\left[\left(\alpha_1\frac{\partial^2\mathcal{O}}{\partial\sigma^2} - \frac{\partial^2 V_t}{\partial\sigma^2}\right)d\langle\sigma\rangle\right.$$
$$\left. + 2\left(\alpha_1\frac{\partial^2\mathcal{O}}{\partial S_t\partial\sigma} - \frac{\partial^2 V_t}{\partial S_t\partial\sigma}\right)d\langle S_t, \sigma\rangle\right]$$

Now we can just plug this equation into equation (3.1) to finally get:

$$Z_T = \int_0^T e^{r_t^d(T-t)}\frac{1}{2}\left[\left(\alpha_1\frac{\partial^2\mathcal{O}}{\partial\sigma^2} - \frac{\partial^2 V_t}{\partial\sigma^2}\right)d\langle\sigma\rangle\right.$$
$$\left. + 2\left(\alpha_1\frac{\partial^2\mathcal{O}}{\partial S_t\partial\sigma} - \frac{\partial^2 V_t}{\partial S_t\partial\sigma}\right)d\langle S_t, \sigma\rangle\right] \tag{3.17}$$

We can use the notation of Chapter 2 and rewrite the equation above as:

$$Z_T = \int_0^T e^{r_t^d(T-t)}\frac{1}{2}\left[\left(\alpha_1\mathcal{W}_t^{\mathcal{O}} - \mathcal{W}_t^V\right)d\langle\sigma\rangle\right.$$
$$\left. + 2\left(\alpha_1\mathcal{X}_t^{\mathcal{O}} - \mathcal{X}_t^V\right)d\langle S_t, \sigma\rangle\right]. \tag{3.18}$$

Equation (3.18) shows that the total error under the Vega-hedging rule depends on:

- The realized quadratic variation of the implied volatility, times the difference between Volga of the position in the hedging option ($\alpha_1\mathcal{W}_t^{\mathcal{O}}$) and Volga of the contingent claim ($\mathcal{W}_t^V$).

- The covariation between the implied volatility and the FX spot rate, times the difference between Vanna of the position in the hedging option ($\alpha_1 \mathcal{X}_t^{\mathcal{O}}$) and Vanna of the contingent claim ($\mathcal{X}_t^V$).

It is clear that the influence, through Vega, of the evolution of implied volatility on the total profits/losses has been removed and only second-order volatility-related Greeks are left playing a role. Nonetheless, it is not possible to establish *a priori* whether these net exposures are large or small.

To get some different insight, we try and express the formula for the total profits/losses in terms of volatility-related Greeks of one option only, namely the contingent claim V_t. We start from equation (3.16) and put forward the following reasoning: since $\mathcal{O}(t, S_t, \sigma)$ is a market price, the drift of its discounted process must be nil under the equivalent martingale measure (analogous to equation (3.8) for V_t). By calculating the drift using Itô's lemma, imposing that it be zero and substituting in equation (3.16) (we still use the fact that $\mathcal{O}$ satisfies the BS PDE), we can write the terminal value of the hedging rule as

$$Z_T = -\int_0^T e^{r_t^d (T-t)} \Big[\mathcal{V}_t \widetilde{\phi} dt + \frac{1}{2} \Gamma_t S_t^2 (\varsigma_t^2 - \sigma^2) dt + \frac{1}{2} \mathcal{W}_t d\langle \sigma \rangle + \mathcal{X}_t d\langle S_t, \sigma \rangle \Big] \tag{3.19}$$

where the usual notation used above applies and we use the fact that, by our choice, $\alpha_1 \frac{\partial \mathcal{O}}{\partial \sigma} = \frac{\partial V_t}{\partial \sigma}$. $\mathcal{V}$, $\mathcal{W}$ and $\mathcal{X}$ are the volatility-related Greeks of the hedged contingent claim V_t, calculated with the implied volatility σ of the hedging option $\mathcal{O}$. It must be stressed that the latter is a true market price, so one can apply the risk-neutral argument and constrain its risk-neutral drift to be zero. On the contrary, V_t is not a market price, since it is calculated by means of the BS formula, but with the implied volatility for $\mathcal{O}$ instead of its own. This means that the process of the discounted value of V_t is not a martingale and its drift is different from zero. That is why, in equation (3.19), the higher-order Greeks Gamma, Volga and Vanna appear whereas in equation (3.10) only Vega is present.

This method of expressing the total hedging error under the Vega-hedging rule has the advantage of quickly detecting the sources of risk once one knows the behaviour of the Greeks of the contingent claim; we do not need to know the net level of Volga and Vanna, as was the case before with equation (3.18). It should be noted that, notwithstanding Vega also contributes to the performance of the Vega-hedging rule when we look at equation (3.19), contrary to the Delta-hedging rule with updating volatility, its contribution is not stochastic so far as we consider only the volatility risk. To be clearer on this point, given the FX spot rate path from time 0 to T (thus, removing the uncertainty regarding S_t), Vega is multiplied by a constant (or a deterministic function of time) $\widetilde{\phi}$ and no stochastic terms appear (as was the case, on the contrary, in equation (3.10).

3.6 HEDGING DELTA, VEGA, VANNA AND VOLGA

We examine the performance of a hedging rule including four instruments: three options and the FX spot rate. They will allow us to hedge the total Delta and all the total volatility-related Greeks: Vega, Vanna and Volga. We name this rule *Vanna–Volga hedging*. It can be implemented under several assumptions, which we will describe separately.

3.6.1 Vanna–Volga hedging with one implied volatility

We start by assuming that all the options involved in the trading strategies are priced by the BS model with the same volatility σ for all of them, and also all the Greeks are calculated accordingly.[16] So, $m = 1$: $s^0 = S_t$, $s^1 = \sigma$ and $n = 4$: $C^0 = S_t$, $C^i = \mathcal{O}^i(t, S_t, \sigma)$ for $i = 1, 2, 3$ and $C^4 = \mathcal{O}^4(t, S_t, \sigma) = V_t$. Once again, we start with equation (3.4) and consider the four terms:

$$\alpha_i \partial_j C^i ds^j, \quad \alpha_i \partial_0 C^i r_t^d s^0$$
$$\alpha_i \tfrac{1}{2} \partial_{jk} C^i d\left\langle s^j, s^k \right\rangle, \quad \alpha_i \tfrac{1}{2} \partial_{00} C^i (\sigma^i s^0)^2$$

Since we assumed that all the σ^i are equal to σ, it can easily be checked that if the following equations hold:

$$\begin{aligned} \alpha_i \partial_j C^i &= 0, \qquad j = 1, 2 \\ \alpha_i \tfrac{1}{2} \partial_{jk} C^i &= 0, \qquad j, k = 1, 2 \end{aligned} \tag{3.20}$$

then all the four terms above are equal to zero and thus $Z_T = 0$ and the replication is perfect. The system (3.20) is made up of six $(2 + 4)$ equations and four variables (recall $\alpha_4 = -1$). Yet, in the second row some equations are redundant by the symmetry of cross-differentiation, yielding five equations and four variables. Besides, by the Vega–Gamma relationship (2.60), we have one more redundancy in the system and we are finally left with four variables and four equations, and the weights α_i can be uniquely determined.

The assumption of a common implied volatility for all the options is at odds with what actually happens in the market, where prices signal different implied volatilities; that is, the presence of a volatility smile. Then we go further and examine the performance of the Vanna–Volga hedging rule in such an environment.

3.6.2 Vanna–Volga hedging with different implied volatilities

Let us assume that we have four hedging tools: the FX spot rate and three options with different strikes, and each option is priced according to its own implied volatility. Thus we have $m = 4$: $s^0 = S_t$, $s^i = \sigma^i$ for $j = 1, 2, 3$ and $n = 4$: $C^0 = S_t$, $C^i = \mathcal{O}^i(t, S_t, \sigma^i)$ for $i = 1, 2, 3$ and $C^4 = \mathcal{O}^4(t, S_t, \sigma) = V_t$, with $\sigma = \sigma_1$ so that it is evaluated with the same implied volatility as options C^1. Consider again equation (3.4). We can start by eliminating some redundancies, since C^0 does not depend on any s^i for $i \geq 1$ and hence also $\partial_{00} = 0$:

$$\begin{aligned} \alpha_i dC^i - \alpha_i C^i r_t^d dt = {} & \alpha_0 (ds^0 - r_t^d s^0 dt) \\ & + \sum_{i=1}^{4} \alpha_i (\partial_j C^i ds^j - \partial_0 C^i r_t^d s^0 dt) \\ & + \sum_{i=1}^{4} \alpha_i \frac{1}{2} (\partial_{jk} C^i d\left\langle s^j, s^k \right\rangle - \partial_{00} C^i (\sigma^i s^0)^2 dt) \end{aligned}$$

[16] This strategy has been analysed by Castagna and Mercurio [22].

We point out the terms with $i = 0$ and $k = 0$:

$$\alpha_i dC^i - \alpha_i C^i r_t^d dt = \alpha_0(ds^0 - r_t^d s^0 dt) + \sum_{i=1}^{4} \alpha_i(\partial_0 C^i ds^0 - \partial_0 C^i r_t^d s^0 dt) + \sum_{i=1}^{4} \alpha_i \sum_{j=1}^{4} \partial_j C^i ds^j + \frac{1}{2}\Bigg[\sum_{i=1}^{4} \alpha_i(\partial_{00} C^i d\langle s^0, s^0\rangle - \partial_{00} C^i (\sigma^i s^0)^2 dt) + 2\sum_{i=1}^{4}\sum_{j=1}^{4} \alpha_i \partial_{j0} C^i d\langle s^j, s^0\rangle + \sum_{i=1}^{4}\sum_{j,k=1}^{4} \alpha_i \partial_{jk} C^i d\langle s^j, s^k\rangle\Bigg]$$

which can be written as

$$\alpha_i dC^i - \alpha_i C^i r_t^d dt = \sum_{i=0}^{4} \alpha_i(\partial_0 C^i ds^0 - \partial_0 C^i r_t^d s^0 dt) + \sum_{i=1}^{4} \alpha_i \sum_{j=1}^{4} \partial_j C^i ds^j + \frac{1}{2}\Bigg[\sum_{i=1}^{4} \alpha_i(\partial_{00} C^i d\langle s^0, s^0\rangle - \partial_{00} C^i (\sigma^i s^0)^2 dt) + 2\sum_{i=1}^{4}\sum_{j=1}^{4} \alpha_i \partial_{j0} C^i d\langle s^j, s^0\rangle + \sum_{i=1}^{4}\sum_{j,k=1}^{4} \alpha_i \partial_{jk} C^i d\langle s^j, s^k\rangle\Bigg]$$

Now, since each C^i depends only on two risk factors, s^0 and s^i, the equation above is simplified as follows:

$$\alpha_i dC^i - \alpha_i C^i r_t^d dt = \sum_{i=0}^{4} \alpha_i(\partial_0 C^i ds^0 - \partial_0 C^i r_t^d s^0 dt) + \sum_{i=1}^{4} \alpha_i \sum_{j=1}^{4} \partial_j C^i ds^j + \frac{1}{2}\Bigg[\sum_{i=1}^{4} \alpha_i \partial_{00} C^i (d\langle s^0\rangle - (\sigma^i s^0)^2 dt) + 2\sum_{i=1}^{4} \alpha_i \partial_{i0} C^i d\langle s^i, s^0\rangle + \sum_{i=1}^{4} \alpha_i \partial_{ii} C^i d\langle s^i\rangle\Bigg]$$

In terms of S_t, V_t, σ^i:

$$\alpha_i dC^i - \alpha_i C^i r_t^d dt = \left(\alpha_0 + \sum_{i=1}^{3} \alpha_i \frac{\partial C^i}{\partial S_t} - \frac{\partial V_t}{\partial S_t}\right)(dS_t - r_t^d S_t dt) + \frac{1}{2}\left[\left(\sum_{i=1}^{3} \alpha_i \frac{\partial^2 C^i}{\partial S_t^2} - \frac{\partial^2 V_t}{\partial S_t^2}\right) d\langle S_t\rangle - \left(\sum_{i=1}^{3} \alpha_i \frac{\partial^2 C^i}{\partial S_t^2}(\sigma^i)^2 - \frac{\partial^2 V_t}{\partial S_t^2}\sigma^2\right) S_t^2 dt\right]$$

$$+\left(\sum_{i=1}^{3}\alpha_i\frac{\partial C^i}{\partial\sigma^i}d\sigma^i-\frac{\partial V_t}{\partial\sigma}d\sigma\right)+\frac{1}{2}\left[\left(\sum_{i=1}^{3}\alpha_i\frac{\partial^2 C^i}{\partial(\sigma^i)^2}d\left\langle\sigma_t^i\right\rangle-\frac{\partial^2 V_t}{\partial\sigma^2}d\left\langle\sigma_t\right\rangle\right)\right.$$
$$\left.+2\sum_{i=1}^{3}\left(\alpha_i\frac{\partial^2 C^i}{\partial S_t\partial\sigma^i}d\left\langle\sigma^i,S_t\right\rangle-\frac{\partial^2 V_t}{\partial S_t\partial\sigma}d\left\langle\sigma,S_t\right\rangle\right)\right]$$

Let us focus on the terms where the first derivatives appear and try to nil them. We have to solve the following system:

$$\alpha_0+\sum_{i=1}^{3}\alpha_i\frac{\partial C^i}{\partial S_t}-\frac{\partial V_t}{\partial S_t}=0$$
$$\sum_{i=1}^{3}\alpha_i\frac{\partial C^i}{\partial\sigma^i}d\sigma^i-\frac{\partial V_t}{\partial\sigma}d\sigma=0$$

It is manifest that when the variations $d\sigma^i$ are independent, no hedging portfolio can be set up so as to completely remove the volatility risk, without considering the fact that the higher-order terms have not been taken into account either. As a first attempt, one may assume that all the implied volatilities have the same increments. This is a very strong hypothesis, but it is worth examining to attain a primal appreciation about the performance of the Vanna–Volga hedging rule, when different volatilities are used. Hence, by assumption, we write the instantaneous hedging error as

$$\alpha_i dC^i-\alpha_i C^i r_t^d dt=\alpha_i\partial_0 C^i(\sigma^i)(ds^0-r_t^d s^0 dt)+\sum_{i=1}^{4}\alpha_i\partial_i C^i(\sigma^i)ds^i$$
$$+\frac{1}{2}\sum_{i=1}^{4}\alpha_i\left[(\partial_{00}C^i(\sigma^i)(d\left\langle s^0\right\rangle-(\sigma^i s^0)^2 dt))\right.$$
$$\left.+2\partial_{i0}C^i(\sigma^i)d\left\langle s^i,s^0\right\rangle+\partial_{ii}C^i(\sigma^i)d\left\langle s^i\right\rangle\right]$$

From now on we make explicit the dependence of the option's prices C^i on the corresponding implied volatilities. To lighten the notation we omit many of the terms that are zero. It is easy to detect the Deltas, the Vegas, Gammas, Vannas and Volgas. Assuming equal $d\sigma^i$ implies that all the $\left\langle s^i,s^0\right\rangle$ are equal and so are all the $\left\langle s^i\right\rangle$. Then, to set the equation above equal to zero, one has to solve the system

$$\alpha_i\partial_0 C^i(\sigma^i)=0$$
$$\sum_{i=1}^{4}\alpha_i\partial_i C^i(\sigma^i)ds^i=0$$
$$\sum_{i=1}^{4}\alpha_i\partial_{00}C^i(\sigma^i)=0$$

$$\sum_{i=1}^{4} \alpha_i \partial_{00} C^i(\sigma^i)(\sigma^i)^2 = 0$$
$$\partial_{i0} C^i(\sigma^i) = 0$$
$$\partial_{ii} C^i(\sigma^i) = 0$$

By the Gamma–Vega relationship for European options:

$$\partial_{00} C^i(\sigma^i)(\sigma^i)^2 = \frac{\sigma_i}{(s^0)^2\tau} \partial_i C^i(\sigma^i)$$

so that the fourth equation in the system becomes

$$\sum_{i=1}^{4} \alpha_i \partial_i C^i(\sigma^i) = 0$$

which is exactly the same as the second equation. Thus, the system can be rewritten as

$$\alpha_i \partial_0 C^i(\sigma^i) = 0$$
$$\sum_{i=1}^{4} \alpha_i \partial_i C^i(\sigma^i) ds^i = 0$$
$$\sum_{i=1}^{4} \alpha_i \partial_{00} C^i(\sigma^i) = 0$$
$$\partial_{i0} C^i(\sigma^i) = 0$$
$$\partial_{ii} C^i(\sigma^i) = 0$$

The constraints above impose the Delta, Vega, Gamma, Vanna and Volga of the portfolio to be zero. Since we have only four hedging tools, it is impossible to solve the system. We choose to release the constraint on Gamma and solve the system for the remaining equation. The final portfolio has an instantaneous hedging error:

$$\alpha_i dC^i - \alpha_i C^i r_t^d dt = \frac{1}{2} \sum_{i=1}^{4} \alpha_i \left[\partial_{00} C^i(\sigma^i)(d\left\langle s^0 \right\rangle - (\sigma^i s^0)^2 dt)) \right]$$

We substitute this equation in equation (3.1):

$$Z_T = \int_0^T e^{r_t^d (T-t)} \frac{1}{2} \left[\sum_{i=1}^{3} \alpha_i \left(\frac{\partial^2 O^i}{\partial S_t^2} (\sigma^i) S_t^2 (\varsigma_t^2 - (\sigma^i)^2) dt \right) - \left(\frac{\partial^2 V_t}{\partial S_t^2} (\sigma^i) S_t^2 (\varsigma_t^2 - \sigma^2) dt \right) \right] \tag{3.21}$$

The result is similar to formula (3.5), where the hedging error for the constant volatility hedging rule is shown. Basically, assuming equal increments in the implied volatilities and adopting a Vanna–Volga hedging rule yields the same performance as adopting a simple constant implied volatility hedging rule, though one has to compare the level of Gamma of the portfolio containing the hedging options with the level of Gamma of the single option (only entering into the portfolio if the constant volatility hedging rule is strictly adopted). It is very likely that the total Gamma will be lower in the Vanna–Volga rule, but it will not be zero. Nevertheless, it should not be forgotten that we made the rather strong assumption of equal variations of implied volatilities, which is not realistic since in practice they evolve according to more complex patterns. This also means that no clear hedging strategy can be designed and besides, the sources of the hedging errors cannot be identified distinctly.

At this stage, the analysis can be extended only by introducing a theory on how to correlate the implied volatilities of options struck at different levels. Such a theory can be derived by observing the actual behaviour of the volatility smile, which must now be defined and examined.

3.7 THE VOLATILITY SMILE AND ITS PHENOMENOLOGY

We now define the volatility smile, as mentioned above, and examine how it typically appears in the market.

Definition 3.7.1. ***Volatility smile.*** *For an expiry T, the volatility smile maps the implied volatilities to a given function $\zeta = f(K)$ of the strike price K. Hence, the smile indicates the volatility parameter to plug into the BS formula struck at level $K = f^{-1}(\zeta)$.*

As a first consequence, the presence of the smile in the market immediately invalidates the BS model, since the latter assumes a constant through strikes, though possibly deterministically dependent on time, implied volatility. Besides, since market operators may experience quite easily that the volatility smile itself is not constant as time elapses, they need to design hedging policies against the sources of risk related to it. In this section we will sketch a toy model to clearly disentangle the types of movements affecting the shape of the smile. To keep things strictly connected to the FX option market, we examine the smile mapped to the Delta of an option, which is a function of the strike price too, thus satisfying Definition 3.7.1. Actually, the liquid structures actively traded in the FX market offer a very intuitive way to tackle the problem in an extremely natural way.

In Chapter 1 we described the ATM **STDL** and the 25 Delta **RR** and **VWB**, and their quotation conventions in terms of implied volatilities (we refer to Section 1.4 in the following). It is straightforward to retrieve from those prices the implied volatility for the ATM strike, which can be considered as the central point of the volatility smile, and for the 25 Delta call and put,[17] which can be considered two symmetric (in terms of Delta) wings of the smile. In fact, recalling the quoting conventions, for a given expiry we can immediately identify three implied volatilities: σ_{ATM} is trivially the quoted volatility for the ATM straddle, whereas

$$\sigma_{25C}(t, T) = \sigma_{ATM}(t, T) + \mathbf{vwb}(t, T; 25) + 0.5\mathbf{rr}(t, T; 25) \tag{3.22}$$

$$\sigma_{25P}(t, T) = \sigma_{ATM}(t, T) + \mathbf{vwb}(t, T; 25) - 0.5\mathbf{rr}(t, T; 25) \tag{3.23}$$

We can use these volatilities as a starting point to also infer the implied volatilities for any other level of Delta, in a very simple framework, which has many drawbacks and is not perfect, but which provides us with a tool to study the main movements of the smile.[18]

[17] From here on, and also in the next chapters, we will adopt the market lore and use the shorthand 25D to mean an option whose strike yields an absolute level of Delta equal to 25%. Moreover, in the following, call and put refer to the base currency.

[18] This interpolation method has been proposed by Malz [46], and actually applied in his empirical analysis.

Assume for a moment that, for a given expiry T, the following holds:

$$\Delta(S_t, t, T, K, P^d(t,T), P^f(t,T), \sigma, -1) = \\ 1 - \Delta(S_t, t, T, K, P^d(t,T), P^f(t,T), \sigma, 1) \quad (3.24)$$

This is not exactly true, since the Delta of the call and the Delta of the put sum not to one but to one times the discount factor of the foreign rate for the option's expiry ($P^f(t,T)$). We also assume for a moment that the ATM quoted by market makers refers to a 50D put. Once again, that is not strictly true, but is a good approximation, at least for an option maturity not too long and if the cost of carry is small (or, which is the same, if the domestic and foreign interest rates are not too different). If these two assumptions hold, then we can say that we have, readily available on the market, the implied volatility for the 25D put, the 50D put (actually, the ATM volatility) and finally the 75D put (actually, the 25D call). We can map, for a given expiry, the implied volatility for any put's Delta running from 0D to 100D, so as to span the entire range of possible values.

The simplest way to interpolate the three implied volatilities is via a second-degree polynomial:

$$\sigma_{\$\Delta\$Put}(t,T) = a \cdot \sigma_{ATM}(t,T) \\ + b \cdot \mathbf{rr}(t,T;25)(\Delta_P - 0.5) + c \cdot \mathbf{vwb}(t,T;25)(\Delta_P - 0.5)^2 \quad (3.25)$$

Since we are assuming that the ATM is the 50D put, we have

$$\sigma_{50Put}(t,T) = a \cdot \sigma_{ATM} = \\ a \cdot \sigma_{ATM}(t,T) + b \cdot \mathbf{rr}(t,T;25) \cdot 0 + c \cdot \mathbf{vwb}(t,T;25) \cdot 0$$

and we set $a = 1$.

Plugging into equation (3.25) the price of the **RR** explicitly (i.e., as a difference of the two 25D volatilities) and recalling that, by assumption, $\sigma_{25C}(t,T) = \sigma_{25P}(t,T)$, we have

$$\mathbf{rr}(t,T,25) = \sigma_{25C}(t,T) - \sigma_{25P}(t,T) = \frac{b}{2} \cdot \mathbf{rr}(t,T;25)$$

implying $b = 2$.

Finally, resorting to the definition of the price of a **VWB** in terms of 25D volatilities, yields

$$\mathbf{vwb}(t,T;25) = 0.5 \cdot (\sigma_{25P}(t,T) + \sigma_{25C}(t,T)) - \sigma_{ATM}(t,T) \\ = 0.25^2 \cdot c \cdot \mathbf{vwb}(t,T;25)$$

and we can set the coefficient $c = 16$.

Hence, equation (3.25) can be written as

$$\sigma_{\$\Delta\$Put}(t,T) = \sigma_{ATM}(t,T) + \\ 2 \cdot \mathbf{rr}(t,T;25)(\Delta_P - 0.5) + 16 \cdot \mathbf{vwb}(t,T;25)(\Delta_P - 0.5)^2 \quad (3.26)$$

This toy model is suitable to understand how the shape of the volatility smile changes. In fact, for a given expiry, one can disentangle three main movements of the smile, which are determined by the three parameters of equation (3.26).

Let us start with a flat smile at 10% implied volatility level, depicted in Figure 3.1 as a continuous line. This smile is produced by equation (3.26), setting $\sigma_{ATM} = 10\%$, $\mathbf{vwb} = 0$ and $\mathbf{rr} = 0$. The first supposed movement is a shift upward or downward of the whole smile, which is produced by a change of the parameter σ_{ATM}. If this is set equal to 11%, the resulting new

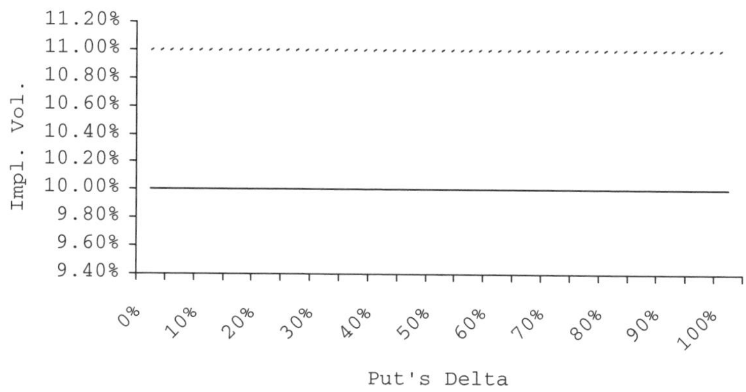

Figure 3.1 Parallel volatility smile movement. Continuous line: 10% implied volatility; dashed line: 11% implied volatility

flat smile is drawn as a dashed line in the figure. Hence, the parameter σ_{ATM} (i.e., the price of an ATM **STDL**) commands the *level* movement: the higher its value, the higher the level of the volatility smile.

The second kind of movement is a change in the curvature of the smile and it is a symmetric movement. In Figure 3.2, the 10% flat smile is depicted as a continuous line, whereas a dashed line draws the new smile with a positive curvature. This is the result of a change in the **vwb** parameter, which is set equal to 0.20% from a starting value of 0 (**rr** is still equal to 0). Therefore, the price of **vwb** commands the *curvature* movement: the higher the value of **vwb**, the more the smile curvature is emphasized.

The third kind of movement is illustrated in Figure 3.3, and it is a change in the slope of the volatility smile. The continuous line is the usual flat smile at the 10% level and the dashed line is the new smile resulting from setting the value of the parameter **rr** (i.e., the price of the **RR**) equal to 0.75% (**vwb** is equal to 0). A greater positive value of **rr** implies a steeper positive slope of the smile.

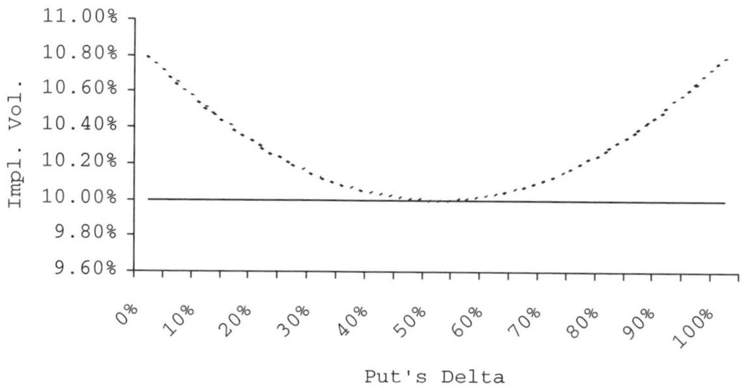

Figure 3.2 Curvature volatility smile movement. Continuous line: 10% flat smile; dashed line: 0.20% **vwb**

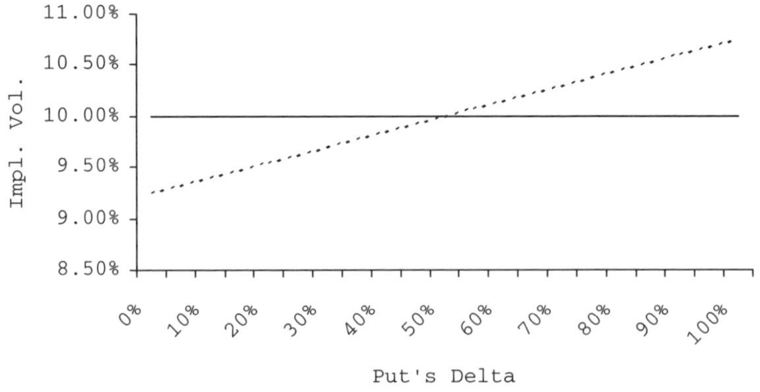

Figure 3.3 Positive slope volatility smile movement. Continuous line: 10% flat smile; dashed line: 0.75% **rr**

The slope can also be negative; for example, in Figure 3.4 the dashed line draws a volatility smile with **rr** set equal to −0.75%. Hence, the price of the **RR** commands the *sign of the slope* of the volatility smile and its *steepness*.

The volatility smile for a given expiry moves according to the three basic movements we have described above. Although it is very useful to disentangle them, one should never forget that in the real world the volatility smile is actually a combined result of the three. In Figure 3.5 the dashed line draws a volatility smile produced by the following set of parameters: $\sigma_{ATM} = 10\%$, **vwb** = 0.20% and **rr** = −0.75%. This is a much more realistic smile.

To recapitulate, the movements of the volatility smile are of three kinds:

- A parallel movement upward or downward, due to a change in the price of the ATM **STDL**, which is expressed as a change of σ_{ATM}.
- A slope movement, due to a change in the **rr** price. That is the same as saying that the difference between the implied volatilities of the 25D call and put varies. The wider the positive (negative) difference, the steeper and more positively (negatively) sloped the smile.

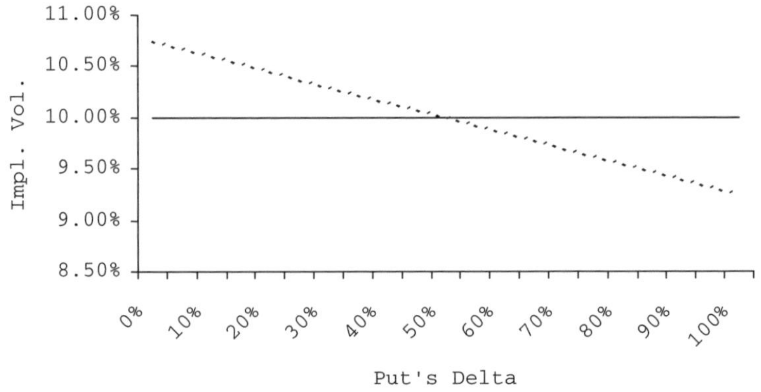

Figure 3.4 Negative slope volatility smile movement. Continuous line: 10% flat smile; dashed line: −0.75% **rr**

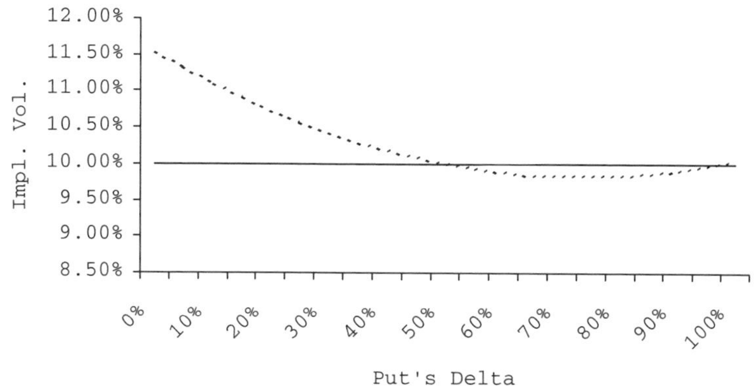

Figure 3.5 Convex and negative slope volatility smile movement. Continuous line: 10% flat smile; dashed line: 0.20% **vwb** and −0.75% **rr**

- A curvature movement, due to a change in the price of the **VWB**, that is the difference between the average of the implied volatilities of the 25D call and put and the ATM **STDL** implied volatility changes. The wider the difference, the more convex the smile.

3.8 LOCAL EXPOSURES TO THE VOLATILITY SMILE

After having sketched the basic movements affecting the volatility smile for a given expiry, the next step is to examine how hedging strategies can be implemented so as to manage the related risks. More specifically: is it possible to get an exposure to these movements by trading specific structures? And, more importantly, is it possible to get an exposure exclusive to one of them? The questions are almost rhetoric and the answer to both of them is: yes, it is. Actually, the main structures quoted by the market (i.e., the ATM **STDL**, **RR** and **VWB**) are the instruments to get exclusive exposures to each of the three movements, as we will show in what follows. We assume, as usual, that we are at time t and the options' expiry is at T. We study the three structures separately, but as a preliminary we first need to examine how exactly to retrieve the strikes for the quoted Deltas.

3.8.1 Retrieving the strikes of the main structures

We mentioned in Chapter 1 that the ATM strike is that one making a straddle Delta-neutral (that is, the total Delta is nil). So, we simply have to find the strike K_{ATM} such that the following relation holds:

$$\begin{aligned}&\Delta(S_t, t, T, K_{ATM}, P^d(t,T), P^f(t,T), \sigma_{ATM}, 1) = \\ &-\Delta(S_t, t, T, K_{ATM}, P^d(t,T), P^f(t,T), \sigma_{ATM}, -1)\end{aligned} \tag{3.27}$$

From the definition of Delta for the call and put,[19] we have

$$P^f(t,T)(t,T)\Phi(d_1) = -P^f(t,T)(t,T)(\Phi(d_1) - 1)$$

[19] See Chapter 2; we also exploit the properties of the normal distribution function.

where the usual notation is used. This implies that

$$2\Phi(d_1) = 1$$

Noting that $\Phi(d_1)$ is the cumulative normal distribution function, the problem reduces to finding the strike K_{ATM} making $d_1 = 0$. Hence:

$$K_{ATM}(t, T) = F(t, T)e^{(0.5\sigma_{ATM}^2(T-t))} \tag{3.28}$$

where, at time t, $F(t, T)$ is the forward price for delivery at T and σ_{ATM} is the ATM implied volatility quoted in the market for the expiry T.

Let us now move on and consider the other two strikes, referring to the 25D call and 25D put. Our task is to find the strikes K_{25C} and K_{25P} such that:

$$\Delta(S_t, t, T, K_{25C}, P^d(t, T), P^f(t, T), \sigma_{25C}, 1) = P^f(t, T)\Phi(d_1^C) = 0.25$$
$$\Delta(S_t, t, T, K_{25P}, P^d(t, T), P^f(t, T), \sigma_{25P}, -1) = P^f(t, T)(\Phi(d_1^P) - 1) = -0.25$$

where

$$d_1^C = \frac{\ln \frac{F(t,T)}{K_{25C}} + \frac{\sigma_{K_{25C}}^2}{2}(T-t)}{\sigma_{K_{25C}}\sqrt{T-t}}$$

$$d_1^P = \frac{\ln \frac{F(t,T)}{K_{25P}} + \frac{\sigma_{K_{25P}}^2}{2}(T-t)}{\sigma_{K_{25P}}\sqrt{T-t}}$$

Now, for the call option we have

$$d_1^C = \Phi^{-1}(0.25/P^f(t, T)) = -\alpha \tag{3.29}$$

where Φ^{-1} is the inverse normal distribution function and $-\alpha$ is the percentile from a standard normal distribution returning a probability equal to $0.25P^f(t, T)$. For the put option, the following must hold:

$$d_1^P = \Phi^{-1}((1 - 0.25)/P^f(t, T)) = \alpha \tag{3.30}$$

where α is again the percentile from a normal distribution function returning the probability $(1 - 0.25)/P^f(t, T)$, recalling the fact that the symmetry of the Normal distribution function yields

$$\Phi^{-1}(1 - x) = -\Phi^{-1}(x)$$

From equations (3.29) and (3.30) we get the two formulae to calculate the strikes on the 25 Delta:

$$K_P \equiv F(t, T)e^{\sigma_{25P}\sqrt{T-t}\Phi^{-1}(0.25/P^f(t,T))+0.5\sigma_{25P}^2(T-t)} \tag{3.31}$$

$$K_C \equiv F(t, T)e^{-\sigma_{25C}\sqrt{T-t}\Phi^{-1}(0.25/P^f(t,T))+0.5\sigma_{25C}^2(T-t)} \tag{3.32}$$

We are now ready to examine the exposure properties featuring each main structure.

3.8.2 ATM straddle exposures

From the definition of an ATM **STDL** provided in Chapter 1 we have, for a given maturity T, the following:

$$\mathbf{STDL} = \mathbf{C}(K_{ATM}) + \mathbf{P}(K_{ATM}) \tag{3.33}$$

where, to lighten the notation, we suppress all the dependencies of the price of an option, except the reference to the strike. We would like to study how the value of this structure is affected by a movement of the volatility smile; since the latter assigns the value of the implied volatility to plug into the BS formula for each level of strike price, we just work with the BS model and calculate the Vega of the ATM **STDL** straddle:

$$\mathcal{V}_{\mathbf{STDL}} = \mathcal{V}_{\mathbf{C}(K_{ATM})} + \mathcal{V}_{\mathbf{P}(K_{ATM})}$$

The subscripts of the two Vegas indicate the option that each of them refers to (we also adopt this notation for the Delta, in this section). Since the call and put are both struck at K_{ATM}, they have the same Vega; we can choose the call option and rewrite the equation above as

$$\mathcal{V}_{\mathbf{STDL}} = 2\mathcal{V}_{\mathbf{C}(K_{ATM})} = 2P^f(t;T)S_t\sqrt{T-t}\frac{1}{2\pi}e^{-\frac{d_1^2}{2}}$$

and, recalling that when $K = K_{ATM}$ then $d_1 = 0$, we get

$$\mathcal{V}_{\mathbf{STDL}} = 2P^f(t;T)S\frac{1}{2\pi}\sqrt{T-t} \tag{3.34}$$

which is always a positive number.

The exposure of the ATM **STDL** to the three main movements of the volatility matrix can be calculated by means of a Taylor expansion. For a parallel shift movement, the expansion yields

$$d\mathbf{STDL} = (\Delta_{\mathbf{C}(K_{ATM})} + \Delta_{\mathbf{P}(K_{ATM})})dS_t + \mathcal{V}_{\mathbf{STDL}}d\sigma_{ATM} + o(S_t, \sigma_{ATM})$$

By definition the Delta of the ATM **STDL** is 0, so that the exposure is linearly proportional to the variation of the ATM volatility:

$$d\mathbf{STDL} \simeq \mathcal{V}_{\mathbf{STDL}}d\sigma_{ATM}$$

Since σ_{ATM} is independent of the other two main volatilities (and their combinations expressed within the risk reversal and butterfly prices), it is trivial to show that the **STDL** is not affected by the movements of the slope and the curvature of the volatility smile.

To recapitulate, the value of an ATM **STDL** long position is influenced only by parallel movements shifting the curve to a different level, all the rest being fixed. Hence, this structure offers the ability to isolate the effect of the parallel movements from the other two kinds of movements, and thus to take exposures only to that.

3.8.3 Risk reversal exposures

From the definition of a 25D **RR** we have

$$\mathbf{RR} = \mathbf{C}(K_{25C}) - \mathbf{P}(K_{25P}) \tag{3.35}$$

The exposure with respect to a parallel shift of the volatility smile can be calculated by a Taylor expansion around the FX spot rate S and the at-the-money volatility σ_{ATM}:

$$d\mathbf{RR} = (\Delta_{\mathbf{C}(K_{25C})} - \Delta_{\mathbf{P}(K_{25P})})dS_t + \mathcal{V}_{\mathbf{RR}} d\sigma_{ATM} + o(S_t, \sigma_{ATM})$$

The Vega of the **RR** with respect to the ATM volatility is

$$\mathcal{V}_{\mathbf{RR}} = \frac{\partial \mathbf{C}}{\partial \sigma_{25C}} \frac{\partial \sigma_{25C}}{\partial \sigma_{ATM}} - \frac{\partial \mathbf{P}}{\partial \sigma_{25P}} \frac{\partial \sigma_{25P}}{\partial \sigma_{ATM}} = \mathcal{V}_{\mathbf{C}(K_{25C})} - \mathcal{V}_{\mathbf{P}(K_{25P})} \tag{3.36}$$

where we used equations (3.22) and (3.23). This is also the sensitivity of the **RR** to a parallel shift of the smile. Since the two strikes have been chosen so that the Delta of both the call and the put have the same value, their Vega is also the same.[20] If the position is Delta-hedged, it is straightforward to see that the exposures to the FX spot rate and to the parallel movements of the smile are nil.

By expanding the value of the **RR** around the spot and the **rr** (that is, the price in volatility terms of a 25D risk reversal), we can calculate the exposure of the structure with respect to a change of the smile's slope:

$$\begin{aligned} d\mathbf{RR} &= (\Delta_{\mathbf{C}(K_{25C})} - \Delta_{\mathbf{P}(K_{25P})})dS_t \\ &\quad + \left(\frac{\partial \mathbf{C}}{\partial \sigma_{25C}} \frac{\partial \sigma_{25C}}{\partial \mathbf{rr}} - \frac{\partial \mathbf{P}}{\partial \sigma_{25P}} \frac{\partial \sigma_{25P}}{\partial \mathbf{rr}} \right) d\mathbf{rr} + o(S_t, \mathbf{rr}) \end{aligned}$$

which yields (resorting once again to equations (3.22) and (3.23))

$$\begin{aligned} d\mathbf{RR} &= (\Delta_{\mathbf{C}(K_{25C})} - \Delta_{\mathbf{P}(K_{25P})})dS_t \\ &\quad + (0.5\mathcal{V}_{\mathbf{C}(K_{25C})} + 0.5\mathcal{V}_{\mathbf{P}(K_{25P})})d\mathbf{rr} + o(S_t, \mathbf{rr}) \end{aligned}$$

Once more, when we consider a Delta-hedged position, the terms in the first bracket are cancelled and we get

$$d\mathbf{RR} \simeq \mathcal{V}_{\mathbf{C}(K_{25C})} d\mathbf{rr} \tag{3.37}$$

where we used the fact that the two $\mathcal{V}$ are equal. So, the value of the **RR** is positively related to the change of the smile's slope ($d\mathbf{rr}$) by a factor equal to the Vega of the call (which is, anyway, equal to the Vega of the put in this case).

Finally, let us study the exposure to the change of the smile's curvature of the **RR**, by expanding its value around the spot and the **vwb** (that is, the price in volatility terms of the Vega-weighted butterfly):

$$\begin{aligned} d\mathbf{RR} &= (\Delta_{\mathbf{C}(K_{25C})} - \Delta_{\mathbf{P}(K_{25P})})dS_t \\ &\quad + \left(\frac{\partial \mathbf{C}}{\partial \sigma_{25C}} \frac{\partial \sigma_{25C}}{\partial \mathbf{vwb}} - \frac{\partial \mathbf{P}}{\partial \sigma_{25P}} \frac{\partial \sigma_{25P}}{\partial \mathbf{vwb}} \right) d\mathbf{vwb} + o(S_t, \mathbf{vwb}) \end{aligned}$$

that is (using the relations (3.22) and (3.23))

$$\begin{aligned} d\mathbf{RR} &= (\Delta_{\mathbf{C}(K_{25C})} - \Delta_{\mathbf{P}(K_{25P})})dS_t \\ &\quad + (\mathcal{V}_{\mathbf{C}(K_{25C})} - \mathcal{V}_{\mathbf{C}(K_{25P})})d\mathbf{vwb} + o(S_t, \mathbf{vwb}) \end{aligned}$$

[20] See Chapter 2 for the Delta–Vega relationship.

and then, after Delta hedging the position so as to eliminate the sum in the first bracket, we have that the **RR** exposure to a change of the smile's curvature is nil:

$$d\mathbf{RR} \simeq 0 \tag{3.38}$$

To sum up, a long **RR** position is influenced only by a change in the slope of the smile, all the rest being fixed. It is then the tool apt to take an exposure to the risk related to the slope movements of the smile, disregarding the other two kinds of movements.

3.8.4 Vega-weighted butterfly exposures

By the definition of a long **VWB** position, we have

$$\mathbf{VWB} = \beta\mathbf{STGL} - \mathbf{STDL} \tag{3.39}$$

The quantity β of the bought 25D **STGL** is chosen such that, considering the sold ATM **STDL**, the total Vega of the structure is nil. We undertake the same analysis as before to study the exposures of the **VWB** by starting with a Taylor expansion around the FX spot rate and the σ_{ATM}:

$$\begin{aligned} d\mathbf{VWB} = {} & [\beta(\Delta_{\mathbf{C}(K_{25C})} - \Delta_{\mathbf{P}(K_{25P})}) - (\Delta_{\mathbf{C}(K_{ATM})} - \Delta_{\mathbf{P}(K_{ATM})})]dS_t \\ & + \mathcal{V}_{\mathbf{VWB}} d\sigma_{ATM} + o(S_t, \sigma_{ATM}) \end{aligned}$$

We need to calculate the Vega with respect to the σ_{ATM}:

$$\mathcal{V}_{\mathbf{VWB}} = \beta\left(\frac{\partial \mathbf{C}}{\partial\sigma_{25C}}\frac{\partial\sigma_{25C}}{\partial\sigma_{ATM}} + \frac{\partial \mathbf{P}}{\partial\sigma_{25P}}\frac{\partial\sigma_{25P}}{\partial\sigma_{ATM}}\right) - \mathcal{V}_{\mathbf{STDL}} = 0$$

Since $\frac{\partial\sigma_{25C}}{\partial\sigma_{ATM}} = \frac{\partial\sigma_{25P}}{\partial\sigma_{ATM}} = 1$, the total Vega with respect to the ATM volatility is zero by construction. Moreover, the total Delta of the **VWB** is zero,[21] and we have that the exposure to a parallel shift of the smile is nil:

$$d\mathbf{VWB} \simeq 0 \tag{3.40}$$

The exposure to a change in the smile's slope is similarly retrieved by the usual Taylor expansion:

$$\begin{aligned} d\mathbf{VWB} = {} & [\beta(\Delta_{\mathbf{C}(K_{25C})} - \Delta_{\mathbf{P}(K_{25P})}) - (\Delta_{\mathbf{C}(K_{ATM})} - \Delta_{\mathbf{P}(K_{ATM})})]dS_t \\ & + \left[\beta\left(\frac{\partial \mathbf{C}}{\partial\sigma_{25C}}\frac{\partial\sigma_{25C}}{\partial\mathbf{rr}} + \frac{\partial \mathbf{P}}{\partial\sigma_{25P}}\frac{\partial\sigma_{25P}}{\partial\mathbf{rr}}\right)\right. \\ & \left. - \left(\frac{\partial \mathbf{C}}{\partial\sigma_{ATM}}\frac{\partial\sigma_{ATM}}{\partial\mathbf{rr}} + \frac{\partial \mathbf{P}}{\partial\sigma_{ATM}}\frac{\partial\sigma_{ATM}}{\partial\mathbf{rr}}\right)\right]d\mathbf{rr} + o(S_t, \mathbf{rr}) \end{aligned}$$

Since $\frac{\partial\sigma_{25C}}{\partial\mathbf{rr}} = 1$, $\frac{\partial\sigma_{25P}}{\partial\mathbf{rr}} = -1$, $\frac{\partial\sigma_{ATM}}{\partial rr} = 0$, and the total Delta of the **VWB** is 0, we once again get

$$d\mathbf{VWB} \simeq 0 \tag{3.41}$$

So the **VWB** is not affected by a change in the smile's slope.

[21] In fact, the ATM **STDL** has zero Delta by definition and the 25D **STGL** contains a call and a put with the same Delta and opposite sign summing up to zero as well.

Finally, we Taylor expand the **VWB** around the FX spot rate and the **vwb**:

$$\begin{aligned} d\mathbf{VWB} &= [\beta(\Delta_{\mathbf{C}(K_{25C})} - \Delta_{\mathbf{P}(K_{25P})}) - (\Delta_{\mathbf{C}(K_{ATM})} - \Delta_{\mathbf{P}(K_{ATM})})]dS_t \\ &+ \left[\beta\left(\frac{\partial\mathbf{C}}{\partial\sigma_{25C}}\frac{\partial\sigma_{25C}}{\partial\mathbf{vwb}} + \frac{\partial\mathbf{P}}{\partial\sigma_{25P}}\frac{\partial\sigma_{25P}}{\partial\mathbf{vwb}}\right)\right. \\ &- \left.\left(\frac{\partial\mathbf{C}}{\partial\sigma_{ATM}}\frac{\partial\sigma_{ATM}}{\partial\mathbf{vwb}} + \frac{\partial\mathbf{P}}{\partial\sigma_{ATM}}\frac{\partial\sigma_{ATM}}{\partial\mathbf{vwb}}\right)\right]d\mathbf{vwb} + o(S_t, \mathbf{vwb}) \end{aligned}$$

which (recalling that $\frac{\partial\sigma_{25C}}{\partial\mathbf{vwb}} = \frac{\partial\sigma_{25P}}{\partial\mathbf{vwb}} = 1$ and $\frac{\partial\sigma_{ATM}}{\partial\mathbf{vwb}} = 0$) yield

$$d\mathbf{VWB} \simeq \beta(\mathcal{V}_{\mathbf{C}(K_{25C})} + \mathcal{V}_{\mathbf{P}(K_{\mathbf{P}})}) = 2\beta\mathcal{V}_{\mathbf{C}(K_{25C})}d\mathbf{vwb} \tag{3.42}$$

where we used the fact that the 25D call and the put have the same Vega. Hence, the value of the **VWB** is positively related to an increase of the smile's curvature by a factor equal to 2β times the Vega of the call.

To sum up, a long **VWB** position is only affected by a change in the curvature of the volatility smile, all the rest being equal; a change in the level or slope of the smile is immaterial. It is the tool best suited to take an exposure to the curvature's movement, the other two movements being ineffective on the value of the structure.

At the end of the analysis above, we can state that each of the three main structures has a particular and specific exposure to one of the three basic movements of the volatility smile. That is, in principle, very useful for the management of an options book.

3.9 SCENARIO HEDGING AND ITS RELATIONSHIP WITH VANNA–VOLGA HEDGING

In Section 3.6 we stopped at a dead-end in the examination of the performance of a Vanna–Volga hedging rule. Now, after we have defined the volatility smile and analysed some features of its dynamics, it is possible to have another look at that hedging rule, although under a different perspective, and explore its effectiveness in hedging a contingent claim.

The set-up is the same as in Section 3.6. To fix things suppose that, in the same spirit as Section 3.7, three stochastic factors affect the dynamics of the smile for a given expiry T: an example has been provided in formula (3.26), which gives the implied volatility for any strike (expressed in terms of the Delta of a put option) and which depends on the ATM implied volatility, the 25D **rr** and the 25D **vwb** or, alternatively, the level, the slope and the convexity of the smile. We already noted that what we examined above is just a toy model, but its basic idea is the same as in more sophisticated specifications of the volatility smile's function. Assume that the risk-neutral dynamics for the three factors are:

$$\begin{aligned} d\sigma_{ATM} &= \widetilde{\phi}^{ATM}dt + \sigma_{ATM}\nu_t^{ATM}dZ_t^{ATM} \\ d\mathbf{rr} &= \widetilde{\phi}^{\mathbf{rr}}dt + \mathbf{rr}\nu_t^{\mathbf{rr}}dZ_t^{\mathbf{rr}} \\ d\mathbf{vwb} &= \widetilde{\phi}^{\mathbf{vwb}}dt + \mathbf{vwb}\nu_t^{\mathbf{vwb}}dZ_t^{\mathbf{vwb}} \end{aligned}$$

where the ATM implied volatility, the 25D **rr** and the 25D **vwb** (hereafter we will omit the reference to the Delta of the latter two structures) are affected by three (possibly correlated) Brownian motions $dZ_t^{\{\cdot\}}$, $\nu_t^{\{\cdot\}}$ being the instantaneous volatility associated with each of them.

We can now reasonably suppose, in a very general form, that the process commanding the evolution of the implied volatility, for a given strike K and expiry T, is a function

$\sigma(K,T) = \sigma_K = g(\sigma_{ATM}, \mathbf{rr}, \mathbf{vwb})$ so that, by Itô's lemma,

$$d\sigma_K = \widetilde{\phi}_t^{\,K} dt + \frac{\partial \sigma_K}{\partial \sigma_{ATM}} \sigma_{ATM} \nu_{ATM} dZ_t^{ATM} + \frac{\partial \sigma_K}{\partial \mathbf{rr}} \mathbf{rr} \nu_t^{\mathbf{rr}} dZ_t^{\mathbf{rr}} + \frac{\partial \sigma_K}{\partial \mathbf{vwb}} \mathbf{vwb} \nu_t^{\mathbf{vwb}} dZ_t^{\mathbf{vwb}} \tag{3.43}$$

The SDE is similar to that derived in a market model setting (see equations (3.12) and (3.11)): we leave the process not fully specified though, since it is not really needed for subsequent analysis. We know from Section 3.4 that the instantaneous error of an updating volatility hedging rule is equal to the difference between the actual variation of the implied volatility and its expected risk-neutral change, times the Vega of the option. If we consider a portfolio containing an FX spot position, three hedging options and the contingent claim to be hedged (as in the Vanna–Volga hedging rule case), and implement an updating volatility hedging rule, we have from equation (3.10):

$$Z_T = -\sum_{i=1}^{4} \int_0^T e^{r_t^d (T-t)} \alpha_i \mathcal{V}_t^i (d\sigma_{K^i} - \widetilde{\phi}^{K^i} dt)$$

where α_i for $i = 1, \ldots, 4$ are the weights of the options entering into the strategy, whose implied volatilities experience an actual variation $d\sigma_{K^i}$ and have a risk-neutral drift $\widetilde{\phi}^{K^i} dt$. By means of equation (3.43) we have

$$Z_T = -\sum_{i=1}^{4} \int_0^T e^{r_t^d (T-t)} \alpha_i \mathcal{V}_t^i \left(\frac{\partial \sigma_{K^i}}{\partial \sigma_{ATM}} \sigma_{ATM} \nu_{ATM} dZ_t^{ATM} + \frac{\partial \sigma_{K^i}}{\partial \mathbf{rr}} \mathbf{rr} \nu_t^{\mathbf{rr}} dZ_t^{\mathbf{rr}} + \frac{\partial \sigma_{K^i}}{\partial \mathbf{vwb}} \mathbf{vwb} \nu_t^{\mathbf{vwb}} dZ_t^{\mathbf{vwb}} \right) \tag{3.44}$$

The total hedging error now contains only three stochastic factors (the prices of the three main structures), as opposed to the original version where each implied volatility could be considered a stochastic factor of its own. Moreover, the three partial derivatives, $\frac{\partial \sigma_{K^i}}{\partial \sigma_{ATM}}$, $\frac{\partial \sigma_{K^i}}{\partial \mathbf{rr}}$ and $\frac{\partial \sigma_{K^i}}{\partial \mathbf{vwb}}$, can be calculated since we are assuming we know the functional form linking each volatility to the three factors. Hence, it is possible to establish the following system:

$$\sum_{i=1}^{3} \alpha_i \mathcal{V}_t^i \frac{\partial \sigma_{K^i}}{\partial \sigma_{ATM}} = \mathcal{V}_t^4 \frac{\partial \sigma_{K^4}}{\partial \sigma_{ATM}}$$

$$\sum_{i=1}^{3} \alpha_i \mathcal{V}_t^i \frac{\partial \sigma_{K^i}}{\partial \mathbf{rr}} = \mathcal{V}_t^4 \frac{\partial \sigma_{K^4}}{\partial \mathbf{rr}}$$

$$\sum_{i=1}^{3} \alpha_i \mathcal{V}_t^i \frac{\partial \sigma_{K^i}}{\partial \mathbf{vwb}} = \mathcal{V}_t^4 \frac{\partial \sigma_{K^4}}{\partial \mathbf{vwb}}$$

The system can be solved for the three quantities α_i for $i = 1, 2, 3$ ($\alpha_4 = -1$): these will make the total hedging error (3.44) equal to zero. To sum up: by imposing a functional dependence of the implied volatilities on the three basic factors, it is possible to perfectly replicate a contingent claim. The framework can easily be extended to include more factors, in which case we need to add more options into our hedging toolkit (whose number will be equal to that of the factors).

3.9.1 Scenario hedging with constant Delta options

In real-life trading in the FX market, options are quoted for strikes expressed in terms of Delta. As illustrated in Chapter 1, the most liquid common structures are the ATM **STDL**, the **RR** and the **VWB**, so that from those the strikes corresponding to the 25 Delta base currency calls and puts can be determined. As for a fixed Delta, the corresponding strike's level changes as the FX spot rate moves and time elapses; this means that the most liquid options for a given fixed expiry are not the same over time. As a consequence, if the three hedging options employed in the scenario rule are conveniently chosen as struck at the three main strikes for each time, then necessarily they change over time.

In the previous analysis we have just considered the case of a constant set of hedging tools (that is, the three options) continuously rebalanced so as to make the entire portfolio insensitive to the volatility smile risk. This strategy has two main flaws:

- The selected options may turn out to become completely meaningless in terms of hedging capability. For example, assume we start with three options struck so as, for a given expiry, to represent the centre and two wings of the smile (as is the case when one chooses the ATM strike and the 25D call and put strikes). As time goes by and the spot moves very far from the initial level, the three strikes can correspond to deep OTM options (and all on the same side, with respect to the FX spot level) on the resulting volatility smile. In this case they will likely have a poor hedging effectiveness for the movements of the volatility smile. Actually, they could still be sufficient to hedge the parallel shifts, but insufficient as far as the other two movements (slope and convexity) are concerned.
- As hinted above, as a strike becomes more and more deep-out-of-the money, the corresponding call and put options get less liquid, thus making the rebalancing more expensive in terms of transaction costs.

From these considerations it is clear that we have to enlarge our examination so as to include the possibility that the set of hedging tools is not restricted to the three starting options. In more detail, we allow for an ever-changing set of options so that at each instant they are those struck at the prevailing levels of ATM, 25D call and 25D put. We begin our strategy with such options at time 0, then in the next instant these options are no longer used as hedging tools, but they still stay in the portfolio and will be considered as claims to be hedged together with the initial contingent claim V_T.

Define the following collection of options:

$$\mathcal{H}_t = \int_0^t \int_0^{+\infty} \sum_{i=1}^{3} \alpha_{i,K}(u) \mathcal{C}_u^i(K) dK du \tag{3.45}$$

Define also the time $\tau_i(K)$ as the (assumed unique) time instant such that $K^i_{\tau_i(K)} = K$. Besides, $\alpha_{i,K}(t)$ is the number of options with strike K held at time t, where K was equal to some K^i_u, $u < t$:

$$d\alpha_{i,K}(t) = x^i_K(t)\delta_{\tau_i(K)}(t)dt \tag{3.46}$$

with $x^i_K(t)$ the weight on the strike K^i_t at time t ($\delta_{\tau_i(K)}(t)$ is the Dirac delta function).

Equation (3.45) defines an accumulating collection of options. Each option is priced at t by an implied volatility $\sigma_{K_u^i}$ corresponding to the strike K_u^i. More specifically, at each instant u three new options enter into this basket. We indicate by $\alpha_{i,K}(t)$ the quantities at t of the options $\mathcal{C}_t^i(K_u^i)$ (for $i = 1, .., 3$) struck such that

$$\begin{aligned}
K_u^1 &= \Delta(S_t, u, T, K_u^1, P^d(u,T), P^f(u,T), \sigma_{25P}, -1) = -0.25 \\
K_u^2 &= F(u,T)e^{(0.5\sigma_{ATM}^2(T-u))} \\
K_u^3 &= \Delta(S_t, u, T, K_u^3, P^d(u,T), P^f(u,T), \sigma_{25C}, 1) = 0.25
\end{aligned}$$

The strikes correspond (given the level of the FX rate S at time u), respectively, to the 25D put, ATM and 25D call. In equation (3.45) we sum[22] all these options from inception of the hedging strategy up to time t; in other words, we have in the collection all the options that we used to nil the sensitivities to the volatility smile at each time $0 \le u \le t$, up to the instant t we are considering. We can define a new contingent claim $\widetilde{V}_t$ as

$$\mathcal{C}^4 = \widetilde{V}_t = V_t - \mathcal{H}_t \tag{3.47}$$

which is simply the difference between the simple European contingent claim V_t and the basket of all the options used as a hedging tool in the past from 0 to t and increasing by three options at each instant. The new contingent claim $\widetilde{V}_t$ still enters into the portfolio with a constant quantity $\alpha_4 = -1$, and this justifies the minus sign for $\mathcal{H}_t$ in equation (3.47): the options collection is actually added to the total portfolio in that way.

Let us now redesign the scenario hedging rule. First we need to calculate the sensitivities of $\widetilde{V}_t$ to the three basic movements. Similarly to what we have done before, we rewrite the total hedging error as

$$\begin{aligned}
Z_T = -\int_0^T e^{r_t^d(T-t)} \Bigg\{ & \sum_{i=1}^{3} \alpha_i \mathcal{V}_t^i \left(\frac{\partial \sigma_{K^i}}{\partial \sigma_{ATM}} \sigma_{ATM} \nu_{ATM} dZ_t^{ATM} \right. \\
& \left. + \frac{\partial \sigma_{K^i}}{\partial \mathbf{rr}} \mathbf{rr} \nu_t^{\mathbf{rr}} dZ_t^{\mathbf{rr}} + \frac{\partial \sigma_{K^i}}{\partial \mathbf{vwb}} \mathbf{vwb} \nu_t^{\mathbf{vwb}} dZ_t^{\mathbf{vwb}} \right) \\
& - \left[\left(\frac{\partial V_t}{\partial \sigma_{K^4}} \frac{\partial \sigma_{K^4}}{\partial \sigma_{ATM}} - \int_0^t \int_0^{+\infty} \sum_{i=1}^{3} \alpha_{i,K}(u) \frac{\partial \mathcal{H}_u}{\partial \sigma_K} \frac{\partial \sigma_K}{\partial \sigma_{ATM}} du dK \right) \sigma_{ATM} \nu_{ATM} dZ_t^{ATM} \right. \\
& + \left(\frac{\partial V_t}{\partial \sigma_{K^4}} \frac{\partial \sigma_{K^4}}{\partial \mathbf{rr}} - \int_0^t \int_0^{+\infty} \sum_{i=1}^{3} \alpha_{i,K}(u) \frac{\partial \mathcal{H}_u}{\partial \sigma_K} \frac{\partial \sigma_K}{\partial \mathbf{rr}} du dK \right) \mathbf{rr} \nu_t^{\mathbf{rr}} dZ_t^{\mathbf{rr}} \\
& \left. + \left(\frac{\partial V_t}{\partial \sigma_{K^4}} \frac{\partial \sigma_{K^4}}{\partial \mathbf{vwb}} - \int_0^t \int_0^{+\infty} \sum_{i=1}^{3} \alpha_{i,K}(u) \frac{\partial \mathcal{H}_u}{\partial \sigma_K} \frac{\partial \sigma_K}{\partial \mathbf{vwb}} du dK \right) \mathbf{vwb} \nu_t^{\mathbf{vwb}} dZ_t^{\mathbf{vwb}} \right] \Bigg\}
\end{aligned} \tag{3.48}$$

[22] We are actually integrating, since we are working in a continuous time setting.

The amounts of the three hedging options at time t are chosen so as to cancel the exposures to the smile movements, by solving the following system:

$$\begin{aligned}
\sum_{i=1}^{3} \alpha_i \mathcal{V}_t^i \frac{\partial \sigma_{K^i}}{\partial \sigma_{ATM}} &= \mathcal{V}_t^4 \frac{\partial \sigma_{K^4}}{\partial \sigma_{ATM}} - A \\
\sum_{i=1}^{3} \alpha_i \mathcal{V}_t^i \frac{\partial \sigma_{K^i}}{\partial \mathbf{rr}} &= \mathcal{V}_t^4 \frac{\partial \sigma_{K^4}}{\partial \mathbf{rr}} - R \\
\sum_{i=1}^{3} \alpha_i \mathcal{V}_t^i \frac{\partial \sigma_{K^i}}{\partial \mathbf{vwb}} &= \mathcal{V}_t^4 \frac{\partial \sigma_{K^4}}{\partial \mathbf{vwb}} - W
\end{aligned} \tag{3.49}$$

where

$$\begin{aligned}
A &= \int_0^t \int_0^{+\infty} \sum_{i=1}^{3} \alpha_{i,K}(u) \frac{\partial \mathcal{H}_u}{\partial \sigma_K} \frac{\partial \sigma_K}{\partial \sigma_{ATM}} du dK \\
R &= \int_0^t \int_0^{+\infty} \sum_{i=1}^{3} \alpha_{i,K}(u) \frac{\partial \mathcal{H}_u}{\partial \sigma_K} \frac{\partial \sigma_K}{\partial \mathbf{rr}} du dK \\
W &= \int_0^t \int_0^{+\infty} \sum_{i=1}^{3} \alpha_{i,K}(u) \frac{\partial \mathcal{H}_u}{\partial \sigma_K} \frac{\partial \sigma_K}{\partial \mathbf{vwb}} du dK
\end{aligned}$$

Hence we can conclude that at each instant t it is possible to perfectly hedge the total portfolio, also under the assumption that the set of hedging tools is not constant over time, as happens in reality, where the most liquid options are those struck corresponding to the ATM level and the 25D call and put. We can further refine the analysis, and carry it much nearer to the market practice, by substituting the three hedging options at each time t with the three main structures. In fact, suppose we want to express the three quantities α_i, $i = 1, 2, 3$, determined as above, in terms of amounts of ATM **STDL**, **RR** and **VWB**. This is possible via the following relationships:

$$\begin{aligned}
\alpha_{ATM} &= \alpha_2 + \frac{1}{\beta} \frac{\alpha_1 + \alpha_3}{2} \\
\alpha_{RR} &= \frac{1}{2}(\alpha_3 - \alpha_1) \\
\alpha_{VWB} &= \frac{1}{\beta} \frac{\alpha_1 + \alpha_3}{2}
\end{aligned} \tag{3.50}$$

Just a few words to make formulae (3.50) clear: the **VWB** amount is determined by averaging the two 25D amounts. Since the market convention is to indicate the amount of the **VWB** via the notional of the ATM **STDL**, the latter is simply the average of the two wing option quantities, divided by the β factor making the butterfly Vega weighted. The amount of the **STDL** is then the original amount (α_2) augmented by the amount of the **STDL** traded (with the opposite sign) in the **VWB**. Finally, the amount of the **RR** is determined via the imbalance between the 25D call and the 25D put, evenly split. It is easy to check that trading the three main instruments as in formulae (3.50) yields the same amounts for α_i, $i = 1, 2, 3$, as in the solution for the system given in formulae (3.49).[23]

An alternative and possibly even easier way is to solve the system (3.49) directly in terms of main traded structures. Recalling the properties of these structures examined in Section 3.8, it is straightforward to establish the system

$$\alpha_{ATM}(2P^f(t;T)S\sqrt{T-t}) = \frac{\partial V_t}{\partial \sigma_{ATM}} - A$$

$$\alpha_{RR}\mathcal{V}_{C(K_{25C})} = \frac{\partial V_t}{\partial \mathbf{rr}} - R$$

$$\alpha_{VWB}2\beta\mathcal{V}_{C(K_{25C})} = \frac{\partial V_t}{\partial \mathbf{vwb}} - W$$

whose solutions are α_{ATM}, α_{RR} and α_{VWB}, respectively: the amounts of ATM **STDL**, **RR** and **VWB** required for zeroing the exposures to the volatility smile movements.

To recapitulate the analysis for scenario hedging:

- We examined how it is possible to infer a possible volatility smile from prices trading in the market.
- We fitted a very simple model to the quotes of the three main structures and identified three basic movements determining the evolution of the volatility smile. We also showed that each of the three basic structures allows for an isolated exposure to only one of the three movements, thus providing for a toolkit to trade the volatility smile.
- Then we moved back to the hedging of the portfolio by means of three options (plus the FX spot rate). Equipped with a reasonable (although not realistic in this case) model describing the evolution of the smile, we assumed that any implied volatility is a function of the prices of the three main structures. We demonstrated that it is possible to nil the hedging error by choosing a function linking the implied volatility for any strike to those for three main strikes.

The problem now shifts to the choice of a function relating each implied volatility to the three main instruments (or, equivalently, to the three main traded volatilities). Its effectiveness in describing the smile for a given expiry is the crucial point for adequate hedging.

Before moving on to the next chapter, we still have to answer a question naturally arising at this point, also (and not secondarily) to justify the title of the current section, that is: what is the relationship between the Vanna–Volga hedging and the scenario hedging rule? Some relationship indeed exists. In fact, to see that, consider equation (3.7), which is the first possible way to express the instantaneous hedging error under the updating volatility hedging rule. It was the starting point for the design of the scenario hedging examined above, although we used the alternative version (equation (3.10)) to express the instantaneous hedging error. Basically, the scenario hedging is tantamount to cancelling the total hedging error under an updating volatility rule adopted for each of the options entering into the portfolio or, equivalently, a zeroing of the sum of four equations of the kind (3.10) each related to one option. But, since the latter is a different, though perfectly equivalent, way of expressing equation (3.7), it means that

[23] Two call options struck at the ATM level give the same exposure as an ATM **STDL**, provided they are Delta-hedged. So the fact that only one type of option enters into the set of hedging tools for the ATM strike does not invalidate the analysis.

the scenario hedging is the same as zeroing the total Vega, Vanna and Volga of the portfolio,[24] exactly as in the Vanna–Volga hedging rule. So, the two rules hinge on the same criteria, although this is not so evident in the scenario rule.

Anyway, it must be stressed that the scenario hedging rule is possible *only* if one is able to devise a smile function with a limited number of factors (three in the case we have examined) that can effectively interpolate amongst all possible strikes for each expiry or, alternatively, that is suitable to satisfactorily capture market prices. This function can be deduced from a proper stochastic volatility model (such as the SABR functional form (2.72), for example) or other sensible model-independent approaches, one of which will be studied extensively in the next chapter, where the problem of building a volatility surface will be tackled.

[24] Actually, Gamma is also cancelled out by scenario hedging, whereas it is still a residual open risk with Vega, Vanna and Volga hedging.

4
The Volatility Surface

4.1 GENERAL DEFINITIONS

In Chapter 3 we defined the volatility smile; we now extend this notion by defining the volatility surface. This is a fundamental building block of market-making activity and risk management, so we devote an in-depth analysis to the building of a consistent volatility surface.[1]

Definition 4.1.1. ***Volatility surface.*** *The volatility surface, or matrix (we will use the two terms without any distinction), is the map of the implied volatilities quoted by the market for plain vanilla options struck at different levels and expiring at different dates. Implied volatility is the parameter σ to plug into the Black–Scholes formula to calculate the price of an option.*

The volatility smile refers to a single expiry, whereas the volatility surface refers to a set of maturities. In practice, the matrix is built according to three main conventions, each prevailing as a standard in the market according to the traded underlying: the *sticky strike*, the *sticky Delta*, and finally the *sticky absolute*. These are simple rules used to conveniently quote and trade options written on different assets and, as such, are not intended to model the evolution of the volatility surface.

Definition 4.1.2. ***Sticky strike rule.*** *When the* sticky strike *rule is effective, implied volatilities are mapped, for each expiry, with respect to the strike prices; this is the rule usually adopted in official markets (e.g., equity options and futures options).*

The name *sticky strike* is related to the fact that implied volatilities are supposed not to change if the underlying asset's price changes. Clearly, that almost never happens, since the volatility matrix is not at all constant in reality. Nevertheless, the assumption is believed to be in force for small movements of the underlying asset. Accordingly, traders quote option prices for specific strikes, and usually in terms of premiums, so that one has to back out the implied volatility from those. A visual example of a sticky strike matrix is given in Table 4.1.

Definition 4.1.3. ***Sticky Delta rule.*** *If the* sticky Delta *rule is adopted, implied volatilities are mapped, for each expiry, with respect to the Delta of the option.*

This rule is usually used in OTC markets (e.g., FX options). The underpinning assumption is that options are priced depending on their Delta, so that when the underlying asset's price moves and the Delta of an option changes accordingly, a different implied volatility has to be plugged into the formula to price an option. The underpinning assumption here is that the implied volatility is constant with respect to the level of the Delta. Table 4.2 shows an example for a sticky Delta matrix: the volatility is mapped against the Delta of a put option on the left of the ATM level (hence for a decreasing level of strikes, given the price of the underlying, moving to the left) and against the Delta of a call option on the right (increasing level of strikes moving to the right).

[1] Much of this chapter is based on the work of Castagna and Mercurio [21].

Table 4.1 Example of a sticky strike matrix

	60	70	80	90	100	110	120	130	140
1M	10.10	10.20	10.30	10.40	10.50	10.60	10.70	10.80	10.90
2M	10.60	10.70	10.80	10.90	11.00	11.10	11.20	11.30	11.40
3M	11.10	11.20	11.30	11.40	11.50	11.60	11.70	11.80	11.90

Definition 4.1.4. ***Sticky absolute rule.*** *The* sticky absolute *rule produces matrices with implied volatilities mapped, for each expiry, in terms of absolute distance, measured in some units of price, from the at-the-money strike. In most cases, under this rule, the ATM strike is set equal to the forward price of the underlying asset.*

This rule, which is in some way a mix of the two described above, prevails in some over-the-counter markets, such as that for swaptions and for bond options. It entails that the implied volatility for a given strike changes along movements in the underlying asset's price, since the absolute distance from the ATM is also different. We represent a stylized volatility surface built according to the sticky absolute rule in Table 4.3.

4.1.1 Arbitrage opportunities under the three different rules

It can be shown that the sticky strike, Delta and absolute rules all produce arbitrage opportunities, should the surface behave as predicted by them. This is the reason why they are mainly regarded as quoting mechanisms and not expressions of actual behaviours of volatility surfaces. We will show here why this is so by means of the risk-neutral process for the implied volatility that we derived in Chapter 3 (in equation (3.14)).

Let us start with the sticky strike rule. This rule implies that the implied volatility for a given strike K and expiry T is, at time t, a deterministic function of the kind

$$\sigma(K, T) = f(t, T, K)$$

If this is the case, then in equation (3.14) ϱ and υ are both equal to zero, since no stochastic term is allowed. Thus, we can write

$$d\sigma(K, T) = \widetilde{\phi}dt = \frac{1}{2\sigma(K, T)\tau}(\sigma^2(K, T) - \varsigma_t^2)dt$$

where $\tau = T - t$. So we have

$$2\sigma(K, T)\tau d\sigma(K, T) - \sigma^2(K, T)dt = -\varsigma_t^2 dt$$

Table 4.2 Example of a sticky Delta matrix

	Δ Put					Δ Call			
	10.0%	20.0%	30.0%	40.0%	ATM	40%	30%	20%	10%
1M	10.30	10.20	10.10	10.00	9.90	10.00	10.10	10.20	10.30
2M	10.40	10.30	10.20	10.10	10.00	10.10	10.20	10.30	10.40
3M	10.50	10.40	10.30	10.20	10.10	10.20	10.30	10.40	10.50

Table 4.3 Example of a sticky absolute matrix

	−150	−100	−75	−50	ATM	+50	+75	+100	+150
1M	10.30	10.20	10.10	10.00	9.90	10.00	10.10	10.20	10.30
2M	10.40	10.30	10.20	10.10	10.00	10.10	10.20	10.30	10.40
3M	10.50	10.40	10.30	10.20	10.10	10.20	10.30	10.40	10.50

or

$$\varsigma_t^2 = -\frac{d(\tau\sigma^2(K, T))}{dt}$$

Hence, the instantaneous volatility ς_t is a function of time only. The only model that is consistent with this is the BS model with a time-dependent implied volatility, which does not allow for any kind of volatility smile. So, the sticky strike rule is not consistent with any arbitrage-free dynamics for the implied volatility.

A similar approach can show why the implied volatility dynamics inferred from a sticky Delta rule is also not admissible. In fact, under this rule, each $\sigma_t(K, T)$ is a deterministic function of the Delta, which is in turn a function of time t, expiry T and the logarithm of the ratio F_t/K (F_t is the forward price at t with maturity at T), so we can write

$$\sigma^2(K, T) = f(t, T, \ln(F_t/K))$$

We know from equation (3.15) that the instantaneous variance is equal to the squared implied volatility for an option struck ATM forward and expiring in the next instant of time. When the time to maturity approaches zero and the strike is equal to the forward price, we have

$$\varsigma_t^2 = \sigma^2(F_t, t) = f^2(t, t, 0)$$

so that the instantaneous variance is simply a function of time. As such, the only model consistent with this setting is once again the BS model with deterministic, time-dependent, instantaneous volatility. We deduce, as before, that the sticky Delta rule does not generate an arbitrage-free drift for an implied volatility. It can be admitted, though, as a more generic rule under which the implied volatility is a function of the time to maturity $(T - t) = \tau$ and the logarithm of the F_t/K ratio. In fact, it is easy to check that the drift (3.14) is just a function of these.

Finally, in a perfectly equivalent fashion, we can show that the sticky absolute rule does not produce arbitrage-free implied volatility dynamics. To see this, consider that under this rule the implied volatility is a function of the time t, expiry T and the (possibly negative) absolute distance x from the forward price level F_t. That is to say:

$$\sigma^2(K, T) = f^2(t, T, F_t + x)$$

For a time to maturity approaching zero and a strike equal to the forward price ($x = 0$), we have

$$\varsigma_t^2 = \sigma^2(F_t, t) = f^2(t, t, F_t)$$

so that the instantaneous volatility is a deterministic function of time t and the forward price F. Local volatility models, such as the lognormal mixture described in Chapter 2 or Dupire's model [26], are the only ones consistent with a deterministic function of that kind. So, we must acknowledge that the sticky absolute rule also cannot generate arbitrage-free implied volatility processes.

Whichever rule prevails, the main problem a market maker has to cope with is the building of a consistent volatility surface for a wide range (in terms of expiries and strikes) of options, given the knowledge of a few prices. The problem is twofold. First, they need a tool to interpolate/extrapolate implied volatilities amongst strikes for a given expiry. Second, they face the problem of the interpolation amongst available expiries. To address the former issue, we introduce the Vanna–Volga (VV) method, which is commonly employed in the FX option market, where three main volatility quotes are typically available for a given conventional maturity. The latter issue is instead tackled by proposing a weighting scheme to consistently include working days, eventful days and holidays.

Before analysing both issues, we first have to choose how to represent and handle a volatility surface in an efficient, intuitive and convenient way, capable of satisfying different instances presented by a financial institution. This is explained in the following section.

4.2 CRITERIA FOR AN EFFICIENT AND CONVENIENT REPRESENTATION OF THE VOLATILITY SURFACE

The representation of the volatility surface is not directly related to the specific conventions of the reference market. Actually, not all the rules we have described in the previous section grant and imply a convenient way of handling the volatility matrix. We list here some critical features that the representation should have:

- **Parsimony**: the representation contains the smallest amount of information needed to retrieve the entire volatility surface for all strikes and expiries.
- **Consistency**: the information contained in the representation is organized consistently along the expiries and strikes, so as to make the integration of missing points, either by interpolation or extrapolation, easily possible.
- **Intuitiveness**: the information provides the user with a clear picture of the shape of the volatility surface, and each piece of the information distinctly affects one specific trait of the volatility surface.

The representation is *parsimonious* if one can devise a suitable interpolation/extrapolation scheme amongst strikes and expiries, which requires only a few points as input. In principle, this seems a hard task to achieve, since for each given expiry, a volatility smile has as many degrees of freedom as considered strikes. However, from an empirical point of view, volatilities do not move independently from one another and, as we have seen in Chapter 3, one may reasonably assume that the degrees of freedom are only three: (i) level, (ii) slope and (iii) convexity. In fact, as a principal component analysis can show, most shape variations can be explained either by a parallel shift of the smile or by a tilt to the right or left or by a relative change of the wings with respect to the central strike. Therefore, three is the minimum number of points, for each expiry, needed to represent these stylized movements: the volatility for the at-the-money strike, that for an out-of-the-money call and that for an out-of-the-money put.[2]

[2] Three points for each expiry can be interpolated by a stochastic volatility model (e.g., Heston's model [37]), although they will typically not be enough to ensure a stable calibration. We will address this issue in what follows,

These strike triplets, one for each expiry, must also be chosen in such a way that the resulting representation is *consistent*. To make things clear, let us think of a very simple volatility surface with only two expiries: one week and ten years. For both expiries, one of the three strikes to choose may be set equal to the current price of the underlying asset (at-the-money spot). This choice is reasonable but not necessarily the best one. In fact, it would be better to replace the two at-the-money spot values with the forward prices at the two expiries, which can be viewed as the expected values of the future underlying asset under suitable measures (the corresponding forward risk-adjusted measures).

Things may even be worse for the other two points, since a meaningful selection criterion likely leads to different values for the two expiries: two chosen strikes may convey a good amount of information regarding the smile for the one-week expiry, but may not be so informative for the ten-year expiry. In fact, what matters (under a probabilistic point of view) is the relative distance of a strike from the central one, possibly expressed in volatility units, which makes the chosen strikes, and their corresponding implied volatilities, comparable throughout the entire range of expiries. A meaningful distance measure, familiar to practitioners, is provided by the Delta of an option (in absolute values), since it is a common indicator used in the market and it has the same signalling power as the relative distance from the at-the-money spot (in units of total standard deviation). For this reason, we will select, for each expiry, the volatility for the at-the-money spot and the 25D call and put. These two Delta levels are introduced because they are almost midway between the centre of the smile and the extreme wings (0D put and 0D call), and also because they are the strikes associated with a high level of Volga,[3] thus containing a good deal of information on the underlying asset's fourth moment, and hence on the curvature of the smile.

Finally, the representation is *intuitive* if it is expressed directly in terms of three qualitative features of the surface, instead of three implied volatilities. These features, already mentioned above, are the level, the steepness and the convexity of the smile for each maturity. We showed in Chapter 3 that the level is measured correctly by the ATM volatility; as for the steepness, we can use the price of the $25D$ **RR**; a good indicator for the convexity is $25D$ **VWB**. In a representation like this one, a user is able to change the shape of the volatility surface by simply changing these three indicators.

As for the set of expiries, a fixed number of maturities expressed as a fraction or multiple of years (and not as a fixed date) is the most intuitive and consistent choice to represent the volatility surface. This makes it easier to compare times in the matrix and is more responsive to the requirements of intuitiveness and consistency.

To sum up the considerations above, a convenient and efficient way to represent the volatility surface can be obtained by organizing the information as follows. For each expiry (expressed as time to maturity and in year units) store the ATM volatility, the **RR** and the **VWB** for the 25D call and put. The ATM can be referred to a strike set equal to the forward price for each expiry. But one could also choose the ATM 0D **STDL**, which is exactly the definition of at-the-moneyness in the FX market. We are rather lucky since the efficient representation we described coincides with the standard way to handle the volatility matrix in the FX market. An example of such a representation, in a stylized form, is provided in Table 4.4.

---

where we describe a robust, consistent and model-independent smile-building method, requiring just the availability of the option prices for three strikes.

[3] The behaviour of Volga (and the other Greeks) will be examined in Chapter 8.

Table 4.4 Stylized representation of a volatility surface in compact form

Expiry	ATM	25D **RR**	25D **VWB**
τ_1	σ_1	$\mathbf{rr}_1$	$\mathbf{vwb}_1$
τ_2	σ_2	$\mathbf{rr}_2$	$\mathbf{vwb}_2$
τ_3	σ_3	$\mathbf{rr}_3$	$\mathbf{vwb}_3$
τ_4	σ_4	$\mathbf{rr}_4$	$\mathbf{vwb}_4$
τ_5	σ_5	$\mathbf{rr}_5$	$\mathbf{vwb}_5$
τ_6	σ_6	$\mathbf{rr}_6$	$\mathbf{vwb}_6$

4.3 COMMONLY ADOPTED APPROACHES TO BUILDING A VOLATILITY SURFACE

Several recipes have been proposed in the literature for the manufacture of a volatility surface, considering the availability of a limited number of options prices. Some of them are simply very general interpolation/smoothing schemes, capable of fitting almost perfectly all available data, provided that no-arbitrage conditions of the resulting matrix are preserved (for instance, see Fengler [27], and the references cited therein). These tools produce good results but they may require many prices to work efficiently, since they are not founded on any valuation model but just on mere no-arbitrage restrictions.

A simpler interpolation method that enjoyed some popularity, especially amongst academics to be honest, is the second-order polynomial function (in Delta) proposed by Malz [46], which we used in Chapter 3 as a toy model to examine stylized movements of the volatility smile (see equation (3.26)). Like the Vanna–Volga[4] approach that we will describe further on, Malz's interpolation needs three basic volatilities in input, that can easily be retrieved from the market quotes of the main structures. This method was devised specifically for the FX options market, and used for an empirical study, but it can be rather easily extended to other markets. As mentioned in Chapter 3, its main flaws are due to the simplifying underpinning assumptions, i.e., the Delta of the call is equal to 1 minus the Delta of the put (which is true only in a zero-foreign-rates environment, in the FX case considered), and the ATM volatility is 50D. But without regard to this criticism, the interpolation (3.26) is a perfect fit to the three points provided and performs quite well in interpolating amongst them; nevertheless, Malz's formula usually underestimates implied volatilities both for low and high put Deltas. Besides, there is no real financial justification for a second-order interpolation amongst the three volatilities, just the mathematical fact that this is the simplest form perfectly fitting them.

A different approach involves the calibration of a stochastic volatility model to available prices, then the entire volatility surface can be built. For instance, a widely adopted choice, also in other markets, is the Heston model [37] we described in Chapter 2, with constant or time-dependent parameters; another choice, very popular in the swaptions market but not often implemented in the FX options market, is the SABR model of Hagan *et al.* [33], which can be used to generate volatility smiles for any expiry and tenor. This model is quite appealing, since in its framework the authors derive an explicit function for equivalent Black–Scholes implied volatilities (see equation (2.72)). Similar to the first approach, the stable calibration of a stochastic volatility model demands many prices and they may not always be available.

[4] Hereafter we will use the shorthand "VV" for "Vanna–Volga".

We will introduce instead a different approach, the aforementioned VV method, which will be studied extensively in the following sections. This approach has several advantages. First, it has a clear financial rationale supporting it, based on a hedging argument leading to its definition. This is shared with other stochastic volatility models, but not with the pure interpolation/smoothing schemes. Second, it requires just three prices per maturity to generate a complete (i.e., for any strike) and consistent smile. Finally, it allows for an automatic calibration to the three input volatilities (derived from market prices), being an explicit function of them. To our knowledge, no other functional form enjoys the same features. Besides, we will show it enjoys some interesting properties which make it very useful for practical purposes.

The interpolation implied by the VV method also yields a very good approximation of the smile induced, after calibration to three available prices, by a stochastic volatility model, especially within the range delimited by the two extreme strikes. A confirmation of this statement will be provided later, when we compare the VV approach to the SABR functional form. This further confirms the choice of the method, since it attains results very similar to those produced by renowned stochastic volatility models, but with a reduced effort and fewer input data required.

4.4 SMILE INTERPOLATION AMONG STRIKES: THE VANNA–VOLGA APPROACH

The VV method is a known empirical procedure that can be used to infer an implied volatility smile from three available quotes for a given maturity. It is based on the construction of locally replicating portfolios whose associated hedging costs are added to the corresponding BS prices so as to produce smile-consistent values. Besides being intuitive and easy to implement, this procedure has a clear financial interpretation, which further supports its use in practice.

In this section, we describe the main features of the VV approach, showing how to construct an implied volatility smile from three given market quotes. We will also provide further motivations and descriptions of the approach to fully show its properties.

4.4.1 The Vanna–Volga approach: general setting

We consider an option market where, for a given maturity T, three basic options are quoted: without loss of generality we assume that the options are all call. We denote the corresponding strikes by K_i, $i = 1, 2, 3$, $K_1 < K_2 < K_3$, and set $\mathcal{K} := \{K_1, K_2, K_3\}$. The market implied volatility associated with K_i is denoted by σ_i, $i = 1, 2, 3$. This setting is consistent with an FX market environment, where three main strikes are dealt, although usually through the three main structures.

The VV method serves the purpose of defining an implied volatility smile that is consistent with the basic volatilities σ_i. The rationale behind it stems from a replication argument in a flat-smile world, where the constant (through strikes) level of implied volatility varies stochastically over time. This argument is presented hereafter, where for simplicity we consider the same type of options, namely calls.

It is well known that in the BS model[5] the payoff of a European call with maturity T and strike K can be replicated by a dynamic Delta-hedging strategy whose value

[5] See Chapter 2.

(comprehensive of the bank account part) matches, at every time t, the option price $\mathbf{C}^{\text{BS}}(t; K, T) = \text{Bl}(S_t, t, T, K, P^d(t,T), P^f(t,T), \sigma, 1)$ where the usual notation applies. We know that σ is the constant BS implied volatility. In real financial markets, however, volatility is stochastic and traders hedge the associated risk by constructing portfolios that are Vega-neutral in a BS (flat-smile) world.

We now make the assumption of flat implied volatilities amongst strikes, but which may fluctuate randomly. We know that this assumption is not consistent with any model, but we use it as a starting point anyway. The presence of three basic options in the market makes it possible to build a portfolio that zeros partial derivatives up to second order. The first step in the VV procedure is the derivation of such a hedging portfolio for the above call with maturity T and strike K. To this end, we set $t = 0$, dropping the argument t in the call prices, and start by finding time-0 weights $x_1(K)$, $x_2(K)$ and $x_3(K)$ such that the resulting portfolio of European calls with maturity T and strikes K_1, K_2 and K_3, respectively, hedges the price variations of the call with maturity T and strike K, up to second order in the underlying and volatility. In fact, denoting respectively by Δ_t and x_i the units of the underlying asset and options with strikes K_i held at time t and setting $\mathbf{C}_i^{\text{BS}}(t) = \mathbf{C}^{\text{BS}}(t; K_i) = \mathbf{C}^{\text{BS}}(t; K_i, T)$, under diffusion dynamics for both S_t and $\sigma = \sigma_t$, we have by Ito's lemma

$$\begin{aligned}
d\mathbf{C}^{\text{BS}}(t;K) &- \Delta_t dS_t - \Delta_t r_t^f S_t dt - \sum_{i=1}^{3} x_i \, d\mathbf{C}_i^{\text{BS}}(t) \\
&= \left[\frac{\partial \mathbf{C}^{\text{BS}}(t;K)}{\partial t} - \sum_{i=1}^{3} x_i \frac{\partial \mathbf{C}_i^{\text{BS}}(t)}{\partial t} - \Delta_t r_t^f S_t\right] dt \\
&+ \left[\frac{\partial \mathbf{C}^{\text{BS}}(t;K)}{\partial S} - \Delta_t - \sum_{i=1}^{3} x_i \frac{\partial \mathbf{C}_i^{\text{BS}}(t)}{\partial S}\right] dS_t \\
&+ \left[\frac{\partial \mathbf{C}^{\text{BS}}(t;K)}{\partial \sigma} - \sum_{i=1}^{3} x_i \frac{\partial \mathbf{C}_i^{\text{BS}}(t)}{\partial \sigma}\right] d\sigma_t \\
&+ \frac{1}{2}\left[\frac{\partial^2 \mathbf{C}^{\text{BS}}(t;K)}{\partial S^2} - \sum_{i=1}^{3} x_i \frac{\partial^2 \mathbf{C}_i^{\text{BS}}(t)}{\partial S^2}\right] (dS_t)^2 \\
&+ \frac{1}{2}\left[\frac{\partial^2 \mathbf{C}^{\text{BS}}(t;K)}{\partial \sigma^2} - \sum_{i=1}^{3} x_i \frac{\partial^2 \mathbf{C}_i^{\text{BS}}(t)}{\partial \sigma^2}\right] (d\sigma_t)^2 \\
&+ \left[\frac{\partial^2 \mathbf{C}^{\text{BS}}(t;K)}{\partial S \partial \sigma} - \sum_{i=1}^{3} x_i \frac{\partial^2 \mathbf{C}_i^{\text{BS}}(t)}{\partial S \partial \sigma}\right] dS_t d\sigma_t
\end{aligned} \tag{4.1}$$

Choosing Δ_t and x_i so as to zero the coefficients of dS_t, $d\sigma_t$, $(d\sigma_t)^2$ and $dS_t d\sigma_t$,[6] the portfolio made of a long position in the call with strike K, short positions in x_i calls with strike K_i, and short the amount Δ_t of the underlying, is locally riskless at time t (no stochastic terms are

---

[6] The coefficient of $(dS_t)^2$ will be zeroed accordingly, due to the relation linking an option's Gamma and Vega in the BS world.

involved in its differential). Using the BS PDE, we then obtain

$$dC^{BS}(t;K) - \Delta_t dS_t - \Delta_t r_t^f S_t dt - \sum_{i=1}^{3} x_i\, dC_i^{BS}(t) =$$
$$r_t^d \left[C^{BS}(t;K) - \Delta_t S_t - \sum_{i=1}^{3} x_i C_i^{BS}(t) \right] dt \tag{4.2}$$

Therefore, when volatility is stochastic and options are valued with the BS formula, we can still have a (locally) perfect hedge, provided that we hold suitable amounts of three more options to rule out the model risk (the hedging strategy is irrespective of the true asset and volatility dynamics, under the assumption of no jumps).[7]

Remark 4.4.1. *The validity of the previous replication argument may be questioned because no stochastic volatility model can produce implied volatilities that are flat and stochastic at the same time. The simultaneous presence of these features, though inconsistent from a theoretical point of view, can however be justified on empirical grounds. In fact, the practical advantages of the BS paradigm are so clear that an option trader may choose to run their book by revaluing and hedging according to a BS flat-smile model, with the ATM volatility being continuously updated to the actual market level.*[8] *This is especially true in the FX market.*

The first step in the VV procedure is the construction of the above hedging portfolio, whose weights x_i are explicitly computed in the following section.

4.4.2 Computing the Vanna–Volga weights and option prices

In most practical applications the constant BS volatility is the ATM one, and also one of the three options will be chosen to be struck at the ATM level; thus, we set $\sigma = \sigma_2$ $(= \sigma_{ATM})$ and $K_2 = K_{ATM}$. Anyway, this is not strictly required and one can actually choose any σ as the constant (through strikes) implied volatility. From equation (4.1), we have that the weights $x_1 = x_1(K)$, $x_2 = x_2(K)$ and $x_3 = x_3(K)$, for which the resulting portfolio of European calls with maturity T and strikes K_1, K_2 and K_3 has the same Vega, Volga and Vanna as the call with strike K, can be found by solving the following system:

$$\begin{aligned}
\frac{\partial C^{BS}}{\partial \sigma}(K) &= \sum_{i=1}^{3} x_i(K) \frac{\partial C^{BS}}{\partial \sigma}(K_i) \\
\frac{\partial^2 C^{BS}}{\partial \sigma^2}(K) &= \sum_{i=1}^{3} x_i(K) \frac{\partial^2 C^{BS}}{\partial \sigma^2}(K_i) \\
\frac{\partial^2 C^{BS}}{\partial \sigma \partial S_0}(K) &= \sum_{i=1}^{3} x_i(K) \frac{\partial^2 C^{BS}}{\partial \sigma \partial S_0}(K_i)
\end{aligned} \tag{4.3}$$

[7] In fact, given that partial derivatives are zeroed up to second order, the sensitivity to possible jumps is reduced considerably, although not completely eliminated.

[8] "Continuously" typically means a daily or slightly more frequent update.

Denoting by $\mathcal{V}(K)$ the Vega of a European option with maturity T and strike K, we can re-express the Vanna and Volga in the following alternative way:

$$\frac{\partial^2 \mathbf{C}^{\mathrm{BS}}}{\partial \sigma^2}(K) = \frac{\mathcal{V}(K)}{\sigma} d_1(K) d_2(K)$$
$$\frac{\partial^2 \mathbf{C}^{\mathrm{BS}}}{\partial \sigma \partial S_0}(K) = -\frac{\mathcal{V}(K)}{S_0 \sigma \sqrt{T}} d_2(K)$$
$$d_2(K) = d_1(K) - \sigma\sqrt{T}$$

We can prove the following:

Proposition 4.4.1. *The system (4.3) always admits a unique solution, which is given by*

$$\begin{aligned} x_1(K) &= \frac{\mathcal{V}(K)}{\mathcal{V}(K_1)} \frac{\ln \frac{K_2}{K} \ln \frac{K_3}{K}}{\ln \frac{K_2}{K_1} \ln \frac{K_3}{K_1}} \\ x_2(K) &= \frac{\mathcal{V}(K)}{\mathcal{V}(K_2)} \frac{\ln \frac{K}{K_1} \ln \frac{K_3}{K}}{\ln \frac{K_2}{K_1} \ln \frac{K_3}{K_2}} \\ x_3(K) &= \frac{\mathcal{V}(K)}{\mathcal{V}(K_3)} \frac{\ln \frac{K}{K_1} \ln \frac{K}{K_2}}{\ln \frac{K_3}{K_1} \ln \frac{K_3}{K_2}} \end{aligned} \tag{4.4}$$

In particular, if $K = K_j$ then $x_i(K) = 1$ for $i = j$ and zero otherwise.

Proof: Writing system (4.3) in the form

$$A \begin{pmatrix} x_1(t;K) \\ x_2(t;K) \\ x_3(t;K) \end{pmatrix} = B$$

straightforward algebra leads to

$$\begin{aligned} \det(A) = {} & \frac{\mathcal{V}(t;K_1)\mathcal{V}(t;K_2)\mathcal{V}(t;K_3)}{S_0\sigma^2\sqrt{T}} \big[d_2(t;K_3)d_1(t;K_2)d_2(t;K_2) \\ & + d_2(t;K_1)d_1(t;K_3)d_2(t;K_3) \\ & - d_1(t;K_1)d_2(t;K_1)d_2(t;K_3) - d_1(t;K_3)d_2(t;K_3)d_2(t;K_2) \\ & - d_2(t;K_1)d_1(t;K_2)d_2(t;K_2) + d_1(t;K_1)d_2(t;K_1)d_2(t;K_2) \big] \\ = {} & \frac{\mathcal{V}(t;K_1)\mathcal{V}(t;K_2)\mathcal{V}(t;K_3)}{S_0\sigma^5 T^2} \ln\frac{K_2}{K_1} \ln\frac{K_3}{K_1} \ln\frac{K_3}{K_2} \end{aligned} \tag{4.5}$$

which is strictly positive since $K_1 < K_2 < K_3$. Therefore, system (4.3) admits a unique solution and (4.4) follows from Cramer's rule. □

We can now proceed to the definition of the VV price, which is consistent with the market prices of the basic options. The above replication argument shows that a portfolio made up of $x_i(K)$ units of the option with strike K_i (and Δ_0 units of the underlying asset) gives a locally perfect hedge in the BS world. The hedging strategy, however, has to be implemented at prevailing market prices, which generates an extra cost with respect to the BS value of the options portfolio. Such cost is to be added to the BS price to produce an arbitrage-free price that is consistent with the quoted option prices $\mathbf{C}^{\text{MKT}}(K_1)$, $\mathbf{C}^{\text{MKT}}(K_2)$ and $\mathbf{C}^{\text{MKT}}(K_3)$.

In fact, in case of a short maturity, i.e., for a small T, equation (4.2) can be approximated as

$$\begin{aligned}&(S_T - K)^+ - \mathbf{C}^{\text{BS}}(K) - \Delta_0[S_T - S_0] - \Delta_0 r_t^f S_0 T\\&- \sum_{i=1}^{3} x_i[(S_T - K_i)^+ - \mathbf{C}^{\text{BS}}(K_i)] \approx r_t^d\left[\mathbf{C}^{\text{BS}}(K) - \Delta_0 S_0 - \sum_{i=1}^{3} x_i \mathbf{C}^{\text{BS}}(K_i)\right]T\end{aligned}$$

so that setting

$$\mathbf{C}(K) = \mathbf{C}^{\text{BS}}(K) + \sum_{i=1}^{3} x_i(K)[\mathbf{C}^{\text{MKT}}(K_i) - \mathbf{C}^{\text{BS}}(K_i)] \tag{4.6}$$

we have

$$\begin{aligned}&(S_T - K)^+ \approx \mathbf{C}(K) + \Delta_0[S_T - S_0] + \Delta_0 r_t^f S_0 T\\&+ \sum_{i=1}^{3} x_i[(S_T - K_i)^+ - \mathbf{C}^{\text{MKT}}(K_i)] + r_t^d\left[\mathbf{C}(K) - \Delta_0 S_0 - \sum_{i=1}^{3} x_i \mathbf{C}^{\text{MKT}}(K_i)\right]T\end{aligned}$$

Therefore, when actual market prices are considered, the option payoff $(S_T - K)^+$ can still be replicated by buying Δ_0 units of the underlying asset and x_i options with strike K_i (investing the resulting cash at rate r_t^d), provided one starts from the initial endowment $\mathbf{C}(K)$.

The quantity $\mathbf{C}(K)$ in equation (4.6) is thus defined as the VV option's premium, implicitly assuming that the replication error is also negligible for longer maturities (we analyse such replication errors below). Such a premium equals the BS price $\mathbf{C}^{\text{BS}}(K)$ plus the cost difference of the hedging portfolio induced by the market implied volatilities with respect to the constant volatility σ. Since we set $\sigma = \sigma_2$, the market volatility for strike K_2, equation (4.6) can be simplified to

$$\mathbf{C}(K) = \mathbf{C}^{\text{BS}}(K) + x_1(K)[\mathbf{C}^{\text{MKT}}(K_1) - \mathbf{C}^{\text{BS}}(K_1)] + x_3(K)[\mathbf{C}^{\text{MKT}}(K_3) - \mathbf{C}^{\text{BS}}(K_3)]$$

When $K = K_j$, $\mathbf{C}(K_j) = \mathbf{C}^{\text{MKT}}(K_j)$, since $x_i(K) = 1$ for $i = j$ and zero otherwise. Therefore, equation (4.6) defines a rule for either interpolating or extrapolating prices from the three option quotes $\mathbf{C}^{\text{MKT}}(K_1)$, $\mathbf{C}^{\text{MKT}}(K_2)$ and $\mathbf{C}^{\text{MKT}}(K_3)$. An analogous interpretation holds for the corresponding implied volatilities $\sigma(K)$, which can be obtained by inverting equation (4.6), for each considered K, through the BS formula. In fact, the VV implied volatility curve $K \mapsto \sigma(K)$ can be obtained by inverting equation (4.6), for each considered K, through the BS formula. Since, by construction, $\sigma(K_i) = \sigma_i$, the function $\sigma(K)$ yields an interpolation/extrapolation tool for the market implied volatilities.

4.4.3 Limit and no-arbitrage conditions

The VV option price has several interesting features that we analyse in the following.

The option price $C(K)$, as a function of the strike K, is twice differentiable and satisfies the following (no-arbitrage) conditions:

(i) $\lim_{K\to 0^+} \mathbf{C}(K) = S_0\, P^f(0,T)$ and $\lim_{K\to +\infty} \mathbf{C}(K) = 0$
(ii) $\lim_{K\to 0^+} \frac{d\mathbf{C}}{dK}(K) = -P^d(0,T)$ and $\lim_{K\to +\infty} K\frac{d\mathbf{C}}{dK}(K) = 0$

These properties, which are trivially satisfied by $\mathbf{C}^{\text{BS}}(K)$, follow from the fact that, for each i, both $x_i(K)$ and $dx_i(K)/dK$ go to zero for $K \to 0^+$ or $K \to +\infty$.

To avoid arbitrage opportunities, the option price $\mathbf{C}(K)$ should also be a convex function of the strike K, i.e., $\frac{d^2\mathbf{C}}{dK^2}(K) > 0$ for each $K > 0$. This property, which is not true in general,[9] holds however for typical market parameters, so that equation (4.6) leads indeed to prices that are arbitrage-free in practice.

Unfortunately, there is no guarantee that the VV price is always positive. In fact, for quite steep smiles, namely for extremely large risk-reversal values, equation (4.6) may become negative. In these situations, which may occur in the current equity markets at extreme strikes, the VV procedure must be handled with care as far as the valuation of the wings is concerned. In most common cases, however, the VV approach yields robust and reliable option prices and volatilities.

4.4.4 Approximating implied volatilities

The specific expression of the VV option price, combined with our analytical formula (4.4) for the weights, allows for the derivation of a straightforward approximation for the VV implied volatility $\sigma(K)$. In fact, by expanding both members of equation (4.6) at first order in $\sigma = \sigma_2$, one has

$$\mathbf{C}(K) \approx \mathbf{C}^{\text{BS}}(K) + \sum_{i=1}^{3} x_i(K)\mathcal{V}(K_i)[\sigma_i - \sigma]$$

which, remembering (4.4) and the fact that $\sum_{i=1}^{3} x_i(K)\mathcal{V}(K_i) = \mathcal{V}(K)$, leads to

$$\mathbf{C}(K) \approx \mathbf{C}^{\text{BS}}(K) + \mathcal{V}(K)\left[\sum_{i=1}^{3} y_i(K)\sigma_i - \sigma\right] \tag{4.7}$$

where

$$y_1(K) = \frac{\ln\frac{K_2}{K}\ln\frac{K_3}{K}}{\ln\frac{K_2}{K_1}\ln\frac{K_3}{K_1}},\quad y_2(K) = \frac{\ln\frac{K}{K_1}\ln\frac{K_3}{K}}{\ln\frac{K_2}{K_1}\ln\frac{K_3}{K_2}},\quad y_3(K) = \frac{\ln\frac{K}{K_1}\ln\frac{K}{K_2}}{\ln\frac{K_3}{K_1}\ln\frac{K_3}{K_2}}$$

Comparing (4.7) with the first-order Taylor expansion

$$\mathbf{C}(K) \approx \mathbf{C}^{\text{BS}}(K) + \mathcal{V}(K)[\sigma(K) - \sigma]$$

one immediately has the following:

[9] One can actually find cases where the inequality is violated for some strike K.

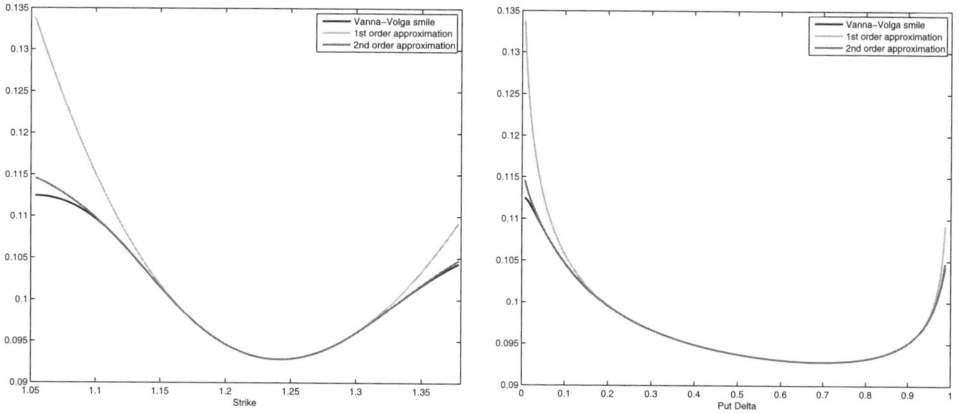

Figure 4.1 EURUSD implied volatilities and their approximations, plotted both against strikes and against EUR put Deltas (in absolute value)

Proposition 4.4.2. *The implied volatility $\sigma(K)$ for the above option with price $\mathbf{C}(K)$ is approximately given by*

$$\sigma(K) \approx \eta_1(K) := \frac{\ln\frac{K_2}{K}\ln\frac{K_3}{K}}{\ln\frac{K_2}{K_1}\ln\frac{K_3}{K_1}}\sigma_1 + \frac{\ln\frac{K}{K_1}\ln\frac{K_3}{K}}{\ln\frac{K_2}{K_1}\ln\frac{K_3}{K_2}}\sigma_2 + \frac{\ln\frac{K}{K_1}\ln\frac{K}{K_2}}{\ln\frac{K_3}{K_1}\ln\frac{K_3}{K_2}}\sigma_3 \tag{4.8}$$

The implied volatility $\sigma(K)$ can thus be approximated by a linear combination of the basic volatilities σ_i, with combinators $y_i(K)$ that sum up to one (as tedious but straightforward algebra shows). It is also easily seen that the approximation is a quadratic function of $\ln K$, meaning that one can resort to a simple parabolic interpolation when log coordinates are used.

Example 4.4.1. *A graphical representation of the goodness of the approximation (4.8) is shown in Figure 4.1, where we show, as an example, the smile for the exchange rate EURUSD, produced by using the following data: $T = 3M$ (= 94 days), $S_0 = 1.205$, $\sigma_{ATM} = 9.05\%$, $\sigma_{RR} = -0.50\%$, $\sigma_{VWB} = 0.13\%$, which lead to $\sigma_{25C} = 8.93\%$, $\sigma_{25P} = 9.43\%$, $K_{ATM} = 1.2114$, $K_{25P} = 1.1733$ and $K_{25C} = 1.2487$. The discount factors used for calculations are, for the US dollar, $P^d = 0.990275201$ and for the euro, $P^f = 0.994585501$.*

The approximation (4.8) is extremely accurate inside the interval $[K_1, K_3]$. The wings, however, tend to be overvalued. In fact, being the functional form quadratic in the log-strike, the no-arbitrage conditions derived by Lee [45] for the asymptotic value of implied volatilities are violated here. This drawback is addressed by a second, more precise, approximation, which is asymptotically constant at extreme strikes, and is obtained by expanding both members of equation (4.6) at second order in $\sigma = \sigma_2$:

$$\mathbf{C}(K) \approx \mathbf{C}^{\mathrm{BS}}(K) + \sum_{i=1}^{3} x_i(K)\left[\mathcal{V}(K_i)(\sigma_i - \sigma) + \frac{1}{2}\frac{\partial^2 \mathbf{C}^{\mathrm{BS}}}{\partial^2 \sigma}(K_i)(\sigma_i - \sigma)^2\right]$$

Comparing this expression with the second-order Taylor expansion

$$\mathbf{C}(K) - \mathbf{C}^{\text{BS}}(K) \approx \mathcal{V}(K)(\sigma(K) - \sigma) + \frac{1}{2}\frac{\partial^2 \mathbf{C}^{\text{BS}}}{\partial^2 \sigma}(K)(\sigma(K) - \sigma)^2$$

one can write

$$\begin{aligned}
&\mathcal{V}(K)(\sigma(K) - \sigma) + \frac{1}{2}\frac{\partial^2 \mathbf{C}^{\text{BS}}}{\partial^2 \sigma}(K)(\sigma(K) - \sigma)^2 \\
&\approx \sum_{i=1}^{3} x_i(K)\left[\mathcal{V}(K_i)(\sigma_i - \sigma) + \frac{1}{2}\frac{\partial^2 \mathbf{C}^{\text{BS}}}{\partial^2 \sigma}(K_i)(\sigma_i - \sigma)^2\right]
\end{aligned}$$

Solving this algebraic second-order equation in $\sigma(K)$ then leads to the following:

Proposition 4.4.3. *The implied volatility $\sigma(K)$ can be better approximated as*

$$\sigma(K) \approx \eta_2(K) := \sigma_2 + \frac{-\sigma_2 + \sqrt{\sigma_2^2 + d_1(K)d_2(K)(2\sigma_2 D_1(K) + D_2(K))}}{d_1(K)d_2(K)} \tag{4.9}$$

where

$$\begin{aligned}
D_1(K) :&= \eta_1(K) - \sigma_2 \\
D_2(K) :&= \frac{\ln\frac{K_2}{K}\ln\frac{K_3}{K}}{\ln\frac{K_2}{K_1}\ln\frac{K_3}{K_1}} d_1(K_1)d_2(K_1)(\sigma_1 - \sigma_2)^2 \\
&\quad + \frac{\ln\frac{K}{K_1}\ln\frac{K}{K_2}}{\ln\frac{K_3}{K_1}\ln\frac{K_3}{K_2}} d_1(K_3)d_2(K_3)(\sigma_3 - \sigma_2)^2
\end{aligned}$$

As we can see from Figure 4.1, the approximation (4.9) is extremely accurate also in the wings, even for extreme values of put Deltas. Its only drawback is that it may not be defined due to the presence of a square-root term. The radicand, however, is positive in most practical applications.

For practical reasons we will expand the approximation around the ATM implied volatility, so that we set $\sigma = \sigma_2 = \sigma_{ATM}$ in expression (4.9).

4.5 SOME FEATURES OF THE VANNA–VOLGA APPROACH

In this section we would like to show some interesting results of the VV method to build a volatility smile so as to fully appraise the main features of the approach. We start by analysing the impact of the assumptions regarding the short time to maturity of the options' portfolio and the hedging error arising for longer expiries. We will then present the implied terminal distribution implicit in option prices generated by the VV approach and finally we will prove two useful results.

4.5.1 Hedging error for longer expiries

The result shown above hinges on a perfectly hedged portfolio strategy, which grants a risk-free return on the initial investment needed to implement it only in case of a short time to maturity. For longer expiries, the argument is no longer valid and the ability to perform a self-financing strategy making the portfolio's return riskless cannot be proved. Anyway, we can try to gauge the hedging error that springs from carrying out the strategy for an arbitrary expiry, assuming a continuous rebalancing. To this end, we proceed as follows.

Assume we run a book with a BS model and continuously update the implied (ATM) volatility to the market level. Consider the time-t hedging portfolio made up of $x_i(t)$ options $\mathbf{C}_i(t)$, $\Delta_t = \dfrac{\partial \mathbf{C}_i(t)}{\partial S}$ shares and an amount β_t in the bank account, whose value is denoted by $\pi(t)$:

$$\pi(t) = \sum_{i=1}^{3} x_i(t; K)\mathbf{C}^{\text{MKT}}(t; K_i) + \Delta_t S_t + \beta_t$$

where we set $\pi(0) = \mathbf{C}^{\text{MKT}}(0; K)$. Assuming that the portfolio is self-financing, we have

$$\begin{aligned} d\pi(t) &= \sum_{i=1}^{3} x_i(t; K)d\mathbf{C}^{\text{MKT}}(t; K_i) + \Delta_t dS_t + \Delta_t r_t^f S_t dt + \beta_t r_t^d dt \\ &= \sum_{i=1}^{3} x_i(t; K)d\mathbf{C}^{\text{MKT}}(t; K_i) + \Delta_t dS_t + \Delta_t r_t^f S_t dt \\ &\quad + \left[\pi(t) - \sum_{i=1}^{3} x_i(t; K)\mathbf{C}^{\text{MKT}}(t; K_i) - \Delta_t S_t\right] r_t^d dt \end{aligned}$$

Denote by ε_t the hedging error at time t:

$$\varepsilon_t = \mathbf{C}(t; K) - \pi(t)$$

We have, remembering the definition (4.6) of $C(t; K)$,

$$\begin{aligned} d\varepsilon_t &= d\mathbf{C}^{\text{BS}}(t; K) + \sum_{i=1}^{3} x_i(t; K)[d\mathbf{C}_i^{\text{MKT}}(t) - dC_i^{\text{BS}}(t)] \\ &\quad + \sum_{i=1}^{3} dx_i(t; K)[\mathbf{C}_i^{\text{MKT}}(t) - \mathbf{C}_i^{\text{BS}}(t)] \\ &\quad + \sum_{i=1}^{3} dx_i(t; K)[d\mathbf{C}_i^{\text{MKT}}(t) - d\mathbf{C}_i^{\text{BS}}(t)] \\ &\quad - \sum_{i=1}^{3} x_i(t; K)d\mathbf{C}_i^{\text{MKT}}(t) - \Delta_t dS_t - \Delta_t r_t^f S_t dt \\ &\quad - \left[\pi(t) - \sum_{i=1}^{3} x_i(t; K)\mathbf{C}_i^{\text{MKT}}(t) - \Delta_t S_t\right] r_t^d dt \end{aligned}$$

Using again equations (4.6) and (4.2) and rearranging terms, we obtain

$$d\varepsilon_t = r_t^d \varepsilon_t dt + \sum_{i=1}^{3} dx_i(t;K)[\mathbf{C}_i^{\text{MKT}}(t) + d\mathbf{C}_i^{\text{MKT}}(t) - \mathbf{C}_i^{\text{BS}}(t) - d\mathbf{C}_i^{\text{BS}}(t)]$$

or, in shorthand notation,

$$d\varepsilon_t = r_t^d \varepsilon_t dt + \sum_{i=1}^{3} dx_i(t;K)[\mathbf{C}_i^{\text{MKT}}(t+dt) - \mathbf{C}_i^{\text{BS}}(t+dt)]$$

This immediately leads to the following:

Proposition 4.5.1. *The total hedging error at maturity T is given by*

$$\varepsilon_T = \sum_{i=1}^{3} \int_0^T e^{\int_t^T r_s^d ds} dx_i(t;K)[\boldsymbol{C}_i^{\text{MKT}}(t+dt) - \boldsymbol{C}_i^{\text{BS}}(t+dt)] \tag{4.10}$$

Equation (4.10) provides us with a useful insight into the accuracy of the replication strategy in a stochastic volatility world: the greater the difference between the market price and the flat-smile price of the three basic options, the higher the total hedging error ε_T. One can see the total hedging error as the sum (the integral in a continuous time setting) of the differences in prices not taken into account by the flat-smile hypothesis (though with a floating ATM implied volatility), times the variations in their quantities in the portfolio. Since only the differences between the true market and the BS prices are relevant when rebalancing is needed, we can reasonably believe that the error is not large, and that it will be larger for very far OTM strikes, since more rebalancing is likely to be expected. Comparisons between the smiles generated by the VV method and by a stochastic volatility model (e.g., Heston's model or the SABR), calibrated to the same set of data, shows that this statement is well grounded.

4.5.2 The implied risk-neutral density and smile asymptotics

The VV price (4.6) is defined without introducing specific assumptions on the distribution of the underlying asset. However, the knowledge of option prices for every possible strike identifies a (unique) risk-neutral density that is consistent with them. In fact, by the general result of Breeden and Litzenberger [11], the risk-neutral density p_T of the asset S_T can be obtained by differentiating twice the option price (4.6):

$$\begin{aligned} p_T(K) = \frac{1}{P^d(0,T)} \frac{\partial^2 \mathbf{C}}{\partial K^2}(K) &= \frac{1}{P^d(0,T)} \frac{\partial^2 \mathbf{C}^{\text{BS}}}{\partial K^2}(K) \\ &+ \frac{1}{P^d(0,T)} \sum_{i\in\{1,3\}} \frac{\partial^2 x_i}{\partial K^2}(K)[\mathbf{C}^{\text{MKT}}(K_i) - \mathbf{C}^{\text{BS}}(K_i)] \end{aligned} \tag{4.11}$$

The first term on the RHS is the lognormal density p_T^{BS} associated with the geometric Brownian motion with drift rate $r^d - r^f$ and volatility $\sigma = \sigma_2$. The second term, which is the deviation from lognormality induced by the VV smile, is more involved and can be calculated by

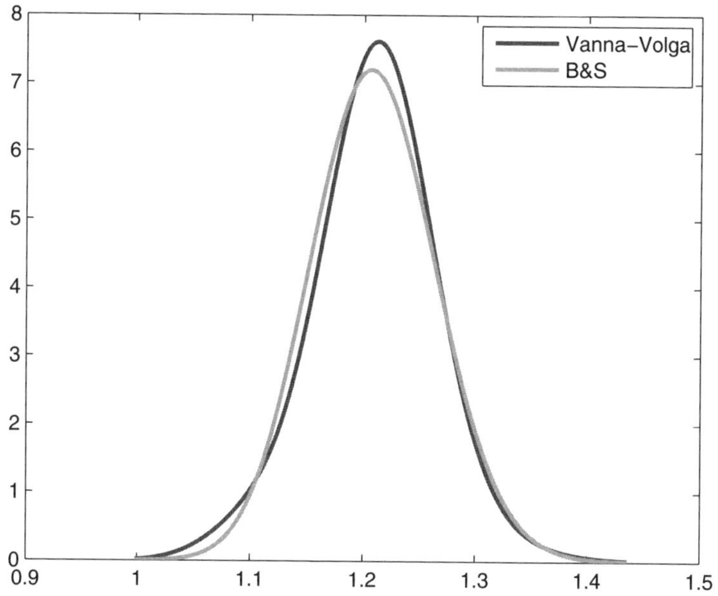

Figure 4.2 Vanna–Volga risk-neutral density compared with the lognormal one coming from the BS model with ATM volatility

differentiating twice the weights (4.4). We obtain:

$$\frac{\partial^2 x_1}{\partial K^2}(K) = \frac{\mathcal{V}(K)}{K^2\sigma^2 T\mathcal{V}(K_1)\ln\frac{K_2}{K_1}\ln\frac{K_3}{K_1}}$$
$$\left[\left(d_1(K)^2 - \sigma\sqrt{T}d_1(K) - 1\right)\ln\frac{K_2}{K}\ln\frac{K_3}{K}\right.$$
$$\left. -2\sigma\sqrt{T}d_1(K)\ln\frac{K_2K_3}{K^2} + \sigma^2 T\left(\ln\frac{K_2K_3}{K^2} + 2\right)\right]$$
$$\frac{\partial^2 x_3}{\partial K^2}(K) = \frac{\mathcal{V}(K)}{K^2\sigma^2 T\mathcal{V}(K_3)\ln\frac{K_3}{K_1}\ln\frac{K_3}{K_2}}$$
$$\left[\left(d_1(K)^2 - \sigma\sqrt{T}d_1(K) - 1\right)\ln\frac{K_2}{K}\ln\frac{K_1}{K}\right.$$
$$\left. -2\sigma\sqrt{T}d_1(K)\ln\frac{K_1K_2}{K^2} + \sigma^2 T\left(\ln\frac{K_1K_2}{K^2} + 2\right)\right]$$

A plot of the risk-neutral density associated with (4.6) is shown in Figure 4.2, where it is compared with the corresponding lognormal density p_T^{BS}.[10]

The analytical expression (4.11) for the VV risk-neutral density allows us to characterize the asymptotic behaviour of the VV implied volatility σ by means of the results in Benaim

[10] A different, though equivalent, expression for such density can be found in Beneder and Baker [5].

and Friz [4]. In fact, it can easily be shown that the density q_T of $\ln S_T$, $q_T(k) = e^k p_T(e^k)$, is a regularly varying function at ∞ in that

$$\lim_{k\to\pm\infty} \frac{q_T(xk)}{q_T(k)} = x^\alpha$$

for some real number α. Moreover, $\ln[q_T(k)]/k$ goes to infinity for $k \to \infty$. Theorems 1 and 2 in Benaim and Friz [4] then lead to the following:

Proposition 4.5.2. *The right and left asymptotic values of the VV implied volatility curve are both equal to $\sigma = \sigma_2$:*

$$\lim_{k\to\pm\infty} \sigma(e^k) = \sigma.$$

4.5.3 Two consistency results

We now state two important consistency results that hold for the option price (4.6) and that give further support to the VV procedure.

The first result is as follows. One may wonder what happens if we apply the VV curve construction method when starting from three other strikes whose associated prices coincide with those coming from formula (4.6). Clearly, for the procedure to be robust, we would want the two curves to coincide exactly. This is indeed the case.

In fact, consider a new set of strikes $\mathcal{H} := \{H_1, H_2, H_3\}$, for which we set

$$\mathbf{C}^{\mathcal{H}}(H_i) = \mathbf{C}^{\mathcal{K}}(H_i) = \mathbf{C}^{\text{BS}}(H_i) + \sum_{j=1}^{3} x_j(H_i)[\mathbf{C}^{\text{MKT}}(K_j) - \mathbf{C}^{\text{BS}}(K_j)] \tag{4.12}$$

where the superscripts $\mathcal{H}$ and $\mathcal{K}$ highlight the set of strikes the pricing procedure is based on, and weights x_j are obtained from $\mathcal{K}$ with formulae (4.4). For a generic strike K, denoting by $x_i(K;\mathcal{H})$ the weights for K that are derived starting from the set $\mathcal{H}$, the option price associated with $\mathcal{H}$ is defined, analogously to (4.6), by

$$\mathbf{C}^{\mathcal{H}}(K) = \mathbf{C}^{\text{BS}}(K) + \sum_{j=1}^{3} x_j(K;\mathcal{H})[\mathbf{C}^{\mathcal{H}}(H_j) - \mathbf{C}^{\text{BS}}(H_j)]$$

where the second term in the sum is now not necessarily zero since H_2 is in general different from K_2. The following proposition states the desired consistency result:

Proposition 4.5.3. *The call prices based on $\mathcal{H}$ coincide with those based on $\mathcal{K}$, namely, for each strike K,*

$$\mathbf{C}^{\mathcal{H}}(K) = \mathbf{C}^{\mathcal{K}}(K) \tag{4.13}$$

Proof: Equality (4.13) holds if and only if

$$\sum_{j=1}^{3} x_j(K;\mathcal{H})[\mathbf{C}^{\mathcal{H}}(H_j) - \mathbf{C}^{\text{BS}}(H_j)] = \sum_{i=1}^{3} x_i(K;\mathcal{K})[\mathbf{C}(K_i) - \mathbf{C}^{\text{BS}}(K_i)]$$

Using equation (4.12) and rearranging terms, the left-hand side can be written as

$$\sum_{j=1}^{3} x_j(K;\mathcal{H})[\mathbf{C}^{\mathcal{H}}(H_j) - \mathbf{C}^{\text{BS}}(H_j)]$$

$$= \sum_{j=1}^{3} x_j(K;\mathcal{H}) \sum_{i=1}^{3} x_i(H_j;\mathcal{K})[\mathbf{C}(K_i) - \mathbf{C}^{\text{BS}}(K_i)]$$

$$= \sum_{i=1}^{3} \left[\sum_{j=1}^{3} x_j(K;\mathcal{H}) x_i(H_j;\mathcal{K}) \right] [\mathbf{C}(K_i) - \mathbf{C}^{\text{BS}}(K_i)]$$

which equals the above equality since, for each strike K and $j = 1, 2, 3$,

$$x_i(K;\mathcal{K}) = \sum_{j=1}^{3} x_j(K;\mathcal{H}) x_i(H_j;\mathcal{K}) \tag{4.14}$$

following from a tedious, but straightforward, application of formulae (4.4) for the weights. □

A second consistency result that can be proven for the option price (4.6) concerns the pricing of European-style derivatives and their static replication. To this end, assume that $h(x)$ is a real function that is defined for $x \in [0, \infty)$, is well behaved at infinity and is twice differentiable. Given the *simple claim* with payoff $h(S_T)$ at time T, we denote by V its price at time 0, when taking into account the whole smile of the underlying at time T. By Carr and Madan [20], we have

$$V = P^d(0, T)h(0) + S_0 P^f(0, T)\, h'(0) + \int_0^{+\infty} h''(K)\mathbf{C}(K)\, dK \tag{4.15}$$

The same reasoning adopted in Section 4.4 on the local hedge of the call with strike K can also be applied to the general payoff $h(S_T)$. We can thus construct a portfolio of European calls with maturity T and strikes K_1, K_2 and K_3, such that the portfolio has the same Vega, Volga and Vanna as the given derivative. Denoting by V^{BS} the claim price under the BS model, this is achieved by finding the corresponding portfolio weights x_1^h, x_2^h and x_3^h, which always exist uniquely, see Proposition 4.4.1. We can then define a new (smile-consistent) price for our derivative as

$$\bar{V} = V^{\text{BS}} + \sum_{i=1}^{3} x_i^h [\mathbf{C}^{\text{MKT}}(K_i) - \mathbf{C}^{\text{BS}}(K_i)] \tag{4.16}$$

which is the obvious generalization of (4.6). Our second consistency result is stated in the following:

Proposition 4.5.4. *The claim price that is consistent with the option price (4.6) is equal to the claim price that is obtained by adjusting its BS price by the cost difference of the hedging portfolio when using market prices $C^{\text{MKT}}(K_i)$ instead of constant volatility prices $\mathbf{C}^{\text{BS}}(K_i)$. In formulae*

$$V = \bar{V}$$

Proof: For each operator $\mathcal{L} \in \left\{\frac{\partial}{\partial\sigma}, \frac{\partial^2}{\partial^2\sigma}, \frac{\partial^2}{\partial\sigma\partial S_0}\right\}$, we have

$$\begin{aligned}\mathcal{L}V^{\text{BS}} &= \mathcal{L}\left[P^d(0,T)h(0) + S_0 P^f(0,T)h'(0) + \int_0^{+\infty} h''(K)\mathbf{C}^{\text{BS}}(K)\,dK\right]\\ &= \int_0^{+\infty} h''(K)\mathcal{L}\mathbf{C}^{\text{BS}}(K)\,dK\end{aligned}$$

which, by definition of the weights $x_i(K)$, becomes

$$\begin{aligned}\mathcal{L}V^{\text{BS}} &= \int_0^{+\infty} h''(K)\sum_{i=1}^{3} x_i(K)\,\mathcal{L}\mathbf{C}^{\text{BS}}(K_i)\,dK\\ &= \sum_{i=1}^{3}\int_0^{+\infty} h''(K)x_i(K)\,\mathcal{L}\mathbf{C}^{\text{BS}}(K_i)\,dK\\ &= \sum_{i=1}^{3}\left[\int_0^{+\infty} h''(K)x_i(K)\,dK\right]\mathcal{L}\mathbf{C}^{\text{BS}}(K_i)\end{aligned}$$

By the uniqueness of the weights x_i^h, we thus have

$$x_i^h = \int_0^{+\infty} h''(K)x_i(K)\,dK, \quad i = 1, 2, 3$$

Substituting into equation (4.16), we get

$$\begin{aligned}\bar{V} &= V^{\text{BS}} + \sum_{i=1}^{3}\left[\int_0^{+\infty} h''(K)x_i(K)\,dK\right][\mathbf{C}^{\text{MKT}}(K_i) - \mathbf{C}^{\text{BS}}(K_i)]\\ &= V^{\text{BS}} + \int_0^{+\infty} h''(K)\sum_{i=1}^{3} x_i(K)[\mathbf{C}^{\text{MKT}}(K_i) - \mathbf{C}^{\text{BS}}(K_i)]\,dK\\ &= V^{\text{BS}} + \int_0^{+\infty} h''(K)[\mathbf{C}(K) - \mathbf{C}^{\text{BS}}(K)]\,dK\\ &= V^{\text{BS}} + [V - V^{\text{BS}}] = V\end{aligned}$$

□

Therefore, if we calculate the hedging portfolio for the claim under flat volatility and add to the BS claim price the cost difference of the hedging portfolio (market price minus constant volatility price), obtaining $\bar{V}$, we retrieve the claim price V exactly as obtained through the risk-neutral density implied by the call option prices that are consistent with the market smile.

4.6 AN ALTERNATIVE CHARACTERIZATION OF THE VANNA–VOLGA APPROACH

The VV approach can be examined from an alternative point of view that offers a different interpretation of the origin of the smile. In fact, one may think that an option is affected by the stochastic nature of the implied volatility via its exposures to Vega, Volga and Vanna, as we have seen above. Now we focus on the fact that each of these exposures implies a cost: it engenders the difference between the price of an option in the BS flat volatility economy, and its price in an economy where a volatility smile is implied in traded prices. The cost is assumed to be constant throughout the entire (infinite) range of strikes, for a given expiry.

We work in the same framework as Section 4.4.1; that is, we are given three strikes and the price of the related options, so that the implied volatility can be retrieved for each of them. We want to infer the costs with respect to the Vega, Vanna and Volga by establishing the following system:

$$\begin{aligned}
\mathbf{C}^{\text{MKT}}(K_1) - \mathbf{C}^{\text{BS}}(K_1) &= y_v \frac{\partial \mathbf{C}^{\text{BS}}}{\partial \sigma}(K_1) + y_w \frac{\partial^2 \mathbf{C}^{\text{BS}}}{\partial \sigma^2}(K_1) + y_x \frac{\partial^2 \mathbf{C}^{\text{BS}}}{\partial \sigma \partial S_0}(K_1) \\
\mathbf{C}^{\text{MKT}}(K_2) - \mathbf{C}^{\text{BS}}(K_2) &= y_v \frac{\partial \mathbf{C}^{\text{BS}}}{\partial \sigma}(K_2) + y_w \frac{\partial^2 \mathbf{C}^{\text{BS}}}{\partial \sigma^2}(K_2) + y_x \frac{\partial^2 \mathbf{C}^{\text{BS}}}{\partial \sigma \partial S_0}(K_2) \\
\mathbf{C}^{\text{MKT}}(K_3) - \mathbf{C}^{\text{BS}}(K_3) &= y_v \frac{\partial \mathbf{C}^{\text{BS}}}{\partial \sigma}(K_3) + y_w \frac{\partial^2 \mathbf{C}^{\text{BS}}}{\partial \sigma^2}(K_3) + y_x \frac{\partial^2 \mathbf{C}^{\text{BS}}}{\partial \sigma \partial S_0}(K_2)
\end{aligned} \tag{4.17}$$

System (4.17) in practice imposes that the difference between the BS price for each of the three options, valued with the market implied volatility, and the BS price valued with a constant (flat) volatility σ, is determined by the three volatility Greeks, Vega, Vanna and Volga, weighted by the respective costs. We indicate by y_v the cost for the Vega, y_w the cost for the Volga and finally y_x the cost for the Vanna exposure. The market prices embed these extra costs with respect to a given σ (which can also be the implied volatility of one of the three options) and by solving the system we infer them. Then these costs can be used to price an option struck at an arbitrary level under the assumption that they are kept constant for every strike; hence, the pricing formula is

$$\mathbf{C}(K) = \mathbf{C}^{\text{BS}}(K) + y_v \frac{\partial \mathbf{C}^{\text{BS}}}{\partial \sigma}(K) + y_w \frac{\partial^2 \mathbf{C}^{\text{BS}}}{\partial \sigma^2}(K) + y_x \frac{\partial^2 \mathbf{C}^{\text{BS}}}{\partial \sigma \partial S_0}(K) \tag{4.18}$$

Besides being quite intuitive, this representation also has the advantage that the weights $y_{\{.\}}$ are independent of the strike K and, as such, can be calculated once and for all. Anyway, it should be stressed that this alternative characterization of the VV approach is perfectly equivalent to the one we have analysed before. Actually, equation (4.18) is just another way of expressing equation (4.6), as proved in the following:

Proposition 4.6.1. *Let x_i for $i := \{1, 2, 3\}$ be the solution of the system (4.4) and y_g, for $g := \{v, w, x\}$, be the solution of the system (4.17). Then the option price (4.6) and the option price (4.18) are equal.*

Proof: From (4.6) and the definition of y_g, we can write

$$\mathbf{C}(K) = \mathbf{C}^{\text{BS}}(K) + \sum_{i=1}^{3} x_i(K) \left[y_v \frac{\partial \mathbf{C}^{\text{BS}}}{\partial \sigma}(K_i) + y_w \frac{\partial^2 \mathbf{C}^{\text{BS}}}{\partial \sigma^2}(K_i) + y_x \frac{\partial^2 \mathbf{C}^{\text{BS}}}{\partial \sigma \partial S_0}(K_i) \right]$$

or

$$\begin{aligned}
\mathbf{C}(K) &= \mathbf{C}^{\text{BS}}(K) \\
&+ y_v \sum_{i=1}^{3} x_i(K) \frac{\partial \mathbf{C}^{\text{BS}}}{\partial \sigma}(K_i) + y_w \sum_{i=1}^{3} x_i(K) \frac{\partial^2 \mathbf{C}^{\text{BS}}}{\partial \sigma^2}(K_i) + y_x \sum_{i=1}^{3} x_i(K) \frac{\partial^2 \mathbf{C}^{\text{BS}}}{\partial \sigma \partial S_0}(K_i)
\end{aligned}$$

By the definition of the solution x_i, the proposition is immediately proved. □

4.7 SMILE INTERPOLATION AMONG EXPIRIES: IMPLIED VOLATILITY TERM STRUCTURE

In the options market a set of maturities are actively traded and provide the market makers with a guide to price options with any expiry. One could first try to use some function fitting, more or less accurately, the given expiries, and then interpolate/extrapolate by means of it. For example, for the FX options market a form of the Heston-type model for instantaneous variance of the underlying asset

$$\varsigma^2(t) = \sigma_\infty^2 + \left(\varsigma_0^2 - \sigma_\infty^2\right) e^{-\kappa t} \tag{4.19}$$

has been proposed to fit the term structure of ATM volatilities. In equation (4.19), the instantaneous variance $\varsigma^2(t)$ evolves toward a long-term average level σ_∞^2 by a mean-reversion speed measured by the parameter κ, starting from an initial level ς_0^2. In order to retrieve the implied volatility for a given expiry, one has to integrate equation (4.19), divide the result by the time to expiry T, and take the square root:

$$\sigma(T) = \sqrt{\frac{\int_0^T \varsigma^2(t)\,dt}{T}} = \sqrt{\sigma_\infty^2 + (\varsigma_0^2 - \sigma_\infty^2)\frac{1 - e^{-\kappa T}}{\kappa T}} \tag{4.20}$$

Although equation (4.19) is qualitatively appealing, usually the fit to the market data is not completely satisfactory, and one must resort to some time dependency of the parameters (or the introduction of a free extra parameter) in order to improve the performance.

Function (4.20) is an example of a parametric form that can be chosen to fit the ATM volatilities in a given options market. However, the problem of finding a suitable parametrization is not fundamental by itself: apart from the arbitrariness of the chosen function in each case, trying to use a function to fit and interpolate/extrapolate implied volatilities may just prove a waste of mental effort without realizing that the starting point is to take the term structures provided by the market as a matter of fact (unless they engender an arbitrage) and simply interpolate between consecutive maturities.[11]

The volatility interpolation between two given expiries needs to be implemented correctly by taking into account the daily variations, and weighting the days with sensible factors. Focusing on the interpolation issue, we would like to stress that the interpolation of the term structure refers only to the ATM volatility, and thus only concerns the level of the surface, if we consider the three basic features of a volatility smile and, by extension, its surface.

Let's start with a set of M standard traded expiries $\mathcal{T} = \{T_1, T_2, ..., T_M\}$. Our problem is to devise a method to interpolate consistently between two contiguous dates. Let T be an expiry date between two dates $T_i \le T \le T_{i+1}$ and $\varsigma(t)$ be the instantaneous volatility of the spot process. The squared implied volatility for expiry T, in a BS world, is given by

$$\sigma^2(T) = \frac{1}{T}\int_0^T \varsigma^2(t)\,dt$$

Such a volatility can be obtained by linearly interpolating the mean variance

$$V(T) = \int_0^T \varsigma^2(t)\,dt = T\sigma^2(T)$$

[11] Extrapolation outside the available range of expiries is a minor issue, normally managed by traders by adding some spread over the last quoted option's maturity.

between its time T_i and time T_{i+1} values. We get

$$\begin{aligned}\int_0^T \varsigma^2(t)dt &= \frac{V(T_{i+1}) - V(T_i)}{T_{i+1} - T_i}(T - T_i) + V(T_i)\\ &= \frac{T_{i+1}\sigma^2(T_{i+1}) - T_i\sigma^2(T_i)}{T_{i+1} - T_i}(T - T_i) + T_i\sigma^2(T_i)\\ &= \frac{T - T_i}{T_{i+1} - T_i}T_{i+1}\sigma^2(T_{i+1}) + \frac{T_{i+1} - T}{T_{i+1} - T_i}T_i\sigma^2(T_i)\end{aligned}$$

and hence

$$\sigma(T) = \sqrt{\frac{T - T_i}{T_{i+1} - T_i}\frac{T_{i+1}}{T}\sigma^2(T_{i+1}) + \frac{T_{i+1} - T}{T_{i+1} - T_i}\frac{T_i}{T}\sigma^2(T_i)} \tag{4.21}$$

This is what we call the *total variance interpolation* method.

As a subsequent step, we then take into account the weighting of the days entering into the interpolation, since holidays and other events may affect the daily volatility heavily. One simple way to account for different weighting of the days is as follows:

- Calculate the number of days N_1 occurring between T_i and T and the number of days N_2 occurring between T_i and T_{i+1}.
- Associate each day with a proper weight w_i:
  - $w_i = 1$ for a normal business day;
  - $w_i > 1$ for holidays in the underlying markets (e.g., in the FX market, it can be set equal to 0.5 if the day is a holiday in one of the two countries involved in the exchange rate, or it can be set at 0 for weekends);
  - $w_i > 1$ for days when special events are expected (e.g., key economic figures are released).
- Set

$$\tau_1 = \frac{\sum_{i=1}^{N_1} w_i}{N_y}, \quad \tau_2 = \frac{\sum_{i=1}^{N_2} w_i}{N_y}$$

  where N_y is the total number of days in the year ($Ny = 365$ or $N_y = 366$).
- Replace $T - T_i$ with τ_1 and $T_{i+1} - T_i$ with τ_2 in the interpolation formula (4.21):

$$\sigma(T) = \sqrt{\frac{\tau_1}{\tau_2}\frac{T_{i+1}}{T}\sigma^2(T_{i+1}) + \frac{\tau_2 - \tau_1}{\tau_2}\frac{T_i}{T}\sigma^2(T_i)} \tag{4.22}$$

The weighting has tangible effects for expiries up to 1 year. After that, it is quite immaterial to use either (4.21) or (4.22).

As mentioned before, the interpolation is used only for the ATM volatilities. If the implied volatility of an OTM option has to be recovered, then first one interpolates by means of (4.22) the ATM volatility, then may use a simple linear interpolation for the risk reversal and butterfly (so as to find the slope and convexity for the intermediate expiry) and finally use the method explained in Section 4.4 to get the consistent volatility for the given strike. The rationale behind this is the following: while the daily volatility (i.e., the second moment of the price returns' distribution) can be affected by the related market activity (so that it changes according to holidays, the release of economic figures, etc.), the higher-order moments (i.e., skewness and kurtosis) are more stable and smoothly changing between expiries. This justifies

Table 4.5 Term structure of ATM implied volatilities traded on 29 March 2004

Expiry	ATM vol.
4/5/2004	12.40%
4/12/2004	11.50%
4/28/2004	11.70%
5/26/2004	11.55%
6/28/2004	11.27%
9/28/2004	11.20%
12/29/2004	11.14%
3/29/2005	11.10%

the weighted interpolation for the ATM volatility, which impacts on the level of the volatility surface and hence the second moment of the price returns' distribution, and also justifies the linear interpolation for the risk reversal and the butterfly, which measure, respectively, the slope and convexity of the volatility surface and hence the skewness and kurtosis of the returns' distribution.

Clearly, in any case and whatever interpolation is used to retrieve the implied volatility for a given strike, the volatility surface must be arbitrage-free. Admissible volatility surfaces are defined in the next section.

Example 4.7.1. *We present an application of the weighted interpolation based on real market data as of* 29 *March 2004, for the EURUSD exchange rate. The ATM volatility for a set of standard maturities is provided in Table 4.5 whereas Figure 4.3 shows the two interpolations obtained by means of (4.21) and (4.22). The effect of the weighting is quite remarkable, considering also that between the* 1*-week and* 2*-week expiries there are Easter holidays, with almost four closed market days in a row. Generally, one can note that the initial linear interpolation produces a sawtooth function, with a collapse of the implied volatility that is*

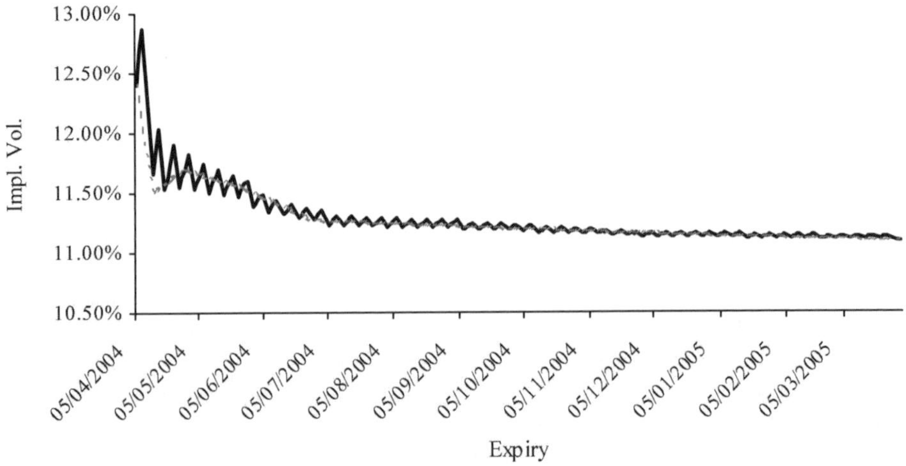

Figure 4.3 Comparison between linear interpolation and weighted interpolation for ATM volatilities. Continuous line: interpolation produced by formula (4.22); dashed line: interpolation produced by formula (4.21)

usually experienced on Mondays since weekends are weighted by zero. Short-dated options are mostly affected by the weighting, and its impact could be even wider than the usual bid/ask spreads.

4.8 ADMISSIBLE VOLATILITY SURFACES

Every volatility surface must satisfy some conditions in order to rule out any arbitrage opportunities exploited by means of static positions set up at time t: in this sense they are necessary and sufficient conditions to declare the volatility surface admissible.

The first condition is a couple of constraints which prevent the possibility of establishing an arbitrage by trading a call spread or a put spread:

$$\frac{\partial \mathrm{Bl}(S_t, t, T, K, P^d(t,T), P^f(t,T), \sigma, \omega)}{\partial K} \mid_{\omega=1} \leq 0 \tag{4.23}$$

$$\frac{\partial \mathrm{Bl}(S_t, t, T, K, P^d(t,T), P^f(t,T), \sigma, \omega)}{\partial K} \mid_{\omega=-1} \geq 0 \tag{4.24}$$

Basically, call options struck at a given level must be worth more than an otherwise identical call struck at a higher price; similarly, a put option must be worth more than an otherwise identical put struck at a lower price.

The second condition sets a constraint on the convexity of the surface at a given maturity, ruling out the possibility of buying a butterfly for nothing or even with a positive income:

$$\frac{\partial^2 \mathrm{Bl}(S_t, t, T, K, P^d(t,T), P^f(t,T), \sigma, \omega)}{\partial K^2} > 0 \tag{4.25}$$

The third condition is on the slope with respect to the time to maturity of the surface. It should not be possible to buy an option and sell an otherwise identical option with a shorter time to maturity without paying a premium:

$$\frac{\partial \mathrm{Bl}(S_t, t, T, K, P^d(t,T), P^f(t,T), \sigma, \omega)}{\partial T} > 0 \tag{4.26}$$

It is worth giving some explanation for the last condition. The Theta of an option is normally a positive function of the time to maturity, and that is exactly what has been expressed in the condition above. Nevertheless, sometimes for deep in-the-money options, and when there is a huge difference between the domestic and foreign interest rates, the Theta could be negatively related to the time to maturity. To avoid this kind of problem, one should check the admissibility of the volatility surface with out-of-the-money options, for which condition (4.26) is always a bounding constraint.

The final two conditions just force the price of a call option struck at 0 to be equal to the forward price discounted by the domestic rate, and the price of a very far out-of-the-money option to be equal to 0. In practice, this means that the implied volatility cannot explode for, when the strike price tends to 0 or infinity,

$$\mathrm{Bl}(S_t, t, T, K, P^d(t,T), P^f(t,T), \sigma, \omega) \mid_{\omega=1} = \frac{S_t}{P^f(t,T)} \tag{4.27}$$

$$\lim_{K \longrightarrow \infty} \mathrm{Bl}(S_t, t, T, K, P^d(t,T), P^f(t,T), \sigma, \omega) \mid_{\omega=1} = 0 \tag{4.28}$$

4.9 TAKING INTO ACCOUNT THE MARKET BUTTERFLY

Up to this point we have not considered a market inconsistency that can safely be disregarded in many situations and configurations of prices, but that can have a deep impact on the volatility surface building in others. We have seen in Chapter 1 the market quoting and trading conventions for the 25D **RR** and **VWB**. From their prices in volatility terms (formulae (1.2) and (1.3)) and the price of the ATM **STDL**, it is straightforward to get the following implied volatilities for the 25D strikes:

$$\sigma_{25P}(t,T) = \sigma_{ATM}(t,T) + \mathbf{vwb}(t,T;25) - 0.5\mathbf{rr}(t,T;25)$$
$$\sigma_{25C}(t,T) = \sigma_{ATM}(t,T) + \mathbf{vwb}(t,T;25) + 0.5\mathbf{rr}(t,T;25)$$

From these (and the ATM **STDL**) implied volatilities, we can calculate the strikes in absolute terms corresponding to the 25D and ATM levels. It should now be stressed that this is not fully consistent with the market standard conventions for trading the **VWB**. In fact, if the market is dealing the ATM **STDL** price at σ_{ATM} and the **VWB** at **vwb** (in volatility terms, for a given expiry), when the latter structure is traded then the two 25D wing strikes are calculated by defining a single volatility disregarding the **RR** price:

$$\sigma_{VWB} = \sigma_{ATM}(t,T) + \mathbf{vwb}(t,T;25) \tag{4.29}$$

The average price is the same as that taking explicitly into account the **RR** price, but equation (4.29) implies a unique average volatility for both the 25D (base currency) call and put instead of two separate volatilities (averaging to the same level anyway). So the two strikes, corresponding to the 25D wings, are

$$\overline{K}_{25P} \equiv F(t,T)e^{\sigma_{VWB}\sqrt{T-t}\Phi^{-1}(0.25/P^f(t,T))+0.5\sigma^2_{VWB}(T-t)} \tag{4.30}$$

$$\overline{K}_{25C} \equiv F(t,T)e^{-\sigma_{VWB}\sqrt{T-t}\Phi^{-1}(0.25/P^f(t,T))+0.5\sigma^2_{VWB}(T-t)} \tag{4.31}$$

whereas, in order to keep things consistent, they should be calculated as

$$K_{25P} \equiv F(t,T)e^{\sigma_{25P}\sqrt{T-t}\Phi^{-1}(0.25/P^f(t,T))+0.5\sigma^2_{25P}(T-t)} \tag{4.32}$$

$$K_{25C} \equiv F(t,T)e^{-\sigma_{25C}\sqrt{T-t}\Phi^{-1}(0.25/P^f(t,T))+0.5\sigma^2_{25C}(T-t)} \tag{4.33}$$

The latter two formulae (with two different implied volatilities for the call and the put) are used when an **RR** is traded, or when a spread ATM vs 25D call (or ATM vs 25D put) is traded. If the market convention for the pair is to pay the premium as a percentage of the base currency, then Procedure 2.2.1 must be run. The following example may help to clarify which practical implications are derived from the butterfly trading market practice.

Example 4.9.1. *Assume we are trading in the USDJPY and the following data are available in the market for the 6-month expiry (183 days):*

S	*102.65*	σ_{ATM}	*11.95%*
P^d	*0.9949767*	rr	*−4.70%*
P^f	*0.98356851*	vwb	*0.12%*

From these data we have that $\sigma_{25C} = 9.72\%$ *and* $\sigma_{25P} = 14.42\%$, *if we use the usual relationships linking the three prices. If one trades a 25D* **RR**, *or asks for a 25D USD call or put, the corresponding strikes would be set equal to*

$$K_{25P} = 94.8708$$

$$K_{25C} = 106.1933$$

The strikes have been calculated by the two volatilities above and by running Procedure 2.2.1 (since according to market conventions for USDJPY, the premium is paid in base currency units and expressed as a percentage of the base currency amount and the Delta includes the premium). The two options are worth (all prices are in US dollar %):

$$\mathbf{C}(K_{25C}, \sigma(K_{25C})) = 1.0560$$
$$\mathbf{P}(K_{25P}, \sigma(K_{25P})) = 1.4847$$

and their sum (i.e., *the 25D strangle) is* **STGL** $= 2.5407$.

If we trade a 25D **VWB** *then we use the unique implied volatility* $\sigma_{VWB} = \sigma_{ATM} + \mathbf{vwb} = 11.95\% + 0.12\% = 12.59\%$, *and the two 25D wing strikes would be*

$$\overline{K}_{25P} = 95.9080 \tag{4.34}$$

$$\overline{K}_{25C} = 107.3774 \tag{4.35}$$

The two options are worth (in US dollar %):

$$\mathbf{C}(\overline{K}_{25C}, \sigma_{VWB}) = 1.3168$$
$$\mathbf{P}(\overline{K}_{25P}, \sigma_{VWB}) = 1.2482$$

and their sum is **STGL** $= 2.5651$.

Now, if we build a volatility smile, via equation (4.9) for example, with the three strikes (the ATM strike is 101.1104, *the others are* K_{25P} *and* K_{25C} *with values as above and the volatilities too are those shown above), and then we price the options referring to the butterfly strikes* $\overline{K}_{25P}$ *and* $\overline{K}_{25C}$, *we will use the proper implied volatilities according to the smile function and the options' prices are*

$$\mathbf{C}(\overline{K}_{25C}, \sigma(\overline{K}_{25C})) = 0.6865$$
$$\mathbf{P}(\overline{K}_{25P}, \sigma(\overline{K}_{25P})) = 1.6950$$

The sum is **STGL** $= 2.3815$. *In this case,* $\sigma(\overline{K}_{25C}) = 9.12\%$ *and* $\sigma(\overline{K}_{25P}) = 14.06\%$ *and they are derived by the interpolating/extrapolating function (4.9).*

To sum up, what does this mean? Basically, if we use a smile function built with the market prices plainly as they deal (without considering actual market conventions for the **VWB**), *and we make prices by means of it, then we can be arbitraged. In fact, if we are asked for a* **VWB**, *we will quote it by using the single volatility* 12.59% *and the cost of the two wings will be* 2.5651 *(we are not interested in the price of the ATM* **STDL** *since it will in any case be priced by the implied volatilility* 11.95%*). If we are asked for a price of the two options separately, we will use the exact implied volatilities provided by the smile function and the total cost will be* 2.3815. *Hence, a counterparty may ask us for a price in a* **VWB** *and they can sell it; afterwards they can ask separately for the two options entering into the* **VWB** *as 25D wings and they can buy them, eventually earning* $2.5651 - 2.3815 = 0.1835\%$ *of the US dollar notional amounts.*

There is clearly a sort of inconsistency resulting from the specific market quoting mechanism producing arbitrage opportunities. We have to find a way to rule this out, making the entire smile arbitrage-free, albeit in line with the prices of the **RR** *and the* **VWB**.

We want to build a volatility surface taking into account all the market conventions. In practice, we want that the two 25D options priced according to the volatility surface we employ have the same value as calculated according to the one-volatility standard (the ATM **STDL** is priced in any case with σ_{ATM}). Thus:

$$\mathbf{C}(\overline{K}_{25C}, \sigma(\overline{K}_{25C})) + \mathbf{P}(\overline{K}_{25P}, \sigma(\overline{K}_{25P})) = \mathbf{C}(\overline{K}_{25C}, \sigma_{VWB}) + \mathbf{P}(\overline{K}_{25P}, \sigma_{VWB}) \tag{4.36}$$

Here we drop the dependence on time and write the option prices as a function only of the strike price and the implied volatility. The right-hand side of equation (4.36) is the sum of the prices of the two options struck at the 25D strikes valued with the implied volatility retrieved via the smile function we used to build the smile. For example, we can use the approximation formula (4.4.3). The left-hand side is the sum of the prices of the same options, valued in this case with the same volatility σ_{VWB}.

Now, if in the market the **VWB** is dealing at the level **vwb**, we want to take properly into account this information in our smile-building process. In practice, we would like to determine which is the correct combination of implied volatilities yielding a volatility smile that satisfies the constraint (4.36). There is one more additional constraint that should be matched – the price of an **RR**, with strikes calculated as in (4.32) and (4.33), must be equal to that dealing in the market: $\mathbf{rr} = \sigma(K_C) - \sigma(K_P)$. To recapitulate: given the market prices σ_{ATM}, **rr** and **vwb**, we have to determine an *equivalent* $\mathbf{vwb}_e$ price so that the smile we build, by means of our predefined interpolation/extrapolation function, matches all the requirements above. The solution to this problem has to be found numerically, by implementing the following procedure:

Procedure 4.9.1. *Equivalent* 25D **VWB** *price for a given price of* 25D **VWB** *dealt in the market.*

1. *For a given expiry, calculate the conventional volatility for the* 25D **VWB**: $\sigma_{VWB} = \sigma_{ATM} + \mathbf{vwb}$ *and the ATM strike:*

$$K_{ATM} = F(t, T)e^{(0.5\sigma^2_{ATM}(T-t))}$$

   In case the market conventions for the pair imply a premium-included Delta, then the ATM level is

$$K_{ATM} = F(t, T)e^{(-0.5\sigma^2_{ATM}(T-t))}$$

   Set $i = 0$ *and* $\mathbf{vwb}^i_e = \mathbf{vwb}$ *(the superscripts refer to the number of the procedure's iterations).*
2. *Retrieve the two* 25D *volatilities in a "consistent" way, i.e.,* $\sigma_{25P} = \sigma_{ATM} + \mathbf{vwb}^i_e - 0.5\mathbf{rr}$ *and* $\sigma_{25C}(t, T) = \sigma_{ATM} + \mathbf{vwb}^i_e + 0.5\mathbf{rr}$.
3. *Calculate the* 25D *strikes with the "consistent" volatilities:*

$$K^i_{25P} = F(t, T)e^{\sigma_{25P}\sqrt{T-t}\Phi^{-1}(0.25/P^f(t,T))+0.5\sigma^2_{25P}(T-t)}$$
$$K^i_{25C} = F(t, T)e^{-\sigma_{25C}\sqrt{T-t}\Phi^{-1}(0.25/P^f(t,T))+0.5\sigma^2_{25C}(T-t)}$$

   If the premiums are a percentage of the base currency amount, then the strikes are recovered by means of Procedure 2.2.1.

4. *Calculate the 25D strikes for the market* **VWB** *(i.e., with the unique σ_{VWB}):*

$$\overline{K}^i_{25P} = F(t,T)e^{\sigma_{VWB}\sqrt{T-t}\Phi^{-1}(0.25/P^f(t,T))+0.5\sigma^2_{VWB}(T-t)}$$
$$\overline{K}^i_{25C} = F(t,T)e^{-\sigma_{VWB}\sqrt{T-t}\Phi^{-1}(0.25/P^f(t,T))+0.5\sigma^2_{VWB}(T-t)}$$

If the premiums are a percentage of the base currency amount, then the strikes are recovered by means of Procedure 2.2.1.

5. *Calculate the difference between the* **STGL** *struck at the market* **VWB** *levels valued with the smile volatility, and the same* **STGL** *valued with the conventional volatility σ_{VWBS}:*

$$\mathcal{S}^i = \boldsymbol{C}(\overline{K}^i_{25C}, \sigma(\overline{K}^i_{25C})) + \boldsymbol{P}(\overline{K}^i_{25P}, \sigma(\overline{K}^i_{25P})) - \boldsymbol{C}(\overline{K}^i_{25C}, \sigma_{VWB}) + \boldsymbol{P}(\overline{K}^i_{25P}, \sigma_{VWB})$$

Shift by one basis point 0.0001 *the equivalent* **VWB** *price:* $\mathbf{vwb}^1_e = \mathbf{vwb}^0_e + 0.0001$ *and set* $dfly^1 = 0.0001$ *(only for the first iteration $i = 0$, for precision's sake). The quantity $dfly^i$ is the variation of* $\mathbf{vwb}_e$ *from iteration $i-1$ to iteration i.*

6. *Increment $i = i + 1$. Perform the same calculations as in steps* 1 *to* 5 *(with the new* $\mathbf{vwb}^{i+1}_e$*) to calculate the new* 25D *volatilities and strikes, and the new difference $\mathcal{S}^i$.*
7. *Calculate the numerical derivatives of the quantity $\mathcal{S}$ with respect to the* $\mathbf{vwb}_e$*:*

$$d\mathcal{S}^i = (\mathcal{S}^i - \mathcal{S}^{i-1})/dfly^i$$

8. *Calculate the new* $\mathbf{vwb}^{i+1}_e = \mathbf{vwb}^i_e - \mathcal{S}^i/d\mathcal{S}^i$ *and* $dfly^{i+1} = -\mathcal{S}^i/d\mathcal{S}^i$.
9. *Iterate from step* 6 *until* $|\mathcal{S}^i - \mathcal{S}^{i-1}| < \epsilon$*, for ϵ suitably small.*

Procedure 4.9.1 yields a $\mathbf{vwb}_e$ which allows us to build a volatility surface consistent with the market prices of both the **RR** and **VWB**. The difference between the quoted **vwb** and the equivalent $\mathbf{vwb}_e$ depends on **rr**; in practice, if the price of the **RR** is smaller than 10% of the ATM volatility level, then the difference is negligible. Nevertheless, for some pairs (such as the USDJPY) with large **rr**, the difference may produce appreciable effects on the options' pricing.

Example 4.9.2. *We return to Example 4.9.1. We apply Procedure 4.9.1 and calculate the equivalent price for the* **VWB** *to use in an arbitrage-free volatility smile function:* $\mathbf{vwb}_e = 0.5133$*, so that the new values for the 25D implied volatilities are* $\sigma(K_{25C}) = 10.11\%$ *and* $\sigma(K_{25P}) = 14.81\%$ *(they are derived by using* $\mathbf{vwb}_e$ *to determine the three volatilities entering into the function (4.9)). The corresponding strikes are*

$$K_{25P} = 94.6993$$
$$K_{25C} = 106.3911$$

The ATM strike is still $K_{ATM} = 101.1104$*. We use once again the approximation (4.9) to build the smile and we now price a* **VWB** *by means of it and compare the sum of the prices of the two wings with the market price, which is* **STGL** $= 2.5651$ *and has been calculated in Example 4.9.1. We have that the new implied volatilities corresponding to the* **vwb** *wings are* $\sigma(\overline{K}_{25C}) = 9.80\%$ *and* $\sigma(\overline{K}_{25P}) = 14.27\%$*. So, if we make a price separately for the two 25D wing options entering into the* **VWB***, we yield*

$$\boldsymbol{C}(\overline{K}_{25C}, \sigma(\overline{K}_{25C})) = 0.6865$$
$$\boldsymbol{P}(\overline{K}_{25P}, \sigma(\overline{K}_{25P})) = 1.6950$$

and the sum is **STGL** = 2.5635. *The difference from the cost of the same options traded via a butterfly is* 0.0016, *which is immaterial in practical terms (it is due to the tolerance error we set in Procedure 4.9.1 at a level ensuring a negligible difference as for trading purposes). Any possible arbitrage is thus prevented.*

4.10 BUILDING THE VOLATILITY MATRIX IN PRACTICE

In the previous sections we have described a set of tools for volatility matrix building. Now we examine a real market situation so as to show how to employ these tools in practice. We consider the EURUSD option market as of 29 February 2008. In Table 4.6 the market prices for the ATM **STDL**, the 25D **RR** and 25D **VWB** are shown. The table also confirms what we have anticipated at the beginning of this chapter, where the criteria for an efficient and convenient representation of the volatility surface are presented. The form that we pointed out as the most preferable is just the one that naturally stems from the quoting mechanism and conventions of the FX option market. The EURUSD FX spot rate we use in the following calculations is 1.5184.

From the prices of the main structures, the volatilities for the ATM and 25D EUR call and put strikes can be calculated immediately in the usual way (by means of the well-known relationships, see formulae (1.2) and (1.3) in Chapter 1); they are given in Table 4.7. We also provide therein the zero-coupon prices needed to perform the calculations in what follows: these are bootstrapped from the money market instruments, namely deposits and interest rate swaps for expiries longer than two years.

The next step is to calculate the strikes referring to the basic structures. We use formula (2.46) (for $\Delta = 0.25$) and the definition of zero Delta **STDL**

$$\begin{aligned}
K_{ATM}(t,T) &= F(t,T)e^{(0.5\sigma_{ATM}^2(T-t))} \\
K_P &= F(t,T)e^{\sigma_{25P}\sqrt{T-t}\Phi^{-1}(0.25/P^f(t,T))+0.5\sigma_{25P}^2(T-t)} \\
K_C &= F(t,T)e^{-\sigma_{25C}\sqrt{T-t}\Phi^{-1}(0.25/P^f(t,T))+0.5\sigma_{25C}^2(T-t)}
\end{aligned} \tag{4.37}$$

Table 4.6 Prices in volatility terms for the EURUSD basic structures dealing in the market as of 29 February 2008

Expiry		ATM	25D RR	25D Fly
O/N	03-mar-08	7.50%	0.50%	0.20%
1W	07-mar-08	11.00%	0.29%	0.20%
2W	14-mar-08	10.40%	0.21%	0.20%
1M	02-apr-08	9.70%	−0.05%	0.20%
2M	02-mag-08	9.65%	−0.20%	0.22%
3M	02-giu-08	9.53%	−0.30%	0.25%
6M	02-set-08	9.33%	−0.40%	0.33%
9M	02-dic-08	9.25%	−0.45%	0.36%
1Y	02-mar-09	9.18%	−0.48%	0.38%
2Y	02-mar-10	8.95%	−0.48%	0.31%
5Y	28-feb-13	8.90%	−0.48%	0.31%
10Y	02-mar-18	8.90%	−0.48%	0.28%

Source: Main brokers' information provider systems.

Table 4.7 Implied volatilities for the ATM and the 25D EUR call and put strikes, and prices of domestic (USD) and foreign (EUR) zero-coupon bonds for EURUSD as of 29 February 2008

Expiry		25D P	ATM	25D C	P^d	P^f
O/N	03-mar-08	7.45%	7.50%	7.95%	0.999737	0.999666
1W	07-mar-08	11.06%	11.00%	11.35%	0.999387	0.999218
2W	14-mar-08	10.50%	10.40%	10.71%	0.998779	0.998429
1M	02-apr-08	9.93%	9.70%	9.88%	0.997132	0.996257
2M	02-mag-08	9.97%	9.65%	9.77%	0.994686	0.992191
3M	02-giu-08	9.93%	9.53%	9.63%	0.992006	0.988242
6M	02-set-08	9.86%	9.33%	9.46%	0.985281	0.977018
9M	02-dic-08	9.84%	9.25%	9.39%	0.975910	0.966284
1Y	02-mar-09	9.80%	9.18%	9.32%	0.970856	0.956071
2Y	02-mar-10	9.50%	8.95%	9.02%	0.949348	0.927723
5Y	28-feb-13	9.45%	8.90%	8.97%	0.840130	0.824089
10Y	02-mar-18	9.41%	8.90%	8.94%	0.643859	0.649933

Source: Main brokers' information provider systems.

For the EURUSD the market conventions are for the option's premium to be paid in numeraire currency pips, so the formulae above are correct. Should the premium be paid in base currency (or, should it be a percentage of the base currency amount), then we have to resort to Procedure 2.2.1 to correctly determine the three strikes. They can be found in Table 4.8. It is worth stressing the fact that, once again by market conventions, the ATM level is the zero Delta **STDL** for expiries up to two years, then for longer expiries it is simply the forward price. We are now endowed with all the data we need to build an entire volatility matrix. We can use formula (4.6) (as we do in this case) or the approximation (4.9) and evaluate an option with any strike. In Tables 4.9 and 4.10 we map the volatility matrix against, respectively, the EUR put and EUR call Delta (the ATM volatility is clearly the same as in Table 4.6). The 25D call and put volatilities are the same as those implied in market quotations, by construction of the VV approach.

Table 4.8 ATM and 25D EUR call and put strikes for EURUSD as of 29 February 2008

Expiry		K_{25P}	K_{ATM}	K_{25C}
O/N	03-mar-08	1.4965	1.5033	1.5107
1W	07-mar-08	1.4882	1.5036	1.5196
2W	14-mar-08	1.4834	1.5040	1.5254
1M	02-apr-08	1.4753	1.5052	1.5355
2M	02-mag-08	1.4670	1.5082	1.5498
3M	02-giu-08	1.4608	1.5107	1.5608
6M	02-set-08	1.4504	1.5193	1.5889
9M	02-dic-08	1.4406	1.5231	1.6071
1Y	02-mar-09	1.4388	1.5329	1.6293
2Y	02-mar-10	1.4255	1.5382	1.6815
5Y	28-feb-13	1.4006	1.5325	1.7396
10Y	02-mar-18	1.4305	1.4892	1.6795

Table 4.9 Volatility matrix for EURUSD as of 29 February 2008 (EUR put partition)

	EUR Put Delta				
Expiry	10.00%	15.00%	20.00%	**25.00%**	35.00%
O/N	7.75%	7.58%	7.50%	**7.45%**	7.43%
1W	11.46%	11.25%	11.13%	**11.06%**	10.98%
2W	10.95%	10.72%	10.58%	**10.50%**	10.41%
1M	10.51%	10.23%	10.05%	**9.93%**	9.78%
2M	10.68%	10.35%	10.13%	**9.97%**	9.77%
3M	10.77%	10.39%	10.12%	**9.93%**	9.68%
6M	11.00%	10.49%	10.12%	**9.86%**	9.53%
9M	11.12%	10.55%	10.13%	**9.83%**	9.47%
1Y	11.17%	10.56%	10.11%	**9.80%**	9.41%
2Y	10.81%	10.22%	9.80%	**9.50%**	9.13%
5Y	11.45%	10.52%	9.87%	**9.45%**	8.90%
10Y	19.09%	14.63%	10.94%	**9.41%**	8.63%

In Figure 4.4 we provide a visual representation of the volatility matrix. The term structure of the ATM volatility is shown on the left-hand side whereas on the right there is the entire volatility surface. The term structure starts at a very low level, since the date we are considering (29 February 2008) is a Friday, which means that the options expiring in one business day (the overnight expiry, denoted "ON" in the tables) have two days (Saturday and Sunday), out of the three days they last, without market activity. Since nobody is willing to pay volatility for days when almost no volatility will presumably occur, the implied volatility is damped on Fridays (though one should consider it is also true that at the opening of the market on the next Monday, prices will at once include, by a jump in levels, all possible information befallen during the weekend).

Table 4.10 Volatility matrix for EURUSD as of 29 February 2008 (EUR call partition)

	EUR call Delta				
Expiry	35.00%	**25.00%**	20.00%	15.00%	10.00%
O/N	7.70%	**7.95%**	8.14%	8.38%	8.71%
1W	11.14%	**11.35%**	11.50%	11.72%	12.03%
2W	10.52%	**10.71%**	10.85%	11.05%	11.36%
1M	9.75%	**9.88%**	9.99%	10.15%	10.41%
2M	9.66%	**9.77%**	9.87%	10.03%	10.29%
3M	9.52%	**9.63%**	9.73%	9.90%	10.19%
6M	9.32%	**9.46%**	9.62%	9.84%	10.23%
9M	9.24%	**9.39%**	9.56%	9.81%	10.25%
1Y	9.17%	**9.32%**	9.51%	9.78%	10.26%
2Y	8.90%	**9.02%**	9.19%	9.43%	9.87%
5Y	8.81%	**8.97%**	9.23%	9.64%	10.41%
10Y	8.90%	**8.94%**	10.45%	15.90%	16.39%

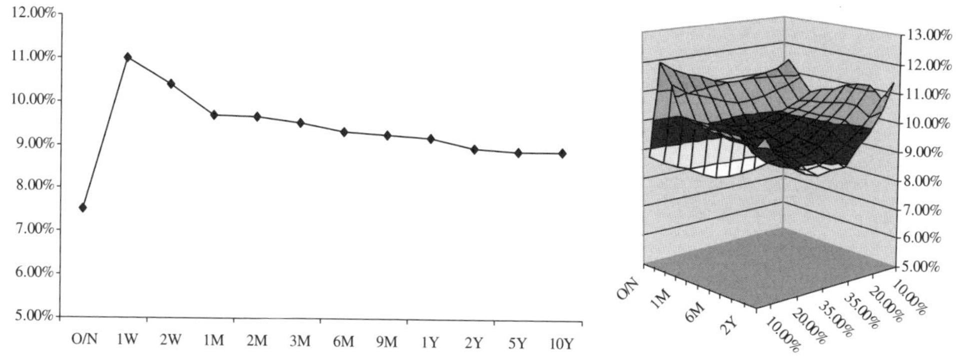

Figure 4.4 ATM volatility term structure and volatility surface for EURUSD as of 29 February 2008

Keeping our attention still on the term structure and its interpolation, in Figure 4.6 we also show how it behaves when a weighted interpolation is applied, instead of the simple linear one, between two contiguous maturities; this is done up to an expiry of one month. In Figure 4.5 we show a snapshot of an electronic sheet where the weights for five calendars are input. The check marks are the holidays in the corresponding countries (including weekends): these days are zero weighted. For 7 March 2008 a "1" is assigned for each calendar, due to a momentous economic event (the Non-farm Payroll figures for the US economy are released on the first Friday of every month) – this overweighting makes the date to account for 0.75

	Holidays					Economic Events					OK	Weights				
Date	target	usa	jap	london	swi	target	usa	jap	london	swi	Date	target	usa	jap	london	swi
29-Feb											29-Feb	0.000	0.000	0.000	0.000	0.000
01-Mar	✓	✓	✓	✓	✓						01-Mar	0.000	0.000	0.000	0.000	0.000
02-Mar	✓	✓	✓	✓	✓						02-Mar	0.000	0.000	0.000	0.000	0.000
03-Mar											03-Mar	0.500	0.500	0.500	0.500	0.500
04-Mar											04-Mar	1.000	1.000	1.000	1.000	1.000
05-Mar											05-Mar	1.500	1.500	1.500	1.500	1.500
06-Mar											06-Mar	2.000	2.000	2.000	2.000	2.000
07-Mar						1	1	1	1	1	07-Mar	2.750	2.750	2.750	2.750	2.750
08-Mar	✓	✓	✓	✓	✓						08-Mar	2.750	2.750	2.750	2.750	2.750
9-Mar	✓	✓	✓	✓	✓						09-Mar	2.750	2.750	2.750	2.750	2.750
10-Mar											10-Mar	3.250	3.250	3.250	3.250	3.250
11-Mar											11-Mar	3.750	3.750	3.750	3.750	3.750
12-Mar											12-Mar	4.250	4.250	4.250	4.250	4.250
13-Mar											13-Mar	4.750	4.750	4.750	4.750	4.750
14-Mar											14-Mar	5.250	5.250	5.250	5.250	5.250
15-Mar	✓	✓	✓	✓	✓						15-Mar	5.250	5.250	5.250	5.250	5.250
16-Mar	✓	✓	✓	✓	✓						16-Mar	5.250	5.250	5.250	5.250	5.250
17-Mar											17-Mar	5.750	5.750	5.750	5.750	5.750
18-Mar											18-Mar	6.250	6.250	6.250	6.250	6.250
19-Mar											19-Mar	6.750	6.750	6.750	6.750	6.750
20-Mar			✓								20-Mar	7.250	7.250	6.750	7.250	7.250
21-Mar	✓			✓	✓						21-Mar	7.250	7.750	7.250	7.250	7.250
22-Mar	✓	✓	✓	✓	✓						22-Mar	7.250	7.750	7.250	7.250	7.250
23-Mar	✓	✓	✓	✓	✓						23-Mar	7.250	7.750	7.250	7.250	7.250
24-Mar	✓			✓	✓						24-Mar	7.250	8.250	7.750	7.250	7.250
25-Mar											25-Mar	7.750	8.750	8.250	7.750	7.750
26-Mar											26-Mar	8.250	9.250	8.750	8.250	8.250
27-Mar											27-Mar	8.750	9.750	9.250	8.750	8.750
28-Mar											28-Mar	9.250	10.250	9.750	9.250	9.250
29-Mar	✓	✓	✓	✓	✓						29-Mar	9.250	10.250	9.750	9.250	9.250
30-Mar	✓	✓	✓	✓	✓						30-Mar	9.250	10.250	9.750	9.250	9.250

Figure 4.5 Weights used in the weighted interpolation of the ATM volatility term structure, up to one month expiry, with weighted interpolation, as of 29 February 2008

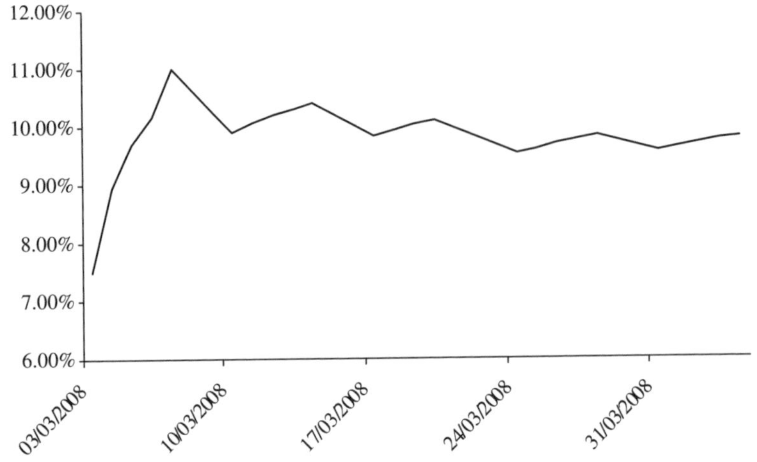

Figure 4.6 EURUSD ATM volatility term structure up to one month expiry, with weighted interpolation, as of 29 February 2008

for each calendar, so that for a pair, say EURUSD, the sum of the weights of the two related currencies is 1.5. Every other "ordinary" business day accounts for 0.5 for any currency, so that when assembling a pair, the sum of the two weights is one. One may easily notice the usual sawtooth behaviour produced by the weekend effect we have just described above, and in fact we weighted all the holidays by zero.

We have not so far taken into account the intrinsic inconsistency implicit in the quoting convention for the **VWB**, whose analysis was conducted in Section 4.9. We employ the procedure described there to calculate the equivalent 25D **VWB** prices originated from the actual market prices in Table 4.6. As already stressed, the quoting inconsistency can safely be disregarded in many market conditions, when the volatility smiles for the different expiries are not too steep, as is the case for the example we are now examining. In fact, Table 4.11 shows the equivalent **VWB** prices so that the sum of the costs (in USD pips) of the two

Table 4.11 Equivalent **VWB** prices for EURUSD and differences with the **VWB** prices dealt in the market, as of 29 February 2008)

Expiry		Equivalent **VWB**	(Equiv. – Mkt) **VWB**
O/N	03-mar-08	0.200%	0.000%
1W	07-mar-08	0.200%	0.000%
2W	14-mar-08	0.200%	0.000%
1M	02-apr-08	0.200%	0.000%
2M	02-mag-08	0.220%	0.000%
3M	02-giu-08	0.250%	0.000%
6M	02-set-08	0.340%	0.010%
9M	02-dic-08	0.370%	0.010%
1Y	02-mar-09	0.390%	0.010%
2Y	02-mar-10	0.320%	0.010%
5Y	28-feb-13	0.320%	0.010%
10Y	02-mar-18	0.255%	−0.022%

Table 4.12 Differences between the volatility matrix built with the equivalent **VWB** and that built with the market **VWB** price for EURUSD, as of 29 February 2008 (EUR put partition)

Expiry	10.00%	15.00%	20.00%	25.00%	35.00%
O/N	0.00%	0.00%	0.00%	0.00%	0.00%
1W	0.00%	0.00%	0.00%	0.00%	0.00%
2W	0.00%	0.00%	0.00%	0.00%	0.00%
1M	0.00%	0.00%	0.00%	0.00%	0.00%
2M	0.00%	0.00%	0.00%	0.00%	0.00%
3M	0.00%	0.00%	0.00%	0.00%	0.00%
6M	0.04%	0.03%	0.02%	0.01%	0.00%
9M	0.04%	0.03%	0.02%	0.01%	0.00%
1Y	0.04%	0.03%	0.02%	0.01%	0.00%
2Y	0.04%	0.03%	0.02%	0.01%	0.00%
5Y	0.06%	0.04%	0.02%	0.01%	0.00%
10Y	−0.46%	−0.35%	−0.11%	−0.02%	0.01%

25D options traded in this structure in the market is the same as that obtained by the smile we built via the interpolation scheme we are using (formula (4.6) in the current example). The differences between equivalent and market **VWB** prices are nil up to six month expiry and, except for 10 years, they are as large as one basis point of volatility. To determine the impact of these differences on the resulting volatility matrices, we show in Tables 4.12 and 4.13 the differences between implied volatilities generated by the equivalent **VWB** prices and those by the market prices. The largest deviations are for more OTM strikes[12] and, since the corresponding options have a small Vega, the impact on their prices is minor.

Finally, to check the efficiency of the VV interpolation scheme, we compare the volatility matrix we produced with that of one of the major market makers for FX options. In Figure 4.7 the UBS's volatility surface as of 29 February 2008 is shown. A quick glance confirms that these volatilities are the same as those we presented in Tables 4.9 and 4.10, at least for practical purposes.

Table 4.13 Differences between the volatility matrix built with the equivalent **VWB** and that built with the market **VWB** price for EURUSD, as of 29 February 2008 (EUR call partition)

Expiry	35.00%	25.00%	20.00%	15.00%	10.00%
O/N	0.00%	0.00%	0.00%	0.00%	0.00%
1W	0.00%	0.00%	0.00%	0.00%	0.00%
2W	0.00%	0.00%	0.00%	0.00%	0.00%
1M	0.00%	0.00%	0.00%	0.00%	0.00%
2M	0.00%	0.00%	0.00%	0.00%	0.00%
3M	0.00%	0.00%	0.00%	0.00%	0.00%
6M	0.00%	0.01%	0.00%	0.03%	0.04%
9M	0.00%	0.01%	0.00%	0.03%	0.04%
1Y	0.00%	0.01%	0.00%	0.03%	0.04%
2Y	0.00%	0.01%	0.00%	0.03%	0.05%
5Y	0.00%	0.01%	0.00%	0.04%	0.07%
10Y	0.00%	−0.02%	0.00%	−0.58%	−0.21%

[12] Clearly, for the 10-year expiry the amount is rather considerable, so that one may not like to neglect the difference between the equivalent and market **VWB** prices.

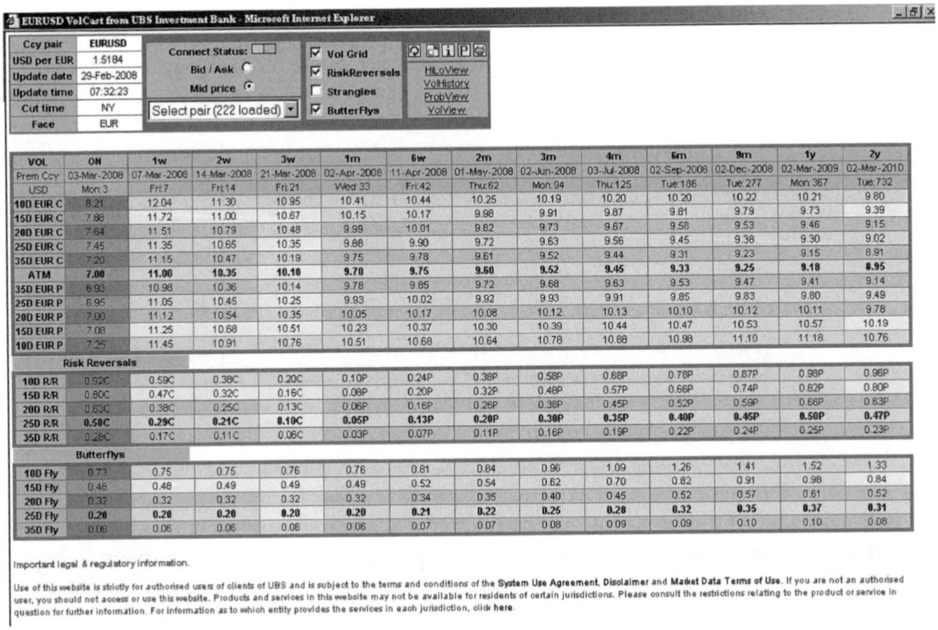

EURUSD VolCast from UBS Investment Bank - Microsoft Internet Explorer

Ccy pair	EURUSD
USD per EUR	1.5184
Update date	29-Feb-2008
Update time	07:32:23
Cut time	NY
Face	EUR

Connect Status:
Bid / Ask
Mid price
Select pair (222 loaded)
Vol Grid
RiskReversals
Strangles
ButterFlys
HiLoView
VolHistory
ProbView
VolView

VOL	ON	1w	2w	3w	1m	6w	2m	3m	4m	6m	9m	1y	2y
Prem Ccy	03-Mar-2008	07-Mar-2008	14-Mar-2008	21-Mar-2008	02-Apr-2008	11-Apr-2008	01-May-2008	02-Jun-2008	03-Jul-2008	02-Sep-2008	02-Dec-2008	02-Mar-2009	02-Mar-2010
USD	Mon:3	Fri:7	Fri:14	Fri:21	Wed:33	Fri:42	Thu:62	Mon:94	Thu:125	Tue:186	Tue:277	Mon:367	Tue:732
10D EUR C	8.21	12.04	11.30	10.95	10.41	10.44	10.25	10.19	10.20	10.20	10.22	10.21	9.80
15D EUR C	7.88	11.72	11.00	10.67	10.15	10.17	9.98	9.91	9.87	9.81	9.79	9.73	9.39
20D EUR C	7.64	11.51	10.79	10.48	9.99	10.01	9.82	9.73	9.67	9.58	9.53	9.46	9.15
25D EUR C	7.45	11.35	10.65	10.35	9.88	9.90	9.72	9.63	9.56	9.45	9.38	9.30	9.02
35D EUR C	7.20	11.15	10.47	10.19	9.75	9.78	9.61	9.52	9.44	9.31	9.23	9.15	8.91
ATM	**7.00**	**11.00**	**10.35**	**10.10**	**9.70**	**9.75**	**9.60**	**9.52**	**9.45**	**9.33**	**9.25**	**9.18**	**8.95**
35D EUR P	6.93	10.98	10.36	10.14	9.78	9.85	9.72	9.68	9.63	9.53	9.47	9.41	9.14
25D EUR P	6.95	11.05	10.45	10.25	9.93	10.02	9.92	9.93	9.91	9.85	9.83	9.80	9.49
20D EUR P	7.00	11.12	10.54	10.35	10.05	10.17	10.08	10.12	10.13	10.10	10.12	10.11	9.78
15D EUR P	7.08	11.25	10.68	10.51	10.23	10.37	10.30	10.39	10.44	10.47	10.53	10.57	10.19
10D EUR P	7.25	11.45	10.91	10.76	10.51	10.68	10.64	10.78	10.88	10.98	11.10	11.18	10.76

Risk Reversals

10D R/R	0.92C	0.59C	0.38C	0.20C	0.10P	0.24P	0.38P	0.58P	0.68P	0.78P	0.87P	0.98P	0.96P
15D R/R	0.80C	0.47C	0.32C	0.16C	0.08P	0.20P	0.32P	0.48P	0.57P	0.66P	0.74P	0.82P	0.80P
20D R/R	0.63C	0.38C	0.25C	0.13C	0.06P	0.16P	0.26P	0.38P	0.45P	0.52P	0.59P	0.66P	0.63P
25D R/R	**0.50C**	**0.29C**	**0.21C**	**0.10C**	**0.05P**	**0.13P**	**0.20P**	**0.30P**	**0.35P**	**0.40P**	**0.45P**	**0.50P**	**0.47P**
35D R/R	0.28C	0.17C	0.11C	0.06C	0.03P	0.07P	0.11P	0.16P	0.19P	0.22P	0.24P	0.25P	0.23P

Butterflys

10D Fly	0.73	0.75	0.75	0.76	0.76	0.81	0.84	0.96	1.09	1.26	1.41	1.52	1.33
15D Fly	0.48	0.48	0.49	0.49	0.49	0.52	0.54	0.62	0.70	0.82	0.91	0.98	0.84
20D Fly	0.32	0.32	0.32	0.32	0.32	0.34	0.35	0.40	0.45	0.52	0.57	0.61	0.52
25D Fly	**0.20**	**0.20**	**0.20**	**0.20**	**0.20**	**0.21**	**0.22**	**0.25**	**0.28**	**0.32**	**0.35**	**0.37**	**0.31**
35D Fly	0.06	0.06	0.06	0.06	0.06	0.07	0.07	0.08	0.09	0.09	0.10	0.10	0.08

Important legal & regulatory information.

Use of this website is strictly for authorised users of clients of UBS and is subject to the terms and conditions of the **System Use Agreement**, **Disclaimer** and **Market Data Terms of Use**. If you are not an authorised user, you should not access or use this website. Products and services in this website may not be available for residents of certain jurisdictions. Please consult the restrictions relating to the product or service in question for further information. For information as to which entity provides the services in each jurisdiction, click **here**.

Figure 4.7 EURUSD volatility matrix published on the Internet by UBS bank, a major market maker for FX options, as of 29 February 2008. (Reproduced with permission.)

We now present an example for the case when the **rr** is high and hence the impact on the difference between the equivalent and market **vwb** is relevant. We consider the case of the USDJPY as of 12 March 2008. The FX spot rate we used for calculation is 102.75. In Table 4.14 market prices for the main structures on canonic expiries are shown. It is manifest that the **rr** is a much higher percentage of the ATM volatility level with respect to the previous

Table 4.14 Prices in volatility terms for the USDJPY basic structures dealing in the market as of 12 March 2008

Expiry		ATM	25D RR	25D Fly
O/N	13-Mar-08	16.00%	−2.30%	0.20%
1W	18-Mar-08	15.05%	−2.26%	0.25%
2W	26-Mar-08	13.15%	−2.75%	0.21%
1M	10-Apr-08	13.95%	−3.70%	0.19%
2M	12-May-08	13.05%	−3.90%	0.20%
3M	12-Jun-08	12.60%	−4.10%	0.21%
6M	11-Sep-08	11.65%	−4.40%	0.21%
9M	12-Dec-08	11.20%	−4.60%	0.22%
1Y	12-Mar-09	10.90%	−4.75%	0.23%
2Y	12-Mar-10	10.20%	−4.63%	0.13%
5Y	12-Mar-13	10.30%	−4.50%	0.14%
10Y	12-Mar-18	10.50%	−4.50%	0.26%

Source: Main brokers' information provider systems.

Table 4.15 Implied volatilities for the ATM and the 25D USD call and put strikes, and prices of domestic (JPY) and foreign (USD) zero-coupon bonds for USDJPY as of 12 March 2008

Expiry		25D P	ATM	25D C	P^d	P^f
O/N	13-Mar-08	17.05%	16.00%	14.83%	0.999986	0.999901
1W	18-Mar-08	16.16%	15.05%	14.09%	0.999913	0.999428
2W	26-Mar-08	14.41%	13.15%	11.91%	0.999771	0.998837
1M	10-Apr-08	15.55%	13.95%	12.21%	0.999399	0.997656
2M	12-May-08	14.72%	13.05%	11.24%	0.998479	0.995118
3M	12-Jun-08	14.34%	12.60%	10.70%	0.997546	0.992916
6M	11-Sep-08	13.49%	11.65%	9.61%	0.994975	0.986023
9M	12-Dec-08	13.12%	11.20%	9.07%	0.991904	0.976914
1Y	12-Mar-09	12.88%	10.90%	8.71%	0.988541	0.971767
2Y	12-Mar-10	11.94%	10.20%	7.99%	0.982237	0.948934
5Y	12-Mar-13	12.01%	10.30%	8.17%	0.947182	0.837498
10Y	12-Mar-18	12.55%	10.50%	8.45%	0.854090	0.642404

Source: Main brokers' information provider systems.

example on the EURSUD. In Table 4.15 we derive the implied volatility for the ATM level and the 25D US dollar call and put and the prices of the discount bonds needed for the calculations.

Now we can calculate which is, for every expiry, the equivalent **VWB** price corresponding to the market one. These are shown in Table 4.16, together with their difference with respect to the corresponding market price. In this case the difference is dramatic and the impact on the building of the entire surface cannot be neglected at all.

To evaluate the impact, we first build a surface for the USDJPY by using the equivalent **VWB** price, as shown in Tables 4.17 and 4.18 (the ATM volatility is clearly the same as in Table 4.14). Then we build the volatility surface with the market **vwb** and calculate the difference from the previous surface; Tables 4.19 and 4.20 contain the results. These confirm that sometimes (especially for OTM strikes) the differences can be larger than the typical

Table 4.16 Equivalent **VWB** prices for USDJPY and differences from the **VWB** prices dealt in the market, as of 12 March 2008

Expiry		Equivalent **VWB**	Equiv − Mkt
O/N	13-Mar-08	0.350%	0.149%
1W	18-Mar-08	0.350%	0.103%
2W	26-Mar-08	0.350%	0.137%
1M	10-Apr-08	0.390%	0.199%
2M	12-May-08	0.420%	0.222%
3M	12-Jun-08	0.450%	0.244%
6M	11-Sep-08	0.490%	0.283%
9M	12-Dec-08	0.530%	0.312%
1Y	12-Mar-09	0.560%	0.333%
2Y	12-Mar-10	0.500%	0.366%
5Y	12-Mar-13	0.600%	0.458%
10Y	12-Mar-18	0.600%	0.345%

Table 4.17 Volatility matrix for USDJPY as of 12 March 2008, built with the equivalent 25D **VWB** prices (USD put partition)

	USD put Delta				
Expiry	10.00%	15.00%	20.00%	25.00%	35.00%
O/N	18.07%	17.70%	17.39%	17.12%	16.64%
1W	17.31%	16.89%	16.53%	16.23%	15.71%
2W	15.56%	15.16%	14.80%	14.49%	13.94%
1M	16.84%	16.41%	16.02%	15.66%	15.00%
2M	16.02%	15.59%	15.20%	14.84%	14.16%
3M	15.65%	15.22%	14.83%	14.47%	13.78%
6M	14.77%	14.36%	13.98%	13.62%	12.92%
9M	14.40%	13.99%	13.61%	13.25%	12.54%
1Y	14.16%	13.76%	13.37%	13.01%	12.29%
2Y	13.36%	12.89%	12.48%	12.08%	11.34%
5Y	13.92%	13.29%	12.72%	12.19%	11.24%
10Y	13.84%	13.73%	13.28%	12.59%	10.71%

Table 4.18 Volatility matrix for USDJPY as of 12 March 2008, built with the equivalent 25D **VWB** prices (USD call partition)

	USD call Delta				
Expiry	35.00%	25.00%	20.00%	15.00%	10.00%
O/N	15.42%	15.03%	14.82%	14.57%	14.26%
1W	14.54%	14.21%	14.05%	13.88%	13.69%
2W	12.50%	12.06%	11.83%	11.56%	11.23%
1M	13.07%	12.43%	12.08%	11.67%	11.15%
2M	12.15%	11.47%	11.10%	10.68%	10.13%
3M	11.68%	10.96%	10.57%	10.12%	9.55%
6M	10.70%	9.90%	9.48%	8.99%	8.40%
9M	10.25%	9.40%	8.94%	8.44%	7.82%
1Y	9.95%	9.05%	8.58%	8.06%	7.44%
2Y	9.21%	8.36%	7.93%	7.46%	6.90%
5Y	9.82%	8.63%	8.12%	7.60%	7.00%
10Y	10.50%	8.80%	6.98%	5.70%	4.67%

Table 4.19 Differences between the volatility matrix built with the equivalent **VWB** and that built with the market **VWB** price for USDJPY as of 3 March 2008 (USD put partition)

Expiry	10.00%	15.00%	20.00%	25.00%	35.00%
O/N	0.34%	0.22%	0.13%	0.07%	0.00%
1W	0.25%	0.17%	0.11%	0.06%	0.01%
2W	0.31%	0.21%	0.14%	0.08%	0.01%
1M	0.41%	0.28%	0.18%	0.11%	0.02%
2M	0.44%	0.30%	0.20%	0.12%	0.02%
3M	0.47%	0.32%	0.21%	0.12%	0.01%
6M	0.50%	0.35%	0.22%	0.13%	0.01%
9M	0.54%	0.37%	0.23%	0.13%	0.00%
1Y	0.55%	0.38%	0.24%	0.12%	−0.01%
2Y	0.63%	0.43%	0.27%	0.15%	0.00%
5Y	0.97%	0.63%	0.37%	0.18%	−0.02%
10Y	1.38%	0.75%	0.32%	0.04%	−0.01%

Table 4.20 Differences between the volatility matrix built with the equivalent **VWB** and that built with the market **VWB** price for USDJPY as of 3 March 2008 (USD Call partition)

Expiry	35.00%	25.00%	20.00%	15.00%	10.00%
O/N	0.09%	0.21%	0.29%	0.41%	0.58%
1W	0.05%	0.12%	0.17%	0.25%	0.37%
2W	0.06%	0.15%	0.22%	0.31%	0.44%
1M	0.09%	0.21%	0.30%	0.40%	0.54%
2M	0.10%	0.23%	0.32%	0.42%	0.56%
3M	0.11%	0.25%	0.34%	0.45%	0.58%
6M	0.13%	0.29%	0.39%	0.49%	0.60%
9M	0.14%	0.32%	0.42%	0.52%	0.62%
1Y	0.15%	0.34%	0.44%	0.54%	0.63%
2Y	0.16%	0.37%	0.48%	0.59%	0.69%
5Y	0.09%	0.46%	0.65%	0.83%	0.99%
10Y	0.00%	0.36%	0.57%	0.61%	0.59%

bid/ask spreads dealing in the market, so that taking the **VWB** prices into account properly is imperative, at least for market-making purposes.

5
Plain Vanilla Options

5.1 PRICING OF PLAIN VANILLA OPTIONS

The pricing of FX plain vanilla options has already been dealt with in Chapter 2, where we sketched the basic features of several models and provided the pricing formulae to evaluate (base currency) call and put options in each of their frameworks. We then referred to other chapters for the details. Here we would just like to stress that the interbank market reference is the BS model, since quoted implied volatilities are relative to this model and also Delta amounts are calculated by the same model. After a deal is struck, the premium (expressed according to the market conventions for the underlying pair) is calculated by the BS formula with the FX spot rate and the interest rates, for the two currencies involved, prevailing in the market, and the agreed implied volatility.

5.1.1 Delayed settlement date

Plain vanilla options are written on the spot FX rate: at expiry the buyer of the option can exercise the right to enter into a spot transaction to buy or sell the notional amount of base currency against the numeraire currency at the strike price. The settlement of this transaction is regulated according to the rules we examined in Chapter 1. Nonetheless, two counterparties may agree to settle the transaction at a different date, for example one month later than the expiry date. In this case the pricing of the option has to take that into account.

While the standard options pricing formulae we have examined up to now assume the underlying rate is the spot FX rate, if the delivery is deferred until a future date, the underlying rate becomes a forward one. The pricing formula, whatever model we are using to evaluate the contract, must be adapted to include this feature. The simple modification we show here allows us to keep all the results we have derived, and it will also be useful in the case of barrier options. In fact, for this kind of exotic options, the modification can be applied in a straightforward way with no difficulties.

Consider a base currency call option with expiry at T. The normal case is when the underlying rate is an FX spot rate whose delivery is on date $T + s$, where s is the number of days after inception of the spot transaction when the settlement occurs, determined by usual market conventions. It is a market practice, though not fully consistent from a logical point of view, to use the standard formulae we have presented in Chapter 2, which means that all the discountings are calculated by means of the domestic and foreign zero-coupon bonds expiring at T: $P^d(t, T)$ and $P^f(t, T)$. Consider now the case when the number of days is $s' > s$, so that the settlement date for the transaction originated by the exercise is $T' = T + s'$. In this case the buyer of the option is actually entering into a forward contract, so that their decision whether to exercise or not will be taken by comparing the forward price, prevailing in the market for delivery at T', with the strike price. The terminal value of the call option is then

$$\mathcal{O}^{ds}(S_T, T; T') = P^d(T, T') \max(F(T, T') - K, 0)$$

where $F(T, T')$ is the fair price of a forward contract starting at the option's expiry date T and with settlement at T'. Discounting by the zero-coupon bond $P^d(T, T')$ is due to the fact that the payoff actually realizes at time T'. We assume, as we have always done in previous chapters, that the interest rates are a deterministic function of time, and write the equation above as

$$\begin{aligned}\mathcal{O}^{ds}(S_T, T; T') &= P^d(T, T') \max\left(S_T \frac{P^f(T, T')}{P^d(T, T')} - K, 0\right)\\ &= P^f(T, T') \max\left(S_T - K \frac{P^d(T, T')}{P^f(T, T')}, 0\right)\end{aligned}$$

where we have simply expressed the forward price in terms of its pricing formula and then performed a naive manipulation. By defining the new price $K' = K \frac{P^d(T,T')}{P^f(T,T')}$, we can write the value of the option at time $t < T$ as the discounted expected terminal value, under the risk-neutral measure Q, times a factor equal to the foreign zero-coupon bond evaluated at T and maturing at T' (i.e., the forward price at time T of a foreign bond maturing at T'):

$$\mathcal{O}^{ds}(S_t, t; T') = P^f(T, T') E^Q[e^{-\int_t^T r_s^d ds} \max(S_T - K', 0)]$$

which, without considering the multiplying factor, is the standard expectation we have met many times before, with the new strike price K' substituting the contract one K. So we can just use all the pricing formulae we have presented, in any model, provided we previously adjust the strike and then multiply by the forward foreign zero-coupon bond price. In case of the BS model, we come up with the following formula:

$$\mathcal{O}^{ds}(S_t, t; T') = P^f(T, T')\mathrm{Bl}(S_t, t, T, K', P^d(t, T), P^f(t, T), \sigma, \omega) \tag{5.1}$$

where we have generalized the payoff so that it can either be a call ($\omega = 1$) or a put ($\omega = -1$). It is possible to rewrite formula (5.1) as an option on a forward contract as follows:

$$\begin{aligned}\mathcal{O}^{ds}(S_t, t; T') &= \mathrm{Bl}^F(F(t, T'), t, T, T', K, P^d(t, T), \sigma, \omega)\\ &= P^d(t, T') \left[\omega F(t, T')\Phi(\omega d_1) - \omega K \Phi(\omega d_2)\right]\end{aligned} \tag{5.2}$$

where

$$\begin{aligned}d_1 &= \frac{\ln \frac{F(t,T')}{K} + \frac{\sigma^2}{2}(T - t)}{\sigma\sqrt{T - t}}\\ d_2 &= d_1 - \sigma\sqrt{T - t}\end{aligned}$$

Just a few remarks to make things perfectly unambiguous:

- The adjusted strike price K' is used only for evaluation purposes and for the option buyer's decision whether to exercise or not upon maturity. The contract strike price remains K.
- The implied volatility to price this option, in case we are employing the BS model, is that corresponding, on the volatility surface, to the option's expiry T. Moreover, the implied volatility should be determined according to the adjusted strike price K'. This means that the implied volatility for the strike K' is interpolated/extrapolated on the volatility smile for expiry T.

Example 5.1.1. *Assume we are pricing a EUR call USD put, expiring in 3 months (or 92 days), and with a standard settlement date 2 days after the expiry. Initial data are the following:*

S	1.4500
K	1.4450
$P^d(0,92d)$	0.992471
$P^f(0,92d)$	0.987847
$P^d(0,122d)$	0.992471
$P^f(0,122d)$	0.987847
σ	9.80%

The discount factors (zero-coupon prices) used in the BS formula for a standard expiry option are just the first two for an expiry of 92 *days into the future. The option's price would be* 273 *USD pips. Assume now we want to price the same options with a delayed settlement date of* 30 *days after the expiry. In this case we have to calculate the discount factors for an expiry of* 122 *days into the future, and they are shown in the table above. We can apply formula* (5.1), *with* $K' = 1.4542$, *and get the new value for the option equal to* 227 *USD pips.*

5.1.2 Cash settlement

Occasionally an FX option can be cash settled upon exercise. The buyer does not receive (call) or deliver (put) the amount of base currency against the numeraire currency amount, but they earn the payoff (i.e., the intrinsic value at expiry) in cash (possibly converted into any currency). Alternatively, if the option is cash settled, the payoff is not simply marked to the market, but immediately realized upon exercise.

If the option has a standard settlement at expiry, the pricing formula is exactly the same as that used to price a European plain vanilla option, in any model. If the settlement is delayed we take it into account, but in a way different from that examined for the delayed settlement of a delivery settled option. In fact, if the settlement is delayed, we do not actually enter into a forward contract, so we simply have to properly discount the payoff up to the settlement date. Assume that a call option expires at time T and it is cash settled at time $T' = T + s$; at time T its value is

$$\mathcal{O}^{cs}(S_T, T; T') = P^d(T, T') \max(S_T - K, 0)$$

The terminal payoff $S_T - K$ (if positive) is permuted into cash and settled at time T', whence the discounting by $P^d(T, T')$. The value at time $t < T$ is the usual discounted expected value under the risk-neutral measure Q:

$$\mathcal{O}^{cs}(S_t, t; T') = P^d(T, T') E^Q[e^{-\int_t^T r_s^d ds} \max(S_T - K, 0)]$$

which can be seen as the expected value of a standard call option multiplied by a factor equal to the domestic zero-coupon bond forward price $P^d(T, T')$. If we adopt the BS model and generalize the payoff so as to consider both call and put, we have

$$\mathcal{O}^{cs}(S_t, t; T') = P^d(T, T') \mathrm{Bl}(S_t, t, T, K, P^d(t, T), P^f(t, T), \sigma, \omega) \tag{5.3}$$

where ω has the usual meaning.

As far as the implied volatility parameter is concerned, the value to plug into formula (5.3) is that interpolated on the volatility smile for the expiry T and a strike equal to K.

5.2 MARKET-MAKING TOOLS

The FX options market making is affected by the structure of the interbank market. Since the latter is very liquid, with extremely narrow dealing bid/ask quotations, and with many technical subtleties (some of which have already been examined in the previous chapters), a set of tools to participate in the market activity is definitely a requisite.

We depicted in Chapter 1 the mechanics of the FX plain vanilla options trading amongst professionals. That implies the quoting of a sticky Delta volatility surface with strikes pointed to as a reference in Delta terms, to be determined after the closing of a deal. The formula to calculate the strike, given the implied volatility, has been provided in Chapter 2 (equation (2.46)), for the premium-paying mode as pips of numeraire currency per base currency unit; Procedure 2.2.1 has to be run, instead, if the premium-paying mode is as a percentage of base currency.[1] Although the natural place within this book to describe these tools is the current section, nonetheless they have been presented beforehand to avoid a forward reference and for clarity's, rather than exposition consistency's, sake. We move on to introduce a couple of other tools.

5.2.1 Inferring the implied volatility for a given strike

Retrieving implied volatility for a given strike is rather straightforward and does not deserve a long examination. Assume we want to determine the implied volatility for an option expiring at T and struck at K. We are not interested in the kind of option, since by the put–call parity both base currency puts and calls struck at the same level are priced by the same implied volatility. We run the following procedure:

Procedure 5.2.1. ***Implied volatility for a given strike.*** *Suppose we have the price of the three basic structures for a given expiry (that is, the ATM* **STDL** *and the 25D* **RR** *and* **VWB***), from which we infer the three volatilities for the ATM and the 25D call and put strikes (σ_{ATM}, σ_{25C} and σ_{25P}).[2] In case we have to price the options expiring on a date between two canonic dates usually quoted in the market, interpolate the prices as explained in Section 4.9.1. To infer the implied volatility at time t for an option struck at K and expiring at T:*

1. *Determine the strikes related to the ATM and the two 25D levels in the usual way:*

$$K_{25P} = F(t,T)e^{\sigma_{25P}\sqrt{T-t}\Phi^{-1}(0.25/P^f(t,T))+0.5\sigma_{25P}^2(T-t)}$$
$$K_{ATM} = F(t,T)e^{(0.5\sigma_{ATM}^2(T-t))}$$
$$K_{25C} = F(t,T)e^{-\sigma_{25C}\sqrt{T-t}\Phi^{-1}(0.25/P^f(t,T))+0.5\sigma_{25C}^2(T-t)}$$

where the usual notation applies. In case the market conventions for the pair imply a premium-included Delta, then run Procedure 2.2.1 for the two 25D strikes, whereas for the ATM level we can use the formula

$$K_{ATM} = F(t,T)e^{(-0.5\sigma_{ATM}^2(T-t))}$$

[1] We omitted the fact (but it should be intuitively implied) that, besides implied volatility, the spot FX rate and the interest rates for the two currencies involved are also given.

[2] We should also have calculated the equivalent butterfly level, given the market **vwb**, as explained in Chapter 4, by means of Procedure 4.9.1.

2. *Retrieve the volatility for the strike K by means of the smile function we are using (for example formula* (4.6) *or the second-order approximation* (4.9)*), in Chapter 4) by using the three basic strikes and the related implied volatilities as calculated in step 1.*

This procedure is also nested in that of the next subsection, which is used more in the interbank market trading activity.

5.2.2 Inferring the implied volatility for a given Delta

Once we have built our volatility matrix and chosen our interpolation function, we are able to infer the implied volatility for any expiry and level of (either base currency put or call) Delta. The procedure could be built on the basis of a Newton–Raphson scheme, but unfortunately this scheme is not robust to any kind of smile configuration. In fact, for sheer increasing (decreasing) smile the convergence is not warranted for any level of Delta of base currency call (put). For such a reason we prefer to devise the procedure below that hinges on a bisection rule: it is likely not the most efficient in any case, but it surely is the most sound in any situation.

Procedure 5.2.2. ***Implied volatility for a given Delta.*** *Suppose we are asked at time t to make a quotation for an (either base currency call or put) option expiring at time T and struck at a level in terms of Delta equal to $\overline{\Delta}$ (the level is taken as absolute without considering the sign). Suppose we have the price of the three basic structures for that expiry, with the same* caveat *as above regarding the equivalent butterfly level and the interpolation between canonic expiries. We run the following steps:*

1. *Determine the strikes related to the ATM and the two 25D levels, as explained in Procedure 5.2.1. Set the counter $i = 1$.*
2. *Calculate a sufficiently far OTM strike K_E that will be the upper (lower) bound of the range which our target strike of the call (put) will lie within. This strike can be set at a four standard deviation distance from the current FX ATM level:*

$$K_E = K_{ATM}(1 + \omega 4\sigma_{ATM}\sqrt{\tau})$$

   where K_{ATM} is calculated as in Procedure 5.2.1 above, and the usual notation applies (in particular, $\omega = 1$ in case of a call or $\omega = -1$ in case of a put). Besides, set $K_C = K_{ATM}$
3. *Calculate a strike level midway between the ATM level and the upper (lower) bound of the call (put) strike:*

$$K^i = K_C + (K_E - K_C)/2$$

   The formula is the same for both the case of a base currency call and put. The superscript i indicates the iteration number.
4. *Retrieve the volatility σ^i for an option struck at K^i and expiring at T by means of the smile function we are using, with the three basic strikes and the related implied volatilities as calculated in step 1.*
5. *Calculate the Delta of the call (put) option struck at K^i and take its absolute value*

$$\Delta^i = \left|\Delta(K^i, \sigma^i, \omega)\right| \tag{5.4}$$

or, if for the pair, market conventions use the premium-included Delta:

$$\Delta^i = \left|\Delta(K^i, \sigma^i, \omega) - Bl(K^i, \sigma^i, \omega)/S_t\right| \tag{5.5}$$

We omitted some arguments of the Delta and the BS pricing formula to lighten the notation.

6. *If the difference between the* Δ^i *and the target Delta* $\overline{\Delta}$ *is positive, that is* $\Delta^i - \overline{\Delta} > 0$, *then set* $K_C = K_i$ *and leave* K_E *unchanged. If* $\Delta^i - \overline{\Delta} < 0$, *then set* $K_E = K_i$ *and leave* K_C *unchanged.*
7. *If the absolute difference between* Δ^i *and the target Delta is acceptably small, that is* $\left|\Delta^i - \overline{\Delta}\right| < \epsilon$, *with* ϵ *suitably small, then the procedure ends. Otherwise, restart from step 3.*

The procedure above is useful in the interbank market when we are asked for a price, since the latter normally refers to an option with a given level of (base currency call or put) Delta and with a certain expiry. If someone asks for the price of an option with the strike referenced in terms of Delta, but the latter is related to numeraire currency instead of base currency, the matter should be dealt using a touch of care. In more detail, the following cases may occur:

1. If the numeraire currency Delta is simply meant as the original base currency Delta, converted into the other currency (and reversing the sign, obviously), then one uses the relation we showed in Chapter 2: $\Delta^{numccy} = -\Delta S_t/K$. Hence, if the price is asked for a numeraire currency Delta equal to Δ^{numccy}, the corresponding base currency Delta is calculated and Procedure 5.2.2 applied.
2. If the numeraire currency Delta is that from the perspective of a trader operating in the numeraire currency country, then this refers to an option priced by the inverse FX rate $S'_t = 1/S_t$, so that $\Delta^{numccy} = -\frac{\Delta_t}{S'_t} + \text{Bl}(1/S'_t)$. This relationship implies that if market conventions quote volatilities for premium-included Delta in the base currency (see Chapter 2 for details), then $\Delta^{numccy} = -\Delta^{pi}$, so that the market maker just has to price an option with the same Delta for a base currency put (call) if a numeraire currency call (put) is requested. If volatilities are quoted for standard base currency Delta, then Δ_t has to be calculated and the corresponding volatility retrieved by Procedure 5.2.2.
3. If the numeraire currency Delta refers to an option priced in the numeraire currency country so that the Delta is calculated for an option priced with inverse FX spot rate, an inverse strike and switched interest rates, then one may use the domestic–foreign symmetry (2.50) of Chapter 2 and obtain the relationship $\Delta^{numccy} = -\frac{\Delta_t S_t}{K} + \frac{\text{Bl}(S_t)}{K}$. Once again, having derived the corresponding base currency Delta, the usual Procedure 5.2.2 applies.

5.2.3 Quoting the Vega-weighted butterfly and the risk reversal

As already mentioned many times, the 25D **VWB** and 25D **RR** are frequently quoted in the market for the canonical expiries, and hence their prices (in volatility terms) are easily available. We now focus on the pricing of these structures for different levels of Delta, provided a given set of prices dealing in the market. We start with the **RR**, since it does not involve a huge effort, whereas we will dwell longer on the **VWB**, which implies some subtleties that must be carefully taken into account.

As usual, assume we are asked to quote an **RR** for a given (symmetric base currency call and put) level of Delta Δ_{RR}. We are at time t and the expiry of the structure is at T. We have built our volatility surface properly from available market prices, so we run Procedure 5.2.2 twice to retrieve the implied volatility for a Δ_{RR} call and put. So, the price of the **RR** will simply be

$$\mathbf{rr}(t, T; \Delta_{RR}) = \sigma_{\Delta_{RR}C} - \sigma_{\Delta_{RR}P}$$

Assume we are now asked a price in volatility terms for a given Δ **VWB**. In this case we have to cope with the reverse problem of that we examined in Section 4.9, where we showed how to deal with specific market quoting conventions for this kind of structure. We assume we have built our surfaces with the equivalent **vwb** prices in the way explained there (i.e., we use $\mathbf{vwb}_e$ in the smile building). To make a quote for a **VWB** whose wings are struck corresponding to any level of Delta, provided we are given the volatility smile, we need the following procedure based on a Newton–Raphson scheme:

Procedure 5.2.3. ***Market* vwb *from a given volatility smile.*** *Suppose we are asked at time t to make a quotation for a* **VWB** *expiring at time T and whose wings are both struck at a level in terms of Delta equal to $\overline{\Delta}$ (the level is taken as absolute without considering the sign). Suppose we have the price of the three basic structures for that expiry, so that we can calculate the equivalent* **VWB** *price* $\mathbf{vwb}_e$ *and build an entire smile for the expiry T. We run the following steps:*

1. *Determine the strikes related to the ATM and the two 25D levels, as explained in Procedure 5.2.1, step 1. Set the counter $i = 0$.*
2. *As a first guess we calculate them by the two 25D implied volatilities:*

$$\sigma_C = \sigma_{25C} = \sigma_{ATM} + 0.5\mathbf{rr} + \mathbf{vwb}_e$$
$$\sigma_P = \sigma_{25P} = \sigma_{ATM} - 0.5\mathbf{rr} + \mathbf{vwb}_e$$

   Calculate the unique implied volatility to use in the **VWB**, *that is: $\sigma^i_{VWB} = \sigma_{ATM} + (\sigma_C + \sigma_P)/2$.*
3. *Calculate the wing's strikes of the* **VWB**:

$$\overline{K}^i_P = F(t, T)e^{\sigma_{VWB}\sqrt{T-t}\Phi^{-1}(\overline{\Delta}/P^f(t,T))+0.5(\sigma^i_{VWB})^2(T-t)}$$
$$\overline{K}^i_C = F(t, T)e^{-\sigma_{VWB}\sqrt{T-t}\Phi^{-1}(\overline{\Delta}/P^f(t,T))+0.5(\sigma^i_{VWB})^2(T-t)}$$

   If the premiums are a percentage of the base currency amount, then the strikes are recovered by means of Procedure 2.2.1.
4. *Retrieve the new implied volatilities referred to the* **VWB** *strikes, that is: $\sigma(\overline{K}^i_C)$ and $\sigma(\overline{K}^i_P)$*
5. *Calculate the difference:*

$$\mathcal{S}^i = \boldsymbol{C}(\overline{K}_{25C}, \sigma(\overline{K}_{25C})) + \boldsymbol{P}(\overline{K}_{25P}, \sigma(\overline{K}_{25P})) - \boldsymbol{C}(\overline{K}_{25C}, \sigma^i_{VWB}) + \boldsymbol{P}(\overline{K}_{25P}, \sigma^i_{VWB})$$

   In case of the first iteration ($i = 1$), shift the unique implied volatility by the amount $d\sigma^i_{VWB} = 0.00005$.
6. *Increment the counter i by 1 and calculate the new $\overline{K}^i_P$ and $\overline{K}^i_C$, and the related implied volatilities according to the smile interpolation scheme as above, and the new difference $\mathcal{S}^i$.*
7. *Calculate the numerical derivatives of the difference:*

$$d\mathcal{S}^i = (\mathcal{S}^i - \mathcal{S}^{i-1})/d\sigma^i_{VWB}$$

8. *Calculate the new $\sigma^{i+1}_{VWB} = \sigma^i_{VWB} - \mathcal{S}^i/d\mathcal{S}^i$ and $d\sigma^{i+1}_{VWB} = -\mathcal{S}^i/d\mathcal{S}^i$.*

9. *Iterate from step* 3 *until* $\left|S^i - S^{i-1}\right| < \epsilon$, *for* ϵ *suitably small. The market price for the* **VWB** *is hence*

$$\mathbf{vwb}(t, T; \overline{\Delta}) = \sigma_{VWB} - \sigma_{ATM}$$

where σ_{VWB} *is the result of the iterative procedure.*

The procedure above is the opposite of Procedure 4.9.1; here we are aiming to infer what is the price of a **VWB** that should be quoted, given the volatility smile built according to the three basic structures prices.[3] In case we want to price a 25D **VWB**, the procedure will yield exactly the dealing market level, provided that the smile includes the equivalent **vwb**; for any other level of Delta, the procedure yields the unique **VWB** volatility σ_{VWB} consistent with the given smile. While in Procedure 4.9.1 we try to build a smile that is consistent with the market quoting conventions for the **VWB**, Procedure 5.2.3 keeps fixed the smile and finds out what is the unique implied volatility to be quoted for a **VWB** struck at any level. The following example will show how the procedure works in practice.

Example 5.2.2. *Assume we are trading in the USDJPY and the following data are available in the market for the 6-month expiry* (184 *days).*

S	*101.95*	σ_{ATM}	*11.95%*
P^d	*0.99496*	rr	*−4.30%*
P^f	*0.98571*	**vwb**	*0.135%*

From these data we can calculate the equivalent 25*D butterfly price:* $\mathbf{vwb}_e = 0.4717$ *(we run Procedure 4.9.1). The two implied volatilities for the* 25*D call and put to be used in the smile function (we still use equation* (4.9)) *are* $\sigma_{25C} = 10.27\%$ *and* $\sigma_{25P} = 14.57\%$ *(note that the* **rr** *is* -4.3%, *consistent with the market price). Assume we are asked to quote a* 10*D* **VWB**, *that is a butterfly whose wing call and put options are stuck corresponding to a Delta of* 10% *(without considering the sign). Provided we have built our smile with* $\mathbf{vwb}_e$, *we run Procedure 5.2.3, obtaining as a result* $\mathbf{vwb}(0, 6M; 10) = 0.9864\%$. *The two strikes can be calulated by means of the usual Procedure 2.2.1, and they are*

$$\overline{K}_{10P} = 90.0188$$
$$\overline{K}_{10P} = 113.7412$$

The corresponding options' prices, calculated by the unique implied volatility for the 10*D* **VWB**, *are worth*

$$\mathbf{C}(\overline{K}_{10C}, \sigma_{10VWB}) = 0.4521$$
$$\mathbf{P}(\overline{K}_{10P}, \sigma_{10VWB}) = 0.4373$$

and their sum is $\mathbf{STGL} = 0.8724$ *(all prices are in USD%, as usual for the USDJPY).*

If we price the two options separately with the volatility retrieved from the smile, we have:

$$\mathbf{C}(\overline{K}_{10C}, \sigma(\overline{K}_{10C})) = 0.0102$$
$$\mathbf{P}(\overline{K}_{10P}, \sigma(\overline{K}_{10P})) = 0.8792$$

[3] From available prices it is possible to determine also the equivalent **vwb** level and enter this in the volatility smile building.

where $\sigma(\overline{K}_{10C}) = 9.19\%$ *and* $\sigma(\overline{K}_{10P}) = 16.60\%$*; the sum is* **STGL** $= 0.8724$*, which is exactly the sum of the prices obtained using the single implied volatility.*

5.3 BID/ASK SPREADS FOR PLAIN VANILLA OPTIONS

The bid/ask spreads of European plain vanilla options are determined by at least three different factors: the FX spot, the interest rates and the FX volatility spreads. The first two factors can be combined together in determining the bid/ask spread of the FX forward price, which is also the only price entering into the BS formula, in the fashion we have rewritten it in Chapter 2. Assume that the FX spot price deals in the market at the two-way price S_b/S_a, where the superscripts a and b indicate (rather intuitively) the bid and ask price. Besides, assume that the domestic and foreign interest rates dealing two-way in the market imply, for a given expiry T, bid/ask prices for the domestic and foreign zero-coupon bonds equal to $P_b^c(t,T)/P_a^c(t,T)$, with $c \in \{d, f\}$. The bid/ask FX forward price is calculated by applying the usual replica argument we have already used in Chapter 1, but considering the fact that in the money market and in the FX market one must trade at the bid/ask prices, and not at mid-market prices. Hence:

$$
\begin{aligned}
F_b(t,T) &= S_b \frac{P_b^f(t,T)}{P_a^d(t,T)} \\
F_a(t,T) &= S_a \frac{P_a^f(t,T)}{P_b^d(t,T)}
\end{aligned}
\tag{5.6}
$$

As for the implied volatility, different choices can be adopted. For a given expiry, assume we have the ATM **STDL** dealing in the market at the two-way price, in volatility terms, equal to $\sigma_b(K_{ATM})/\sigma_a(K_{ATM})$ and set $\mathbf{BA}(K) = \sigma_a(K) - \sigma_b(K)$; that is, $\mathbf{BA}(K)$ is the bid/ask spread for the implied volatility for strike K.

The first, trivial, choice is to keep the bid/ask constant throughout all the range of possible strikes and equal to the ATM **STDL** spread, so that $\mathbf{BA}(K) = \mathbf{BA}(K_{ATM}) = \overline{k}$. This method is adopted in the interbank market practice, at least for most liquid options (i.e., those struck at the ATM level and up to the 25D level for call and put) and pairs. Since OTM options have a lower Vega than ATM ones, the bid/ask in absolute premium terms (whichever of the four ways[4] it is expressed) will be smaller for the former options, which is sensible in some respect since their value is also smaller. In fact, we have that the corresponding premium's bid/ask spread (for both a call and a put option) is

$$
\mathbf{C}(K;\sigma_a(K)) - \mathbf{C}(K;\sigma_b(K)) = \mathbf{P}(K;\sigma_a(K)) - \mathbf{P}(K;\sigma_b(K)) \approx \mathbf{BA}(K)\mathcal{V}(K)
$$

A second choice is to keep constant the bid/ask spreads as a percentage of the premium. Let the value of the ATM straddle be $\mathbf{STDL}_c = \mathbf{C}(K;\sigma_c(K_{ATM})) + \mathbf{P}(K;\sigma_c(K_{ATM}))$, with $c \in \{b, a, m\}$, denoting respectively the bid, the ask and the mid-price or value of the implied volatility (the forward we use in the pricing is the mid-market value). For a given (call or put)

[4] See Chapter 1 for details.

option struck at K, we impose the following condition:

$$\frac{\mathbf{C}(K;\sigma_a(K)) - \mathbf{C}(K;\sigma_b(K))}{\mathbf{C}(K;\sigma_m(K))} \approx \frac{\mathbf{BA}(K)\mathcal{V}(K)}{\mathbf{C}(K;\sigma_m(K))}$$

$$= \frac{2\mathbf{BA}(K_{ATM})\mathcal{V}(K_{ATM})}{\mathbf{C}(K_{ATM};\sigma_m(K_{ATM})) + \mathbf{P}(K_{ATM};\sigma_m(K_{ATM}))}$$

or, for a put option:

$$\frac{\mathbf{P}(K;\sigma_a(K)) - \mathbf{P}(K;\sigma_b(K))}{\mathbf{P}(K;\sigma_m(K))} \approx \frac{\mathbf{BA}(K)\mathcal{V}(K)}{\mathbf{P}(K;\sigma_m(K))}$$

$$= \frac{2\mathbf{BA}(K_{ATM})\mathcal{V}(K_{ATM})}{\mathbf{C}(K_{ATM};\sigma_m(K_{ATM})) + \mathbf{P}(K_{ATM};\sigma_m(K_{ATM}))}$$

Hence the bid/ask spread $\mathbf{BA}(K)$ is

$$\mathbf{BA}(K) = \mathbf{C}(K;\sigma_m(K))\frac{2\mathbf{BA}(K_{ATM})\mathcal{V}(K_{ATM})}{\mathcal{V}(K)\mathbf{STDL}_m} \tag{5.7}$$

and an analogous formula for the put options, with $\mathbf{P}(K;\sigma_m(K))$ instead of $\mathbf{C}(K;\sigma_b(K))$. It is advisable to use the approach to determine the bid/ask spread for OTM options and then apply the same spread to the corresponding ITM struck at the same level.

Once the implied volatility bid/ask spread has been determined, we have all the information we need to quote the bid/ask spread for the plain vanilla options. Namely, for a base currency call option, with a premium in numeraire currency pips, we have

$$\begin{aligned} \mathbf{C}_b(K,T) &= \mathrm{Bl}(S_b, t, T, K, P_a^d(t,T), P_b^f(t,T), \sigma_b, 1) \\ \mathbf{C}_a(K,T) &= \mathrm{Bl}(S_a, t, T, K, P_b^d(t,T), P_a^f(t,T), \sigma_a, 1) \end{aligned} \tag{5.8}$$

where the subscript, as usual, indicates the bid or ask level of the financial variable or parameter. In practice, we choose the bid/ask level so as to get the highest and lowest possible call options price. This is rather evident for the implied volatility, since the call option is a monotone increasing function of this parameter. As for the forward, this is the result of the combination of the spot price and the two zero-coupon bonds; by recalling the definitions above, we have that the bid FX forward price enters into the option's pricing formula for the bid, whereas the ask FX forward price is plugged into the formula for the ask.

A similar reasoning leads to the definition of the bid and ask price for European put options, and yields the following:

$$\begin{aligned} \mathbf{P}_b(K,T) &= \mathrm{Bl}(S_a, t, T, K, P_b^d(t,T), P_a^f(t,T), \sigma_b, -1) \\ \mathbf{P}_a(K,T) &= \mathrm{Bl}(S_b, t, T, K, P_a^d(t,T), P_b^f(t,T), \sigma_a, -1) \end{aligned} \tag{5.9}$$

The options' premiums are expressed in formulae (5.8) and (5.9) as numeraire currency pips; the conversion relationships, described in Chapter 1, can then be applied and thus one gets the bid/ask spreads for the other ways to express premiums.

Some market conventions have to be described so as to fully explain the actual quoting mechanism. First, as seen in Chapter 1, amongst professional market participants options are traded Delta-hedged: this means that the spot price does not affect the total price of the entire package, since what is gained/lost on one side, is perfectly compensated on the other. Besides, bid/ask spreads for the interest rates (and hence for the zero-coupon bonds) are neglected. All in all, only the implied volatility bid/ask affects the option's price.

The volatility bid/ask is applied only on one side when options combinations are traded. For example, if a market maker is asked for a quote in a call spread, only one of the two options is quoted with bid/ask (for volatility), and the other is left with a single value and it is said that it is *choice*. Moreover, if the combination is required in Vega-weighted amounts (that is, one of the two sides is asked in a given amount and the other is determined so as to make the total position Vega-weighted, according to the BS model), then the implied volatility bid/ask is reduced, because one is actually trading second-order exposures (see Chapter 3 for more detail).

As a consequence of the above criteria, the three main structures are dealt in the market as follows:

- The ATM **STDL** is quoted as a bid/ask volatility spread.
- The **RR** is quoted as an implied volatility spread to be applied only to one of the two options entering into the structure (usually the bought one), while the other is priced by using a mid-market level of implied volatility. The spread is tighter than that dealing for straight positions, such as an ATM **STDL**.
- The **VWB** is quoted as a bid/ask spread to be applied only to the wing options entering into the structure, while the ATM **STDL** is priced by the current mid-market implied volatility; since the strategy yields an exposure to just the convexity of the curve, the spread is much lower than the ATM **STDL**'s one.

5.4 CUTOFF TIMES AND SPREADS

As already mentioned in Chapter 1, plain vanilla options traded in the market amongst professional operators are of the European type and they can be exercised upon expiry date at a given time that is set at 10:00 AM, New York time. They are hence referred to as *NY cut*. Implied volatility dealing in the market is related to such European options; anyway, any other time can be chosen, for a given expiry, as a cutoff for the options. In fact, another commonly traded time is 10:00 AM, Tokyo time (whence *TK cut*), especially in the Far East market.

The way the market makers deal with the different cutoffs is rather simple: it is clear that an option featured with TK cut lasts less time than a standard NY cut option. In normal conditions the difference between Tokyo and New York time is 14 hours, and one should also consider the fact that NY cut options expire after most economic figures and data are released; that is, during the European morning hours for the European economy and 8:30 New York time for the US economy, besides the figures released in the Far East countries before then. All of this is accounted for by assuming a higher implied volatility for the NY cut as a consequence of the larger amount of information that can be exploited by the buyer. More generally speaking, provided that NY cut is the standard market convention, a spread is added on the implied volatilities applying for options with such an expiry: $\sigma_{OC}(K, T) = \sigma_{NYC}(K, T) + cs(T)$, where the implied volatility $\sigma_{OC}(K, T)$ for an option expiring at T at some OC cutoff is equal to the standard NY cut volatility plus the cutoff spread $cs(T)$. The spread is time-dependent and it is higher for short-dated options (one week and shorter maturities) and fades out as the maturity lengthens.

A special cutoff that deserves attention and some care too is the ECB fixing one. Every day the European Central Bank asks for quotes for the main pairs (against the euro) to major market makers; the quotes are averaged out and then published. This occurs at 14:15 Frankfurt time but the process lasts a few minutes, so communication of the actual fixings to the market is at around 14:20. This means that for some five minutes the option's buyer does not really know whether to exercise or not if the strike is very near to the market level; on the other hand, the seller is in the unpleasant situation of not being sure whether to hedge or not the probable exercise. Luckily enough, this kind of cutoff is applied for very liquid pairs, so that one can be quite sure that the published fixing is basically the market level dealing in the market at 14:15 Frankfurt time and thus they can undertake the proper actions, although the official fixing appears on the information providers' screens only a little later. Moreover, the ECB fixing cut is preferred by non-professional customers, such as corporates, because it is an official way to set a price within an OTC market. Nonetheless, it is not really liked in the interbank market, where options of such a feature are traded only when one has to hedge big customers' flows and mainly involving barrier and digital options. We will examine the latter later on in this chapter, and it will be clear that their risk is not changed dramatically (either positively or negatively) with the ECB fixing cutoff, and the only way to hedge their risk is to sell or buy them back. The effect of the ECB fixing cutoff is more interesting in the barrier options' case, because the feature is extended to the barrier monitoring too, thus becoming discretely rather than continuously monitored. The following chapters will cover these issues, amongst others.

As for the European options, as mentioned above, the quickest and easiest way to cope with the ECB fixing risk, from a market-maker perspective, is to act as if it were announced at 14:15 and assume it is equal to the then current market level for the reference pair. After publication the risk is $S_{ECB} \neq S_{t_E}$, where S_{ECB} is the ECB fixing for the reference pair and S_{t_E} is the level dealing in the market for the same pair at 14:15. Assuming we start from an unhedged condition, should a market maker have wrongly hedged, they would unwind the position by trading at the market level at the time of the publication S_{t_e}, thus realizing a profit or a loss, in absolute terms, equal to $|S_{t_e} - S_{t_E}|$. It is easy to check that a buyer will realize a profit in this case, whereas the seller will suffer a loss. Now, assuming that (i) the usual delay is around five/ten minutes, (ii) the volatility is that of an ordinary day (it could be estimated historically or based on the implied volatilities), and finally (iii) the probability (calculated at the start of the contract) of the FX spot rate being around the strike rate at expiry is nil in practice, then the expected loss to charge to the selling price of the option has no economic impact. Clearly, in real market activity, a few pips can be added to the option's selling price, but this mark-up depends rather on the instinct of the market maker (and their price-setting power) than on a financial model.

5.5 DIGITAL OPTIONS

We examine digital options in this chapter because, although considered to be exotic contracts (and they can actually be deemed the most difficult payoff to hedge), they are somehow strongly connected to European plain vanilla options. In fact, their payoff is of the European kind, being totally path-independent, their price can be calculated unambiguously by means of plain vanilla options prices or, alternatively, of the volatility smile for the corresponding maturity.

Definition 5.5.1. ***Digital option FX option contract.*** *An XXXYYY digital option is a contract paying one unit of the XXX or YYY currency if the FX spot rate observed at expiry is strictly* *above (digital call) or below (digital put) a given strike price. The amount is paid at the settlement date.*

The type of option (i.e., call or put) depends just on whether the non-zero payoff is above or below the strike price at maturity, whereas the amount of either currency to be delivered is an element of the contract to be defined during the bargaining process, and that clearly affects the price. In the interbank market there are no strict conventions about the amounts of the two currencies involved in a pair that should be delivered, so they are always explicitly declared. As a loose rule implied from the observation of market activity, the amount to be delivered is in euros for pairs against this currency, and in US dollars if the latter is one of the pair's currencies (for EURUSD the deliverable amount is in most cases euro-denominated). The price is expressed as a percentage of the deliverable amount.

5.5.1 Digital options pricing: the static replica approach

We first examine how to price a digital option in model-independent fashion and then how to properly include the smile effects in the value. Let us consider a digital option, on the pair XXXYYY, at time t with expiry at T and struck at K; assume that it is a digital call paying one unit of YYY if the FX spot rate at maturity is above the level K. One may consider as usual the pair XXXYYY as the price of the asset XXX (base currency) expressed in YYY units (numeraire currency) and, by resorting to the tools we introduced in Chapter 2 (formula (2.13)), they can write the pricing formula as

$$\mathbf{Dc}_n(S_t, t; T, K) = E^Q\left[e^{-\int_t^T r_s^d ds}\mathbf{1}_{\{\mathbf{S_T}>\mathbf{K}\}}\right] \tag{5.10}$$

Equation (5.10) is the risk-neutral discounted expected value of one YYY unit conditioned on the fact that the option expires in-the-money; that is, the FX spot rate at T is above K: $\mathbf{1}_{\{S_T>K\}}$ is the indicator function equal to one if the condition in the curly brackets at the subscript is verified, and zero otherwise. The discounting is operated continuously at the domestic rate r^d, which is the rate referring to the numeraire (domestic) currency. In mathematical terms, the payoff can be seen as a Heaviside function calculated in K. The subscript n indicates the currency denomination of the payoff, which is in the numeraire currency in this case.

As a first attempt to solve the digital call pricing problem, we try to find a method to replicate its payoff by means of plain vanilla options. In theory, this should be possible since digital options are not path-dependent, just as for European plain vanilla options. To this end, define the following portfolio:

$$\pi(t) = \frac{1}{2\Delta K}[\mathbf{C}(K - \Delta K) - \mathbf{C}(K + \Delta K)] \tag{5.11}$$

The portfolio π is long an amount of $1/(2\Delta K)$ European (base currency) call options struck at level $K - \Delta K$ and is short the same amount of European (base currency) call options struck at $K + \Delta K$; ΔK is a value arbitrarily chosen. It should be clear from the context, but for clarity's sake we specify that K is the strike price of the digital call we are replicating. To lighten the notation, we drop all the arguments of the plain vanilla pricing functions. The payoff of π at T, which is the expiry of the replicating options and the digital call as well, will be, depending on the level of the FX spot rate S_T,

$$\pi(T) = \begin{cases} 0 & \text{if } S_T \leq K - \Delta K \\ 0 < \frac{1}{2\Delta K}[S_T - (K - \Delta K)] < 1\text{YYY} & \text{if } K - \Delta K < S_T \leq K + \Delta K \\ \frac{1}{2\Delta K}[(K + \Delta K) - (K - \Delta K)] = 1\text{YYY} & \text{if } S_T > K + \Delta K \end{cases}$$

It is easy to check that the portfolio attains a perfect replica of the digital payoff (i.e., 1 YYY) only if the FX spot rate is greater than $K + \Delta K$ at expiry. If it is between the two strikes, the payoff of the portfolio is less than 1 YYY, so the replica is not sufficient to match the digital payoff. Anyway, it should be noted that the digital option pays off 1 YYY when $S_T > K$, whereas the portfolio has a positive payoff also when the spot is above $K - \Delta K$, so that when it is below K the replica yields more than a digital call, thus compensating for the fact that it yields less when $K < S_T < K + \Delta K$. If we let ΔK tend to zero, the possible sub-replicating range $K < S_T < K + \Delta K$ shrinks,[5] and the replica will more and more perfectly match the digital payoff:

$$\lim_{\Delta K \to 0} \pi(T) = \lim_{\Delta K \to 0} \frac{1}{2\Delta K}[\mathbf{C}(K - \Delta K) - \mathbf{C}(K + \Delta K)] = \mathbf{1}_{\{S_T > K\}} = \mathbf{Dc}_n(S_T, T)$$

To tie up what we have just seen above, a theoretically perfect replica of a digital call option is possible by trading an infinitely narrow (base currency) call spread struck around the digital strike K (the difference between the two strikes being an infinitesimal amount ΔK) in an infinite amount $(1/(2\Delta K))$. In practice, it is not possible to trade such a structure, since granularity[6] of prices and above all transaction costs would make the strategy definitely unfeasible.

In practice the static replica is widely used for pricing purposes and is also employed somehow for hedging purposes. Clearly, the approach is adapted in order to make it a viable tool, and this is done in two respects: (i) the choice of the width of the range between the two European call options $2\Delta K$, which should be set so that it is possible to trade in the market (although with some limitations) and the amount of the replicating structure $1/(2\Delta K)$ is not huge; (ii) the replica is built in the most convenient way for the market maker.

As for the first issue, the width of the range $2\Delta K$ is usually set well below 1 figure, because of the high competitiveness of the FX market and hence the proneness towards the theoretical fair price, which we have seen obtained above via a tight spread around the digital strike.

As for the second issue, we observe that the replica has some flaws when it is centred around the digital's strike, and for some FX spot rate levels S_T it does not fully replicate the digital's payoff (though for some other levels it is over-replicating it, so that as a whole the worst cases balance the best cases). In practice, the range $2\Delta K$ is offset with respect to the centre K, so that the replica perfectly pays off the same amount as the digital when the latter expires in-the-money. We make this point clearer: assume we want to be sure that the call spread pays off the exact amount 1 YYY when $S_T > K$. This is possible if we offset the range of the strikes and trade the following static replica portfolio:

$$\pi(t) = \frac{1}{2\Delta K}[\mathbf{C}(K - 2\Delta K) - \mathbf{C}(K)] \tag{5.12}$$

---

[5] Also the super-replicating range $K - \Delta K < S_T < K$ shrinks with $\Delta K \to 0$.

[6] Strike prices cannot be set at totally arbitrary levels since market conventions for FX rate quotations imply the smallest price fraction that is possible to trade: see Chapter 1.

whose terminal value is

$$\pi(T) = \begin{cases} 0 & \text{if } S_T \le K - 2\Delta K \\ 0 < \frac{1}{2\Delta K}[S_T - (K - 2\Delta K)] < 1\text{YYY} & \text{if } K - 2\Delta K < S_T \le K \\ \frac{1}{2\Delta K}[K - (K - 2\Delta K)] = 1\text{YYY} & \text{if } S_T > K \end{cases}$$

The portfolio thus perfectly replicates the digital's payoff, but there is a range ($K - 2\Delta K < S_T \le K$) yielding a positive payoff, even though the digital is always worth nil within it, which is wider than that of the centred case we examined above. The call spread costs more in this case, however small we choose ΔK, and hence the corresponding replica price of the digital will be higher. It is manifest that when a market maker sells a digital call, they want to price it as a call spread with the displaced range $2\Delta K$ as just seen, so that they can buy the spread in the market and hedge the short digital position. The digital value so determined – that is, set equal to the call spread – always pays off as the digital, or more than that, and is said to be "in over-hedge for the offer". The reason for such a denomination is evident: the call spread is over-hedging the digital, since it grants a perfect covering of the digital's exposure at expiry, and besides it yields a positive economic result in some cases. The "offer over-hedge" price is the maximum offer price a digital should be traded at in the market, provided that market participants agree on the width of the strike range $2\Delta K$.

Now assume the opposite case, and we trade a call spread struck as follows:

$$\pi(t) = \frac{1}{2\Delta K}[\mathbf{C}(K) - \mathbf{C}(K + 2\Delta K)] \tag{5.13}$$

whose terminal value is

$$\pi(T) = \begin{cases} 0 & \text{if } S_T \le K \\ 0 < \frac{1}{2\Delta K}[S_T - K] < 1\,\text{YYY} & \text{if } K < S_T \le K + 2\Delta K \\ \frac{1}{2\Delta K}[(K + 2\Delta K) - K] = 1\,\text{YYY} & \text{if } S_T > K + 2\Delta K \end{cases}$$

Such a call spread never attains the digital's payoff when the latter expires in-the-money, unless the FX spot rate S_T reaches a level $K + 2\Delta K$. There is a range for the terminal FX spot rate ($K < S_T \le K + 2\Delta K$) within which the call spread is sub-replicating the digital payoff; this range is wider than that in the centred case. This call spread costs less than that centred around K, and also the corresponding digital replica value will be lower. Suppose a market maker buys a digital call and they set up as a hedge a short position in a call spread struck the way we have just shown: its total payoff will not match the digital's payoff up to the FX spot rate S_T equal to $K + 2\Delta K$, so that they will earn the amount paid by the digital call – only partially giving it up to compensate for the losses suffered in the call spread position. We thus have a way to determine the minimum bid price we can buy the digital at, given the width of the range $2\Delta K$, and it is equal to the call spread struck with the displacement on the upper strike. This price is said to be "in over-hedge for the bid", for manifest reasons.

It should be noted that in the normal market activity bid/ask prices for digital options are never set so that they fully reflect the over-hedge value of the call spread for the bid or ask side. Competition amongst market makers pushes prices to a centred replica level, hence making the bid/ask spread narrower, although in some market conditions (e.g., with a great supply or a great demand) the spread may swerve on either side, or ultimately just widen to the two over-hedge prices.

A very general pricing formula for the digital call option, encompassing all the considerations we have made above, is the following:

$$\mathbf{Dc}_n(S_t, t; T, K) = \frac{1}{2\Delta K}[\mathbf{C}(K - 2oh\Delta K) - \mathbf{C}(K + 2(1 - oh)\Delta K)] \quad (5.14)$$

where $\mathbf{C}(K)$ is the price at t of a European call option struck at K and expiring at T; oh is the over-hedge displacement parameter and it may vary from 0 to 1. When it is equal to 0, the digital call is priced in full bid over-hedge and the replica clashes with that in formula (5.13); when it is equal to 1, we have the offer over-hedge price, the replica matching that in formula (5.12); when it is 0.5, we have the centred replica price, equation (5.14) becoming equal to (5.11). Given the width of the range $2\Delta K$, the two extreme replica values are attained by setting, respectively, $oh = 0$ and $oh = 1$.

We will now examine very quickly the pricing of a digital put option. It can be written as

$$\mathbf{Dp}_n(S_t, t; T, K) = E^Q\left[e^{-\int_t^T r_s^d ds}\mathbf{1}_{\{S_T < K\}}\right] \quad (5.15)$$

The idea to price it hinges on the static replica via a put spread, in a completely analogous way to the digital call case, so that we will not linger on repeating it all in detail. A general formula considering both the width of the put spread strike range and the over-hedge displacement is

$$\mathbf{Dp}_n(S_t, t; T, K) = \frac{1}{2\Delta K}[\mathbf{P}(K + 2oh\Delta K) - \mathbf{P}(K - 2(1 - oh)\Delta K)] \quad (5.16)$$

where $\mathbf{P}(K)$ is the price at t of a European put option struck at K and expiring at T; oh is the over-hedge displacement parameter and it has the same meaning as in formula (5.14): when it is 0, one gets the bid over-hedge price whereas the offer over-hedge is obtained by setting it at 1, $oh = 0.5$ yielding the centred replica value.

The digital options payoff denominated in the base currency can be expressed in terms of a payoff denominated in the numeraire currency: it is enough to consider that for a pair XXXYYY, at any time t, 1 XXX = S_t YYY. Thus the price of a base-currency-denominated digital call option can be written as

$$\mathbf{Dc}_b(S_t, t; T, K) = E^Q\left[e^{-\int_t^T r_s^d ds} S_T \mathbf{1}_{\{S_T > K\}}\right] \quad (5.17)$$

whereas the digital put option is

$$\mathbf{Dp}_b(S_t, t; T, K) = E^Q\left[e^{-\int_t^T r_s^d ds} S_T \mathbf{1}_{\{S_T < K\}}\right] \quad (5.18)$$

The usual notation applies. The subscript b indicates that the amount paid if the option expires in-the-money is denominated in the base currency. Equations (5.17) and (5.18) show that the paid amount is denominated in the numeraire currency and is variable, depending on the terminal FX spot rate S_T. More precisely, it is exactly equal to the terminal FX rate, so that, when converted into base currency units, it is equal to 1 XXX.

There are some different ways to approach the problem of the pricing of such digital options. In other markets it would simply be seen as an asset-or-nothing digital, delivering at expiry, if in-the-money, exactly the asset instead of an amount of money. In the FX market things can be examined under a slightly different perspective, but clearly they are perfectly consistent with the asset-or-nothing valuation.

Since we are interested in finding a static replica of the digital option, let us start with a base currency digital call option and consider the following. (i) When the digital expires when the FX spot rate is exactly equal to the strike level, 1 XXX $= K$ YYY. If we try to replicate a base currency digital call with K numeraire currency digital calls with the same expiry and strike as of the former, the two payoffs are identical in this case.[7] (ii) When $S_T \geq K$ the numeraire-currency-denominated amount of the previous digital is not enough to match one unit of base currency. In fact, K/S_T XXX < 1 for $S_T > K$ and to make up for this insufficient replication, we need a supplementary payoff equal to $S_T - K$. In this case the total amount paid in numeraire currency would be $K + (S_T - K) = S_T$ YYY, or 1 XXX, which is what we need to replicate the base currency digital call. The supplementary payoff, paid only when $S_T > K$, is easily seen to be that of a European call option, so a static replica for the base currency digital call is

$$\mathbf{Dc}_b(S_t, t; T, K) = K\mathbf{Dc}_n(S_t, t; T, K) + \mathbf{C}(S_t, t; K, T) \tag{5.19}$$

where, as usual, $\mathbf{C}(S_t, t; K, T)$ is the value at time t of a base currency European call expiring at T and struck at K.

The case of a base currency digital put option can be tackled in a similar way: (i) K units of a numeraire currency digital put would match the payoff of an otherwise identical base currency digital put, when the terminal FX rate is equal to the strike rate K; (ii) when $S_T < K$, the numeraire currency digital is super-replicating the base currency digital, since K/S_T XXX > 1 in this case. We eliminate this excessive payoff by a negative supplementary amount equal to $-(S_T - K)$, so that the total payoff will be $K - (K - S_T) = S_T$ YYY, or 1 XXX, as required to match the base currency digital put's paid amount. The supplementary payoff, paid only when the FX spot rate in T is lower than the strike level, is attained by a short position in a base currency European put option. Hence, the replica is given by

$$\mathbf{Dp}_b(S_t, t, T, K) = K\mathbf{Dp}_n(S_t, t; T, K) - \mathbf{P}(S_t, t; K, T) \tag{5.20}$$

and the usual notation applies.

After having examined how to price all the versions of available digital options via a static replica of plain vanilla options, we list the main advantages of this approach:

1. The replica price is model-independent and allows us to define a digital options price simply by retrieving plain vanilla prices available in the market. In other words, knowledge of the market volatility smile for a given expiry univocally allows for the pricing of a digital option.
2. The inclusion of the smiles effects is automatic, since the replica portfolio is set up by considering market prices of the component options.
3. The hedging of the (nasty) digital option payoff (*pin risk*) is somehow suggested by the replication portfolio and it can be operated by liquid instruments.
4. The digital value depends on the over-hedge parameter and on the width of the range between the strike prices of the call (or put) spread; these can be controlled by the market maker and adjusted according to the changing market conditions, thus allowing for a greater control over the bid/ask spread setting.

[7] We are changing the definition of in-the-moneyness slightly so that the payoff is paid if the terminal FX rate is equal to or greater than the strike level ($S_T \geq K$).

5.5.2 Digital options pricing in specific model settings

The replica approach can be used within any model setting. One can calibrate a model to market volatility smiles and then use the plain vanilla options prices produced by the model itself to build the replica portfolio, thus determining the digital option value too. The "goodness" of the fit clearly affects the digital pricing too, and some care should be taken to check whether the model European options prices entering into the portfolio reflect actual prices dealing in the market.

When the BS is used to price plain vanilla options, the assumption of constant volatility is disregarded and we plug into the formula, for given strikes and expiry, the implied volatility inferred from the volatility surface. The digital options pricing can be performed as usual by means of the replication argument, but some further observations can be made. To fix things, let us start by building a European call spread so as to replicate a numeraire currency digital call option struck at K and expiring at T. We consider a spread replication fully in over-hedge for the bid ($oh = 0$) so that we have

$$\mathbf{Dc}_n^{\mathrm{BS}}(S_t, t, T, K) = \frac{1}{2\Delta K}\Big[\mathrm{Bl}(S_t, t, T, K, P^d(t, T), P^f(t, T), \sigma(K), 1) \\ - \mathrm{Bl}(S_t, t, T, K + 2\Delta K, P^d(t, T), P^f(t, T), \sigma(K + 2\Delta K), 1)\Big]$$

The options entering into the call spread are valued by means of the BS formula, by plugging each of them into the proper implied volatility retrieved by the volatility smile built by means of the prices dealt in the market. Let us set $\widetilde{\Delta K} = 2\Delta K$ and let $\widetilde{\Delta K}$ tend to zero. We have the following:

$$\mathbf{Dc}_n^{\mathrm{BS}}(S_t, t, T, K) = -\frac{\partial \mathrm{Bl}(S_t, t, T, K, P^d(t, T), P^f(t, T), \sigma(K), 1)}{\partial K} = \\ P^d(t, T)N(d_2) - \mathcal{V}(S_t, t, T, K, P^d(t, T), P^f(t, T), \sigma(K), 1)\frac{\partial \sigma(K)}{\partial K} \quad (5.21)$$

This is the theoretical price of a digital call option obtained by the limit of an infinitesimally narrow call spread, by exploiting the BS formula and the market volatility smile. The digital call is equal to the value calculated as if we were in a flat-smile environment ($P^d(t, T)N(d_2)$) plus a quantity equal to the Vega of a call option struck at the strike price K, times a factor given by the slope of the volatility smile function at the strike level ($\partial\sigma(K)/\partial K$). It is worth noticing that the flat-smile component of the price is calculated by using the implied volatility corresponding to the strike K, that is $\sigma(K)$. We refer to the flat-smile environment just to indicate the fact that ($P^d(t, T)N(d_2)$) would be the digital value if one volatility $\sigma(K)$ dealt in the market and we did not hint at the ATM volatility. Since the Vega of a European plain vanilla option is always positive, the digital call's value is abated in the presence of an upward-sloping volatility smile, whereas the reverse occurs when the volatility smile is downward-sloping.

An analogous formula can be derived for numeraire currency digital put options (in this case $oh = 1$):

$$\mathbf{Dp}_n^{\mathrm{BS}}(S_t, t; T, K) = \frac{\partial \mathrm{Bl}(S_t, t, T, K, P^d(t, T), P^f(t, T), \sigma(K), -1)}{\partial K} = \\ P^d(t, T)(N(-d_2)) + \mathcal{V}(S_t, t, T, K, P^d(t, T), P^f(t, T), \sigma(K), -1)\frac{\partial \sigma(K)}{\partial K} \quad (5.22)$$

The interpretation is exactly the same as in the digital option case, but it should be stressed that for digital options the slope of the volatility smile has an opposite effect on its value. In fact, an upward-sloping smile makes the digital option worth more and a downward-sloping smile makes it cheaper.

It is straightforward to derive pricing formulae for base currency digital options within the BS model, by just adding the value of European options, according to what we have seen above. For base currency digital calls:

$$\begin{aligned}\mathbf{Dc}_b^{\mathrm{BS}}(S_t, t; T, K) = K\mathbf{Dc}_n^{\mathrm{BS}}(S_t, t; T, K) \\ + \mathrm{Bl}(S_t, t, T, K, P^d(t, T), P^f(t, T), \sigma(K), 1)\end{aligned} \tag{5.23}$$

and for base currency digital puts:

$$\begin{aligned}\mathbf{Dp}_b^{\mathrm{BS}}(S_t, t; T, K) = K\mathbf{Dp}_n^{\mathrm{BS}}(S_t, t; T, K) \\ - \mathrm{Bl}(S_t, t, T, K, P^d(t, T), P^f(t, T), \sigma(K), -1)\end{aligned} \tag{5.24}$$

If we wish to price digital options in the LMUV,[8] the valuation formulae are easily retrieved. For example, a digital call options value is

$$\mathbf{Dc}_c^{\mathrm{UV}}(S_t, t; T, K) = \sum_{i=1}^{N} \lambda_i \mathbf{Dc}_c^{\mathrm{BS}}(S_t, t; T, K) \tag{5.25}$$

where $c \in \{n, b\}$. A similar formula can be used for digital put options, whose value will be the λ_i weighted average of BS values. In this case the BS formula is the "pure" one, which does not consider the smile:

$$\mathbf{Dc}_c^{\mathrm{BS}}(S_t, t; T, K) = P^d(t, T)N(d_2)$$

Example 5.5.1. *Assume we have the following market data in the EURUSD option market (the EURUSD spot rate is* 1.4000*):*

	ATM	*25D RR*	*25D VWB*	P^d	P^f
O/N	*18.50%*	*−0.03%*	*0.20%*	*0.999936*	*0.999936*
1W	*12.50%*	*0.00%*	*0.20%*	*0.999558*	*0.999558*
2W	*12.40%*	*−0.30%*	*0.20%*	*0.999089*	*0.999089*
1M	*11.85%*	*−0.40%*	*0.24%*	*0.997743*	*0.997743*
2M	*11.55%*	*−0.50%*	*0.26%*	*0.995373*	*0.995373*
3M	*11.05%*	*−0.60%*	*0.30%*	*0.992471*	*0.992471*
6M	*10.70%*	*−0.75%*	*0.37%*	*0.985050*	*0.985050*

We want to price a European digital call, struck at 1.4500 *expiring in* 6 *months (*182 *days). The volatility smile for the* 6*-month expiry has been built via the VV method of Chapter 4, and besides we calibrated the LMUV model presented in Chapter 2 to the data in the table above.*[9] *First we price the digital by a replica approach, choosing* $\Delta K = 0.05$ *and* $h = \{0, 0.5, 1\}$ *(formula* (5.14)*). Then we price the same option by the BS model, simply by plugging in the*

[8] See Section 2.5.2.

[9] More details on how to calibrate the LMUV model are provided in Chapter 8.

volatility corresponding to the strike 1.4500 *inferred from the smile, and add the adjustment due to the slope of the smile (formula* (5.21)*). Finally we provide the price of the LMUV model. The results are shown in the following table:*

Method	*Price*
Replica $\Delta K = 0.05$ *and* $h = 0$ *(bid over-hedge)*	*23.22%*
Replica $\Delta K = 0.05$ *and* $h = 0.5$ *(centred)*	*24.83%*
Replica $\Delta K = 0.05$ *and* $h = 1$ *(ask over-hedge)*	*26.51%*
BS price	*26.06%*
BS price smile slope adjusted	*24.87%*
LMUV	*24.95%*

It is easy to see that the centred replica, the BS model with full account of the smile and the LMUV model agree almost perfectly on the price of the digital. This is not surprising, since we are dealing with a European payoff – for these, only the volatility smile matters. The first two methods just take the smile exactly as an input, whereas the LMUV model has a very good smile-fitting capability, so that it also agrees on European-style options.

5.5.3 Delayed cash settlement date

Digital options can also be settled on a delayed date later than the standard one determined according to the market conventions.[10] It is rather easy to handle this feature, after we have examined it for European plain vanilla options.

Assume a digital call expiring in T and settling the cash amount (either denominated in numeraire or base currency) in $T' = T + s$, where s is a given number of days. The option's value in T is

$$\mathbf{Dc}_c^{cs}(S_T, T; T, K, T') = P^d(T, T')\mathbf{1}_{\{S_T < K\}}$$

and at any time $t < T$:

$$\begin{aligned}\mathbf{Dc}_c^{cs}(S_t, t; T, K, T') &= P^d(T, T')E^Q\left[e^{-\int_t^T r_s^d ds}\mathbf{1}_{\{S_T > K\}}\right] \\ &= P^d(T, T')\mathbf{Dc}_c^{cs}(S_t, t; T, K)\end{aligned} \tag{5.26}$$

Equation (5.26) sets the value of a delayed settled digital call equal to an otherwise identical digital call times a factor equal to the T'-expiring zero coupon bond price at time T (the subscript $c = \{n, b\}$, since the payout amount can be denominated in either currency). Digital put options have exactly similar formulae.

5.5.4 Bid/ask spreads

Bid/ask spreads for digital options can be set in two fashions. A first simple, but not so uncommon, way is to establish for a given expiry a fixed percentage spread and apply it to any

[10] See Chapter 1 for details of the market rules to calculate settlement dates.

digital option however struck. A second way is to calculate the spread as a result of the bid/ask spread of the replication portfolio. The latter method should be more consistent, although it must be admitted that on the interbank market amongst professionals the former method seems mostly to be adopted.

We focus on the second method, since the first one is rather trivial. The bid/ask spread is a consequence of the bid/ask spread of the options entering into the replicating portfolio. Clearly, should we calculate the spread for the theoretically perfect replica, with an infinitely narrow distance between the two strikes, we would get a huge, unfeasible (in the sense that we could not use it in real dealing activity) spread. If we try to replicate the digital by means of a viable European plain vanilla portfolio, then the digital bid/ask spread result is more sensible. Besides, to also take into account the market conventions for setting the bid/ask spreads for plain vanilla structures (see Section 5.3), we should keep one leg of the European call (or put) spread fixed in terms of price by using one constant implied volatility (i.e., the mid of the two volatilities dealing in the market), whereas we calculate the bid/ask for the second leg by inputting the two implied volatilities dealing for the corresponding strike and expiry. Usually, one also keeps constant the implied volatility for the supplementary plain vanilla option needed to replicate a digital paying off a base-currency-denominated amount. We provide the formulae to retrieve the bid/ask prices for the numeraire digital call and put:

$$\mathbf{Dc}_{n\_b}(S_t, t; T, K) = \frac{1}{2\Delta K}[\mathbf{C}(K - 2oh\Delta K; \sigma_m(K - 2oh\Delta K)) \\ -\mathbf{C}(K + 2(1 - oh)\Delta K; \sigma_a(K - 2oh\Delta K))]$$

$$\mathbf{Dc}_{n\_a}(S_t, t; T, K) = \frac{1}{2\Delta K}[\mathbf{C}(K - 2oh\Delta K; \sigma_m(K - 2oh\Delta K)) \\ -\mathbf{C}(K + 2(1 - oh)\Delta K; \sigma_b(K - 2oh\Delta K))]$$

The subscript m referred to σ means that we take the mid-market value between the bid and ask levels. Similarly for digital puts:

$$\mathbf{Dp}_{n\_b}(S_t, t; T, K) = \frac{1}{2\Delta K}[\mathbf{C}(K - 2oh\Delta K; \sigma_m(K - 2oh\Delta K)) \\ -\mathbf{C}(K + 2(1 - oh)\Delta K; \sigma_a(K - 2oh\Delta K))]$$

$$\mathbf{Dp}_{n\_a}(S_t, t; T, K) = \frac{1}{2\Delta K}[\mathbf{P}(K + 2oh\Delta K; \sigma_m(K - 2oh\Delta K)) \\ -\mathbf{P}(K + 2oh\Delta K; \sigma_b(K - 2oh\Delta K))]$$

In the case of base currency digital calls:

$$\mathbf{Dc}_{b\_b}(S_t, t; T, K) = K\mathbf{Dc}_{n\_b}(S_t, t; T, K) + \mathbf{C}_b(S_t, t; K, T)$$

$$\mathbf{Dc}_{b\_a}(S_t, t; T, K) = K\mathbf{Dc}_{n\_a}(S_t, t; T, K) + \mathbf{C}_a(S_t, t; K, T)$$

whereas for digital puts:

$$\mathbf{Dp}_{b\_b}(S_t, t, T, K) = K\mathbf{Dp}_{n\_b}(S_t, t, T, K) - \mathbf{P}_a(S_t, t; K, T)$$

$$\mathbf{Dp}_{b\_a}(S_t, t, T, K) = K\mathbf{Dp}_{n\_a}(S_t, t, T, K) - \mathbf{P}_b(S_t, t; K, T)$$

5.5.5 Quotation conventions

As already mentioned above, the digital option premiums are quoted in the market as a percentage of the notional amount. The formulae we have derived produce a premium expressed in numeraire currency units (p_{numccy} using the notation introduced in Chapter 1), so we need to convert them in the proper format by means of conversion rules slightly different from those seen for plain vanilla options. Let dnp_{numccy} and $dbp_{baseccy}$ be, respectively, the numeraire and base currency digital option premiums calculated as above. The corresponding market premium will be

$$dnp_{numccy\%} = 100 \times dnp_{numccy}$$
$$dbp_{baseccy\%} = 100 \times \frac{dnp_{numccy}}{S_t}$$

where the notation is as usual.

5.6 AMERICAN PLAIN VANILLA OPTIONS

American features for plain vanilla options are not so common in the FX market, but sometimes they can be requested by customers.

Definition 5.6.2. ***American plain vanilla FX option contract.*** *An XXXYYY American plain vanilla option contract is equal to an otherwise identical European plain vanilla option, but for the possibility of exercising it any time before maturity.*

The valuation of an American option is not possible by a closed-form formula, not even in the BS environment. Many attempts to price it via analytical approximations have been proposed, but none are really satisfying, except those entailing numerical procedures that make them comparable to other classic numerical methods to calculate the price of an option (i.e., trees, finite differences, etc.). Let us examine a possible valuation in the BS setting by a trinomial tree, then we hint at how to operate a valuation in a stochastic volatility environment. We will not dwell too much on the theoretical foundations of American option pricing, because that would be beyond the scope of this book (and, besides, the subject has been studied extensively and thoroughly in a huge number of articles and technical papers).

5.6.1 Valuation of American plain vanilla options in a BS setting

Assume we are in a BS economy such as that described in Chapter 2. To evaluate an American option we choose to resort to a trinomial tree, which means that first we have to devise a discrete approximation for the process (2.16) in Chapter 2, so as to allow the building of a tree. We must impose that the parameters are time-independent, i.e., $r_t^d = r^d$, $r_t^f = r^f$ and $\varsigma_t = \sigma$. In our experience, the following approximation works satisfactorily well: the time to expiry of the option is $\tau = T - T$ and we divide it into n sub-periods of length $\Delta t = \tau/n$. We start from a value of the FX spot rate equal to S_t and suppose that it can move into the next interval of time by three jumps u, m and d with given probabilities p_u, p_m and p_d, so that in time $t_1 = t + \Delta t$ it has three possible values. The jumps are defined as

$$\begin{aligned} m &= \mu V^2 \\ u &= X + \sqrt{X^2 - m^2} \\ d &= X - \sqrt{X^2 - m^2} \end{aligned} \tag{5.27}$$

where

$$
\begin{aligned}
V &= e^{\sigma^2 \Delta t} \\
\mu &= e^{(r^d - r^f)\Delta t} \\
X &= 0.5\mu(V^4 + V^3)
\end{aligned}
\tag{5.28}
$$

This definition of the jumps allows for a recombining tree, which is a desirable property to ensure a non-explosive number of nodes going ahead in time and thus a fast numerical computation. The probabilities associated with each jump are

$$
\begin{aligned}
p_u &= \frac{m\,d - \mu(m+d) + \mu^2 V}{(u-d)(u-m)} \\
p_m &= \frac{\mu(u+d) - u\,d - \mu^2 V}{(u-m)(m-d)} \\
p_d &= \frac{u\,m - \mu(m+u) + \mu^2 V}{(u-d)(m-d)}
\end{aligned}
\tag{5.29}
$$

Suppose now we want to price at time t an American option struck at K, with expiry in T. To start the numerical procedure we just have to set the values of the option for each terminal node in the tree. Let us indicate by $\mathcal{A}O(i, j)$ the value of the option in the node (i, j). At time $T = n\,\Delta t$ we have

$$\mathcal{A}O(1 + i + j, n) = \max[\omega(u^{(j)} m^{(i-j)} d^{(n-1-i)} S_t - K), 0]$$

for $i = \{0, \ldots, n-1\}$ and $j = \{0, \ldots, i\}$; $\omega = 1$ if we are pricing a call option and -1 if a put option.

We can now proceed backwards to the layer $L = n - 1$, and in each node we calculate the value of the option as the expected value of the option in the three nodes sprung into the next interval of time from it:

$$
\begin{aligned}
\mathcal{A}O(j + i + 1, L) = e^{-r^d \Delta t}\big(&p_u \mathcal{A}O(j + 1 + i + 2, L + 1) + \\
&p_m \mathcal{A}O(j + 1 + i + 1, L + 1) + p_d \mathcal{A}O(j + 1 + i, L + 1)\big)
\end{aligned}
$$

for $i = \{0, \ldots, L-1\}$ and $j = \{0, \ldots, i\}$. Once we have the value of the option for the node, we must verify the optimality of the early exercise, so that we replace the value of the option in the node by the following:

$$\mathcal{A}O^*(j + i + 1, L) = e^{-r^d \Delta t} \max[\omega(u^{(j)} m^{(i-j)} d^{(n-1-i)} S_t - K), \mathcal{A}O(j + i + 1, L)]$$

We proceed backwards by decreasing L by 1 until $L = 0$. For practical purposes a number of n sub-intervals equal to 60 attains an acceptable degree of accuracy for the price.

5.6.2 Pricing of American plain vanilla options with the volatility smile

The value σ used in the numerical procedure above should be the ATM volatility. In practice, one uses the implied volatility corresponding to the strike as if pricing a European option. This is not correct, since we should take into account the entire volatility smile in a more proper way.

We could adopt one of the stochastic volatility models we have examined in Chapter 2, and then apply one numerical procedure. If we opt for the LMUV we can simply value the

American option as a combination of two BS prices, so that the computational burden is just doubled, since we have to run the backward recursion on the tree twice.

The bid/ask spread can be calculated by using the bid or ask volatility in the numerical procedure, calculated in one of the ways shown above for European plain vanilla options.

Example 5.6.1. *We want to price a* 6*-month (or* 182 *days) American EUR call USD put struck at* 1.4000*, and we use market data as in Example 5.5.1 (EURUSD spot rate is also* 1.4000*).*

We run the numerical procedure we have described and get a premium of 361 *USD pips, by using an implied volatility of* 10.64%*, which is the same as we would infer from the market data in the table, should we price an equivalent European option (we use the VV approach to build the smile). The premium for such a European EUR call USD put is* 350 *USD pips, so that the premium for the American feature is* 11 *USD pips*

We calibrate an LMUV model to the market data and get that the option price is 364 *USD pips, not too far from the value we have calculated by assuming a flat volatility smile (though with a level of volatility corresponding to that of a European option struck at the same level).*

6
Barrier Options

6.1 A TAXONOMY OF BARRIER OPTIONS

Barrier options are the most commonly traded kind of exotic options in the FX market. They are employed in structures devised to hedge the FX risk of the cash flows of a corporate, and to take exposures to sophisticated views on the FX spot rates by speculators. As such they engender the most relevant risks of the book of a typical market maker. We will start with the taxonomy of a different kind of barrier option, including also the touch-type exotic products in this broad category.

Let us start with barrier options. The main feature, common to all these kinds of exotic contracts, is the presence of a barrier whose breaching triggers a given event.

Definition 6.1.1. ***Barrier FX option contract.*** *An XXXYYY barrier option is a contract in all respects equal to an otherwise identical plain vanilla option, the only difference being that the terminal payoff is contingent on the knocking of a predefined level by the underlying FX spot rate.*[1]

More specifically, *knock-in* options pay the terminal value only if, during the life of the contract, the barrier is breached at least once, whereas *knock-out* options pay their value at expiry only if the barrier level is never touched. If the barrier is set at a level with respect to which the terminal value of the option is out-of-the-money, the contract is considered a *standard* barrier; on the contrary, if the terminal value is in-the-money then the contract is denominated as a *reverse* barrier. The position of the trigger level with respect to the starting FX rate identifies *up* or *down* barriers.

It is possible to set more barriers, both with a knock-in or a knock-out feature (respectively, *double-knock-in* and *double-knock-out*), but nothing prevents us from setting one of the barriers as a knock-in and the other as a knock-out level (*knock-in–knock-out*). Besides, the knock-out level can be contingent on the breaching of the knock-in level (*first-in-then-out*).

The monitoring frequency of the barrier is generally *continuous*, although it may be preferred by some customers to set the monitoring on a *discrete* frequency, usually on the basis of a more or less "official" fixing. For example, for parity involving the euro, the daily ECB fixing can be used. Less frequent monitoring, such as weekly or monthly observations, are much less common. With respect to the life of the contract, the barrier can be monitored from start-up to a given time or from a given time to expiry, or only for a specified period after the start and before the expiry: in these cases we have *windows* barriers. When the trigger level is monitored only at the expiry of the contract, the barrier is named *at-expiry*; it is rather straightforward to realize that in this case the only meaningful position of the barrier is where the option expires in-the-money. More convoluted combinations of the observation period are possible, but extremely rare in the FX market.

---

[1] Actually, some second-generation barrier options have a payoff contingent on a second FX rate or another financial variable (*external barriers*)

Table 6.1 Taxonomy of barrier options

Barrier	Call/put	Bets
W/r to moneyness	standard/reverse	–
W/r to the starting FX rate	up/down; in/out; first-in-then-out	–
Number	single/double	touch/double-touch
Cancel/activate	in/out	/no
Monitoring frequency	continuous/discrete	continuous/discrete
Monitoring period	/window	/window

The breaching of the barrier may also produce or cancel the payment of a given amount of money. This kind of contract is often referred to as a *bet*.

Definition 6.1.2. ***Bet FX option contract.*** *An XXXYYY bet option is a contract paying a given amount denominated in one of the two currencies involved in the underlying pair*[2] *contingent on the knocking of a predefined level by the underlying FX spot rate. The payment may occur at the time when the barrier is breached, or at expiry.*

In the *one-touch* and *double-touch* contracts the breaching of the barrier (or, respectively, one of the two barriers) triggers the payment of the notional amount. The payment may occur at the very time the level is touched (*at-hit*) or at the end of the contract (*at-expiry*). The no-touch and double-no-touch contracts pay the notional amount if, during the life of the contract, the level of the barrier (or, respectively, the levels of the two barriers) have never been touched by the underlying FX rate.

In Table 6.1 we give a synopsis of the taxonomy we have presented above.

6.2 SOME RELATIONSHIPS OF BARRIER OPTION PRICES

Similarly to plain vanilla options, some useful relationships can be established for barrier options also and they can be used for pricing and sometimes also for hedging purposes.

Some relations are the same as for plain vanilla options, and we will refer to the equations presented in Chapter 2. Namely, the put–call parity (2.47) applies fully for a call option and a put option expiring on the same date, with the same strike and with the same barrier level. Put–call symmetry (2.48) and foreign–domestic symmetry (2.50) apply also for a put and a call both contingent on the triggering of the same barrier.

Peculiar to barrier options is the knock-in–knock-out parity. This relationship states that the sum of two otherwise identical knock-in and knock-out options (with trigger level H) is equal to a plain vanilla option expiring on the same date (T) and struck at the same level (K) as the barrier options:

$$\mathbf{KIC}(K, T, H) + \mathbf{KOC}(K, T, H) = \mathbf{C}(K, T) \tag{6.1}$$

$$\mathbf{KIP}(K, T, H) + \mathbf{KOP}(K, T, H) = \mathbf{P}(K, T) \tag{6.2}$$

The proof of the relation is rather obvious and we leave it to the reader. Needless to say, an arbitrage strategy could be established should the relationship not hold in the market.

[2] It is nevertheless possible to have a payment denominated in any other currency.

Equations (6.1) and (6.2) are often used in practice for pricing knock-in options. In fact, as we will show later on in this chapter, many rules and techniques to gauge and take into account specific risks, related to barrier contracts, have been devised by market makers specifically for knock-out options. As a consequence, the corresponding knock-in options can be valued by means of the knock-in–knock-out parity, given also the price of a corresponding plain vanilla option.

6.3 PRICING FOR BARRIER OPTIONS IN A BS ECONOMY

Assume we are in a BS economy as designated in Chapter 2.[3] We know that in this economy a contingent claim is the solution to the basic PDE (2.12). Let us define the following transformations:

$$\begin{cases} x = \ln \dfrac{S}{S_0} + \alpha_t \Rightarrow S = S_0 e^{x-\alpha_t} \\ \Pi = \mathcal{O} e^{\beta_t} \\ \tau = \tau_t \end{cases} \tag{6.3}$$

with α_t, β_t and τ_t functions to be determined (we assume that τ_t is invertible, and we will verify it after we have derived the result). By rewriting the PDE (2.12) in terms of the variables (x, τ), we have

$$\frac{\varsigma_t^2}{2}\frac{\partial^2 \Pi}{\partial x^2} - \frac{\varsigma_t^2}{2}\frac{\partial \Pi}{\partial x} + (r_t^d - r_t^f)\frac{\partial \Pi}{\partial x} + \dot{\alpha}_t \frac{\partial \Pi}{\partial x} + \dot{\tau}_t \frac{\partial \Pi}{\partial \tau} - \Pi(\dot{\beta}_t + r_t^d) = 0 \tag{6.4}$$

We try to simplify equation (6.4) by setting

$$\begin{cases} \dot{\beta}_t = -r_t^d \\ \dot{\alpha}_t = -(r_t^d - r_t^f - \dfrac{\varsigma_t^2}{2}) \\ \dot{\tau} = -\varsigma_t^2 \end{cases} \tag{6.5}$$

which means that, for a given reference time T^*, we set

$$\begin{cases} \beta_t = \displaystyle\int_t^{T^*} r_s^d ds \\ \alpha_t = \displaystyle\int_t^{T^*} (r_s^d - r_s^f - \frac{\varsigma_s^2}{2}) ds \\ \tau = \displaystyle\int_t^{T^*} \varsigma_s^2 ds \end{cases}$$

This choice allows us to rewrite equation (6.6) as a standard one-dimensional diffusion equation:

$$\frac{\partial \Pi}{\partial \tau} = \frac{1}{2}\frac{\partial^2 \Pi}{\partial x^2} \tag{6.6}$$

It is worth noticing that equation (6.6) is written in reverse time τ instead of physical time t since $\dot{\tau}_t < 0$, which also verifies the assumption of an invertible function regarding τ that we

[3] We refer to what has been outlined previously; the notation is also the same, when it is not explicitly modified. The entire section is based on the work of Rapisarda [54]).

stated above. The fundamental solution of equation (6.6) is Green's function:

$$G_0((x', \tau') \to (x, \tau)) = \frac{1}{\sqrt{2\pi(\tau - \tau')}} \exp\left[-\frac{(x - x')^2}{2(\tau - \tau')} \right] \tag{6.7}$$

with the property that for any function $\Pi(x', 0)$, the function

$$\Pi(x, \tau) = \int dx' \Pi(x', 0) G_0((x', 0) \to (x, \tau)) \tag{6.8}$$

is a solution of equation (6.6). If we write equation (6.8) in terms of the original variables (S, t), we get

$$G_0((S', t') \to (S, t)) = \frac{e^{-\int_t^{t'} r_s^d ds}}{\sqrt{2\pi \int_t^{t'} \varsigma_s^2 ds}} \exp\left[-\frac{(\ln \frac{S}{S'} + \int_t^{t'} (r_s^d - r_s^f - 0.5\varsigma_s^2) ds)^2}{2 \int_t^{t'} \varsigma_s^2 ds} \right] \tag{6.9}$$

This function represents the solution of the PDE (6.4) for a free boundary condition; that is, only under the condition that the function goes to zero smoothly at infinity for all times. Thus, the pricing of European payoffs is rather straightforward. For example, a plain vanilla call option's value is

$$\mathbf{C}(S, T) = \int_{-\infty}^{\infty} d\xi \, G_0(x, T; \xi, 0)(S_0 e^{\xi} - K)^+$$

yielding the standard BS formula (2.28). The problem is much more complex if we want to price a contingent claim with different boundary conditions, such as a barrier option. In this case Green's function, related to the absorbing boundary condition, has to be built.

6.3.1 The diffusion equation under single absorbing boundaries

One technique that is widely used in the world of physics is the so-called *method of images*. We build a Green's function for a PDE under either absorbing or reacting boundary conditions (Dirichlet or von Neumann, respectively) from the Green's function for the free case. An absorbing boundary (Dirichlet boundary condition) is a surface in $(x; t)$ space where Green's function is equal to zero. A rejecting boundary (von Neumann boundary condition) is a surface where the first spatial derivative $\partial P / \partial x$ goes to zero.

Our goal is to price a European option with a barrier at price H. We could choose as reference level $S_0 = H$ in the system (6.3) and seek a propagator of the form

$$G((x', \tau') \to (x, \tau)) = G_0((x', \tau') \to (x, \tau)) + \zeta(x') G_0((z(x'), \tau') \to (x, \tau)) \tag{6.10}$$

with $\zeta(x_0)$ located in the inhibited region. First, we try to find a profile κ_τ where this combination of free-boundary-condition Green's functions vanishes:

$$\begin{aligned}
0 &= G((x', \tau') \to (x, \tau)) = G_0((x', \tau') \to (x, \tau)) + \zeta(x') G_0((z(x'), \tau') \to (x, \tau)) = 0 \\
&\Longleftrightarrow \exp\left[-\frac{(\kappa_\tau - x')^2}{2(\tau - \tau')} \right] + \zeta(x') \exp\left[-\frac{(\kappa_\tau - z(x'))^2}{2(\tau - \tau')} \right] = 0 \\
&\Longleftrightarrow \ln(-\zeta(x')) = \frac{2\kappa_\tau (x' - z(x)) + z^2(x') - x'^2}{2(\tau - \tau')} \\
&\Longleftrightarrow \kappa_\tau = \frac{\ln(-\zeta(x'))}{x' - z(x')} (\tau - \tau') + \frac{x' + z(x')}{2}
\end{aligned}$$

Note that we did not make any assumption on the sign of x'; that is, on whether the barrier is up or down. This will be useful in deriving a general formula for barriers.

A precise choice of $z(x')$ and $\zeta(x')$ is now in order. The latter is determined by noting that, since the integration of the payoff function is performed over x' and the barrier level should not move with the initial condition x', we must have

$$\frac{\ln(-\zeta(x'))}{x' - z(x')} = \beta$$

where β is a constant. It is rather easy to check that the only functional form for the (log of the) barrier κ_τ consistent with the hypothesis of a Green's function of the form (6.10) under (time-dependent) BS dynamics is

$$\kappa_\tau = \frac{x' + z(x')}{2} + \beta(\tau - \tau')$$

It should be stressed that κ_τ represents the barrier level in returns space as a function of reverse time τ. This approach thus introduces a specific time dependence of the barrier (we just recall that the original barrier is set at a constant price level H, which means that $\kappa_\tau = 0$). Switching back to physical time t, the actual barrier level implied by this approach is

$$\tilde{H}_t = H \exp\left(- \int_t^T (r_s^d - r_s^f - (1 + 2\beta)\frac{\varsigma_s^2}{2} ds \right) \tag{6.11}$$

The most natural choice for the function $z(x')$ is $z(x') = -x'$, so that $\kappa_\tau = \beta(\tau - \tau')$, $\zeta(x') = e^{-2\beta x'}$.

The physical interpretation of the choice above is the following: we want the Green's function to be just a linear combination of two free-boundary Green's functions. Since the physical process described by equation (6.6) is that of a simple one-dimensional diffusion, one can view equation (6.8) as the solution where a unit amount of the diffusing substance ("charge") is deposited in x' at time τ' and then let diffuse according to the PDE. On the other hand, equation (6.10) is nothing but the independent diffusion of two amounts of substance deposited at time τ' in x' and $z(x')$, respectively. The amount deposited in x' integrates initially to one, whereas the amount in $z(x')$ integrates to $\zeta(x')$. Since we want $G((x';\tau') \to (x;\tau)) = \delta(x - x')$ (where $\delta(x - x')$ is the Dirac delta function), we need to ensure that the position $z(x')$ of the image charge is in the inaccessible region, or $z(x') \geq \kappa'_\tau$.[4]

6.3.2 Dealing with a constant barrier

The constraint on the implied shape of the barrier makes this method in theory not suitable to deal with the case of a constant barrier. In any case, no closed-form formulae are available in general for constant barrier options in the presence of time-dependent dynamical parameters governing the evolution of the underlying's price. Therefore, we can still resort to this approach provided that we set the barrier profile κ_τ as close as possible to the constant barrier value. The idea is to use the amount of image charge $\zeta(x')$ (or, equivalently, the parameter β) so that the curve κ_τ is "as straight as possible", and this can be achieved by minimizing with respect

[4] For the interested reader, an analysis of the exactness of the mirror image approximation of Green's functions can be found in Rapisarda [54].

to β the quantity

$$\chi^2(\beta) = \int_{t_1}^{t_2} \left(\ln \frac{\tilde{H}_t}{H} \right)^2 dt \tag{6.12}$$

assuming that the barrier extends from physical time t_1 to physical time $t_2 \geq t_1$. By recalling that the constant barrier level in returns space is set to 0, the optimal choice of β will thus be given by

$$\frac{\partial \chi^2}{\partial \beta^*} = 0 \Longleftrightarrow \beta^* = \frac{\int_{t_1}^{t_2} (\int_t^{t_2} (r_s^d - r_s^f - \frac{\varsigma_s^2}{2}) ds)(\int_t^{t_2} \varsigma_s^2 ds) dt}{\int_{t_1}^{t_2} (\int_t^{t_2} \varsigma_s^2 ds) dt} \tag{6.13}$$

It is worth noticing that equation (6.13) reduces to $\beta^* = \frac{r_s^d - r_s^f - \frac{\varsigma_s^2}{2}}{\varsigma_s^2}$ in the case of a constant barrier.

We are now ready to provide pricing formulae for the different types of barrier options.

6.4 PRICING FORMULAE FOR BARRIER OPTIONS

The pricing of a barrier option can be performed in the usual fashion as in Chapter 2. The price at time t is the expected value of the terminal payoff under the risk-neutral measure. We will provide a very general formula, so as to include all types of first-generation exotic barrier options. In order to do that, we set the following notation:

	+1	−1
ω	call	put
θ	down	up
ζ	out	in

and

$$\begin{cases} v_t = r_t^d - r_t^f - \frac{\varsigma_t^2}{2} \\ d_1(\tilde{S}, X, \tilde{T}) = \dfrac{\ln \frac{\tilde{S}}{X} + \int_t^{\tilde{T}} (r_s^d - r_s^f + \frac{\varsigma_s^2}{2}) ds}{\sqrt{\int_t^{\tilde{T}} \varsigma_s^2 ds}} \\ d_2(\tilde{S}, X, \tilde{T}) = \dfrac{\ln \frac{\tilde{S}}{X} + \int_t^{\tilde{T}} (r_s^d - r_s^f - \frac{\varsigma_s^2}{2}) ds}{\sqrt{\int_t^{\tilde{T}} \varsigma_s^2 ds}} \end{cases}$$

The value of a barrier option at time t expiring in T and contingent on the barrier level H can thus be written:

$$\begin{aligned} &\mathcal{B}^{\mathrm{BS}}(S_t, t, T, K, P^d(t,T), P^f(t,T), H, \omega, \theta, \zeta) \\ &= E^Q\left[e^{-\int_t^T r_s^d ds} (\omega S_T - \omega K)^+ \left[\frac{1-\zeta}{2} + \zeta \mathbf{1}_{\{\theta S_{t'} > \theta H, \forall t' \in [t,T]\}} \right] \right] \end{aligned} \tag{6.14}$$

Hence, by calculating the expectation in equation (6.14) by means of Green's function and the terminal value of the payoff, we have:[5]

$$
\begin{aligned}
&\mathcal{B}^{\text{BS}}(S_t, t, T, K, P^d(t,T), P^f(t,T), H, \omega, \theta, \zeta) \\
&= \omega P^d(t,T)\Bigg[\frac{1-\zeta}{2}\Bigg\{S_t e^{\int_t^T v_s + \frac{\varsigma_s^2}{2}ds}\,\Phi\Bigg(\omega\frac{\ln\frac{S_t}{K} + \int_t^T v_s + \varsigma_s^2 ds}{\sqrt{\int_t^T \varsigma_s^2 ds}}\Bigg) \\
&-K\Phi\Bigg(\omega\frac{\ln\frac{S_t}{K} + \int_t^T v_s ds}{\sqrt{\int_t^T \varsigma_s^2 ds}}\Bigg)\Bigg\} \\
&+\zeta\Bigg\{S_t e^{\int_t^T v_s + \frac{\varsigma_s^2}{2}ds}\Bigg(\Phi\Bigg(\omega\frac{\max[\omega\theta\infty, 0] - \ln\frac{S_t}{H} - \int_t^T v_s + \varsigma_s^2 ds}{\sqrt{\int_t^T \varsigma_s^2 ds}}\Bigg) \\
&-\Phi\Bigg(\frac{\theta\max[\theta\ln\frac{K}{H}, 0] - \ln\frac{S_t}{H} - \int_t^T v_s + \varsigma_s^2 ds}{\sqrt{\int_t^T \varsigma_s^2 ds}}\Bigg)\Bigg) \\
&-K\Bigg(\Phi\Bigg(\omega\frac{\max[\omega\theta\infty, 0] - \ln\frac{S_t}{H} - \int_t^T v_s ds}{\sqrt{\int_t^T \varsigma_s^2 ds}}\Bigg) \\
&-\Phi\Bigg(\frac{\theta\max[\theta\ln\frac{K}{H}, 0] - \ln\frac{S_t}{H} - \int_t^T v_s ds}{\sqrt{\int_t^T \varsigma_s^2 ds}}\Bigg)\Bigg) \\
&-\tilde{H}_t\left(\frac{\tilde{H}_t}{S_t}\right)^{1+2\beta} e^{\int_t^T v_s + \frac{\varsigma_s^2}{2}ds}\Bigg(\Phi\Bigg(\omega\frac{\max[\omega\theta\infty, 0] - \ln\frac{\tilde{H}_t^2}{S_t H} - \int_t^T v_s + \varsigma_s^2 ds}{\sqrt{\int_t^T \varsigma_s^2 ds}}\Bigg) \\
&-\Phi\Bigg(\frac{\theta\max[\theta\ln\frac{K}{H}, 0] - \ln\frac{\tilde{H}_t^2}{S_t H} - \int_t^T v_s + \varsigma_s^2 ds}{\sqrt{\int_t^T \varsigma_s^2 ds}}\Bigg)\Bigg) \\
&+K\left(\frac{\tilde{H}_t}{S_t}\right)^{2\beta}\Bigg(\Phi\Bigg(\frac{\omega\max[\omega\theta\infty, 0] - \ln\frac{\tilde{H}_t^2}{S_t H} - \int_t^T v_s ds}{\sqrt{\int_t^T \varsigma_s^2 ds}}\Bigg) \\
&-\Phi\Bigg(\frac{\theta\max[\theta\ln\frac{K}{H}, 0] - \ln\frac{\tilde{H}_t^2}{S_t H} - \int_t^T v_s ds}{\sqrt{\int_t^T \varsigma_s^2 ds}}\Bigg)\Bigg)\Bigg\}\Bigg]
\end{aligned}
\tag{6.15}
$$

When the parameters are constant, equation (6.15) reduces to the standard formulae for a BS economy that can be found, for example, in Zhang [64].

Via equation (6.15) we can price the different kinds of barrier options. We quickly present the list and refer to the section at the beginning of this book for the notation we use:

$$
\begin{aligned}
&\mathbf{UOC}^{\text{BS}}(S_t, t, T, K, H) = \mathcal{B}^{\text{BS}}(S_t, t, T, K, P^d(t,T), P^f(t,T), H, 1, -1, 1) \\
&\mathbf{DOC}^{\text{BS}}(S_t, t, T, K, H) = \mathcal{B}^{\text{BS}}(S_t, t, T, K, P^d(t,T), P^f(t,T), H, 1, 1, 1)
\end{aligned}
$$

[5] The pricing formula is also from Rapisarda [54].

$$
\begin{aligned}
\mathbf{UIC}^{\text{BS}}(S_t, t, T, K, H) &= \mathcal{B}^{\text{BS}}(S_t, t, T, K, P^d(t,T), P^f(t,T), H, 1, -1, -1)\\
\mathbf{DIC}^{\text{BS}}(S_t, t, T, K, H) &= \mathcal{B}^{\text{BS}}(S_t, t, T, K, P^d(t,T), P^f(t,T), H, 1, 1, -1)\\
\mathbf{UOP}^{\text{BS}}(S_t, t, T, K, H) &= \mathcal{B}^{\text{BS}}(S_t, t, T, K, P^d(t,T), P^f(t,T), H, 1, -1, 1)\\
\mathbf{DOP}^{\text{BS}}(S_t, t, T, K, H) &= \mathcal{B}^{\text{BS}}(S_t, t, T, K, P^d(t,T), P^f(t,T), H, -1, 1, 1)\\
\mathbf{UIP}^{\text{BS}}(S_t, t, T, K, H) &= \mathcal{B}^{\text{BS}}(S_t, t, T, K, P^d(t,T), P^f(t,T), H, -1, -1, -1)\\
\mathbf{DIP}^{\text{BS}}(S_t, t, T, K, H) &= \mathcal{B}^{\text{BS}}(S_t, t, T, K, P^d(t,T), P^f(t,T), H, -1, 1, -1)
\end{aligned}
$$

6.5 ONE-TOUCH (REBATE) AND NO-TOUCH OPTIONS

One-touch (rebate) options are similar to European digitals in that their payoff is one unit of the notional amount denominated in either of the two currencies involved in the underlying FX rate; the difference with respect to a digital option is that the amount is paid if, at any time until expiry, the underlying FX spot breaches a given barrier level. The payment can occur immediately as the spot rate touches the barrier (one-touch at hit) or alternatively at maturity of the contract (one-touch at expiry).

Assume we want to price at time t a one-touch option at expiry, with barrier level set at H and expiring in T, with the initial FX spot rate equal to S_t. The payoff is one unit of the numeraire currency, paid in T if the barrier is breached at any time in the interval $[t, T]$. The price is then

$$
\begin{aligned}
\mathbf{OTE}_n^{\text{BS}}(S_t, t, T, P^d(t,T), P^f(t,T), H, \theta) &= P^d(t,T)\left\{\Phi\left(\theta\frac{\ln\frac{H}{S_t} - \int_t^T \upsilon_s ds}{\sqrt{\int_t^T \varsigma_s^2 ds}}\right)\right.\\
&\left. + \left(\frac{\tilde{H}_t}{S_t}\right)^{2\beta}\Phi\left(\theta\frac{\ln\frac{\tilde{H}_t^2}{S_t H} + \int_t^T \upsilon_s ds}{\sqrt{\int_t^T \varsigma_s^2 ds}}\right)\right\}
\end{aligned}
\tag{6.16}
$$

where $\theta = \pm 1$ depending on whether the barrier level is above or below the initial FX spot rate price. When the amount paid at the end is in base currency units, the pricing formula is

$$
\begin{aligned}
\mathbf{OTE}_b^{\text{BS}}(S_t, t, T, P^d(t,T), P^f(t,T), H, \theta) &= S_t P^f(t,T)\left\{\Phi\left(\theta\frac{\ln\frac{H}{S_t} - \int_t^T \upsilon_s + \varsigma_t^2 ds}{\sqrt{\int_t^T \varsigma_s^2 ds}}\right)\right.\\
&\left. + \left(\frac{\tilde{H}_t}{S_t}\right)^{2\beta+2}\Phi\left(\theta\frac{\ln\frac{\tilde{H}_t^2}{S_t H} + \int_t^T \upsilon_s + \varsigma_t^2 ds}{\sqrt{\int_t^T \varsigma_s^2 ds}}\right)\right\}
\end{aligned}
\tag{6.17}
$$

The value of a one-touch option paid at the hitting time of the barrier is more complex. First we need the following result:

Proposition 6.5.1. (*Rapisarda* [54]). *In a deterministic interest rate economy, the replicating portfolio for an option that pays one unit of currency when a barrier H is hit within the time* *interval* $[0; T]$ *is*

$$\Pi_T = \boldsymbol{1}_{\{\exists\tau\in[0;T]|\theta S_\tau\geq\theta H_\tau\}} - \int_0^T dt \frac{1}{P^d(0,T)} \frac{dP^d(0,t)}{dt} 1_{\{\theta S_\tau\geq\theta H_\tau, \tau\in[0,t]\}} \tag{6.18}$$

where $\boldsymbol{1}$ *is the indicator function.*

Proof: The portfolio value can be represented in terms of the first hitting time

$$t_H^* = \inf\{t \geq 0 | \theta S_t \geq \theta H_t\}$$

as

$$\Pi_T = \mathbf{1}_{\{t_H^*\leq T\}} - \frac{1}{P^d(0,T)} \int_{\min\{t_H^*,T\}}^T dt \frac{dP^d(0,t)}{dt}$$

Direct integration of this expression proves the theorem when analysing separately the two cases $t_H^* \leq T$ and $t_H^* > T$. □

Approximating the straight barrier by the curved barrier of equation (6.11), the first hitting time becomes

$$t_H^* = \inf\{t \geq 0 | \theta S_\tau \geq \theta \tilde{H}_\tau\}$$

so that the argument can be repeated as before, yielding

$$\begin{aligned}\mathbf{OTH}_n^{\text{BS}}\,(S_t,t,T,P^d(t,T),P^f(t,T),H,\theta) &= \mathbf{OTE}_n(S_t,t,T;H,\theta) \\ &+ \int_t^T r_s^d \mathbf{OTE}_n(S_t,t,s,P^d(t,T),P^f(t,T),H,\theta)ds\end{aligned} \tag{6.19}$$

When the parameters are constant, equation (6.19) reduces to a closed-form formula:

$$\begin{aligned}\mathbf{OTH}_n^{\text{BS}}(S_t,t,T,P^d(t,T),P^f(t,T),H,\theta) = P^d(t,T)&\left\{\left(\frac{H}{S_t}\right)^{a+b}\Phi\left(\theta\frac{\ln\frac{H}{S_t}+b\sigma^2(T-t)}{\sigma\sqrt{T-t}}\right)\right. \\ &\left.+\left(\frac{H}{S_t}\right)^{a-b}\Phi\left(\theta\frac{\ln\frac{H}{S_t}-b\sigma^2(T-t)}{\sigma\sqrt{T-t}}\right)\right\}\end{aligned} \tag{6.20}$$

where $a = (r^d - r^f - 0.5\sigma^2)/\sigma^2$ and $b = \sqrt{(r^d - r^f - 0.5\sigma^2)^2 + 2r^d\sigma^2}/\sigma^2$.

If the payoff is one unit of the base currency, formula (6.20) can easily be modified to calculate the price of the options. It is enough to consider that when the barrier level is touched at time t^*, $S_{t^*} = H$ and 1 XXX= H YYY. Hence

$$\begin{aligned}&\mathbf{OTE}_b^{\text{BS}}\,(S_t,t,T,P^d(t,T),P^f(t,T),H,\theta) \\ &= H\mathbf{OTE}_n(S_t,t,T,P^d(t,T),P^f(t,T),H,\theta)\end{aligned} \tag{6.21}$$

A no-touch option pays off one unit of either base or numeraire currency at expiry T if the FX spot rate never breaches the barrier level H. Its price at time t can be calculated simply by the one-touch option value; in case the payoff is one unit of numeraire currency, the price is

$$\begin{aligned}\mathbf{NT}_n^{\mathrm{BS}}&(S_t, t, T, P^d(t,T), P^f(t,T), H, \theta)\\ &= P^d(t,T) - \mathbf{OTE}_n^{\mathrm{BS}}(S_t, t, T, P^d(t,T), P^f(t,T), H, \theta)\end{aligned} \tag{6.22}$$

whereas if the notional amount is expressed in base currency, the price is

$$\begin{aligned}\mathbf{NT}_b^{\mathrm{BS}}&(S_t, t, T, P^d(t,T), P^f(t,T), H, \theta)\\ &= P^f(t,T)S_t - \mathbf{OTE}_b^{\mathrm{BS}}(S_t, t, T, P^d(t,T), P^f(t,T), H, \theta)\end{aligned} \tag{6.23}$$

6.6 DOUBLE-BARRIER OPTIONS

We need to extend the analysis for the single absorbing state that we showed above so as to include a second absorbing state.[6] The results will then be used to price double-barrier options.

6.6.1 Two absorbing states

In the presence of two absorbing barriers, L and U with $L \leq U$ in the space of prices, we measure returns with respect to the reference level $S_0 = L$ in system (6.3). We set $l = \ln U/L$ and the mirror image solution is

$$\begin{aligned}G((x', \tau') \to (x, \tau)) = \sum_{n=-\infty}^{+\infty} \Big[&\zeta_n(x') G_0((2nl - x', \tau') \to (x, \tau))\\ &+ \xi_n(x') G_0((2nl + x', \tau') \to (x, \tau))\Big]\end{aligned} \tag{6.24}$$

Setting $\zeta_n(x') = -e^{2n\beta l + 2\beta x'}$ and $\xi_n(x') = e^{-2n\beta l}$, the accessible region is delimited from below and above by

$$\begin{cases} \kappa_\tau^L = \beta(\tau - \tau') \\ \kappa_\tau^U = l + \beta(\tau - \tau') \end{cases} \tag{6.25}$$

in the return space, and

$$\begin{cases} \tilde{L}_t = L \exp[-\int_t^T (r_s^d - r_s^f - (1+2\beta)\frac{\varsigma_s^2}{2})ds] \\ \tilde{U}_t = U \exp[-\int_t^T (r_s^d - r_s^f - (1+2\beta)\frac{\varsigma_s^2}{2})ds] \end{cases} \tag{6.26}$$

in the price space. Hence, Green's function can be written as

$$\begin{aligned}G((x', \tau') \to (x, \tau)) = \sum_{n=-\infty}^{+\infty} e^{-2n\beta l}\Big[&G_0((2nl + x', \tau') \to (x, \tau))\\ &+ e^{+2\beta x'} G_0((2nl - x', \tau') \to (x, \tau))\Big]\end{aligned} \tag{6.27}$$

The optimal parameter β is that in equation (6.13)

[6] Details in this case are also given in Rapisarda [54].

6.6.2 Pricing formula for double-barrier options

The value of a double-barrier option at time t expiring in T and contingent on the upper barrier level U and lower barrier level L during the time period $[t \leq t^*, T^* \leq T]$ can thus be written

$$\begin{aligned} &\mathcal{DB}^{\text{BS}}\,(S_t, t, T, K, P^d(t,T), P^f(t,T), L, U, \omega, \zeta) \\ &\quad = E^Q\left[e^{-\int_t^T r_s^d ds}(\omega S_T - \omega K)^+\left(\frac{1-\zeta}{2} + \zeta\mathbf{1}_{(L<S_t'<U, \forall t' \in [t,T])}\right)\right] \end{aligned} \tag{6.28}$$

It is then possible to show that the pricing formula is

$$\begin{aligned} &\mathcal{DB}^{\text{BS}}(S_t, t, T, K, P^d(t,T), P^f(t,T), L, U, \omega, \zeta) \\ &= \omega P^d(T,t)\frac{1-\zeta}{2}\left\{S_t e^{\int_t^T v_s + \frac{\varsigma_s^2}{2} ds}\Phi\left(\omega\frac{\ln\frac{S_t}{K} + \int_t^T (v_s + \varsigma_s^2)ds}{\sqrt{\int_t^T \varsigma_s^2 ds}}\right)\right. \\ &\left. -K\Phi\left(\omega\frac{\ln\frac{S_t}{K} + \int_t^T v_s + ds}{\sqrt{\int_t^T \varsigma_s^2 ds}}\right)\right\} \\ &+\zeta\sum_{n=-\infty}^{+\infty}\left(\frac{L}{U}\right)^{2n\beta}\{A_1 - B_1 + C_1 + D_1 - A_2 + B_2 - C_2 - D_2\} \end{aligned} \tag{6.29}$$

where

$$\begin{aligned} A_1 = S_t e^{\int_t^T v_s + \frac{\varsigma_s^2}{2} ds}\left(\frac{L}{U}\right)^{2n}&\left(\Phi\left(\frac{\omega\max[\omega\infty, 0] - \ln\frac{S_t}{L} - \int_t^T v_s + \varsigma_s^2 ds + 2n\ln\frac{U}{L}}{\sqrt{\int_t^T \varsigma_s^2 ds}}\right)\right. \\ &\left.-\Phi\left(\frac{\max[\ln\frac{K}{L}, 0] - \ln\frac{S_t}{L} - \int_t^T v_s + \varsigma_s^2 ds + 2n\ln\frac{U}{L}}{\sqrt{\int_t^T \varsigma_s^2 ds}}\right)\right) \end{aligned}$$

$$\begin{aligned} B_1 = K&\left(\Phi\left(\frac{\omega\max[\omega\infty, 0] - \ln\frac{S_t}{L} - \int_t^T v_s ds + 2n\ln\frac{U}{L}}{\sqrt{\int_t^T v_s^2 ds}}\right)\right. \\ &\left.-\Phi\left(\frac{\max[\ln\frac{K}{L}, 0] - \ln\frac{S_t}{L} - \int_t^T v_s ds + 2n\ln\frac{U}{L}}{\sqrt{\int_t^T \varsigma_s^2 ds}}\right)\right) \end{aligned}$$

$$\begin{aligned} C_1 = -\tilde{L}_t\left(\frac{\tilde{L}_t}{S_t}\right)^{1+2\beta} &e^{\int_t^T v_s + \frac{\varsigma_s^2}{2} ds}\left(\frac{U}{L}\right)^{(1+2\beta)2n} \\ &\left(\Phi\left(\frac{\omega\max[\omega\infty, 0] - \ln\frac{\tilde{L}_t^2}{S_t L} - \int_t^T v_s + \varsigma_s^2 ds - 2n\ln\frac{U}{L}}{\sqrt{\int_t^T \varsigma_s^2 ds}}\right)\right. \\ &\left.-\Phi\left(\frac{\max[\ln\frac{K}{L}, 0] - \frac{\tilde{L}_t^2}{S_t L} - \int_t^T v_s + \varsigma_s^2 ds - 2n\ln\frac{U}{L}}{\sqrt{\int_t^T \varsigma_s^2 ds}}\right)\right) \end{aligned}$$

$$D_1 = K\left(\frac{\tilde{L}_t}{S_t}\right)^{2\beta}\left(\frac{U}{L}\right)^{4n\beta}\left(\Phi\left(\frac{\omega\max[\omega\infty,0] - \ln\frac{\tilde{L}_t^2}{S_tL} - \int_t^T v_s ds - 2n\ln\frac{U}{L}}{\sqrt{\int_t^T \varsigma_s^2 ds}}\right)\right.$$

$$\left. -\Phi\left(\frac{\max[\ln\frac{K}{L},0] - \frac{\tilde{L}_t^2}{S_tL} - \int_t^T v_s ds - 2n\ln\frac{U}{L}}{\sqrt{\int_t^T \varsigma_s^2 ds}}\right)\right)$$

$$A_2 = S_t e^{\int_t^T v_s + \frac{\varsigma_s^2}{2} ds}\left(\frac{L}{U}\right)^{2n}\left(\Phi\left(\frac{\omega\max[\omega\infty,0] - \ln\frac{S_t}{L} - \int_t^T v_s + \varsigma_s^2 ds + (2n+1)\ln\frac{U}{L}}{\sqrt{\int_t^T \varsigma_s^2 ds}}\right)\right.$$

$$\left. -\Phi\left(\frac{\max[\ln\frac{K}{U},0] - \frac{S_t}{L} - \int_t^T v_s + \varsigma_s^2 ds + (2n+1)\ln\frac{U}{L}}{\sqrt{\int_t^T \varsigma_s^2 ds}}\right)\right)$$

$$B_2 = K\left(\Phi\left(\frac{\omega\max[\omega\infty,0] - \ln\frac{S_t}{L} - \int_t^T v_s ds + (2n+1)\ln\frac{U}{L}}{\sqrt{\int_t^T \varsigma_s^2 ds}}\right)\right.$$

$$\left. -\Phi\left(\frac{\max[\ln\frac{K}{L},0] - \ln\frac{S_t}{L} - \int_t^T v_s^2 ds + (2n+1)\ln\frac{U}{L}}{\sqrt{\int_t^T \varsigma_s^2 ds}}\right)\right)$$

$$C_2 = -\tilde{L}_t\left(\frac{\tilde{L}_t}{S_t}\right)^{1+2\beta} e^{\int_t^T (v_s + \frac{\varsigma_s^2}{2})ds}\left(\frac{U}{L}\right)^{(1+2\beta)2n}$$

$$\left(\Phi\left(\frac{\omega\max[\omega\infty,0] - \ln\frac{\tilde{L}_t^2}{S_tL} - \int_t^T (v_s + \varsigma_s^2)ds - (2n-1)\ln\frac{U}{L}}{\sqrt{\int_t^T \varsigma_s^2 ds}}\right)\right.$$

$$\left. -\Phi\left(\frac{\max[\ln\frac{K}{L},0] - \frac{\tilde{L}_t^2}{S_tL} - \int_t^T (v_s + \varsigma_s^2)ds - (2n-1)\ln\frac{U}{L}}{\sqrt{\int_t^T \varsigma_s^2 ds}}\right)\right)$$

$$D_2 = K\left(\frac{\tilde{L}_t}{S_t}\right)^{2\beta}\left(\frac{U}{L}\right)^{4n\beta}\left(\Phi\left(\frac{\omega\max[\omega\infty,0] - \ln\frac{\tilde{L}_t^2}{S_tL} - \int_t^T v_s ds - (2n-1)\ln\frac{U}{L}}{\sqrt{\int_t^T \varsigma_s^2 ds}}\right)\right.$$

$$\left. -\Phi\left(\frac{\max[\ln\frac{K}{L},0] - \frac{\tilde{L}_t^2}{S_tL} - \int_t^T v_s ds - (2n-1)\ln\frac{U}{L}}{\sqrt{\int_t^T \varsigma_s^2 ds}}\right)\right)$$

Via equation (6.15) we retrieve pricing formulae for the different kinds of double-barrier options; in this case we also refer to the section at the beginning of this book for the notation we use:

$$\mathbf{DKOC}^{\text{BS}}(S_t, t, T, K, L, U) = \mathcal{DB}^{\text{BS}}(S_t, t, T, K, P^d(t,T), P^f(t,T), L, U, 1, 1)$$
$$\mathbf{DKIC}^{\text{BS}}(S_t, t, T, K, L, U) = \mathcal{DB}^{\text{BS}}(S_t, t, T, K, P^d(t,T), P^f(t,T), L, U, 1, -1)$$
$$\mathbf{DKOP}^{\text{BS}}(S_t, t, T, K, L, U) = \mathcal{DB}^{\text{BS}}(S_t, t, T, K, P^d(t,T), P^f(t,T), L, U, -1, 1)$$
$$\mathbf{DKIP}^{\text{BS}}(S_t, t, T, K, L, U) = \mathcal{DB}^{\text{BS}}(S_t, t, T, K, L, P^d(t,T), P^f(t,T), U, -1, -1)$$

6.7 DOUBLE-NO-TOUCH AND DOUBLE-TOUCH OPTIONS

Double-no-touch (**DNT**) options pay at expiry the notional amount, denominated in either currency involved in the underlying pair, contingent on the event that neither the (upper or lower) barrier has been breached during the life of the contract. The pricing of these contracts can be performed in the usual fashion, by calculating the present value of the expected terminal payoff, under a risk-neutral measure. Nevertheless, since we have already derived the pricing formulae for double-barrier options, we can exploit these and hence value double-no-touch options via a static replica argument.

Assume we want to price at time t a **DNT** expiring in T, paying one unit of numeraire currency if the underlying spot FX rate remains in the range identified by the two barriers $L < U$. Clearly, for the option to be worth something, the staring FX spot rate must satisfy $L < S_t < U$. Consider a portfolio long a double-knock-out call and double-knock-out put struck, respectively, at the lower and the barrier and in a base currency notional amount equal to the difference between the two barriers. It is easy to check that this portfolio will yield at expiry, if neither barrier has been breached during the life of the contract, a payoff equal to one unit of numeraire currency. So the **DNT**'s price is

$$\begin{aligned}\mathbf{DNT}_n^{\mathrm{BS}}&(S_t, t, T; L; U)\\ &= \frac{\mathbf{DKOC}^{\mathrm{BS}}(S_t, t, T, L, L, U) + \mathbf{DKOP}^{\mathrm{BS}}(S_t, t, T, U, L, U)}{U - L}\end{aligned} \tag{6.30}$$

If we want to price the same **DNT** as before but with a payoff denominated in base currency units, we can still resort to a static replica approach. It is enough to consider that at expiry, the terminal FX spot rate being within the range between the two barriers, one unit of base currency is equal to $L + (S_T - L)$ numeraire currency units. Besides, we want that the payoff is nil outside the range at expiry and if either barrier had been breached at least once before. So we set up a replication portfolio consisting of an L times **DNT** plus a **DKOC** struck at the lower barrier and with the same barriers as the **DNT** we want to price. Then we have that the price of a **DNT** paying at expiry one unit of base currency is

$$\mathbf{DNT}_b(S_t, t, T; L; U) = L\mathbf{DNT}_n(S_t, t, T; L, U) + \mathbf{DKOC}(S_t, t, T, L, L, U) \tag{6.31}$$

Double-touch options pay one unit of either currency involved in the underlying FX spot rate if either the upper or the lower barrier has been breached at least once up to expiry of the contract. If the payment occurs at maturity of the contract, it is easy to value the double-touch by setting up a replication portfolio of a zero-coupon bond and a double-no-touch. Assume we want to price at time t a **DTE** expiring in T, paying one unit of numeraire currency if the underlying spot FX rate touches one of the two barriers $L < U$. The price is

$$\mathbf{DTE}_n(S_t, t, T, L, U) = P^d(t, T) - \mathbf{DNT}_n(S_t, t, T, L; U) \tag{6.32}$$

If the **DTE** is the same as above but the payoff is one unit of base currency, by the same token we set up a replication portfolio and get

$$\mathbf{DTE}_b(S_t, t, T, L, U) = P^f(t, T)S_t - \mathbf{DNT}_b(S_t, t, T, L, U) \tag{6.33}$$

6.8 PROBABILITY OF HITTING A BARRIER

As will be clear later on, it is useful to derive formulae for the probability of hitting one or two barriers in a given period of time, within the BS model with possibly time-dependent parameters. Actually, given the pricing formulae for bets, probabilities can be calculated rather easily. We note here that we derive risk-neutral probability, since we use the risk-neutral drift.

We start with the case of one barrier. Assume we are at time t when the FX spot rate is S_t and we want to know the probability that before time T a barrier level H, located either above or below S_t, is breached. We denote by t_H^* the first hitting time. The probability can be expressed formally as

$$\Pr(t_H^* < T) = E^Q[\mathbf{1}|\theta S_{t'} > \theta H, \forall t' \in [t, T]]$$

By inspection, it is easy to see that this is the price of a one-touch option paying one unit of numeraire currency at expiry, without any discounting. Then we may resort to the pricing formula for this contract (equation (6.16)), and get

$$\Pr(t_H^* < T) = \frac{\mathbf{OTE}_n}{P^d(t, T)} \tag{6.34}$$

In fact, we will use more often the so-called *survival probability*, which is the probability that the FX spot rate does not hit the barrier level. The name is due to the fact that usually it is calculated with reference to knock-out barriers. Clearly, this is

$$\Pr(t_H^* > T) = 1 - \frac{\mathbf{OTE}_n}{P^d(t, T)} \tag{6.35}$$

Let us now move on to examine the case for two barriers. It is more convenient in this case to start with the survival probability, so we want to compute the probability that the FX spot price stays in a range identified by a lower L and an upper U barrier up to time T. We indicate by $t_{U,L}^*$ the first time when one of the two barriers is breached, so we have

$$\Pr(t_{U,L}^* > T) = E^Q[\mathbf{1}|L < S_{t'} < U, \forall t' \in [t, T]]$$

Also in this case, inspection reveals that the probability above is equal to the undiscounted price of a double-no-touch paying one unit of numeraire currency if the FX spot rate deals within the range up to expiry T, and hence we get

$$\Pr(t_H^* > T) = \frac{\mathbf{DNT}_n}{P^d(t, T)} \tag{6.36}$$

and the probability that the first hitting time is before T:

$$\Pr(t_H^* < T) = 1 - \frac{\mathbf{DNT}_n}{P^d(t, T)} \tag{6.37}$$

6.9 GREEK CALCULATION

Although the Greeks we have shown in Chapter 2 for plain vanilla options are available in closed form also for barrier options, within the BS setting, nevertheless the formulae are so convoluted that it is easier to calculate them numerically, without any substantial loss of computing time.

Assume the exotic option $\mathcal{E}^{\text{BS}}(S_t, t, \sigma_{ATM})$ is valued by the BS model with implied volatility σ_{ATM} (usually set at a level equal to the at-the-money strike, as indicated by the subscript). The two Greeks related to the underlying FX spot rate can be calculated as follows:

$$\Delta_t^{\mathrm{BS}}(S_t, t, \sigma_{ATM}) = \frac{\mathcal{E}^{\mathrm{BS}}(S_t + \Delta S, t, \sigma_{ATM}) - \mathcal{E}^{\mathrm{BS}}(S_t - \Delta S, t, \sigma_{ATM})}{2\Delta S} \tag{6.38}$$

$$\Gamma_t^{\mathrm{BS}}(S_t, t, \sigma_{ATM}) = \frac{\mathcal{E}^{\mathrm{BS}}(S_t + \Delta S, t, \sigma_{ATM}) + \mathcal{E}^{\mathrm{BS}}(S_t - \Delta S, t, \sigma_{ATM}) - 2\mathcal{E}^{\mathrm{BS}}(S_t, t, \sigma_{ATM})}{\Delta S^2} \tag{6.39}$$

where ΔS is set at a suitably small level, such as $0.005S_t$.

The Vega-related derivatives can be calculated by the same token:

$$\mathcal{V}_t^{\mathrm{BS}}(S_t, t, \sigma_{ATM}) = \frac{\mathcal{E}^{\mathrm{BS}}(S_t, t, \sigma_{ATM} + \Delta\sigma) - \mathcal{E}^{\mathrm{BS}}(S_t, t, \sigma_{ATM} - \Delta\sigma)}{2\Delta\sigma} \tag{6.40}$$

$$\mathcal{W}_t^{\mathrm{BS}}(S_t, t, \sigma_{ATM}) = \frac{\mathcal{E}^{\mathrm{BS}}(S_t, t, \sigma_{ATM} + \Delta\sigma) + \mathcal{E}^{\mathrm{BS}}(S_t, t, \sigma_{ATM} - \Delta\sigma) - 2\mathcal{E}^{\mathrm{BS}}(S_t, t, \sigma_{ATM})}{\Delta\sigma^2} \tag{6.41}$$

$$\begin{aligned}\mathcal{X}_t^{\mathrm{BS}}(S_t, t, \sigma_{ATM}) = {} & [\mathcal{E}^{\mathrm{BS}}(S_t + \Delta S, t, \sigma_{ATM} + \Delta\sigma) - \mathcal{E}^{\mathrm{BS}}(S_t - \Delta S, t, \sigma_{ATM} + \Delta\sigma) \\ & -\mathcal{E}^{\mathrm{BS}}(S_t + \Delta S, t, \sigma_{ATM} - \Delta\sigma) + \mathcal{E}^{\mathrm{BS}}(S_t - \Delta S, t, \sigma_{ATM} - \Delta\sigma)]/(4\Delta\sigma\Delta S)\end{aligned} \tag{6.42}$$

Although the Vega is usually expressed in trading systems as the sensitivity of the options' values to a tilt of 1% of the implied volatility, when we come to barrier options this notion is not fit at all for the hedging needs. Given the large value of the second-order derivatives with respect to the volatility, choosing such an amount in calculating the numerical derivatives would yield a considerable approximation error. As such, we suggest setting $\Delta\sigma = 0.01\%$ so as to compute a more precise derivative.

6.10 PRICING BARRIER OPTIONS IN OTHER MODEL SETTINGS

In Chapter 2 we reviewed, besides the BS setting, a few other models capable of coping with the presence of a volatility smile in the market. We can also price the barrier options we have examined above by them. In most cases, closed-form formulae are not available, so we must resort to numerical procedures, such as finite differences and Monte Carlo simulations. We have to note, though, that convergence is rather slow and this hinders the practical use of these models for book revaluation and hedging purposes. In fact, FX options books typically contain tens and sometimes hundreds of thousands of contracts, and calculation speed and accuracy is a crucial issue.

The only model, amongst those presented, allowing for a closed-form pricing, when this is available in a BS environment, is the LMUV model. We saw in Chapter 2 that within this setting a plain vanilla option is simply the weighted average of the BS prices, the weights being the probability attached to each scenario. The same result applies also for barrier options, and exotic options broadly speaking. In general, if $\mathcal{E}(S_t, t)$ is the price of an exotic option, its price in the LMUV model is

$$\mathcal{E}^{\mathrm{UV}}(S_t, t) = \sum_{i=1}^{n} \lambda_i \mathcal{E}^{\mathrm{BS}}(S_t, t) \tag{6.43}$$

where $\mathcal{E}^{\mathrm{BS}}(S_t, t)$ is the BS price of the exotic contract.

6.11 PRICING BARRIERS WITH NON-STANDARD DELIVERY

Two non-standard delivery types can be agreed upon in a barrier contract, as for a plain vanilla contract: a delayed settlement date and a cash delivery. We have analysed these issues extensively for plain vanilla options, and the results presented in Chapter 5 apply also in the case of barrier options, so in what follows we will quickly examine how to deal with these features.

6.11.1 Delayed settlement date

Consider a barrier option at time t expiring in T and with delivery of the underlying $T' = T + s'$, where the number of days s' is greater than the standard number, usually equal to two business days. In this case the buyer of the option is actually entering into a forward contract, so that their decision whether to exercise or not will be taken by comparing the forward price, prevailing in the market for delivery T', with the strike price. The terminal value of the call option is then

$$\begin{aligned}&\mathcal{B}^{ds}\,(S_T, T, T, T', K, P^d(t,T), P^f(t,T), H, \omega, \zeta, \theta)\\&\quad = P^d(T,T')\max(\omega S_T - \omega K)\end{aligned}$$

We can perform the same calculation we have seen in the case of plain vanilla options with delayed settlement (see Chapter 5) considering also the fact that the terminal payoff is contingent on the barrier event. Eventually we come up with a similar adjustment of the standard barrier options evaluation formulae so as to include the new feature, and we then have

$$\begin{aligned}&\mathcal{B}^{ds}\,(S_t, T, T, T', K, P^d(t,T), P^f(t,T), H, \omega, \zeta, \theta)\\&\quad = P^f(T,T')\mathcal{B}(S_T, t, T, K', P^d(t,T), P^f(t,T), H, \omega, \zeta, \theta)\end{aligned} \tag{6.44}$$

where $K' = K\frac{P^d(T,T')}{P^f(T,T')}$. In practice, in case of a delayed settlement clause, we can still value the barrier option by the ordinary pricing formula for standard settlement, by multiplying the latter times a factor equal to the price of a foreign zero-coupon bond price expiring in T' and valued in T, and by using the adjusted strike price K' instead of the original K. It is worth noting that the strike of the contract is still K, whereas K' is only used for evaluation purposes and for the buyer's decision whether to exercise or not.

6.11.2 Cash settlement

Cash settlement delivery for a barrier option can be handled similarly as for plain vanilla options. Assume that a barrier option expires at time T and it is cash settled at time $T' = T + s$. At time T its value is

$$\mathcal{B}^{cs}(S_T, T, T, T', K, P^d(t,T), P^f(t,T), H, \omega, \zeta, \theta) = P^d(T,T')\max(\omega S_T - \omega K, 0)$$

where ω depends as usual on the kind of option. The terminal payoff $\omega S_T - \omega K$ (if positive) is permuted in cash and settled at time T', so that the discounting is performed by multiplying the amount by the zero-coupon price bond $P^d(T,T')$. The value at time $t < T$ is the usual discounted expected value under the risk-neutral measure Q, and we can use the standard pricing formulae, with the adjustment due to the factor $P^d(T, T')$,

$$\begin{aligned}\mathcal{B}^{cs}&(S_t, t, T, T', K, P^d(t, T), P^f(t, T), H, \omega, \zeta, \theta)\\&= P^d(T, T')\mathcal{B}(S_t, t, T, K', P^d(t, T), P^f(t, T), H, \omega, \zeta, \theta)\end{aligned} \tag{6.45}$$

The touch-type barrier options, which naturally pay off at expiry a cash amount, denominated in either currency involved in the underlying pair, can be handled according to the criteria used for barrier options. Clearly, the only touch options we are interested in are those paying not at hitting time, but rather at a different time which can be later than the expiry. In this case we can use the standard pricing formulae for the one-touch at expiry, no-touch, double-no-touch and double-touch at expiry, and adjust them by a factor equal to $P^d(T, T')$.

6.12 MARKET APPROACH TO PRICING BARRIER OPTIONS

Market makers have developed many skills in trading and managing barrier options. As a consequence, they have devised a set of tools and rules of thumb to include in the pricing many risks that are not taken into account by standard models. Most of the ideas that we will examine below are strictly related to the BS model, which is still the reference setting for the market, nevertheless some of them can be applied to any model one should adopt for pricing and hedging purposes.

6.12.1 Inclusion of the smile: the Vanna–Volga approach for barrier options

The presence of a smile in the implied volatility makes the BS model not suited to consistently price exotic options. Yet, as the plain vanilla pricing formula is tweaked by (inconsistently) applying a different volatility parameter to each strike level, thus taking into account the smile, similarly the basic BS formulae[7] are adjusted so as to include the smile effect in the pricing. The adjustment is not so easy and univocally operated as in the plain vanilla case, but the basic idea underlying it can be referred to the same essential concepts, which we are going to analyse.

Assume that we are in a BS framework and, for simplicity's sake, that the parameters are constant, although the analysis can also be extended to the time-dependent parameter case. To make things concrete, assume that we have an exotic contract (either a knock-out barrier option or a bet) $\mathcal{E}(S_t, t, \sigma_t)$, whose payoff is contingent on the breaching of a barrier level H by the FX spot rate. Similar to Chapter 4, we further assume that the implied volatility σ is also a stochastic process affecting the contract's price.[8] By means of Itô's lemma we may derive the differential equation commanding the evolution of $\mathcal{E}(S_t, t, \sigma_t)$, given the dynamics of the FX spot rate and of the implied volatility, although in this case we take into account the event of the barrier's knocking. We define

$$t_H^* = \inf\{t \geq 0 | \theta S_t \geq \theta H\}$$

[7] The BS formulae are those presented above, in their time-dependent parameter version.

[8] See Chapter 3 for a market model of the implied volatility.

as the first time the FX spot S_t knocks the level H. It is possible to show[9] that

$$E^Q[P^d(0,T)(S_T-K)^+\mathbf{1}_{\{t_H^*>T\}}|\mathcal{F}_t] = e^{-\int_0^{t\wedge t_H^*} r_s^d ds}\mathcal{E}(S_{t\wedge t_H^*}, t\wedge t_H^*, \sigma_{t\wedge t_H^*})$$

The differential of the discounted value process can be written

$$\begin{aligned} d(e^{-\int_0^t r_s^d ds}\mathcal{E}(S_t,t,\sigma_t)) = e^{-\int_0^t r_s^d ds}\Big(& -r_t^d\mathcal{E} + \mathcal{E}_t + (r_t^d - r_t^f)S_t\mathcal{E}_S + \frac{1}{2}\varsigma_t^2 S_t^2\mathcal{E}_{SS} \\ & +\widetilde{\phi}_t\mathcal{E}_\sigma + \frac{1}{2}\nu_t^2\mathcal{E}_{\sigma\sigma} + \rho_t\nu_t\varsigma_t S_t\mathcal{E}_{\sigma S}\Big)dt \\ & +e^{-\int_0^t r_s^d ds}\Big(\varsigma_t S_t\mathcal{E}_S dW_t^Q + \nu_t\mathcal{E}_\sigma dZ_t^Q\Big) \end{aligned}$$

where the subscripts indicate the partial derivatives and the notation, for the parameters of the risk-neutral processes for the FX spot rate and the implied volatility, is the usual one. By integrating from 0 to $t\wedge t_H^*$:

$$\begin{aligned} e^{-\int_0^{t\wedge t_H^*} r_s^d ds}\,\mathcal{E}(S_{t\wedge t_H^*}, t\wedge t_H^*, \sigma_{t\wedge t_H^*}) = \int_0^{t\wedge t_H^*} & e^{-\int_0^s r_u^d du}\Big(-r_s^d\mathcal{E} + \mathcal{E}_s \\ & +(r_s^d - r_s^f)S_s\mathcal{E}_S + \frac{1}{2}\varsigma_s^2 S_s^2\mathcal{E}_{SS} \\ & +\widetilde{\phi}_s\mathcal{E}_\sigma + \frac{1}{2}\nu_s^2\mathcal{E}_{\sigma\sigma} + \rho_s\nu_s\varsigma_s S\mathcal{E}_{\sigma S}\Big)ds \\ & +\int_0^{t\wedge t_H^*} e^{-\int_0^s r_u^d du}\Big(\varsigma_s S_s\mathcal{E}_S dW_s^Q + \nu_s\mathcal{E}_\sigma dZ_s^Q\Big) \end{aligned}$$

Since a stopped martingale is a martingale, the stopped discounted value process is a martingale as well.

We want to price the exotic contract by the same approach as that followed in Chapter 4. There we priced a plain vanilla option expiring at time T and struck at an arbitrary level K by means of three basic options, whose price was assumed to be known. The idea here is to set up a perfectly hedged portfolio containing the exotic contract, the three basic options and an amount of underlying FX spot to cancel the Delta exposure. The three basic options are actively traded and we assume they are all calls: the corresponding strikes are denoted by $K_i, i = 1, 2, 3$, $K_1 < K_2 < K_3$, and set $\mathcal{K} := \{K_1, K_2, K_3\}$. The market implied volatility associated with K_i is $\sigma_i, i = 1, 2, 3$.

The difference arising in pricing an exotic contract is due to the fact that the value process for the latter is stopped at $t\wedge t_H^*$, whereas the three basic options used for the hedging are standard European contracts expiring in any case in T. We would like those options to stop in $t\wedge t_H^*$ as well as the exotic contract, but this would be possible only if their payoff were contingent on the breaching of a barrier too, which is not the case by assumption. To cope with this situation we make the following observation:

$$E^Q[P^d(t,T)(S_T-K)^+\mathbf{1}_{t_H^*>T}|\mathcal{F}_t] \cong E^Q[P^d(t,T)(S_T-K)^+|\mathcal{F}_t]\Pr(t_H^*>T) \quad (6.46)$$

The equation above simply states that an exotic option (in this case a knock-out barrier) is approximately equal to a standard European option with the same expiry and strike, times the probability that the barrier is not breached before the maturity or, alternatively, the survival

[9] See, for example, Shreve [59], Chapter 7.

probability of the option. Then we have a way to still resort to standard plain vanilla options to build a perfectly hedged portfolio and derive the price of the exotic contract by an arbitrage argument. To mimic the price of an exotic option contingent on the barrier level H, we take an amount of a corresponding European contract multiplied by a factor $\varpi = \Pr(t_H^* > T)$, which we assume to be a constant.

We have to find the time-0 weights $x_1(K)$, $x_2(K)$ and $x_3(K)$ such that the resulting portfolio of (survivor probability) European calls with maturity T and strikes K_1, K_2 and K_3, respectively, hedges the price variations of the exotic contract $\mathcal{E}^{\text{BS}}(t; H)$ with maturity T and barrier level H, up to second order in the underlying and volatility.[10] In fact, denoting respectively by Δ_t and x_i the units of the underlying asset and options with strikes K_i held at time t and setting $\mathbf{C}_i^{\text{BS}}(t) = \mathbf{C}^{\text{BS}}(t; K_i) = \mathbf{C}^{\text{BS}}(t; K_i, T)$, under diffusion dynamics both for S_t and $\sigma = \sigma_t$, we have by Itô's lemma

$$
\begin{aligned}
& d\mathcal{E}^{\text{BS}}(t; H) - \Delta_t dS_t - \Delta_t r_t^f S_t dt - \sum_{i=1}^{3} x_i d\mathbf{C}_i^{\text{BS}}(t) \\
&= \left[\frac{\partial \mathcal{E}^{\text{BS}}(t; H)}{\partial t} - \varpi \sum_{i=1}^{3} x_i \frac{\partial \mathbf{C}_i^{\text{BS}}(t)}{\partial t} - \Delta_t r_t^f S_t \right] dt \\
&+ \left[\frac{\partial \mathcal{E}^{\text{BS}}(t; H)}{\partial S_t} - \Delta_t - \varpi \sum_{i=1}^{3} x_i \frac{\partial \mathbf{C}_i^{\text{BS}}(t)}{\partial S_t} \right] dS_t \\
&+ \left[\frac{\partial \mathcal{E}^{\text{BS}}(t; H)}{\partial \sigma} - \varpi \sum_{i=1}^{3} x_i \frac{\partial \mathbf{C}_i^{\text{BS}}(t)}{\partial \sigma} \right] d\sigma_t \\
&+ \frac{1}{2} \left[\frac{\partial^2 \mathcal{E}^{\text{BS}}(t; H)}{\partial S_t^2} - \varpi \sum_{i=1}^{3} x_i \frac{\partial^2 \mathbf{C}_i^{\text{BS}}(t)}{\partial S_t^2} \right] (dS_t)^2 \\
&+ \frac{1}{2} \left[\frac{\partial^2 \mathcal{E}^{\text{BS}}(t; H)}{\partial \sigma^2} - \varpi \sum_{i=1}^{3} x_i \frac{\partial^2 \mathbf{C}_i^{\text{BS}}(t)}{\partial \sigma^2} \right] (d\sigma_t)^2 \\
&+ \left[\frac{\partial^2 \mathcal{E}^{\text{BS}}(t; H)}{\partial S_t \partial \sigma} - \varpi \sum_{i=1}^{3} x_i \frac{\partial^2 \mathbf{C}_i^{\text{BS}}(t)}{\partial S_t \partial \sigma} \right] dS_t d\sigma_t
\end{aligned}
\tag{6.47}
$$

We just notice that ϖ is constant and common for all the European contracts. Choosing Δ_t and x_i so as to zero the coefficients of dS_t, $d\sigma_t$, $(d\sigma_t)^2$ and $dS_t d\sigma_t$, at time $t = 0$:

$$
\begin{aligned}
\frac{\partial \mathcal{E}^{\text{BS}}}{\partial \sigma}(H) &= \varpi \sum_{i=1}^{3} x_i(K) \frac{\partial \mathbf{C}^{\text{BS}}}{\partial \sigma}(K_i) \\
\frac{\partial^2 \mathcal{E}^{\text{BS}}}{\partial \sigma^2}(H) &= \varpi \sum_{i=1}^{3} x_i(K) \frac{\partial^2 \mathbf{C}^{\text{BS}}}{\partial \sigma^2}(K_i) \\
\frac{\partial^2 \mathcal{E}^{\text{BS}}}{\partial \sigma \partial S_0}(H) &= \varpi \sum_{i=1}^{3} x_i(K) \frac{\partial^2 \mathbf{C}^{\text{BS}}}{\partial \sigma \partial S_0}(K_i)
\end{aligned}
\tag{6.48}
$$

[10] We add the superscript BS to stress the fact that we use the BS formulae.

The portfolio made up of a long position in the call with strike K, short positions in x_i calls with strike K_i and short the amount Δ_t of the underlying, should ideally be locally riskless at time t (no stochastic terms are involved in its differential). Nonetheless, since for barrier options the Vega–Gamma relationship holds in its general version (2.59), we have not cancelled out completely the Gamma exposure. In fact, we are left with the following:

$$\begin{aligned} d\mathcal{E}^{\text{BS}}(0;\,H) &- \Delta_0 dS_0 - \Delta_0 r_0^f S_0 dt - \varpi \sum_{i=1}^{3} x_i\, d\mathbf{C}_i^{\text{BS}}(0) \\ &= \left[\frac{\partial \mathcal{E}^{\text{BS}}(0;\,H)}{\partial t} - \varpi \sum_{i=1}^{3} x_i \frac{\partial \mathbf{C}_i^{\text{BS}}(0)}{\partial t} - \Delta_0 r_0^f S_t\right] dt - \frac{1}{\tau}(r_0^d - r_0^f)\frac{\partial \Pi_0}{\partial r_0^f}(dS_0)^2 \end{aligned} \tag{6.49}$$

where Π_t is the total portfolio and we used the general Gamma–Vega relationship (2.59) in Chapter 2, the BS PDE and the fact that the Delta of the portfolio has been zeroed. Unfortunately, unlike the plain vanilla case, the portfolio is not locally perfectly risk-free. The last term is the quadratic variation of the FX spot rate times a factor depending on the foreign Rho of the total portfolio and the domestic and foreign interest rates. The hedging argument does not hold, but we claim that the last term in (6.49) is very small (or anyway we just neglect it) and, at least when the two interest rates are not too different, we can safely assume that. However, in Chapter 8 we will verify that actually the hedged portfolio has a small Gamma and that the assumption is not recklessly unreasonable.

We may now find the VV price which is consistent with the market prices of the basic options. The above replication argument shows that a portfolio made up of $x_i(K)$ units of the option with strike K_i and Δ_0 units of the underlying asset gives a locally perfect hedge in a BS setting (if we neglect the term with the quadratic variation). Since the hedging strategy has to be operated at prevailing market prices, it generates differential costs with respect to the BS values. Such differences have to be added to the BS price to produce an arbitrage-free price that is consistent with the quoted option prices $\mathbf{C}^{\text{MKT}}(K_1)$, $\mathbf{C}^{\text{MKT}}(K_2)$ and $\mathbf{C}^{\text{MKT}}(K_3)$.

Assuming a short time to maturity, i.e., a small $\tau = T$, equation (6.49) can be approximated as

$$\begin{aligned} &(S_T - K)^+ \mathbf{1}_{\{t_H^* > T\}} - \mathcal{E}^{\text{BS}}(H) - \Delta_0[S_T - S_0] - \Delta_0 r_0^f S_0 T \\ &\quad -\varpi \sum_{i=1}^{3} x_i[(S_T - K_i)^+ - \mathbf{C}^{\text{BS}}(K_i)] \approx r_0^d \left[\mathbf{C}^{\text{BS}}(K) - \Delta_0 S_0 - \varpi \sum_{i=1}^{3} x_i \mathbf{C}^{\text{BS}}(K_i)\right] T \end{aligned}$$

so that setting

$$\mathcal{E}(H) = \mathcal{E}^{\text{BS}}(H) + \varpi \sum_{i=1}^{3} x_i(K)[\mathbf{C}^{\text{MKT}}(K_i) - \mathbf{C}^{\text{BS}}(K_i)] \tag{6.50}$$

we have

$$\begin{aligned} &(S_T - K)^+ \mathbf{1}_{\{t_H^* > T\}} \approx \mathcal{E}(H) + \Delta_0[S_T - S_0] + \Delta_0 r_0^f S_0 T \\ &\quad +\varpi \sum_{i=1}^{3} x_i[(S_T - K_i)^+ - \mathbf{C}^{\text{MKT}}(K_i)] + r_0^d \left[\mathbf{C}(K) - \Delta_0 S_0 - \varpi \sum_{i=1}^{3} x_i \mathbf{C}^{\text{MKT}}(K_i)\right] T \end{aligned}$$

Therefore, when actual market prices are considered, the option payoff $(S_T - K)^+$ can still be replicated by buying Δ_0 units of the underlying asset and x_i options with strike K_i and investing the resulting cash at rate r^d, provided one starts from the initial endowment $\mathcal{E}(K)$.

The quantity $\mathcal{E}(K)$ in equation (6.50) can be defined as the VV option's premium, implicitly assuming that the replication error is also negligible for longer maturities. Such a premium equals the BS price $\mathcal{E}^{BS}(H)$ plus the differential costs of the hedging portfolio induced by the market implied volatilities that are different from the constant volatility σ. We can then state the following:

Proposition 6.12.1. *Let x_i for $i := \{1, 2, 3\}$ be the solution of the system* (6.48)*: equation* (6.50) *is the new VV exotic option price consistent with the market smile implied by the three basic options with strike K_i for $i := \{1, 2, 3\}$. Moreover, if we set $\sigma = \sigma_2$, i.e., the market volatility for strike K_2, equation* (6.50) *can be simplified to*

$$\mathcal{E}(H) = \mathcal{E}^{BS}(H) + \varpi\{x_1(K)[C^{MKT}(K_1) - C^{BS}(K_1)] + x_3(K)[C^{MKT}(K_3) - C^{BS}(K_3)]\} \tag{6.51}$$

In practice, the VV approach allows us to calculate a smile-adjusted exotic price by means of three basic options, which are also in this case the 25D call and put and the ATM call (or put). These options are the building blocks of the three main structures dealt in the market (the ATM **STDL**, the 25D **RR** and the 25D **VWB**). The reference implied volatility is normally set equal to the ATM level, so that if K_i is the ATM strike, $\sigma = \sigma_2 = \sigma_{\text{ATM}}$, thus justifying the use of equation (6.51).

Remark 6.12.1. *It is worth stressing the fact that we use, in the VV approach, the three strikes K_{25P}, K_{ATM}, K_{25C} retrieved by the respective implied volatilities σ_{25P}, σ_{ATM}, σ_{25C}. These volatilities are consistently defined as seen in Chapter 4, after having run Procedure 4.9.1 to calculate the equivalent* 25D *Vega-weighted butterfly price.*

Some considerations are in order:

- The VV exotic option price we have derived above is for the knock-out option (or a bet paying if the barrier is breached). The knock-in (and other kinds of single bets) can be derived by the usual relationships linking their prices.
- We made some assumptions besides those underpinning the VV approach for the plain vanilla options. The assumption with the greater impact is formula (6.46).
- One of the main flaws of the approach is including the smile in the pricing, while assuming a constant volatility to calculate the survival probability, since standard BS formulae are used with a constant volatility equal to the implied volatility for the ATM strike.
- The path-dependent nature of the exotic options is only roughly taken into account via the VV approach.
- The method can also be employed to pricing double barrier options and double no-touch, provided that the survival probability takes into account both barrier levels.

Although the VV approach to pricing exotic options can be criticized in many respects, likely even more than its use for plain vanilla options, it should nonetheless be noted that the method works surprisingly well and it is extremely satisfactory for market environments where not too steep volatility smiles manifest, such as is usually the case for the EURUSD, as an example.

An alternative characterization of the VV price is possible also for exotic options. In fact, we can express the adjusted price as the sum of the Vega, Vanna and Volga exposures of the contract, each weighted with its cost, inferred from the available market prices of the three basic options, and taking into account the survival probability. We then have the following:

Proposition 6.12.2. *Let x_i for $i = \{1, 2, 3\}$ be the solution of the system* (6.48) *and y_g, for $g \in \{v, w, x\}$, be the solution of the system* (4.17) *of Chapter 4. Then the option price* (6.50) *and the option price*

$$\mathcal{E}(H) = \mathcal{E}^{BS}(H) + \varpi\left[y_v\frac{\partial\mathcal{E}}{\partial\sigma}(H) + y_w\frac{\partial^2\mathcal{E}}{\partial\sigma^2}(H) + y_x\frac{\partial^2\mathcal{E}}{\partial\sigma\,\partial S_0}(H)\right] \tag{6.52}$$

are equal.

The proof of Proposition 6.12.2 is in practice the same as for Proposition 4.6.1, so we omit it.

Example 6.12.1. *Assume we have the following market data in the EURUSD option market (the EURUSD spot rate is* 1.4000*):*

	ATM	*25D RR*	*25D VWB*	P^d	P^f
O/N	*12.00%*	*−0.03%*	*0.20%*	*0.999808*	*0.999890*
1W	*12.50%*	*0.00%*	*0.20%*	*0.999555*	*0.999207*
2W	*12.40%*	*−0.30%*	*0.20%*	*0.999100*	*0.998382*
1M	*11.85%*	*−0.40%*	*0.24%*	*0.997688*	*0.996374*
2M	*11.55%*	*−0.50%*	*0.26%*	*0.995253*	*0.992382*
3M	*11.05%*	*−0.60%*	*0.30%*	*0.992345*	*0.987979*
6M	*10.70%*	*−0.60%*	*0.30%*	*0.985089*	*0.975875*

We also calibrate to these data the LMUV model of Chapter 2.[11]

Suppose we want to price a 6-month (or 182-day) expiry barrier EUR call USD put, struck at 1.4100 *and with barrier level at* 1.5000*. The BS price and Greeks are:*

Price	*Vega*	*Volga*	*Vanna*
0.0040	*−0.071018*	*1.299674*	*−0.590212*

We solve the system (6.48) *and then apply formula* (6.46)*. We get the following results for the smile adjustment:*

	Strike	*Quantity (1)*	*MKT-BS (2)*	*Sur. prob. (3)*	*Adj. (1) × (2) × (3)*
25D P	*1.3204*	*0.6448*	*0.00189*	*69%*	*0.0008*
ATM	*1.3908*	*– 1.0015*	*0*	*69%*	*0.0000*
25D C	*1.4614*	*0.3815*	*0*	*69%*	*0.0000*
				VV smile adj.	*0.0008*

In the table we show the strikes of the three basic hedging options (i.e., the ATM and the two 25D wings), the quantities needed to nil all the volatility-related exposures, the barrier option's survival probability $\Pr(t_H^* > T)$ *and finally the adjustment due to each option and the total. The 25D call option produces no adjustment in this example since its volatility is equal to the ATM (*10.70%*, see the table above with market data). The total smile adjustment is 8 USD pips.*

[11] In Chapter 8 the calibration LMUV will be explained in more detail.

We summarize all the results in the following table, where we also show the price obtained by the LMUV model (all quantities are in US dollars):

BS price	*VV smile adj.*	*VV approach price*	*LMUV price*
0.0040	*0.0008*	*0.0048*	*0.0053*

The VV approach's price is slightly lower than the LMUV's one.

6.12.2 The Vanna–Volga approach for barrier options: variations on the theme

The VV approach for barrier options that we have described in the previous section follows the ideas for the VV approach applied to plain vanilla options. The crucial point is the set-up of a perfectly hedged portfolio under the assumption of one stochastic implied volatility.[12] Actually the VV method can be employed in different ways, and some of them are likely very popular amongst practitioners. We would like to stress that in general those variations have a weaker degree of internal consistency, from a theoretical point of view, than the VV approach we examined. Nonetheless, it is worth studying them since, in the end, we are in any case dealing with approximations (which should never be forgotten) and they may prove to work well for practical purposes.

We start with what we name the *market VV approach* because it retrieves the inputs from the market prices of the basic structures dealing in the market; that is, the 25D **RR** and **VWB**.[13] Moreover, this variation follows the characterization of the exotic option's price in terms of Vega-related costs (i.e., equation (6.52)), but with a difference with respect to what we have done above. Namely, only the costs for the Volga and the Vanna are considered, whereas the Vega cost is assumed to be nil (actually it is small, but not exactly zero). These two costs are extracted from the market prices of the **RR** and **VWB** without solving any system.

Assume at time $t = 0$ we are given, for a given expiry T, the prices, in terms of implied volatility, of the three basic structures, so that we are able to find the three implied volatilities σ_{ATM}, σ_{25C} and σ_{25P},[14] and hence, by means of them, we can retrieve the three basic strikes K_{ATM}, K_{25C} and K_{25P}.[15] Define the following quantities:

$$\mathcal{X}^{RR} = \frac{\partial \mathbf{C}(K_{25C}, \sigma_{25C})}{\partial S_0 \partial \sigma_{25C}} - \frac{\partial \mathbf{P}(K_{25P}, \sigma_{25P})}{\partial S_0 \partial \sigma_{25P}} \tag{6.53}$$

$$\widetilde{\mathcal{W}}^{VWB} = \frac{\partial^2 \mathbf{C}(K_{25C}, \sigma_{25C})}{\partial \sigma_{25C}^2} + \frac{\partial^2 \mathbf{P}(K_{25P}, \sigma_{25P})}{\partial \sigma_{25P}^2} \tag{6.54}$$

Equation (6.53) is Vanna of the risk reversal, whereas equation (6.54) is an approximation for Volga of the **VWB**, since the second derivatives with respect to the implied volatility of the ATM **STDL** are missing. This is due to the small value of Volga for an options struck ATM.

[12] The VV approach under such assumptions was first studied in Castagna and Mercurio [22].

[13] Wystup [62] presents an analysis of the market VV approach to include the smile in the pricing of one-touch options.

[14] For the moment we do not consider the correct definition of the **VWB** wings' implied volatility, see Chapter 4 on that point.

[15] The reader should refer to formula (2.46) and Procedure 2.2.1 in Chapter 2.

Even better, if the ATM is referred to a zero-Delta straddle with premium included, then Volga is just zero.

Remark 6.12.2. *It is worth noticing that, for each instrument, all derivatives are calculated with respect to the market implied volatility (in the VV approach, on the contrary, only one volatility was used for all calculations).*

We can now define the cost for Vanna and the cost for Volga in following way:

$$y_x = \frac{[\mathbf{C}(K_{25C}, \sigma_{25C}) - \mathbf{P}(K_{25P}, \sigma_{25P})] - [\mathbf{C}(K_{25C}, \sigma_{ATM}) - \mathbf{P}(K_{25P}, \sigma_{ATM})]}{\mathcal{X}^{RR}} \tag{6.55}$$

$$y_w = \frac{[\mathbf{C}(K_{25C}, \sigma_{25C}) + \mathbf{P}(K_{25P}, \sigma_{25P})] - [\mathbf{C}(K_{25C}, \sigma_{ATM}) + \mathbf{P}(K_{25P}, \sigma_{ATM})]}{\widetilde{\mathcal{W}}^{VWB}} \tag{6.56}$$

Similarly to before, the Vanna cost is defined as the difference between the **RR** valued with market implied volatility and the same structure valued with the ATM volatility, per unit of Vanna of the **RR**. By the same token, the Volga cost is the difference of the **VWB** valued with the market volatilities and the same structure valued with the ATM volatility, per unit of (approximated) Volga.[16]

We are now able to state the following:

Proposition 6.12.3. *Let y_g, for $g \in \{w, x\}$, be the Vanna and Volga costs calculated as in equations* (6.55) *and* (6.56). *The market VV exotic option price is defined as*

$$\mathcal{E}(H) = \mathcal{E}^{BS}(H) + \varpi \left[y_w \frac{\partial^2 \mathcal{E}}{\partial \sigma_{ATM}^2}(H) + y_x \frac{\partial^2 \mathcal{E}}{\partial \sigma_{ATM} \partial S_0}(H) \right] \tag{6.57}$$

where ϖ is the survival probability.

We notice that Proposition 6.12.3 refers to knock-out barriers and bet contracts paying when the barrier is breached. The usual relationships are used for other contracts; the proposition applies also for double no-touch options.

Some observations for the market VV approach:

- The market VV is similar to the VV approach, in its version in equation (6.52), although the choice to use different volatilities to calculate the Greeks is less theoretically consistent.
- The choice of using the market volatilities referring to each strike simplifies calculations for options whose underlying parity conventions imply a pure Delta (e.g., EURUSD). Actually, the two 25D wings have the same Vega (when the market implied volatility is used) and hence very similar Volga and Vanna, so that the **RR** has almost no Volga whereas the **VWB** has almost no Vanna. In practice, one neglects the small Vanna and Volga.
- The above considerations are no longer valid when the underlying parity conventions imply a premium included in Delta (e.g., USDJPY). In this case options with the same Delta do not yield the same Vega. This means that the **RR** has some Volga and the **VWB** has some Vanna that could be greater than the case of pure Delta. Neglecting these amounts involves an error that is related to the degree of (either positive or negative) steepness and convexity of the implied volatility smile. The standard VV approach, on the other hand, does not make any

[16] The straddle options are missing because their contribution is zero, by assumption.

simplifying assumption about the values of Vega, Volga and Vanna for the options involved in hedging.

- The market VV approach can be modified slightly in such a way that only the ATM implied volatility is used for all calculations, thus making it more similar to the standard VV approach. Unfortunately, in this case the approximation error made in separately extracting the Vanna and Volga costs from the **RR** and **VWB** is much larger, since the two wing strikes will no longer yield the same (25%) Delta and the same Vega, which allows for the computations above. In practice, the assumption that the **RR** has only a Vanna exposure and the **VWB** has only a Volga exposure is stronger when using a single volatility to calculate the volatility-related Greeks. The steeper and more convex the volatility smile (i.e., the difference amongst the three input volatilities), the greater the error.
- The market VV approach can be used to extrapolate/interpolate the smile, but the properties we have examined in Chapter 4 for the standard VV approach no longer hold, and besides it is not ensured that the method will retrieve exactly the three basic implied volatilities.

In Chapter 4 we analysed the actual market definition of **VWB**, which is the (unique) implied volatility to use for the wing options and how to calculate the wing strikes. Since in the market VV approach the basic structures are used to imply the Vanna and Volga costs, then it would be better to correctly take into account the market conventions, so that equation (6.54) modifies as follows:

$$\widetilde{\mathcal{W}}^{VWB} = \frac{\partial^2 \mathbf{C}(K_{VWB}, \sigma_{VWB})}{\partial \sigma^2_{VWB}} + \frac{\partial^2 \mathbf{P}(K_{VWB}, \sigma_{VWB})}{\partial \sigma^2_{VWB}} \tag{6.58}$$

This means that one uses the one implied σ_{VWB} to calculate the strikes, the option values and the Volga of the **VWB**. Accordingly, we have that the Volga cost is

$$y_w = \frac{[\mathbf{C}(K_{VWB}, \sigma_{VWB}) + \mathbf{P}(K_{VWB}, \sigma_{VWB})] - [\mathbf{C}(K_{VWB}, \sigma_{ATM}) + \mathbf{P}(K_{VWB}, \sigma_{ATM})]}{\widetilde{\mathcal{W}}^{VWB}} \tag{6.59}$$

Example 6.12.2. *Suppose market prices and data are those of Example 6.12.1 and we want to calculate the smile adjustment by the market VV approach. We first compute the prices for the 25D call and put options, their Vanna and Volga, then we compute these quantities for the 25D* **RR** *and* **VWB**. *The table below summarizes the results:*

	Volga	*Vanna*	*Mkt premium*	*ATM vol. premium*
25D C	1.3901	2.1465	0.0153	0.0153
25D P	1.0366	−1.6007	0.0175	0.0157
RR		3.7472	−0.0022	−0.0004
VWB	2.4267		0.0328	0.0310

The quantities y_x and y_w are easily derived: $y_x = -0.00048$ and $y_w = 0.00075$. The survival probability and the volatility-related Greeks are those in Example 6.12.1, so that the adjustment to the BS price in formula (6.57) is 0.0009, very similar to the amount obtained via the standard VV approach.

We can also test the impact of using the market definition of **VWB**. *In this case we use* **vwb** $= 0.30$ *and* $\sigma_{VWB} = 11.00\%$. *The table below shows the new values for the required inputs:*

	Volga	*Vanna*	*Mkt premium*	*ATM vol. premium*
25D C	*1.3549*	*2.0923*	*0.0157*	*0.0148*
25D P	*1.0677*	*−1.6487*	*0.0170*	*0.0161*
VWB	*2.4267*		*0.0327*	*0.0309*

The Volga cost changes slightly: $y_w = 0.00076$, *but the effect on the VV adjustment is not significant for practical purposes.*

The basic market VV approach can be modified in a variety of ways, each of them more or less justified by the market-making experience. In general, these modified versions can be summarized in the following formula for the adjusted exotic option price:

$$\mathcal{E}(H) = \mathcal{E}^{\text{BS}}(H) + \varpi\left[\phi_v y_v \frac{\partial \mathcal{E}}{\partial \sigma_{ATM}}(H) + \phi_w y_w \frac{\partial^2 \mathcal{E}}{\partial \sigma_{ATM}^2}(H) + \phi_x y_x \frac{\partial^2 \mathcal{E}}{\partial \sigma_{ATM}\partial S_0}(H)\right] \tag{6.60}$$

where ϕ_v, ϕ_x and ϕ_w more or less give weights to the costs of the respective Vega-related exposures. The costs can be calculated either by solving a system, as in the VV approach, or by considering the **RR** and the **VWB** separately, as in the market VV approach. In this way, if one deems that Vanna is more important than Volga and Vega, then a heavier weight can be assigned to the Vanna cost. Moreover, one may choose to assign time-dependent weights to reflect the importance of the different exposures depending on the time to maturity. Let us examine some specific cases.

Some market makers believe that the cost for convexity should affect the price for long expiry options rather more than for short expiry options. This can be translated into a time-dependent weight of the kind

$$\phi_w = b(1 - e^{-a\tau})$$

where a and b can be calibrated to market conditions and to exotic option prices available. Such a parametrization of ϕ_w tends to 0 as the expiry approaches ($\tau \to 0$) and to b for very long maturities. Similar time-dependent weights can also be devised for the Vega and Vanna costs.

Along the same lines, some practitioners think that some exposures can be considered as fungible for all kinds of contracts, both plain and exotic, whereas Vanna has non-fungible features, since it does not really vanish in proximity to the barrier, in case of a knock-out option, in contrast to the other two Greeks (Vega and Volga). This means that a different weighting should be applied and, namely, equal to one for Vega and Volga, without any survival probability weighting, whereas the weight for Vanna should depend on the type of barrier and thus tend to zero for knock-out options (i.e., the adjustment should tend to zero as the FX spot rate approaches the barrier, so as to ensure that the zero-value condition is warranted). The weight for Vanna can be the survival probability, for example, so we have the following set of weights:

$$\phi_w = \frac{1}{\varpi}, \quad \phi_v = \frac{1}{\varpi}, \quad \phi_x = 1$$

In the same spirit, taking an average of the no-weighting and survival-probability-weighting for Vega and Volga, the following weights can be employed:[17]

$$\phi_w = \frac{1}{2\varpi} + \frac{1}{2}, \quad \phi_v = \frac{1}{2\varpi} + \frac{1}{2}, \quad \phi_x = 1$$

6.12.3 Slippage at the barrier level

Delta-hedging when the FX spot rate is near the barrier level and the time to expiry of the option is short can be a difficult task. We will examine later on the behaviour of Delta in these situations, and it will be clear where the difficulties arise. For the moment, as an intuition, it is enough to hint at the following: when a market maker is short a reverse knock-out option, they will typically be long (short) a possibly huge amount of the underlying FX pair, for Delta-hedging purposes, when the spot rate is around the down (up) barrier. As the barrier level is breached, they will have to unwind the Delta-hedging position by selling (buying back) the underlying FX amount, with a declining (rising) spot rate. In such an event, the order to place in the market is a *stop-loss* (i.e., close the position for an adverse movement of the FX spot rate), and this will typically produce an additional cost known as *slippage*. The stop-loss will be executed only after the specified level is traded in the market, so that in most cases the order is executed at a worse price than the stop-loss level. If the hedger places the stop-loss order at the barrier (i.e., when they need to unwind the Delta-hedge position after the triggering of the barrier), the difference between this level and the actual price at which the closing of the position is executed generates the slippage cost.

The market maker has to include the slippage in the pricing of the barrier option. Assume we want to price a knock-out option: one may impose that the value of the option at the barrier level is not nil, but has some residual value so as to make up for the slippage cost borne by the hedger. In practice, the boundary condition at the barrier level $\mathcal{B}(H, t, T; K, H, \omega, 1, \theta) = 0$ is replaced by

$$\mathcal{B}^*(H, t, T, K, P^d(t, T), P^f(t, T), H, \omega, 1, \theta) = -x\% H \frac{\partial \mathcal{B}^*}{\partial S_t} \tag{6.61}$$

where $x\%$ is the expected slippage cost, expressed as a percentage of the FX spot level at the barrier H. It could be positive or negative depending on whether, respectively, the barrier is above or below the starting FX spot rate. If $x\%$ is, for example, set at 1% and the barrier level is 200, this means that the order is expected to actually be executed at an FX spot rate distant $200 \times 1\% = 2$ numeraire currency units from the stop-loss level 200 (equal to the barrier). The minus sign on the right-hand side of equation (6.61) is due to the fact that the cost is referred to a position in the underlying FX that is the opposite of Delta.

The slippage cost can thus be included in the pricing of the barrier option by valuing a different contract with a slightly different condition when the FX spot rate breaches the trigger level. To price this contract set $\Delta H = x\% H$ and $\mathcal{B}^*$ as the value of the contract with the new feature we want to determine. We can rewrite the equation above as

$$\mathcal{B}^*(H, t; T; K, H, \omega, 1, \theta) + \Delta H \frac{\partial \mathcal{B}^*}{\partial S_t} = 0 \tag{6.62}$$

[17] This adjustment has been proposed by Fisher [28]. The author further refines the survival probability computation by taking the average of the risk-neutral domestic and foreign values.

Since, for an ordinary barrier with knock-out trigger at $H^* = H + \Delta H$, when the FX spot rate $S_t = H$ we have

$$\mathcal{B}(H, t, T, K, P^d(t, T), P^f(t, T), H^*, \omega, 1, \theta) + \Delta H \frac{\partial \mathcal{B}}{\partial S_t} \approx$$
$$\mathcal{B}(H^*, t, T, K, P^d(t, T), P^f(t, T), H^*, \omega, 1, \theta) = 0 \qquad (6.63)$$

by inspection (assuming that[18] $\frac{\partial \mathcal{B}^*}{\partial S_t} = \frac{\partial \mathcal{B}}{\partial S_t}$) we immediately get that $\mathcal{B}^*(H, t; T; K, H, \omega, 1, \theta) \approx \mathcal{B}(H, t; T; K, H^*, \omega, 1, \theta)$, so that the expected value (given the current FX spot rate) of the slippage cost can be included in the pricing by valuing an otherwise equal barrier option, by setting the trigger at a new level $H^* = (1 + x\%)H$. The slippage cost is then defined as[19]

$$\begin{aligned} \mathbf{slg} = &\mathcal{B}(S_t, t, T, K, P^d(t, T), P^f(t, T), H^*, \omega, 1, \theta) \\ &-\mathcal{B}(S_t, t, T, K, P^d(t, T), P^f(t, T), H, \omega, 1, \theta) \end{aligned} \qquad (6.64)$$

Some considerations are in order:

- The option we considered above is a knock-out barrier. Knock-in options should be valued by means of the knock-out–knock-in parity.
- The inclusion of the slippage cost increases the value of the option, since the barrier level is shifted further from the starting FX spot rate. This can be consistent with the fact that the slippage cost is borne by the hedger short the barrier option, so that they sell the contract at a higher price – thus compensating for it. It is not unambiguously clear whether the slippage cost also has to be included when the market maker is bidding the barrier contract, since when they are long the option it is possible to place *take-profit* orders on the barrier level, which eventually could also be executed at better prices,[20] hence producing an unexpected positive windfall. In any case it is possible to partially exploit this exposure, but no sure gain can be extracted from it. As such, the buyer of a reverse knock-out option should not take into account the unwinding of the Delta-hedge position at the breaching of the barrier and the slippage cost should be added asymmetrically in the bid/ask spread on the offer side.[21] In practice, since a market maker is usually a seller of knock-out options, the slippage cost is simply added to the theoretical fair value of the contract and then the bid/ask spread is added algebraically.
- The inclusion of the slippage has a much greater impact on reverse barriers than on standard barriers, and for short-term contracts than for long term. This is also intuitive, and in accordance with the fact that the Delta for a reverse knock-out expiring in a short period can be extremely large compared to an option expiring in a longer period, and to a standard barrier option.
- The slippage percentage $x\%$ may depend on (i) the underlying pair – the scanter its general liquidity, the greater the slippage; (ii) the specific level of the barrier – some levels may be considered psychological and many stop-loss orders can be expected to be placed there,

[18] The assumption is not strong, since $x\%$ is usually very small and well below 1%. It should be stressed anyway that the arguments of the two dervatives are different.

[19] In a much more formal and thorough framework, Shreve *et al.* [60, 61] derive a more precise result, although our less exact formula (6.64) works well for practical purposes.

[20] According to our market experience, we can remember just a couple of cases when that actually occurred. In general, take-profit orders are executed at the specified level for the very mechanics of the spot rate trading.

[21] That is, to the ask price.

causing a larger slippage cost; (iii) the notional amount of the order – bigger orders are usually executed at a worse level.[22]

The slippage cost can also be included in the pricing of the bets. Similar to the case of barrier options, the slippage cost can be calculated by pricing the contract at two different levels of the barrier. It should be stressed that for one-touch options, moving the barrier further from the starting FX spot rate will imply a lower price, so that the slippage cost will be negative, thus decreasing the fair value when included. This is consistent with the fact that the hedger with a long position in the one-touch needs to place a stop-loss in the market to unwind their Delta hedge when the barrier level is breached,[23] so that, rightly enough, the buyer of a one-touch should be compensated for this additional cost borne by requiring a discount on the fair price.

As for double-no-touch options, on the other hand, shifting the barrier levels further away from the starting FX spot level will produce a higher price and then a positive slippage cost to be added to the fair value. Also in this case the procedure is consistent with the fact that the seller of the **DNT** will use stop-loss orders to unwind the Delta hedge, thus requiring a higher price to make up for this additional cost. For other bet contracts similar considerations can be made, but we leave them to the reader as an exercise to better understand the mechanics of the Delta-hedge activity when barriers are breached.

Example 6.12.3. *We want to calculate the slippage cost for the option in Example 6.12.3. We assume that the presumable slippage when the barrier is breached is* 10 *USD pips, or* 0.07% *of the barrier level. The slippage cost is* **slg** = 0.0001, *derived as follows:*

Slippage(%H)	*Price H*	*Price H**	**slg**
0.07%	*0.0040*	*0.0041*	*0.0001*

where the two Price columns show the barrier's price calculated with the original barrier $H = 1.5000$ *and the shifted one* $H^* = 1.5010$.

6.12.4 Delta-hedging near the barrier level

We will see later that Delta-hedging is a difficult task when the FX spot rate is near the barrier level and the time to maturity of the contract is short. This risk is taken into account by the BS (and also other) models, but it is underestimated for the assumptions that generally underpin the model itself, i.e., a continuous path of the FX spot rate without jumps and an absence of transaction costs. Market makers make up for this lacking appraisal by the BS model with some alternative measures, which will be analysed in this sub-section and, in some respects, also in the following two.

Consider the case of a knock-out option struck at K and contingent on the barrier level H. When the time to maturity is long (say, one year) it can reasonably be argued that its value is not noticeably affected by the prolongation or abbreviation of the time to maturity by one day, and this can be held for any level of the underlying spot rate, also when it trades near the

[22] The amount of the stop-loss order to unwind the Delta-hedge position is strictly related to the amount of the implicit one-touch of a barrier; this will be examined below.

[23] We recall that for barrier options the stop-loss order has to be placed by the seller: accordingly, the slippage is positive and increases the fair price of the contract when included.

barrier. On the other hand, if the expiration is approaching (say, in five days), the sensitivity of the option's price to the lengthening or shortening of the time to maturity by one day is appreciable and will depend also on the position of the FX spot rate with respect to the trigger level. The higher the sensitivity, the more untamed the changes of the option's price with respect to the movements of the underlying and the passing of time. This in turn means that Delta rebalancing is more difficult, since the Delta is sheerly unstable.

The considerations above boil down to the employment of the sensitivity of the barrier option's price to a small variation of the time to expiry (i.e., one day) as an indicator of the risk related to the Delta-hedging activity. The shorter the period to expiry and the nearer the current spot rate is to the barrier level, the heftier is the risk. We have formally that the hedging risk is

$$\begin{aligned}\mathbf{hdg} = {} & \mathcal{B}(S_t, t, T, K, P^d(t,T), P^f(t,T), H, \omega, 1, \theta) \\ & -\mathcal{B}(S_t, t, T+1/365, K, P^d(t, T+1/365), P^f(t, T+1/365), H, \omega, 1, \theta)\end{aligned} \tag{6.65}$$

The quantity **hdg** may enter into the pricing of a knock-out in a weighted fashion, so that it affects the price more for short-dated than for long-dated contracts, since the risk is higher in the latter case.

Example 6.12.4. *The hedging risk's cost for the option in Example 6.12.1 is quite negligible, since repricing the same option by shifting the expiry forward one day yields a difference of* 0.02 *USD pips, which is not significant for practical purposes, so that we have in this case* **hdg** $= 0$.

Should we calculate the hedging risk quantity when the time to expiry is 1 month, and the EURUSD spot rate is 1.4800*, we would get* **hdg** $= 0.0002$.

6.12.5 Implicit one-touch and gearing

A long or short position in a reverse knock-out option somehow implies an implicit position in a one-touch option. Assume, as an example, we have a **UOC** struck at K contingent on a knock-out level $H > K$; besides, assume we are on the last day of the life of the contract, just an instant before expiry. When the barrier is breached, the buyer of the option is giving away the payoff they would realize if they could exercise the option, equal to $(H - K)$. In practice, this is the same as if they had a short position in a one-touch option paying away the intrinsic value amount at the barrier. The greater the intrinsic value, and then the amount paid by the implicit one-touch, the higher the risk borne by the holder of the reverse knock-out option.

On the other hand, the seller of the option, who is typically a market maker and a hedger, will have to cope with a dangerous situation as well. In fact, although they are long the implicit one-touch, in dynamically hedging this position near the barrier and with the expiry approaching, they will face very unstable exposures to the underlying FX spot rate with an exceedingly sheer Gamma profile, which can hardly be deemed a comfortable situation. The larger the amount paid by the implicit one-touch, the more difficult the plight of the hedger. Since, in most cases, the market maker is a seller of reverse knock-outs, the implicit one-touch risk is charged in the selling price as an additional cost.

To sum up, define the implicit one-touch amount as

$$\mathbf{iot} = |H - K| \tag{6.66}$$

which is the absolute distance, measured in units of numeraire currency, between the barrier level and the strike. We take the absolute difference because this is the amount paid by the implicit one-touch. This factor may enter into the pricing of a barrier option in a weighted (possibly time-dependent) fashion.

Remark 6.12.3. *It should be clear, but is anyway worth stressing, that the implicit one-touch risk refers only to reverse knock-out options, whereas such risk does not affect the price of standard barriers.*

Related to the implicit one-touch, in some respects, is the gearing of the exotic option. This is the difference between the theoretical value of a plain vanilla option and an otherwise identical barrier option.[24] The gearing reflects the risk that, the barrier not being knocked, the barrier's value changes approaching the corresponding plain vanilla value. The greater the gearing, the larger this movement, which in turn will entail a substantial alteration of the Greeks' exposure and hence the need for rebalancing, which can be difficult and expensive, in particular with reference to the Vega-related derivatives. It is also clear that in this case the costs are suffered by the hedger/market maker, so that the gearing will affect the value of the barrier by increasing its price. We define the gearing formally as

$$\begin{aligned}\mathbf{grn} = &\ \mathrm{Bl}(S_t, t, T, K, P^d(t,T), P^f(t,T), \sigma_{ATM}, \omega) \\ &-\mathcal{B}^{\mathrm{BS}}(S_t, t, T, K, P^d(t,T), P^f(t,T), H, \omega, \theta, \zeta)\end{aligned} \tag{6.67}$$

In formula (6.67) the barrier is priced with the term structure of the ATM volatilities or with the same σ_{ATM} if a constant-parameter BS model is chosen. It should be stressed that the smile is not taken into account in calculating the gearing. Once computed, the gearing should enter into the pricing of the barrier option with a time-dependent weight, increasing as the time to maturity shortens. This is due to the fact that the pace with which the barrier's value approaches the plain vanilla one is more intense the shorter the time to maturity.

Remark 6.12.4. *The implicit one-touch is a risk pertaining only to reverse knock-out options, whereas the gearing is inherent to both reverse and standard knock-outs. Besides, the two risks can be considered complementary in that the implicit one-touch is a measure of the unstable Greeks' exposure when the spot moves near the barrier, as the option's expiry approaches; the gearing risk is related to a stale FX spot rate activity by reflecting the magnitude of the migration of the barrier's value towards the corresponding plain vanilla value.*

Example 6.12.5. *We still refer to Example 6.12.1 and calculate the implicit one-touch and gearing for the barrier option described therein. The implicit one-touch is simply* $\mathbf{iot} = |1.5000 - 1.4100| = 0.0900$ *US dollars.*

The gearing can easily be calculated as follows:

Implied vol.	*Plain vanilla*	*Barrier*
10.70%	*0.0271*	*0.0040*

so that $\mathbf{grn} = 0.0232$.

[24] We recall that the theoretical value of a plain vanilla option is always greater than that of an otherwise identical barrier option, so that the gearing is always a positive number.

A possible choice for the weights of the Delta hedge near the barrier, the implicit one-touch and the gearing risks is the following:

$$w = ae^{-b\tau} \tag{6.68}$$

Clearly, the weights can be different for each of the three risk measures, by choosing different parameters.

6.12.6 Vega-hedge rebalancing

The inclusion of the smile by the VV method (and its variations) is based on the idea of including the costs to set up the hedging portfolio. These costs are given by the difference between the options price computed by the BS formula with their respective implied volatilities dealing in the market, and the same price computed with an ATM volatility. The implicit assumption is that the cost to build the initial hedging portfolio is enough, in the sense that the composition of the latter will not change as the spot moves and the time passes until maturity. Clearly, this is a strong assumption, which can reasonably be held only for short expiries. Mapping the Vega profile for the barrier option can be a useful tool to understand how much Vega-hedge rebalancing we should expect in the future, if some FX spot rate levels trade in the market.

We are interested, besides, in the starting FX spot level and the associated Vega-related exposures that contribute to the total value of the contract, and also the other FX spot levels yielding momentous risk profiles. These can be summarized in the levels referring to the maximum and minimum value of the barrier option's Vega. It is worth noticing that in these points the contract's Vanna is zero, this coming from the fact that it is the first derivative of Vega with respect to the spot price, so that there is no adjustment due to this Greek. On the other hand, Volga is not necessarily nil, so an adjustment to the theoretical BS value may occur, but we should know the expected future shape of the smile and that can be rather difficult. Therefore, we choose to focus on the main exposure, that is Vega, and determine the amount of variation of the exotic option's value due to the change of the implied volatility we are using at the starting valuation's time, and of the volatility entering into the pricing formula when Vega is at its extreme. The basic assumption we make is that the future level of the ATM implied volatility (to plug into the BS formula) is the one that can be inferred from the current volatility smile. We try to clarify this point better by showing the details of the procedure.

Procedure 6.12.1. *We aim to find the extreme values of the barrier option's Vega and determine the consequent adjustment to the BS price. We operate the following steps:*

1. *Given the current spot rate S_t at the valuation's time t, seek the levels S_{min} and S_{max} where Vega reaches, respectively, maximum and the minimum value. This amounts to seeking the FX spot levels that yield a Vanna equal to zero. To determine if this is a maximum or a minimum, we should also check the sign of the second derivative of the Vega with respect to the spot, but we are not really interested in that information.*
2. *Calculate the levels of the ATM strikes related to S_{min} and S_{max}. From the definition of the ATM strike, we would actually also need the implied volatility, but in the end such a degree of precision is excessive, for the very reason that we make other stronger assumptions that may produce even bigger errors than those arising from a slight mis-specification of the ATM strike. So, we simply choose to set them equal to the forward price, given the*

prevailing interest rates:

$$X_{min} = S_{min}\frac{P^f(t,T)}{P^d(t,T)}$$
$$X_{max} = S_{max}\frac{P^f(t,T)}{P^d(t,T)}$$

Comparing the two equations above with the definition of the ATM strike in formula (3.28), *we can see that an approximation has been made.*

3. *Determine the implied volatilities σ_{min} and σ_{max} to use when the ATM strike is, respectively, X_{min} and X_{max}. We assume that they will be equal to the implied volatility we can infer from the current smile for options struck at these levels. To this end we employ Procedure 5.2.1.*
4. *Compute the Vega cost adjustment of a plain vanilla option for the maximum and minimum strike levels as follows:*

$$\Delta\mathbf{C}(K_e) = \mathbf{C}(S_e, X_e, \sigma_e) - \mathbf{C}(S_e, X_e, \sigma_{\text{ATM}})$$

   where $e \in \{max, min\}$.
5. *Calculate Vega of the plain vanilla and Vega of the barrier option for levels of the FX spot rate equal to S_{min} and S_{max}: $\mathcal{V}_{C(S_e,X_e)}$ and $\mathcal{V}_{B(S_e)}$, for $e \in \{max, min\}$.*
6. *The final Vega adjustment to apply to the barrier option is*

$$\mathbf{vad} = \left(\Delta\mathbf{C}(S_{min}, X_{min})\frac{\mathcal{V}_{B(S_{min})}}{\mathcal{V}_{C(S_{min},X_{min})}} + \Delta\mathbf{C}(S_{max}, X_{max})\frac{\mathcal{V}_{B(S_{max})}}{\mathcal{V}_{C(S_{max},X_{max})}}\right)w_a \quad (6.69)$$

   The weight w_a in equation (6.69) *can be time-dependent and a possible choice is to set it equal to the probability of the FX spot rate to reach the levels X_{min} and X_{max}.*

The adjustment is basically based on the idea of formula (6.52), where one suppresses the cost arising from the Vanna and Volga exposures and just considers the Vega exposure. In fact, for each strike, the Vega adjustment is equal to the Vega cost $\Delta\mathbf{C}/\mathcal{V}_C$ inferred from the plain vanilla option times the barrier Vega $\mathcal{V}_B$. As hinted above, since Vanna of the barrier is zero when the spot is equal to the strikes K_{min} and K_{max}, only the Volga adjustment is actually being neglected.

To calculate the plain vanilla and barrier Vegas one may choose to use the current ATM volatility, as one does when employing formula (6.52), or one may choose the volatilities related to the strikes X_{min} and X_{max}, similar to the market VV approach.

Example 6.12.6. *We calculate the Vega-hedge rebalancing cost for the barrier option in Example 6.12.1. We run Procedure 6.12.1 and find the two levels of the FX spot rate associated with the maximum and minimum value of the barrier option's Vega (Vega is computed with the ATM implied volatility set at* 10.70%*). We also calculate the strikes X_{min} and X_{max}, and have the following results:*

S_{max}	S_{min}	X_{max}	X_{min}	$\mathcal{V}_{B(S_{max})}$	$\mathcal{V}_{B(S_{min})}$
1.2613	*1.4235*	*1.2494*	*1.4101*	*0.021080*	*−0.078022*

We can now calculate the premiums and Vega related to the plain vanilla options: we use EUR call USD put options and Vega is computed with the current ATM implied volatility:

S	*X*	*Smile vol.*	*ATM vol.*	*C smile vol.*	*C ATM vol.*	ΔC	*Vega*
1.2613	*1.2494*	*12.23%*	*10.70%*	*0.0424*	*0.0371*	*0.0053*	*0.346418*
1.4235	*1.4101*	*10.62%*	*10.70%*	*0.0416*	*0.0419*	*−0.0003*	*0.390973*

We have the input we need to plug into formula (6.69) *and compute a Vega-rebalancing cost of* **vad** = 0.0004 *US dollars, if we set* $w_a = 1$.

We can now determine the exotic option price according to the market approach. It will simply be the sum of all the adjustments we have shown above:

$$\mathcal{E}(0; H) = \mathcal{E}^{\text{BS}}(0; H) + \mathbf{sml} + \mathbf{slg} + w_h \mathbf{hdg} + w_i \mathbf{iot} + w_g \mathbf{grn} + w_a \mathbf{vad} \qquad (6.70)$$

where **sml** is the VV adjustment calculated with one of the methods examined above.

Example 6.12.7. *We can price the barrier option in Example 6.12.1 with all the adjustments we have described above, by setting the respective weights as in the table below, where the LMUV model's price is also shown for comparison:*

	(1)	*w (2)*	*(1) × (2)*
BS price	*0.0040*	*1.0000*	*0.0040*
sml	*0.0008*	*1.0000*	*0.0008*
slg	*0.0001*	*1.0000*	*0.0001*
hdg	*0.0000*	*0.2500*	*0.0000*
iot	*0.0900*	*0.0030*	*0.0003*
grn	*0.0232*	*0.0050*	*0.0001*
vad	*0.0004*	*1.0000*	*0.0004*
Market approach price			*0.0057*
LMUV price	*0.0053*		

It is worth noticing that the only adjustments that are not also applicable to the LMUV price are the VV smile and the Vega-hedge rebalancing, since these costs should already be taken into account by the stochasticity of the volatility. If we consider the BS price with only these two adjustments we get exactly 53 *USD pips, that is the LMUV price. The costs* **slg**, **hdg**, **iot** *and* **grn** *can also be added to the LMUV model's price, clearly with the due modifications (i.e., all quantities must be calculated by using the LMUV model instead of the BS model).*

6.13 BID/ASK SPREADS

The bid/ask spread for an exotic (barrier) option, different from plain vanilla options, is not dealt in the market in terms of BS implied volatility, but expressed in absolute terms with respect to the fair options price. It should take into account all the risks we have examined above and that are entering into the pricing. Some of these risks are more important for longer expiries, while others should be weighted more for short maturities. The experience of the market-making activity and the style of hedging could also impact on the bid/ask spread associated with each risk.

The first source of the bid/ask spread is the risk referring to the Vega-related exposure, which is strictly connected to the smile adjustment **sml**. The spread can be defined according to the different variations of the VV approach. Let us start with the standard VV approach that yields formula (6.51). We have the quantities of the three basic options that we have to buy/sell so as to keep the total portfolio perfectly hedged. The bid/ask of the exotic option could be defined simply as the absolute sum of the bid/ask for each of the plain vanilla options entering into the hedge portfolio, retrieved from the volatility surface as in Chapter 4. We should anyway take into account that usually the three options can be traded in the market as a spread, which dramatically reduces bid/ask costs,[25] and besides the three separate amounts can be converted into the amount of the three basic structures by employing the relationships

$$
\begin{aligned}
x_{ATM} &= x_2 + \frac{1}{\beta}\frac{x_1 + x_3}{2} \\
x_{RR} &= \frac{1}{2}(x_3 - x_1) \\
x_{VWB} &= \frac{1}{\beta}\frac{x_1 + x_3}{2}
\end{aligned}
$$

where x_1, x_3, x_3 are the amounts of the options struck, respectively, at K_{25P}, K_{ATM}, K_{25C}, the other $x_{\{.\}}$ are the quantities of the structures indicated by the subscript, and β is the ratio to make the **VWB** Vega-neutral. We are not considering the market definition of **VWB** here, but this approximation is rather innocuous for the current purpose. We can now apply the bid/ask referring to each structure, which is half the spread dealing in the market, so that we have the absolute spread in terms of numeraire currency units:

$$
\begin{aligned}
s_{\mathbf{sml}} = \frac{1}{2}[&|x_{ATM}|\mathbf{BA}(\text{ATM})\mathcal{V}(K_{ATM}) \\
&+|x_{RR}|\mathbf{BA}(\mathbf{RR})\mathcal{V}(K_{25C}) + |x_{VWB}|\beta\mathbf{BA}(\mathbf{VWB})\mathcal{V}(K_{25C})]
\end{aligned}
\tag{6.71}
$$

Remark 6.13.1. *The quantity x_2 usually refers to the ATM strike option, so that actually it does not affect the exotic option price in that it does not contribute to any adjustment (see equation* (6.51)*). When determining the bid/ask spread, the quantity x_2 must be included, since the ATM option enters into the hedging portfolio and the bid/ask spread that has to be paid in the market should be charged in the bid/ask of the exotic. In formula* (6.71)*, x_2 enters implicitly in the ATM straddle quantity x_{ATM}.*

The quantity of **VWB** *that the hedger has to trade (x_{VWB}) is expressed in terms of ATM* **STDL**, *according to market conventions. The bid/ask spread is applied on the wing options (see Chapter 5 for bid/ask quoting conventions for the main structures), whose total quantity is $x_{VWB}\beta$, evenly split. This is why the factor β appears in equation* (6.71).

The spreads are all multiplied by the Vega of the ATM and 25D calls for simplicity (the ATM and 25D puts Vegas have the same value).

Example 6.13.1. *We determine the bid/ask spread for the barrier option in Example 6.12.1. From the hedging quantities of the hedging options shown therein, we have the amount of the*

[25] See Chapter 5 for the market bid/ask conventions when dealing spread structures.

three main instruments to trade in the market. The ratio to have a Vega-neutral butterfly is $\beta = 1.24$. The following table summarizes the results:

	Quantity	*Vega*	**BA**	*BA barrier*
ATM **STDL**	*0.587690218*	*0.384793604*	*0.30%*	*0.00068*
25*D* **RR**	*0.131634034*	*0.310504432*	*0.15%*	*0.00006*
25*D* ***VWB***	*0.413813961*	*0.310504432*	*0.05%*	*0.00008*
1/2 Total				*0.00041*

So the amount to be added and subtracted from the mid-market value is 4 *USD pips.*

By the same token, if we are pricing the exotic via a generalized market VV approach as in formula (6.60), we are given the quantity of **RR** and **VWB** to trade as a hedge, i.e., y_x and y_x respectively. In this case we also have to take into account the bid/ask spread for the ATM volatility level, which is not explicitly included in the formula and which refers to the Vega exposure of the barrier. Thus, we first calculate the quantities for each of the basic instruments as follows:

$$x_{ATM} = \frac{\frac{\partial \mathcal{E}}{\partial \sigma_{ATM}}}{\mathcal{V}(K_{ATM})}$$

$$x_{RR} = \frac{\frac{\partial^2 \mathcal{E}}{\partial \sigma_{ATM} \partial S}}{\mathcal{X}^{RR}}$$

$$x_{VWB} = \frac{1}{\beta} \frac{\frac{\partial^2 \mathcal{E}}{\partial^2 \sigma_{ATM}^2}}{\widetilde{\mathcal{W}}^{VWB}}$$

The spread can be determined as

$$s_{\mathbf{sml}} = \frac{1}{2} \Big[\gamma x_{ATM} \mathbf{BA}(\text{ATM}) \mathcal{V}(K_{ATM}) + \phi_x x_{RR} \mathbf{BA}(\mathbf{RR}) \mathcal{V}(K_{25C}) + \phi_w x_{VWB} \beta \mathbf{BA}(\mathbf{VWB}) \mathcal{V}(K_{25C}) \Big] \quad (6.72)$$

where $\gamma \geq 1$ is a multiplying factor to enlarge the bid/ask spread, given the higher volatility risks related to the exotic contract. We also kept the weights $\phi_{\{.\}}$ referring to the Vanna and Volga exposures.

All other risks are not directly related to the bid/ask spread directly observable in the market, as for the Vega-related risk. In this case we must provide for a spread just as a (possibly time-dependent) function of their single values. Let us start with the same sequence as above, considering the slippage at the barrier. Its cost is already included in the fair exotic price, so it is a sort of double counting to also add a specific bid/ask for it. Delta hedging near the barrier and gearing may cause a bid/ask spread generated by their values weighted by a time-dependent function:

$$s_{\mathbf{hdg}} = w_{\mathbf{hdg}}^{ba} \mathbf{hdg} \quad (6.73)$$

$$s_{\mathbf{grn}} = w_{\mathbf{grn}}^{ba} \mathbf{grn} \quad (6.74)$$

where each $w_{\{.\}}^{ba} = ae^{-b\tau}$, each with its own parameters a and b. On the other hand, the implicit one-touch and Vega-hedge rebalancing can be assumed to produce a bid/ask spread as a simple percentage of their values:

$$s_{\text{iot}} = x_{\text{iot}}\%\mathbf{iot} \tag{6.75}$$

$$s_{\text{vad}} = x_{\text{vad}}\%\mathbf{vad} \tag{6.76}$$

Finally, the bid/ask spread for the exotic contract contingent on barrier H is the sum of all the spreads above:

$$\mathbf{BA}(H) = s_{\text{sml}} + s_{\text{hdg}} + s_{\text{grn}} + s_{\text{iot}} + s_{\text{vad}} \tag{6.77}$$

which is symmetrically added to and subtracted from the fair mid-market price in equation (6.70).

Example 6.13.9. *We complete the pricing of the option in Example 6.12.1 by determining the full bid/ask spread. The following table shows the spread for the additional risks:*

	(1)	*w (2)*	*(1) × (2)*
hdg	*0.0000*	*0.0125*	*0.0000*
iot	*0.0900*	*0.0010*	*0.0001*
grn	*0.0232*	*0.0003*	*0.0000*
vad	*0.0004*	*0.0100*	*0.0000*
		Total	*0.0001*

So we have that the total bid/ask spread is $\mathbf{BA}(H) = 0.0004 + 0.0001 = 0.0005$ *US dollars.*

6.14 MONITORING FREQUENCY

In previous sections we examined barrier and bet contracts whose payoff is contingent on the breaching of a given level by the FX spot rate. The monitoring of the price in the market is continuous, in that it is enough that it is traded in a good size[26] when one of the main marketplaces is open (basically, weekends are not considered in the monitoring).

Barriers can also be discretely monitored, with some predefined frequency. The most common alternative to continuous monitoring, especially for pairs against the euro, is the daily frequency referenced to the ECB fixing.[27] Less usually, the monitoring may be set at a weekly or monthly fixing. Monitoring only at expiry deserves special treatment, and we defer its examination to the next chapter, since what we will present here does not apply to this feature. Unfortunately, closed-form formulae to evaluate such contracts do not exist, so one has to resort to some numerical scheme to properly take into account the discrete monitoring: Monte Carlo, trees or finite differences are the most widely adopted. An alternative is the analytical approximation provided by Broadie *et al.* [16, 17] and by Kou [42].[28] It works well for practical purposes for daily frequency, then for lower frequencies the accuracy of the approximation deteriorates and it is worth employing one of the numerical procedures we mentioned above.

Assume we have an exotic contract contingent on the barrier level H and monitored m times in one year. The following proposition holds:

[26] By "good size" is meant an amount of base currency that can be considered twice or three times the minimum amount traded by professional market makers. For example, for the EURUSD it is 3 million euros.

[27] See Section 5.4 for the ECB fixing.

[28] We refer to those articles for the proofs of the results we show here.

Proposition 6.14.1. *Let $\mathcal{E}(H)$ be the price of an exotic option contingent on the barrier level H, and $\mathcal{E}_m(H)$ be the price of an otherwise identical exotic option with annual period frequency $1/m$ (i.e., monitored at m equally spaced points until expiry). Then for the discrete monitored exotic options, we have the approximation*

$$\mathcal{E}_m(H) = \mathcal{E}(He^{\pm\beta\sigma\sqrt{\tau/m}}) + o(1/\sqrt{\tau}) \tag{6.78}$$

with + for a barrier level above the starting FX spot rate at the evaluation time, and − for a barrier level above the starting FX spot rate. The constant

$$\beta = -\frac{\zeta(1/2)}{\sqrt{2\pi}} \approx 0.5826$$

with ζ being the Riemann zeta function.

For the proof, see Kou [42]. The approach can be used for any kind of contract dependent on a single barrier, but it can also safely be employed to calculate the adjustment for contracts dependent on two barriers (see Horfelt [38] for a discussion on the extension of the method).

One of the difficulties with discrete monitored barriers, faced by the hedger, is the unwinding of the Delta hedge after breach of the barrier levels. This is a momentous issue for reverse knock-out options with a short time to maturity. In fact, if the FX spot rate touches the barrier between two observation times defined by the frequency period (e.g., one ECB fixing and that of the following day), then they have to decide whether to close the Delta-hedge spot position in the underlying FX rate, thus assuming that the spot will not revert to the levels where the option is still alive, or leave the position unchanged. The problem is partially solved by using the pricing formula with adjustment (6.78), which implicitly suggests keeping on Delta hedging even for levels above (or below) the contract barrier level H, although the problem is simply shifted to the adjusted level $He^{\pm\beta\sigma\sqrt{\tau/m}}$. Once this level is reached, again, one has to choose whether to unwind or not the Delta position.

In order to cope with this problem and to include the related risks in the pricing of discrete barrier options, we propose the following Delta-hedging strategy for a discrete barrier option (we assume we are working with knock-out options):

Strategy 6.14.1. *The market maker completely unwinds the Delta-hedge positions whenever the barrier level $He^{\pm\beta\sigma\sqrt{\tau/m}}$ is breached as they were hedging a continuously monitored barrier (the pricing formula in this case evaluates the contracts as zero, and the Delta is nil); if the FX spot rate reverts so that the contract is back in the "live" region, then the Delta hedge suggested by the pricing formula is set up again.*

This strategy has also been proposed for plain vanilla options, with reference to the strike price, and it is called *stop-loss-start-gain* (SLSG). Clearly this rule implies some costs that should be borne, since Delta is traded (for example, in case of a **UOC**) at some level of the FX rate $S_{t^*} = He^{\pm\beta\sigma\sqrt{\tau/m}} + \varepsilon$, and it is set up again at a level $S_{t^*} = He^{\pm\beta\sigma\sqrt{\tau/m}} - \varepsilon$. Letting $\varepsilon \to 0$ we have that the expected cost of the rebalancing of this strategy is equal to the so-called *expected local time* of the FX spot rate's process during a given period τ.[29] As far as discrete barriers are concerned, the period is given by the monitoring frequency.

[29] See Carr and Jarrow [18]. The local time is the amount of time spent around a given level by the FX spot rate, in an interval of time.

To make things concrete, let us consider a reverse knock-out call option with barrier H, daily monitored. It is clear that we perform the (SLSG) Delta-hedging strategy only if the FX spot is around the (adjusted) barrier level and for the period between two observations, i.e., one day in this case. It is a well-known result that the local time for an SLSG strategy operated with one unit of underlying, in a given period and for a given level of the FX spot rate, can be measured by the time value of plain vanilla option struck at the former level and expiring in the same time interval (i.e., one day in our case). So, provided that the FX rate reaches the adjusted barrier level $S_t = He^{\beta\sigma\sqrt{\tau/m}}$, the local time will be the time value of (either a call or a put) plain vanilla option struck at a level equal to the barrier and maturing in one day:

$$\Lambda = \mathrm{Bl}(He^{\beta\sigma\sqrt{\tau/m}}, 0, 1/365, He^{\beta\sigma\sqrt{\tau/m}}, P^d(0, 1/365), P^f(0, 1/365), \sigma, \omega) \quad (6.79)$$

where $\omega = 1$ if the barrier level is above the FX spot rate at time $t = 0$, or $\omega = -1$ otherwise. Equation (6.79) evaluates the expected local time assuming that we are in a BS environment. We can use the current market value for the interest rates and set σ equal to the current overnight level. We are interested, though, in finding the value of the local time for an SLSG strategy operated with an amount Δ_t (Delta of the exotic option), which is time-dependent. To this end, we make the simplifying assumption that the local time for each day is constant, and express it as a percentage of the adjusted barrier $\widehat{\Lambda} = \Lambda/(He^{\pm\beta\sigma\sqrt{\tau/m}})$. At any time t we then have that the expected local time (or, alternatively, the expected rebalancing cost around the barrier level) is $\Delta_t\widehat{\Lambda}He^{\pm\beta\sigma\sqrt{\tau/m}}$.

By a reasoning similar to that for the slippage cost of a continuous barrier, we want that when the barrier is breached, the option is worth an amount equal to zero plus a value compensating for the loss due to the local time at the barrier during one day (the Delta amount held to hedge has the opposite sign of the mathematical first derivatives with respect to the spot):

$$\mathcal{B}^*(He^{\beta\sigma\sqrt{\tau/m}}, t, T, K, P^d(t,T), P^f(t,T), He^{\beta\sigma\sqrt{\tau/m}}, \omega, 1, \theta) = -\Delta\widehat{\Lambda}He^{\beta\sigma\sqrt{\tau/m}} \quad (6.80)$$

and by repeating the same argument as above for the slippage cost, we have

$$\begin{aligned}\mathbf{mtg} = &\ \mathcal{B}(S_t, t, T, K, P^d(t,T), P^f(t,T), \widetilde{H}^*, \omega, 1, \theta) \\ &-\mathcal{B}(S_t, t, T, K, P^d(t,T), P^f(t,T), \widetilde{H}, \omega, 1, \theta)\end{aligned} \quad (6.81)$$

where $\widetilde{H} = He^{\pm\beta\sigma\sqrt{\tau/m}}$ and $\widetilde{H}^* = (1+\widehat{\Lambda})\widetilde{H}$.

Equation (6.81) can also be employed for lower frequencies, as weekly or monthly observation periods, by changing the expiry of the option in (6.79), although it is more appropriate to resort to numerical procedures, as mentioned above. On the other hand, equation (6.81) can also be used for standard knock-outs, double knock-outs and bet contracts.

Example 6.14.1. *Assume that the barrier option in Example 6.12.1 is monitored daily. Then the adjusted barrier is* 1.5049 *and the option's value is* 0.0046 *US dollars.*

To determine the discrete monitoring cost, we first have to compute the Λ*, which is equal to a plain vanilla EUR call USD put option expiring in one day, struck at* 1.5049 *and evaluated with a spot rate at the same level as the strike (we use the O/N implied volatility* 12.50%*). Its price is 37 USD pips; that is,* 0.25% *of the adjusted barrier level* 1.5049*. The new barrier*

$\widetilde{H}^* = 1.5086$, *so that the difference between a barrier option valued with the level* 1.5049 *and the adjusted one* 1.5086 *yields* **mtg** $= 0.0005$ *US dollars; that is, almost* 11% *of the theoretical price of* 46 *USD pips. This percentage is in line with what some traders "feel" they should charge as a discrete monitoring cost, and also with other ways to determine empirically the latter, such as the approach explained in Becker and Wystup [3].*

7 Other Exotic Options

7.1 INTRODUCTION

In this chapter we examine a varied range of exotic contracts. They are less frequently traded in the market, yet deserve a detailed treatment for pricing and risk management. Some of them can simply be derived by a static replication argument by means of standard plain vanilla options (e.g., volatility swaps and barrier options monitored at expiry, denominated *at-end* or *at-expiry* barriers) or by some other tricks allowing for the use of already derived formulae for other contracts (e.g., first-in-then-out barriers). For some others, specific pricing formulae have to be devised (e.g., forward start options and compound options).

We start with barrier options monitored at expiry, ideally carrying on and completing the analysis of the previous chapter.

7.2 AT-EXPIRY BARRIER OPTIONS

Barrier options monitored only at expiry can be either knock-in or knock-out, but they can only be of the reverse kind. Actually, it is easy to see that if the barrier is set at a level where the option is out-of-the-money at expiry, and whose effect operates only at the end of the contract, then the exotic option is exactly equal to an otherwise identical plain vanilla option. The pricing of at-expiry barrier options can be performed by means of plain vanilla options and digitals. They have been analysed at length in Chapter 5, so we effortlessly derive pricing formulae.

Definition 7.2.1. ***At-expiry barrier FX option contract.*** *An XXXYYY at-expiry barrier option is a contract in all respects equal to an otherwise identical barrier option, the only difference being that the barrier is monitored only at maturity. At this time the option can be exercised only if the terminal FX spot rate is between the strike price and the barrier, in the knock-out's case, or above or below the barrier level (depending on whether the option is, respectively, a base currency call or put), in the knock-in's case.*

We start with a knock-out at-expiry call option expiring in T and struck at K, contingent on the barrier $H > K$. Its terminal payoff can be written as

$$\mathbf{KOCE}(K, T, H) = \max[S_T - K; 0]\mathbf{1}_{\{S_T < H\}} \tag{7.1}$$

which can be decomposed in turn in terms of two plain vanilla options and a digital option as follows:

$$\mathbf{KOCE}(K, T, H) = \mathbf{C}(K, T) - \mathbf{C}(H, T) - (H - K)\mathbf{Dc}_n(H, T) \tag{7.2}$$

which is equal to a call spread struck at K and H, plus a digital call struck at H paying a numeraire currency amount $H - K$. The pricing formula at time t, in a BS environment, is

$$\begin{aligned}\mathbf{KOCE}^{\text{BS}}(S_t, t, T, K, H) = {} & \text{Bl}(S_t, t, T, K, P^d(t, T), P^f(t, T), \sigma(K), 1) \\ & - \text{Bl}(S_t, t, T, H, P^d(t, T), P^f(t, T), \sigma(H), 1) \\ & - (H - K)\mathbf{Dc}_n^{\text{BS}}(S_t, t, T, H)\end{aligned} \tag{7.3}$$

It should be stressed that the smile is properly taken into account in the pricing formula (7.3), both in the plain vanilla contracts (valued by the correct implied volatility σ inferred from market prices) and in the digital call (valued as we described in Chapter 5).

The knock-in can be priced straightforwardly by means of the relationships (6.1) and (6.2) of Chapter 6, which still hold. Therefore, we have that a knock-in at-expiry call is

$$\begin{aligned}\mathbf{KICE}^{\text{BS}}(S_t, t, T, K, H) &= \mathbf{C}(K, T) - \mathbf{KOCE}(S_t, t, T, K, H)\\ &= \text{Bl}(S_t, t, T, H, P^d(t, T), P^f(t, T), \sigma(H), 1) \\ &+ (H - K)\mathbf{Dc}_n^{\text{BS}}(S_t, t, T, H)\end{aligned} \tag{7.4}$$

By the same token we may obtain the pricing formulae for the put options. The knock-out at-expiry put is

$$\begin{aligned}\mathbf{KOPE}^{\text{BS}}(S_t, t, T, K, H) &= \text{Bl}(S_t, t, T, K, P^d(t, T), P^f(t, T), \sigma(K), -1)\\ &- \text{Bl}(S_t, t, T, H, P^d(t, T), P^f(t, T), \sigma(H), -1)\\ &- (K - H)\mathbf{Dp}_n^{\text{BS}}(S_t, t, T, H)\end{aligned} \tag{7.5}$$

whereas the knock-in put is

$$\begin{aligned}\mathbf{KIPE}^{\text{BS}}(S_t, t, T, K, H) &= \text{Bl}(S_t, t, T, H, P^d(t, T), P^f(t, T), \sigma(H), -1)\\ &+ (K - H)\mathbf{Dp}_n^{\text{BS}}(S_t, t, T, H)\end{aligned} \tag{7.6}$$

Remark 7.2.1. *At-expiry barrier option prices are model-independent in that they are completely determined by the current market prices of the plain vanilla options. In fact, the digital option entering into the decomposition of the terminal payoff is also totally derived by the plain vanilla option prices. So any model, if perfectly fitting market prices (i.e., the current market volatility smile for the barrier option's expiry) will yield exactly the same price as the BS model, when employed by plugging the market implied volatilities into the formulae and with proper pricing of the digital.*

Bid/ask spreads are calculated similarly to what we have seen for plain vanilla and digital options. To avoid wide spreads and adhere to market conventions, we may keep fixed one of the two options entering into the replica portfolio, so that we have, for a knock-out call, for example:

$$\mathbf{KOCE}_b(K, T, H) = \mathbf{C}_b(K, T) - \mathbf{C}_m(H, T) - (H - K)\mathbf{Dc}_{n\_b}(H, T) \tag{7.7}$$

$$\mathbf{KOCE}_a(K, T, H) = \mathbf{C}_a(K, T) - \mathbf{C}_m(H, T) - (H - K)\mathbf{Dc}_{n\_a}(H, T) \tag{7.8}$$

where b, a, m indicate, respectively, the bid, ask and mid price. On the other hand, for knock-in call options:

$$\mathbf{KICE}_b(K, T, H) = \mathbf{C}_m(K, T) - \mathbf{KOCE}_a(S_t, t, T, K, H) \tag{7.9}$$

$$\mathbf{KICE}_a(K, T, H) = \mathbf{C}_m(K, T) - \mathbf{KOCE}_b(S_t, t, T, K, H) \tag{7.10}$$

The put option bid/ask prices are calculated in similar fashion. The delayed and cash settlement features are easily handled in the same way as described in Chapter 5 for plain vanilla and digital options.

7.3 WINDOW BARRIER OPTIONS

Definition 7.3.1. ***Window barrier FX option contract.*** *An XXXYYY window barrier option is a contract in all respects equal to an otherwise ordinary barrier option, except for the fact that the barrier is active only for a specified period* (window) *included between the start and maturity of the contract. Hence, such an option is characterized by three basic instants in time: time t_1 when the barrier starts being effective, time t_2 when the barrier stops being effective, and time T when the option expires.*

In order to derive a pricing formula for this contract, we first need to derive the pricing formula for a particular kind of window barrier, whose barrier's effectiveness starts in $t_1 = t$, i.e., at inception of the contract, and $t_2 \leq T$ is when the barrier's effectiveness stops. The valuation can be performed in a BS setting and the general pricing formula is:[1]

$$\begin{aligned}
\mathcal{WB}^{\mathrm{BS}}(S_t, t, T, K, H, \omega, \theta, \zeta, t, t_2) &= \omega P^d(t, T) \\
&\times \Bigg\{ S e^{\int_t^T v_s + \frac{\varsigma_s^2}{2} ds} \Phi_2\Big(\theta\zeta d_1(S_t, H, t_2), \omega d_1(S_t, K, T), \omega\theta\zeta\rho\Big) \\
&- K\Phi_2\Big(\theta\zeta d_2(S_t, H, t_2), \omega d_2(S_t, K, T), \omega\theta\zeta\rho\Big) \\
&- e^{\int_t^T v_s + \frac{\varsigma_s^2}{2} ds}\left(\frac{\widetilde{H}_t}{S_t}\right)^{2\beta}\left(\frac{\widetilde{H}_t^2}{S_t}\right)\Phi_2\Big(\theta d_1(\frac{\widetilde{H}_t^2}{S_t}, H, t_2), \omega d_1(\frac{\widetilde{H}_t^2}{S_t}, K, T), \omega\theta\rho\Big) \\
&+ K\left(\frac{\widetilde{H}_t}{S_t}\right)^{2\beta}\Phi_2\Big(\theta d_2(\frac{\widetilde{H}_t^2}{S_t}, H, t_2), \omega d_2(\frac{\widetilde{H}_t^2}{S_t}, K, T), \omega\theta\rho\Big)\Bigg\}
\end{aligned} \tag{7.11}$$

The notation is the same as that introduced in Chapter 6, except for the additional parameter $\rho = \sqrt{\frac{\int_t^{t_2} \varsigma_s^2 ds}{\int_t^T \varsigma_s^2 ds}}$ and for $\Phi_2(x, y, \rho)$ denoting the bivariate normal distribution function.

We can use formula (7.11) for the general window barrier case so that the price of a window barrier option reduces to the computation of cumulative trivariate normal distribution functions. A compact formula is then

$$\begin{aligned}
\mathcal{WB}^{\mathrm{BS}}(S_t, t, T, K, H, \omega, \theta, \zeta, t_1, t_2) &= \omega P^d(t, T) \\
&\times \Bigg\{ H e^{\int_{t_1}^T v_s + \frac{\varsigma_s^2}{2} ds} F\Bigg(\ln\frac{S_t}{H}, \int_t^{t_1} \varsigma_s^2 ds, \frac{\theta}{\sqrt{\int_{t_1}^{t_2} \varsigma_s^2 ds}}, \frac{\theta\int_{t_1}^{t_2} v_s + \varsigma_s^2 ds}{\sqrt{\int_{t_1}^{t_2} \varsigma_s^2 ds}}, \frac{\omega}{\sqrt{\int_{t_1}^{T} \varsigma_s^2 ds}}, \\
&\omega\frac{\ln\frac{H}{K} + \int_{t_1}^T v_s + \varsigma_s^2 ds}{\sqrt{\int_{t_1}^T \varsigma_s^2 ds}}, \omega\theta\zeta\rho, 1\Bigg) \\
&- KF\Bigg(\ln\frac{S_t}{H}, \int_t^{t_1} \varsigma_s^2 ds, \frac{\theta}{\sqrt{\int_{t_1}^{t_2} \varsigma_s^2 ds}}, \frac{\theta\int_{t_1}^{t_2} v_s ds}{\sqrt{\int_{t_1}^{t_2} \varsigma_s^2 ds}}, \frac{\omega}{\sqrt{\int_{t_1}^{T} \varsigma_s^2 ds}}, \omega\frac{\ln\frac{H}{K} + \int_{t_1}^T v_s ds}{\sqrt{\int_{t_1}^T \varsigma_s^2 ds}}, \omega\theta\zeta\rho, 0\Bigg) \\
&- e^{\int_{t_1}^T v_s + \frac{\varsigma_s^2}{2} ds}\left(\frac{\widetilde{H}_{t_1}}{H}\right)^{2\beta}\frac{\widetilde{H}_{t_1}^2}{H}
\end{aligned}$$

[1] This formula, as well as the next one for a general window barrier option, has been derived by Rapisarda [54].

$$F\left(\ln\frac{S_t}{H}, \int_t^{t_1} \varsigma_s^2 ds, -\frac{\theta}{\sqrt{\int_{t_1}^{t_2} \varsigma_s^2 ds}}, \theta\frac{\ln\frac{\widetilde{H}_{t_1}^2}{H^2} + \int_{t_1}^{t_2} v_s + \varsigma_s^2 ds}{\sqrt{\int_{t_1}^{t_2} \varsigma_s^2 ds}}, -\frac{\omega}{\sqrt{\int_{t_1}^{T} \varsigma_s^2 ds}}, \omega\frac{\ln\frac{\widetilde{H}_{t_1}}{HK} + \int_{t_1}^{T} v_s + \varsigma_s^2 ds}{\sqrt{\int_{t_1}^{T} \varsigma_s^2 ds}}, \omega\theta\rho, -(1+2\beta)\right) + K\left(\frac{\widetilde{H}_{t_1}}{H}\right)^{2\beta}$$

$$F\left(\ln\frac{S_t}{H}, \int_t^{t_1} \varsigma_s^2 ds, -\frac{\theta}{\sqrt{\int_{t_1}^{t_2} \varsigma_s^2 ds}}, \theta\frac{\ln\frac{\widetilde{H}_{t_1}^2}{H^2} + \int_{t_1}^{t_2} v_s ds}{\sqrt{\int_{t_1}^{t_2} \varsigma_s^2 ds}}, -\frac{\omega}{\sqrt{\int_{t_1}^{T} \varsigma_s^2 ds}}, \omega\frac{\ln\frac{\widetilde{H}_{t_1}^2}{HK} + \int_{t_1}^{T} v_s ds}{\sqrt{\int_{t_1}^{T} \varsigma_s^2 ds}}, \omega\theta\rho, -2\beta\right)\Bigg\} \tag{7.12}$$

where

$$\begin{aligned} &F(x_t, \tau_t, A, B, C, D, \rho, \eta) \\ &= \exp\left[\frac{\eta^2\tau_t}{2} + \eta x\right]\frac{1}{\sqrt{2\pi}}\int_{-\infty}^{b_1} \exp\left[-\frac{\widetilde{x}}{2}\right]\Phi_2\left(\frac{b_2 - r_{21}\widetilde{x}}{\sqrt{1-r_{21}^2}}, \frac{b_3 - r_{31}\widetilde{x}}{\sqrt{1-r_{31}^2}}, \rho\right)d\widetilde{x} \\ &= \exp\left[\frac{\eta^2\tau_t}{2} + \eta x\right]\Phi_3[\mathbf{b}, R] \end{aligned}$$

with $\Phi_2(a, b, \rho)$ the bivariate normal distribution function

$$\begin{cases} r_{21} = -\dfrac{A\sqrt{\tau_t}}{\sqrt{1+A^2\tau_t}} \\ r_{31} = -\dfrac{C\sqrt{\tau_t}}{\sqrt{1+C^2\tau_t}} \\ b_1 = \dfrac{d-(x+\eta\tau_t)}{\sqrt{\tau_t}} \\ b_2 = [B + A(x+\eta\tau_t)]\sqrt{1-r_{21}^2} \\ b_3 = [D + C(x+\eta\tau_t)]\sqrt{1-r_{31}^2} \\ r_{32} = \rho\sqrt{(1-r_{21}^2)(1-r_{31}^2)} + r_{21}r_{31} \\ \rho = \dfrac{r_{32} - r_{31}r_{21}}{\sqrt{(1-r_{21}^2)(1-r_{31}^2)}} \end{cases}$$

$\mathbf{b} = (b1; b2; b3)$ and $R = (r_{ij})$ denoting the vector of independent entries of a three-dimensional correlation matrix. The parametrization used for the trivariate distribution function is that by Genz [32].

The price in formula (7.12) does not include the smile effects. We could use the market approach (as explained in Chapter 6 for standard barrier options) to determine the adjustments to take the smile into account, and possibly incorporate all other risks. Nevertheless, the nature of the window barrier options entails a more thorough treatment of the term structure of the volatility, so that it is advisable to price this kind of option with a stochastic volatility model. In this case, numerical procedures will be required, unless one employs the LMUV model – thus obtaining a closed-form formula which is the weighted average of the BS prices (see Chapter 2, formula (2.28), where the price for the plain vanilla option should be replaced by (7.12)).

The bid/ask spreads can be calculated by the market approach for standard barrier options. The rougher treatment of the risks, related to the window barriers, has a less dangerous impact in this case. If the window barrier has a delayed or cash settlement feature, we can simply apply the same treatment as for standard barrier contracts (see Chapter 6).

7.4 FIRST–THEN AND KNOCK-IN–KNOCK-OUT BARRIER OPTIONS

Barrier options can be contingent on the breaching of two barriers, as in the double-barrier case, but one of the two barrier levels can produce a knock-in and the other a knock-out level: in practice, an option must first be activated and then it can be cancelled. The second level may be an activating barrier as well, so that both barriers must be breached, in the given sequence, to yield a plain vanilla option.

Definition 7.4.1. ***First–then barrier FX option contract.*** *An XXXYYY first–then barrier option is a contract in all respects equal to an otherwise identical double-barrier option, the only difference being that one of the two barrier levels knocks-in the option and must be reached first, the other barrier level knocks-out or knocks-in the option, provided that it has been activated (i.e., provided that the knock-in level has been breached some time before during the life of contract).*

To evaluate this contract within a BS environment is rather simple, since we may resort to the put–call symmetry (2.49) of Chapter 2, which also holds for barrier options in the following version:[2]

$$\begin{aligned}&\mathcal{B}^{\text{BS}}(S_t, t, T, K, P^d(t,T), P^f(t,T), H, 1, 1, -1)\\&\quad= \frac{K}{S_t}\mathcal{B}^{\text{BS}}\left(S_t, t, T, \frac{S_t^2}{K}, P^f(t,T), P^d(t,T), \frac{S_t^2}{H}, -1, -1, -1\right)\end{aligned} \tag{7.13}$$

A down-and-in call is equal to an up-and-in put option, with a modified strike and barrier level, times the ratio of the strike price to the FX spot rate. It should also be noted that the discount factors have been inverted. For the other cases, we have

$$\begin{aligned}&\mathcal{B}^{\text{BS}}(S_t, t, T, K, P^d(t,T), P^f(t,T), H, 1, -1, -1)\\&\quad= \frac{K}{S_t}\mathcal{B}^{\text{BS}}\left(S_t, t, T, \frac{S_t^2}{K}, P^f(t,T), P^d(t,T), \frac{S_t^2}{H}, -1, 1, -1\right)\end{aligned} \tag{7.14}$$

$$\begin{aligned}&\mathcal{B}^{\text{BS}}(S_t, t, T, K, P^d(t,T), P^f(t,T), H, 1, 1, 1)\\&\quad= \frac{K}{S_t}\mathcal{B}^{\text{BS}}\left(S_t, t, T, \frac{S_t^2}{K}, P^f(t,T), P^d(t,T), \frac{S_t^2}{H}, -1, -1, 1\right)\end{aligned} \tag{7.15}$$

$$\begin{aligned}&\mathcal{B}^{\text{BS}}(S_t, t, T, K, P^d(t,T), P^f(t,T), H, 1, -1, 1)\\&\quad= \frac{K}{S_t}\mathcal{B}^{\text{BS}}\left(S_t, t, T, \frac{S_t^2}{K}, P^f(t,T), P^d(t,T), \frac{S_t^2}{H}, -1, 1, 1\right)\end{aligned} \tag{7.16}$$

[2] These relationships and the formulae for the first–then options are derived by Haug [36].

For the sake of completeness, we also present here the put–call symmetry for double-barrier options, although we will not use the result in what follows:

$$\begin{aligned}&\mathcal{DB}^{\text{BS}}(S_t, t, T, K, P^d(t,T), P^f(t,T), L, U, 1, 1)\\&= \frac{K}{S_t}\mathcal{DB}^{\text{BS}}\left(S_t, t, T, \frac{S_t^2}{K}, P^f(t,T), P^d(t,T), \frac{S_t^2}{L}, \frac{S_t^2}{U}, -1, 1\right)\end{aligned} \tag{7.17}$$

$$\begin{aligned}&\mathcal{DB}^{\text{BS}}(S_t, t, T, K, P^d(t,T), P^f(t,T), L, U, 1, -1)\\&= \frac{K}{S_t}\mathcal{DB}^{\text{BS}}\left(S_t, t, T, \frac{S_t^2}{K}, P^f(t,T), P^d(t,T), \frac{S_t^2}{L}, \frac{S_t^2}{U}, -1, -1\right)\end{aligned} \tag{7.18}$$

By means of these relationships we are able to find pricing formulae for a wide range of first–then barriers. Let us start with a first-down-then-up-and-in call. The option's buyer holds a standard up-and-in call with barrier $U > L$ and strike K if the underlying FX spot rate asset first hits a lower barrier L. We can employ the up-and-in call/down-and-in put barrier symmetry (7.14) and build a static hedge perfectly replicating the contract we want to price:

$$\begin{aligned}&\mathcal{FTB}^{\text{BS}}(S_t, t, T, K, P^d(t,T), P^f(t,T), L, U, 1, 1, -1)\\&= \frac{K}{L}\mathcal{B}^{\text{BS}}\left(S_t, t, T, \frac{L^2}{K}, P^f(t,T), P^d(t,T), \frac{L^2}{U}, -1, 1, -1\right)\end{aligned} \tag{7.19}$$

where $\mathcal{FTB}^{\text{BS}}(S_t, t, T, K, P^d(t,T), P^f(t,T), L, U, \omega, \theta, \zeta)$ is the price of a call ($\omega = 1$) first-down ($\theta = 1$) then up-and-in ($\zeta = -1$), struck at K and expiring in T, with lower and upper barrier levels equal to, respectively, L and U. The static hedge works as follows: a (numerarire currency) quantity K/L of standard down-and-in put options with strike L^2/K and barrier L^2/U will expire worthless if the FX spot rate never reaches the lower level L, and this is also what happens to a first-down-then-up-and-in call; if the FX spot rate breaches the lower barrier L at some time between t and T, the value of the K/L down-and-in put will exactly match the value of the up-and-in call, by the symmetry relationship. In this case we sell the down-and-in put and buy the up-and-in call, with no extra profit or loss. We are in the same condition as if we had bought the first-down-then-up-and-in call and then the static hedge perfectly replicates the first-then contract we are examining, thus also providing its value at time t.

By the same token we can derive pricing formulae for the other kinds of first-then barrier options. The first-up-then-down-and-in call is

$$\begin{aligned}&\mathcal{FTB}^{\text{BS}}(S_t, t, T, K, P^d(t,T), P^f(t,T), L, U, 1, -1, -1)\\&= \frac{K}{U}\mathcal{B}^{\text{BS}}\left(S_t, t, T, \frac{U^2}{K}, P^f(t,T), P^d(t,T), \frac{U^2}{L}, -1, -1, -1\right)\end{aligned} \tag{7.20}$$

The first-down-then-up-and-in put is

$$\begin{aligned}&\mathcal{FTB}^{\text{BS}}(S_t, t, T, K, P^d(t,T), P^f(t,T), L, U, -1, 1, -1)\\&= \frac{K}{L}\mathcal{B}^{\text{BS}}\left(S_t, t, T, \frac{L^2}{K}, P^f(t,T), P^d(t,T), \frac{L^2}{U}, 1, 1, -1\right)\end{aligned} \tag{7.21}$$

The first-up-then-down-and-in put is

$$\begin{aligned}&\mathcal{FTB}^{\text{BS}}(S_t, t, T, K, P^d(t,T), P^f(t,T), L, U, -1, -1, -1)\\&= \frac{K}{U}\mathcal{B}^{\text{BS}}\left(S_t, t, T, \frac{U^2}{K}, P^f(t,T), P^d(t,T), \frac{U^2}{L}, 1, -1, -1\right)\end{aligned} \tag{7.22}$$

The knock-out barrier can be priced by means of the knock-in–knock-out relationship (6.2) of Chapter 6. Hence we have that a first-down-then-up-and-out call, for example, is

$$\begin{aligned}&\mathcal{FTB}^{\mathrm{BS}}(S_t, t, T, K, P^d(t,T), P^f(t,T), L, U, 1, -1, 1)\\&= \mathrm{Bl}(S_t, t, T, K, P^d(t,T), P^f(t,T), \sigma_{ATM}, 1)\\&- \mathcal{FTB}^{\mathrm{BS}}(S_t, t, T, K, P^d(t,T), P^f(t,T), L, U, 1, -1, -1)\end{aligned} \quad (7.23)$$

The other three knock-out barrier options corresponding to formulae (7.23), (7.21), (7.22) can be priced in an analogous fashion.

Remark 7.4.1. *The static hedges we have devised to price first–then barrier options are only theoretical and their performance is spoilt in practice by the fact that we will not find an underlying FX rate with the domestic interest rate inverted with the foreign, as implied by the symmetry relationships we have shown above. Nevertheless, the pricing is correct and the usual Greeks can be used as for hedging purposes, although a dynamical hedge is required. The static hedge will be possible for those pairs whose underlying currencies have very similar (or equal, in the best of cases) interest rates.*

The knock-in–knock-out (or in–out) barrier options, similarly to first-then barrier contracts, have two barrier levels, one of which has a knock-in effect while the other produces a knock-out result. Contrary to the first-then barrier, in–out levels need not be breached in a specific sequence and their effectiveness is independent one from the other; the option can either be first knocked in and then out or simply knocked out. The pricing of these contracts is straightforward, and a simple static hedge (with no *caveat* as above) is employed. A general formula to price an in–out option struck at K, expiring in T, with barrier levels L and U, is

$$\begin{aligned}&\mathcal{IOB}^{\mathrm{BS}}(S_t, t, T, K, P^d(t,T), P^f(t,T), L, U, \omega, \zeta)\\&= \mathbf{1}_{\{\zeta=-1\}}\mathcal{B}^{\mathrm{BS}}(S_t, t, T, K, P^d(t,T), P^f(t,T), U, \omega, -1, 1)\\&+ \mathbf{1}_{\{\zeta=1\}}\mathcal{B}^{\mathrm{BS}}(S_t, t, T, K, P^d(t,T), P^f(t,T), L, \omega, 1, 1)\\&- \mathcal{DB}^{\mathrm{BS}}(S_t, t, T, K, P^d(t,T), P^f(t,T), L, U, \omega, -1)\end{aligned} \quad (7.24)$$

where $\omega = \pm 1$ depending on whether the option is a call or a put, and $\zeta = \pm 1$ depending on whether the lower barrier is "in" (and the upper is "out") or "out" (and the upper is "in"). So, as an example, if we want to price a down-in-up-out call option, we have

$$\begin{aligned}&\mathcal{IOB}^{\mathrm{BS}}(S_t, t, T, K, P^d(t,T), P^f(t,T), L, U, 1, 1)\\&= \mathcal{B}^{\mathrm{BS}}(S_t, t, T, K, P^d(t,T), P^f(t,T), H, 1, -1, 1)\\&- \mathcal{DB}^{\mathrm{BS}}(S_t, t, T, K, P^d(t,T), P^f(t,T), L, U, 1, -1)\end{aligned}$$

If the activating lower barrier L is never reached, then the option expires worthless; if it is reached before the upper barrier U, then the double knock-out is cancelled, and a standard up-and-out call remains in the replication portfolio; if the upper barrier is breached at any time, both options are knocked out and the portfolio expires worthless. Therefore, the replica perfectly matches the payoff of the down-in-up-out call option.

The pricing of the first–then and in–out barrier options can also be performed within other frameworks. As usual, numerical procedures will be the main tool, unless one employs the LMUV model. The use of these models is required if one wants to include the smile effects in the pricing. Alternatively, one may use the market approach to price standard barrier options (described in Chapter 6) to take into account the smile effects and other risks. Also, the bid/ask spread can be determined in a way similar to that adopted for standard barriers. Delayed and cash settlement features may be dealt with by means of formulae (6.44) and (6.45) of Chapter 6, therefore, we need to modify the strike to K' and multiply by $P^f(T, T')$ when applying the symmetry relationships.

7.5 AUTO-QUANTO OPTIONS

We examine here the case of an auto-quanto option, leaving to future analysis the more general case of a quanto option.

Definition 7.5.1. ***Auto-quanto option contract.*** *An XXXYYY (plain vanilla) auto-quanto option is equal to an otherwise identical plain vanilla option, but for the fact that it pays out at maturity T the amount $[\omega(S_T - K)]^+$ in XXX foreign currency units, which is equivalent to $[\omega(S_T - X)]^+ S_T$ in YYY domestic currency units, where as usual $\omega = 1$ for a call and $\omega = -1$ for a put.*

In practice, an auto-quanto option is in all respects equal to a plain vanilla option, except for the fact that the terminal payoff is denominated in the foreign instead of the domestic (numeraire) currency. We just stress the fact that the payoff is not converted into foreign currency units at expiry, in which case it would be $[\omega(S_T - X)]^+/S_T$.

The pricing of an auto-quanto within a BS economy can be performed quite easily.[3] First, we need to derive the dynamics of the FX spot rate under a new numeraire, which we choose to be $\overline{S}_t = S_t \exp\left(\int_0^t r_u^f du\right)$. Under the associated measure $Q^{\overline{S}}$, the dynamics of S_t is

$$dS_t = (r_t^d - r_t^f + \varsigma_t^2)S_t dt + S_t \varsigma_t dW_t^{Q^{\overline{S}}} \tag{7.25}$$

We assume that the FX spot rate follows a dynamics as in the SDE (2.16), Chapter 2, under the equivalent risk-neutral measure.

We know that the price of a European claim can be calculated in general terms as in (2.14) of Chapter 2, under the risk-neutral measure, i.e., using the domestic deposit as numeraire. If we use $\overline{S}_t$ as numeraire, the valuation of a claim is

$$\begin{aligned} \mathcal{O}_t &= \overline{S}_t E^{Q^{\overline{S}}}\left[\frac{\mathcal{O}_T}{\overline{S}_T}|\mathcal{F}_t\right] \\ &= S_t e^{-\int_t^T r_u^f du} E^{Q^{\overline{S}}}\left[\frac{\mathcal{O}_T}{S_T}|\mathcal{F}_t\right] \end{aligned} \tag{7.26}$$

Since for the auto-quanto $\mathcal{O}_T = [\omega(S_T - X)]^+ S_T$, it is convenient to use formula (9.33) and the associated dynamics for the FX spot rate (7.25), to derive the pricing formula in the BS model:

$$\begin{aligned} &\mathcal{AQ}^{\mathrm{BS}}(S_t, t, T, K, P^d(t,T), P^f(t,T), \sigma, \omega) \\ &= \omega S_t P^f(t,T)\Big[F(t,T)e^{\sigma^2(T-t)}\Phi(\omega d_1) - K\Phi(\omega d_2)\Big] \end{aligned} \tag{7.27}$$

[3] We follow here the derivation in Mercurio [49].

where

$$d_1 = \frac{\ln \frac{F(t,T)}{K} + \frac{3}{2}\sigma^2(T-t)}{\sigma\sqrt{T-t}}$$
$$d_2 = d_1 - \sigma\sqrt{T-t}$$

and

$$\sigma = \sqrt{\frac{\int_t^T \varsigma_s^2 ds}{T-t}}$$

The pricing formula (7.27) clearly does not take into account the implied volatility smile. Since an auto-quanto option is a European payoff, we can use the static replica approach for a general payoff $h(S_T)$ (equation (4.15) of Chapter 4). Hence, auto-quanto call and put prices can be written in terms of plain vanilla call and put prices as follows:

$$\mathcal{AQ}(S_t, t, T, K, 1) = 2\int_K^{+\infty} \mathbf{C}(K)\,dK + K\mathbf{C}(K)$$
$$\mathcal{AQ}(S_t, t, T, K, -1) = K\mathbf{P}(K) - 2\int_0^K \mathbf{P}(K)\,dK \tag{7.28}$$

where $\mathbf{P}(K)$ is the put price with strike K and maturity T, i.e., $\mathbf{P}(K) = \mathbf{C}(K) - S_t\, e^{-\int_t^T r_s^f ds} + K\, e^{-\int_t^T r_s^d ds}$, and the last argument in the function $\mathcal{AQ}(\cdot)$ is 1 for call and -1 for put options. By means of the static replica (7.28) and by considering market prices for the plain vanilla options (i.e., by plugging the market implied volatility referring to each strike K into the formulae), we can price the auto-quanto option consistently with the smile.

We can also avoid calculating the integral of the static replication if we build the smile by the VV approach explained in Chapter 4. In this case we may resort to the second consistency result of equation (1.16) and therefore calculate the smile-consistent auto-quanto price by the VV approach.

Example 7.5.1. *In what follows we verify, with real market data, that the auto-quanto option prices* (7.28) *equal the prices derived via* (4.16) *of Chapter 4, coming from the VV hedging arguments. To this end we use the market data as of* 1 *July 2005, as reported in Tables 7.1 and 7.2. The underlying FX rate is set at* 1.2050.

Our calculations are reported in Table 7.3, where auto-quanto option prices calculated with hedging arguments, i.e., with formula (4.16), *are compared with the static replication prices* (7.28) *that are obtained by using* 500 *and* 3000 *steps and, respectively, a constant strike step of* 0.15% *and* 0.25%.[4] *The percentage differences between these prices are also shown.*

Table 7.1 Market data as of 1 July 2005

Expiry		P^d	P^f
3M	03/10/2005	0.9902752	0.9945049
1Y	03/07/2006	0.9585801	0.9785056

[4] The integrals in the system (7.28) can of course be calculated with more efficient procedures. Here, however, we only want to show the correctness of the VV pricing procedure numerically.

Table 7.2 Strikes and volatilities corresponding to the three main Deltas, as of 1 July 2005

Delta	3M		1Y	
25Δ put	1.1733	9.43%	1.1597	9.65%
ATM	1.2114	9.05%	1.2355	9.40%
25Δ call	1.2487	8.93%	1.3148	9.43%

The purpose of this example is also to show that auto-quanto option prices can be derived, consistently with the market smile, by using only three European options and not a continuum of strikes, as implied by (7.28).

The bid/ask spread for an auto-quanto can be calculated by considering the bid/ask spread for the corresponding VV hedging portfolio, or by calculating formula (7.28) with the bid/ask volatilities, depending on which approach we chose to price the contract.

Remark 7.5.1. *The price of an auto-quanto option is usually expressed as a percentage of the base currency amount. The prices derived above are p_{numccy}, so that they must be transformed into $p_{baseccy\%}$ for quoting purposes.*

Table 7.3 Comparison of quanto option prices obtained through formulae (4.16) of Chapter 4 and (7.28)

Strike	1.1750		1.2050		1.2350	
Expiry	3M	1Y	3M	1Y	3M	1Y
			VV hedging arguments			
Call	4.8917	8.7404	2.8409	6.7434	1.4301	5.0545
Put	0.7935	1.8740	1.7173	2.8031	3.2812	4.0401
			Static replication (500 steps)			
Call	4.8963	8.7275	2.8460	6.7381	1.4325	5.0548
Pct diff.	0.005	−0.013	0.005	−0.005	0.002	0.000
Put	0.7877	1.8690	1.7145	2.8005	3.2750	4.0396
Pct diff.	−0.006	−0.005	−0.003	−0.003	−0.006	0.000
			Static replication (3000 steps)			
Call	4.8916	8.7383	2.8433	6.7434	1.4311	5.0570
Pct diff.	0.000	−0.002	0.002	0.000	0.001	0.002
Put	0.7885	1.8711	1.7164	2.8034	3.2785	4.0433
Pct diff.	−0.005	−0.003	−0.001	0.000	−0.003	0.003

7.6 FORWARD START OPTIONS

Forward start options can be any type of option whose inception is delayed at a future date t_1 later than the evaluation date t. The contract must have some feature to be determined in the future, in order to be meaningful and distinguished from an otherwise identical contract. Typically, the strike is set at the start date t_1 as a function of the underlying FX spot rate. In what follows we will focus on forward start plain vanilla options. Forward start barrier options can be treated in a similar fashion.

Definition 7.6.1. ***Forward start option contract.*** *An XXXYYY forward start option is an option contract starting at a future date $t_1 > t$, t being the evaluation date, and expiring in T; the strike price is determined at the starting date t_1 as a function of the market FX spot rate S_{t_1}: $K = f(S_{t_1})$.*

Forward start contracts may also be barrier or bet options. In this case, besides the strike, the barrier level is also a function of the market FX spot rate S_{t_1}: $H = g(S_{t_1})$.

The function of the FX spot rate is in practice of two kinds: (i) a given percentage α of the FX spot rate in t_1 (i.e., $K = \alpha S_{t_1}$); (ii) the FX spot rate in t_1 plus or minus an absolute difference α (i.e., $K = S_{t_1} \pm \alpha$). The pricing within the BS model is rather easy in the first case, whereas it involves a numerical integration in the second case. We first discuss the forward start plain vanilla contracts, then we adapt the analysis to the forward start exotic contracts case.

When the strike is determined as a given percentage of the FX spot rate at the start date, at time t_1 the forward start option becomes a standard plain vanilla option, expiring in T and struck at αS_{t_1} (we also consider the fact that the settlement of the underlying option can be non-standard in $T' = T + s'$, where $s' > s$ with s being the standard settlement):[5]

$$
\begin{aligned}
&\mathcal{FS}^{\mathrm{BS}}(S_{t_1}, t_1, t_1, T, T', \alpha S_{t_1}, P^d(t_1, T), P^f(t_1, T), \sigma_{t_1,T}, \omega)\\
&\quad = P^f(T, T')\mathrm{Bl}(S_{t_1}, t_1, T, \alpha' S_{t_1}, P^d(t_1, T), P^f(t_1, T), \sigma_{t_1,T}, \omega)\\
&\quad = S_{t_1} P^f(T, T')\mathrm{Bl}(1, t_1, T, \alpha', P^d(t_1, T), P^f(t_1, T), \sigma_{t_1,T}, \omega)
\end{aligned}
$$

where $\alpha' = \alpha \frac{P^d(T,T')}{P^f(T,T')}$. In the second line above we exploited the first-degree homogeneity property of the BS formula. At time t we have to calculate the discounted expectation of the value above, which reduces at the discounted expected value of S_{t_1} times the value of the BS formula (which is a constant in this case). The value of the forward start plain vanilla option is then

$$
\begin{aligned}
&\mathcal{FS}^{\mathrm{BS}}(S_{t_1}, t, t_1, T, T', \alpha S_{t_1}, P^d(t_1, T), P^f(t_1, T), \sigma_{t_1,T}, \omega)\\
&\quad = S_t P^f(t, T')\mathrm{Bl}(1, t_1, T, \alpha', P^d(t_1, T), P^f(t_1, T), \sigma_{t_1,T}, \omega)
\end{aligned}
\tag{7.29}
$$

where $\omega = \pm 1$ depending on whether the option is a base currency call or a put. We would like to stress the fact that the BS formula is computed with forward zero-coupon bond prices. These can easily be derived from the current term structure of interest rates.[6] More important is the parameter $\sigma_{t_1,T}$; that is, the forward implied volatility. We will dwell upon this issue below.

Remark 7.6.1. *In the FX market it is rather common, amongst professionals, to trade forward start 0 Delta straddles (defined as usual). This structure is built by a forward start call and put, struck at the ATM level determined with market rates and volatilities prevailing in the market in t_1. It is easy to check that the structure is a specific case of the more general rule to set the strike as a percentage of the FX spot rate S_{t_1}. Actually, according to the definition of*

[5] The cash settlement case is rather easy to handle, and we leave it as an exercise for the reader.

[6] In fact, $P(t_1, T) = \frac{P(t,T)}{P(t,t_1)}$.

ATM, we have that

$$K = S_{t_1} \frac{P^f(t_1, T)}{P^d(t_1, T)} e^{0.5\sigma^2_{t_1,T}(T-t_1)}$$

or

$$K = S_{t_1} \frac{P^f(t_1, T)}{P^d(t_1, T)} e^{-0.5\sigma^2_{t_1,T}(T-t_1)}$$

if the premium is included in the Delta. So, the forward start ATM straddle is the sum of a forward start call and put whose strike will be defined in t_1 as a percentage of S_{t_1} equal to

$$\alpha_t = \frac{P^f(t_1, T)}{P^d(t_1, T)} e^{0.5\sigma^2_{t_1,T}(T-t_1)}$$

or, if the premium is included in the Delta,

$$\alpha_t = \frac{P^f(t_1, T)}{P^d(t_1, T)} e^{-0.5\sigma^2_{t_1,T}(T-t_1)}$$

The pricing poses no particular problems, although the particular feature of the contract must be taken into account for risk management purposes. In more detail, while in a standard forward start option α is set as constant at the inception of the contract, in the forward start ATM straddle α is not explicitly defined and it is not constant at all, being a function of both domestic and foreign interest rates, as well as of the forward implied volatility $\sigma_{t_1,T}$ (whence the subscript t of α to stress that).

If the strike is determined in terms of a given distance α (a positive or negative number) from the FX spot rate, in t_1 we have that the forward start option is worth

$$\begin{aligned}
&\mathcal{FS}^{\text{BS}}(S_{t_1}, t_1, t_1, T, T', S_{t_1} + \alpha, P^d(t_1, T), P^f(t_1, T), \sigma_{t_1,T}, \omega) \\
&= P^f(T, T')\text{Bl}(S_{t_1}, t_1, T, (S_{t_1} + \alpha)\frac{P^d(T, T')}{P^f(T, T')}, P^d(t_1, T), P^f(t_1, T), \sigma_{t_1,T}, \omega)
\end{aligned}$$

In this case we cannot exploit the homogeneity property of the BS formula, so that to calculate the discounted expected value at time t we must resort to a numerical integration:

$$\begin{aligned}
&\mathcal{FS}^{\text{BS}}(S_{t_1}, t, t_1, T, T', S_{t_1} + \alpha, P^d(t_1, T), P^f(t_1, T), \sigma_{t_1,T}, \omega) \\
&= P^d(t, t_1)P^f(T, T') \int_{-\infty}^{\infty} \text{Bl}\Bigg(F(t, t_1)e^{-\frac{\sigma^2_{t_1}}{2}(t_1-t)+\sigma_{t_1}\sqrt{t_1-t}x}, t_1, T, \\
&(F(t, t_1)e^{-\frac{\sigma^2_{t_1}}{2}(t_1-t)+\sigma_{t_1}\sqrt{t_1-t}x} + \alpha)\gamma, P^d(t_1, T), P^f(t_1, T), \sigma_{t_1,T}, \omega \Bigg)\varphi(x)dx \qquad (7.30)
\end{aligned}$$

where

$$\varphi(x) = \Phi'(x) = \frac{1}{\sqrt{2\pi}} e^{-\frac{x^2}{2}}$$

and $\gamma = \frac{P^d(T,T')}{P^f(T,T')}$. Although a numerical integration is required, the computation is very quick.

Remark 7.6.2. *When the strike is determined as a percentage of the FX spot rate in t_1, only the forward implied volatility $\sigma_{t_1,T}$ enters into the pricing formula (equation (7.29)). When the strike is determined in terms of absolute positive or negative difference from the FX spot rate* *in t_1, the implied volatility σ_{t_1} up to the start date t_1 is also required (equation (7.30)). Clearly, this is because in the first case we just need the expected value of S_{t_1}, while in the second case we need to integrate over all possible future values, which requires solving the SDE describing the dynamics of the FX spot rate, which in turn involves knowledge of the integrated volatility up to t_1.*

The most momentous parameter to price forward start options is the forward implied volatility $\sigma_{t_1,T}$. In the BS model we just need to determine one value, since it is well known that within that framework the volatility smile is not existent.[7] We proceed in the same fashion as in Section 4.7, and adopt a similar notation. Assume $t = 0$, and define

$$V(T) = \int_0^T \varsigma^2(t)\,dt = T\sigma^2(T)$$

and

$$V(t_1, T) = \int_{t_1}^T \varsigma^2(t)\,dt = (T - t_1)\sigma^2(t_1, T)$$

where $\varsigma^2(t)$ is the instantaneous time-dependent variance of the FX spot rate process, $\sigma^2(T) \equiv \sigma_T^2$ is the mean variance, and $\sigma^2(t_1, T) \equiv \sigma_{t_1,T}^2$ is the forward mean variance. The following relationship is immediate:

$$V(T) = V(t_1) + V(t_1, T)$$

so that the forward implied volatility can be derived as

$$\sigma(t_1, T) = \sqrt{\frac{\sigma^2(T)T - \sigma^2(t_1)t_1}{T - t_1}} \tag{7.31}$$

7.6.1 Including the volatility smile in the pricing

As mentioned above, the BS model assumes no volatility smile and therefore just one forward implied volatility parameter (and an implied volatility up to time t_1 in some cases) is required to price a forward start option. If we want to take into account the volatility smile that actually manifests in the market, we have some choices at our disposal: (i) a stochastic volatility model, (ii) an adapted VV approach or (iii) an *ad hoc* procedure based on a static replication approach.

As far as the choice of a stochastic volatility model is concerned, once we have calibrated its parameters to the current volatility surface, we can price forward start options by means of numerical procedures (in practice, a Monte Carlo simulation). If we adopt an LMUV we can exploit the result of formula (2.88) in Chapter 2, which also holds for this kind of contract, and thus we use a closed-form pricing formula.

The adapted VV and the static replication approach deserve some more attention. We start by examining the VV approach: basically, we use the same ideas as described in Chapters 4 and 6. We assume we want to hedge a forward start option at a time t, starting in t_1 and expiring in T. Our aim is to build a portfolio perfectly hedged against the movements of the underlying FX spot rate (Delta hedge) and the Vega-related risk (Vega, Vanna, Volga hedge). If the Delta hedge implies no particular difficulty, the volatility-related risks need to be treated with some

[7] We will see later how to deal with forward volatility smiles.

care. Actually, when deriving the Vega, Vanna and Volga of formula (7.29) or (7.30), we can do that with respect to the forward implied volatility $\sigma_{t_1,T}$, but this is not what we need, since we are going to build the hedge with plain vanilla options, which depend on spot implied volatilities. We can calculate the three Vega-related Greeks with respect to $\sigma^2(t_1)$ and $\sigma^2(T)$, for a total of six derivatives, to be hedged with three options expiring in t_1 and three options expiring in T.[8] In practice, we have

$$\mathcal{V}^{\text{BS}}_{\sigma_{t_1}} = \sum_{i=1}^{3} x_i(K)\frac{\partial \mathbf{C}^{\text{BS}}}{\partial \sigma_{t_1}}(K_i, t_1)$$

$$\mathcal{X}^{\text{BS}}_{\sigma_{t_1}} = \sum_{i=1}^{3} x_i(K)\frac{\partial^2 \mathbf{C}^{\text{BS}}}{\partial \sigma_{t_1}\partial S_t}(K_i, t_1)$$

$$\mathcal{W}^{\text{BS}}_{\sigma_{t_1}} = \sum_{i=1}^{3} x_i(K)\frac{\partial^2 \mathbf{C}^{\text{BS}}}{\partial \sigma^2_{t_1}}(K_i, t_1)$$

$$\mathcal{V}^{\text{BS}}_{\sigma_T} = \sum_{j=1}^{3} x_j(K)\frac{\partial \mathbf{C}^{\text{BS}}}{\partial \sigma_T}(K_j, T)$$

$$\mathcal{X}^{\text{BS}}_{\sigma_T} = \sum_{j=1}^{3} x_j(K)\frac{\partial^2 \mathbf{C}^{\text{BS}}}{\partial \sigma_T\partial S_t}(K_j, T)$$

$$\mathcal{W}^{\text{BS}}_{\sigma_T} = \sum_{j=1}^{3} x_j(K)\frac{\partial^2 \mathbf{C}^{\text{BS}}}{\partial \sigma^2_T}(K_j, T)$$

where $\mathcal{V}^{\text{BS}}_{\{\cdot\}}$, $\mathcal{W}^{\text{BS}}_{\{\cdot\}}$, $\mathcal{X}^{\text{BS}}_{\{\cdot\}}$ are, respectively, Vega, Volga and Vanna of the forward start option with respect to the implied volatility indicated in the subscript, and $\mathbf{C}^{\text{BS}}(K, t)$ is a plain vanilla call option struck at K and expiring in t. The three options for the two expiries t_1 and T are struck at the levels corresponding to the strikes of the three basic structures (the ATM and the two 25D wings). Finally, σ_{t_1} and σ_T are the ATM implied volatilities for the corresponding expiries indicated in the subscript.

The system above can be solved separately in two sub-systems of three equations for each of two expiries. Thus we come up with a pricing formula that strongly resembles that in equation (4.6) of Chapter 4 and provides an adjustment over the BS price to take into account the smile effects:

$$\begin{aligned}\mathcal{FS}(t, t_1, T) = \mathcal{FS}^{\text{BS}}(t, t_1, T)&\\ + \sum_{i=1}^{3} x_i(K)[\mathbf{C}^{\text{MKT}}(K_i, t_1) - \mathbf{C}^{\text{BS}}(K_i, t_1)]&\\ + \sum_{j=1}^{3} x_j(K)[\mathbf{C}^{\text{MKT}}(K_j, T) - \mathbf{C}^{\text{BS}}(K_j, T)]&\end{aligned} \tag{7.32}$$

where we have omitted some of the arguments in the function $\mathcal{FS}^{\text{BS}}$ to lighten the notation.

[8] The six derivatives can be calculated analytically for pricing formula (7.29), whereas a numerical derivation is required for formula (7.30).

Remark 7.6.3. *Besides all the usual assumptions underpinning the VV approach for plain vanilla options, when applying it to the forward start contracts we also make the supplementary assumption that all the mixed second derivatives with respect to the two implied volatilities are nil. This assumption can have a smaller impact when the period between the forward start and the expiry of the option is long, so that a decorrelation between the movements of the two related implied volatilities may be more marked than that prevailing when the period is short.*

Example 7.6.1. *Consider the market data for the EURUSD as in Example 6.12.1 in Chapter 6. We want to price a plain vanilla EUR call USD put starting in 3 months (or 94 days) and expiring after 3 months from the start (or 182 days from today). The strike will be set in 3 months as a percentage of the FX spot rate dealing at that time and it will be equal to* $K = 1.05\,S_{t_1}$. *We calculate the BS flat-smile price and also the VV smile adjustments as explained above. The following table summarizes the results:*

BS price	*Fwd vol.* t_{t_1}, T	*VV adj.* t_{t_1}	*VV adj. T*	*VV adj. price*
0.0053	*10.31%*	*−0.00061*	*0.00344*	*0.00715*

We now analyse the case when a static replication approach is used. The basic formula to replicate a general payoff $h(S_t)$ at given time t (by means of standard plain vanilla options) is equation (4.15) in Chapter 4. We can also use it to replicate a forward start option at time t_1. We will focus on the case when the strike is set in terms of an absolute positive or negative difference from the FX spot rate S_{t_1}, which is trickier than the other case when it is set as a percentage of the S_{t_1}. Let us denote by $\sigma_{t_1,T}(S_{t_1} + \alpha)$ the forward implied volatility of an option struck at $K = S_{t_1} + \alpha$, provided that the FX spot rate is S_{t_1}. We have to replicate the payoff $h(S_{t_1}) = \mathcal{FS}^{\text{BS}}(S_{t_1}, t, t_1, T, T', (S_{t_1} + \alpha)\gamma, P^d(t_1, T), P^f(t_1, T), \sigma_{t_1,T}, \omega)$ (γ is defined as above). When α is negative, there may be some scenarios of S_{t_1} such that the forward strike K may turn out to be negative. To consistently take into account this occurrence, it is convenient to modify the payoff in the following way:[9]

$$h(S) = \mathcal{FS}^{\text{BS}}(S, (S+\alpha)\gamma, \sigma_{t_1,T}((S+\alpha)\gamma), \omega)\mathbf{1}_{\{S_{t_1}+\alpha>0\}} \\ -\alpha\gamma\mathbf{1}_{\{S_{t_1}+\alpha\le 0\}}\mathbf{1}_{\{\omega=1\}} \tag{7.33}$$

so that the replication is

$$\mathcal{FS}(S_{t_1}, t, t_1, T, T', (S_{t_1}+\alpha)\gamma, \omega) = P^d(t, t_1)h(F(t, t_1)) \\ + \int_0^{F(t,t_1)} h''(x)\mathbf{P}(S_t, x, t_1)dx + \int_{F(t,t_1)}^{\infty} h''(x)\mathbf{C}(S_t, x, t_1)dx \tag{7.34}$$

where $\mathbf{P}$ and $\mathbf{C}$ are prices of plain vanilla options struck at x and expiring in t_1, dealing in the market at time t with the current FX spot rate S_t. Clearly, since we need a continuum of strikes, these prices can be derived once we have defined an entire volatility smile for the expiry t_1 by means of a smile interpolation/extrapolation function, such as formula (4.9) of Chapter 4. The problem we now have to cope with is that, in order to replicate a correct payoff, we need to know $\sigma_{t_1,T}((S+\alpha)\gamma)$; that is, we need to build a forward implied volatility smile.

[9] When the strike is set in t_1 as a percentage of the FX spot rate, the payoff can be safely defined as $h(S_{t_1}) = \mathcal{FS}^{\text{BS}}(S_{t_1}, t, t_1, T, T', \alpha' S_{t_1}, P^d(t_1, T), P^f(t_1, T), \sigma_{t_1,T}, \omega)$, where the notation defined above applies.

7.6.2 Forward implied volatility smiles

If we price forward start options by a stochastic volatility model, we do not need to model the forward volatility smile explicitly, since it is implicitly determined by the dynamics for the instantaneous volatility and the correlation (if any) between this and the FX spot rate. This is the case, for example, when we employ the Heston model or the LMUV model. We can just judge whether the implicit forward volatility smiles are realistic and they depict a reasonable behaviour of the market.

A forward volatility smile is also implicit in the VV approach: we invert formula (7.32) and back out $\sigma_{t_1,T}(K)$ for all the range of possible strikes, so also in this case we do not have to worry in modelling the forward smile. Only when we use a static replication approach (formula (7.34)) do we need to describe such a variable, since it enters into the formula and plain vanilla option prices in the market convey no information about that.

The simplest way to cope with the determination of the forward volatility smile is to adopt a strict control over its future evolution.[10] Assume we are at time 0 and that, for a given strike K, the forward volatility $\sigma_{t_1,T}(K)$ between t_1 and T is a function of the three basic volatilities, such as in equation (4.9) in Chapter 4:

$$\sigma_{t_1,T}(K) = f(\sigma_{t_1,T}(K_{ATM}), \sigma_{t_1,T}(K_{25C}), \sigma_{t_1,T}(K_{25P}))$$

which can be rewritten, without loss of generality, in terms of market prices of the three basic structures:[11]

$$\sigma_{t_1,T}(K) = f(\sigma_{t_1,T}(K_{ATM}), \mathbf{rr}(t_1, T; 25), \mathbf{vwb}(t_1, T; 25)) \tag{7.35}$$

We now have to determine the forward values of the market prices for the three main structures. As for the ATM volatility, we can simply resort to equation (7.31). As for the other two variables, we have a rather free choice, but the most reasonable one is likely to assume that their future values will be the same as today for an expiry corresponding to time between the forward start and the expiry of the contract:

$$\mathbf{rr}(t_1, T; 25) = \mathbf{rr}(0, T - t_1; 25)$$
$$\mathbf{vwb}(t_1, T; 25) = \mathbf{vwb}(0, T - t_1; 25)$$

Remark 7.6.4. *It is almost superfluous to notice that the tools we have described above can be employed to also price forward start digital options. Namely, we have shown in Chapter 5 how to price spot start digital options via a replication approach by means of plain vanilla options. The same approach will allow the pricing of forward start digital options by means of forward start plain vanilla options, whose price is derived as we saw above.*

7.6.3 Forward start barrier and bet options

We can easily fit the framework and tools we have analysed above for forward start plain vanilla options to the case of forward start exotic options (i.e., barrier and bet options, examined in Chapter 6).

---

[10] This approach to propagate forward volatility smiles is very similar to that proposed by Rebonato in [55], Chapter 17.

[11] We can use, as a first approximation, equations (3.22) and (3.23) in Chapter 3. For a proper treatment of the three market quotes, and how to translate them into the three basic implied volatilities for the ATM and the two 25D wings, see Section 4.9.

Assume we are within the BS framework and want to price a forward start barrier option at time t, whose strike and barrier are determined in t_1 as a given function of the FX spot rate at that date: at time t_1 the forward start option becomes a standard barrier option, expiring in T.[12] Then, when the strike is set as a percentage α of S_{t_1} and the barrier as a percentage η, we have in t_1:

$$\begin{aligned}&\mathcal{FSB}^{\text{BS}}(S_{t_1}, t_1, t_1, T, T', \alpha S_{t_1}, P^d(t_1, T), P^f(t_1, T), \eta S_{t_1}, \omega, \theta, \zeta)\\&= P^f(T, T')\mathcal{B}^{\text{BS}}(S_{t_1}, t_1, t_1, T, T', \alpha' S_{t_1}, P^d(t_1, T), P^f(t_1, T), \eta S_{t_1}, \omega, \theta, \zeta)\\&= S_{t_1} P^f(T, T')\mathcal{B}^{\text{BS}}(1, t_1, t_1, T, T', \alpha', P^d(t_1, T), P^f(t_1, T), \eta, \omega, \theta, \zeta)\end{aligned}$$

We exploit also in this case the homogeneity properties of the BS pricing formula for barrier options. The pricing is straightforward and in closed-formula form, analogous to formula (7.29) for forward start plain vanilla options:

$$\begin{aligned}&\mathcal{FSB}^{\text{BS}}(S_{t_1}, t, t_1, T, T', \alpha S_{t_1}, P^d(t_1, T), P^f(t_1, T), \eta S_{t_1}, \omega, \theta, \zeta)\\&= S_t P^f(t, T')\mathcal{B}^{\text{BS}}(1, t, t_1, T, T', \alpha', P^d(t_1, T), P^f(t_1, T), \eta, \omega, \theta, \zeta)\end{aligned} \tag{7.36}$$

If the strike and the barrier are determined in terms of a given distance, respectively, α and η (either positive or negative numbers) from the FX spot rate, in t_1 we have that the forward start barrier option is worth

$$\begin{aligned}&\mathcal{FSB}^{\text{BS}}(S_{t_1}, t_1, t_1, T, T', S_{t_1} + \alpha, P^d(t_1, T), P^f(t_1, T), S_{t_1} + \eta, \omega, \theta, \zeta)\\&= P^f(T, T')\mathcal{B}^{\text{BS}}(S_{t_1}, t_1, T, (S_{t_1} + \alpha)\frac{P^d(T, T')}{P^f(T, T')}, P^d(t_1, T), P^f(t_1, T),\\&\quad S_{t_1} + \eta, \omega, \theta, \zeta)\end{aligned}$$

In this case we need to resort once again to a numerical integration:

$$\begin{aligned}&\mathcal{FSB}^{\text{BS}}(S_{t_1}, t_1, t_1, T, T', S_{t_1} + \alpha, P^d(t_1, T), P^f(t_1, T), S_{t_1} + \eta, \omega, \theta, \zeta)\\&= P^d(t, t_1)P^f(T, T')\int_{-\infty}^{\infty} \mathcal{B}^{\text{BS}}\Bigg(F(t, t_1)e^{-\frac{\sigma_{t_1}^2}{2}(t_1-t)+\sigma_{t_1}\sqrt{t_1-t}x}, t_1, T,\\&(F(t, t_1)e^{-\frac{\sigma_{t_1}^2}{2}(t_1-t)+\sigma_{t_1}\sqrt{t_1-t}x} + \alpha)\gamma, P^d(t_1, T), P^f(t_1, T),\\&(F(t, t_1)e^{-\frac{\sigma_{t_1}^2}{2}(t_1-t)+\sigma_{t_1}\sqrt{t_1-t}x} + \eta), \omega, \theta, \zeta)\Bigg)\varphi(x)dx\end{aligned} \tag{7.37}$$

The notation is the same as that used for the forward start plain vanilla case.

The extension of the two formulae above to the case of double-barrier options and bet options is rather easy, and we will not dwell on it here. The inclusion of the smile, as usual, can be achieved either by a consistent stochastic volatility model, or by one of the two market-oriented approaches we have sketched above for the forward start plain vanilla case.

7.6.4 Dealing with notional amounts expressed in numeraire currency

All the formulae we have seen above, both for forward start plain vanilla and exotic options, refer to a contract whose underlying is one unit of the base currency. It may happen that two counterparties agree that the notional refers to a given amount of numeraire currency. This

[12] Also in this case, we consider the fact that the settlement of the underlying option can be non-standard in $T' = T + s'$, where $s' > s$ with s being the standard settlement.

is not a problem for spot start options, since one unit of base currency notional is equal to K units of numeraire currency notional. Unfortunately, this is no longer the case for forward start options, since we do not know exactly what is the strike of the option until t_1. To cope with this problem, we have to modify the pricing formulae slightly according to the following reasoning: at the forward start date t_1 one base currency notional will be equal to $K = f(S_{t_1})$ of numeraire currency units. Therefore, assuming we have to price a forward start whose strike is set as a percentage of the FX spot price S_{t_1}, we have

$$\begin{aligned}&\mathcal{F}S_n^{\text{BS}}(S_{t_1}, t_1, t_1, T, T', \alpha S_{t_1}, P^d(t_1, T), P^f(t_1, T), \sigma_{t_1,T}, \omega)\\&= \frac{1}{\alpha S_{t_1}}\mathcal{F}S^{\text{BS}}(S_{t_1}, t_1, t_1, T, T', \alpha' S_{t_1}, P^d(t_1, T), P^f(t_1, T), \sigma_{t_1,T}, \omega)\end{aligned}$$

where $\alpha' = \alpha\frac{P^d(T,T')}{P^f(T,T')}$. In the second line above we exploited the first-degree homogeneity property of the BS formula. At time t we have to calculate the discounted expectation of the value above, which reduces to the discounted expected value of S_{t_1} times the value of the formula above (which is a constant in this case). The value of the forward start plain vanilla option is then

$$\begin{aligned}&\mathcal{F}S_n^{\text{BS}}(S_{t_1}, t, t_1, T, T', \alpha S_{t_1}, P^d(t_1, T), P^f(t_1, T), \sigma_{t_1,T}, \omega)\\&= \frac{1}{\alpha}P^d(t, T')\text{Bl}(1, t_1, T, \alpha', P^d(t_1, T), P^f(t_1, T), \sigma_{t_1,T}, \omega)\end{aligned} \tag{7.38}$$

When the strike is determined in terms of a given distance α from the FX spot rate S_{t_1}, we have that in t_1:

$$\begin{aligned}&\mathcal{F}S_n^{\text{BS}}(S_{t_1}, t_1, t_1, T, T', S_{t_1} + \alpha, P^d(t_1, T), P^f(t_1, T), \sigma_{t_1,T}, \omega)\\&= \frac{1}{S_{t_1} + \alpha}P^f(T, T')\text{Bl}\left(S_{t_1}, t_1, T, (S_{t_1} + \alpha)\frac{P^d(T, T')}{P^f(T, T')}, P^d(t_1, T), P^f(t_1, T), \sigma_{t_1,T}, \omega\right)\end{aligned}$$

In this case we still have to compute the expectation in t via a numerical integration:

$$\begin{aligned}&\mathcal{F}S_n^{\text{BS}}(S_{t_1}, t, t_1, T, T', S_{t_1} + \alpha, P^d(t_1, T), P^f(t_1, T), \sigma_{t_1,T}, \omega)\\&= P^d(t, t_1)P^f(T, T')\int_{-\infty}^{\infty}\frac{1}{\alpha + F(t, t_1)e^{-\frac{\sigma_{t_1}^2}{2}(t_1-t)+\sigma_{t_1}\sqrt{t_1-t}x}}\\&\text{Bl}\Bigg(F(t, t_1)e^{-\frac{\sigma_{t_1}^2}{2}(t_1-t)+\sigma_{t_1}\sqrt{t_1-t}x}, t_1, T,\\&(F(t, t_1)e^{-\frac{\sigma_{t_1}^2}{2}(t_1-t)+\sigma_{t_1}\sqrt{t_1-t}x} + \alpha)\gamma, P^d(t_1, T), P^f(t_1, T), \sigma_{t_1,T}, \omega\Bigg)\varphi(x)dx\end{aligned} \tag{7.39}$$

where the notation applies as above.

By the same token we can also price forward start exotic options. The inclusion of the smile is operated in the same way as above.

7.7 VARIANCE SWAPS

Variance swaps are contracts with a particular payoff:

Definition 7.7.1. ***Variance swap contract.*** *A variance swap is a contract paying out at maturity T the difference between the realized variance of the underlying asset and a fixed* *level (swap variance rate). The latter is the swap variance making nil the value of the contract at inception. The swap variance level is conventionally expressed as volatility on an annual basis (the number of days can be 365 or a different number, say 255, to take into account business days only), and the realized variance is calculated by contractually specifying the fixing and monitoring frequency (usually daily).*

Hence, the terminal payoff (for one unit of notional) can be written as follows:

$$\mathcal{VS}(T,T) = \frac{365}{n}\sum_{i=1}^{n}\left(\ln\frac{S_i}{S_{i-1}}\right)^2 - \sigma_{VAR}^2 \tag{7.40}$$

where 365 is the number of days used for annualizing, n is the number of days until the expiry T of the contract, S_i is the underlying fixing price at time t_i and σ_{VAR} is the strike volatility. As commonly done in the financial literature for ease of calculation, we assume we can replace the realized variance with its continuous-time limit:[13]

$$\frac{365}{n}\sum_{i=1}^{n}\left(\ln\frac{S_i}{S_{i-1}}\right)^2 \approx \frac{1}{T}\int_0^T \varsigma_t^2 dt$$

The value at time 0 of the variance swap is the (risk-neutral) expected value of the terminal payoff:

$$\mathcal{VS}(0,T) = P^d(0,T)E\left[\frac{1}{T}\int_0^T \varsigma_t^2 dt - \sigma_{VAR}^2\right]$$

By definition, at inception:

$$\sigma_{VAR}^2 = E\left[\frac{1}{T}\int_0^T \varsigma_t^2 dt\right]$$

The pricing of this contract is trivial within the BS environment, since the variance swap rate is simply the (one) squared implied volatility for the relevant expiry. This clearly does not take into account the volatility smile, and so we need some method to include it in the pricing. One method is a replication approach: it can be shown[14] that the variance contract can be perfectly statically replicated by a continuum of options, with strikes in the range running from 0 to infinity. Assume that at time 0 we want to price a variance swap expiring in T. By replicating with a continuum of plain vanilla options a log-contract and by Delta hedging this portfolio, the total P&L of the strategy is exactly the right-hand side of (7.40). Hence, the swap strike is given by

$$\sigma_{VAR} = \sqrt{2\frac{1}{P^d(0,T)T}\left(\int_0^{F(0,T)}\frac{1}{K^2}\mathbf{P}(K)dK + \int_{F(0,T)}^{\infty}\frac{1}{K^2}\mathbf{C}(K)dK\right)} \tag{7.41}$$

where $F(0,T)$ is the forward FX spot price at time 0 for delivery in T and $\mathbf{P}(K)$ and $\mathbf{C}(K)$ denote the put and call option prices with strike K and expiry in T, dealing in the market. It is very unlikely that all the prices will be available in the market, but we can derive an entire

[13] The assumption implies no loss of generality, since it can be shown that the monitoring frequency does not affect the price of the variance swap; see, for example, Carr *et al.* [19].

[14] See Carr and Madan [20].

Table 7.4 EURUSD ATM volatilities, 25D **RR** and **VWB** for 3M and 1Y expiries, as of 1 July 2005

	ATM	25D **rr**	25D **vwb**
3M	9.37%	−0.50%	0.17%
1Y	9.55%	−0.23%	0.17%

Source: Bloomberg.

smile from the basic market quotes and then price the options in formula (7.41) by means of it.

If we use the VV approach to build the vol surface, we can exploit the second consistency result of equation (4.16) in Chapter 4, since the variance swap is a European payoff. So we can use, as an alternative to the static replication approach, the VV pricing based on the Vega-related Greeks hedging argument. In order to apply the VV approach to the present case, we need to calculate its BS (flat-smile) price and Vega, Vanna and Volga sensitivities. In a BS environment, as mentioned above, the expected variance is simply the implied volatility squared, the latter being common to all options expiring at time T. Assuming this is the at-the-money volatility σ_{ATM}, it will be the swap strike as well, since it makes 0 the value of the contract at the start. As for the Vega, Vanna and Volga, we immediately have

$$\begin{aligned}
\mathcal{V}S^{\text{BS}}(0, T) &= P^d(0, T)\left[\sigma_{ATM}^2 - \sigma_{VAR}^2\right] \\
\frac{\partial \mathcal{V}S^{\text{BS}}(0)}{\partial \sigma_{ATM}} &= 2P^d(0, T)\sigma_{ATM} \\
\frac{\partial^2 \mathcal{V}S^{\text{BS}}(0)}{\partial \sigma_{ATM}\partial S_0} &= 0 \\
\frac{\partial^2 \mathcal{V}S^{\text{BS}}(0)}{\partial \sigma_{ATM}^2} &= 2P^d(0, T)
\end{aligned}$$

We then solve the usual system by equating the Vega-related Greeks of the variance swap to the corresponding Greeks of the hedging portfolio built with the three basic options. The final price is given by using formula (4.16) in Chapter 4. The static replication and the Vanna–Volga method yield the same results, thanks to Proposition 4.5.4.

Example 7.7.1. *We calculate the strike volatility of two variance swaps on the EURUSD FX rate, with market data as of* 1 *July 2005 (the spot rate is 1.2050, see also Tables 7.4 and 7.5). The first contract expires in* 3 *months (94 days) and the second in* 1 *year (367 days). The numerical integration is performed by a Gauss–Lobatto scheme, whereas the Vanna–Volga method has been described above. Table 7.6 shows the results and makes clear that the Vanna–Volga method produces outputs virtually indistinguishable from those implied by the static replication approach, with the main advantage that the former requires no numerical integration.*

Table 7.5 Discount factors as of 1 July 2005

Expiry		USD	EUR
3M	03-Oct-05	0.990275201	0.994585501
1Y	01-Jul-06	0.962184069	0.979390945

Table 7.6 Variance swap strike volatilities

Expiry	VV	Static replication
3M	9.738%	9.738%
1Y	9.914%	9.914%

A final note on the bid/ask spread for a volatility swap. Since they can be priced via a replication portfolio containing options with the same sign (i.e., if we want to buy (sell) a volatility swap, we will be long (short) all the options), we can calculate a bid (ask) price by pricing the replicating options by bid (ask) implied volatilities.

7.8 COMPOUND, ASIAN AND LOOKBACK OPTIONS

It is beyond the scope of this book to examine all possible exotic options that can be traded in the FX market. Some of them are not common, such as compound options. These contracts can be valued in closed-form formulae in the BS economy, they depend on the forward volatility and the contribution of the smile can be approximated by one of the methods we have described for forward starting options. Compound options, being options to enter into a forward starting contract, are strongly dependent on the volatility of the volatility (i.e., they have a big Volga exposure).

Asian options are more common than compound options, and they can be priced in closed-form in the BS environment for some types of contractual features. Unfortunately, the kinds of Asian contracts usually traded in the market do not allow for a closed-form formula, so that one must resort to Monte Carlo simulations to price them. The same considerations apply for lookback options. Since there is now an enormous number of papers and articles dealing with such issues, we simply refer to them for the details.[15]

The best way to include the smile in the pricing of Asian and lookback options is to fit a stochastic volatility model to market data and run a numerical procedure. The VV approach to include the smile effect, when theoretically possible because closed-form formulae are available, does not perform satisfactorily well, even if some modifications are brought in.

The hedging of Asian and lookback options is not particularly difficult since payoffs are smooth, at least in the typically traded structures.

[15] A simple search on the web will produce a long and interesting list of works, most of them freely available.

8

Risk Management Tools and Analysis

8.1 INTRODUCTION

In the previous chapters we have analysed specific issues related to the pricing of FX contracts. We have not fully examined the peculiar risks associated with those contracts and how to manage them. The aim of this chapter is to describe some tools to monitor, detect and measure the most relevant risks. Besides, we also show how to employ them in practice and which are the risk profiles, connected to the main types of contracts traded in the FX market, that may be identified by means of them.

The analysis will be carried out along two lines, assuming that we are working either in a BS world or in a stochastic volatility environment. Each of the two cases entails specific risks that should be managed. As we know from Chapter 2, there are many stochastic volatility models but we presented just a few of them that can be used to price FX options. In this chapter we will choose the LMUV model, in its extended version, as an example of how to run an FX option book in a stochastic volatility setting. The reasons for this choice are manifold: we just hint here at the fact that the LMUV is very easy to implement and it allows a closed-form pricing also for exotic contracts whenever corresponding closed-form formulae are available in the BS model.

We start with a brief description of how to implement the LMUV model and calibrate it to a given set of market data.

8.2 IMPLEMENTATION OF THE LMUV MODEL

We assume that the exchange rate dynamics evolves according to the uncertain volatility model (with uncertain interest rates) that we have described in Section 2.5.2.[1]

We just recall that the intuition behind the LMUV model is as follows: the exchange rate process is nothing but a BS geometric Brownian motion, where the asset volatility and (domestic and foreign) risk-free rates are unknown in the next instant of time, and one assumes different (joint) scenarios for them. We adopt the extended version of the model, within which both interest rates and volatility are stochastic in the simplest possible manner.

The advantages of the LMUV model can then be summarized in the following points: (i) explicit dynamics; (ii) explicit marginal density at every time (mixture of lognormals with different means and standard deviations); (iii) explicit option prices (mixtures of BS prices) and, more generally, explicit formulae for European-style derivatives at the initial time; (iv) explicit transition densities, and hence future option prices; (v) explicit (but approximated) prices for barrier options and other exotics; (vi) potentially perfect fitting to any (smile-shaped or skew-shaped) implied volatility curves or surfaces. Other models can be chosen, such as Heston's, with time-dependent parameters, although many of the alluring advantages we have just listed may be lost (mainly, the analytical tractability).

---

[1] This section and the following one, dealing with the implementation of the LMUV model in practice, are based on the work of Bisesti *et al.* [7].

The LMUV model can be fitted to market data in an easy way. The inputs we need are:

1. The FX spot rate S_0.
2. The volatility matrix. This surface is built based on market prices of the three main structures, by means of the tools we have examined in Chapter 4.
3. The domestic and foreign discount factors (or, equivalently, the zero-coupon prices) for the same expiries as in the volatility matrix.

In order to fit both the domestic and foreign discount factors exactly at the initial time, the following no-arbitrage constraints must be imposed:[2]

$$\sum_{i=1}^{N} \lambda_i e^{-\int_0^t r_i^d(u)\,du} = P^d(0,t)$$

$$\sum_{i=1}^{N} \lambda_i e^{-\int_0^t r_i^f(u)\,du} = P^f(0,t) \tag{8.1}$$

Our calibration is then performed by minimizing the sum of squared percentage differences between model and market volatilities of the 25D puts, ATM puts and 25D calls, while respecting the constraint (8.1), for the set of strikes referring to each expiry. We let the remaining points of the surface be determined by the model. We will see that when volatility matrices are built in a consistent way, the fitting is reasonably accurate. Since the procedure will be fed with matrices in the sticky Delta form, the set of strikes will be different for each expiry.

Given the high degrees of freedom at hand, we set the number of scenarios $N = 2$ and resort to a non-parametric estimate of the functions r^f and ς, assuming at the same time a deterministic domestic rate r^d. Moreover, we assume r_i^f and ς_i to be constant over each interval defined by consecutive expiries. In such a way, we can apply an iterative procedure and calibrate one implied volatility curve at a time, starting from the first maturity and up to the last. This procedure turns out to be extremely fast. Sticking to only two scenarios and assuming uncertainty only in the FX spot rate, instantaneous volatility and foreign rates are sufficient in most cases to achieve a perfect calibration to the three main volatility quotes for all maturities simultaneously.

Such a perfect fit holds true for many different specifications of the probability parameter λ_i (i.e., the probability of each scenario occurring), for a single expiry. One could use this parameter and then choose an optimal λ_i by considering the calibration of the overall implied volatility matrix.

Example 8.2.1. *We consider an example of calibration to real market FX data of the EURUSD, as of* 12 *February 2004, when the spot exchange rate was* 1.2832.

In Table 8.1 we report the market quotes of EURUSD σ_{ATM}, 25D **rr** *and* 25D *vwb for the relevant maturities from one week (1W) to two years (2Y), while in Table 8.2 we report the corresponding domestic and foreign discount factors (zero-coupon bond prices).*

The implied volatility surface that is built with the VV method from the basic volatility quotes is shown in Table 8.3 and in Figure 8.1, where for clarity we plot the implied volatility in terms of (base currency EUR) put Deltas ranging from 5% to 95% and for the same maturities as in Table 8.1.

[2] We can safely use the same λ's for both the domestic and foreign risk-neutral measures, since such probabilities do not change when changing measure due to the independence between the Brownian motion entering into the FX spot rate dynamics and (r^d, r^f, σ). The notation is the same as in Chapter 2.

Table 8.1 EURUSD volatility quotes for the ATM **STDL** and the 25D **RR** and **VWB**, as of 12 February 2004

	ATM	25D **rr**	25D vwb
1W	11.75%	0.50%	0.190%
2W	11.60%	0.50%	0.190%
1M	11.50%	0.60%	0.190%
2M	11.25%	0.60%	0.210%
3M	11.00%	0.60%	0.220%
6M	10.87%	0.65%	0.235%
9M	10.83%	0.69%	0.235%
1Y	10.80%	0.70%	0.240%
2Y	10.70%	0.65%	0.255%

Table 8.2 Domestic and foreign discount factors for the relevant expiries

	τ (in years)	$P^d(0, T)$	$P^f(0, T)$
1W	0.0192	0.999804	0.999606
2W	0.0384	0.999595	0.999208
1M	0.0877	0.999044	0.998179
2M	0.1726	0.998083	0.996404
3M	0.2493	0.997187	0.994803
6M	0.5014	0.993959	0.989548
9M	0.7589	0.990101	0.984040
1Y	1.0110	0.985469	0.978479
2Y	2.0110	0.960102	0.951092

Table 8.3 EURUSD volatility matrix as of 12 February 2004

	10D **P**	25D **P**	35D **P**	ATM	35D **C**	25D **C**	10D **C**
1W	11.96%	11.69%	11.67%	11.75%	11.94%	12.19%	12.93%
2W	11.81%	11.54%	11.52%	11.60%	11.79%	12.04%	12.78%
1M	11.60%	11.39%	11.39%	11.50%	11.72%	11.99%	12.77%
2M	11.43%	11.16%	11.15%	11.25%	11.48%	11.76%	12.60%
3M	11.22%	10.92%	10.90%	11.00%	11.23%	11.52%	12.39%
6M	11.12%	10.78%	10.76%	10.87%	11.12%	11.43%	12.39%
9M	11.04%	10.72%	10.71%	10.83%	11.09%	11.41%	12.39%
1Y	11.00%	10.69%	10.68%	10.80%	11.06%	11.39%	12.38%
2Y	11.02%	10.63%	10.60%	10.70%	10.94%	11.28%	12.34%

In Table 8.4 we show the calibration errors in absolute terms: the model fits the three main volatilities perfectly for each maturity and performs quite well for almost every level of Delta. The performance degenerates for extreme wings, but it can safely be avowed that it is not impaired substantially; in this case the larger error is 0.10%, which is acceptable since it is related to a 10Δ *call.*

In Figure 8.2 we report the resulting absolute differences (between model and market volatilities), where the zero calibration error corresponding to the basic quotes is highlighted explicitly. Once again, we plotted the errors for levels of put Deltas in order to make the figure clearer.

Perfect calibration to the basic volatility quotes is essential for a breakdown of the sensitivities to the volatility surface's movements along the strike and maturity dimensions. This is sort

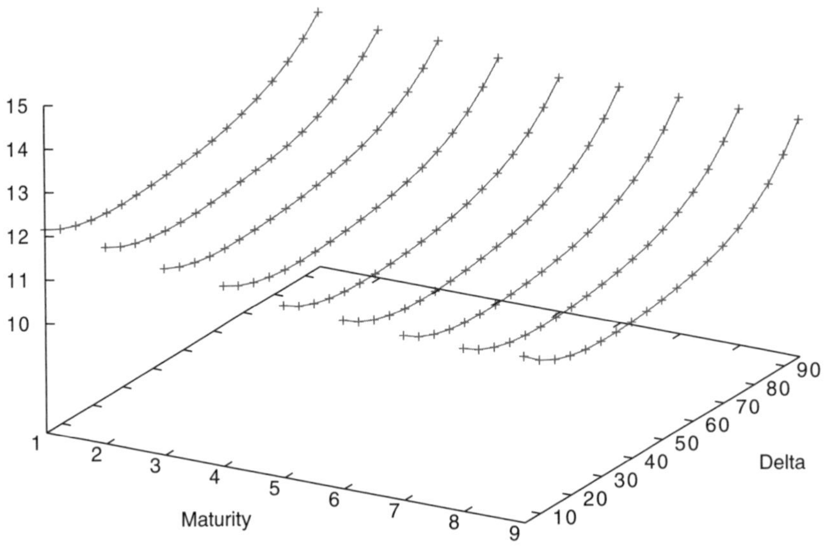

Figure 8.1 EURUSD implied volatilities surface (in percentage points) as of 12 February 2004

of equivalent to Vega in the BS model (and we will also use the term Vega in referring to it in the LMUV model, although with a slight abuse of terminology). This bucketing is extremely helpful to marker makers/risk managers of options books, since it allows them to understand where their volatility risk is concentrated. The possibility of such a Vega breakdown is a clear advantage of the LMUV model. In general, the calculation of bucketed sensitivities is neither straightforward nor even possible when we depart from the BS world. In fact, classic and widely used stochastic volatility models, like Heston's [37] (especially in its original time-constant version), cannot produce bucketed sensitivities and a trader is typically compelled to resort to a dangerous and unnatural parameter hedging or an overall Vega hedge based on a parallel shift of the implied volatility surface.

In sub-section 8.2.2 below, we will show how to calculate a volatility sensitivity breakdown and, accordingly, how to hedge a book of exotic options in terms of plain vanilla instruments.

Table 8.4 Absolute differences (in percentage points) between model and market implied volatilities

	10D **P**	25D **P**	35D **P**	ATM	35D **C**	25D **C**	10D **C**
1W	0.00%	0.00%	0.00%	0.00%	0.00%	0.00%	0.07%
2W	0.00%	0.00%	0.00%	0.00%	0.00%	0.00%	0.07%
1M	−0.01%	0.00%	0.00%	0.00%	0.00%	0.00%	0.07%
2M	0.00%	0.00%	0.00%	0.00%	0.00%	0.00%	0.08%
3M	0.00%	0.00%	0.00%	0.00%	0.00%	0.00%	0.08%
6M	0.00%	0.00%	0.01%	0.00%	0.00%	0.00%	0.09%
9M	0.00%	0.00%	0.01%	0.00%	0.00%	0.00%	0.10%
1Y	0.00%	0.00%	0.01%	0.00%	0.00%	0.00%	0.10%
2Y	0.00%	0.00%	0.01%	0.00%	−0.01%	0.00%	0.10%

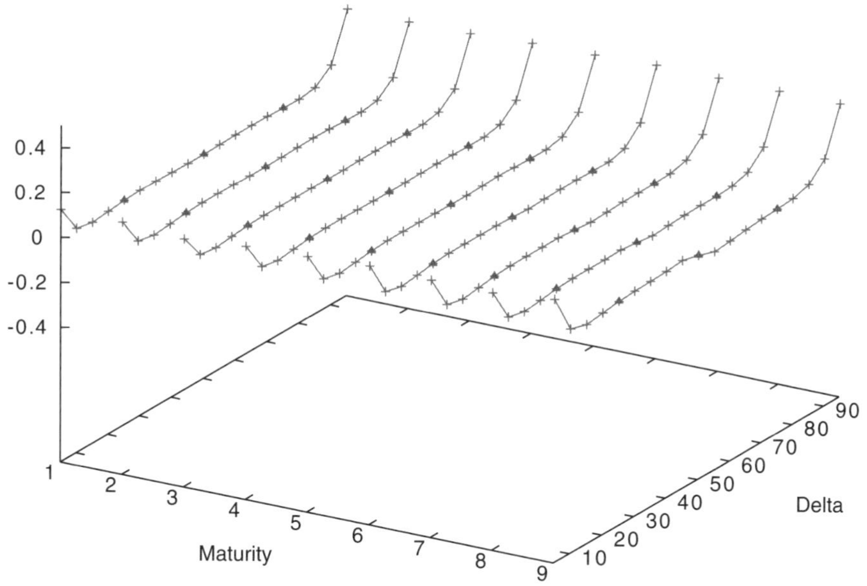

Figure 8.2 Absolute differences (in percentage points) between model and market implied volatilities

8.2.1 The forward volatility surfaces

The quality of calibration to implied volatility data is usually insufficient as a criterion for judging the goodness of an alternative to the BS model. In fact, a trader is also interested in the evolution of future volatility surfaces, which are likely to have a strong impact both in the pricing and especially in the hedging of exotic options.

Once the deterministic (time-dependent) volatility ς and interest rates r^d and r^f are drawn at time ε, we know that the model behaves as a BS geometric Brownian motion, thus leading to flat implied volatility curves for each given maturity. This may be a disturbing feature, even though there is no economical reason why a smile cannot flatten in the future. One should also consider that, although the smile is supposed to vanish after a very short period of time, the forward implied volatility smile is not at all flat in the model. Actually, one can analyse forward implied volatility surfaces and judge whether they show reasonable behaviour.

A forward implied volatility is defined as the volatility parameter to plug into the BS formula for forward starting options to match the model price. We have examined the forward start contacts pricing in Chapter 7. We assume that the forward start plain vanilla strike is set at the future date as a percentage of the FX spot rate. The pricing formula to use in this case is equation (7.29). We can infer the forward implied volatility for a given strike at the forward start date as the parameter $\sigma_{t_1,T}$ that matches the option price today (t_1 is the forward start date and T is the expiry of the option).

In Figure 8.3 we show the 3-month forward volatility surface that is implied by the calibration of the example in the previous section. Such a surface is the graph of function $\sigma_{t_1,T}$ for different values of T and percentages of the FX spot rate α, with T_1 set to 0.25 (3-months). For a more consistent plot and a better homogeneity of values, we actually decided to replace α with Delta, thus using different α's for different maturities. The α for a given maturity T and Delta was calculated as the moneyness of the plain vanilla option with the same Delta and the same

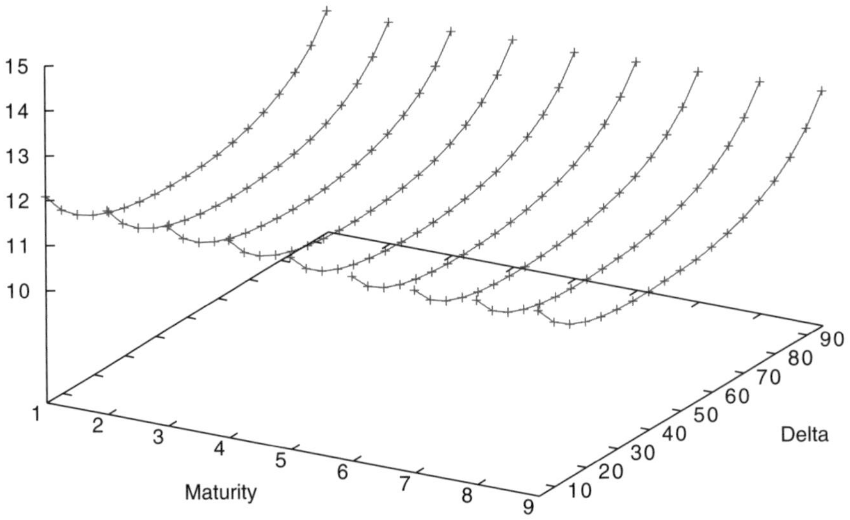

Figure 8.3 The 3-month forward volatility surface

time to maturity $T - t_1$. In Table 8.5 we compare the ATM volatilities as of 12 February 2004 and the implied ATM volatility 3-months forward. The level of the surface, as is clear from the ATM volatilities, keeps a regular term structure. The shape of the surface also looks consistent with the initial surface.

Similar plots can be obtained by considering different forward start dates T. This provides an empirical support for the LMUV model, since its forward volatility surfaces are regular and realistic in that they do not differ too much from the initial one.

As a further example, in Figure 8.4 we show the evolution of the 3-month forward volatility over time. To this end, we set $T = t_1 + 0.25$ and considered the forward implied volatility curves for $T \in \{1W, 2W, 1M, 2M, 3M, 6M, 9M, 1Y, 2Y\}$. The evolution in this case is also sensible and realistic; the shape of the smile keeps the features usually observed in the market.

Table 8.5 Comparison between ATM implied volatilities as of 12 February 2004 and ATM implied volatilities starting in 3 months forward

	12 February 2004	3-month fwd
1W	11.75%	10.63%
2W	11.60%	10.63%
1M	11.50%	10.63%
2M	11.25%	10.64%
3M	11.00%	10.65%
6M	10.87%	10.66%
9M	10.83%	10.65%
1Y	10.80%	10.63%
2Y	10.70%	10.62%

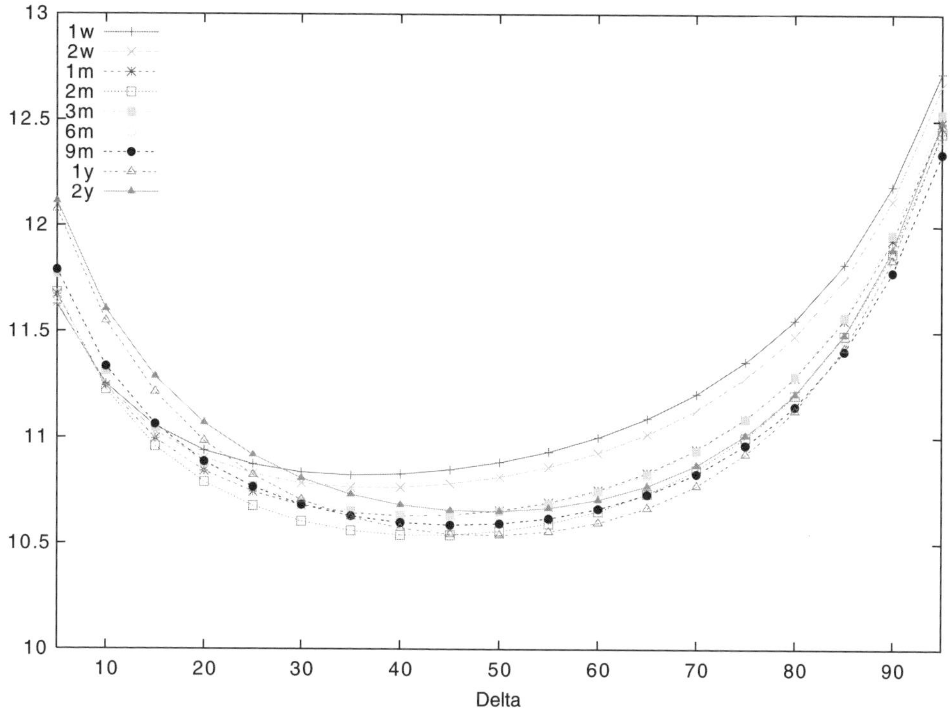

Figure 8.4 Evolution of the 3-month forward volatility over time

8.2.2 Calculating the sensitivity to the movements of the volatility surface

The LMUV can be used efficiently for valuing an entire options book. This is because, contrary to the known stochastic volatility models, most of the FX derivatives can here be valued in closed form. Our practical experience is that it takes less than a minute to value a book with 10 000 options, half of them exotics, including the time devoted to calibration.

The consistent valuation of their book is not, however, the only concern of an options trader. An even more important issue is in fact due to hedging.

In what follows we will show how to calculate the sensitivities, and how to hedge the changes of a portfolio's value due to changes in the volatility surface, within the LMUV framework. Our hedging procedure is based on the concept of a Vega bucketing and reflects what a trader is willing to do in practice.

As already explained, in the LMUV model, a Vega breakdown is possible thanks to the model capability of exactly reproducing the quotes of the basic instruments and hence the implied volatilities of the ATM and the two 25D wings. In practice, it is meaningful to hedge the typical movements of the market implied volatility curves. From the analysis in Chapter 3 and based on the VV approach to building a volatility smile, we can reasonably assume that three basic movements affect the smile, for a given expiry. Therefore, we start from the three basic prices for each maturity (the ATM and the two 25D call and put volatilities), and calculate the contract's sensitivities to: (i) a parallel shift of the three volatilities; (ii) a change in the **rr** (i.e., the difference between the two 25D wings); (iii) an increase in the **vwb** (i.e., of the two wings with fixed ATM volatility).[3] In this way we should be able to capture the effect of a parallel, a twist and a convexity movement of the implied volatility surface.[4] Once these sensitivities are calculated, it is straightforward to hedge the related exposure via plain vanilla options, namely the ATM calls, 25D calls and 25D puts for each expiry; then these quantities can easily be translated into amounts of main instruments traded in the market. To sum up the ideas we have just discussed, we state the following procedure:

Procedure 8.2.1. ***Calculation of the sensitivities to the volatility surface movements.*** *Assume we have calibrated the LMUV model to current market rates and basic volatilities. We calculate the sensitivity of a contract to a change in the level of the volatility surface for a given expiry:*

1. *Shift the relevant ATM volatility by a fixed amount $\Delta\sigma_{ATM}$, say* 10 *basis points; the* 25*D* **rr** *and* **vwb** *are kept fixed.*
2. *Generate a new smile corresponding to the tilted ATM value, by the VV method.*
3. *Fit the model to the tilted surface by a new calibration and calculate the new price of the contract, π_{NEW} corresponding to the newly calibrated parameters. Denoting by π_{INI} the initial price of the contract, its sensitivity to the ATM volatility change is thus calculated as*
$$\frac{\pi_{NEW} - \pi_{INI}}{\Delta\sigma}$$
For a better sensitivity we can also calculate the contract's price under a shift of $-\Delta\sigma_{ATM}$. However, if $\Delta\sigma_{ATM}$ is small enough (though not too small), the improvement tends to be negligible.
4. *Repeat steps 1 to 3 by tilting first the* **rr** *price (say, 10 basis points) and then the* **vwb** *price (say,* 5 *basis points), so as to also calculate the contract's sensitivities to a change in the slope and convexity of the smile for the same expiry.*
5. *Repeat steps 1 to 4 for all expiries in the volatility matrix.*

The procedure is quite robust due to the extreme flexibility of the LMUV model, which derives from the time-dependent nature of its parameters. From our experience we can affirm that the calibration to a tilted surface reaches perfect convergence by keeping the λ parameter constant, for reasonable changes.[5]

A further approach that can be used for hedging is the classic *parameter hedging*. In this case, one calculates the variations of the contract with respect to the parameters of the model, namely the forward volatilities ς_t and the foreign forward rates r_t^f, which are the ones used to calibrate the volatility surface. We assume that the parameter λ is constant.[6]

If we have a number n of hedging instruments equal to the number of parameters (in our case three options for each expiry), we can solve a linear system $Ax = b$, where b is a $(n \times 1)$ vector with the contract's sensitivities obtained by an infinitesimal perturbation of the n parameters, and A is the $(n \times n)$ matrix whose ith row contains the variations of the n hedging instruments with respect to the ith parameter. The instruments we use are, as before,

[3] This is actually equivalent to calculating the sensitivities with respect to the basic market quotes.

[4] We refer to Section 3.7 for a description of volatility smile phenomenology.

[5] We recall that we are employing a two-scenario LMUV, so that $\lambda = \lambda_1$ and $\lambda_2 = 1 - \lambda_1$.

[6] This can be justified by the fact that λ turns out to mainly accommodate the convexity of the volatility surface, which, as measured by the **vwb**, is typically very stable in the market. Besides, the effect of a change in convexity is also well captured by the difference between the volatilities in the two scenarios (when $N = 2$).

the ATM puts (or calls), 25D calls and 25D puts for each expiry. Since the model is able to perfectly fit the price of these hedging instruments, we have a one-to-one relation between the sensitivities of the contract with respect to the model parameters, and its variations with respect to the hedging instruments. More formally, denoting by π the option's price, by p the model parameters vector and by R the market data vector, we have

$$\frac{d\pi}{dR} = \frac{\partial\pi}{\partial R} + \frac{\partial\pi}{\partial p}\frac{\partial p}{\partial R}$$

Exact calibration therefore allows an exact calculation of the matrix $\partial p/\partial R$.

Example 8.2.2. *We price two barrier options by the LMUV model. We consider a* **UOC** *and a* **DOP**. *Valuations are based on the EURUSD market data shown in Table 8.6 (they are real market data as of* 31 *March 2004; we use the EURUSD spot rate set at* 1.2183*).*

Table 8.6 Market data for EURUSD as of 31 March 2004

	ATM	25D **rr**	25D **vwb**	$P^d(0, T)$	$P^f(0, T)$
1W	13.50%	0.00%	0.19%	0.9997974	0.9996036
2W	11.80%	0.00%	0.19%	0.9995851	0.9992202
1M	11.95%	0.05%	0.19%	0.9991322	0.9983883
6M	11.30%	0.20%	0.23%	0.9941807	0.9902598
9M	11.23%	0.23%	0.23%	0.9906808	0.9855211
1Y	11.20%	0.25%	0.24%	0.9866905	0.9807808
2Y	11.10%	0.20%	0.25%	0.9626877	0.9550092

We first price the two options with the BS model, then calculate the related adjustments by the VV approach and finally compare the adjusted prices with those implied by the LMUV model. We simply use a combination of BS barrier option formulae, plugging in for each scenario the integrated volatility corresponding to the contract's expiry. A more precise formula should take into account the term structure of the implied volatility and the formulae presented in Chapter 6. In our example this is not steep, and our pricing formula is satisfyingly accurate.[7] *The results are displayed in Table 8.7. The first option is a EUR call USD put struck at* 1.2250 *with knock-out at* 1.3100*, expiring in* 6 *months. The BS price is* 0.0041 *US dollars and the VV adjustment to this theoretical value is positive and equal to* 0.0006 *US dollars. The LMUV model evaluates this option at* 0.0049 *US dollars. The second option is a EUR put USD call struck at* 1.2000 *and knocked out at* 1.0700*, expiring in* 3 *months. The BS price is* 0.0169 *US dollars and, in this case, the market adjustment is negative and equal to* −0.0021 *US dollars. Also, the LMUV model produces a price lower than that of the BS model and analogous to market practice. Hence, the model seems to be (at least on barrier options) consistent with market adjustments and prices.*

An example is presented on how to also use the LMUV model in the management of an options book.

The hedging of the barrier options, in terms of plain vanilla options, is shown under both the scenarios and parameter hedging procedures; we also present a BS-based hedging portfolio for both options. We assume that both exotics have a nominal of 100 000 000 *US dollars and calculate the nominal values of the ATM EUR puts and 25D wings that hedge them.*

[7] Basically, we use the pricing formulae of Chapter 6 with constant parameters.

Table 8.7 LMUV model prices compared with BS and BS+market adjustments

	BS value	BS+VV adj.	LMUV
UOC	0.0041	0.0047	0.0049
DOP	0.0169	0.0148	0.0150

Table 8.8 shows the hedging portfolio suggested by the BS model; the expiry of the hedging plain vanilla options is the same as the related barrier option and the quantities are chosen so as to match the exposures, as explained in the previous paragraph.

In Table 8.9 we show the hedging quantities calculated according to the LMUV model with the scenario approach. The expiry of the hedging plain vanilla options is once again the same as the corresponding barrier options. It is noteworthy that both the sign and order of magnitude of the hedging options are similar to those of the BS model.

Table 8.8 Quantities of plain vanilla options to hedge the barrier options according to the BS model

	25D put	25D call	ATM put
UOC	79 008 643	54 195 790	−127 556 533
DOP	−400 852 806	−197 348 566	496 163 095

Table 8.9 Quantities of plain vanilla options to hedge the barrier options according to the LMUV model with the scenario approach

	25D put	25D call	ATM put
UOC	76 409 972	42 089 000	−117 796 515
DOP	−338 476 135	−137 078 427	413 195 436

In Tables 8.10 and 8.11 we show the results with a parametric approach. In this case we have a portfolio made up of options expiring on each main maturity, though the amounts are all negligible but those for the maturity of the related barrier option. Also in this case, the signs and order of magnitude of the hedging amounts seem to agree with those obtained by the BS model and the LMUV model with a scenario approach. This should be considered a nice feature of the model we are proposing, since it is next to the market practice and can be implemented and used without significant effort from a trader's point of view.

Table 8.10 Quantities of plain vanilla options to hedge the 6-month up-and-out call according to the LMUV model with the parametric approach

	25D put	25D call	ATM put
1W	5	49	−34
2W	5	−4	5
1M	21	14	−30
2M	−27	−28	43
3M	15	39	−37
6M	77 737 033	44 319 561	−116 151 192

Table 8.11 Quantities of plain vanilla options to hedge the 3-month down-and-out put according to the LMUV model with the parametric approach

	25D put	25D call	ATM put
1W	−11	244	−169
2W	−150	−226	288
1M	−34	78	−49
2M	24	−6	−19
3M	−334 326 734	−145 863 908	397 433 268

8.3 RISK MONITORING TOOLS

Many tools must be designed to run an FX options book. Some of them are standard and used in different markets, some others are specific to the technicalities of the FX market and to the features of the kind of contracts traded therein. In what follows we present a review of what we deem imperative tools to monitor the several risks.

8.3.1 FX spot rate-related Greeks

Delta and Gamma are the two Greeks common to any model and used to monitor and manage the underlying FX spot risk. We have already shown in Chapter 2 how they are calculated within the BS and other model settings, and how they are modified in the FX options market. Here we consider some more issues related to these Greeks, shifting our attention to a more aggregate point of view.

The Delta of an FX option book is simply the sum of all the Deltas of the contracts entering into it. When a book contains options on different pairs, it is wise to consider the total Delta for each them, without trying any form of intra-pair netting. Typically, the total Delta is expressed in the same way as it is in the market; that is, it is a pure Delta or a premium-included Delta, depending on how the premium is quoted in the market (i.e., respectively, in numeraire currency pips or base currency notional percentage). This general (not mandatory) rule has an exception when we deal with pairs, one of whose constituent currencies is the same as that used to calculate the general profit and loss of the book. We try to clarify that: assume a market maker's institution has a balance sheet denominated in euros, then the P&L of the FX options book will also very likely be calculated in euros. All the options on pairs against the euro will be Delta-hedged so as to protect against the variations of the book's value due to changes of the underlying FX spot rate, and besides, so as to preserve the value of the stock of the premium expressed in terms of euros. This is tantamount to saying that the Delta has to be calculated including the premium, although the market conventions do not imply this kind of Delta. In the case of a EURUSD pair, for instance, the premium is expressed in terms of US dollar (numeraire currency) pips, and therefore a pure Delta is exchanged in the market when an option is traded. Nevertheless, a European market maker (with a book evaluated in euros) will use a premium-included Delta when managing the FX spot-related risk of their portfolio.

Although not essential, the Delta for each pair can be bucketed for different predefined standard expiries (e.g., 1W, 1M, 3M, 6M, ...) and this can be of some help to the risk manager. A linear interpolation for the options expiring between two bucketing dates can be used to allocate the amount of Delta on the previous and subsequent buckets.

One issue is related to Delta originated from the barrier and bets contracts: as already mentioned several times, when a barrier is breached a gap occurs in the Delta position, due to the fact that either the contract expires (knock-out options or bets) or transforms into a different contract (knock-in options). The gap has to be monitored in terms of the amount that has to be traded in the market so as to offset the change caused by the knocking of the barrier. We also have to take into account the Delta exchange agreed upon by the two counterparties at inception of the contract.[8]

Example 8.3.1. *Consider a portfolio containing a short position in an up-and-out EURUSD call and a long position in a one-touch:*

Type	*Strike*	*Barrier*	*Expiry*	*Notional EUR*
UOC	*1.3900*	*1.4800*	*2M*	*−50 000 000*
OTH		*1.3700*	*2W*	*1 000 000*

Assume we evaluate the options by the BS model. We have two Delta gaps to manage, equal to:

Delta gap	*Amount EUR*
1.4800	*−17 500 000*
1.3700	*36 550 000*

The gap is determined simply by considering which is the Delta of the option's position just before the barrier is breached (say, at 0.1% *distance) and then after the breach. The* **UOC** *enters into the portfolio as a short position and therefore Delta is positive near the barrier. When this is knocked, Delta disappears and, assuming the position was Delta-hedged, a correspondng amount, with the reverse sign, has to be traded into the market. In practice, a stop-loss order for* 17.5 *million EUR has to be placed in the market at the EURUSD FX spot level* 1.4800*. A similar reasoning applies also to the one-touch position.*

The Delta gap is model-dependent. In fact, assume we are managing the book by the LMUV model. The amount is modified as follows:

Delta gap	*Amount EUR*
1.4800	*−23 180 000.00*
1.3700	*37 830 000.00*

Assume now that we have agreed with the counterparty of the **UOC** *to exchange Delta if the barrier is breached. The amount is usually determined on the basis of the BS formula*

[8] See Chapter 1 for a description of the market conventions when trading exotic options in the interbank market.

calculating the gap when the contract is dealt. Suppose that the gap was 15 million EUR. The market maker has to deduct this amount from the Delta gap risks, since when the barrier level trades the options knock out and they receive 15 million euros from the counterparty. The residual risk is then 2.5 million EUR if they run the book by a BS model and 8.18 million EUR if an LMUV model is used.

Gamma is expressed as trader's Gamma (see Chapter 2, equation (2.38)). This quantity signals the change of the Delta amount after a movement of 1% of the FX spot rate. Gamma can be bucketed similarly to Delta, and a linear interpolation can be employed for options expiring within two bucket dates.

8.3.2 Cash-settled options

A risk management system should detect cash-settled options since this feature affects Delta at the expiry of the contract. Usually, on the last day of the life of the contract, Delta is measured according to the terminal payoff. This means that for a plain vanilla option, for example, Delta is the full notional amount (either in base or numeraire currency, depending on how we are expressing the Greek) if the option is in-the-money, and it is nil if the option is out-of-the money. If the option expires in-the-money, the option's buyer exercises the option and they actually receive or deliver the base against the numeraire notional, so that their terminal position in the pair is exactly that indicated by Delta before expiry. If the option is cash-settled and ends in-the-money, upon the holder's exercise, only the difference between the strike and the final FX spot price, times the base currency amount, is paid by the option's seller. Therefore, after expiry there is a change in the total Delta of the book exactly equal to the cash-settled Delta, since no exchange of the notional amount occurs.[9] The risk manager has to trade in the FX spot market to restore the Delta exposure, and this has to be signalled by the risk monitoring system.

Example 8.3.2. *A market maker is short 50 million euros of EUR call USD put struck at 1.5000, cash settled. Assume the FX spot rate at the option's expiry is 1.5100. After expiry there will be a jump in the Delta position of the book of +50 000 000 euros, or −75 500 000 US dollars (−50 000 000 × 1.5100), since the option's Delta = −100% × 50 000 000 euros just before expiry, and it will cancel since there will be no delivery but only a cash payment of 500 000 euros from the seller to the buyer. If the terminal FX spot rate is 1.4900, the option expires worthless and no change in the Delta position will manifest, since the option's Delta = 0 in this case.*

Therefore, the risk monitoring system should signal a change of the Delta's position of +50 000 000 euros if the FX spot rate is above the strike price 1.5000 and zero otherwise.

8.3.3 Volatility-related Greeks and sensitivities

The sensitivity with respect to the volatility is strongly dependent on the model one adopts to manage the risks of the FX options book. When a stochastic or local volatility model is chosen, it is more convenient to express the volatility-related sensitivities with respect to the main options market prices, which is in fact the same as expressing them in terms of volatility

[9] The statement should be corrected slightly, since a change occurs in the currency in which the cash settlement is paid.

surface movements.[10] Therefore, we show the main tools in case we use the BS model and when we use the other models presented in Chapter 2.

It is well known that the BS model assumes a flat volatility smile and a non-stochastic, possibly time-dependent, instantaneous volatility. In such an environment, the sensitivities to the volatility, albeit inconsistent and superfluous in theory, are provided by Vega, Vanna and Volga. They allow us to hedge the changes in the one (ATM) implied volatility for each expiry, at the first and second order (Vega and Volga), and against movements of the FX spot rate (Vanna). The bucketing of these Greeks should be handled with more care than Delta and Gamma. In fact, the correct allocation on the various time pillars of the sensitivities value has a significant impact on the hedging of the related risks by means of options expiring on the most suitable dates. According to the way the implied volatility is interpolated between two (actively traded) market dates,[11] we use the following weights to assign to two contiguous buckets, T_i and T_{i+1}, the split amount of the total Vega of a given option with maturity T:

$$w_i = \frac{T_{i+1} - T}{T_{i+1} - T_i} \frac{T_i}{T} \frac{\sigma(T_i)}{\sigma(T)}$$

$$w_{i+1} = \frac{T - T_i}{T_{i+1} - T_i} \frac{T_{i+1}}{T} \frac{\sigma(T_{i+1})}{\sigma(T)}$$

The same weights can also be used to split the total amount of Vanna and Volga between two buckets.

If we adopt a stochastic volatility model or a local volatility model, we express the volatility-related sensitivities in terms of price changes of the main traded options for each expiry, or equivalently in terms of basic movements of the volatility smile. More specifically, assume we adopt the LMUV model and run Procedure 8.2.1 to calculate the exposures, for each bucket, to the three basic smile movements: the parallel shift, the change of the slope and the change of the curvature. For any option, and in general for the entire portfolio, we will be able to measure how its value modifies as a consequence of the occurrence of one of the movements. We do not need any particular weighting scheme for splitting the total exposure between two contiguous buckets, since the recalibration to a tilted volatility surface in Procedure 8.2.1 will provide the suitable allocation implicitly.

Once we have built a panel of Vega, Vanna and Volga (BS model), or of sensitivities to the volatility smile's movements (LMUV model), for an entire options book, we can calculate the quantities of the three basic options (ATM, and the two 25D wings) to hedge the exposures. In case we are employing the BS model, we can solve a system so as to nil for each expiry the total Vega, Vanna and Volga. In case we are using an LMUV model, we simply measure for each bucket the sensitivity of each of the three basic options to the three smile movements and then solve once again a system to nil the exposures. The hedging amounts can then be translated into the main instruments (ATM **STDL**, 25D **RR** and 25D **VWB**) by means of formula (3.50) in Chapter 3. Although satisfactory in most practical situations, we should anyway stress the fact that in this way the amounts of the three basic instruments are not precise, since we are not considering the correct definition of **VWB**.[12] To circumvent this (usually small) error, we

---

[10] We know from the analysis of Chapter 3 that it is possible to hedge against the changes of the volatility smile for a given expiry, by a number of options equal to the number of factors determining the smile itself.

[11] See Chapter 4.

[12] See Chapter 4 for a discussion of how to properly deal with the actual **VWB** traded in the market.

could calculate the sensitivities of the three main structures directly (then consider the actual **VWB** traded in the market) to the three basic instruments (ATM, and the two 25D wings), and then solve the system to nil the volatility-related exposures, thus yielding the amounts of main instruments needed for hedging.

8.3.4 Barrier implicit one-touch, bets and digitals

An FX options book contains mainly, amongst its exotic contracts, barrier options, bets and digitals. All those options have a typical risk due to discontinuity of their payoffs, usually named *pin-risk* for the way it manifests when mapping the value of the contract at expiry. It is very useful to monitor the amount of the pin-risk, by a risk monitoring tool that recognizes it throughout the entire book and shows the related amount and expiry date of the contract.

As far as barrier options are concerned, the implicit one-touch has to be determined. This refers only to reverse knock-out options (i.e., the barrier is set at a level at which the option is in-the-money at expiry) and we have already seen it in Chapter 6, when analysing the market approach to pricing barrier options. For a given contract the implicit one-touch is defined as

$$\mathbf{iot} = -|H - K| \times N \tag{8.2}$$

where N is the base currency notional amount. The negative sign is due to the fact that when a trader is long the reverse knock-out option, they are actually short the implicit one-touch, since the breaching of the barrier is equivalent to an outflow of cash equal to the (absolute) intrinsic value between the barrier and the strike price.

It should be stressed that the implicit one-touch, as well as the option's payoff, is expressed in terms of numeraire currency and this is not always convenient for hedging and risk management purposes. In more detail, the reason why it is important to monitor such risk is that it can also be hedged with other contracts, such as other barrier options expiring on the same date and with the same barrier (though with a different strike) or, as usually happens, with one-touch options. Now, it may very often happen that bets (and therefore one-touches) have payoffs denominated in base currency amounts as market standard. For example, this is the case for EURUSD, whose one-touches are traded amongst professionals with a euro-denominated payout. Also, USDJPY one-touches have a market standard payout denominated in the base currency (i.e., US dollars). Since we would like to know how much one-touch we should trade with a professional to hedge the implicit one-touch risk, it is better to express it in base currency terms for those pairs whose market standard is to trade base-currency-denominated bets. Equation (8.2) will simply modify as follows:

$$\mathbf{iot} = -\frac{|H - K| \times N}{H}$$

since upon the barrier, one base currency unit is equal to $1/H$ numeraire currency units.

The pin-risk of a bet contract is given by the notional amount, however denominated, in case of one-touches (either paid at expiry or at hitting time),

$$\mathbf{ot} = N \tag{8.3}$$

If the contract's amount is denominated in numeraire currency, it is worth converting it into a base currency amount when the market standard is defined in such a way, thus:

$$\mathbf{ot} = N_{numccy} \times H$$

For the no-touch option the implicit one-touch is

$$\mathbf{ot} = -N \tag{8.4}$$

or, if we want to convert it into a numeraire-currency-denominated contract:

$$\mathbf{ot} = -N_{numccy} \times H$$

Double no-touches have pin-risks referring to the two upper and lower barrier levels. They are equal to the notional amount and, since the contract expires worthless when one of the two barriers is breached, a long **DNT** position implies a short implicit one-touch exposure on both levels. Assuming that the payout is denominated in base currency, we have that the implicit one-touch risk is

$$\mathbf{iot} = -N \tag{8.5}$$

If the notional amount is denominated in numeraire currency, the conversion depends on the level, so that we have

$$\mathbf{iot} = -N \times U$$

for the upper barrier, and

$$\mathbf{iot} = -N \times L$$

for the lower barrier. Double-touches simply have reverse sign to double-no-touches.

Example 8.3.3. *Assume a market maker has a position of* 75 *million EUR of a EURUSD* **UOC** *expiring on* 15 *December* 2008*, struck at* 1.4200 *and with a barrier at* 1.6000*. The implicit knock-out is*

$$\mathbf{iot} = -|1.6000 - 1.4200| \times 75\,000\,000 = 13\,500\,000\ USD$$

Since in the market standard EURUSD one-touches are denominated in EUR amounts, we prefer to express the implicit one-touch in euro units:

$$\mathbf{iot} = -\frac{|1.6000 - 1.4200|}{1.6000} \times 75\,000\,000 = 8\,437\,500\ EUR \tag{8.6}$$

The trader could try to hedge this pin-risk by trading a one-touch option with the same expiry and paying at hit an amount of 8 437 000 *EUR.*

If the market maker has on his portfolio a short position in a no-touch expiring on the same date as the barrier options above, and paying 8 437 000 *EUR at maturity if the barrier is never breached, then they could consider this as an alternative to trading the one-touch, although (as is manifest from the pricing formulae) the implicit one-touch of a no-touch contract is paid at expiry. If the time to maturity is not so long, that makes no great difference in practice, although a one-touch paid at hit better serves the hedging purpose.*

Assume now the market maker is short one **DNT** *contract paying at the* 6*-month expiry* 1 *million EUR if either barrier never trades (we set the lower level at* 1.3900 *and the higher level at* 1.5700*). They are implicitly long two one-touch contracts expiring in* 6 *months, one with a barrier at* 1.3900 *and the other equal to* 1.5700*, both paying* 1 *million EUR. It is evident that this kind of hedge is rough (although useful in practice) since, once one of the two levels is breached, the* **DNT** *expires and so does the corresponding one-touch, but the other one-touch is still alive, thus engendering a new pin-risk that has to be managed. In most cases, since the* *market moved definitely in one direction, this risk is quite negligible; nevertheless, it has to be monitored and hedged.*

DTE *should be Delta in the same fashion as the* **DNT**, *but one-touches paying at expiry are a more appropriate hedge.*

We now move on to consider the pin-risk related to digital options. As before, this is the notional amount of the contract, expressed according to the market standard for the pair. For the EURUSD, as an example, the standard payout is expressed in euros. Differently from the pin-risk referring to exotic options, for digital options it can change sign during the life of the contract. Actually, while breaching of the barrier entails termination of the contract for an exotic option, crossing of the digital's strike price, prior to maturity, does not trigger any specific event. Nevertheless, depending on whether the FX spot rate is above or below the strike, the pin-risk may have a positive or negative value that switches sign when the FX spot rate crosses the strike level.

To be more precise, in case of a digital call, the digital pin-risk is defined as

$$\mathbf{dig}_c = \mathbf{1}_{S_t<K} N - \mathbf{1}_{S_t\geq K} N \tag{8.7}$$

and for a digital put:

$$\mathbf{dig}_p = \mathbf{1}_{S_t>K} N - 1_{S_t\leq K} N \tag{8.8}$$

Take, for instance, a digital call. If the FX spot rate is below the strike, the pin-risk is positive, since if the spot is above the strike at expiry, the notional amount is received. This risk can be hedged by an identical digital option, with the opposite position. Assume now that the FX spot rate is above the strike. The risk is that at expiry the payoff will not be paid if the spot moves below the strike level. Therefore, the pin-risk has a negative sign in this case, and it can be hedged either by selling the digital call, as before, or by buying a digital put expiring on the same date and with the same notional, providing the good hedge for the pin-risk as can be seen by inspecting equations (8.7) and (8.8).

The pin-risk in the equations above is in base currency units. This is the proper way to deal with digital options paying an amount denominated in base currency. When the amount is denominated in numeraire currency, we can convert the risk by dividing by the strike, but we should remember also the static replication formulae (5.23) and (5.24) in Chapter 5, when trying to hedge the pin-risk with an option denominated in the other currency of the pair. This is a little trickier than the exotic bets.

Example 8.3.4. *Assume the market maker has on their book a EURUSD digital call expiring in* 4 *months and paying* 1 *million EUR if the FX spot rate is above* 1.5700 *at maturity, with a current level of* 1.4300. *The pin-risk today is*

$$\mathbf{dig}_c = 1\,000\,000\ EUR$$

To hedge the risk the market maker could either sell the same digital call or buy a digital put, with the same expiry and notional.

Assume now that the notional is denominated in USD. In the market the EURUSD standard is for EUR-denominated amounts, so we prefer to express the risk in euros. We have:

$$\mathbf{dig}_c = \frac{1\,000\,000\ USD}{1.5700} = 636\,942.68\ EUR$$

To hedge the pin-risk in the market, the trader can sell a digital call with a notional amount of 636 943 *EUR and then, by considering equation (5.23), buy also a* 1 *million EUR plain vanilla call option.*

8.3.5 Interest rate-related Greeks

The monitoring of the sensitivity of an option's value to changes in the domestic and foreign interest rates is operated in a fashion similar to the methods we have described above. We also consider the cases separately when the options book is managed by the BS model and by the LMUV model.

We have shown in Chapter 2 the domestic and foreign Rhos for the BS model. We would like to remark on the fact that the sensitivity is with respect to a change in the time-average interest rate up to the option's expiry, within an environment where interest rates are deterministically time-dependent. The bucketing can be performed by calculating the derivatives with respect to the time-averaged integrated interest rates up to expiry of the option, and then allocating the total Rho amount on the contiguous expiries with weights determined via a linear interpolation. More specifically, for either a domestic or foreign interest rate we have

$$R(T) = \int_0^T r(t)\,dt = T\bar{r}(T)$$

with $\bar{r}(T) = (\int_0^T r(s)ds)/T$. If we linearly interpolate between two time buckets T_i and T_{i+1}:

$$\begin{aligned}\int_0^T r(t)dt &= \frac{R(T_{i+1}) - R(T_i)}{T_{i+1} - T_i}(T - T_i) + R(T_i) \\ &= \frac{T_{i+1}\bar{r}(T_{i+1}) - T_i\bar{r}(T_i)}{T_{i+1} - T_i}(T - T_i) + T_i\bar{r}(T_i) \\ &= \frac{T - T_i}{T_{i+1} - T_i}T_{i+1}\bar{r}(T_{i+1}) + \frac{T_{i+1} - T}{T_{i+1} - T_i}T_i\bar{r}(T_i)\end{aligned}$$

and hence

$$\bar{r}(T) = \frac{T - T_i}{T_{i+1} - T_i}\frac{T_{i+1}}{T}\bar{r}(T_{i+1}) + \frac{T_{i+1} - T}{T_{i+1} - T_i}\frac{T_i}{T}\bar{r}(T_i)$$

so that the weights to allocate to the Rhos are

$$\begin{aligned}w_i &= \frac{T_{i+1} - T}{T_{i+1} - T_i}\frac{T_i}{T} \\ w_{i+1} &= \frac{T - T_i}{T_{i+1} - T_i}\frac{T_{i+1}}{T}\end{aligned}$$

If we employ an LMUV model, we could exploit its properties and calculate the Rhos as a linear combination of BS Rhos. For the domestic Rho this is quite straightforward:

$$\begin{aligned}\mathrm{Rho}^{d\,\mathrm{UV}} &= \lambda \mathrm{Rho}^d(S_t, t, T, K, P^d(t,T), P_1^f(t,T), \sigma_1, \omega) \\ &\quad + (1-\lambda)\mathrm{Rho}^d(S_t, t, T, K, P^d(t,T), P_2^f(t,T), \sigma_2, \omega) \qquad (8.9)\end{aligned}$$

where the subscripts refer to the volatilities and foreign interest rates used in the two scenarios. The weights to allocate Rho into two contiguous buckets are the same as above.

As for the foreign Rho, this is a little trickier but it can be shown that it is

$$\text{Rho}^{f\,\text{UV}} = (1-\lambda)\text{Rho}^f(S_t, t, T, K, P^d(t,T), P_2^f(t,T), \sigma_2, \omega)\frac{\partial \bar{r}_2^f}{\partial \bar{r}^f} \tag{8.10}$$

The problem here is that we cannot calculate analytically the quantity $\partial \bar{r}_2^f / \partial \bar{r}^f$, so that we are forced to compute the foreign Rho numerically. This is operated by shifting the foreign rate for a given bucket expiry by a small amount, say 10 basis points, recalibrating the model to the new set of input data, then revaluing the option (or the entire book), and finally calculating the numerical derivative. In this case, when performing the bucketing for all the expiries by tilting one by one all the foreign interest rates, the allocation between contiguous buckets is implicitly determined by the procedure.

We also dwell some time here on the hedging of the Rhos. This can be achieved by money market instruments, such as deposits in both currencies involved in the pair, FX swaps and cross-currency swaps for long-dated options. FX swaps are by far the preferred tool employed by risk managers, since they allow for an exposure to interest rates without any FX spot rate risk (if it is "no par", see Chapter 1 for more detail). We can calculate the Rhos of the FX swap from its definition as the sum of an outright minus a spot contract, that is

$$\mathbf{Fsw}(t,T) = \mathbf{Fw}(t,T) - S_t$$

The Rhos in a BS environment are

$$\frac{\partial \mathbf{Fsw}(t,T)}{\partial \bar{r}_t^d} = \tau \overline{F} P^d(t,T)$$

and

$$\frac{\partial \mathbf{Fsw}(t,T)}{\partial \bar{r}_t^f} = -\tau S_t P^f(t,T)$$

where $\overline{F}$ is the contract forward price. Delta is

$$\frac{\partial \mathbf{Fsw}(t,T)}{\partial S_t} = P^f(t,T) - 1$$

If the forward contract is "no par", then we know it is

$$\mathbf{Fsw}(t,T) = \frac{1}{P^f(t,T)}\mathbf{Fw}(t,T) - S_t$$

The Rhos in a BS environment are

$$\frac{\partial \mathbf{Fsw}(t,T)}{\partial \bar{r}_t^d} = \tau \overline{F}\frac{P^d(t,T)}{P^f(t,T)}$$

and

$$\frac{\partial \mathbf{Fsw}(t,T)}{\partial \bar{r}_t^f} = -\tau \overline{F}\frac{P^d(t,T)}{\overline{P}^f(t,T)}$$

Table 8.12 Domestic and foreign zero-coupon bond prices (discount factors) used in the simulations

Expiry	P^d	P^f
O/N	0.99994	0.99989
1W	0.99955	0.99922
2W	0.99910	0.99840
1M	0.99793	0.99655
2M	0.99508	0.99205
3M	0.99261	0.98806
6M	0.98501	0.97580
9M	0.97728	0.96353
1Y	0.96898	0.95088

where P^f dividing the forward contract is the factor adjustment to the final exchanged amount so as to make the contract hedged against the FX spot at expiry. Delta is

$$\frac{\partial \mathbf{Fsw}(t, T)}{\partial S_t} = 0$$

In the LMUV model the Rhos can be computed as for other Greeks: the domestic Rho is simply the linear combination of the corresponding BS Greek, with foreign interest rates and volatilities referred to the two scenarios. The foreign Rho is correctly computed numerically by recalibrating the model, as explained above.

8.4 RISK ANALYSIS OF PLAIN VANILLA OPTIONS

We now examine in more depth the risk exposures of plain vanilla options, and more specifically of the three main instruments traded in the market. The analysis is carried out both in a BS flat-smile environment and in an LMUV model, focusing on some subtle implications deriving from the market conventions. For a general discussion of the exposures of the main instruments to the volatility surface, we refer to Chapter 3.

We will use the following market data, which reflect a typical situation in the EURUSD market: the spot rate at time $t = 0$ is 1.4000, and the zero-coupon prices are those shown in Table 8.12.

The volatility surface is built with the VV method and the input data shown in Table 8.13.

8.4.1 ATM straddle

In a BS environment with flat smile, the ATM **STDL** is the structure allowing exposure to Vega, without any exposure to the other two volatility-related Greeks, Vanna and Volga.[13] It is manifest (see Figure 8.5, right-hand side) that at the starting level[14] of 1.4000, which yields an ATM level of 1.3904, the Vega of a long ATM **STDL** is at its maximum, whereas the other two Greeks (Figures 8.6 and 8.7, right-hand side) show zero or negligible values.

[13] Actually, a small Volga exposure is produced by the ATM **STDL**, unless the Delta is calculated including the premium; this does not happen for all pairs.

[14] The strike levels given Delta are calculated by means of the formulae and the procedure shown in Chapter 2.

Table 8.13 Implied volatilites for the main strikes used in the simulations

	25D P	ATM	25D C
O/N	13.15%	13.00%	13.15%
1W	11.10%	11.00%	11.20%
2W	10.80%	10.75%	11.00%
1M	10.27%	10.25%	10.52%
2M	10.00%	10.00%	10.30%
3M	9.77%	9.80%	10.12%
6M	9.98%	10.00%	10.36%
9M	10.08%	10.10%	10.48%
1Y	10.19%	10.20%	10.59%

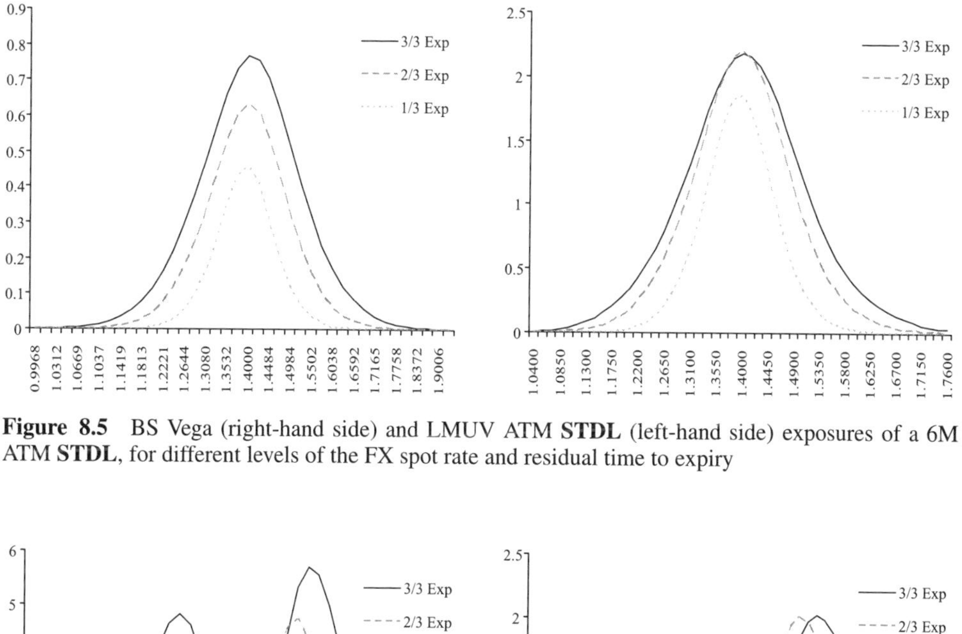

Figure 8.5 BS Vega (right-hand side) and LMUV ATM **STDL** (left-hand side) exposures of a 6M ATM **STDL**, for different levels of the FX spot rate and residual time to expiry

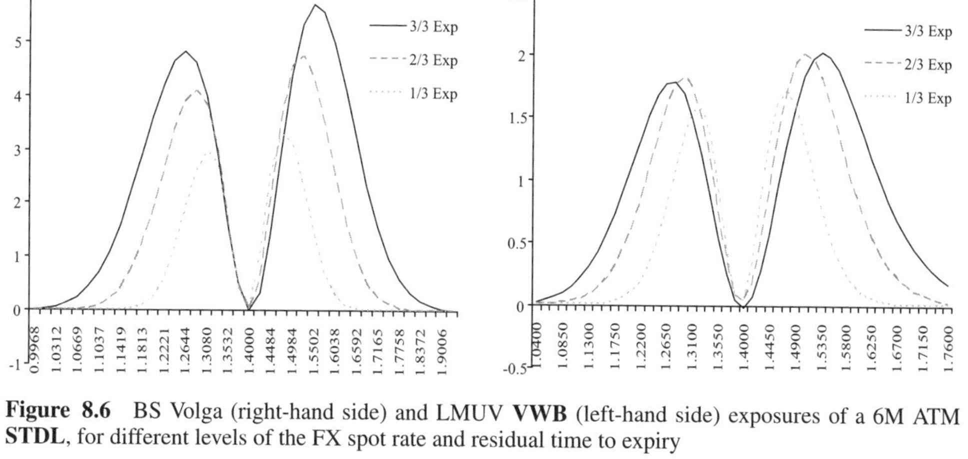

Figure 8.6 BS Volga (right-hand side) and LMUV **VWB** (left-hand side) exposures of a 6M ATM **STDL**, for different levels of the FX spot rate and residual time to expiry

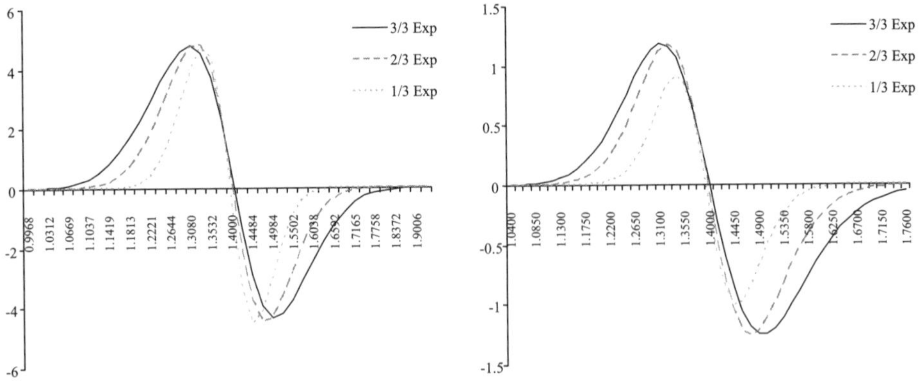

Figure 8.7 BS Vanna (right-hand side) and LMUV **RR** (left-hand side) exposures of a 6M ATM **STDL**, for different levels of the FX spot rate and residual time to expiry

The exposures are strongly dependent on the FX spot. Vega is declining as the spot moves from the starting level, and this is confirmed by the shape of Vanna in Figure 8.7, right-hand side, which is negative on the right-hand side and positive on the left-hand side. Also, Volga changes with the FX spot rate, becoming increasingly positive as the spot moves in either direction, up to a maximum, then declining with further movements. The profile is symmetrical.

Considering the evolutions of the three exposures as the time to maturity decreases, it can be seen that the profile of all the three Greeks keeps the same shape at a lower level (in the figures, Vega, Vanna and Volga are drawn when the time to maturity is six (3/3), four (2/3) and two (1/3) months to maturity). Given the three exposures above, it is evident that a long position in an ATM **STDL** is a second-moment play, since it will gain value if the (expected) volatility of the FX spot rate increases.

If we want to manage the risk of our portfolio by means of the LMUV model, then we can analyse the exposures of the ATM **STDL** in terms of the three basic instruments, that is to say: the ATM **STDL** itself, the 25D **RR** and the 25D **VWB**. In Figure 8.5, left-hand side, the exposure equivalent to the ATM **STDL** is plotted for different levels of Delta and for a shortening time to maturity (as above). It is quite tautological to say that an ATM **STDL** made up of one call and one put is equivalent to two ATM **STDLs** at the starting FX rate.[15] The same exposure as the FX spot move is more interesting and its shape is, not surprisingly, similar to the shape of Vega in the BS framework. Also, the behaviour as the time to expiry decreases shows the same pattern.

Very similar considerations can be made for the exposures of the ATM **STDL** in terms of the **VWB** and **RR** shown, respectively, in Figures 8.6 and 8.7, left-hand side. The shapes resemble the BS Greeks exposures both in the space and time dimension. The analogy between Vega and the ATM **STDL** exposure, Volga and the **VWB** exposure, and Vanna and the **RR** exposure also confirms the analysis of Chapter 3, which anticipated the results we are now showing from a more tangible perspective.

Since the exposures to the **RR** and **VWB** are zero, the ATM **STDL** is a smile-level play within an LMUV setting.

[15] We recall from Chapter 1 that one unit of ATM **STDL** is built from a half base currency amount of put options and a half amount of call options according to market conventions.

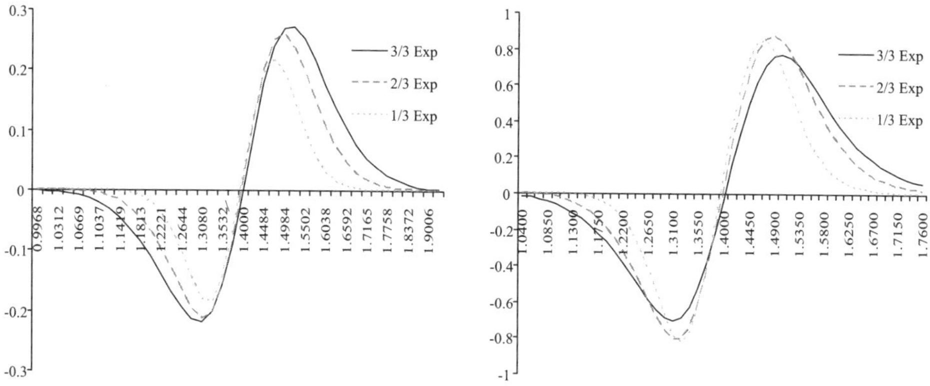

Figure 8.8 BS Vega (right-hand side) and LMUV ATM **STDL** (left-hand side) exposures of a 6M **RR**, for different levels of the FX spot rate and residual time to expiry

8.4.2 Risk reversal

We move on to analyse the **RR**, starting as usual from the BS setting. The Vega of a long position in this structure (long one unit of base currency 25D call and short the same amount of 25D put option) is shown in Figure 8.8, right-hand side. From an initial nil Vega exposure, when the FX spot rate increases, a corresponding higher Vega results, whereas the opposite occurs when the spot declines, according to a symmetrical though specular pattern. This is obviously confirmed by the Vanna exposure of the **RR**, which is plotted in Figure 8.10, right-hand side. This is positive but decreasing, both for higher and lower values than the starting FX spot rate, becoming negative for wide variations of the underlying and then approaching zero.

The time behaviour of the **RR** is very regular, as the ATM in the sense that the profiles of both the Vega and Vanna exposures retain their shapes, but they have lower values for shorter time to maturity and with maximum and minimum points corresponding to a nearer level of the FX spot rate.

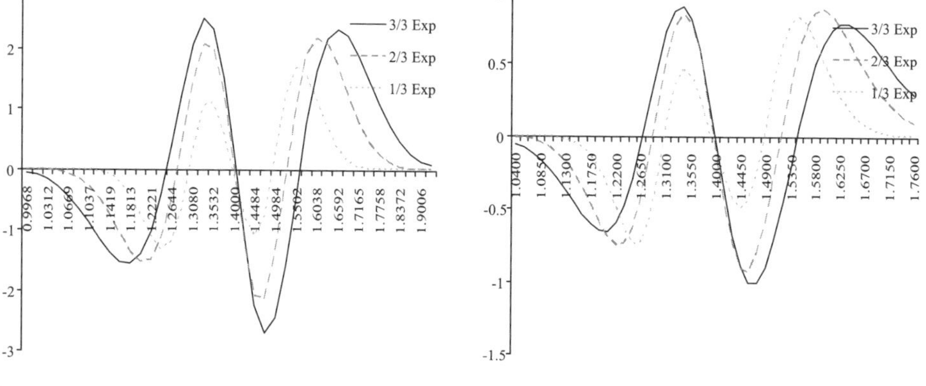

Figure 8.9 BS Volga (right-hand side) and LMUV **VWB** (left-hand side) exposures of a 6M **RR**, for different levels of the FX spot rate and residual time to expiry

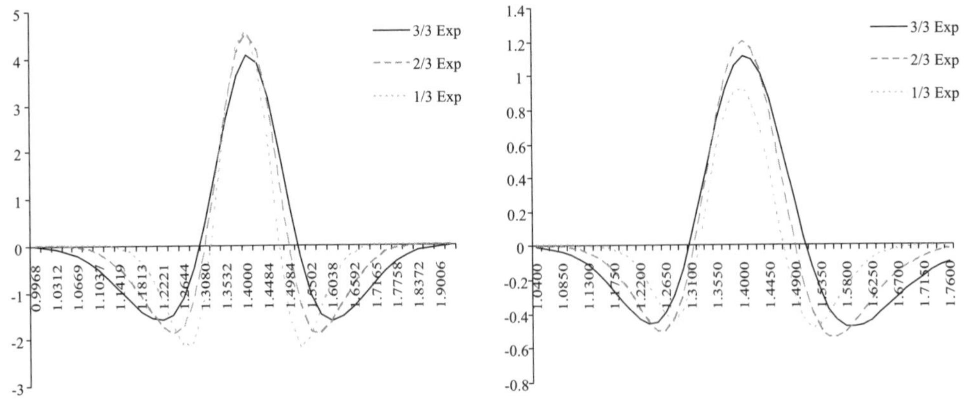

Figure 8.10 BS Vanna (right-hand side) and LMUV **RR** (left-hand side) exposures of a 6M **RR**, for different levels of the FX spot rate and residual time to expiry

Finally, the Volga of the **RR**, plotted in Figure 8.9, right-hand side, shows a rather interesting behaviour, starting from a zero value when the structure is set up, then becoming sharply negative (positive) as the FX spot rate soars (plunges). As usual, as expiry approaches, the basic shape of the exposure is kept with shrinking FX spot rate ranges between the maximum and minimum and generally lower values. It should be stressed that we are working in a sort of laboratory environment, since we are assuming that no skew appears in the market, so that our risk management system reproduces market conditions exactly. This is not usually the case, so we will determine the 25D strikes for the **RR** by plugging into the formulae the related market implied volatility. When we revalue the options with a flat smile (10% in our example), the two options will not be exactly struck at a 25D level, the difference being directly proportional to the (absolute) steepness of the smile (or, alternatively, the **rr** price). The final effect will be that at the starting FX spot level the Vega position will not be zero, but will be slightly positive or negative depending on the sign of **rr**.

Example 8.4.1. *Given the market data as shown at the beginning of this section, we have that the Vega of a 6M* **RR***, according to market implied volatilities extracted from the price of the three main structures, is the following:*

	Strike	*Market volatility*	*Market vega*	*Flat-smile vega*
25D P	*1.3282*	*9.98%*	*−0.308007*	*−0.308241*
25D C	*1.4584*	*10.35%*	*0.308007*	*0.302745*
RR *net Vega:*			*0.000000*	*−0.005496*

The flat-smile Vega is calculated by the single common volatility equal to the ATM **STDL** *for the 6M expiry, i.e.,* 10%.

Another market convention prevents us from enjoying the rather nice feature of the 25D **RR**: for those pairs whose options' Delta is calculated in the market with included premium, the strikes will not exactly refer to the pure 25D BS Delta, even in the theoretical presence of a flat smile. Also in this case, the initial Vega exposure will be slightly different from zero. In real market activity one or both effects may be operating.

Example 8.4.2. *Assume that the 25D strikes for a EURUSD 6M* **RR** *are calculated with the (non-standard) market convention of including the premium in Delta. In this case we have the following net Vega:*

	Strike	*Volatility*	*Vega*	*Flat-smile Vega*
25D P	*1.3249*	*9.99%*	*0.300769*	*0.300931*
25D C	*1.4522*	*10.31%*	*−0.319057*	*−0.315028*
RR *net Vega:*			*−0.018289*	*−0.014097*

This example is rather virtual for the EURUSD and it only serves the purpose of showing that even calculating the Vega with market volatilities, the **RR** *is no longer Vega-neutral when the premium is included. The slightly different volatilities for the 25D strikes are due to the fact that we are still using a volatility surface built with prices referred to Deltas without premium inclusion.*

For all those pairs whose premiums are included in Delta, such as the USDJPY, the example applies also in reality.

The long 25D **RR** is a Vanna play, since it has (almost, in reality) zero Vega and Volga exposures, and a positive Vanna. It is a strategy that earns money if the third moment of the FX spot rate increases.

When we examine the **RR** in an LMUV setting and calculate its exposures in terms of the three basic traded instruments, we still observe a strict analogy between Vega, Vanna, Volga and, respectively, the ATM **STDL**, 25D **RR** and 25D **VWB** exposures. This is manifest in Figures 8.8, 8.9 and 8.10, left-hand side. In practice, we can repeat the same considerations made before for the corresponding Greeks.

Basically, the third moment play of the BS model translates into a smile-steepening play in an LMUV model.

8.4.3 Vega-weighted butterfly

Finally we examine the 25D **VWB**: the BS Vega, Volga and Vanna are plotted in Figures 8.11, 8.12 and 8.13, right-hand side. The Vega, similarly to the 25D **RR**, is by construction equal to zero at the starting FX spot level, increasing up to a maximum as the latter moves, then declining towards zero. This is reflected by the Vanna exposure, which starts from a zero value and switches sign accordingly with lower and higher levels of the FX spot rate. The time behaviour of Vega is partially similar to the other structures we have seen before, but it should be stressed that if the FX spot rate is stale, the total Vega changes sign, becoming more and more negative as the expiry approaches. This is due to the fact that the Vega weighting factor indicating the **STGL** quantity to trade against an **STDL** is fixed at the initial value, but it should actually be increased to preserve Vega-neutrality. The negative Vega exposure of the **STDL** is heavier than the positive Vega exposure of the **STGL** as time goes by.

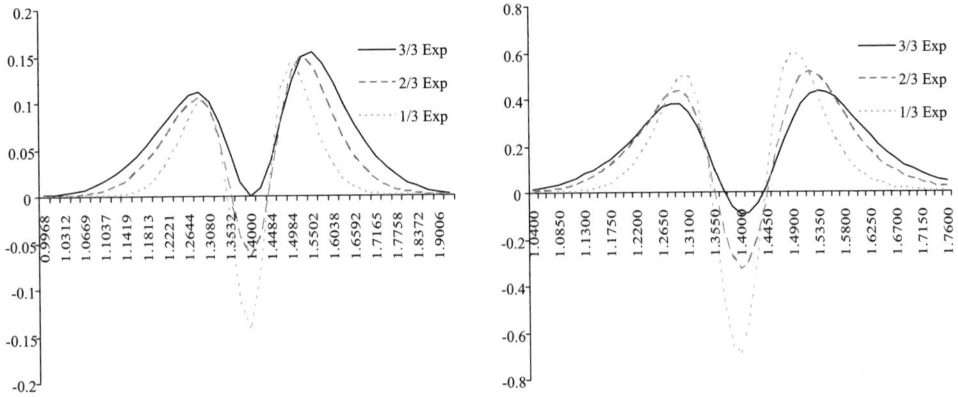

Figure 8.11 BS Vega (right-hand side) and LMUV ATM **STDL** (left-hand side) exposures of a 6M **VWB**, for different levels of the FX spot rate and residual time to expiry

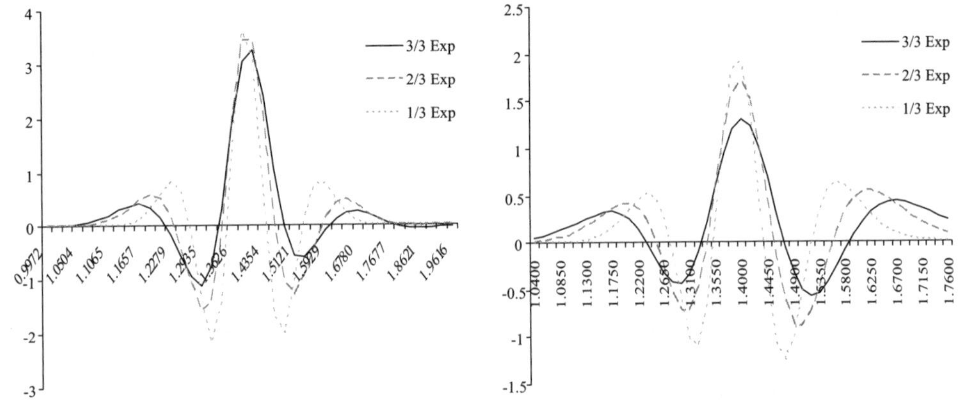

Figure 8.12 BS Volga (right-hand side) and LMUV **VWB** (left-hand side) exposures of a 6M **VWB**, for different levels of the FX spot rate and residual time to expiry

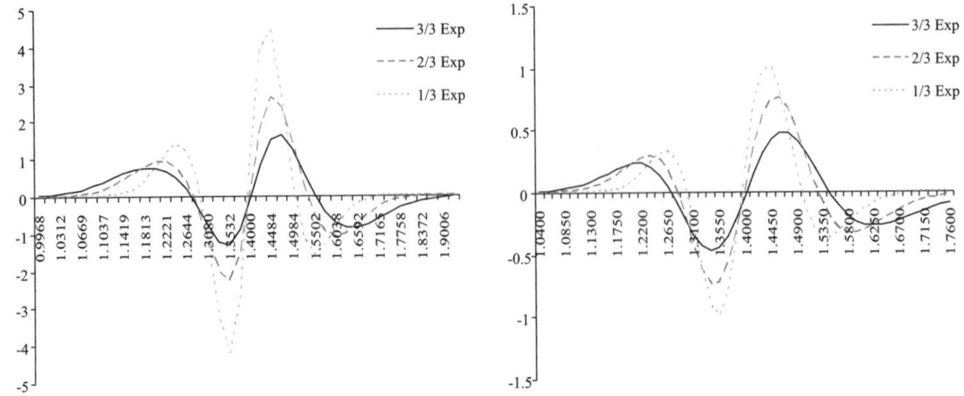

Figure 8.13 BS Vanna (right-hand side) and LMUV **RR** (left-hand side) exposures of a 6M **VWB**, for different levels of the FX spot rate and residual time to expiry

Volga is positive at the starting FX spot level, and is at its maximum. It declines as the underlying moves to also become negative for relatively moderate excursions of the underlying. The time evolution of the Volga is quite surprising, since its starting value for a **VWB** seems to be very feebly affected by the approach of expiry.

Also for the **VWB** the nice feature of a zero Vega and Vanna exposure and a positive Volga are lost when things come down to real market activity. In fact, the presence of a smile will produce non-symmetrical wings in terms of Delta when revaluing the structure within a BS flat-smile setting. This will result in a not-exact Vega weighting factor,[16] thus obtaining a slightly negative total Vega exposure. Moreover, a positive or negative steepness of the smile (**rr** $\neq 0$) will make the starting **RR** value different from zero.

Example 8.4.3. *Assume we are trading a 6M* **VWB** *in the market. Given the market data we have also used in the previous example and the market conventions for this structure, the volatility price is* 10.17% ((9.98% + 10.36%)/2) *and the 25D wing strikes are calculated with this volatility as well as the Vega weighting factor (rounded to* 1.24 *for practical purposes). The net Vega we have according to the market convention volatilities and the true smile volatilities that we have to apply to the strikes is the following:*

	Strike	**VWB** *vol.*	**VWB** *Vega*	*Smile vol.*	*Smile Vega*
ATM C	*1.3905*	*10.00%*	*−0.381795*	*10.00%*	*−0.381795*
ATM P	*1.3905*	*10.00%*	*−0.381795*	*10.00%*	*−0.381795*
25D P	*1.4571*	*10.17%*	*0.381928*	*10.17%*	*0.379163*
25D C	*1.3272*	*10.17%*	*0.381928*	*10.17%*	*0.384991*
VWB *net Vega (weighting ratio:* 1.24*):*			*0.000266*		*0.000564*

The **VWB** *has a negligible Vega according to the market volatility and it is still quite small and nil for practical purposes, even when we consider the true volatility, interpolated on the smile, that we should plug into the BS formula to calculate the Vega. Nonetheless, it is remarkable that the value more than doubled in the second case. The steeper the smile, the larger the net Vega exposure of the* **VWB** *when passing from the market convention volatilities to the smile volatilities. Moreover, it should be stressed that in any case the* **VWB** *will not be Vega-neutral in the flat volatility environment, if we choose to adopt the BS model or manage our portfolio's risks.*

Notwithstanding this imperfection, the 25D **VWB** is basically a Volga play and it is a good strategy to set up to earn on an increase of the fourth moment of the distribution of the FX spot rate.

The analysis of the 25D **VWB** in the LMUV model is shown in Figures 8.8, 8.9 and 8.10, left-hand side. Not surprisingly, we still have the same analogy as before for the Vega, Volga and Vanna exposures. The starting negative value of the ATM **STDL** is due to the fact that the market Vega weighting factor is not exactly what makes nil the former exposure in the LMUV model. The same considerations apply for the exposure to the 25D **RR**, which is almost zero.

[16] The Vega weighting factor is exact when considering the Vegas calculated by the market volatility, but it is not the same as the Vega weighting factor determined by all Vegas calculated with the same (flat) volatility.

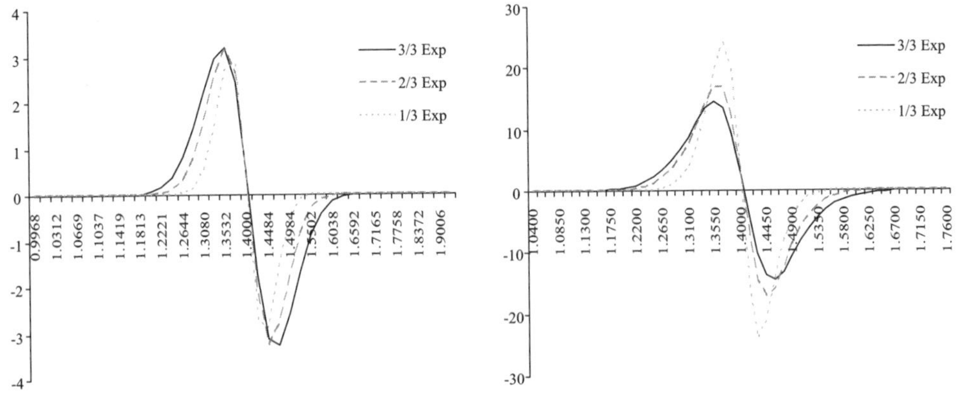

Figure 8.14 BS Vega (right-hand side) and LMUV ATM **STDL** (left-hand side) exposures of a 2M digital call option, for different levels of the FX spot rate and residual time to expiry

Clearly, the most relevant exposure is the **VWB** one. In the LMUV model, the fourth moment play of the BS model corresponds to a smile convexity play.

8.5 RISK ANALYSIS OF DIGITAL OPTIONS

Digital options are likely the most difficult to hedge payoffs to market makers. Their pin-risk is also shared by one-touch options, but for the latter it is always possible that the breaching of the barrier makes the contract end before expiry, and if this occurs rather early, the knocking implies no damage in terms of Delta-hedging and managing of the Vega-related Greeks. Unfortunately, this is not the case for digital options, since they stay alive up to expiry and hedging can become extremely toilsome if the FX spot hovers around the strike in the last few days before the end of the contract.

As an example, we analyse the risks referred to a 1 EUR digital call option with 2-month expiry and struck at 1.4000 (the other market data are the usual, shown at the beginning of Section 8.4). The value in the BS model is 46.65% of the notional and its smile-adjusted value[17] is at 45.53%. The LMUV model prices the same contract at 45.43% of the notional, in very strict accordance with the smile-adjusted value (we recall that the price of a digital is actually model-independent, given the entire volatility smile for a given expiry).

In Figure 8.14 we start by analysing the behaviour of Vega (right-hand side) and of the ATM **STDL** exposures in the LMUV model. We can still observe a strong resemblance between the two exposures as for the three main structures examined above. Besides, the profile is similar to that produced by a short **RR**, as is also clear from a comparison of the Volga and **VWB** (Figure 8.15), Vanna and **RR** exposures (Figure 8.16) and the corresponding exposures for an **RR** (Figures 8.9 and 8.10). This can be understood rather easily, since we have seen in Chapter 5 that a digital option can actually be valued via a certain amount of plain vanilla option spread by buying a lower strike contact and selling a higher strike one.

The Gamma of a digital option is shown in Figure 8.17. The profile is similar both in the BS and the LMUV model, and it is important to stress the fact that the pin-risk generates an

[17] See Formula (5.21) in Chapter 5.

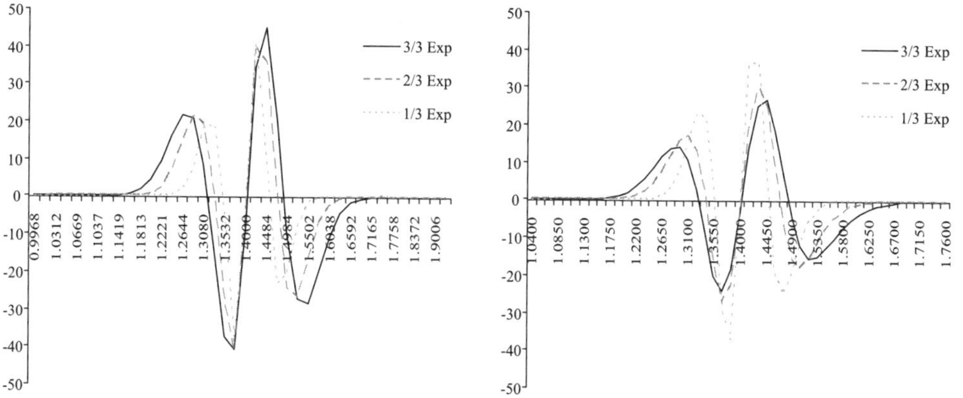

Figure 8.15 BS Volga (right-hand side) and LMUV **VWB** (left-hand side) exposures of a 2M digital call option, for different levels of the FX spot rate and residual time to expiry

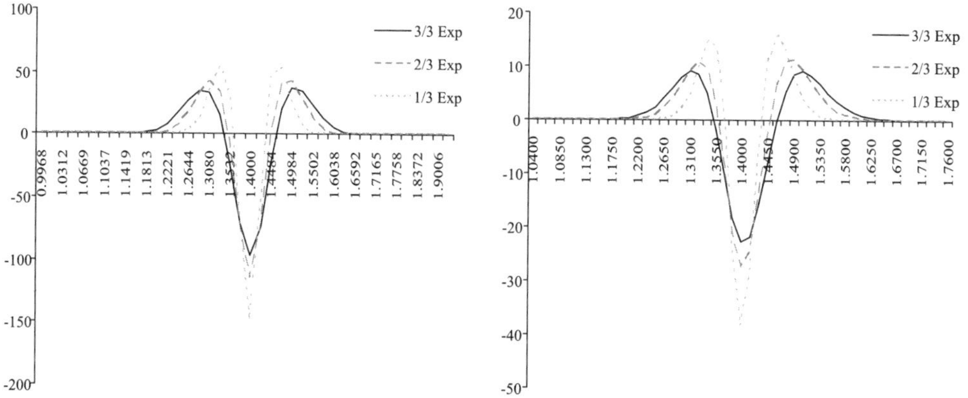

Figure 8.16 BS Vanna (right-hand side) and LMUV **RR** (left-hand side) exposures of a 2M digital call option, for different levels of the FX spot rate and residual time to expiry

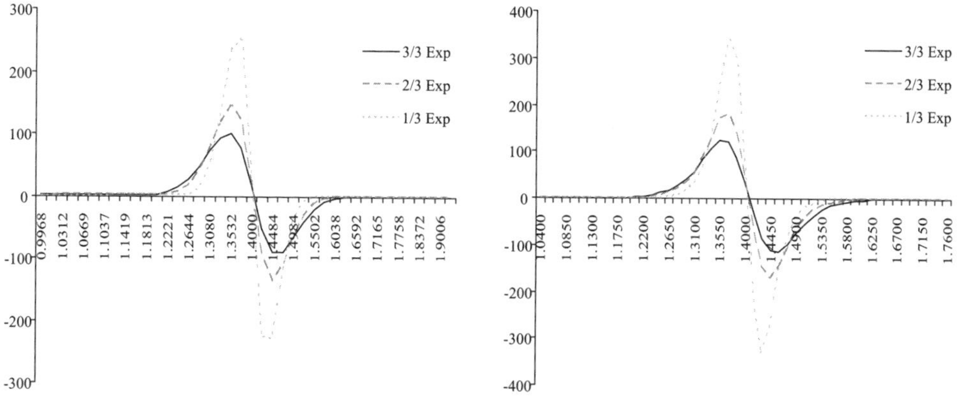

Figure 8.17 BS Gamma (right-hand side) and LMUV Gamma (left-hand side) of a 2M digital call option, for different levels of the FX spot rate and residual time to expiry

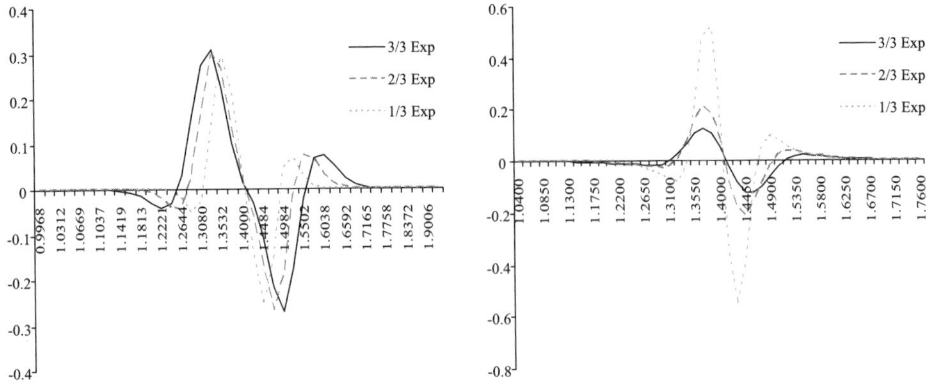

Figure 8.18 BS Vega (right-hand side) and LMUV ATM **STDL** (left-hand side) exposures of a 2M digital call option hedged by a static replication portfolio, for different levels of the FX spot rate and residual time to expiry

explosive behaviour of this Greek as the time to expiry shortens, which generates the main problem to hedgers. This risk can actually be mitigated by some hedging strategies that we are going to examine, although not fully eliminated except by reversing the position in the digital contract.

The first hedge we can set up for a position in the digital call is based on the static replication portfolio. In this case we know that the contract can be thought of as equivalent to a call option spread struck around 1.4000 plus a call option struck at 1.4000 (see equation (5.19)). We chose spread strikes of 1.3900 and 1.4100 (that means a centred replica with no over-hedge), which yields an amount of 70 million EUR of notional.[18] We show the performance of this hedge in Figures 8.18, 8.19 and 8.20. All exposures are drastically reduced and almost equal to zero for the starting FX level of 1.4000, except for the BS Vanna and the LMUV **RR**. The hedge does guarantee a zero exposure for all levels of the FX rate, but if we think that it is a static replica matching (on average) the digital payoff, then we can just set it up and forget about it, without hedging any possibly different exposure arising before the expiry (it is anyway strongly advised to follow this policy only if the replica has been built to be an over-hedge). Hence, the hedger would also disregard Delta and the changes in this Greek indicated by Gamma, which is shown in Figure 8.21.

The static replication hedge can be rather difficult to set up, for a variety of reasons: firstly, the spread should be tightly struck around the digital's strike, and the tighter it is, the larger the notional amount will be (such a kind of spread is rarely quoted in the market); secondly, the replica should ideally be in over-hedge, so that the hedger just "forgets" about it, but by doing so, the price of the digital contract (assuming that the market maker is transferring the over-hedge into it) could be worse than other competitors' prices. An alternative to the static replication hedge is provided by the hedge of the three Vega-related Greeks, if we adopt the BS model, or the exposures to the three basic instruments, if we use the LMUV model.

The performance of such hedges is shown in Figures 8.22, 8.23 and 8.24. Before noting some considerations about that, we warn that we just want to gauge the efficiency and stability of the hedge without taking into account the possibility of rebalancing. The sources of profit

[18] See Chapter 5.

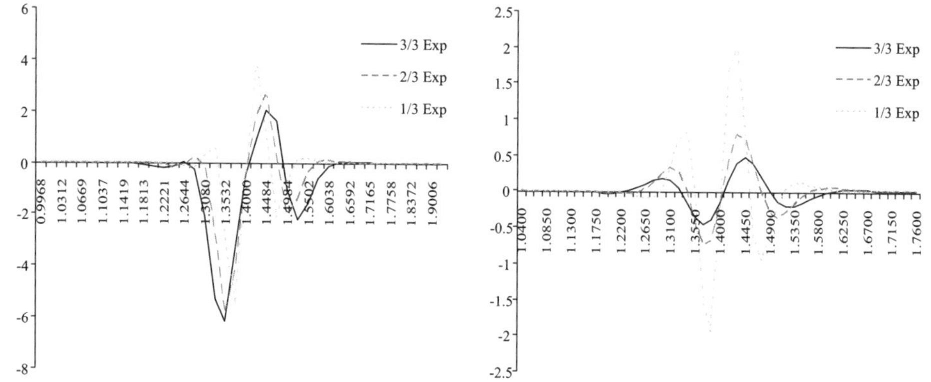

Figure 8.19 BS Volga (right-hand side) and LMUV **VWB** (left-hand side) exposures of a 2M digital call option hedged by a static replication portfolio, for different levels of the FX spot rate and residual time to expiry

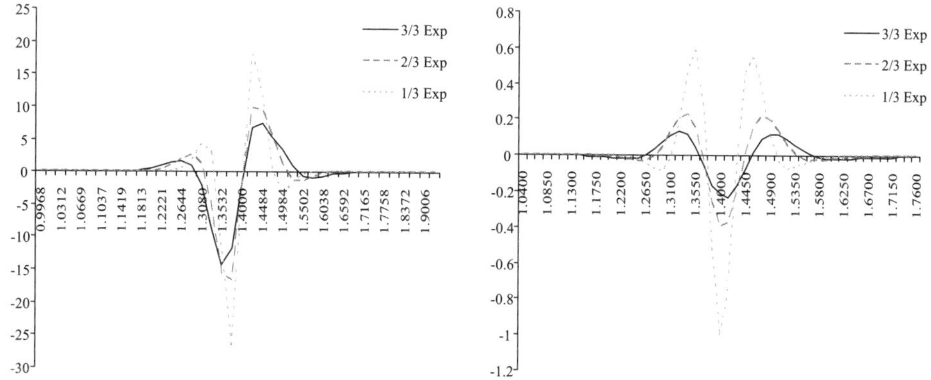

Figure 8.20 BS Vanna (right-hand side) and LMUV **RR** (left-hand side) exposures of a 2M digital call option hedged by a static replication portfolio, for different levels of the FX spot rate and residual time to expiry

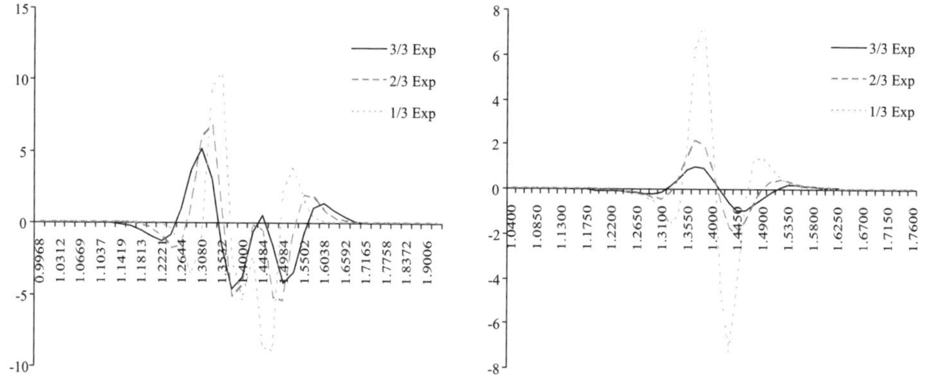

Figure 8.21 BS Gamma (right-hand side) and LMUV Gamma (left-hand side) exposures of a 2M digital call option hedged by a static replication portfolio, for different levels of the FX spot rate and residual time to expiry

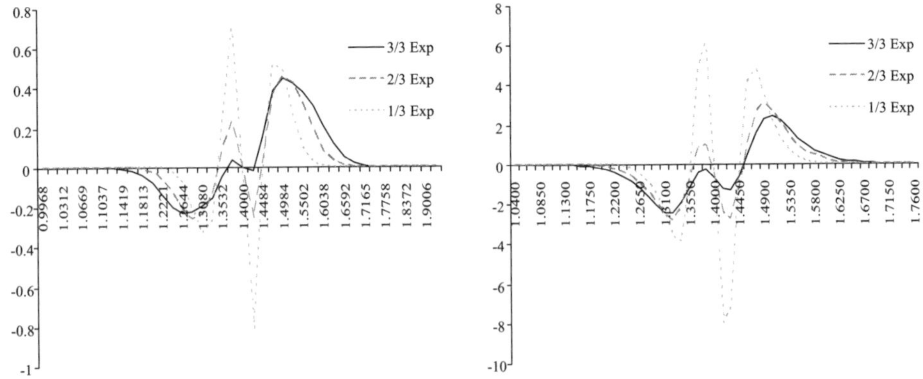

Figure 8.22 BS Vega (right-hand side) and LMUV ATM **STDL** (left-hand side) exposures of a 2M digital call option hedged by a Vega–Vanna–Volga matching, for different levels of the FX spot rate and residual time to expiry

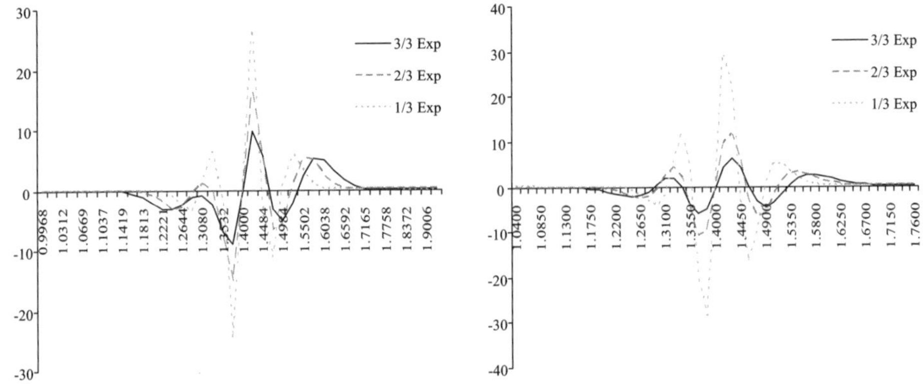

Figure 8.23 BS Volga (right-hand side) and LMUV **VWB** (left-hand side) exposures of a 2M digital call option hedged by a Vega–Vanna–Volga matching portfolio, for different levels of the FX spot rate and residual time to expiry

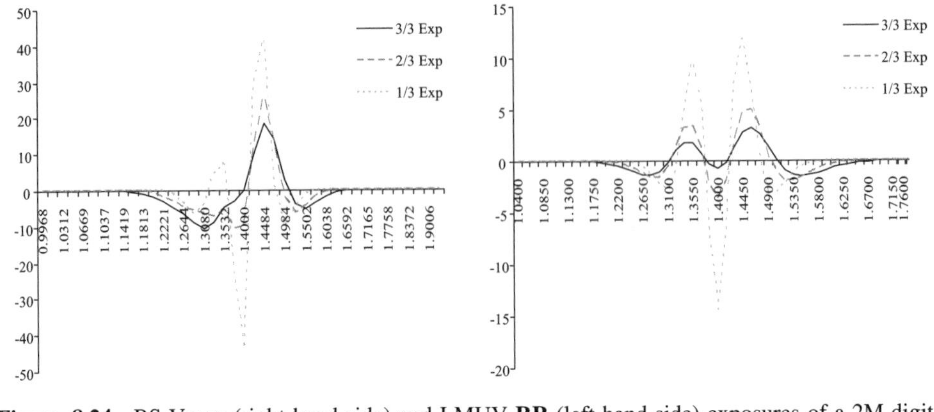

Figure 8.24 BS Vanna (right-hand side) and LMUV **RR** (left-hand side) exposures of a 2M digital call option hedged by a Vega–Vanna–Volga matching portfolio, for different levels of the FX spot rate and residual time to expiry

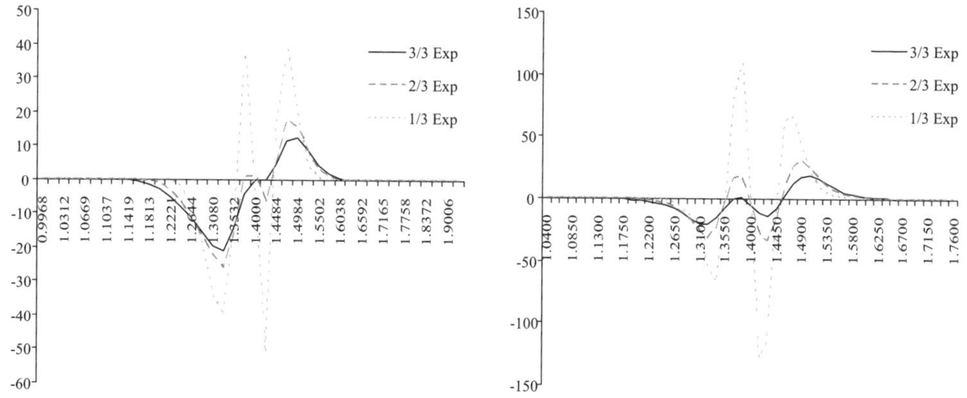

Figure 8.25 BS Gamma (right-hand side) and LMUV Gamma (left-hand side) exposures of a 2M digital call option hedged by a Vega–Vanna–Volga matching portfolio, for different levels of the FX spot rate and residual time to expiry

and loss arising from this activity have been examined thoroughly and deeply in Chapter 3 and we refer to this also for the remainder of this chapter, as far as the Vega–Vanna–Volga and the three instruments' exposure hedging is concerned.[19]

The efficiency of the hedging can be judged satisfactory, in both cases, since the general levels of the exposures are reduced for all levels of the FX spot rate. Clearly, by construction, all the exposures are nil for the starting FX spot level of 1.4000, although this value is not retained as it moves away from this point. A rebalancing is also needed as expiry approaches, both in the BS and LMUV models, and the Gamma of the entire portfolio (shown in Figure 8.25) is affected strongly by the digital pin-risk. In this case we cannot disregard Delta-hedging, and thus Gamma is the main problem the hedger has to cope with near expiry, if the FX spot rate is around the strike. Anyway, as a partial but scarcely soothing compensation, the sharp profile of Gamma is concentrated in a tight range around the strike, narrowing as the time to expiry shortens.

8.6 RISK ANALYSIS OF EXOTIC OPTIONS

We will examine the risks of the typical exotic options traded in the FX market. We know that almost 90% of these are barrier and bet contracts. We will not analyse all the possible kinds of contracts, but select some examples that we deem representative of the major risks a hedger has to face. Also in this case we use the market data shown at the beginning of Section 8.4.

8.6.1 Barrier options

Reverse knock-out options are likely the worst typology for a market maker. They entail the management of different risks, related to the implicit one-touch (pin-risk), the rather wild behaviour of the volatility-related exposures as expiry approaches (when the FX spot rate is

[19] It is worth recalling that the three instruments' exposure hedging is the scenario hedging in Chapter 3.

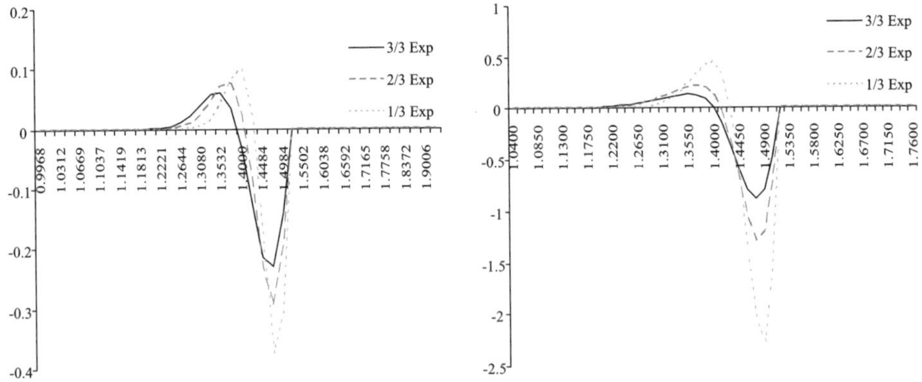

Figure 8.26 BS Vega (right-hand side) and LMUV ATM **STDL** (left-hand side) exposures of a 3M UOC for different levels of the FX spot rate and residual time to expiry

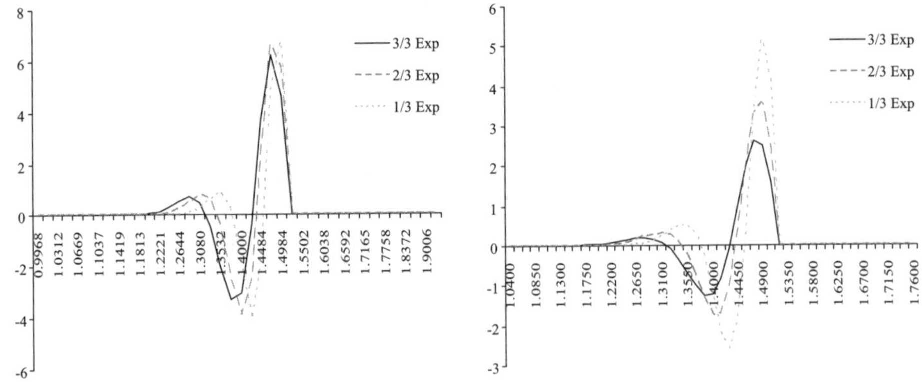

Figure 8.27 BS Volga (right-hand side) and LMUV **VWB** (left-hand side) exposures of a 3M UOC option for different levels of the FX spot rate and residual time to expiry

near the barrier level), and the Delta gap when the barrier is breached. This is also the reason why we analysed the pricing of such contracts rather extensively in Chapter 6.

The reverse knock-out we consider is a 3-month expiry UOC, struck at 1.4200 and with barrier at 1.5200: its value in the BS model is 0.84 USD pips, which with the Vanna–Volga adjustment[20] reduces to 0.73 USD pips.[21] In the LMUV model the price is in practice the same: 0.74 USD pips. In Figures 8.26, 8.27 and 8.28, the BS Vega, Volga and Vanna, together with their corresponding ATM **STDL**, **VWB** and **RR** equivalent, are shown.

Vega is very small for the starting FX spot level 1.4000, and switches sign from positive (on the left) to negative (on the right) when the spot rate changes. The same also happens to the ATM **STDL** exposure. The more worrying feature to a hedger is the rather acute and swinging profile of Volga and of the **VWB** equivalent exposures. This would make a sole Vega or ATM hedging rather unstable when the general level of the smile (i.e., the ATM volatility) changes.

[20] See equation (6.51) in Chapter 6.

[21] We disregard all other adjustments examined in Chapter 6, some of which can also be applied to the LMUV model price.

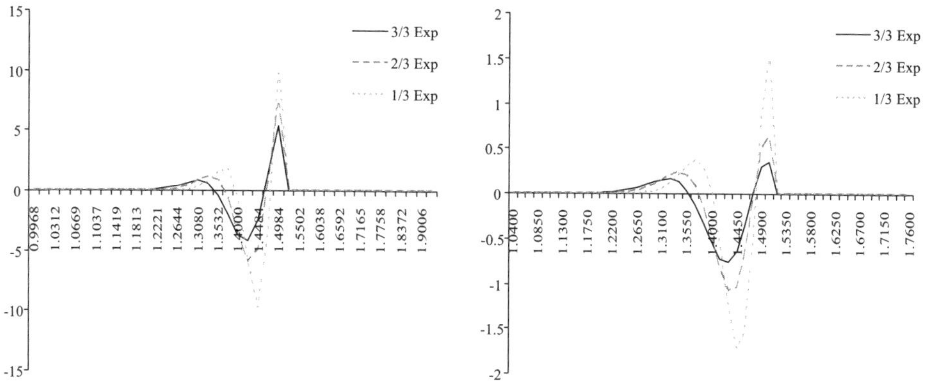

Figure 8.28 BS Vanna (right-hand side) and LMUV **RR** (left-hand side) exposures of a 3M UOC option for different levels of the FX spot rate and residual time to expiry

Finally, the Gamma produced by both the BS and LMUV models is plotted in Figure 8.29. In this case particular attention should be paid when the time to expiry is short and the FX spot rate is near the barrier, since this Greek becomes increasingly negative, making the Delta hedge a difficult task.

We try to reduce the volatility risks by Vega–Vanna–Volga hedging in the BS model, or scenario hedging (exposures to the three main smile movements) in the LMUV model. We set up the hedging portfolio by a suitable combination of options struck at the ATM level and the two 25D wings. We notice here that in all figures the hedging portfolio is not dismantled when the barrier level 1.5200 is breached (and the options stop living), so as to appreciate what happens if the hedger does not unwind the plain vanilla options portfolio. The risk profiles are plotted in Figures 8.30 to 8.33.

It is manifest that all the risks have a more stable profile, except when the FX spot rate is near the barrier, where the hedging plain vanilla options portfolio is not able to tame the brute behaviour of the reverse knock-out exposures. The worsening of the hedging ability also occurs as time elapses and expiry approaches. In both cases a rebalancing of the hedging options is required, with all the implications examined in Chapter 3.

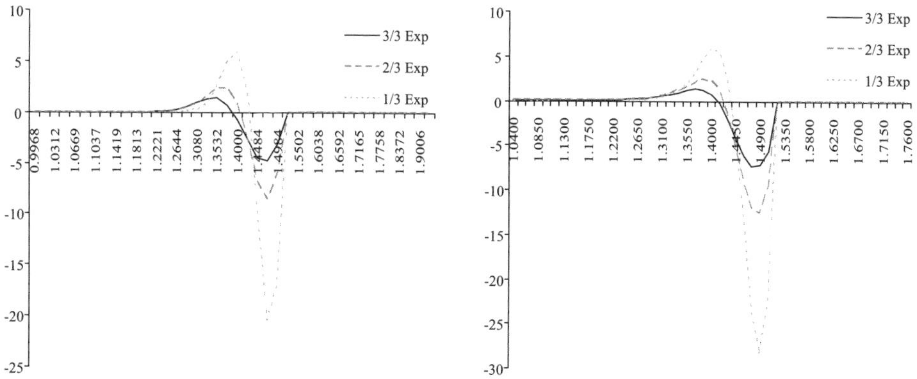

Figure 8.29 BS Gamma (right-hand side) and LMUV Gamma (left-hand side) exposures of a 3M UOC option for different levels of the FX spot rate and residual time to expiry

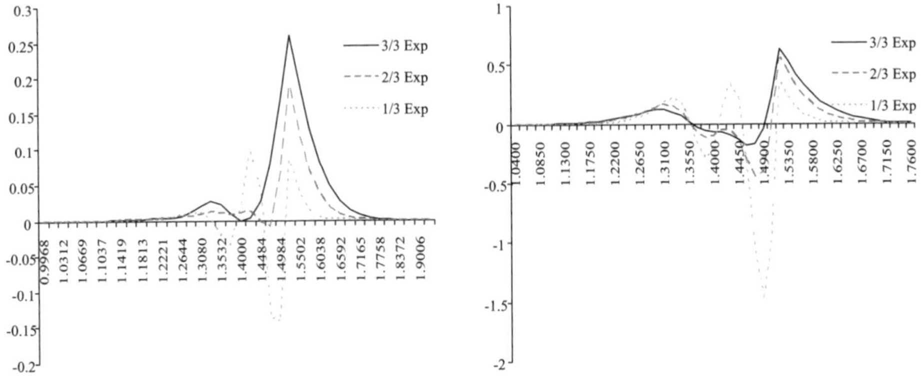

Figure 8.30 BS Vega (right-hand side) and LMUV ATM **STDL** (left-hand side) exposures of a 3M UOC option hedged by a Vega–Vanna–Volga matching, for different levels of the FX spot rate and residual time to expiry

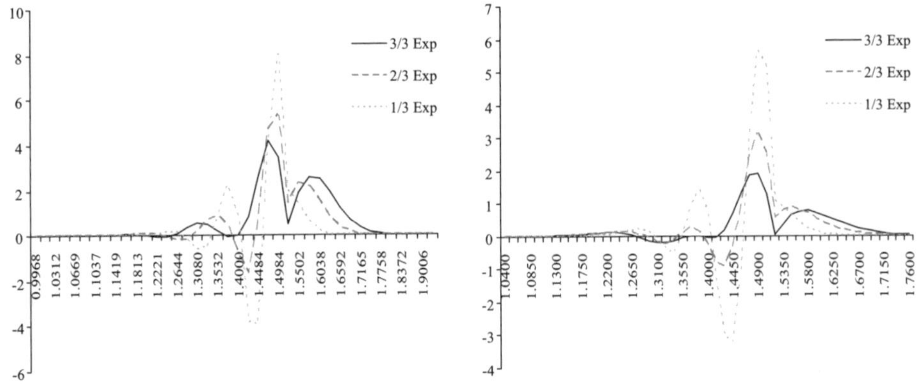

Figure 8.31 BS Volga (right-hand side) and LMUV **VWB** (left-hand side) exposures of a 3M UOC option hedged by a Vega–Vanna–Volga matching portfolio, for different levels of the FX spot rate and residual time to expiry

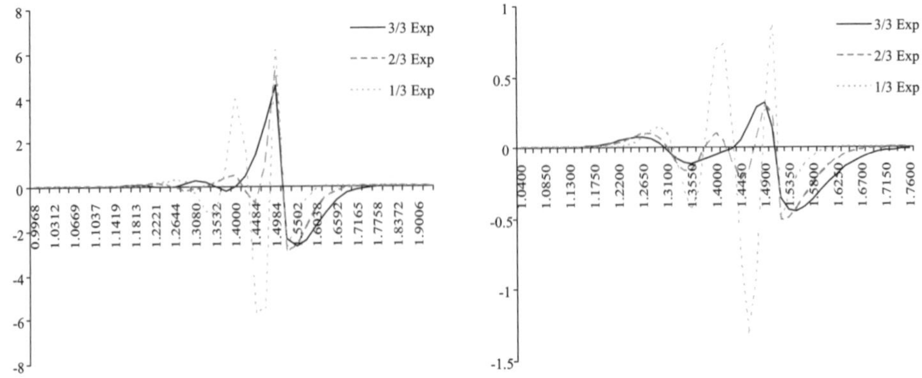

Figure 8.32 BS Vanna (right-hand side) and LMUV **RR** (left-hand side) exposures of a 3M UOC option hedged by a Vega–Vanna–Volga matching portfolio, for different levels of the FX spot rate and residual time to expiry

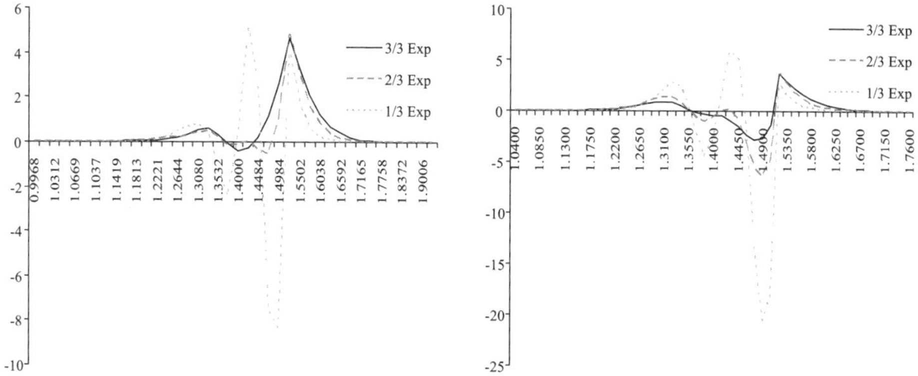

Figure 8.33 BS Gamma (right-hand side) and LMUV Gamma (left-hand side) exposures of a 3M UOC option hedged by a Vega–Vanna–Volga matching portfolio, for different levels of the FX spot rate and residual time to expiry

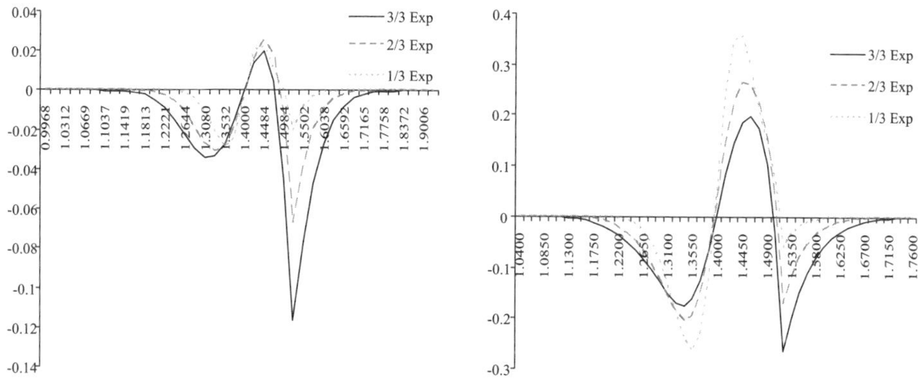

Figure 8.34 BS Vega (right-hand side) and LMUV ATM **STDL** (left-hand side) exposures of a 3M UOC option hedged by a Vega–Vanna–Volga matching portfolio and for the implicit one-touch, for different levels of the FX spot rate and residual time to expiry

We can test whether a specific hedge of the implicit one-touch option can improve the general hedging efficiency. To that end we insert into the portfolio an **OTH** paying 0.10 USD when 1.5200 is knocked.[22] Then the combination of the three basic options is revised so as to consider the new volatility-related risks in both the BS and LMUV models, after the inclusion of the **OTH**. In Figures 8.34 to 8.37 the risks related to this enhanced portfolio are shown.

The profiles are smooth enough and near zero both in the BS and in the LMUV model. Gamma is much lower, and it even changes sign when the expiry and barrier are near in time and space, becoming positive and at more manageable levels. In general, the specific hedge of the implicit one-touch improves significantly the risk management, and this is not surprising since we are in practice eliminating the main source of "exoticism" in the reverse knock-out, i.e., the discontinuity in the payoff and its sudden drop to zero from the intrinsic value (the absolute difference between the barrier and the strike).

[22] See equation (8.2).

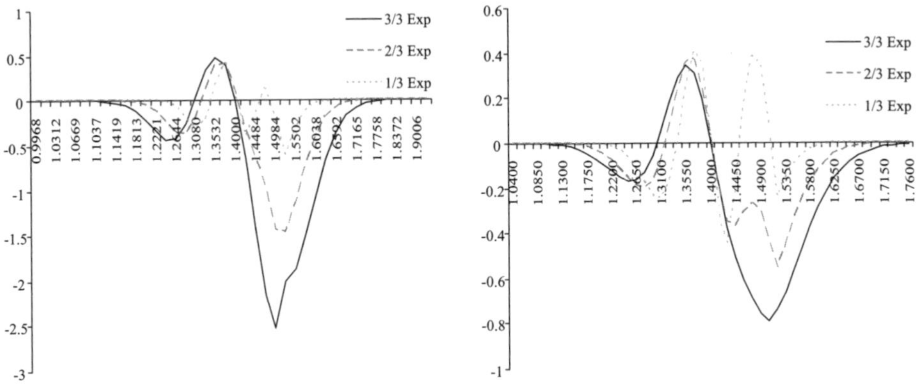

Figure 8.35 BS Volga (right-hand side) and LMUV **VWB** (left-hand side) exposures of a 3M UOC option hedged by a Vega–Vanna–Volga matching portfolio and for the implicit one-touch, for different levels of the FX spot rate and residual time to expiry

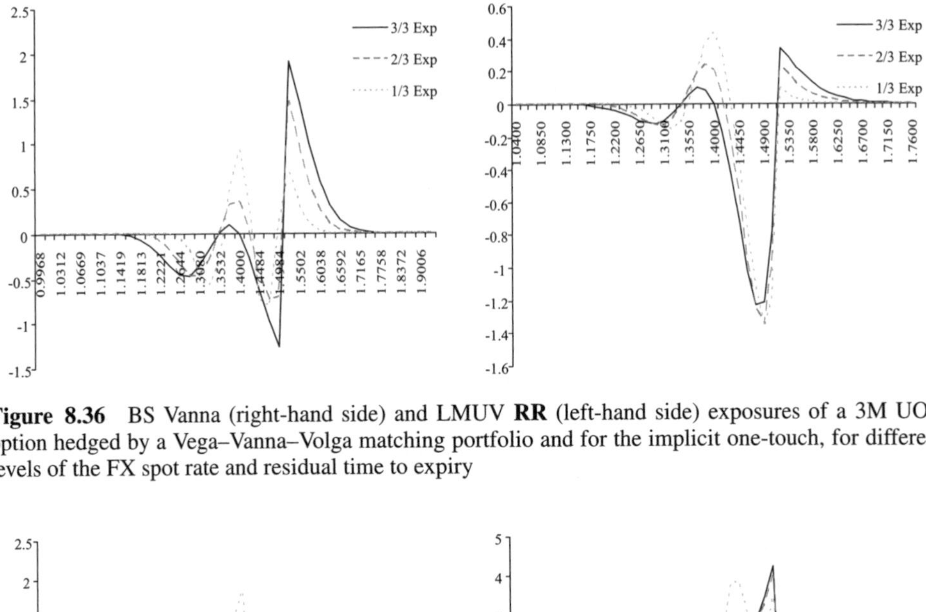

Figure 8.36 BS Vanna (right-hand side) and LMUV **RR** (left-hand side) exposures of a 3M UOC option hedged by a Vega–Vanna–Volga matching portfolio and for the implicit one-touch, for different levels of the FX spot rate and residual time to expiry

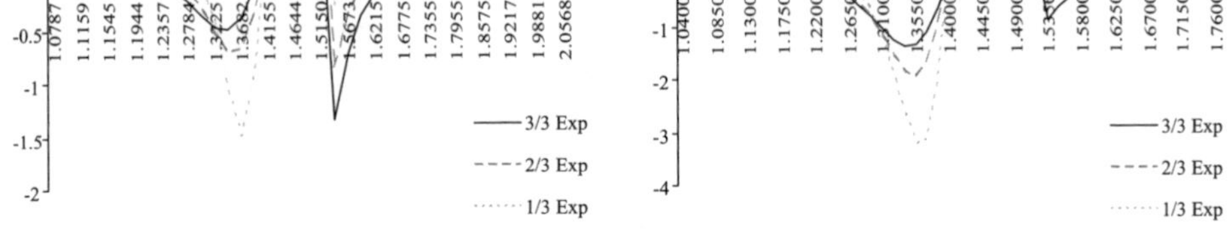

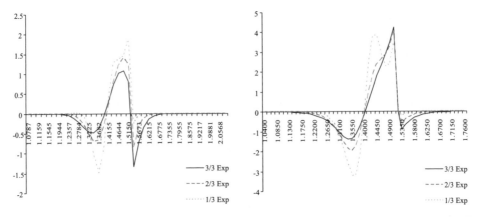

Figure 8.37 BS Gamma (right-hand side) and LMUV Gamma (left-hand side) exposures of a 3M UOC option hedged by a Vega–Vanna–Volga matching portfolio and for the implicit one-touch, for different levels of the FX spot rate and residual time to expiry

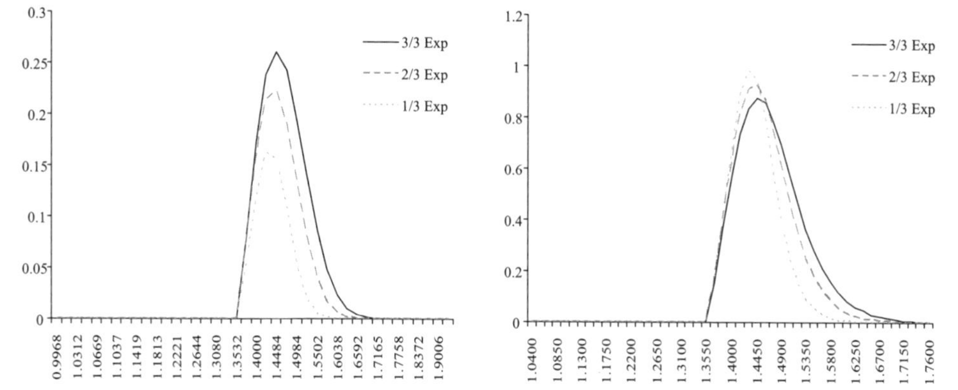

Figure 8.38 BS Vega (right-hand side) and LMUV ATM **STDL** (left-hand side) exposures of a 3M DOC for different levels of the FX spot rate and residual time to expiry

The other type of barrier option worth analysing is a **DOC**, as an example of a knock-out option. The expiry is still 3 months as for the reverse knock-out above, it is struck at 1.4300 and the barrier is 1.3600. The BS value is 116 USD pips, and if adjusted to include the smile effects with the VV approach we get 117. The same option in the LMUV model is worth 116 USD pips, confirming that the volatility smile has a very limited impact on the price.

Knock-out options are easier to manage than reverse knock-out options. No implicit one-touch (pin-risk) is embedded in the contract, and the risk profiles of the volatility exposures make the point clear. These are shown in Figures 8.38, 8.39 and 8.40. The Vega and ATM **STDL** exposure are not so different from a plain vanilla option's Vega and ATM **STDL** exposure, and like the latter they are always positive, just dropping to zero when the barrier is breached. The time behaviour is regular as well, preserving the basic shape and with a lowering general level as the expiry nears. As a consequence, the other two volatility-related risks (in the BS and LMUV models) show regular patterns similar to those produced by an

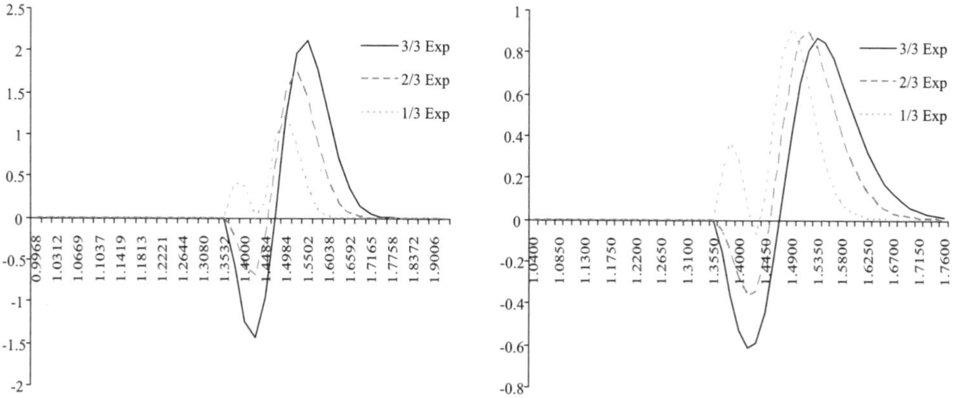

Figure 8.39 BS Volga (right-hand side) and LMUV **VWB** (left-hand side) exposures of a 3M DOC option for different levels of the FX spot rate and residual time to expiry

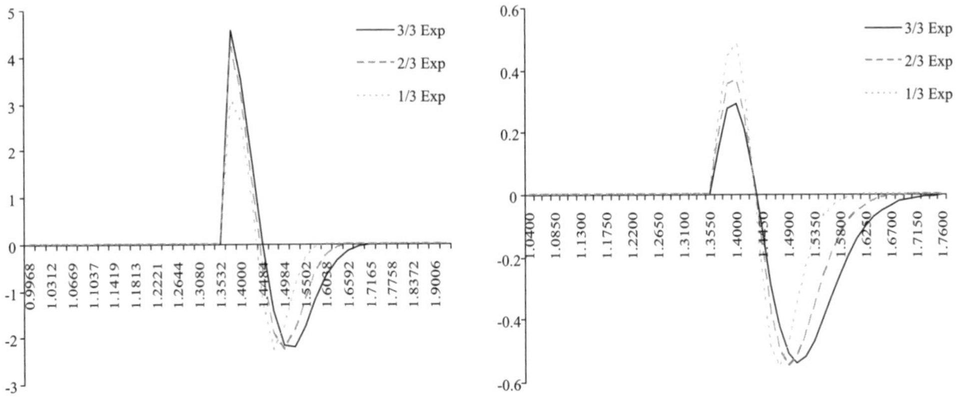

Figure 8.40 BS Vanna (right-hand side) and LMUV **RR** (left-hand side) exposures of a 3M DOC option for different levels of the FX spot rate and residual time to expiry

equivalent plain vanilla contract. Finally, Gamma (plotted in Figure 8.41) has no particularly worrisome traits and implies a rather ordinary hedging activity.

We can test if the hedging of a **DOC** option is stable in the BS and LMUV environments, by setting up the usual portfolio of three basic options (which may be expressed in terms of quantity of the three main traded instruments) and assume it is held up to maturity. The resulting volatility risk profiles are plotted in Figures 8.42 to 8.44; the levels are very near to zero for a safe range of FX spot prices, although rebalancing is needed for large moves and as time elapses. On the lower side, for FX spot rates below 1.3600, the closing of all the positions in the plain vanilla options after breaching of the barrier would eliminate the non-zero exposures shown in the figures.

Gamma of the hedged portfolio in Figure 8.45 is smooth and no explosive feature shows up for short time to maturity. As for Vega and the ATM **STDL** exposure, the hedged portfolio's Gamma switches sign from positive to negative when the FX spot rate moves towards the barrier level.

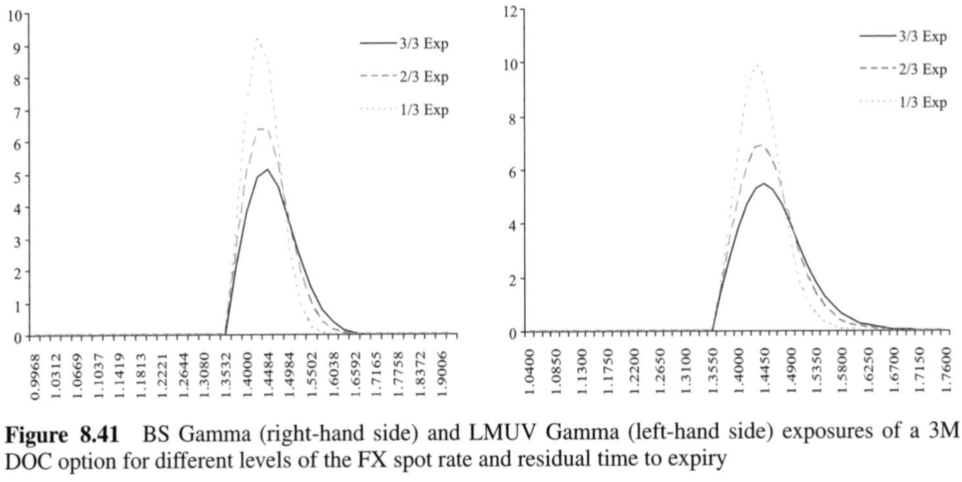

Figure 8.41 BS Gamma (right-hand side) and LMUV Gamma (left-hand side) exposures of a 3M DOC option for different levels of the FX spot rate and residual time to expiry

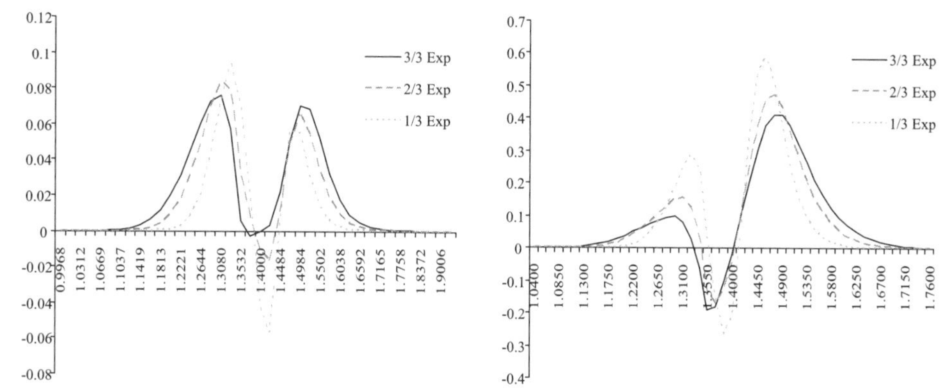

Figure 8.42 BS Vega (right-hand side) and LMUV ATM **STDL** (left-hand side) exposures of a 3M DOC option hedged by a Vega–Vanna–Volga matching, for different levels of the FX spot rate and residual time to expiry

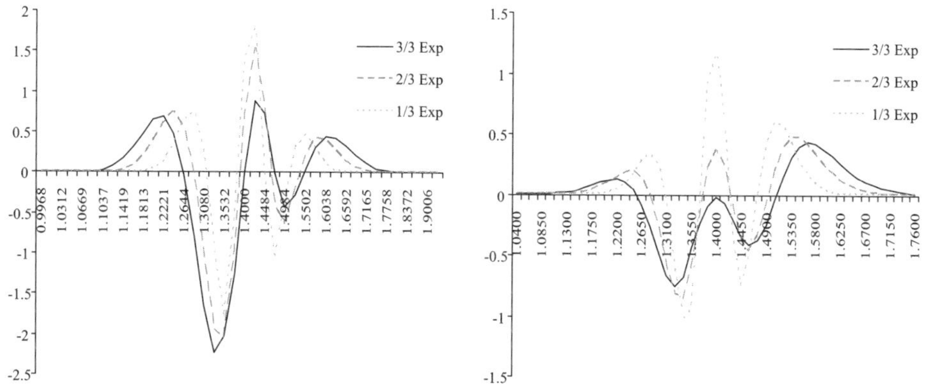

Figure 8.43 BS Volga (right-hand side) and LMUV **VWB** (left-hand side) exposures of a 3M DOC option hedged by a Vega–Vanna–Volga matching portfolio, for different levels of the FX spot rate and residual time to expiry

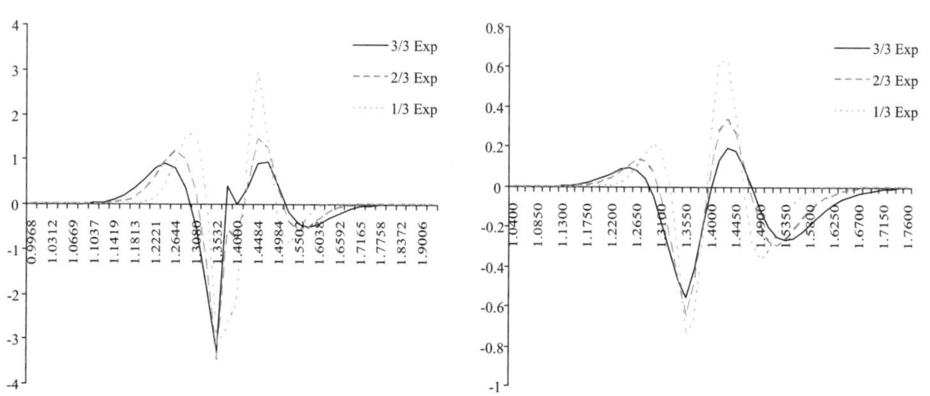

Figure 8.44 BS Vanna (right-hand side) and LMUV **RR** (left-hand side) exposures of a 3M DOC option hedged by a Vega–Vanna–Volga matching portfolio, for different levels of the FX spot rate and residual time to expiry

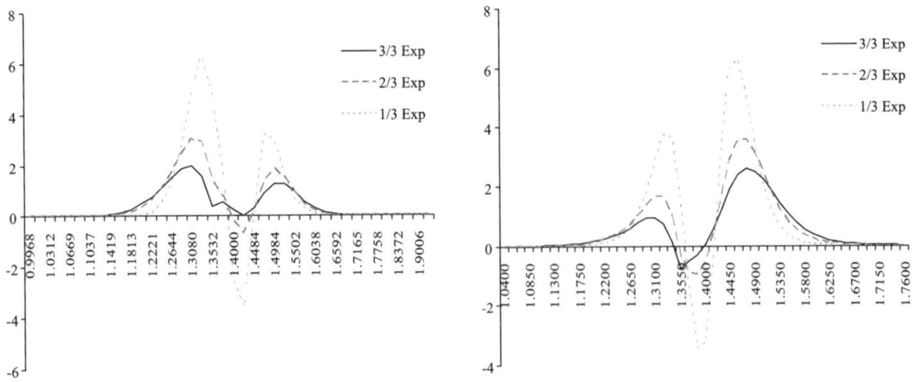

Figure 8.45 BS Gamma (right-hand side) and LMUV Gamma (left-hand side) exposures of a 3M DOC option hedged by a Vega–Vanna–Volga matching portfolio, for different levels of the FX spot rate and residual time to expiry

8.6.2 Double-barrier options

Double-barrier options are a sort of combination, in terms of risk, of a reverse knock-out and a knock-out option since one of the barriers implies an implicit one-touch (pin-risk), whereas the other is usually set at an out-of-the money level.[23] As a case study for the double-knock-out option, we choose a 3-month expiry **DKOP**, struck at 1.4000 with lower and upper barriers equal to, respectively, 1.3600 and 1.4800. The BS value of such an option is 84 USD pips,[24] and when we apply the VV smile adjustment we get 89 USD pips.[25] The LMUV model values this option at 93 USD pips. It is worth noticing here that in general the market prices of exotic options are such that the fourth moment exposure, reflected by the **VWB** exposure in stochastic volatility models, has a lighter contribution to the value, more in accordance with a VV adjustment (based on a static hedging portfolio without considering any particular dynamics for the volatility) than with a stochastic volatility model. We will see that other contracts with high fourth moment exposures (e.g., **DNT**) also have a significantly higher price in a stochastic volatility framework than in the BS environment with VV adjustments.

In Figures 8.46 to 8.49 we have a picture of the profiles of the volatility-related risks and Gamma. The noticeable feature of Vega and the ATM **STDL** exposure is that a long position in the **DKOP** produced a short position relative to both risks, for almost the entire range included between the barriers, with a very limited positive exposure for values of the FX spot rate near the upper barrier. Also, Volga and the **VWB** risks should be watched carefully, since they are quite negatively large, although very rapidly reverting towards zero and eventually changing sign. This shape of the profile implies a difficult hedging activity of the volatility risks, with

[23] This is not always true since we can trade a double knock-out with a strike set at a level outside the range limited by the two barrier levels (e.g., EUR put USD call strike 1.6000, barriers 1.3000 and 1.5000, with a reference FX spot rate of 1.4000). These kinds of double barrier options have produced some unexpected outcomes in the life of the author of this book, and ultimately they can be considered the first cause of its writing.

[24] We still use the market date of Section 8.4.

[25] Also in this case we neglect all other adjustments examined in Chapter 6, which can also be applied to the LMUV model price in some cases.

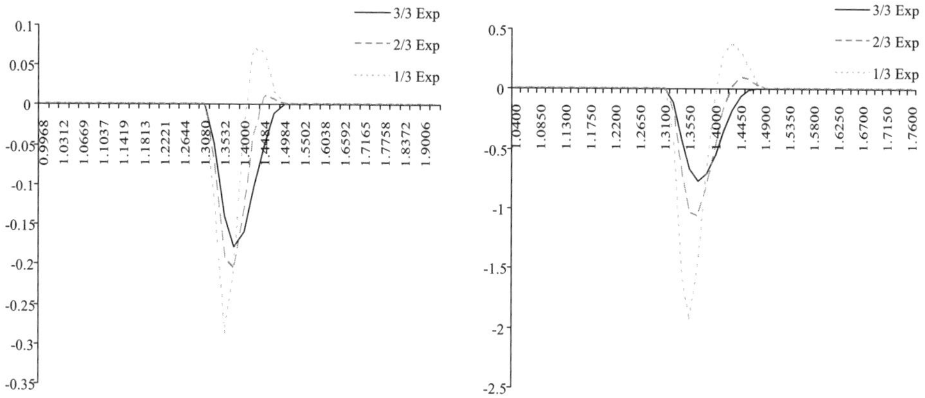

Figure 8.46 BS Vega (right-hand side) and LMUV ATM **STDL** (left-hand side) exposures of a 3M **DKOP** for different levels of the FX spot rate and residual time to expiry

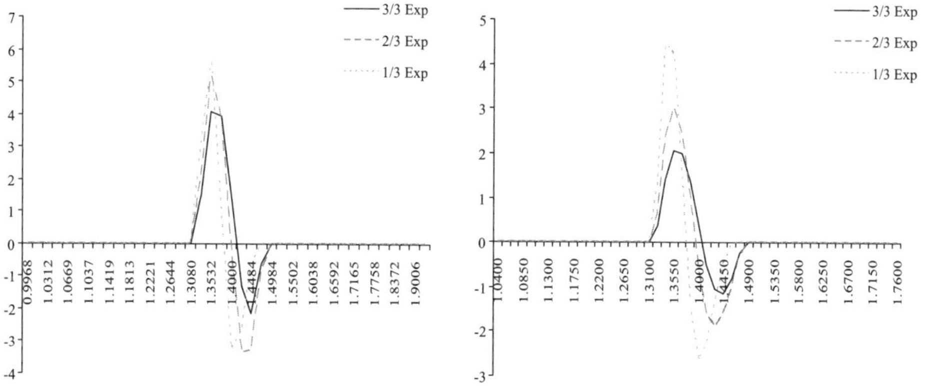

Figure 8.47 BS Volga (right-hand side) and LMUV **VWB** (left-hand side) exposures of a 3M **DKOP** option for different levels of the FX spot rate and residual time to expiry

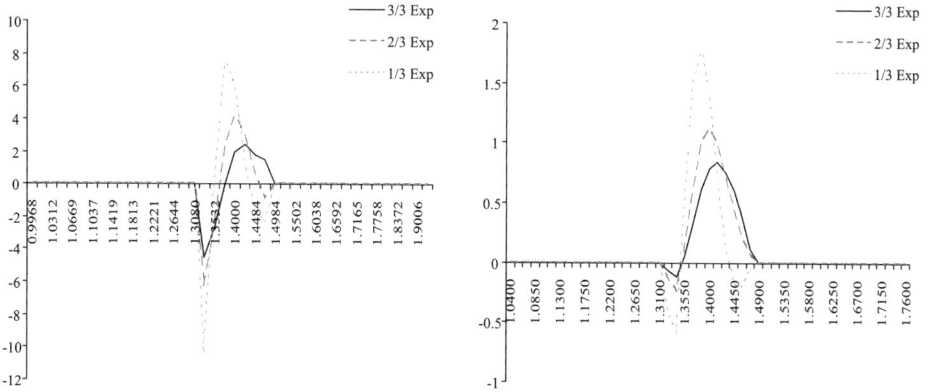

Figure 8.48 BS Vanna (right-hand side) and LMUV **RR** (left-hand side) exposures of a 3M **DKOP** option for different levels of the FX spot rate and residual time to expiry

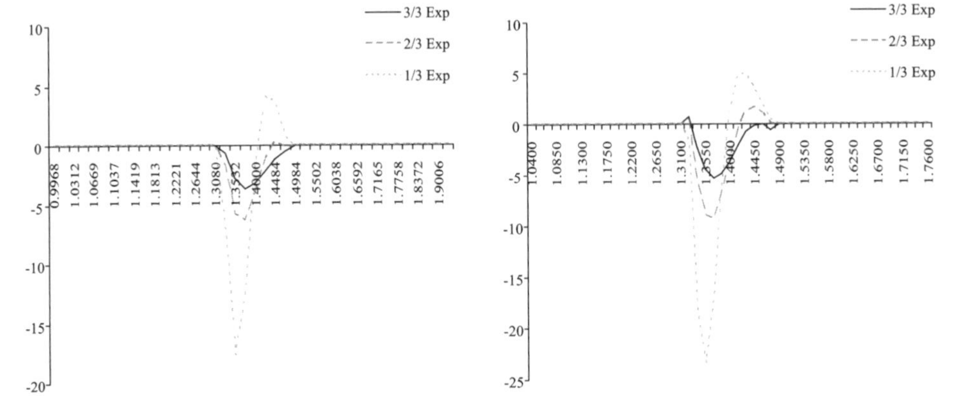

Figure 8.49 BS Gamma (right-hand side) and LMUV Gamma (left-hand side) exposures of a 3M **DKOP** option for different levels of the FX spot rate and residual time to expiry

remarkable instability caused also by the movements of the ATM implied volatility and in general of the volatility smile.

Gamma is explosive when expiry approaches, and the FX is near the lower barrier (the reverse knock-out one). In this case the double knock-out behaves like a reverse knock-out and a costly and tiring Delta-hedging activity is required.

We examine how the Vega–Vanna–Volga hedging and scenario hedging perform in Figures 8.50 to 8.53. Both in the BS and LMUV models the exposures are reduced, but they are not stable as the spot moves and as time elapses, even causing a switch of sign for the same level of the FX spot rate. A frequent, and likely expensive, rebalancing has to be expected from a position in a double-knock-out. Gamma is significantly smoothened for almost the entire range delimited by the barriers, but it still has a disturbing behaviour for short time to maturity. As with reverse knock-out, the hedging can be improved if the implicit one-touch is hedged, thus also reducing the Gamma-related risks.

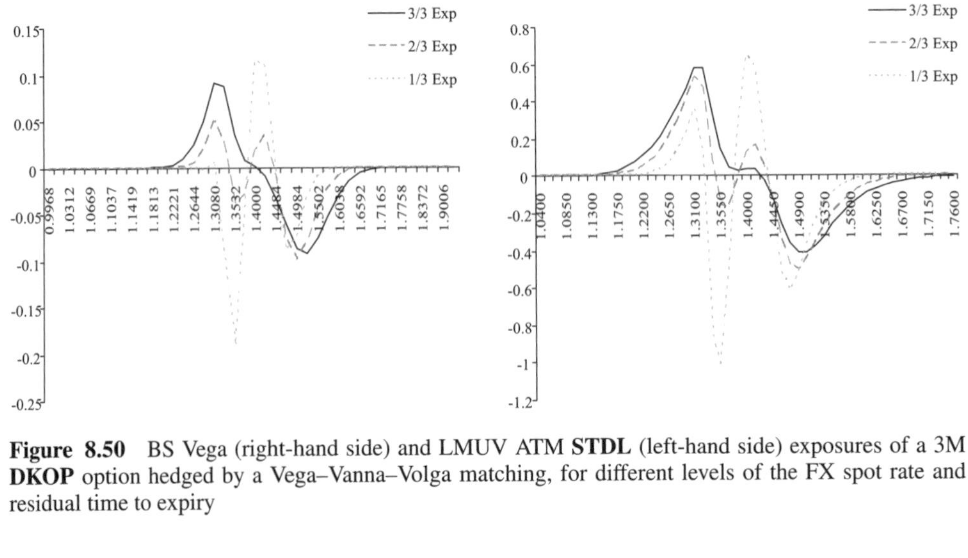

Figure 8.50 BS Vega (right-hand side) and LMUV ATM **STDL** (left-hand side) exposures of a 3M **DKOP** option hedged by a Vega–Vanna–Volga matching, for different levels of the FX spot rate and residual time to expiry

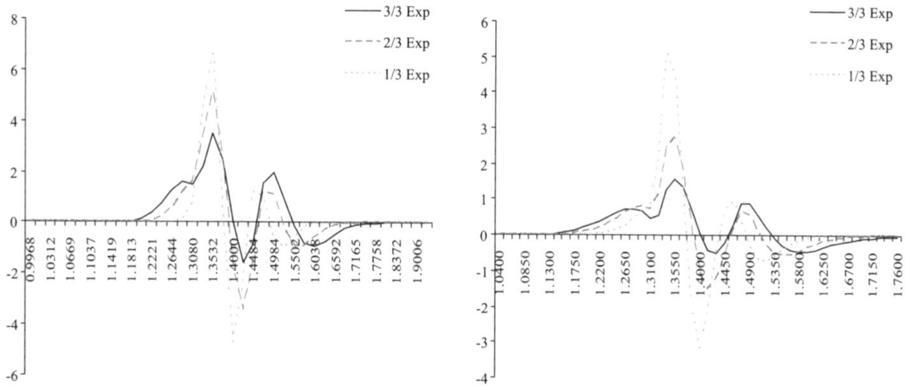

Figure 8.51 BS Volga (right-hand side) and LMUV **VWB** (left-hand side) exposures of a 3M **DKOP** option hedged by a Vega–Vanna–Volga matching portfolio, for different levels of the FX spot rate and residual time to expiry

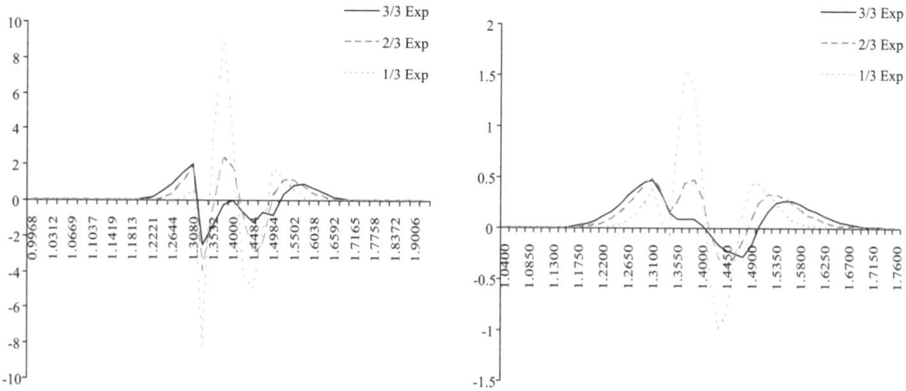

Figure 8.52 BS Vanna (right-hand side) and LMUV **RR** (left-hand side) exposures of a 3M **DKOP** option hedged by a Vega–Vanna–Volga matching portfolio, for different levels of the FX spot rate and residual time to expiry

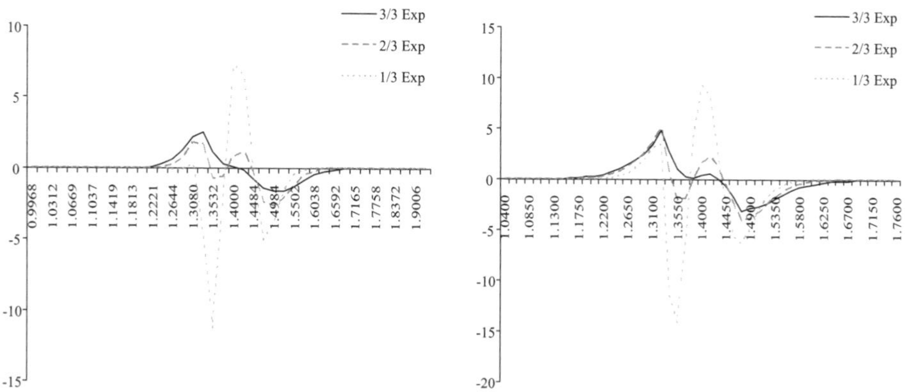

Figure 8.53 BS Gamma (right-hand side) and LMUV Gamma (left-hand side) exposures of a 3M **DKOP** option hedged by a Vega–Vanna–Volga matching portfolio, for different levels of the FX spot rate and residual time to expiry

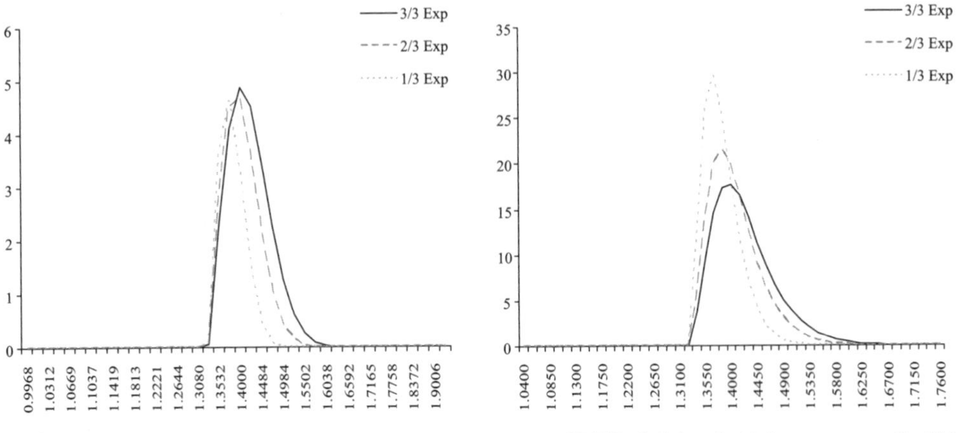

Figure 8.54 BS Vega (right-hand side) and LMUV ATM **STDL** (left-hand side) exposures of a 3M **OTH** for different levels of the FX spot rate and residual time to expiry

8.6.3 Bet options

We choose as typical examples of bet options a one-touch and a double no-touch. They are the most traded bet contracts in practice, since they allow hedging of the implicit one-touch risk and provide a great exposure to Volga and the **VWB** (mainly the double-no-touch is employed for this purpose).

We start by examining a 2-month expiry **OTH** paying 1 USD if the barrier level 1.3300 is breached. Its price in the BS model is 33% of the notional amount. When we apply the VV adjustment we get 31.97% and this price is very near that produced by the LMUV model: 31.72%. The volatility-related exposures for such a contract are shown in Figures 8.54 to 8.56, and Gamma is plotted in Figure 8.57.

Vega and the ATM **STDL** do not have a particularly strange profile. Most of the problems rather derive from Volga and the **VWB** exposure, which are high. Besides, Gamma shows the

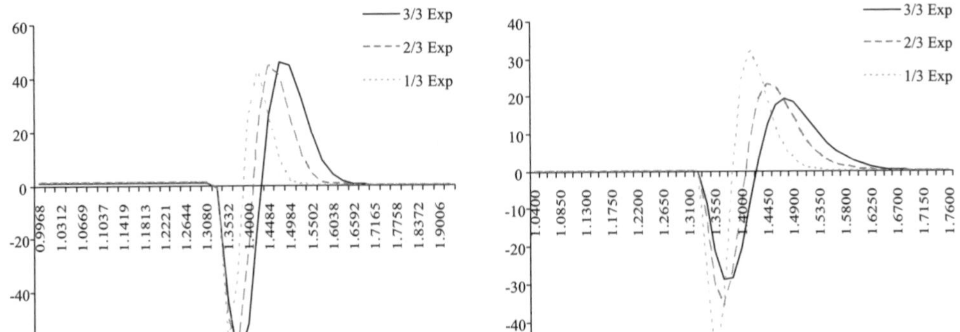

Figure 8.55 BS Volga (right-hand side) and LMUV **VWB** (left-hand side) exposures of a 3M **OTH** option for different levels of the FX spot rate and residual time to expiry

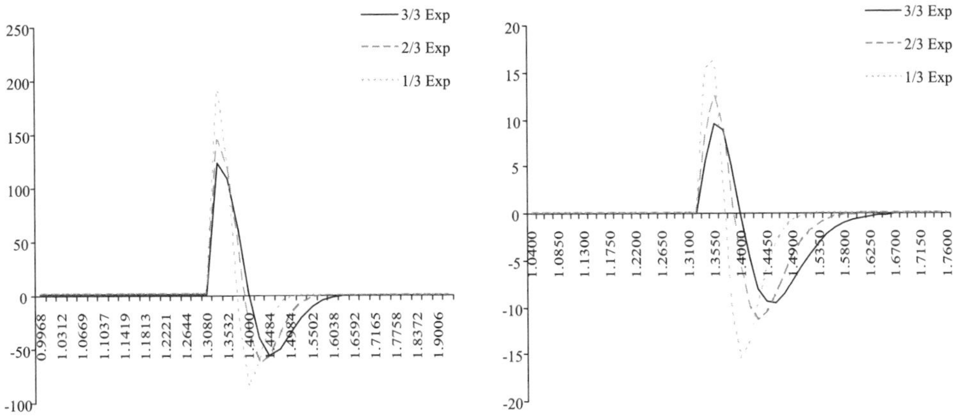

Figure 8.56 BS Vanna (right-hand side) and LMUV **RR** (left-hand side) exposures of a 3M **OTH** option for different levels of the FX spot rate and residual time to expiry

usual difficult behaviour for short expiries and near the barrier, due to the pin-risk. This risk can be eliminated either by naively reversing the position or by trading a reverse knock-out with suitable strike and barrier.

To verify the stability of the Vega–Vanna–Volga hedging and scenario hedging, we look at Figures 8.58 to 8.61. As usual, the reduction of all the exposures is manifest, but the rebalancing is unavoidable for a large move of the FX spot rate and, anyway, when the time to expiry shortens. This is also true for Gamma, which still keeps on showing a worrisome behaviour for the hedger, who could be compelled to do some tiring and difficult Delta-hedging activity. Clearly, dismantling the hedging plain vanilla options portfolio after breaching of the barrier would eliminate the exposures plotted in the figures for FX spot rates below 1.3300.

Finally, we examine a 2-month expiry **DNT**, with 1.3400 and 1.4600 barrier levels, paying 1 USD at expiry if neither barrier is breached. The BS price is 25.25% of the notional amount,

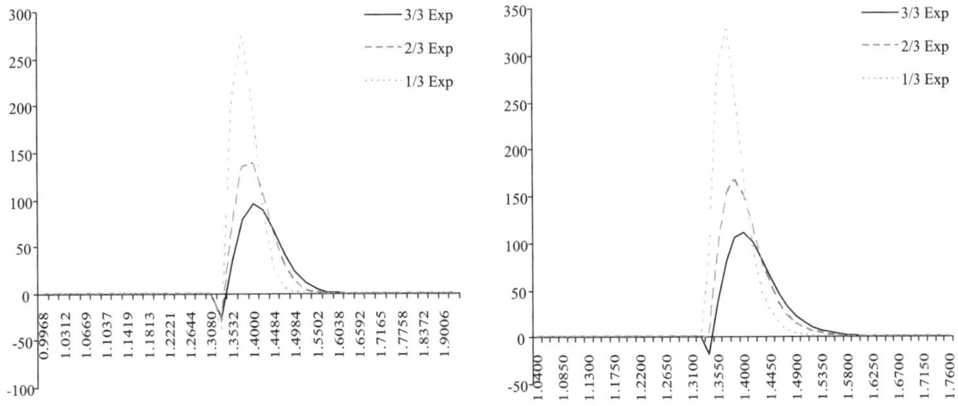

Figure 8.57 BS Gamma (right-hand side) and LMUV Gamma (left-hand side) exposures of a 3M **OTH** option for different levels of the FX spot rate and residual time to expiry

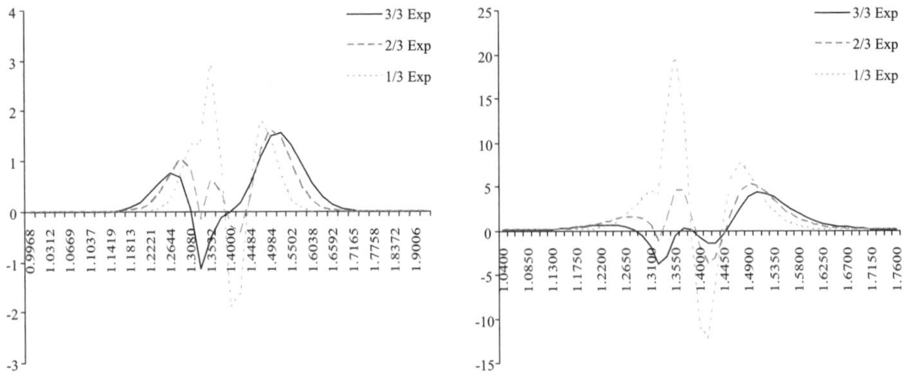

Figure 8.58 BS Vega (right-hand side) and LMUV ATM **STDL** (left-hand side) exposures of a 3M **OTH** option hedged by a Vega–Vanna–Volga matching, for different levels of the FX spot rate and residual time to expiry

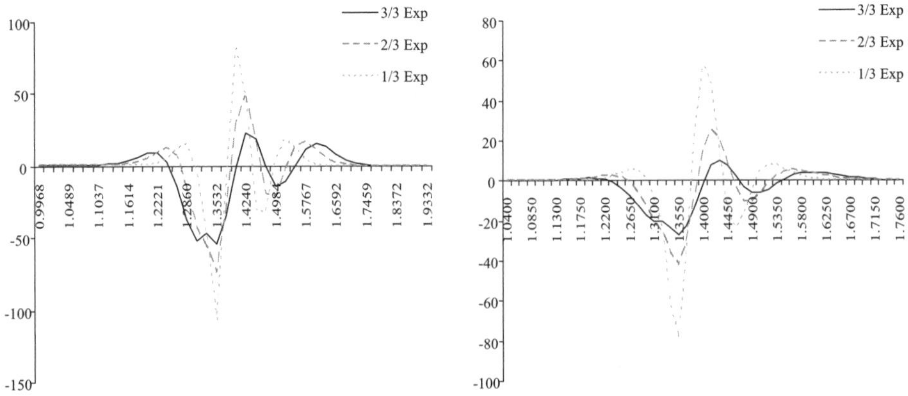

Figure 8.59 BS Volga (right-hand side) and LMUV **VWB** (left-hand side) exposures of a 3M **OTH** option hedged by a Vega–Vanna–Volga matching portfolio, for different levels of the FX spot rate and residual time to expiry

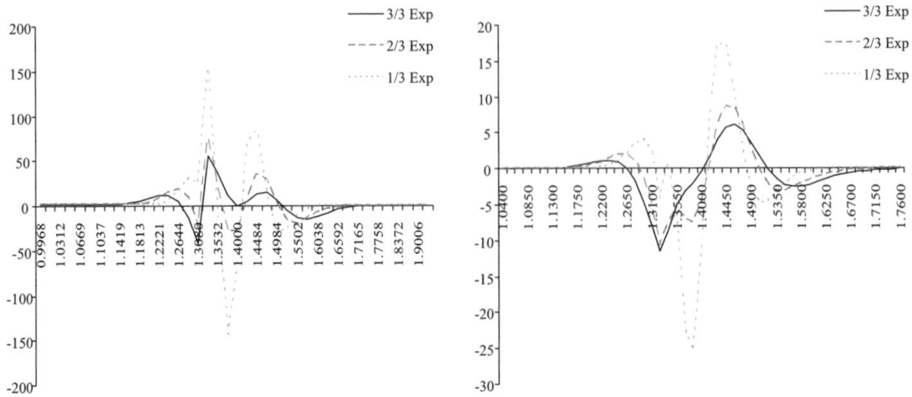

Figure 8.60 BS Vanna (right-hand side) and LMUV **RR** (left-hand side) exposures of a 3M **OTH** option hedged by a Vega–Vanna–Volga matching portfolio, for different levels of the FX spot rate and residual time to expiry

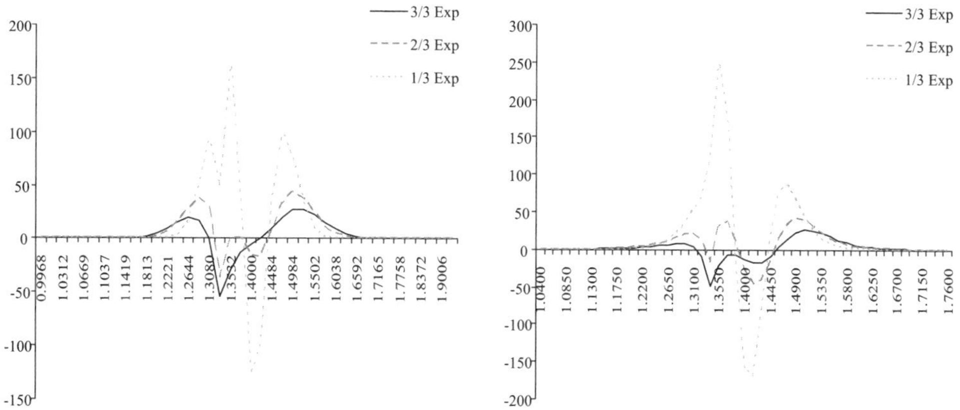

Figure 8.61 BS Gamma (right-hand side) and LMUV Gamma (left-hand side) exposures of a 3M **OTH** option hedged by a Vega–Vanna–Volga matching portfolio, for different levels of the FX spot rate and residual time to expiry

which becomes 27.91% with VV adjustments. The LMUV model prices the same contract higher, at 30.89%, confirming what we have written above on the contribution to the value by the fourth moment exposure within a stochastic volatility framework.

Figures 8.62 to 8.65 show the volatility-related and Gamma exposures. The features are the negative Vega and ATM **STDL** exposure linked with the high value of negative Volga and **VWB** exposure. Also, Gamma is rather awful since it becomes increasingly negative when expiry approaches.

Let us test how the Vega–Vanna–Volga hedging and scenario hedging perform with this kind of exotic option. Figures 8.66 to 8.69 show the resulting risk profiles. In this case it is easy to see that Vega and the ATM **STDL** exposures are very near to zero for moderate changes in the FX spot rate, whereas the hedging worsens when it approaches both barriers, according to a symmetrical pattern. The levels do not increase dramatically as time elapses, except when the

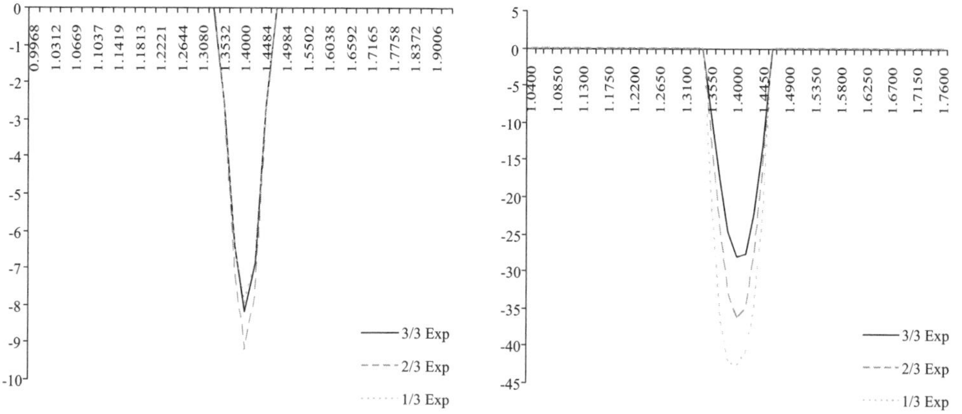

Figure 8.62 BS Vega (right-hand side) and LMUV ATM **STDL** (left-hand side) exposures of a 3M **DNT** for different levels of the FX spot rate and residual time to expiry

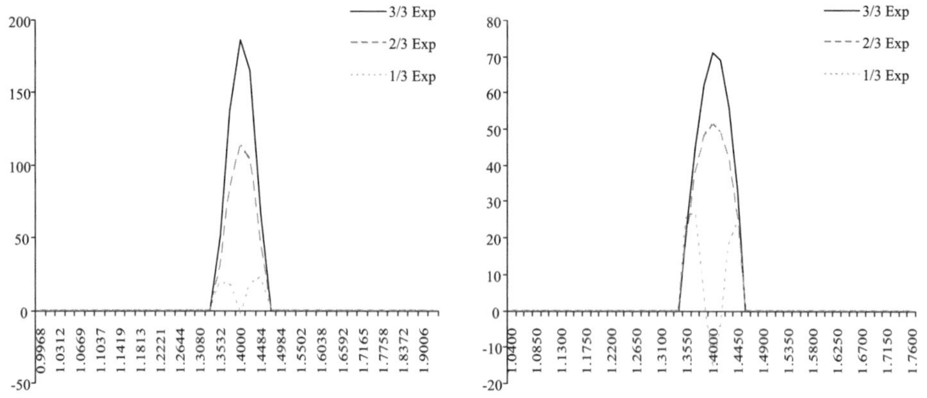

Figure 8.63 BS Volga (right-hand side) and LMUV **VWB** (left-hand side) exposures of a 3M **DNT** option for different levels of the FX spot rate and residual time to expiry

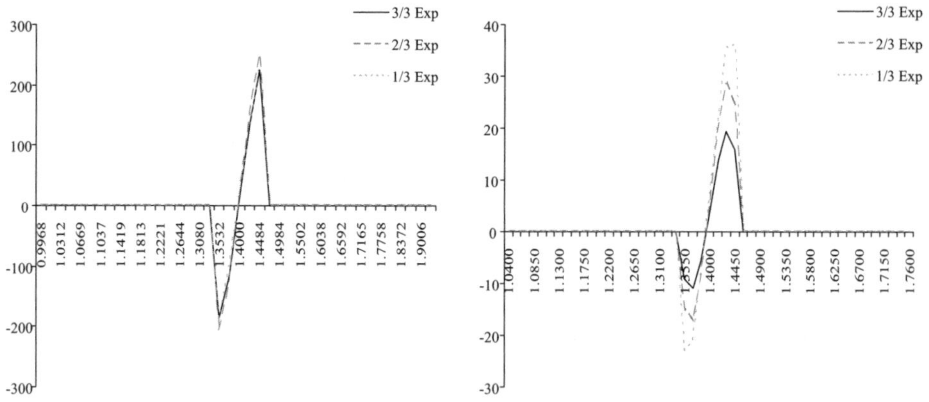

Figure 8.64 BS Vanna (right-hand side) and LMUV **RR** (left-hand side) exposures of a 3M **DNT** option for different levels of the FX spot rate and residual time to expiry

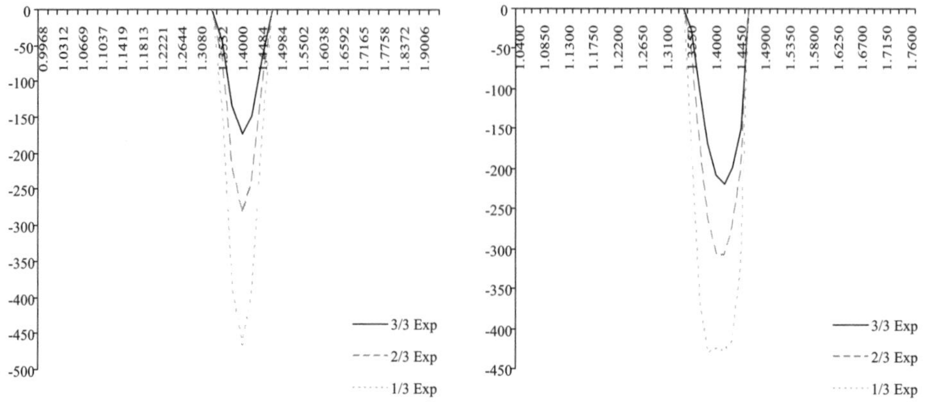

Figure 8.65 BS Gamma (right-hand side) and LMUV Gamma (left-hand side) exposures of a 3M **DNT** option for different levels of the FX spot rate and residual time to expiry

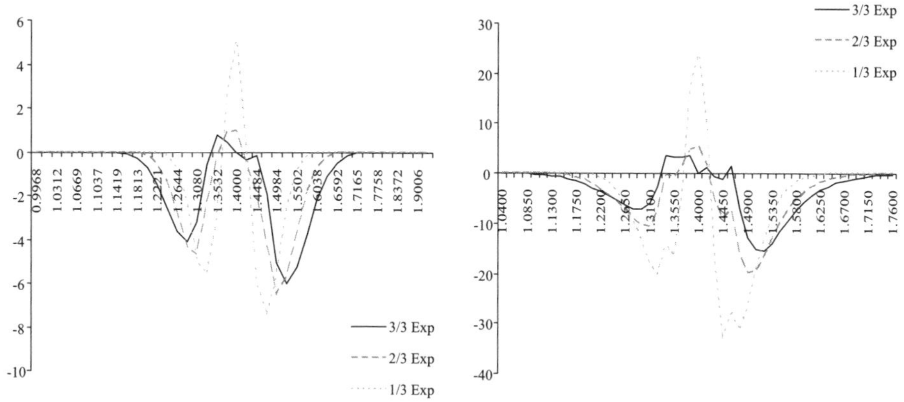

Figure 8.66 BS Vega (right-hand side) and LMUV ATM **STDL** (left-hand side) exposures of a 3M **DNT** option hedged by a Vega–Vanna–Volga matching, for different levels of the FX spot rate and residual time to expiry

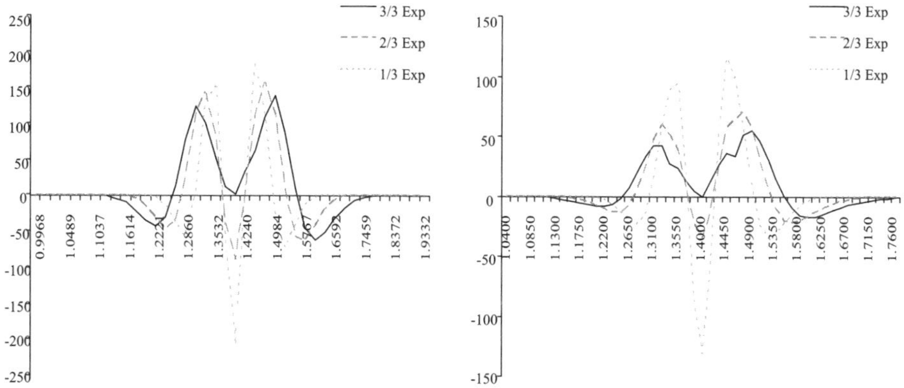

Figure 8.67 BS Volga (right-hand side) and LMUV **VWB** (left-hand side) exposures of a 3M **DNT** option hedged by a Vega–Vanna–Volga matching portfolio, for different levels of the FX spot rate and residual time to expiry

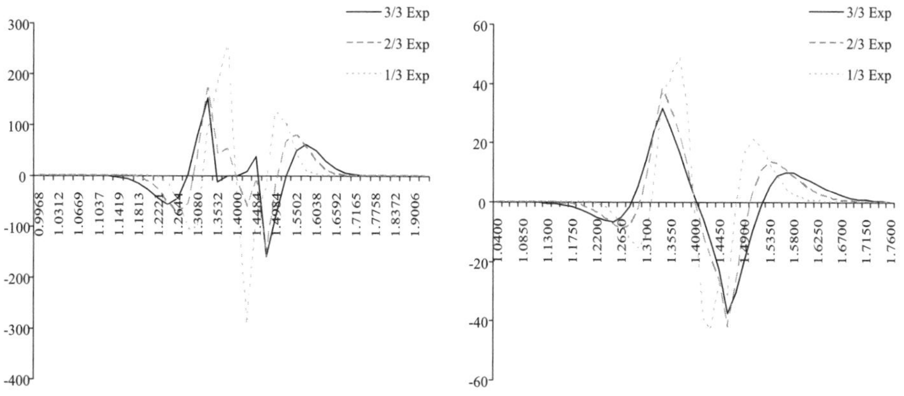

Figure 8.68 BS Vanna (right-hand side) and LMUV **RR** (left-hand side) exposures of a 3M **DNT** option hedged by a Vega–Vanna–Volga matching portfolio, for different levels of the FX spot rate and residual time to expiry

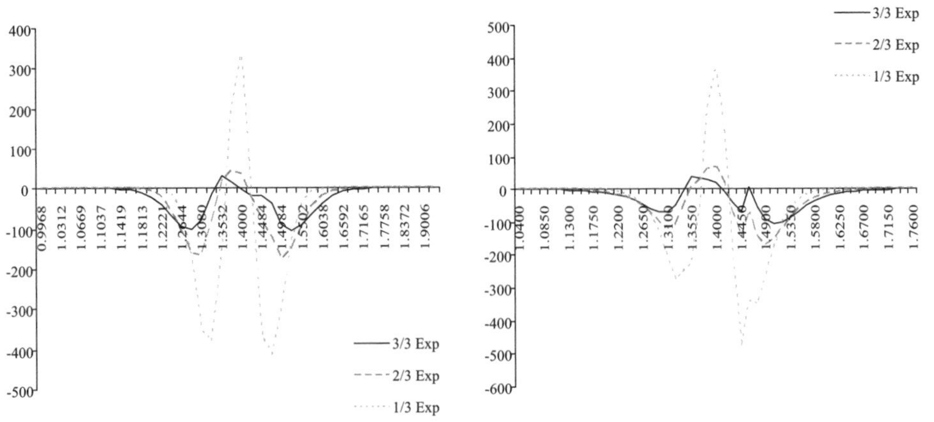

Figure 8.69 BS Gamma (right-hand side) and LMUV Gamma (left-hand side) exposures of a 3M **DNT** option hedged by a Vega–Vanna–Volga matching portfolio, for different levels of the FX spot rate and residual time to expiry

spot is stale at the starting level 1.4000. In this case both exposures we are examining become exceedingly positive. The same considerations also apply for Volga and **VWB** and for Vanna and **RR** exposures, and for Gamma as well. Rebalancing of the hedging plain vanilla portfolio is required in any case.

9

Correlation and FX Options

9.1 PRELIMINARY CONSIDERATIONS

It is not within the scope of this book to extend the analysis to those contracts usually embedded in structured financial products and that consider currencies as an asset class. Such contracts are typically based on baskets of currencies often with averaging (Asian) features, and they are similar to those structures commonly traded in the equity markets. In most cases, a strong dependence on the correlation amongst all the involved pairs marks these kinds of options, and a great deal of theory has been developed for their pricing and (to a lesser extent, to be frank) hedging.

We will not dwell on the subject of the currencies as an asset class, but nevertheless correlation in the FX market deserves special attention for the tight links that can be established amongst pairs, at least those built from a triplet of currencies. As usual, care should be taken because some concepts may be misleading, as we will see in what follows. We start by analysing how correlation can be dealt with in a BS world, and then we expand the results to an economy where the volatility smiles appear in the market.

9.2 CORRELATION IN THE BS SETTING

Assume we are in the BS economy described in Chapter 2, and that three pairs are traded: XXX, YYY and ZZZ. It is possible to build three pairs: XXXYYY, ZZZYYY and XXXZZZ.[1] The dynamics are given by the following SDEs:

$$dS_t^{XY} = \left(r_t^Y - r_t^X\right) S_t^{XY} dt + \varsigma_t^{XY} S_t^{XY} dZ_t^{XY} \tag{9.1}$$

$$dS_t^{XZ} = \left(r_t^Z - r_t^X\right) S_t^{XZ} dt + \varsigma_t^{XZ} S_t^{XZ} dZ_t^{XZ} \tag{9.2}$$

and

$$dS_t^{ZY} = \left(r_t^Y - r_t^Z\right) S_t^{ZY} dt + \varsigma_t^{ZY} S_t^{ZY} dZ_t^{ZY} \tag{9.3}$$

The single superscripts indicate the currency by referring to the first letter, and the double superscripts indicate, by the same token, the pair. The Brownian motions are all correlated. For example, the Brownian motions affecting the prices of the pairs XXXYYY and ZZZYYY are correlated as

$$dZ_t^{XY} dZ_t^{ZY} = \rho^{XY,ZY} dt \tag{9.4}$$

Other Brownian motions are similarly correlated: just substitute XY and ZY with two other pairs in equation (9.4).

[1] Actually, we could also build another three pairs by reversing the definition of the base/numeraire currency. We are assuming that the three pairs in the text are those actually traded according to market conventions.

From a purely mathematical point of view, the following relationship may be established:

$$S_t^{XZ} = \frac{S_t^{XY}}{S_t^{ZY}} \tag{9.5}$$

That is, it is possible to find the value of the pair S_t^{XZ} once the other two are known. As mentioned above, given the definition of the FX spot rate, the price of the first currency appearing in the label in terms of the second one is a simple mathematical truth. Nonetheless, we will shortly see that the relation also has a financial foundation, based on an arbitrage argument. Equation (9.5) holds if the pair XXXYYY is traded in the market, but if the convention is for the YYYXXX quotation then the three FX spot rates are linked in this way:

$$S_t^{ZX} = \frac{S_t^{ZY}}{S_t^{XY}} \tag{9.6}$$

Example 9.2.1. *Let XXX=EUR, YYY=JPY and ZZZ=USD, and assume that the EURJPY FX spot rate is* $S^{EJ} = 150.00$ *and that USDJPY* $S^{UJ} = 100.00$. *Then the EURUSD rate is*

$$S_t^{EU} = \frac{S_t^{EJ}}{S_t^{UJ}} = \frac{150.00}{100.00} = 1.5000 \tag{9.7}$$

Although it is not the market standard, we can also calculate the FX spot rate for the USDEUR quotation:

$$S_t^{UE} = \frac{S_t^{UJ}}{S_t^{EJ}} = \frac{100.00}{150.00} = 0.6667 \tag{9.8}$$

One would be tempted to also derive the dynamics for S^{XZ} form (9.5), by applying Itô's lemma. This is possible, but the resulting SDE is not that commanding in the evolution of S^{XZ}, but slightly different, as will be clear below. For the moment, let us examine how it is possible to build a portfolio containing S^{ZY} and S^{XY} so as to replicate the profits and losses flowing from a position in the S^{XZ} pair. Consider the following portfolio:

$$\Pi_{t_0} = x_1 S_{t_0}^{XY} + x_2 S_{t_0}^{ZY} \tag{9.9}$$

We do not calculate the derivatives with respect to S^{ZY} and S^{XY}, as one could be inspired to do. Instead, we set $x_1 = 1$ and $x_2 = -S_{t_0}^{XZ}$, which are the amounts corresponding, respectively, to the base currency and the numeraire currency exchanged when trading one unit of S^{XZ}. The portfolio Π_{t_0} evolves in an interval of time equal to $t_1 - t_0$ as

$$\Delta\Pi_{t_0} = \Delta S_{t_0}^{XY} - S_{t_0}^{XZ} \Delta S_{t_0}^{ZY} \tag{9.10}$$

It is worth noticing that the variations of both the value Π_{t_0} in equation (9.9) and $\Delta\Pi_{t_0}$ in equation (9.10) are denominated in YYY units. Since the value of S^{XZ} and its variations are expressed in terms of ZZZ units, we convert the value of the portfolio in ZZZ at the S^{ZY} spot rate, thus obtaining

$$\frac{1}{S_{t_1}^{ZY}} \Delta\Pi_{t_0} = \frac{1}{S_{t_1}^{ZY}} \left[\Delta S_{t_0}^{XY} - S_{t_0}^{XZ} \Delta S_{t_0}^{ZY}\right] ZZZ \tag{9.11}$$

where the ZZZ indicates, in a rather disturbing way for those strictly observing mathematical notation, that we are now dealing with amounts denominated in the ZZZ currency. After some algebraic manipulations, we finally come up with

$$\frac{1}{S_{t_1}^{ZY}}\Delta\Pi_{t_0} = \frac{S_{t_1}^{XY} - S_{t_0}^{XY}}{S_{t_1}^{ZY}} - \frac{S_{t_0}^{XY}}{S_{t_0}^{ZY}}\frac{S_{t_1}^{ZY} - S_{t_0}^{ZY}}{S_{t_1}^{ZY}} = \left(S_{t_1}^{XZ} - S_{t_0}^{XZ}\right)\ ZZZ \tag{9.12}$$

which shows how the portfolio Π_{t_0} is equal, at time t_1, to the variation of the spot rate S^{XZ}, in ZZZ units after having converted it by the $S_{t_1}^{ZY}$ spot rate in t_1. At time t_0 from equation (9.12), we immediately get

$$\frac{1}{S_{t_0}^{ZY}}\Pi_{t_0} = 0 \tag{9.13}$$

Equation (9.5) follows as a direct consequence, thus showing that the mathematical truism also has a financial foundation based on a no-arbitrage argument. We can similarly prove, along the same line of reasoning, that $S_{t_0}^{ZX}$ can also be replicated by a portfolio containing $S_{t_0}^{XY}$ and $S_{t_0}^{ZY}$ and in this way we can confirm equation (9.5).

Some other results can be derived from the replicating portfolio we have examined. In more detail, by applying Itô's lemma, we derive the SDE commanding the evolution of the replication portfolio:

$$d\Pi_t = \left[\left(r_t^Y - r_t^X\right) S_t^{XY} - \left(r_t^Y - r_t^Z\right) S_t^{XZ} S_t^{ZY}\right] dt + \varsigma_t^{XY} S_t^{XY} dZ_t^{XY} - \varsigma_t^{ZY} S_t^{XZ} S_t^{ZY} dZ_t^{ZY} \tag{9.14}$$

By the no-arbitrage argument, the following must hold:

$$\frac{1}{S_{t_0}^{ZY}} E[d\Pi_t] = E\left[dS_t^{XZ}\right] \Leftrightarrow \mu^{\Pi} = \mu^{XZ} \tag{9.15}$$

where μ is the drift of the process indicated by the superscript. Hence, in a risk-neutral world, we have that the two drifts are

$$\mu^{\Pi} = \mu^{XZ} = S_t^{XZ}(r_t^Z - r_t^X) \tag{9.16}$$

which is also confirmed by equation (9.14). On the other hand, the variance of the processes must also be equal:

$$\frac{1}{(S_{t_0}^{ZY})^2}\ Var[d\Pi_{t_0}] = Var[dS_t^{XZ}] \tag{9.17}$$

It is straightforward to check that the relationship linking the two quantities is

$$(S_t^{XZ})^2[(\varsigma_t^{XY})^2 + (\varsigma_t^{ZY})^2 - 2\rho^{XY,ZY}\varsigma_t^{XY}\varsigma_t^{ZY}]dt = (S_t^{XZ})^2(\varsigma_t^{XZ})^2 dt \tag{9.18}$$

We recall that we are in a BS economy, so the implied volatilities for an option starting in 0 and expiring in T are obtained by integrating the (possibly time-dependent) instantaneous volatilities and averaging them over the entire period considered:

$$\frac{1}{T}\int_0^T (\varsigma_s^{XZ})^2 dt = \frac{1}{T}\int_0^T \left[(\varsigma_s^{XY})^2 + (\varsigma_s^{ZY})^2 - 2\rho^{XY,ZY}\varsigma_s^{XY}\varsigma_s^{ZY})\right] ds \tag{9.19}$$

Adopting the usual notation, we have

$$(\sigma^{XZ})^2 T = \left[(\sigma^{XY})^2 + (\sigma^{ZY})^2 - 2\rho^{XY,ZY}\sigma^{XY}\sigma^{ZY}\right] T \tag{9.20}$$

If the pair is quoted as ZX instead of XZ, we may prove that its implied volatility is linked to the other two volatilities as

$$(\sigma^{ZX})^2 T = \left[(\sigma^{XY})^2 + (\sigma^{ZY})^2 + 2\rho^{XY,ZY}\sigma^{XY}\sigma^{ZY} \right] T \tag{9.21}$$

If the implied volatilities of the three pairs are available in the market, we can infer the correlation implied by them:

$$\rho^{XY,ZY} = \frac{(\sigma^{XY})^2 + (\sigma^{ZY})^2 - (\sigma^{XZ})^2}{2\sigma^{XY}\sigma^{ZY}} \tag{9.22}$$

or, if S^{ZX} is quoted,

$$\rho^{XY,ZY} = \frac{(\sigma^{XZ})^2 - (\sigma^{XY})^2 - (\sigma^{ZY})^2}{2\sigma^{XY}\sigma^{ZY}}$$

Example 9.2.2. *We show an example of how the replication portfolio works in practice. Assume the following prices are dealing in the market at times t_0 and t_1:*

	t_0	t_1
EURJPY	*150.00*	*151.00*
USDJPY	*100.00*	*101.50*
EURUSD	*1.5000*	*1.4877*

Moreover, assume that the EURUSD price is derived by a no-arbitrage argument from the other two pairs EURJPY and USDJPY. Namely, we want to replicate the performance of a long position in one million EURUSD. We build a portfolio as explained above, i.e., one million long EURJPY and $S^{EU}_{t_0} = 1.5000$ million short USDJPY. Table 9.1 provides a picture of the situation at time t_0 and at time t_1. In the first column, in the upper part of the table, we show how much one million EUR is worth at each time, in terms of USD. The profits and losses

Table 9.1 Replication of the EURUSD spot rate by a portfolio of EURJPY and USDJPY spot rates

				P&L	
	EUR	USD	JPY	JPY	USD
(1) EURUSD					
t_0	1 000 000.00	1 500 000.00			
t_1	1 000 000.00	1 487 684.73			−12 315.27
(2) EURJPY					
t_0	1 000 000.00		150 000 000.00		
t_1	1 000 000.00		151 000 000.00	1 000 000.00	9 852.22
(3) USDJPY					
t_0		−1 500 000.00	−150 000 000.00		
t_1		−1 500 000.00	−152 250 000.00	−2 250 000.00	−22 167.49
			Total (2) + (3)	−1 250 000.00	−12 315.27

of this position are shown in the right-hand side of the table, in USD units (−120 315.27), clearly calculated as the difference between the final and initial values of one million EUR.

In the lower part of the table, the replication portfolio is shown (EUR and USD columns) as well as the equivalent value in JPY. The profits and losses of both these pairs are in JPY, and they are collected in the column JPY on the right-hand side of the table (−1 250 000 JPY), converted into USD at the rate prevailing in t_1 (1.4877)*, thus showing that the portfolio is actually replicating the EURUSD position.*

Let us now come back to the idea, just alluded to above, of deriving the dynamics for S^{XZ} by applying Itô's lemma directly to equation (9.5), employing the dynamics in formulae (9.2) and (9.3). That would yield

$$d\left(\frac{S_t^{XY}}{S_t^{ZY}}\right) = d\mathcal{S}_t^{XZ} = (r_t^Z - r_t^X + (\varsigma_t^{ZY})^2 - \rho^{XY,ZY}\varsigma_t^{XY}\varsigma_t^{ZY})\mathcal{S}_t^{XZ}dt + \varsigma_t^{XY}\mathcal{S}_t^{XZ}dZ_t^{XY} - \varsigma_t^{ZY}\mathcal{S}_t^{XZ}dZ_t^{ZY} \tag{9.23}$$

We have indicated the ratio as the new pair resulting from the ratio as $\mathcal{S}_t^{XZ}$, so as to distinguish it from S_t^{XZ}, since actually it is something different. In fact, what we have just derived in equation (9.23) is the dynamics for the pair S_t^{XZ} quantoed (**not** converted, as above) into YYY units. This is a new asset, not directly tradeable in the market, but that can be replicated by a dynamic trading strategy (as opposed to a static one, in the case above) involving the two pairs S_t^{XY} and S_t^{ZY}. It is worth noticing that it is possible to intuitively see that $\mathcal{S}_t^{XZ}$ is an asset whose value is denominated in YYY currency units, since both pairs utilized in the trading strategy have YYY as numeraire currency. Hence, the profits and losses generated by trading them are denominated in this currency. The quantities to use to set up the replication portfolio are

$$\Pi_{t_0} = x_1 S_{t_0}^{XY} - x_2 S_{t_0}^{ZY} \tag{9.24}$$

where

$$x_1 = \frac{\partial\left(\frac{S_{t_0}^{XY}}{S_{t_0}^{ZY}}\right)}{\partial S_{t_0}^{XY}} = \frac{1}{S_{t_0}^{ZY}} \text{ and } x_2 = \frac{\partial\left(\frac{S_{t_0}^{XY}}{S_{t_0}^{ZY}}\right)}{\partial S_{t_0}^{ZY}} = -\frac{S_{t_0}^{XY}}{(S_{t_0}^{ZY})^2}.$$

The dynamic trading strategy entails a rebalancing, and its effectiveness depends as usual on the range of factors we have analysed in Chapter 3. Before checking how the replication works with a practical example, we just hint at the fact that in case we replicate the reverse pair S_t^{ZX}, that would yield the dynamics

$$d\left(\frac{S_t^{ZY}}{S_t^{XY}}\right) = d\mathcal{S}_t^{ZX} = (r_t^X - r_t^Z + (\varsigma_t^{XY})^2 - \rho^{ZY,XY}\varsigma_t^{ZY}\varsigma_t^{XY})\mathcal{S}_t^{ZX}dt + \varsigma_t^{ZY}\mathcal{S}_t^{ZX}dZ_t^{ZY} - \varsigma_t^{XY}\mathcal{S}_t^{ZX}dZ_t^{XY} \tag{9.25}$$

which is the SDE commanding the evolution of the S_t^{ZX} FX spot rate quantoed in YYY units.

Example 9.2.3. *We show here how the replication strategy works in practice for the quantoed* $\mathcal{S}_t^{XZ}$*. We use the same pairs and market data as in Example 9.2.2. We are then replicating the EURUSD spot rate in JPY units and the portfolio weights in equation* (9.31) *are* $x_1 = \frac{1}{S_{t_0}^{UJ}} = \frac{1}{100.00}$ *and* $x_2 = -\frac{S_{t_0}^{EJ}}{(S_{t_0}^{UJ})^2} = -\frac{150.00}{100.00^2}$.

Table 9.2 EURUSD spot rate quantoed in JPY, by dynamic trading of a portfolio of EURJPY and USDJPY spot rates

				P&L	
	EUR	USD	JPY	JPY	USD
(1) EURUSD					
t_0	1 000 000.00	1 500 000.00			
t_1	1 000 000.00	1 487 684.73			−12 315.27
(2) EURJPY					
t_0	10 000.00		1 500 000.00		
t_1	10 000.00		1 510 000.00	10 000.00	98.52
(3) USDJPY					
t_0		−15 000.00	−1 500 000.00		
t_1		−15 000.00	−1 522 500.00	−22 500.00	−221.67
			Total (2) + (3)	−12 500.00	−123.15

Table 9.2 shows the notional one has to trade in EURJPY and USDJPY to replicate one million EURUSD quantoed in JPY. The third column on the left-hand side displays the values of those notional amounts in JPY terms. The profits and losses arising from this strategy are on the right-hand side. Different from the example above, the JPY columns show a value very similar to the USD columns for the EURUSD (upper side of the table), thus confirming that we are actually replicating the EURUSD's performance but in JPY terms (or alternatively, we are quantoing the EURUSD). The error is due to the discrete rebalancing and the convex feature of the S_t^{XY}/S_t^{ZY} payoff. The USD column proves that we are not at all replicating the EURUSD, as was the case in Example 9.26.

The volatility of the process (9.23) is

$$(\sigma^{XZ})^2 = (\sigma^{XY})^2 + (\sigma^{ZY})^2 - 2\rho^{XY,ZY}\sigma^{XY}\sigma^{ZY} \tag{9.26}$$

This is the same as that derived above for the static replication portfolio of the spot rate S^{XZ}, and actually many people derive the volatility of the latter from the quantoed process, although in our opinion it is better to keep things distinct, even if this causes clashes in the same result.

We may now wonder if the quantoed process in equation (9.23), which has not been derived by standard arguments, coincides with that derived by standard arguments.[2] To examine this point further, we first note that by following the same reasoning as above, we can easily get the volatility for the process σ^{XY} as a function of the volatilities of the other two pairs and their correlation:

$$(\sigma^{XY})^2 = (\sigma^{XZ})^2 + (\sigma^{ZY})^2 + 2\rho^{XZ,ZY}\sigma^{XZ}\sigma^{ZY} \tag{9.27}$$

Trivial algebra allows us to establish, from formulae (9.26) and (9.27), that

$$(\sigma^{ZY})^2 - \rho^{XY,ZY}\sigma^{XY}\sigma^{ZY} = -\rho^{XZ,ZY}\sigma^{XZ}\sigma^{ZY} \tag{9.28}$$

By substituting equation (9.28) into equation (9.23), we finally obtain

$$dS_t^{XZ} = (r_t^Z - r_t^X - \rho^{XZ,ZY}\sigma^{XZ}\sigma^{ZY})S_t^{XZ}dt + \varsigma_t^{ZY}S_t^{XZ}dZ_t^{ZY} - \varsigma_t^{XY}S_t^{XZ}dZ_t^{XY} \tag{9.29}$$

[2] See, for example, Hull [39].

The route usually followed to determine the drift adjustment is: (i) take the process for the asset one wishes to “quanto” (i.e., S^{XZ} in our case); (ii) take the volatility of the new numeraire currency in which one wants the quantoed asset to be denominated (i.e., S^{ZY}), and the correlation between this currency and the asset; (iii) correct the asset's drift by introducing a correction that is equal to the covariance between the asset's and the new numeraire currency's returns (the sign of the correction depends on whether the new numeraire currency is the base or the numeraire currency in the pair – in our case it is negative). In the present case in which the S^{XZ} process has to be quantoed in YYY units,[3] this route leads to drift adjustments for the process of S^{XZ} shown in equation (9.29), which is the same as that determined by the ratio S^{XY}/S^{ZY}, by also considering the fact that one may set $\varsigma_t^{ZY} dZ_t^{ZY} - \varsigma_t^{XY} dZ_t^{XY} = \varsigma_t^{XZ} dZ_t^{XZ}$, and thus yield

$$dS_t^{XZ} = \left(r_t^Z - r_t^X - \rho^{XZ,ZY}\sigma^{XZ}\sigma^{ZY}\right) S_t^{XZ} dt + S_t^{XZ}\varsigma_t^{XZ} dZ_t^{XZ} \tag{9.30}$$

The replication portfolio now contains S^{XZ} and S^{ZY}:

$$\Pi_{t_0} = x_1 S_{t_0}^{XZ} - x_2 S_{t_0}^{ZY} \tag{9.31}$$

The quantities to use are

$$x_1 = \frac{\partial\left(\frac{S_{t_0}^{XZ}}{S_{t_0}^{ZY}}\right)}{\partial S_{t_0}^{XY}} = \frac{1}{S_{t_0}^{ZY}} \text{ and } x_2 = \frac{\partial\left(\frac{S_{t_0}^{XZ}}{S_{t_0}^{ZY}}\right)}{\partial S_{t_0}^{ZY}} = -\frac{S_{t_0}^{XZ}}{(S_{t_0}^{ZY})^2}$$

Example 9.2.4. *In this example we show that the quantoed spot rate can be replicated by a portfolio containing spot contracts on the pair to be quantoed and the pair to translate the numeraire currency into the new one. We still work with the same pairs and market values as in Example 9.2.2. We wish to replicate the EURUSD spot rate quantoed in JPY, for an amount of one million EUR; the quantities of the two pairs to be used in this case are:* $x_1 = \frac{1}{S_{t_0}^{UJ}} = \frac{1}{100.00}$ *and* $x_2 = -\frac{S_{t_0}^{EU}}{(S_{t_0}^{UJ})^2} = -\frac{1.5000}{100.00^2}$.

Table 9.3 shows the results. As before, the columns on the right-hand side display the amount held in each pair and the value expressed in the corresponding numeraire currencies. On the left-hand side we can see that the performance in JPY of the portfolio is very close to the performance of the EURUSD in US dollars. It is worth noticing that the replica is less approximate than that attained by setting up a portfolio containing EURJPY and USDJPY pairs – that being a suggestion to adopt the hedging tools arising from a classic quanto adjustment argument, rather than these.

9.3 CONTRACTS DEPENDING ON SEVERAL FX SPOT RATES

Some contracts may depend on several FX spot rates. We examine only those depending on two rates and more specifically, a quanto plain vanilla. Many more types of contracts can be introduced, with many exotic features (e.g., barriers), but here we just want to give some flavour of the problems one has to cope with when trading such instruments.

[3] We just recall here that S^{XZ}/S^{YZ} $ZZZ = S^{XZ}$ YYY.

Table 9.3 EURUSD spot rate quantoed in JPY, by dynamic trading of a portfolio of EURUSD and USDJPY spot rates

				P&L	
	EUR	USD	JPY	JPY	USD
(1) EURUSD					
t_0	1 000 000.00	1 500 000.00			
t_1	1 000 000.00	1 487 684.73			−12 315.27
(2) EURJPY					
t_0	10 000.00	15 000.00			
t_1	10 000.00	14 876.85		−12 500.00	−123.15
(3) USDJPY					
t_0		150.00	22 500.00		
t_1		150.00	22 650.00	150.00	1.48
			Total (2) + (3)	−12 350.00	−121.67

Let us assume that an option $\mathcal{O}^Y$ whose payoff at expiry T is denominated in YYY units, depends on two spot rates. Its price at time t, in very general terms, can be written

$$\mathcal{O}_t(S_t^{XY}, S_t^{ZY}) = E^{Q^Y}\left[e^{-\int_t^T r_s^Y ds} f(S_T^{XY}, S_T^{ZY})|\mathcal{F}_t\right] \tag{9.32}$$

Equation (9.32) simply states that the price of a contract that is a function of several currencies is its expected value at expiry under the risk-neutral measure Q^Y, where the superscripts indicate that the payoff is denominated in YYY currency units. The expected terminal value is discounted with the domestic interest rate r_t^Y. By means of a change of numeraire, shifting from the risk-neural domestic money market deposit to $\overline{S}_t = S_t e^{-\int_t^T r_u^Y du}$ as a new numeraire, the valuation of a claim is

$$\begin{aligned}\mathcal{O}_t &= \overline{S}_t E^{Q^{\overline{S}}}\left[\frac{\mathcal{O}_T}{\overline{S}_T}|\mathcal{F}_t\right] \\ &= S_t e^{-\int_t^T r_u^Y du} E^{Q^{\overline{S}}}\left[\frac{\mathcal{O}_T}{S_T}|\mathcal{F}_t\right]\end{aligned} \tag{9.33}$$

This can be useful to price contracts such as a quanto plain vanilla option, which we define as follows:

Definition 9.3.1. ***Quanto option contract.*** *An XXXYYY (plain vanilla) quanto option pays out at maturity T the amount $[\omega(S_T^{XZ} - K^{XZ})]^+$ denominated in a third currency YYY, which is equivalent to $[\omega(S_T^{XZ} - K^{XZ})]^+/S_T^{ZY}$ or $[\omega(S_T^{XZ} - K^{XZ})]^+ S_T^{YZ}$ in YYY domestic currency, depending on whether the market quoting convention for the YYY and ZZZ currencies is, respectively, ZZZYYY or YYYZZZ. As usual, $\omega = 1$ for a call and $\omega = -1$ for a put.*

In a BS economy, we can price this contract in a closed-form formula. Assume we have an option on the quantoed process S_t^{XZ}. From equation (9.23) we know that it is a function of the spot rates S_t^{ZY} and S_t^{XY}. The (ATM) implied volatilities involved in the process are those referring to these spot rates, since they enter into the drift of the process dS_t^{XZ}, and also, by setting $\varsigma_t^{ZY} dZ_t^{ZY} - \varsigma_t^{XY} dZ_t^{XY} = \varsigma_t^{XZ} dZ_t^{XZ}$, the implied volatility for the FX spot rate S_t^{XZ}. The strike is K^{XZ}, whose superscript indicates that it refers to the quantoed pair XXXZZZ. We may then write

$$\begin{aligned}
&QO_Y(S_t^{XY}, S_t^{ZY}, t, T, K^{XZ}, P^X(t,T), P^Y(t,T), P^Z(t,T), \sigma^{XY}, \sigma^{ZY}, \sigma^{XZ}) = \\
&\quad QE^{Q^Y}\left[e^{-\int_t^T r_s^Y ds}(\omega S_T^{XZ} - \omega K^{XZ})^+ / S_T^{ZY}\right] ZZZ \\
&\quad QE^{Q^Y}\left[e^{-\int_t^T r_s^Y ds}\left(\omega \frac{S_T^{XY}}{S_T^{ZY}} - \omega K^{XZ}\right)^+\right] YYY
\end{aligned}$$

where Q is a fixed quanto factor. The third line in the equation above indicates that we have changed (not converted) the denomination of the terminal payoff from the XXX to the YYY currency. It is possible to calculate this expectation explicitly, and then yield

$$\begin{aligned}
&QO_Y(S_t^{XY}, S_t^{ZY}, t, T, K^{XZ}, P^X(t,T), P^Y(t,T), P^Z(t,T), \sigma^{XY}, \sigma^{ZY}, \sigma^{XZ}) = \\
&\quad QP^Y(t,T)\left[\omega S_t^{XZ} e^{\mu^{XZ}\tau}\Phi(\omega d_1) - \omega K^{XZ}\Phi(\omega d_2)\right] \qquad (9.34)
\end{aligned}$$

where $\mu^{XZ} = r_t^Z - r_t^X + (\sigma^{ZY})^2 - \rho^{XY,ZY}\sigma^{XY}\sigma^{ZY}$. Moreover,

$$\begin{aligned}
d_1 &= \frac{\ln \frac{S_t^{XZ} e^{\mu^{XZ}}(T-t)}{K^{XZ}} + \frac{1}{2}(\sigma^{XZ})^2(T-t)}{(\sigma^{XZ})^2\sqrt{(T-t)}} \\
d_2 &= d_1 - \sigma_T\sqrt{(T-t)}
\end{aligned}$$

and

$$\sigma^{XZ} = \sqrt{\frac{(\int_t^T \varsigma_s^{XZ} ds)^2}{T-t}}$$

Alternatively, we could express the quanto adjustment as $\mu^{XZ} = r_t^Z - r_t^X - \rho^{XZ,ZY}\sigma^{XZ}\sigma^{ZY}$ if the quoting convention for the currencies YYY and ZZZ is S^{ZY} or $\mu^{XZ} = r_t^Z - r_t^X + \rho^{XZ,YZ}\sigma^{XZ}\sigma^{YZ}$ in case it is S^{YZ}. The implied volatility could also be written as a function of the other two implied volatilities:

$$\sigma^{XZ} = \sqrt{(\sigma^{XY})^2 + (\sigma^{ZY})^2 - 2\rho^{XY,ZY}\sigma^{XY}\sigma^{ZY}}$$

The different ways to express the input are equivalent, but their choice can depend on the availability of reliable market prices. This should entail no problem for most liquid pairs, but in some cases it might be easier to retrieve volatilities for some pairs rather than for others.

We go not further in analysing other kinds of quanto contracts. It is possible to derive closed-form formulae for barrier quanto options, external barrier options (i.e., contracts not necessarily quantoed, but whose payoff determined by a given pair is contingent on the breaching of a barrier on a different pair), Asian quanto and multi-pair contracts quantoed in one currency.[4] We deem it more important to outline a possible general treatment of the smile for options depending on several FX spot rates.

[4] See Kwok and Wong [43] for a discussion and for closed-form formulae on these kinds of contracts.

9.4 DEALING WITH CORRELATION AND VOLATILITY SMILE

The most sound theoretical way to deal with an economy where many FX spot rates are quoted and where in their respective options market a volatility smile manifests, is to extend a stochastic volatility model (such as one of those examined in Chapter 2) so as to describe in a consistent fashion a multi-FX rate environment. In this case one of the main issues is how to correctly and consistently build a correlation matrix. We just note the fact that for each spot rate a correlation exists not only with its own (stochastic) volatility, but also between pairs of spot rates and between each spot rate and all the other volatilities. A tool to build such a complex object in a robust way is given by Kahl and Gunther [41]: they consider a general method for a multidimensional stochastic volatility model.

An alternative, though less thorough, method from a theoretical perspective is to extend the VV method to a multi-FX rate. We will sketch this extension below, and examine how to include the (multiple) smile effects in options depending on several FX spot rates.[5]

9.4.1 Vanna–Volga extension

Assume we are in a BS world where three pairs are traded and we want to price an option depending on these. An example could be the quanto plain vanilla option we have shown above: equation (9.33) indicates that such a contract depends on the three implied volatilities associated with the three pairs. We can compute the Vega corresponding to each of the three implied volatilities in the usual way, by calculating the first derivative with respect to each volatility. That would yield

$$\mathcal{V}^{XY} = \frac{\partial \mathcal{O}_t^Y}{\partial \sigma^{XY}}, \quad \mathcal{V}^{ZY} = \frac{\partial \mathcal{O}_t^Y}{\partial \sigma^{ZY}}, \quad \mathcal{V}^{XZ} = \frac{\partial \mathcal{O}_t^Y}{\partial \sigma^{XZ}} \frac{1}{S_t^{ZY}} \tag{9.35}$$

In equation (9.35) the first two derivatives measure the change in the option's value due to a change in the implied volatilities σ^{XY} and σ^{ZY}. This change is expressed in YYY currency units, since the options price is denominated in such currency. Also the last Vega, with respect to σ^{XZ}, is originally expressed in YYY units, but we prefer to convert it into ZZZ units, since we are going to hedge this risk with plain vanilla options on the XXXZZZ pair, whose price is expressed in ZZZ units. This is the reason why $\mathcal{V}^{XZ}$ is divided by the spot rate S_t^{ZY}.[6]

Now we have to define the other volatility-related Greeks. Let us consider Vanna: it is the first derivative of Vega with respect to the underlying spot rate. For $\mathcal{V}^{XY}$ it is straightforward to calculate the derivatives with respect to S^{XY}, but it cannot be neglected that this Vega is also a function of the other spot rate S^{ZY}. To account for that we need a tool to link the variations of S^{XY} to those in S^{ZY}. Assuming, just for this purpose, that the drifts of S^{XY} and S^{ZY} are equal to zero, we can establish the relationship

$$\begin{aligned} E[dS_t^{ZY}|dS_t^{XY}] &= \sigma^{ZY} S_t^{ZY} E[dZ_t^{ZY}|dZ_t^{XY}] \\ &= \sigma^{ZY} S_t^{ZY} \rho^{XY,ZY} dZ_t^{XY} = \rho^{XY,ZY} \frac{\sigma^{ZY} S_t^{ZY}}{\sigma^{XY} S_t^{XY}} dS_t^{XY} \end{aligned} \tag{9.36}$$

[5] The original idea of the VV extension first appeared in Beneder and Baker [5]. We basically hinge on their work, with some slight differences and some minor corrections.

[6] Clearly, market conventions could be that the option prices on XXXZZZ are expressed as a percentage of the base currency XXX. Nonetheless, we can always choose, without any loss of generality, to express them in ZZZ units for our purposes, although in opposition to market quotation standards.

Equation (9.36) shows that the expected change of the spot rate S^{ZY}, conditional on a given change of S^{XY}, is equal to the latter times a factor depending on the correlation between the two pairs, and proportional to the ratio of their price volatilities. An analogous relationship can also be identified between other couples of pairs, and we can then exploit that to calculate the Vanna in a multi-FX setting. We have

$$\mathcal{X}^{XY} = \frac{\partial \mathcal{V}^{XY}}{\partial S_t^{XY}} + \rho^{XY,ZY} \frac{\sigma^{ZY} S_t^{ZY}}{\sigma^{XY} S_t^{XY}} \frac{\partial \mathcal{V}^{XY}}{\partial S_t^{ZY}} \tag{9.37}$$

We are thus defining Vanna as the first derivative of Vega with respect to the corresponding FX spot rate, i.e., in formula (9.37) we calculate the derivative of $\mathcal{V}^{XY}$ with respect to S^{XY}, but consider also the variations of the spot rate S_t^{ZY} given a variation of S^{XY}, whence the second addend in the equation. By the same token we can define Vanna for Vega with respect to σ^{ZY} as

$$\mathcal{X}^{ZY} = \frac{\partial \mathcal{V}^{ZY}}{\partial S_t^{ZY}} + \rho^{XY,ZY} \frac{\sigma^{XY} S_t^{XY}}{\sigma^{ZY} S_t^{ZY}} \frac{\partial \mathcal{V}^{ZY}}{\partial S_t^{XY}} \tag{9.38}$$

At this stage, apparently, we have calculated all possible Vannas of the option, since the FX spot rates entering into the function of the price are just S_t^{XY} and S_t^{ZY}. Nevertheless, we can link the movements of these two pairs to the spot rate S_t^{XZ} similarly to equation (9.36). Hence we have that Vanna with respect to S_t^{XZ} is calculated with respect to the variations of S_t^{XY} and S_t^{ZY}, conditioned on the variations of S_t^{XZ}. We then get

$$\mathcal{X}^{XZ} = \rho^{XY,XZ} \frac{\sigma^{XY} S_t^{XY}}{\sigma^{XZ} S_t^{XZ}} \frac{\partial \mathcal{V}^{XZ}}{\partial S_t^{XY}} + \rho^{ZY,XZ} \frac{\sigma^{ZY} S_t^{ZY}}{\sigma^{XZ} S_t^{XZ}} \frac{\partial \mathcal{V}^{XZ}}{\partial S_t^{ZY}} \tag{9.39}$$

and we have completed the analysis for Vannas. It is worth noticing[7] that the definition of the multi-FX Vannas we have just provided is consistent with the change of base currency. We know from Chapter 2, equation (2.50), the relationship between the price of an option calculated by choosing either of the two currencies as the base one (domestic–foreign symmetry). Also, the Greeks must be consistent with that relationship, and this is what happens with the Vannas as defined in equations (9.37), (9.38) and (9.39). Not all the definitions of Vanna, although reasonable, enjoy such a property. For instance, as noted by Beneder and Baker [5], an independence copula modelling the joint density distribution of two FX spot rates would not guarantee that the domestic–foreign symmetry holds for Vanna.

We now move on to the Volgas: their definition is somewhat similar to the case of the Vanna, although here we take into account the correlations between couples of implied volatilities:

$$\mathcal{W}^{XY} = \frac{\partial \mathcal{V}^{XY}}{\partial \sigma^{XY}} + \varrho^{XY,ZY} \frac{\nu^{ZY} \sigma_t^{ZY}}{\nu^{XY} \sigma^{XY}} \frac{\partial \mathcal{V}^{XY}}{\partial \sigma^{ZY}} + \varrho^{XY,XZ} \frac{\nu^{XZ} \sigma_t^{XZ}}{\nu^{XY} \sigma^{XY}} \frac{\partial \mathcal{V}^{XY}}{\partial \sigma^{XZ}} \tag{9.40}$$

In this case we have defined conditional variations of the implied volatilities σ^{ZY} and σ^{XZ} given a variation of σ^{XY}, similarly to what we have done above for the spot rates. In this case we are not able to retrieve all the inputs we need from the market prices. In fact, in equation (9.40), $\varrho^{XY,ZY}$ and $\varrho^{XY,XZ}$ are the correlations between, respectively, σ^{XY} and σ^{ZY}, and σ^{XY} and σ^{XZ}. Besides, $\nu^{\{\cdot\}}$ is the volatility of the implied volatility indicated in the superscript. Both $\varrho^{\{\cdot,\cdot\}}$ and $\nu^{\{\cdot\}}$ cannot be inferred directly from market prices, and estimates on historical data are needed. This makes the extended VV method somewhat less self-concluded than it is in

[7] This is proved in Beneder and Baker [5].

the standard mono-FX case we have examined in previous chapters, but the impact of these parameters is actually limited so we do not need to worry too much about the precision of the values we are using.

For the other two Volgas we operate in the same way, and we have

$$\mathcal{W}^{ZY} = \frac{\partial \mathcal{V}^{ZY}}{\partial \sigma^{ZY}} + \varrho^{ZY,XY} \frac{\nu^{XY}\sigma_t^{XY}}{\nu^{ZY}\sigma^{ZY}} \frac{\partial \mathcal{V}^{ZY}}{\partial \sigma^{XY}} + \varrho^{ZY,XZ} \frac{\nu^{XZ}\sigma_t^{XZ}}{\nu^{ZY}\sigma^{ZY}} \frac{\partial \mathcal{V}^{ZY}}{\partial \sigma^{XZ}} \tag{9.41}$$

and

$$\mathcal{W}^{XZ} = \frac{\partial \mathcal{V}^{XZ}}{\partial \sigma^{XZ}} + \varrho^{XZ,XY} \frac{\nu^{XY}\sigma_t^{XY}}{\nu^{XZ}\sigma^{XZ}} \frac{\partial \mathcal{V}^{XZ}}{\partial \sigma^{XY}} + \varrho^{XZ,ZY} \frac{\nu^{ZY}\sigma_t^{ZY}}{\nu^{XZ}\sigma^{XZ}} \frac{\partial \mathcal{V}^{XZ}}{\partial \sigma^{ZY}} \tag{9.42}$$

Remark 9.4.1. *Since Vega, $\mathcal{V}^{XZ}$, for the S^{XZ} pair is expressed in ZZZ currency units, also the related Vanna $\mathcal{X}^{XZ}$ and Volga $\mathcal{W}^{XZ}$ are denominated in the same ZZZ currency. For all of these Greeks we use XXXZZZ plain vanilla options for hedging purposes.*

We are now able to define a portfolio capable of hedging all the volatility-related Greeks we have just defined for the multi-FX option we are considering. Namely, as for the XXXYYY pair, we can establish the following system:

$$\begin{aligned}
\mathcal{V}^{XY} &= \sum_{i=1}^{3} x_i^{XY} \mathcal{V}_i(K_i^{XY}) \\
\mathcal{X}^{XY} &= \sum_{i=1}^{3} x_i^{XY} \mathcal{X}_i(K_i^{XY}) \\
\mathcal{W}^{XY} &= \sum_{i=1}^{3} x_i^{XY} \mathcal{W}_i(K_i^{XY})
\end{aligned} \tag{9.43}$$

In system (9.43) we equate the quanto option's Vega, Vanna and Volga, with respect to the XXXYYY pair, to the same Greeks of a portfolio of three plain vanilla options written on the same pair. We indicate that by inserting as an argument of all the Greeks' functions, the strikes referred to the XXXYYY pair by the superscript XY. The plain vanilla options are, as usual, the ATM and the two 25D wings. A similar system is also solved for the other two pairs, thus obtaining the quantities needed to make the entire portfolio locally riskless. By an argument similar to that used in Chapter 4, we may deduce that the smile-adjusted price for the quanto option is

$$\begin{aligned}
\mathcal{QO}_Y = \mathcal{QO}_Y^{\text{BS}} &+ \sum_{i=1}^{3} x_i^{XY} [\mathbf{C}^{\text{MKT}}(K_i^{XY}) - \mathbf{C}^{\text{BS}}(K_i^{XY})] \\
&\sum_{i=1}^{3} x_i^{ZY} [\mathbf{C}^{\text{MKT}}(K_i^{ZY}) - \mathbf{C}^{\text{BS}}(K_i^{ZY})] \\
&\sum_{i=1}^{3} x_i^{XZ} [\mathbf{C}^{\text{MKT}}(K_i^{XZ}) - \mathbf{C}^{\text{BS}}(K_i^{XZ})] S_t^{ZY}
\end{aligned} \tag{9.44}$$

Equation (9.44) shows that the adjusted price is equal to the BS flat volatility price plus the difference between the real market price and the flat volatility price of each hedging option, weighted by its amount. We just remark the fact that the differences for the plain vanilla options on the XXXZZZ pair are in ZZZ units, so that they are converted into YYY units (which the price QO_Y is expressed in) by multiplying them by the spot rate S_t^{ZY}.

By the same token we can also price other kinds of contracts depending on several spot rates, including external barrier options. For Asian options, as we have already mentioned in Chapter 7, the VV approach does not perform very well.

Example 9.4.1. *Assume we want to price a EUR call USD put expiring in* 6 *months (or* 182 *days), struck at* 1.5000 *and quantoed in JPY. The quanto factor* $Q = 100$. *Market data for the level of the spot rates and the discount factors (zero-coupon bond prices) are the following:*

S^{EJ}	S^{UJ}	$P^U(0,6M)$	$P^E(0,6M)$	$P^J(0,6M)$
140.0000	*101.00*	*0.975878*	*0.9850498*	*0.99481527*

From the options market quotes, the three main volatilities and strikes for all the pairs involved in the pricing of the quanto options are:

	EURUSD		
	25D P	*ATM*	*25D C*
6M	*11.30%*	*10.70%*	*10.70%*

	USDJPY		
	25D P	*ATM*	*25D C*
6M	*12.89%*	*11.00%*	*9.71%*

	EURJPY		
	25D P	*ATM*	*25D C*
6M	*12.30%*	*10.40%*	*9.15%*

We can immediately price the flat-smile price for the quanto contract by means of formula (9.34), *and we get that the option is worth* 1.1379 *JPY. To include the smile* *effects in the pricing, we first calculate the volatility-related Greeks for all the pairs (these Greeks are calculated considering the quanto factor $Q = 1$), assuming the following set of parameters:*

$\rho^{EJ,UJ}$	50.00%
$\rho^{EJ,EU}$	40.00%
$\rho^{EU,UJ}$	−60.00%
ν^{EJ}	25.00%
ν^{UJ}	30.00%
ν^{EU}	20.00%
$\varrho^{EJ,UJ}$	70.00%
$\varrho^{EJ,EU}$	85.00%
$\varrho^{EU,UJ}$	90.00%

The strikes and the Greeks for the USDJPY are

Strike	Vega	Volga	Vanna
98.78	27.6825	0.0000	0.0000
103.64	23.9929	72.8746	1.8905
93.364	20.1029	106.6341	−1.8604

and for the EURUSD we have

Strike	Vega	Volga	Vanna
0.3846	1.4032	0.0000	0.2775
0.3097	1.4752	1.4126	2.1771
0.3020	1.3313	1.2174	−1.7879

Finally, the strikes (Delta with premium included) and the volatility-related Greeks for the EURJPY are

Strike	Vega	Volga	Vanna
38.7449	138.25	0.0000	0.0000
33.4468	144.70	109.2378	2.0192
27.8228	130.90	162.5658	−2.0125

The Greeks for the quanto option with respect to the three pairs are summarized in the following table:

Pair	*Vega*	*Volga*	*Vanna*
EURJPY	*−0.0077*	*−0.1332*	*−0.0005*
USDJPY	*0.0234*	*0.2180*	*−0.0024*
EURUSD	*0.0027*	*0.0188*	0.0252

Then we apply formula (9.44) and we have that the final VV-adjusted quanto option price is 0.70 *JPY.*

9.5 LINKING VOLATILITY SMILES

An interesting byproduct of the extension of the VV method to the multi-FX case is that we are able to link the volatility smile of two pairs, say XXXZZZ and ZZZYYY, to a third one, say XXXYYY. It is particularly useful to infer the smile of less liquid pairs from two liquid ones. Usually, for minor currencies, the most liquid cross rate is against the US dollar and also (for options) more prices are available for this one. Since we also have the (extremely) liquid pair EURUSD and the option prices for it, we can infer the volatility smile of the less liquid currency also for the cross against the euro.

To make things concrete, assume we want to price at time t a plain vanilla option on the (illiquid) XXXYYY pair with strike K^{XY} and expiry in T. We know from Section 9.2 that the spot rate S_t^{XY} can be replicated by means of a portfolio containing a proper amount of S_t^{XZ} and S_t^{ZY}. By recalling the results obtained, there we can write the value of the plain vanilla option on XXXYYY as:

$$\begin{aligned} \mathcal{O}_t(S_t^{XZ}, S_t^{ZY}) &= E^{Q^Y}\left[e^{-\int_t^T r_s^Y ds} f\left(S_T^{XZ}, S_T^{ZY}\right)|\mathcal{F}_t\right] \\ &= E^{Q^Y}\left[e^{-\int_t^T r_s^Y ds}(\omega((x_1 S_T^{XZ} + x_2 S_T^{ZY}) - K^{XY}))^+|\mathcal{F}_t\right] \\ &= \mathrm{Bl}(S_t^{XY}, t, T, K^{XY}, P^Y(t,T), P^X(t,T), \sigma_T^{XY}, \omega) \end{aligned} \quad (9.45)$$

where we can express the implied volatility for the pair S^{XY} in terms of the volatilities for the other two pairs:

$$\sigma^{XY} = \sqrt{(\sigma^{XZ})^2 + (\sigma^{ZY})^2 + 2\rho^{XZ,ZY}\sigma^{XZ}\sigma^{ZY}} \quad (9.46)$$

Since we are assuming we do not have a liquid market for the XXXYYY pair with reliable options prices, we cannot infer the correlation $\rho^{XZ,ZY}$ via an equation of the kind (9.22), since we are missing σ^{XY}, which is just what we want to infer from the prices in the more liquid markets. So, a crucial input in this case is $\rho^{XZ,ZY}$ and some guess, or historical data-based estimate, is needed to assign a value to it. Given this value, we can calculate the Vegas for the option:

$$\mathcal{V}^{ZY} = \frac{\partial \mathcal{O}_t^Y}{\partial \sigma^{ZY}}, \quad \mathcal{V}^{XZ} = \frac{\partial \mathcal{O}_t^Y}{\partial \sigma^{XZ}} \frac{1}{S_t^{ZY}}$$

The Vegas are only with respect to σ^{ZY} and σ^{XZ}, different from the quanto option that depends on three implied volatilities. Also in this case, the Vega with respect to σ^{XZ} is converted into ZZZ units since we will use plain vanilla on the XXXZZZ pair to hedge it. For the Vannas we apply the definition we have introduced in Section 9.4.1, so that we have

$$\mathcal{X}^{ZY} = \frac{\partial \mathcal{V}^{ZY}}{\partial S_t^{ZY}} + \rho^{XZ,ZY} \frac{\sigma^{XZ} S_t^{XZ}}{\sigma^{ZY} S_t^{ZY}} \frac{\partial \mathcal{V}^{ZY}}{\partial S_t^{XZ}}$$

and

$$\mathcal{X}^{XZ} = \frac{\partial \mathcal{V}^{XZ}}{\partial S_t^{XZ}} + \rho^{XZ,ZY} \frac{\sigma^{ZY} S_t^{ZY}}{\sigma^{XZ} S_t^{XZ}} \frac{\partial \mathcal{V}^{XZ}}{\partial S_t^{ZY}}$$

The Volgas are also defined as in the previous section:

$$\mathcal{W}^{ZY} = \frac{\partial \mathcal{V}^{ZY}}{\partial \sigma^{ZY}} + \varrho^{ZY,XZ} \frac{\nu^{XZ} \sigma_t^{XZ}}{\nu^{ZY} \sigma^{ZY}} \frac{\partial \mathcal{V}^{ZY}}{\partial \sigma^{XZ}}$$

and

$$\mathcal{W}^{XZ} = \frac{\partial \mathcal{V}^{XZ}}{\partial \sigma^{XZ}} + \varrho^{ZY,XZ} \frac{\nu^{ZY} \sigma_t^{ZY}}{\nu^{XZ} \sigma^{XZ}} \frac{\partial \mathcal{V}^{XZ}}{\partial \sigma^{ZY}}$$

The correlation between the implied volatilities and the volatilities of the latter has to be provided externally, since they cannot by any means be inferred from the market prices. Given the Vannas and the Volgas, we build a portfolio of three XXXYYY plain vanilla options (ATM and the two 25D wings), so as to hedge the volatility-related exposures with respect to σ^{XY}:

$$\begin{aligned}
\mathcal{V}^{XY} &= \sum_{i=1}^{3} x_i^{XY} \mathcal{V}_i(K_i^{XY}) \\
\mathcal{X}^{XY} &= \sum_{i=1}^{3} x_i^{XY} \mathcal{X}_i(K_i^{XY}) \\
\mathcal{W}^{XY} &= \sum_{i=1}^{3} x_i^{XY} \mathcal{W}_i(K_i^{XY})
\end{aligned} \tag{9.47}$$

We do the same for the exposures with respect to σ^{XZ}, by adding three XXXZZZ plain vanilla options to the portfolio, in suitable quantities so as to nil the risks. Once we have solved the systems to determine the quantities, we can finally get the smile-adjusted price for the XXXYYY option:

$$\mathcal{O} = \mathcal{O}^{\text{BS}} + \sum_{i=1}^{3} x_i^{ZY} [\mathbf{C}^{\text{MKT}}(K_i^{ZY}) - \mathbf{C}^{\text{BS}}(K_i^{ZY})] \sum_{i=1}^{3} x_i^{XZ} [\mathbf{C}^{\text{MKT}}(K_i^{XZ}) - \mathbf{C}^{\text{BS}}(K_i^{XZ})] S_t^{XY} \tag{9.48}$$

The interpretation of equation (9.48) is the same as that we gave for equation (9.44). The BS flat volatility price $\mathcal{O}^{BS}$ is calculated by plugging in equation (9.46), once we input the required value for $\rho^{XZ,ZY}$.

Example 9.5.2. *We show an example of how to link the EURJPY to the USDJPY and EURUSD smile volatilities, for a* 6*-month expiry. We assume that the market data are those in the following tables:*

S^{EU}	S^{UJ}	$P^U(0,6M)$	$P^E(0,6M)$	$P^J(0,6M)$
1.3861	*101.00*	*0.975878*	*0.9850498*	*0.99481527*

The data for the three main strikes' volatilities are the same as in Example 9.4.1. We also consider two sets of parameters for the correlation amongst implied volatilities and for the volatilities of implied volatilities, to test their impact on the shape of the smile:

	Set 1	*Set 2*
$\rho^{EU,UJ}$	*−60.00%*	*−60.00%*
$\varrho^{EU,UJ}$	*70.00%*	*90.00%*
ν^{EU}	*20.00%*	*30.00%*
ν^{UJ}	*25.00%*	*50.00%*

We want to price three options written on the EURJPY and struck at 140.00, 150.00 *and* 130.00*, expiring in* 6 *months. The inputs we need for our cross-currency VV approach are the volatility-related Greeks, defined as above. With respect to the EURUSD, they are*

Strike	*Vega*	*Volga*	*Vanna*
140.00	*0.1615*	*1.4465*	*0.1875*
130.00	*0.1013*	*1.5290*	*−0.3231*
150.00	*0.0871*	*1.5919*	*0.4544*

The same Greeks with respect to the USDJPY are

Strike	*Vega*	*Volga*	*Vanna*
140.00	*18.2172*	*41.7270*	*0.1949*
130.00	*11.4341*	*110.1253*	*−0.6195*
150.00	*9.8321*	*132.1492*	*0.6993*

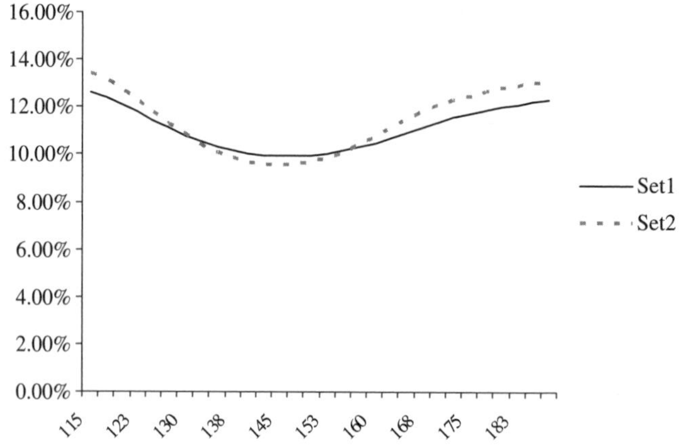

Figure 9.1 EURJPY volatility smiles for the 6-month expiry, obtained from the EURUSD and USDJPY volatility smiles by means of the extended VV approach with the two sets of parameters listed in the text.

Finally, the prices obtained via formula (9.48), *for the two sets of parameters, are*

		Set 1		*Set 2*	
Strike	*Flat vol. price*	*VV adj. price*	*Impl. smile vol.*	*VV adj. price*	*Impl. smile vol.*
140.00	*3.1451*	*3.2311*	*9.93%*	*3.1293*	*9.67%*
130.00	*0.8583*	*1.15920*	*10.89%*	*1.1090*	*10.70%*
150.00	*0.6101*	*0.6487*	*9.89%*	*0.6117*	*9.72%*

We can use the VV smile function (9.48) *to produce the entire volatility smiles, in terms of strikes, and Figure 9.1 plots them. Clearly, we can infer from the strikes corresponding to the ATM and the two 25D levels, the volatilities to use for the three main instruments, and hence the related prices (in terms of volatility):* σ_{ATM}, **rr** *and* **vwb**.

References

[1] M. Abramowitz and I.A. Stegun. *Handbook of Mathematical Functions*. National Bureau of Standards, Applied Mathematics Series 55, 10th edition, 1972.

[2] H. Albrecher, P. Mayer, W. Schoutens and J. Tistaert. The little Heston trap. *Wilmott Magazine*, 1:83–92, 2005.

[3] C. Becker and U. Wystup. On the cost of delayed currency fixing announcements. *Working Paper, HfB Business School of Finance and Management*, 2005.

[4] S. Benaim and P. Friz. Regular variation and smile asymptotics. *Mathematical Finance*, 19(1):1–12, 200.

[5] R. Beneder and G. Baker. Pricing multi-currency options with smile. *ABN AMRO Bank Internal Report*, 2005.

[6] Y.Z. Bergman. A characterization of self-financing portfolio strategies. *IBER Working Paper, University of California Berkeley*, 113, 1981.

[7] L. Bisesti, A. Castagna and F. Mercurio. Consistent pricing and hedging of an FX options book. *Kyoto Economic Review*, 1(75):65–83, 1997.

[8] P. Bjerksund and G. Stensland. American exchange options and a put–call tranformation: a note. *Journal of Business Finance and Accounting*, 5(20):761–764, 1993.

[9] F. Black and M. Scholes. The pricing of options and corporate liabilities. *Journal of Political Economy*, 81:637–654, 1973.

[10] A. Brace, B. Goldys, F. Klebaner and R. Womersley. Market model of stochastic implied volatility with application to the BGM. *Working Paper, UNSW*, 2001.

[11] D.T. Breeden and R.H. Litzenberger. State-contingent claims implicit in option prices. *Journal of Business*, 51:621–651, 1978.

[12] D. Brigo and F. Mercurio. A mixed-up smile. *Risk Magazine*, 9:123–126, 2000.

[13] D. Brigo and F. Mercurio. Analytical models for volatility smiles and skews. *Banca IMI Internal Report*, 2000.

[14] D. Brigo and F. Mercurio. *Interest Rate Model, Theory and Practice*. Springer, 2nd edition, 2006.

[15] D. Brigo, F. Mercurio and F. Rapisarda. Smile at the uncertainty. *Risk Magazine*, 5:97–101, 2004.

[16] M. Broadie, P. Glasserman and S.G. Kou. A continuity correction for discrete barrier options. *Mathematical Finance*, 7:325–349, 1997.

[17] M. Broadie, P. Glasserman and S.G. Kou. Connecting discrete and continuous path-dependent options. *Finance and Stochastics*, 3:55–82, 1999.

[18] P.P. Carr and R.A. Jarrow. The stop-loss start-gain paradox and option valuation: a new decomposition into intrinsic value and time value. *Review of Financial Studies*, 3(3):469–492, 1990.

[19] P.P. Carr, K. Lewis and D.B. Madan. On the nature of options. *Working Paper available at http://www. math.nyu.edu/research/carrp/papers/pdf/nature5.pdf*, 1999.

[20] P.P. Carr and D.B. Madan. Towards a theory of volatility trading. In *New Estimation Techniques for Pricing Derivatives*. Risk Publication, 1998.

[21] A. Castagna and F. Mercurio. Building implied volatility surfaces from the available market quotes: a unified approach. In *Volatility as an Asset Class*, pages 3–59. Risk Books, 2007.

[22] A. Castagna and F. Mercurio. The vanna–volga method for implied volatilities. *Risk*, 20(1):106–111, 2007.
[23] C.J. Corrado and T.W. Miller. A note on a simple, accurate formula to compute implied standard deviations. *Journal of Banking and Finance*, 20:595–603, 1996.
[24] J.C. Cox, J.E. Ingersoll and S.A. Ross. A theory of the term structure of interest rates. *Econometrica*, 53:385–467, 1985.
[25] T. Daglish, J. Hull and W. Suo. Volatility surfaces: theory, rules of thumb, and empirical evidence. *Quantitative Finance*, 5(7):507–524, 2007.
[26] B. Dupire. Pricing with a smile. *Risk*, 7:18–20, 1994.
[27] M.R. Fengler. Arbitrage-free smoothing of the implied volatility surface. *SFB 649 Discussion Paper, Humboldt University, Berlin*, 19, 2005.
[28] T. Fisher. Variations on the vanna–volga adjustment. *Bloomberg, Quantitative Research and Development, FX Team*, 0, 2007.
[29] M. Forde. Static hedging of barrier options under the SABR model and local volatility model with non-zero interest rates. *Doctoral Thesis, School of Mathematics*, University of Bristol, 2005.
[30] M.B. Garman and S.W. Kohlhagen. Foreign currency option values. *Journal of International Money and Finance*, 2:231–237, 1983.
[31] H. Geman, N. El Karoui and J.C. Rochet. Changes of numeraire, changes of probability measures and pricing of option. *Journal of Applied Probability*, 32:443–458, 1995.
[32] A. Genz. Numerical computation of rectangular bivariate and trivariate normal and t probabilities. *Working Paper available at http://www.sci.wsu.edu/math/faculty/genz/homepage*, 2001.
[33] P.S. Hagan, D. Kumar, A.S. Lesniewski and D.E. Woodward. Managing smile risk. *Wilmott Magazine*, 9:84–108, 2002.
[34] J.M. Harrison and S. Pliska. Martingales and arbitrage in multiperiod securities markets. *Journal of Economic Theory*, 20:381–408, 1979.
[35] J.M. Harrison and S. Pliska. Martingales and stochastic integrals in the theory of continuous trading. *Stochastic Processes and their Applications*, 11:215–260, 1981.
[36] E.G. Haug. Barrier put–call transformations. *Working Paper, Tempus Financial Engineering*, 1999.
[37] S.L. Heston. A closed-form solution for options with stochastic volatility with applications to bond and currency options. *Review of Financial Studies*, 6:327–343, 1993.
[38] P. Horfelt. Extension of the corrected barrier approximation by Broadie, Glasserman and Kou. *Finance and Stochastics*, 7(2):231–243, 2003.
[39] J. Hull. *Options, Futures, and Other Derivatives*. Prentice-Hall, 7th edition, 2008.
[40] F. Jamshidian. An exact bond option pricing formula. *The Journal of Finance*, 44:205–209, 1989.
[41] C. Kahl and M. Gunther. Complete the correlation matrix. *Working Paper*, 2005.
[42] S.G. Kou. On pricing of discrete barrier options. *Working Paper, Department of IEOR*, Columbia University, 2001.
[43] Y.K. Kwok and H.Y. Wong. Currency-translated foreign equity options with path-dependent features and their multi-asset extensions. *International Journal of Theoretical and Applied Finance*, 3(2):257–278, 2000.
[44] O. Ledoit and P. Santa-Clara. Relative pricing of options with stochastic volatility.*University of California-Los Angeles Finance Working Paper 9-98*, 1998.
[45] R.W. Lee. The moment formula for implied volatility at extreme strikes. *Mathematical Finance*, 14(3):469–480, 2004.
[46] A. Malz. Estimating the probability distribution of the future exchange rate from option prices. *Journal of Derivatives*, Winter:18–36, 1997.
[47] S. Manaster and G. Koehler. The calculation of implied variance from the Black–Scholes model: a note. *The Journal of Finance*, 32:227–230, 1982.
[48] F. Mercurio. A multi-stage uncertain volatility model. *Banca IMI Internal Report available at http://www.fabiomercurio.it/UncertainVol.pdf*, 2002.
[49] F. Mercurio. Pricing and static replication of FX quanto options. *Banca IMI Internal Report availablehttp://www.fabiomercurio.it/fwdstartquanto.pdf*, 2003.
[50] F. Mercurio. A simple uncertain volatility model. *Banca IMI Internal Report*, 2004.
[51] R.C. Merton. Theory of rational option pricing. *Bell Journal of Economics and Management Science*, 1(4):141–183, 1973.

[52] S. Mikhailov and U. Noegel. Heston's stochastic volatility model implementation, calibration and some extensions. *Wilmott Magazine*, 1:74–79, 2005.

[53] V.V. Piterbarg. Mixture of models: a simple recipe for a . . . hangover? *Bank of America Internal Report*, 2003.

[54] F. Rapisarda. Pricing barriers on underlyings with time-dependent parameters. *Banca IMI Internal Report*, 2003.

[55] R. Rebonato. *Volatility and Correlation, The Perfect Hedger and the Fox*. John Wiley & Sons, 2nd edition, 2004.

[56] O. Reiss and U. Wystup. Computing option price sensitivities using homogeneity and other tricks. *The Journal of Derivatives*, 2(9):41–53, 2001.

[57] G. Sartorelli. Hedging errors for unknown underlying evolution. *Private Communication*, 2005.

[58] P. Schonbucher. Market model for stochastic implied volatility. *Philosophical Transactions of the Royal Society*, 357(1758):2071–2092, 1999.

[59] S.E. Shreve. *Stochastic Calculus for Finance II*. Springer, 2004.

[60] S.E. Shreve, U. Schmock and U. Wystop. Valuation of exotic options under short selling constraints. *Finance and Stochastics*, 6(2), 2002.

[61] S.E. Shreve, U. Schmock and U. Wystop. Valuation of exotic options under short selling constraints. In *Foreign Exchange Risk*. Risk Publications, 2002.

[62] U. Wystop. The market price of one-touch options in foreign exchange markets. *Derivatives Week*, 12(13) 8–9, 2003.

[63] U. Wystup. *FX Options and Structured Products*. John Wiley & Sons, 2006.

[64] P.G. Zhang. *Exotic Options: A Guide to Second Generation Options*. World Scientific, 1997.

Index

act/360 day count convention, concepts 2–4
act/365 day count convention, concepts 2–4
admissible trading strategies
concepts 24–5, 114, 115–16
definition 24
admissible volatility surfaces, concepts 114, 115–16
American FX options
concepts 11, 152–4
definition 152
LMUV 153–4
pricing 152–4
stochastic volatility models 152, 153–4
volatility smiles 153–4
analytical approximation, concepts 191–2
approximated implied volatilities, vanna–volga approach 102–4, 121–9
arbitrage strategy
barrier options 156–7, 172–4
outright contracts 4–7, 9
volatility surfaces 92–4, 102, 116–20
arbitrage-free prices, concepts 24–5, 38–41, 102, 114–20
Asian options
see also exotic FX...
concepts 11, 215, 269, 277, 281–2
definition 215
pricing 215, 281
asset classes 269
asset-or-nothing valuations 146–7
asymmetric volatility smiles *see* volatility skew
asymptotic behaviour of VV implied volatilities 106–10
at-expiry barrier options
see also double-touch...; one-touch...
concepts 155–6, 162–4, 171, 195–6
definition 155, 156, 162, 195
pricing 195–6
at-hit barrier options
see also double-touch...; one-touch...
concepts 156, 162–4
definition 156, 162
at-the-money (ATM), concepts 15, 16–19, 42–5, 53, 67, 75–90, 92–129, 134–50, 168–9, 175–81, 185–8, 189–91, 206–12, 214–15, 218–68, 276–86
ATM straddles (STDLs)
bid/ask spreads 139–41
concepts 16–19, 53, 75–90, 95–129, 134–50, 175–81, 189–91, 206–12, 214–15, 218–68
critique 116–20
real market situations 120–9, 177–81, 218–68
risk management tools 236–68
volatility smiles 75–90, 116–29, 134–50, 175–81, 189–91, 214–15, 218–68
volatility surfaces 95–129, 189–91, 218–68
attainable claims, concepts 23–5
AUD (Australian dollar) 2, 3, 6
auto-quanto options
concepts 11, 202–4, 205–12, 273–7, 280–3
definition 202
pricing 202–4, 205–12, 273–7, 280–3
vanna–volga approach 203–4

BA *see* bid/ask spreads
Bachelier model 44
bankruptcy 5–6
banks 1–19
barrier options
see also double...; exotic FX...; no-touch...; one-touch...; reverse...
arbitrage strategy 156–7, 172–4
bid/ask spreads 182–3, 188–91, 196, 199, 201–2
Black–Scholes options pricing model 157–62, 167–88, 195–202, 225–31
cash settlement 170–1, 202
concepts 11, 13–14, 15–16, 40, 53–4, 58, 155–94, 195–202, 210–12, 225–34, 249–68, 275–7

barrier options (*Cont.*)
constant barriers 159–62
definition 155–6
delayed settlement dates 170–1, 202
delta hedging 172–88, 190–3, 201–2, 213–15
diffusion equation under single absorbing boundaries 158–62, 164–6
expiry dates 155–6, 213–15, 231–4, 249–68
the Greeks 168–88
implied volatilities 168–9, 171–88, 201–2
knock-in–knock-out parity 156–7, 182–3, 201–2
LMUV 169, 177, 188, 198–9, 201–2, 225–7
market pricing approach 171–88, 199
monitoring frequencies 155–6, 191–4, 195–6, 213–15, 225–34
non-standard delivery dates 170–1
numerical procedures 169, 191–2, 198–9
pricing 156–94, 195–202, 210–12, 225–34, 249–68, 275–7
pricing formula 160–2
probability of hits 167–8
relationships 156–7
risk management tools 231–4, 249–68
slippage costs 181–3, 193–4
SLSG 192–4
survival probability concepts 168, 173–81
triggers 155–94, 195–202
types 155–6, 195–202, 225–7
uses 155–7
vanna–volga approach 171–91
vega-hedge rebalancing 186–91, 251–4, 268
base currencies
see also foreign currencies
concepts 1–19, 32–41, 136–9, 143–54, 270–86
definition 1–2
base currency percentage, FX option premiums 13–19, 32–3, 38–41
base currency units, FX option premiums 13–19, 32–3, 38–41, 134
Basket options
see also exotic FX...
concepts 11
Becker and Wystup model 194
Benaim and Friz results 107–8
bet options
see also barrier... ; double-no-touch... ; double-touch... ; exotic... ; no-touch... ; one-touch...
concepts 15–16, 156, 171–88, 193–4, 205, 210–12, 228–34, 262–8
definition 156
forward start plain/barriers 205, 210–12
risk management tools 231–4, 262–8
biases, market makers 58–9
bid/ask spreads (BA)
barrier options 182–3, 188–91, 196, 199, 201–2
concepts 134, 139–41, 145–7, 150–1, 182–3, 188–91, 196, 199, 201–2, 204
variance swaps 215
binary options *see* digital options
Biseti findings 217
bivariate normal distributions, concepts 197–9
Black–Scholes economy, concepts 21–31, 157–62
Black–Scholes options pricing model (BS) 14–15, 17, 21–55, 58, 60–7, 70, 75–6, 91–4, 96–115, 131–54, 157–62, 167–88, 195–215, 217–27, 234–68, 269–75
see also Greeks
American FX options 152–4
assumptions 21–2, 26, 29, 33–4, 59–61, 75–6
barrier options 157–62, 167–88, 195–202, 225–31
concepts 14–15, 17, 21–55, 58, 60–7, 70, 75–6, 91–4, 96–115, 131–54, 157–62, 167–88, 195–215, 217–27, 234–68, 269–75
correlations 269–75, 281
critique 26, 29, 33, 58, 75–6, 99, 171
definition 29–31
digital options 148–50
formula 29–31, 38–41, 171
outright parameter 29–55
relationships 38–41
risk management tools 229–68
time-homogeneous property 38–9, 205–6, 211–12, 221–7
uses 29, 33–4, 35, 75–6, 91–2, 96–9, 131–54, 157–62, 167–88, 217–27, 234–68, 269–75
volatility smiles 58, 75–6, 91–4, 96–115, 208–12
volatility surfaces 91–4, 96–115, 218–27
book value (bv), concepts 33–4
bootstrap procedures, concepts 5–7, 120–9
Breeden and Litzenberger risk-neutral density results 106–7
Brigo and Mercurio model 27–8, 45–7
Broadie *et al* 191–2
Brownian motion 21–55, 67, 84–90, 106–10, 217–27, 269–75
BS *see* Black–Scholes options pricing model
bucketing 220–7, 230–6
building approaches, volatility surfaces 91–7, 120–9
butterflies 17–19, 53, 75–90, 95–129, 134–50, 175–81, 189–91, 210–12, 214–15, 218–68
buy and sell backs *see* FX swaps
bv *see* book value

CAD 2, 3–4, 6, 14
  EURCAD 14
  USDCAD 3–4, 14
call FX options
  see also FX options
  barrier options 156–94, 195–202
  concepts 10–19, 29–55, 60–90, 91–129, 131–54, 156–94, 195–202
  put–call parity 38–41, 134–9, 156–7
  put–call symmetry 38–41, 156–7, 199–200
  RR 17–19, 75–90, 120–9, 134–50, 175–81, 189–91
Canadian dollar *see* CAD
canonic settlement dates, concepts 11–19, 134–9
capitalization 7
caps 44
Carr and Madan 109, 213
cash settlement
  concepts 133, 150, 170–1, 202, 229
  risk management tools 229
CEV *see* constant elasticity of variance
CHF 2, 3, 6, 14
  EURCHF 14
  GBPCHF 14
  USDCHF 14
choice 141
closed-form formulae 53–5, 163–4, 168–9, 191–2, 207–15, 217–68, 277
collateralized loans
  see also FX swaps
  concepts 10
competition in the FX market 1, 145–6
complete markets 21–55
compound options
  concepts 195, 215
  definition 215
consistency representation criteria, volatility surfaces 94–6, 108–10, 116–20
constant barrier options
  see also barrier...
  concepts 159–60
constant elasticity of variance (CEV)
  concepts 44–5
  definition 44
constant-parameter version of the Heston stochastic volatility model 41–3, 96
continuous financial modelling, concepts 21–55, 87, 213–14
continuously-monitored barrier options, concepts 155–6, 191–4, 213–14
conventions, FX markets 1–4, 6–7, 13–14, 32–3, 75–6, 91–4, 116–21, 131–54, 276–7
correlations 67, 84–90, 198–9, 269–86
  Black–Scholes options pricing model 269–75, 281
  concepts 269–86
  the Greeks 278–86
  linked volatility smiles 283–6
  pricing 269–86
  quanto options 273–7
  several FX spot rates 275–7
  vanna–volga approach 278–86
  volatility smiles 278–86
counterparty risks 5–7, 9–10, 30–1
Cox, Ingersoll and Ross (CIR) 41
Cramer's rule 100–1
currencies
  see also FX...
  conventions 1–4, 131–54
  major currencies 1–19
curvature movements of volatility smiles 75–84, 86–90, 94–9, 106–10, 113–15, 148–9, 175–6, 220–7, 240–68
cutoff times, concepts 11, 141–2
CZK (Czech koruna) 2

Danish krone *see* DKK
day counts
  concepts 1–19
  definition 1–2
  examples 2, 3–4
day periods, expiry/settlement concepts 11–19, 131–3
default probabilities 5–7, 9–10, 30–1
default risks 5–7, 9–10, 30–1
  outright contracts 5–7, 9–10
  recovery rates 10, 30–1
delayed settlement dates 131–3, 150, 170–1, 202
delivery dates *see* settlement dates
delta
  see also FX spot...; gamma; premium-included...
  concepts 15, 16–19, 29–55, 63–5, 70–84, 86–90, 91–129, 134–9, 169, 172–88, 206–12, 218–68
  definition 31–3, 227
  implied volatilities 75–84, 86–90, 91–4, 95–6, 134–9, 172–88
  risk management tools 227–31, 238–68
  scenario hedging 86–90, 218–27, 263–8
  sticky delta rule 91–4, 134, 218–27
  uses 31–3, 86–90, 91–4, 135–9, 172–88, 227–31
  volatility smiles 75–84, 86–90, 91–4, 95–6, 134–9, 172–88
delta hedging
  see also dynamic hedging
  barrier options 172–88, 190–3, 201–2, 213–15
  concepts 15, 16–19, 29–55, 61–90, 97–9, 140–1, 181–4, 190–3, 201–2, 207–12, 213–15, 263–8
  rule 63–5

delta–vega relationship
  concepts 40–1, 69–70
  definition 40
deterministic financial modelling 21–55, 75–6, 93–4, 132–3, 162–3
diffusion processes 45–55, 158–62, 173–88
  see also Fokker–Planck equation
digital options
  see also exotic FX...
  bid/ask spreads 145–7, 150–1
  Black–Scholes options pricing model 148–50
  call digital option pricing formula 146–7, 151
  concepts 11, 142–52, 195–6, 210–12, 231–4, 244–9
  definition 142–3
  delayed cash settlement date 150
  European plain vanilla FX options 142–52
  LMUV 149–50
  over-hedge parameter 145–50
  pricing 142–52, 195–6, 210–12, 231–4, 244–9
  put digital option pricing formula 146–7, 151
  quotation conventions 152
  risk management tools 231–4, 244–9
  specific pricing model settings 148–50
  static replica pricing approach 143–9, 246–9
  volatility smiles 142–52
Dirac delta function 86–90
  see also Heaviside function
Dirichlet boundary conditions 158
discount factors
  see also pure discount bonds
  concepts 5–7, 23–55, 64–7, 70, 131–3, 172–88, 199–200, 205–12, 214–15, 218–68, 281–2
  LMUV 218–68
discretely-monitored barrier options, concepts 155–6, 191–4
DKK 2, 3
DNT *see* double-no-touch options
domestic currencies
  see also numeraire currencies
  concepts 1–19, 27–8, 38–41
  definition 1–2
double knock-in/out barrier options
  see also barrier... ; exotic FX... ; knock...
  concepts 11, 155–6, 166–7, 193–4, 258–62
  definition 155–6, 166
  pricing 166–7, 193–4, 258–62
double-barrier options
  concepts 11, 15–16, 155–6, 164–6, 175, 199–200, 211–12, 258–62
  definition 164–6
  pricing 164–6, 175, 211–12, 258–62
  risk management tools 258–62
double-no-touch options
  see also barrier... ; exotic FX...
  concepts 11, 15–16, 156, 167–8, 171, 175, 178–9, 183, 232–4, 258–68
  definition 156, 167
  pricing 167, 168, 171, 175, 178–9, 183, 232–4, 258–68
  risk management tools 232–4, 258–68
double-touch options
  see also barrier... ; exotic FX...
  concepts 11, 15–16, 156, 167, 171, 232–4
  definition 156, 167
  pricing 167, 171, 232–4
down barrier options
  concepts 155–94, 199–202, 226–7, 255–8
  definition 155–6
drift 23–55, 65–7, 70, 85–90, 93–129, 275–86
DTE *see* double-touch options
Dupire's model 93–4
dynamic hedging
  see also delta hedging; hedging
  concepts 53–5, 57–90, 97–102, 108–10, 140–1, 201–2
  constant implied volatilities 61–3, 65–6, 74–5, 86–90, 99–102, 108–10, 171–88
  marking-to-market 57–9, 63–7
  model requirements 53–5, 57–9
  profits and losses 55, 57–90
  revaluation rule 57–61, 99
  updating implied volatilities 63–7, 85–90, 99, 105–10
  vanna–volga approach 70–5, 84–90, 94–129

EBS interbank platform 1
ECB *see* European Central Bank
economic news 113–15, 122–9
efficient/convenient representation criteria, volatility surfaces 94–7
Einstein summation convention 59
end-of-month rule, expiry/settlement concepts 12
equivalent martingale measure (EMM), concepts 24–5, 26–8, 60, 65–7
EUR 1–19, 30, 32–3, 103–4, 114, 120–6, 132–3, 143, 149, 154, 175–9, 188, 193–4, 209–12, 214–15, 218–68, 270–86
  USDEUR 270–1
EURCAD 14
EURCHF 14
EURGBP 14
Euribor 30–1
EURJPY 4–19, 272–86
European Central Bank (ECB) 141–2, 155, 191–2
European plain vanilla FX options
  see also FX options
  concepts 10–19, 22–4, 29–55, 142–52, 275–86
  definition 10–11
  digital options 142–52
  risk management tools 236–44

EURUSD 1–19, 32–3, 103–4, 114, 120–6, 132–3, 143, 149, 154, 175–9, 188, 193–4, 209–12, 214–15, 218–68, 270–86
EURZAR 14
even FX swaps *see* par FX swaps
exercise, FX options 11–19, 141–2, 152–4
exotic FX options
  see also Asian . . . ; barrier . . . ; bet . . . ; first-generation . . . ; FX options; second-generation . . . ; vega hedging
  concepts 10–11, 13–14, 15–16, 29, 50–2, 53–4, 155–94, 195–215, 275–7
  definition 10–11
  LMLV/LMUV uses 50–2, 149–50, 169, 177, 188, 198–9, 201–2
  pricing 29, 50–2, 53–4, 156–94, 195–202, 275–7
  risk management tools 231–4, 249–68
  types 10–11, 15–16, 155–6, 195–215
expected local times of the FX spot rate's process 192–3
expiry dates
  barrier options 155–6, 213–15, 231–4, 249–68
  FX options 11–19, 91–129, 131–3, 141–2, 155–6, 213–15, 217–68
extended LMUV model 51–3, 217–68
  see also lognormal mixture uncertain volatility model
external barriers
  see also exotic FX options
  concepts 11

Feynman–Kac formula
  concepts 23–5, 27–8
  definition 23
figure
  see also pips
  concepts 2–4
  definition 2
filtered probability space 21–55
financial risk hedging
  see also hedging rule
  concepts 57–9
finite-difference methods 169, 191–2
first-generation FX exotic options, concepts 11
first-in-then-out barrier options
  concepts 155–6, 195, 199–202
  definition 155, 199
  pricing 199–202
first–then barrier options
  concepts 156, 199–202
  definition 199
  pricing 199–202
five-digit numbers, FX rates 2–4
floors 44
Fokker–Planck equation
  see also diffusion . . .
  concepts 45–6
foreign currencies
  see also base currencies; FX . . .
  concepts 1–19, 38–41
  definition 1–2
foreign–domestic symmetry
  concepts 38–41, 156–7
  definition 38
forward contracts *see* outright contracts
forward points (Fpts)
  concepts 6–7, 8–10
  definition 6–7
forward start plain/barriers
  see also exotic FX options
  bet options 205, 210–12
  compound options 215
  concepts 11, 195, 204–12, 215, 221–7
  definition 204–5
  numeraire currencies 211–12
  pricing 204–12, 221–7
  volatility smiles 207–12, 221–7
Fpts *see* forward points
free boundary conditions 158–62
Fsw *see* FX swaps
FX markets
  competition in the FX market 1, 145–6
  concepts 1–19
  conventions 1–4, 6–7, 13–14, 32–3, 75–6, 91–4, 116–21, 131–54, 276–7
  definition 1
  trading centres 1
FX options
  see also American . . . ; call . . . ; European . . . ; exotic . . . ; options pricing; put . . .
  bid/ask spreads 134, 139–41, 145–7, 150–1, 182–3, 188–91, 196, 199, 201–2, 204
  concepts 10–19, 21–55, 57–90, 131–54, 269–86
  correlations 67, 84–90, 198–9, 269–86
  definition 10–11
  examples 12–13, 15–16, 17–19
  exercise 11–19, 141–2, 152–4
  expiry dates 11–19, 91–129, 131–3, 141–2, 155–6, 213–15, 217–68
  main traded structures 16–19, 218–27
  market standard quotation practices 14–19, 29, 32–3, 131–54, 199
  portfolios 16–17, 21–55, 59–90
  premiums 13–19, 32–3, 38–41, 101–2, 120–9, 134–54, 174–88
  settlement dates 11–19, 131–3, 141–2, 170–1
  types 10–11

FX rates
  see also base currencies; FX options; numeraire currencies; pairs; tags
  concepts 1–19, 21, 23–55, 57–90, 131–54, 155–94, 205–12, 227–68, 275–86
  definition 1–2, 205
  examples 1–4
  five-digit numbers 2–4
  stochastic volatility 21, 26–8
FX spot contracts
  see also delta; gamma
  bid/ask spreads 139–41
  concepts 1–19, 29–55, 57–90, 94–129, 131–54, 155–94, 195–202, 218–68, 269–86
  definition 2–3
  FX swaps definition 7–8
FX swaps
  see also collateralized loans
  concepts 2, 7–10, 30–1
  definition 7–9
  examples 7–8, 9–10
  FX spot contracts 7–10
  hedgers 9
  outright contracts 7–10
  pricing 7–10, 30–1
  risks 8–9
  trading platforms 7–8
  users 9

gamma
  see also delta
  concepts 33–4, 42, 51, 62–3, 64–7, 70, 169, 174–5, 184–6, 229, 244–68
  definition 33–4
  risk management tools 229, 244–68
  trader's gamma 33, 229
  uses 33–4
Gatarek, M. 54
Gauss–Lobatto scheme 214–15
GBP 2, 3, 6, 14
  EURGBP 14
GBPCHF 14
GBPJPY 14
GBPUSD 14
gearing, one-touch (rebate) options 184–6
Geman *et al* 27–8
general framework, concepts 57, 59–90
geometric Brownian motion, concepts 44–5, 48–9, 106–10, 217–27
Girsanov's theorem
  see also risk-neutrality
  concepts 25, 26–8, 49
the Greeks
  see also delta; rho; theta; vanna; vega; volga
  barrier options 168–88
  bucketing 220–7, 230–6
  concepts 29, 31–55, 64–7, 68–70, 168–81, 201–2, 207–12, 214–15, 227–68, 278–86
  correlations 278–86
  definitions 31–5, 67
  profits and losses 65, 70, 213–15, 227–31
  risk management tools 227–68
Green's function 158–64

Haug 199
Heaviside function
  see also Dirac delta function
  concepts 143–4
hedging
  see also delta . . . ; dynamic . . . ; gamma; vega . . .
  barrier options 155, 156–7
  concepts 9, 21–55, 57–90, 91–129, 139–41, 143–9, 155, 162–94, 195–215, 217–68
  constant implied volatilities 61–3, 65–6, 74–5, 86–90, 99–102, 108–10, 171–88
  LMUV 45, 48–55, 149–50, 153–4
  marking-to-market 57–9, 63–7
  parameter hedging 224–7
  profits and losses 55, 57–90, 227–31
  replicating strategies 21–55, 57–90, 91–129, 139–41, 143–9, 162–94, 195–215, 246–9, 258–68, 270–86
  scenario hedging 84–90, 218–27, 263–8
  tools 57–90, 217–68
  updating implied volatilities 63–7, 85–90, 99, 105–10
  vanna–volga approach 70–5, 84–90, 94–129, 149–50, 171–91
  volatility smiles 79–84
hedging errors
  concepts 61–3, 64–7, 69–70, 73–5, 84–90, 104–10
  longer expiries 104–5
hedging rule
  concepts 57–90
  definition 57, 65
Heston stochastic volatility model
  concepts 41–4, 54–5, 96, 106, 112–13, 210–12, 217–27
  constant-parameter version 41–3, 96
  definition 41–2
  time-dependent parameters 42–3, 96, 217–18
  volatility surfaces 96, 106, 112–13, 217–27
HKD 2, 3, 6
holidays 113–15, 122–9
Hong Kong dollar *see* HKD

implicit one-touch risk, concepts 184–6, 231–4, 249–54, 260–8

implied volatilities
  see also vanna; vega; volatility smiles; volatility surfaces; volga
  approximated implied volatilities 102–4, 121–9
  asymptotic behaviour of VV implied volatilities 106–10
  barrier options 168–9, 171–88, 201–2
  BS critique 33–4
  concepts 14–19, 29–55, 57–90, 91–129, 131–54, 168–9, 171–88, 205–12, 217–68, 271–86
  correlations 271–86
  delta 75–84, 86–90, 91–4, 95–6, 134–9, 172–88
  forward start plain/barriers 205–12, 221–7
  hedging with constant implied volatilities 61–3, 65–6, 74–5, 86–90, 99–102, 108–10, 171–88
  hedging with updating implied volatilities 63–7, 85–90, 99, 105–10
  market model 66–7, 85–90, 172–80, 199, 217–68
  retrieval methods 35–7, 60–1, 75–6, 91, 111, 120–9, 134–9, 189–91
  sticky absolute rule 91–4
  sticky delta rule 91–4, 134, 218–27
  sticky strike rule 91–4
  term structures 112–15, 122–9, 198–9
  vanna–volga approach 71–5, 84–90, 94–129, 149–50, 154, 171–91, 203–4, 207–12, 218–68, 278–86
in-the-money FX options 11, 115, 155–94, 229
incomplete markets, concepts 26–8
indices 57
instantaneous volatilities 26–55, 62–7, 84–90, 92–129, 230–1
interbank platforms, concepts 1, 11–19, 131, 134–9
interest rate derivatives
  concepts 27–8, 44–5, 120–9
  SABR model 44–5
  volatility smiles 44–5
interest rate risks, concepts 8–10
interest rate swaps 120–9
interest rate symmetry, definition 39
interest rates 8–10, 21–55, 120–9, 131–54, 162–4, 217–68
  see also Euribor; Libor; rho
  bid/ask spreads 139–41
  stochastic foreign interest rates 52–3
Internet platforms for clients 1
intuitiveness representation criteria, volatility surfaces 94–6
ISDA 11
Ito's lemma
  see also Taylor expansion
  concepts 22–5, 26–8, 60–1, 65, 67, 85–90, 98–9, 171–2, 173–4, 271, 273

Jamshidian 27
Japanese yen *see* JPY
JPY 2, 3–19, 36, 116–20, 126–9, 138–9, 231–2, 241, 270–86
  EURJPY 4–19, 272–86
  GBPJPY 14
  USDJPY 4–19, 36, 116–20, 126–9, 138–9, 231–2, 241, 270–86
jumps 43, 123–9, 152–4

Kahl and Gunther model 278
knock-in–knock-out (in–out) barrier options, concepts 156, 199, 201–2
knock-in–knock-out parity 156–7, 182–3, 201–2
knock-in/out barrier options
  see also barrier . . . ; double . . . ; exotic FX . . .
  concepts 11, 155–94, 195–6, 228–34, 249–54, 255–62
  definition 155–6
Kou model 191–2
kurtosis 113–15

labels
  see also tags
  concepts 1–19
  definition 1–2
Libor 30
linked volatility smiles 283–6
LMLV *see* lognormal mixture local volatility model
LMUV *see* lognormal mixture uncertain volatility model
loans, outright contracts 4–7, 9–10, 30–1
local exposures to volatility smiles 79–84, 97–110
local volatilities, concepts 45–55, 93–4, 229–31
lognormal mixture local volatility model (LMLV)
  concepts 45–55, 93–4
  critique 50–1
  definition 45–7
  LMUV contrasts 50–3
lognormal mixture uncertain volatility model (LMUV)
  American FX options 153–4
  barrier options 169, 177, 188, 198–9, 201–2, 225–7
  benefits 50–5, 217–27
  concepts 45, 48–55, 149–50, 153–4, 169, 177, 188, 198–9, 201–2, 207–12, 217–68
  critique 50–5, 217–27

lognormal mixture uncertain (*Cont.*)
definition 48–9
digital options 149–50
exotic FX options 50–2, 149–50, 169, 177, 188, 198–9
extensions 51–3, 217–68
implementation methods 217–27
LMLV contrasts 50–3
market data 217–68
rho 234–6
risk management tools 228–68
London trading centre 1
long positions 4–7, 17–19
lookback options, definition 215

Malz's formula, volatility surfaces 96–7
margin agreements 31
marginal densities, mixture approach to modelling 45–55, 217–68
market makers
biases 58–9
concepts 1–19, 53, 57–9, 91–4, 134–54, 157, 171–88, 217–68
risk management 53–5, 195–215, 217–68
tools 134–9, 171–88, 217–68
market model for implied volatilities 66–7, 85–90, 172–88, 199, 217–68
market pricing approach, barrier options 171–88
market standard quotation practices, FX options 14–19, 29, 32–3, 131–3, 152
market-to-model tools, concepts 58–9
marking-to-market 57–9, 63–7
martingales 21–55, 60, 65–7, 70, 172–88
see also equivalent...
concepts 24–5, 26–8, 49–50, 60, 65–7
mean variance 112–15, 207–12
mean-reversion, concepts 41–4, 112–14
Mercurio, F. 27–8, 45–9, 177
Merton, R. 29
method of images
concepts 158–62
definition 158
mixture approach to modelling
see also lognormal mixture...
concepts 45–55, 217–27
model risks
see also hedging rule; options pricing...
concepts 54–5, 57
money markets, concepts 1–19, 120–9
monitoring frequencies, barrier options 155–6, 191–4, 195–6, 213–15, 225–34
monotonic behaviour 37, 140–1
Monte Carlo simulations, concepts 47, 169, 191–2, 207, 215
month/year periods, expiry/settlement concepts 12–19

New York trading centre 1
New Zealand dollar *see* NZD
Newton–Raphson method, concepts 35–7, 135–9
nil currency exposures 8
no-arbitrage conditions
concepts 24–5, 38–41, 102, 114–20, 218–27, 272–5
vanna–volga approach 102, 218–27
no-touch options
see also barrier...; exotic FX...
concepts 11, 15–16, 156, 163–4, 171, 231–4, 258–62
definition 156, 163–4
pricing 163–4, 171, 231–4, 258–62
NOK 2, 6
non-par FX swaps, concepts 7–10
non-standard delivery dates, barrier options 170–1
normal distributions 79–84, 197–8
Norwegian kroner *see* NOK
NT *see* no-touch options
numeraire currencies
see also domestic currencies
concepts 1–19, 27–8, 32–41, 120–9, 130–1, 133, 140–1, 211–12, 231–4, 270–86
definition 1–2
forward start plain/barriers 211–12
options pricing theory 27–8, 211–12, 231–4, 270–86
numeraire currency percentage, FX option premiums 13–19, 32–3, 38–41
numeraire currency units, FX option premiums 13–19, 32–3, 38–41, 121–9, 134, 140–1
numerical procedures 47, 53–5, 169, 191–2, 198–9, 207–8, 215
see also finite-difference methods; Monte Carlo simulations
barrier options 169, 198–9
NY Cut denominations, FX options exercise 11, 141–2
NZD 2, 3, 6

ODEs *see* ordinary differential equations
OIS swap rates 31
one-touch (rebate) options
see also barrier...; exotic FX...
concepts 11, 15–16, 156, 162–4, 168, 171, 184–6, 231–4, 249–54, 262–8
definition 156, 162–4
gearing 184–6
implicit positions 184–6, 231–4, 260–8
pricing 162–4, 168, 171, 184–6, 231–4, 249–54, 262–8
risk management tools 231–4, 249–54, 262–8
options *see* FX options

options pricing theory
  see also FX options . . . ; Greeks; pricing
  concepts 2, 4–7, 10–19, 21–55, 57–90, 91–129, 131–55, 211–12, 231–4, 270–86
  model requirements 53–5, 57–9, 163–4, 168–9, 191–2, 207–15
ordinary differential equations (ODEs) 60–1
OTC markets 1, 14–15, 31, 91–4, 142
  definition 1
  margin agreements 31
OTE *see* one-touch (rebate) options
out-of-the-money FX options (OTM) 11, 15, 63, 86–90, 94–5, 106, 113–15, 127–9, 135–9, 140–1, 155–94
outright contracts
  arbitrage strategy 4–7, 9
  Black–Scholes options pricing model parameters 29–55
  concepts 2–3, 4–10, 16–19, 25, 29–55, 92–4, 131–3
  default risks 5–7, 9–10
  definition 4–5, 8–9, 25
  examples 7, 9–10, 25
  FX swaps definition 7–8
  hedgers 9
  pricing 4–7, 25, 29–31, 92–4, 131–3
  quotation conventions 6–7
  risks 5–7, 8–9
  speculators 9
  users 9
over-hedge parameter, digital options 145–50

pairs
  see also FX rates; tags
  concepts 1–19, 21–55, 142, 269–86
  correlations 269–86
  definition 1–2
par FX swaps, concepts 7–10
parameter hedging, concepts 224–7
parsimonious representation criteria, volatility surfaces 94–6
partial differential equations (PDEs)
  see also Black–Scholes . . .
  concepts 23–55, 61, 65–7, 70, 157–62, 174–5
path-dependency 11, 13–14, 15–16, 40–1, 53–4, 58, 142, 155–94, 271–2
  see also barrier options
perfect markets 21–55, 59–61
pi *see* premium-included delta
piecewise-constant parameters 42–3
pin risk 147–8, 231–4, 244–62
pips
  see also figure
  concepts 2–4, 13–19, 121–9, 134, 140–1, 154, 193–4
  definition 2
plain vanilla FX options *see* European . . . ; FX options
PLN (Polish zloty) 2
portfolios
  FX options 16–17, 21–55, 59–90
  replicating strategies 21–55, 57–90, 91–129, 139–41, 143–9, 162–94, 195–215, 246–9, 258–68, 270–86
  valuations 59–61
premium-included delta (pi)
  concepts 32, 35–7, 41, 134–9, 241
  definition 32, 136
premiums for FX options
  concepts 13–19, 32–3, 38–41, 101–2, 120–9, 134–54, 174–88
  conventions 13–14, 32–3, 120–1
  implied volatilities 14–19
present values 8–10, 30–55
pricing
  see also Greeks
  American FX options 152–4
  Asian options 215, 281
  at-expiry barrier options 195–6
  auto-quanto options 202–4, 205–12, 273–7, 280–3
  barrier options 156–94, 195–202, 210–12, 225–34, 249–68, 275–7
  Black–Scholes options pricing model 14–15, 17, 21–55, 58, 60–7, 70, 75–6, 91–2, 96–115, 131–54, 157–62, 167–88, 195–215, 217–27, 234–6, 269–75
  concepts 2, 4–7, 10–19, 21–55, 57–90, 91–129, 131–55
  correlations 269–86
  digital options 142–52, 195–6, 210–12, 231–4, 244–9
  double knock-in/out barrier options 166–7, 193–4, 258–62
  double-barrier options 164–6, 175, 211–12, 258–62
  double-no-touch options 167, 168, 171, 175, 178–9, 183, 232–4, 258–68
  double-touch options 167, 171, 232–4
  exotic FX options 29, 50–2, 53–4, 156–94, 195–202
  finite-difference methods 169, 191–2
  first-in-then-out barrier options 199–202
  forward start plain/barriers 204–12, 221–7
  FX swaps 7–10, 30–1
  Heston stochastic volatility model 41–4, 54–5, 96, 106, 112–13, 210–12, 217–27, 278
  knock-in–knock-out (in–out) barrier options 156, 199, 201–2
  LMLV 45–55

pricing (*Cont.*)
LMUV 45, 48–55, 149–50, 153–4, 169, 177, 188, 198–9, 201–2, 207–12, 217–68
lookback options 215
marking-to-market 57–9, 63–7
mixture approach 45–55, 217–27
Monte Carlo simulations 47, 169, 191–2, 207, 215
no-touch options 163–4, 171, 231–4, 258–62
numeraire currencies 27–8, 211–12, 231–4, 270–86
one-touch (rebate) options 162–4, 168, 171, 184–6, 231–4, 249–54, 262–8
outright contracts 4–7, 25, 29–31, 92–4, 131–3
quanto options 202–4, 205–12, 273–7, 280–3
SABR model 44–5, 90, 96–7, 106
stochastic volatility 21, 26–8, 41–4, 54–5, 68–70, 90, 96–9, 152, 153–4, 171–88, 198–9, 210–12
window barrier options 197–9
profits and losses
the Greeks 65, 70, 213–15, 227–31
trading strategies 55, 57–90, 269–86
pure discount bonds 5–7, 25, 131–3
see also discount factors
put FX options
see also FX options
barrier options 156–94, 195–202
concepts 10–19, 29–55, 75–90, 91–129, 131–54, 156–94, 195–202, 281–6
RR 17–19, 75–90, 120–9, 134–50, 175–81, 189–91
put–call parity
concepts 38–41, 134–9, 156–7
definition 38
put–call symmetry
concepts 38–41, 156–7, 199–200
definition 38

quanto options
see also exotic FX...
concepts 11, 202–4, 205–12, 273–7, 280–3
correlations 273–7, 280–3
definition 202
pricing 202–4, 205–12, 273–7, 280–3
quotation conventions 6–7, 14–19, 29, 32–3, 75–6, 91–4, 116–21, 131–54, 276–7

Radon–Nikodym derivative, concepts 24–5, 27–8
Rapisarda, F. 162–4
realized instantaneous variance 62–7, 93–4, 112–14, 212–15
rebate options *see* one-touch (rebate) options
Rebonato, R. 210
recovery rates, default risks 10, 30–1
redundant claims, concepts 22–4
rehedging concepts 62–90
replicating strategies 21–55, 57–90, 91–129, 139–41, 143–9, 162–94, 195–215, 246–9, 258–68, 270–86
residual open risks 90
Reuters Dealing 1, 2–3, 7, 15–16, 17
revaluation rule
concepts 57–61, 99
definition 57–8
reverse barrier options
see also barrier...
concepts 155–6, 182–6, 231–4, 249–54, 258–62, 273–5
definition 155
implicit one-touch risk 184–6, 231–4, 249–54, 260–2
risk management tools 231–4, 249–54, 258–62
rho
see also interest rates
concepts 34–5, 42, 234–6
definition 34
LMUV 234–6
risk management tools 234–6
Riemann zeta function 192
risk management 53–5, 195–215, 217–68
see also hedging
barrier options 231–4, 249–68
bet options 231–4, 262–8
Black–Scholes options pricing model 229–68
cash settlement 229
concepts 217–68
digital options 231–4, 244–9
exotic FX options 231–4, 249–68
FX spot rate-related Greeks 227–9, 238–68
the Greeks 227–68
interest rate-related Greeks 234–6
LMUV 228–68
plain vanilla FX options 236–44
RR 238–68
STDLs 236–68
tools 217, 227–68
volatility-related Greeks 229–31, 236–68
VWBs 237–68
risk reversal strategy (RR)
concepts 17–19, 53, 75–90, 95–129, 134–50, 177–81, 189–91, 210–12, 214–15, 218–68
critique 116–20
definition 17
delta levels 136–9, 218–27
real market situations 120–9, 177–81, 218–68
risk management tools 238–68
volatility smiles 75–90, 113–15, 116–29, 134–50, 175–81, 189–91, 210–12, 214–15, 218–68
volatility surfaces 95–129, 218–68
risk-free rates 21–55, 217–27

risk-neutrality
  see also Girsanov's theorem
  concepts 23–55, 60, 65–7, 84–90, 106–10, 160–2, 168, 170–1, 172–88, 213–15, 276–86
  definition 23–4, 27
  vanna–volga approach 106–10
risks
  FX swaps 8–9
  outright contracts 5–7, 8–9
RR *see* risk reversal strategy

SABR model
  concepts 44–5, 90, 96–7, 106
  definition 44–5
  properties 44
  vanna–volga approach 97, 106
  volatility surfaces 96–7, 106
Sartorelli, Giulio 57
sawtooth functions 114–15, 124–5
scenario hedging
  see also volatility smiles
  analysis summary 89–90
  concepts 84–90, 218–27, 263–8
  constant delta options 86–90
  vanna–volga approach 84–90, 218–27
SDEs *see* stochastic differential equations
second-generation FX exotic options, concepts 11
SEK 2, 3, 6
self-financing strategies
  concepts 21–5, 26–8, 51, 57–61, 104–10, 144–6
  definition 21–2, 59–60
self-quanto options *see* auto-quanto options
sensitivities *see* Greeks
settlement dates
  cash settlement 133, 150, 170–1, 202, 229
  concepts 1–19, 131–3, 141–2, 170–1
  definition 1–2
  delayed settlement dates 131–3, 150, 170–1, 202
  examples 1–4
  FX options 11–19, 131–3, 141–2, 170–1
short positions 4–7, 17–19, 62–3, 66, 145–6, 228–31
Sidney trading centre 1
simple compounding, concepts 2, 7
Singapore trading centre 1
slippage costs, concepts 181–3, 193–4
slope movements of volatility smiles 75–84, 86–90, 94–9, 106–10, 113–15, 148–9, 175–6, 220–7, 240–68
SLSG *see* stop-loss-start-again
South African rand *see* ZAR
speculators
  barrier options 155
  outright contracts 9
standard settlement dates, concepts 11–19, 131–3, 141–2, 170–1
static replica pricing approach 143–9, 195–215, 246–9, 258–62, 273–5
STDLs *see* ATM straddles; straddles
steepness of volatility smiles 75–84
sticky absolute rule
  see also volatility surfaces
  arbitrage opportunities 92–4
  concepts 91–4
  definition 92
sticky delta rule
  see also delta; volatility surfaces
  arbitrage opportunities 92–4, 218
  concepts 91–4, 134, 218–27
  definition 91–2
sticky strike rule
  see also strike prices; volatility surfaces
  concepts 91–4
  definition 91
stochastic differential equations (SDEs) 21–55, 85–90, 202–3, 207–12, 270–1
stochastic foreign interest rates, concepts 52–3
stochastic volatility economy, concepts 26–8, 68–70, 97–9, 171–88
stochastic volatility models
  see also lognormal mixture uncertain volatility model
  American FX options 152, 153–4
  concepts 21, 26–8, 41–4, 68–70, 90, 96–9, 106, 152, 153–4, 198–9, 210–12, 217–68, 278
  Heston stochastic volatility model 41–4, 54–5, 96, 106, 112–13, 210–12, 217–27
  SABR model 44–5, 90, 96–7, 106
  volatility surfaces 96–9, 106, 112–13, 217–27, 278
stop-loss orders, barrier options 181–3, 192–3
stop-loss-start-again (SLSG) 192–4
straddles (STDLs)
  see also ATM straddles; vega-weighted butterflies
  concepts 16–19, 53, 75–90, 95–129, 134–50, 175–81, 189–91, 206–12, 214–15, 218–68
  implied volatilities 16–19, 53, 75–90, 95–129, 134–50, 175–81, 189–91, 206–12, 214–15, 218–68
  real market situations 120–9, 177–81, 218–68
strangles
  see also vega-weighted butterflies
  concepts 17–19, 83–4

strike prices 14–19, 29–55, 75–90, 91–129, 131–54, 195–215, 278–86
see also volatility smiles; volatility surfaces
retrieval methods 35–7, 80–4, 120–9, 134–9, 189–91
sticky strike rule 91–4
survival probability, concepts 168, 173–81
swap variance rates, concepts 213–15
swaptions 44
Swedish krona see SEK
Swiss franc see CHF

'T +' convention
see also settlement dates
concepts 1–4, 131–3
definition 1–2
tags
see also FX rates; labels
concepts 1–19
definition 1–2
Taylor expansion 81–4, 102–4
see also Ito's lemma
term structures of implied volatilities, volatility surfaces 112–15, 122–9, 198–9
terminal values
barrier options 155–94
self-financing strategies 21–5, 26–8, 32–3, 51, 57–61, 104–10, 131–3, 144–6
theta, concepts 115
three-months expiry (3M) 7–8, 15–16
time to maturity 39–41, 91–129, 183–4
time-dependent parameters 21, 42–5, 93–4, 96, 152–3, 171–2, 185–91, 217–18, 230–1, 271–2
time-homogeneous property, Black–Scholes options pricing model 38–9, 205–6, 211–12, 221–7
Tokyo Cut denominations, FX options exercise 11, 141–2
Tokyo trading centre 1
tools
hedging 57–90, 217–68
market makers 134–9, 217–68
risk management 217, 227–68
total variance interpolation method, concepts 113–15
trader's gamma
see also gamma
concepts 33, 229
definition 33
trading books 29, 33, 57–9, 217–68
trading centres, major trading centres 1
trading strategies 21–55, 57–90, 269–86
transaction costs 59–61
triggers, barrier options 155–94, 195–202
trinomial trees 152–4, 191

UK pound see GBP
uncertain volatility
see also lognormal mixture uncertain volatility model
concepts 45, 48–55, 149–50, 153–4, 169, 177, 188, 198–9, 201–2, 207–12, 217–68
underlying 14–15, 17, 21–55, 131–54, 155–94, 195–215
uneven/split/change FX swaps see non-par FX swaps
up barrier options
concepts 155–94, 199–202, 226–7
definition 155–6
USD 1–19, 30, 32–3, 36, 103–4, 114, 116–29, 132–3, 138–9, 143, 149, 154, 175–9, 183–6, 188, 193–4, 209–12, 214–15, 218–68, 270–86
EURUSD 1–19, 32–3, 103–4, 114, 120–6, 132–3, 143, 149, 154, 175–9, 188, 193–4, 209–12, 214–15, 218–68, 270–86
GBPUSD 14
USDCAD 3–4, 14
USDCHF 14
USDEUR 270–1
USDJPY 4–19, 36, 116–20, 126–9, 138–9, 231–2, 241, 270–86
USDZAR 14

vanna
concepts 34–5, 41, 42, 64–7, 70–5, 84–90, 94–129, 149–50, 154, 171–91, 203–4, 207–12, 215, 218–68, 278–86
definition 34
risk management tools 229–31, 236–68
vanna–volga approach
alternative viewpoints 110–11
approximated implied volatilities 102–4, 121–9
asymptotic behaviour of VV implied volatilities 106–10
auto-quanto options 203–4
barrier options 171–91
benefits 97
concepts 70–5, 84–90, 94–129, 149–50, 154, 171–91, 203–4, 207–12, 215, 218–68, 278–86
consistency results 108–10
correlations 278–86
cost of exposures 110–11
definition 70–1, 97–102
general setting 97–9
interesting results 104–10
linked volatility smiles 283–6
no-arbitrage conditions 102, 218–27
option prices 99–102, 109–10, 121–9

risk-neutrality 106–10
SABR model 97, 106
scenario hedging 84–90, 218–27
variance swaps 214–15
volatility smiles 84–90, 97–110, 149–50, 154, 171–91, 203–4, 207–12, 215, 218–68, 278–86
volatility surfaces 94–129, 218–68
weights 99–102, 109–11, 121–9, 180–1
variance interpolation method, concepts 113–15
variance swaps
bid/ask spreads 215
concepts 212–15
definition 212–13
vanna–volga approach 214–15
volatility smiles 213–15
vega
see also implied volatilities; volga
barrier options 169, 186–91
concepts 15–19, 29, 34, 42, 53, 64–7, 68–90, 95–129, 134–50, 169, 174–81, 185–91, 207–12, 214–15, 218–68, 278–86
correlations 278–86
definition 34
linked volatility smiles 283–6
risk management tools 229–31, 236–68
vega hedging
see also exotic FX options
barrier options 186–91
concepts 15–19, 29, 34–5, 68–90, 186–91, 220–7, 249–68
definition 68–9
rebalancing 186–8, 246–9, 251–4, 268
vega–gamma relationship
concepts 39–41, 69–70, 71–5, 174–5
definition 39–40, 69
vega–vanna–volga matching portfolios 246–68
vega-weighted butterflies (VWBs)
see also straddles; strangles
bid/ask spreads 139–41
concepts 17–19, 53, 75–90, 95–129, 134–50, 175–81, 189–91, 210–12, 214–15, 218–68
critique 116–20
delta levels 136–9, 218–27
risk management tools 237–68
volatility smiles 75–90, 113–15, 116–20, 124–9, 134–50, 175–81, 189–91, 210–12, 214–15, 218–68
volatility surfaces 95–129, 189–91, 218–68
volatilities
see also implied . . . ; vanna; vega; volga
concepts 14–19, 26–55, 57–90
volatility matrix *see* volatility surfaces
volatility risk, concepts 27–8, 57–90, 220–68
volatility skew, concepts 51–3, 113–15, 217–18
volatility smiles
see also implied volatilities; strike prices
American FX options pricing 153–4
asymptotic behaviour of VV implied volatilities 106–10
ATM STDLs 75–90, 116–29, 134–50, 175–81, 189–91, 214–15, 218–68
Black–Scholes options pricing model 58, 75–6, 91–4, 96–115, 208–12
concepts 42–5, 50–5, 58–90, 91–129, 132–3, 142–52, 175–91, 201–4, 207–12, 217–68, 278–86
correlations 278–86
curvature movements 75–84, 86–90, 94–9, 106–10, 113–15, 148–9, 175–6, 220–7, 240–68
definition 75–6, 91–2
delta 75–84, 86–90, 91–4, 95–6, 134–9, 172–88
digital options 142–52
forward start plain/barriers 207–12, 221–7
hedging strategies 79–84
interest rate derivatives 44–5
interpolation amongst available expiries 94, 96–101, 112–29, 132–3
linked volatility smiles 283–6
LMUV 218–27
local exposures 79–84, 97–110
market inconsistency issues 116–20
movements 75–84, 86–90, 94–9, 106–10, 113–15, 148–9, 175–6, 220–7, 240–68
phenomenology 75–9
risk 86–90
RR 75–90, 113–15, 116–29, 134–50, 175–81, 189–91, 210–12, 214–15, 218–68
scenario hedging 84–90, 218–27
slope movements 75–84, 86–90, 94–9, 106–10, 113–15, 148–9, 175–6, 220–7, 240–68
trading specific structures 75–84, 175–88
vanna–volga approach 84–90, 97–110, 149–50, 154, 171–91, 203–4, 207–12, 215, 218–68, 278–86
variance swaps 213–15
VWBs 75–90, 113–15, 116–20, 124–9, 134–50, 175–81, 189–91, 210–12, 214–15, 218–68
volatility spreads, bid/ask spreads 139–41
volatility surfaces
see also implied volatilities; sticky . . . ; strike prices
admissible volatility surfaces 114, 115–16
arbitrage opportunities 92–4, 102, 116–20
ATM STDLs 95–129, 189–91, 218–68
Black–Scholes options pricing model 91–4, 96–115, 218–27

volatility surfaces (*Cont.*)
building approaches 91–110, 120–9
concepts 19, 57–90, 91–129, 132–3, 217–68
consistency representation criteria 94–6, 108–10, 116–20
definitions 67, 91–2
efficient/convenient representation criteria 94–7
EURUSD real world example 120–6, 218–68, 281–6
forward volatility surfaces 221–7
Heston stochastic volatility model 96, 106, 112–13, 217–27
interpolation amongst available expiries 94, 96–101, 112–29, 132–3
intuitiveness representation criteria 94–6
LMUV 218–27
Malz's formula 96–7
market inconsistency issues 116–20
parsimonious representation criteria 94–6
real market situations 120–9, 218–68
RR 95–129, 218–68
SABR model 96–7, 106
stochastic volatility models 96–9, 106, 112–13, 217–27, 278
term structures of implied volatilities 112–15, 122–9, 198–9
USDJPY real world example 126–9
vanna–volga approach 94–129, 218–68
VWBs 95–129, 189–91, 218–68
volatility trading, concepts 57–90
volatility of the volatility, compound options 215
volga
see also implied volatilities; vega
compound options 215
concepts 34–5, 41, 42, 64–7, 69–75, 84–90, 94–129, 149–50, 154, 171–91, 203–4, 207–12, 215, 218–68, 278–86
correlations 278–86
definition 34
linked volatility smiles 283–6
risk management tools 229–31, 236–68
vanna–volga approach 70–5, 84–90, 94–129, 149–50, 154, 171–91, 203–4, 207–12, 215, 218–68, 278–86
von Neumann boundary conditions 158–9
VV *see* vanna–volga approach
VWBs *see* vega-weighted butterflies

week periods, expiry/settlement concepts 12–19
weights, vanna–volga approach 99–102, 109–11, 121–9, 180–1
Wilmott, Paul 54
window barrier options
concepts 11, 155–6, 197–9
definition 155, 197
pricing 197–9
window knock-in/out barrier options
see also exotic FX...
concepts 11, 155–6, 197–9

ZAR 2, 14
EURZAR 14
USDZAR 14
zero-coupon bonds 5, 29–55, 120–9, 131–3, 140–1, 167, 170–1, 205–12, 218–27, 236–68, 281–2
Zhang 161

Index compiled by TERRY HALLIDAY (HallidayTerence@aol.com)